POETS OF THE ITALIAN DIASPORA

Poets of the Italian Diaspora

⇢ A Bilingual Anthology

Edited by LUIGI BONAFFINI
and JOSEPH PERRICONE

Fordham University Press | New York | 2014

Fordham University Press has no responsibility
for the persistence or accuracy of URLs for external
or third-party Internet websites referred to in this
publication and does not guarantee that any content
on such websites is, or will remain, accurate or
appropriate.

Fordham University Press also publishes its books
in a variety of electronic formats. Some content that
appears in print may not be available in electronic
books.

Library of Congress Cataloging-in-Publication Data

Poets of the Italian diaspora : a bilingual anthology /
edited by Luigi Bonaffini and Joseph Perricone. —
First edition.
     pages cm
   Includes bibliographical references.
   ISBN 978-0-8232-3253-6 (cloth : alk. paper) —
ISBN 978-0-8232-3254-3 (pbk. : alk. paper)
   1. Italian poetry—19th century.   2. Italian
poetry—20th century.   3. Italian literature—
Foreign authors.   4. Immigrants' writings, Italian.
   5. Italians—Foreign countries.   I. Bonaffini, Luigi,
editor of compilation.   II. Perricone, Joseph, 1946–
editor of compilation.

   PQ4213.A8P66   2013
   851'.7'08—dc23

                                        2013012329

Printed in the United States of America
16 15 14   5 4 3 2 1
First edition

Contents

Belgium

Introduction

Brazil

Introduction

Canada

Introduction

Switzerland

Introduction

United States

Introduction

Italian Roots in Global Soil

SANTE MATTEO

This anthology, the first to bring together the poetry of Italians dispersed throughout the world, is a remarkable pioneering work that marks a milestone in Italian studies and lays the foundation for a new academic discipline: the study of the literature of the Italian diaspora.

Italian American studies, of which this project is an offshoot and an extension, is itself a relatively new field that came into its own as a mainstream academic discipline during the last two decades of the twentieth century, though there were earlier isolated pioneering programs, such as the Italian American studies minor at Queens College established in 1973. It took considerable time and effort to identify and gather a coherent literary corpus of primary texts and to get them published or republished to make them available to readers and to students in university courses. It took even longer to produce a supporting body of critical and theoretical studies that made it possible to analyze and appreciate the rediscovered and newly minted texts that have come to constitute "Italian American" literature.

Much of the critical and theoretical enterprise has been devoted to negotiating the differences and the tensions between traditional "Italian" culture and the "Italian American" experience: that is between the so-called high culture that is usually the content of university courses in Italian—for example, Dante, Petrarch, Boccaccio, Machiavelli, Leonardo, and Michelangelo—and the so-called low culture that is more frequently evoked in testimonials of the Italian American immigrant experience: *nonna*'s kitchen, *nonno*'s vegetable garden in the backyard, *zia*'s spaghetti sauce (or gravy, depending on where you live) and meatballs, *zio*'s heroic efforts to raise a fig tree in the forbidding climate of North America.

The gap between Italian studies and Italian American studies initially seemed to be unbridgeable for many scholars. Academic Italianists, whether raised and educated in America or "imported" from Italy, promoted standard Italian language and canonical Italian literature and art in the classroom and in their scholarship. Some of them seemed uncomfortable to be linked with Italian American communities. They were perhaps amused or irrititated by Italian Americans who mistook the distorted dialect words they knew, passed down and mutilated through several generations, for the genuine dialect of provenance, or worse, for standard Italian. They were alienated from Italian American associations that seemed to revel in nostalgia and a sentimental attachment to an outdated image of agricultural Italian life that bore little resemblance to contemporary reality in metropolitan Italy. Members of Italian American associations, for their part, kept their distance from academic Italianist organizations and tended to resent the apparent disdain with which Italian scholars and intellectuals dismissed their experience and their interests. Before the founding in 1966 of the American Italian Historical Association (AIHA), which holds annual conferences and publishes studies to address precisely such issues, there was little dialogue and much mistrust between the two sides.

That rift has been greatly reduced, initially in the social sciences, thanks to the scholars of AIHA and the pioneering work of social historians, such as Donna Gabaccia, who has studied Italian migration in the United States and elsewhere on the globe, and subsequently in the field of literature and the creative arts, thanks to the bridge-building efforts of such scholars and writers as Helen Barolini, Robert Viscusi, Daniela Gioseffi, Edwige Giunta, Fred Gardaphé, Anthony Tamburri, Paolo Giordano, Peter Carravetta, and Mary Jo Bona, to mention only a few who have managed to embrace both traditional academic content and the cultural production of lived experience in the theoretical and critical apparatus they have elaborated to analyze Italian American literary texts, as well as in their own creative works, poetry, plays, and narrative fiction. Thanks to such scholars, including the editors of this volume, Luigi Bonaffini and Joe Perricone, Italian American studies has won a place as a legitimate discipline alongside that of national literatures in the American academy (despite ongoing arguments as to whether it should be housed in Italian or English departments).

The next step is to go global. Links between particular branches of the Italian diaspora—American, Australian, Venezuelan, Argentinean, and so on—and their Italian roots have already been addressed locally in each country where Italians migrated. Now this book provides a view of all the branches simultaneously, indeed of the whole global forest where Italian roots have spread and flourished, giving us the poetic voices of the Italian diaspora from around the planet.

On my bookshelf there are two Italian books from a used bookstore in Cincinnati, Ohio—sister city to Rome; built on hills overlooking a river, in this case the Ohio, and named after the famous citizen-soldier Cincinnatus, the farmer-general who put down the sword for the plow in times of peace but laid down his plow to take up the sword when Rome needed him to fight. At the top of both front covers is the heading "Scuole italiane all'estero" (Italian Schools Abroad), and at the bottom, the name of the publisher: "Libreria dello Stato" (in this case probably best rendered as The State's Bookshelf). One book is titled *Letture: Classe IV* (Readings: Fourth Grade). Over the title is an image of a hilltop town: a handful of stone houses with red-tiled roofs, clustered around a church and its lofty Romanesque campanile, with a garland of swallows flying around it. The caption under the drawing reads *"Il luogo natio"* (The place of birth). The other book is called *Sole d'Italia: Letture: Classe V* (Sun of Italy: Readings: Fifth Grade). The image here, also above the title, is of a stylized statuary bust of a woman's head with a laurel wreath and above it a crown in the form of a Romanesque castle, with a five-pointed star hovering over it. It is labeled "La Patria" (The Fatherland or Motherland, take your pick).

The books were published in Rome and apparently distributed to "Italian" communities abroad. The year of publication is listed as "Anno IX" (Year Nine, or better yet, the Ninth). That would be 1930–31, the ninth year of the Fascist era (year I dating from October 29, 1922, when Mussolini assumed power as prime minister after the March on Rome). Inside the back covers of the books there is a map of the Roman Empire, a reminder of the glory to be resurrected by Mussolini's Third Rome. As a confirmation of the outreach of Fascist Rome to foreign communities with Italian enclaves, in Cincinnati's Eden Park, a cultural and botanical venue in a scenic setting overlooking the majestic Ohio River and the Kentucky coast on the far bank, there is a bronze copy of the famous Capitoline statue of the she-wolf suckling the twins Romulus and Remus, presented to the city of Cincinnati by "il Governatore di Roma" (the governor of Rome) in Year X, the year following the publication of the books.

Inside the front covers there is another map: not a national map of Italy, as one might perhaps expect, but a map of the world, with Italy smack in the middle (in fact, cut by the crease between the two facing pages). It is in four colors: blue-green for the seas; white for landmasses; black for borders, major rivers, and names of countries; and red for Italy and Italian territories. The legend says, "*Italiani viventi oltre confine*" (Italians living outside the borders). It shows the Boot in solid red and the Italian colonies in Africa in red stripes (Libya in the north and Eritrea and Somalia in the Horn of Africa in the east; Ethiopia, or Abyssinia, had not yet been conquered).

The most interesting feature on the map, however, is the dozens of clusters of red dots dispersed throughout the world that represent other Italian settlements, identified as "*Dislocazione degli italiani negli Stati esteri*" (dislocation of Italians in foreign states). These clusters are widely and thickly dispersed throughout North and South America (with the "Italian" population in these areas listed as 3,912,416 in North America and 3,762,168 in South America) as well as in the rest of Europe (1,265,841), excluding the Nordic countries. Somewhat surprisingly, there are many other clusters, smaller and more widely spaced, in other, unexpected parts of the world: in sub-Saharan Africa (188,702); in Australia (27,567), where, of course, many tens of thousands more would migrate after World War II; and in Asia (9,674), including several clusters in China, two in India, two in Siam and Indochina, and two lonely isolated dots in Japan.

Why dwell in such detail on these bibliographic relics from a bygone and repudiated age? Because it is commonplace to claim that, until very recently, Italian authors and statesmen largely ignored the phenomenon of mass emigration from Italy between 1880 and 1920, shortly after the nation was unified and created in 1861. Recently, thanks to scholars such as Franceso Durante, present in this volume, the phenomenon has been revived and studied extensively in books, TV documentaries, the popular press, and movies, such as *Nuovomondo* (*The Golden Gate*, 2006). This attention is likely prompted in large measure by the recent phenomenon of massive immigration into Italy from many parts of the world, a century after Italians' massive emigration out of the country to diverse regions. Clearly, however, as these two serendipitously discovered books suggest, this renewed interest in Italian emigration is not a brand-new phenomenon that has emerged after more than a century of complete neglect, as is often claimed, but rather a resurgence of interest after half a century of relative silence.

The Fascist regime was apparently fully aware of the outward migration of so many newly minted Italians and made a concerted effort to put a positive spin on the phenomenon, presenting it not as an embarrassing sign of the new nation's inability to support all its citizens but as part of a colonizing process whose aim was to spread Italian civilization through-out the world. Italian emigrants were to be perceived and appreciated as emissaries of "Italian culture," indeed of the Italian or Latin "race." Furthermore, they were to see themselves in this light, since these books were meant to be used abroad, within Italian immigrant communities. The fifth-grade reader begins with an appeal "*Ai Giovani*" (to the youth) by Benito Mussolini. Il Duce urges young Italians living in other countries to do their part to make sure that the twentieth century will come to recognize Rome, the center of Latin civilization, as the "*faro di luce per tutte le genti*" (the beacon of light for all peoples).

The subsequent silence about emigration that took hold after the fall of the Fascist regime, despite another large wave of emigration in the two decades following World War II, may be a reaction to this "imperialist" interpretation of the phenomenon's significance. The reluctance to acknowledge and speak about the massive migratory movement of Italians to other parts of the world may have resulted from an antifascist backlash that produced an aversion to embrace any notion that could be construed as promoting an "Italian" national or racial identity. This same newfound anti-imperialist and antinationalistic impulse may have also fueled some of the initial resistance to Italian American studies: a fear of being labeled "nationalistic," if not "fascistic," for accepting a notion of "Italianness" as a legitimate psychosocial category used to characterize behavior, beliefs, customs, or aspects of artistic and literary production.

I confess to sharing that resistance at first. The notion of *italianità*, central to Fred Gardaphé's, Paolo Giordano's, and Anthony Tamburri's enterprise to identify and promote Italian American literature and its study when they founded Bordighera Press in 1989 and the journal *VIA* (*Voices in Italian Americana*) in 1990, made me uncomfortable. It seemed to echo Mussolini's call to *latinità*. Nevertheless, as the discipline of Italian American studies has matured and its concepts have been refined, it has become clear that what is meant by *italianità*, at least as Gardaphé and company define it, is not an essentialist biological or genetic set of characteristics but a sociocultural construct that takes form only as people of Italian origin and their descendants, as bearers of sociocultural baggage of a particular kind, set up shop in a new environment, deploying the cultural heritage they have brought with them or have inherited from their ancestors. It is the interplay of the old and the new, the roots and the branches, that defines this hyphenated culture and makes it so rich and resonant.

Mussolini the imperial salesman pushed high culture to promote nationalist pride: Caesar and Dante. The current notion of *italianità* in an Italian American context embraces low culture as well, the quotidian and the demotic, as do many of the poems in this anthology. Still, as Robert Viscusi has convincingly demonstrated in *Buried Caesars, and Other Secrets of Italian American Writing* (2006), the imperialist impulse that informs Roman and Western history should not be dismissed or undervalued, for it is a constitutive component of what might be called the Italian imaginary or mindset, whether it belongs to Italians living in Italy or to Italian Americans, and presumably to Italian Australians, Italian Brazilians, and so on. The imperialist dream that haunts Italians as well as all Europeans, also descendants of the Romans, should not be denied or ignored, nor blindly followed, he claims, but should be studied and understood. Shakespeare's Marc Antony, he reminds us, did not in fact come to bury Caesar, as Viscusi insists, but indeed to praise him, and in so doing to introduce and plant his memory, or his ghost, as the agent of empire that still haunts Western culture.

This anthology of poetry of the Italian diaspora reflects the tension between the centrifugal impulse to leave one's home and seek other lands of opportunity and the countervailing centripetal impulse to remain home-bound or to return homeward: in short, wanderlust versus nostalgia as fundamental urges of the human experience. It is primarily the interplay between these two opposite yet complementary impulses that makes this collection of poems so *captivating* and so *moving*, to use terms suggestive of the opposing tug of centripetal and centrifugal inclinations.

There are, as one would expect, poems that evoke aspects of a common core or rootedness, no matter where they are written: the sounds, odors, vistas, countryside, church, food, customs of the village left behind; memories of mothers suckling their babies, of grandparents and aunts and uncles helping a toddler take his or her first steps. The images are similar and so are the emotions they evoke, regardless of the language and the country in which they are written: for example, "La mia terra" and "Homecoming" (Luigi Strano, Australia), "Il pane" (Giacomo Scotti, Istria and Fiume in the Balkans).

There are also poems that evoke the different and the exotic: experiences and realities unique to the land of the emigrants' destination: the South American "Pampa" (Dino Campana, Argentina), "The Cry of the Kookaburra" (Alberto Avolio, Australia), "A stae trupicale/Noon Summer in the Tropics" with its luxuriant vegetation and hot tropical sun

(Ermanno Minuto, Brazil), "The Valleys of Caracas" full of "concrete and *ranchitos*" (Valeriano Garbin, Venezuela).

Italian American literature and Italian American studies have already given us a taste, an idea, of how cultural paradigms come together, how they clash and combine, endure and shift, and in so doing come to create new cultural paradigms. This anthology shows us how this process works on a global scale. In a sense it represents the completion of the Ulyssean journey that was aborted in Dante's *Inferno*. Dante's Ulysses and his companions founder at sea after crossing the Pillars of Hercules. Italian emigrants, on the contrary, as new, more successful Ulyssean voyagers, have managed to reach their far-flung destinations, even unto the antipodes. In providing us the poetic testaments of these latter-day Odysseys, this anthology provides us with Odysseus's two-eyed, stereoscopic vision that gave him the advantage over the isolated, monocular Cyclops, who with no experience of the world outside his island and with only one eye could not see the the things of the world in perspective.

As we move from poem to poem, from one language to another, vicariously traveling from country to country, we too are "translated" (transported) out of our home turf, out of ourselves: like Ulysses, whose travels through the Mediterranean over a twenty-year period afflicted him with great nostalgia but also gained him the ability to see his world in perspective, to compare one place with another, one society with another, one belief system with another. The Cyclops, by contrast, confined to his island, never acquired the migrant's second eye, the depth perception necessary to see beyond the surface of things, to understand causes, effects, consequences, tangents, differences, or alternatives.

It is precisely this migration, movement out of our initial situation, which gives us binocular vision, or the ability to perceive what lies beside or beyond the surface. Reading is a form of migration, a mental activity that transports us into other realities. The journey through the poetry of the Italian diaspora provided in this anthology allows readers to replicate Ulysses's voyage from land to land, with poems that evoke anew the lost homeland with nostalgia, accompanied by poems that present the novelty and surprise of new environments. The experience allows us to see in stereoscope, with imagery and perceptions that juxtapose the point of departure with the point of arrival: the old and familiar with the new and different, the traditional with the exotic.

With one eye we glimpse the far horizons that pulled us in varied directions and turned us into strangers in strange lands, while we keep the other eye on the social and cultural roots of our origin, which we share in common with all other diasporic Italians, all in some manner still and forever *paesani*, whether Australians, Balkans, or South Americans. This stereoscopic vision, engendered by migration and the diasporic experience, is the gift of insight that this volume offers to all of us.

Seven Points on Poetry of the Italian Diaspora

FRANCESCO DURANTE

1. Emigration is, without a doubt, an important and dramatic process. Indeed, its impact is such that those who undertake this passage are somehow naturally endowed with a degree of poetic authority. Their memories of and reflections on this experience merit documentation, and their resultant documents merit a level of critical regard that might even seem disproportionate with regard to certain qualitative aspects of their works. In other words, to comprehend and evaluate the output of these small groups who move with uncertain steps in new spheres, one must go beyond the traditional method of mapping out their writings and establishing connections among them. One must also consider them as the precious, budding expressions of a new culture's first moment. As such, one must come to accept that their literary products in some cases might seem poor or anachronistic, or at any rate beneath the contemporary standards held by the apparently higher culture of their country of origin, in this case Italy. The dilettante or perhaps somewhat derivative nature of some of their writings, therefore, cannot and must not be evaluated in parallel with concurrent tendencies in the motherland. For what they document is a yet-incomplete and unstructured passage, a suspended reality that is at once no longer Italian and not yet—at least not fully— something else. Within this ambiguous territory of incipient transformation and evolving identities, the words that map the territory acquire value and weight.

2. For the most part, the poems produced by such writers reveal their origins in necessity. These are not writers who have pursued normal literary careers, nor have they had significant recognition in academic or publishing circles. What moves them to become vocal is the extraordinary nature of their experience, granting them a degree of authenticity that transcends even their most exasperated, stylistically exaggerated modes of expression. For many of these men and women, life is founded

upon labor, primarily manual labor, and their poetry is thus reflective of a fundamental *verità*, an essential truth, even where their expressions seem to turn away from the toil and disgust around them in favor of capturing the mysterious echoes of unreal dreams. It is thus important to not only perceive this dynamic, but to understand its necessity.

3. Though at times executed en masse, the act of expatriation is an absolutely singular experience, one whose irreducible singularity is nonetheless, and in fact perforce, expressed through a plurality of voices. This circumstance should itself suffice to underscore the necessity and motives behind an anthology such as this, but it is also indicative of the truly epic, indeed choral resonance of such writings. With particular regard to the great waves of emigration that took place in the nineteenth and twentieth centuries, these expressive characteristics attain also a social and political scope as the men and women giving voice to their struggles seek to reaffirm a sense of dignity and lay the groundwork for a better future. One might even say that a certain Promethean connotation is part and parcel of the poetry of expatriation of every era in so far as it conveys—live and in real time—the realizations, awakenings, hopes, and expectations of its practitioners.

4. This poetics still speaks Italian, but it is clear that it will soon become multilingual. To be sure, the expatriate eventually needs to borrow terms and expressions from his host country to properly express feelings and experiences in his new world. Thus this poetics, whose moment of birth invariably coincides with its moment of detachment from its motherland, relies on the Italian language as a sort of residual resource of identity, perhaps even the only such available resource. Yet the expatriate is also aware that this resource is a circumstantially limited means of expression. For him or her, writing in Italian is tantamount to entering, in a literary sense, a blind alleyway; whatever he or she produces is at once peripheral and eccentric to Italian literary spheres, as well to the literary spheres of his or her host country. As such, whatever literary output emerges therefrom immediately falls short of its literary aims of communicating, transmitting, and contributing to the creation of a cohesive community. As a result, these poets quickly realize the need to make radical shifts, at least in terms of their themes, to ensure that their words are not only heard by those whose lives they recount, but also somehow reflective of them.

5. What results from this is a sort of idiolect suspended between two worlds, and it is precisely herein that the heroic choice of emigration

poetry lies. One might liken the precariousness of this literary space to a response to Nietzsche's invitation, in *The Gay Science*, to build a house at the foot of a volcano, for within this space, creativity and expression might at times amount only to insignificant repetition, but they will more often become an integral and irrevocable part of that most crucial moment for members of a diaspora: the final dream they dreamed before liquefying themselves into a new identity.

6. The German concepts of *Gastarbeiterliteratur* (guest worker or migrant literature) and *Gastarbeiterdeutsch* (guest worker German) help to define, in an effective, albeit objectively ghettoizing way, the fulcrum, the *ubi consistam*, of this poetry and literature. It is of course a provisory definition in that it evaluates writers according to categories that lie outside of their writing activities (before being considered writers, many of them are first and foremost laborers), and because it is based on an idea of extraneity, of a certain foreignness that is neither stable nor permanent, and can be overcome through the existential journeys of individuals, or through the increasingly complex cultural heredity that passes from one generation to the next. Through this process, a decisive encounter, or perhaps collision, with the new language is inevitable; once Italian is no longer sufficient, the expatriate must master the new language if s/he hopes to tweak it properly according to her/his expressive needs. This requires the uprooting of one language and the acquisition of another, a process that begins when the uprooting appears to be only physical and does not yet seem to entail an exchange of original identity for a new one. This holds for multiple historical contexts, and it is as valid for the end of the nineteenth century as it is for the middle of the twentieth.

7. Precariousness, tentativeness, risk, identity conflicts, and consequently hybrid natures: All of these things factor into the fundamentally experimental character of expatriate poetry, even when (as I have stated several times already, and as the reader of this book might initially think) this same poetry seems to be an attempt to recapture or echo the traditions and modes of the writers' nation of origin, Italy. Two things are at play in these works: the establishment of a new and seminal voice, and a voice that consumes itself in the name of supposed continuity. Expatriate poetry invents new worlds as it reinvents antique ones, employing memory with obsessive selectivity, aggrandizing that which is small and rendering diminutive that which is large. It is the field of a battle that is at once valorously fought and valorously lost.

Acknowledgments

A volume of this magnitude would not have been possible without the support and assistance of a considerable number of people whom the editors herewith thank sincerely. In particular we would like to express our gratitude to Dr. Dominic Balestra, who as Dean of Faculty at Fordham first encouraged us to pursue this project, and to Robert Oppedisano, who initially approved it for Fordham University Press. Additional thanks go to Dr. Robert Himmelberg for his supportive subvention as Dean of Faculty. A word of appreciation is also due to Dr. Paolo Spedicato for his help in Brazil and, last but not least, to Dr. Sarafina De Gregorio for her assiduous and insightful work and suggestions in the revisions of the manuscript.

Special recognition is given to Paul D'Agostino for his contributions as Assistant Editor.

POETS OF THE ITALIAN DIASPORA

Argentina

Argentina

GABRIEL CACHO MILLET

Italian poetry in the twentieth century in Argentina is intimately connected with immigration. Millions of foreigners settled there throughout the 1950s. From Italy, people rarely arrived who represented that other spirit of its consummate civilization and of its perennial art, which it nurtures and takes care of.

In general, the people who landed in the most southerly seaport in South America were poor and at times not well educated. According to Dino Campana, the orphic poet from Marradi, Italians went to Argentina because "it was easier to make a living there." Thus the verses of the five poets presented in this section are gifts of the labor of life; they all made a living, or got by, by performing the most humble tasks. And they discovered their poetic vocations along the way: Alfredo Bufano while shining shoes in the streets of Buenos Aires and later working in a bookstore; Antonio Aliberti while working in his barber shop and dreaming of the island where he could not grow up nor ever return; the antifascist Severino Di Giovanni as a gardener and flower seller before becoming an editor running articles against the organization of power and private ownership at his own newspaper. With his anarchist friends, he began to put into practice the theories of his Russian idol, Mikhail Bakunin, and those of his precursors, theorists and pre-anarchist philosophers such as William Godwin and Proudhon, as well as others who contributed to the doctrine, including Reclus, Grave, and Tolstoy. Di Giovanni's anarchism, according to Oscar D'Angelo, "foresaw a horizontal social structure and a social development without violence, but in order to create this anarchist society, violence was necessary. Violence was necessary only to obtain a just society without violence: violence to construct a society without violence, a society without social classes, violence to fight violence." As such, Osvaldo Bayer, Di Giovanni's biographer, was able to designate him "the idealist of violence."

It is not easy to envision a veritable poetics in this man of action and thought from Abruzzi. Certainly, in his short life he read, together with his anarchist theorists, Shakespeare, Shelley, and, among the Italians, Carducci and D'Annunzio, in addition to minor poets and freethinkers such as Rapisardi and Novatore. It is also true that he spoke ill of Gentile and Pirandello: In the philosopher he saw a theorist of fascism, while in the playwright and Nobel Prize winner he saw a messenger of Mussolini taking his theater around the world.

Severino Di Giovanni was executed by a firing squad in Buenos Aires in 1931. He was twenty-nine years old. When he was arrested, he was in the midst of preparing an elegant, two-volume edition of the works of Elisée Reclus. As he was leaving the printing shop, a few policemen informed him that he was under arrest. At the end of an adventurous chase, having left behind a few dead bodies and sensing that he was lost, he pointed his gun at his own chest. He fired but did not die. At his trial prior to his execution, he declared to the presidents: "I don't intend to avoid any responsibility. As any good player, I know I have lost and I am ready to pay." Here, a nocturne and a fragment, "Hymn to Dynamite" (to the dynamite, that is, with which Gino Lucetti tried to eliminate, without success, the dictator and father of fascism, Benito Mussolini), evidence Di Giovanni's first utterances in what might be considered his poetic voice.

Antonio Porta, from Calabria, wrote only in Spanish and so cannot be included in the present anthology. Like Di Giovanni, he was an editor affiliated with leftist Italo-Argentinian groups, anarchists and socialists. In his words: "In every way, my side is left. I was born on that side." In 1943, Antonio Porta published a book entitled *Voces* (*Voci/Voices*), hailed triumphantly in France by its most alert reader, Roger Caillois, and declared a masterpiece by Henry Miller and André Breton. In his land, few people are aware of his work. Daringly, the publisher Il Grappolo recently published an Italian translation of *Voces*. The collection of short poems, aphorisms, and "words that attempt to say what cannot be said" (Laura Pariani) was written originally in Spanish.

J. Rodolfo Wilcock, born in Argentina (although his mother was of Swiss-Italian origins), was able to earn a degree in engineering. He was the most privileged of the four poets mentioned here, and he distinguished himself further as a member of the group of Borges, Bioy Casares, and Silvina Ocampo. He belongs to the other mind of Italy, the cultured one that looks toward Europe. As any Argentine deserving respect, he is "a European in exile," according to the well-known definition coined by Borges. It is for this reason that, in 1958, he decided to end his exile in the town where he was born, go back definitively to Italy, change country and language, and "begin to write in a sort of Italian." Ricardo H. Herrera asks whether Wilcock made such a decision because he felt expelled from the political reality of Perón or, instead, because he was attracted by the roots of his tradition. The critic's answer is both, "expelled and attracted." At any rate, he is a son of the diaspora who returned to his homeland.

Dino Campana also felt that his destiny was Europe, but his stay in Argentina for a little over one year made him part of the Italian immigration experience, albeit in a transitory way. The best poetry that he produced in this period consists of Orphic reflections on the mysteries of the pampas, modifications of the countryside through the labor of a humble worker (*obrero del riel*) or of a railway digger (*peón de vía*). It is not the view of a tourist come from the Old World to photograph the New. For Campana, in the pampas, the "vast fatherland," life finds again for "an instant the contact with the forces of the cosmos." He is a poet of the diaspora, even though he remains one of the most unsettling visionary poets of the twentieth century in Italy.

In his prose poems, brief segments appear in Spanish. Though rather awkward, these words are never mixed up with the Italian text. Thus his language does not turn into the *cocoliche*, a jargon that mixes Italian and Spanish and is the major expressive vehicle of the *sainete*, a theatrical form that was popular during the immigration period.

In describing and narrating what he sees in the urban centers, the author of the *Orphic Songs* depicts scenes of corruption, of thieves (*lunfa*) without, however, appropriating their speech (*lunfardo*), which, with the passing of time, becomes part of the common language of Buenos Aires and is found frequently in the tangos.

Campana, in *Fantasia su un quadro di Ardengo Soffici*, writes surprisingly in his language about a painting by Ardengo Soffici, re-creating the rhythms of the tango that he had learned while playing the piano in the meeting places of the crime-ridden areas of Buenos Aires when he needed money. The piano, at times accompanied by the flute or the violin, was the instrument most frequently used for the tango, not the guitar, which is used instead in the countryside for the more classical *tango-canción*.

The tango leaves the periphery and enters the urban world when, in 1914, news comes from Paris that it was played by the municipal board in its repertory. The tango that Campana plays on the piano is already the "sad thought of a dance" (A. Discepolo), "the soft lullaby" (Gadda); it is not the tango of the peasants that Campana has heard when he says, in *The Night*: "I thought I was learning the grieving of the guitars there in the hovel of studs and metal on the fanciful grounds of the city." The guitars "on the fanciful grounds of the city" tell of the "mythology of courage" of the "marginalized," as Borges and Bioy Casares would say. There, the "dregs of the sea" are active in the silver sea of the pampas. Campana, in his "Dualism: Open Letter to Manuelita Etchegarray," describes "wretched fierce men, unknown men locked in their sullen will, bloody stories soon forgotten suddenly living in the night again, weaving around me the history of the young fierce city." The "dregs" or "rejects" that Campana describes in this piece are rightfully those that "the guitars commemorate" humbly with a tango or a song, and that the piano in a café or a bordello can no longer commemorate because their deeds are no longer mythical and take place in little dwellings and furnished rooms of the city's outskirts. They are topics for the crime news—no longer for Borges and Bioy Casares, but for Roberto Arlt. Once in the city, the "rejects" blend in with the newcomers off the boats and compose, together, the tale of the city, the "implacable conqueror, burning with a bitter fever of money and immediate happiness."

Moreover, the writers of tango lyrics of the 1920s and 1930s are known for their commitment to explore thoroughly the consciences of their companions. For this reason it should come as no surprise that they included words not proper to *rioplatense*, the Spanish of the Rio de la Plata area. The lyricists of the tangos included Italian words in their songs, and in some cases even entire sentences from immigrant groups that, in some instances, consist of real verses. Although these lyricists are not, strictly speaking, poets of the diaspora, their verses document words and expressions related to the immigrant experience.

Alfredo Bufano also utilizes material from Italian immigration heritage, yet he claimed to have been born in Guaymallén de Mendoza because he wanted to be known only as an Argentine poet and writer. In the two selections that exemplify his work in this anthology, "El viajero" (The Traveler) and "Égloga" (Idyll), Bufano cannot deny his origins. He cites Leopardi in Italian and imitates, in Italian verses, the answers that a peasant provides to the poet's questions concerning the harvest.

Over the years, Bufano translated D'Annunzio's poetry into Spanish for the review *Nosotros* (1907–43), which, along with *Martín Fierro* (1924–27) and *Sur* (1931–81), provided essential material for reconstructing the historical course that Italian literature took in Argentina. They documented the realization of a classic canon of Italian literature: the presence in Argentinian literature of the Italian and European avant-garde, and the establishment of modern cultural models of remarkable prestige from World War II to today (Alejandro Patat).

⇥ Dino Campana (1885–1932)

Dino Campana was born in Marradi (Florence, Italy) on August 20, 1885, and died in the mental institution of Castel Pulci in Scandicci (Florence), after fourteen years of confinement, on March 1, 1932. His vagabond and tormented life carried him to Argentina in 1907 because, there, it was "easier to make a living." Campana was twenty-three when he boarded the ship carrying in his pocket a copy of *Leaves of Grass* and a 38mm Belgian gun on his belt. If it is true that, during that voyage toward the unknown, he wanted as companions a book by Whitman and a gun, this alone says a great deal about the objectives of the immigrant and the idea he had of the New World.

On an October morning in 1907, Campana glimpsed "the sea capital of the new continent" as the ship moved slowly on "a yellow sea" (caused by the green waters of the Atlantic mixing with the muddy waters of the Rio de la Plata). He also saw some compatriots, Italian immigrants dressed as gauchos, throwing oranges "in Buenos Aires style" to the newcomers while a boy, a "son of freedom," saluted him, a gesture that he alone seems to have seen.

Down there in Argentina, Campana, a laborer, a railway digger with "Orphic" visions that "sunny happiness" had pointed out to him in the Mediterranean, continued "across the paths of the sky I followed mankind's adventurous journey toward happiness through the centuries," reading, standing up in an open wagon, the story of the "knights" of the Pampas, a story of living or dead written in the heavens. A poet of Mediterranean origin, Campana could not but carry with him his knowledge of antiquity and the baroque: In the sky of the Pampas he discovered "arabesques" and heard the "melodramatic moans." On the shores of the Mediterranean, albeit not in the area envisioned by him as an illusory South, was born the God of the three monotheistic religions; on these other shores there was "no God" that might disturb the infinite sky with

9

its shadow, not even that "unknown God" that the Greeks worshipped so as not to forget anyone. Man was alone, free and "reconciled with nature, ineffably sweet and frightening." Down there, before the poet's eyes, "through the mysterious force of a barbarian myth" were re-created "figurations of a most ancient free life, of enormous solar myths, of massacres of orgies." In the Pampas he rediscovered for an instant the contact "with the forces of the cosmos." There, an "adorable Creole" loved him.

In America, Campana does not invoke help from any local poet. Leopoldo Lugones, close reader of Dante (as well as of D'Annunzio), had already published, in 1906, *La guerra gaucha* (*The Gaucho War*), but Campana never mentions the gaucho, the natural enemy of the Indios, in his recreation of the deeds of the Indios, dead and alive, "who charged forward in lightning charge to reconquer their dominion of freedom" (Pampas). There are no traces of any reading of *Martín Fierro* (1872) by José Hernandez, more of a myth than just a book on the adventures of the gaucho. During the time that Campana lived in Buenos Aires, Rubén Darío, the father of Spanish modernism, also lived there after he had published two books of poetry that would have been of interest to Campana: *Cantos de vida y esperanza* (*Songs of Life and Hope*, 1905) and *El canto errante* (*The Wandering Song*, 1907). It seems that Campana never heard of him. The only author of the New World that he cites explicitly and claims to "adore" is the North American Walt Whitman. But Campana was not going through Whitman's America; that is not what he was trying to understand. *Leaves of Grass* is not a travel book for the Pampas. He will need that book later to identify with the boy "whose innocent blood had been shed" in order to conclude his *Canti orfici* (1914; *Orphic Songs*, 2003).[1]

Viaggio a Montevideo

da *Canti orfici*

Io vidi dal ponte della nave
I colli di Spagna
Svanire, nel verde
Dentro il crepuscolo d'oro la bruna terra celando
Come una melodia:
D'ignota scena fanciulla sola
Come una melodia
Blu, su la riva dei colli ancora tremare una viola . . .
Illanguidiva la sera celeste sul mare:
Pure i dorati silenzii ad ora ad ora dell'ale
Varcaron lentamente in un azzurreggiare: . . .
Lontani tinti dei varii colori
Dai più lontani silenzi!
Ne la celeste sera varcaron gli uccelli d'oro: la nave
Già cieca varcando battendo la tenebra
Coi nostri naufraghi cuori
Battendo la tenebra l'ale celeste sul mare.
Ma un giorno
Salirono sopra la nave le gravi matrone di Spagna
Da gli occhi torbidi e angelici
Dai seni gravidi di vertigine. Quando
In una baia profonda di un'isola equatoriale
In una baia tranquilla e profonda assai più del cielo notturno
Noi vedemmo sorgere nella luce incantata
Una bianca città addormentata
Ai piedi dei picchi altissimi dei vulcani spenti
Nel soffio torbido dell'equatore: finché
Dopo molte grida e molte ombre di un paese ignoto,
Dopo molto cigolìo di catene e molto acceso fervore
Noi lasciammo la città equatoriale
Verso l'inquieto mare notturno.
Andavamo andavamo, per giorni e per giorni: le navi
Gravi di vele molli di caldi soffi incontro passavano lente:
Sì presso di sul cassero a noi ne appariva bronzina

Voyage to Montevideo

from *Orphic Songs and Other Poems*

I saw from the deck of the ship
The hills of Spain
Vanish, while in the green
Within the golden twilight the dark earth concealed
Almost a melody:
Almost a blue melody
Of solitary unknown youthful scene,
On the bank of the hills still trembling a viola . . .
The pale-blue evening languished on the sea:
From time to time the golden silences of wings
Also crossed slowly in the deepening blue . . .
Distant tinged with various colors
From the most distant silences
The golden birds crossed in the sky-blue evening: the ship
Already blind
Crossing beating the darkness
With our shipwrecked hearts
The wings beating the pale-blue darkness on the sea.
But one day
Aboard ship came the solemn matrons of Spain
With turbid angelic eyes
With breasts heavy with vertigo. When
In a deep bay of an equatorial island
In a bay much more tranquil and deep than the nocturnal sky
We saw in the enchanted light rise
A white city asleep
At the foot of the highest peaks of the dead volcanoes
In the turbid breath of the equator: until
After much shouting and many shadows of an unknown country,
After much clattering of chains and much burning fervor
We left the equatorial city
Toward the restless nocturnal sea.
We went on and on, for days and days: the ships
Heavy with sails slackened by warm breezes slowly went by:

Una fanciulla della razza nuova,
Occhi lucenti e le vesti al vento! ed ecco: selvaggia a la fine di
un giorno che apparve
La riva selvaggia là giù sopra la sconfinata marina:
E vidi come cavalle
Vertiginose che si scioglievano le dune
Verso la prateria senza fine
Deserta senza le case umane
E noi volgemmo fuggendo le dune che apparve
Su un mare giallo de la portentosa dovizia del fiume,
Del continente nuovo la capitale marina.
Limpido fresco ed elettrico era il lume
Della sera e là le alte case parevan deserte
Laggiù sul mar del pirata
De la città abbandonata
Tra il mare giallo e le dune . . .
. . . .

Near the upper deck a bronze-colored girl
Of the new race appeared to us,
Eyes shining and clothes in the wind! and then: savage at day's end
The savage shore appeared to us down there over the boundless
    ocean:
And I saw the dunes unfurl
Like whirling Mares
Toward the endless prairie
Deserted without human houses
And as the dunes fled we turned, for the marine capital
Of the new continent appeared on a sea yellow
With the prodigious abundance of the river.
Limpid fresh and electric was the light
Of evening, and there the tall houses seemed deserted
Down there on the sea of the pirate
Of the abandoned city
Between the yellow sea and the dunes . . .

. . . .

Dualismo
(Lettera aperta a Manuelita Etchegarray)

Voi adorabile creola dagli occhi neri e scintillanti come metallo in fusione, voi figlia generosa della prateria nutrita di aria vergine voi tornate ad apparirmi col ricordo lontano: anima dell'oasi dove la mia vita ritrovò un istante il contatto colle forze del cosmo. Io vi rivedo Manuelita, il piccolo viso armato dell'ala battagliera del vostro cappello, la piuma di struzzo avvolta e ondulante eroicamente, i vostri piccoli passi pieni di slancio contenuto sopra il terreno delle promesse eroiche! Tutta mi siete presente esile e nervosa. La cipria sparsa come neve sul vostro viso consunto da un fuoco interno, le vostre vesti di rosa che proclamavano la vostra verginità come un'aurora piena di promesse! E ancora il magnetismo di quando voi chinaste il capo, voi fiore meraviglioso di una razza eroica, mi attira non ostante il tempo ancora verso di voi! Eppure Manuelita sappiatelo se lo potete: *io non pensavo, non pensavo a voi: io mai non ho pensato a voi*. Di notte nella piazza deserta, quando nuvole vaghe correvano verso strane costellazioni, alla triste luce elettrica io sentivo la mia infinita solitudine. La prateria si alzava come un mare argentato agli sfondi, e rigetti di quel mare, miseri, uomini feroci, uomini ignoti chiusi nel loro cupo volere, storie sanguinose subito dimenticate che rivivevano improvvisamente nella notte, tessevano attorno a me la storia della città giovine e feroce, conquistatrice implacabile, ardente di un'acre febbre di denaro e di gioie immediate. Io vi perdevo allora Manuelita, perdonate, tra la turba delle signorine elastiche dal viso molle inconsciamente feroce, violentemente eccitante tra le due bande di capelli lisci nell'immobilità delle dee della razza. Il silenzio era scandito dal trotto monotono di una pattuglia: e allora il mio anelito infrenabile andava lontano da voi, verso le calme oasi della sensibilità della vecchia Europa e mi si stringeva con violenza il cuore. Entravo, ricordo, allora nella biblioteca: io che non potevo Manuelita io che non sapevo pensare a voi. Le lampade elettriche oscillavano lentamente. Su da le pagine risuscitava un mondo defunto, sorgevano immagini antiche che oscillavano lentamente coll'ombra del paralume e sovra il mio capo gravava un cielo misterioso, gravido di forme vaghe, rotto a tratti da gemiti di melodramma: larve che si scioglievano mute per rinascere a vita inestinguibile nel silenzio pieno delle profondità meravigliose del destino. Dei ricordi perduti, delle immagini si componevano già morte mentre era più profondo il silenzio. Rivedo ancora Parigi, Place d'Italie, le baracche, i car-

Dualism
(Open Letter to Manuelita Etchegarray)

You adorable Creole with black eyes sparkling like molten metal, you generous daughter of the grassland nourished by virgin air, you appear to me once more with the distant memory: soul of the oasis where for a moment my life came into contact again with the forces of the cosmos. Once more I see you, Manuelita, the small face armed with the combative wing of your hat, the ostrich feather rolled and swaying heroically, your small steps full of contained energy on the ground of heroic promises! You are all present before me slender and nervous. The powder sprinkled like snow on your face consumed by an inner fire, your rose-colored dress that proclaimed your virginity like a dawn full of promises! And still the magnetism of when you bowed your head, you wonderful flower of a heroic race, still draws me toward you regardless of time! And yet Manuelita you must know if you can: *I did not think, I did not think of you: I never thought of you.* At night in the deserted square, when wandering clouds coursed toward strange constellations, under the sad electric light I felt my infinite solitude. The grassland rose like a silvery sea in the background, and flotsam of that sea, wretched fierce men, unknown men locked in their sullen will, bloody stories soon forgotten suddenly living in the night again, weaving around me the history of the young fierce city, implacable conqueror, burning with the acrid fever of money and instant pleasures. I would lose you then Manuelita, forgive me, among the throng of supple young ladies with soft faces unconsciously fierce, violently exciting between the two bands of smooth hair in the immobility of the goddesses of the race. The silence was punctuated by the monotonous trot of a patrol: and then my unrestrainable yearning would go far away from you, toward the calm oases of old Europe's sensibility, and violently wring my heart. I would go then, I remember, into the library: I who was not able I who didn't know how to think of you. The electric lamps swayed slowly. Up from the pages a dead world sprang back to life, ancient images arose, swaying slowly with the shadow of the lampshade, and above my head weighed a mysterious sky, heavy with vague forms, rent now and then by melodramatic moans: ghosts dissolving silently to be reborn to inextinguishable life in the silence full of the wonderful depths of destiny. Lost memories, images were forming already dead as the silence grew deeper. I see Paris again, Place d'Italie, the

rozzoni, i magri cavalieri dell'irreale, dal viso essiccato, dagli occhi perforanti di nostalgie feroci, tutta la grande piazza ardente di un concerto infernale stridente e irritante. Le bambine dei Bohémiens, i capelli sciolti, gli occhi arditi e profondi congelati in un languore ambiguo amaro attorno dello stagno liscio e deserto. E in fine Lei, dimentica, lontana, l'amore, il suo viso di zingara nell'onda dei suoni e delle luci che si colora di un incanto irreale: e noi in silenzio attorno allo stagno pieno di chiarori rossastri: e noi ancora stanchi del sogno vagabondare a caso per quartieri ignoti fino a stenderci stanchi sul letto di una taverna lontana tra il soffio caldo del vizio noi là nell'incertezza e nel rimpianto colorando la nostra voluttà di riflessi irreali!

E così lontane da voi passavano quelle ore di sogno, ore di profondità mistiche e sensuali che scioglievano in tenerezze i grumi più acri del dolore, ore di felicità completa che aboliva il tempo e il mondo intero, lungo sorso alle sorgenti dell'Oblio! E vi rivedevo Manuelita poi: che vigilavate pallida e lontana: voi anima semplice chiusa nelle vostre semplici armi.

So Manuelita: voi cercavate la grande rivale. So: la cercavate nei miei occhi stanchi che mai non vi appresero nulla. Ma ora se lo potete sappiate: io dovevo restare fedele al mio destino: era un'anima inquieta quella di cui mi ricordavo sempre quando uscivo a sedermi sulle panchine della piazza deserta sotto le nubi in corsa. Essa era per cui solo il sogno mi era dolce. Essa era per cui io dimenticavo il vostro piccolo corpo convulso nella stretta del guanciale, il vostro piccolo corpo pericoloso tutto adorabile di snellezza e di forza. E pure vi giuro Manuelita io vi amavo e vi amo e vi amerò sempre più di qualunque altra donna . . . dei due mondi.

booths, the caravans, the lean horsemen of the unreal, their shriveled faces, their eyes piercing with fierce longings, the whole square burning in a hellish concert, shrill and irritating. The little girls of the Bohemians, their hair loose, their eyes bold and deep, frozen in an ambiguous bitter languor around the smooth and deserted pond. And finally She, oblivious, distant, love, her gypsy face in the wave of sounds and lights taking on the hue of an unreal enchantment: and we in silence around the pond full of reddish glimmers: and we still weary from the dream wandering aimlessly through unknown places until we stretched out wearily on the bed of a distant tavern amid the warm breath of vice, we there in the uncertainty and regret tingeing our wantonness with unreal reflections!

And so those hours of dream passed far away from you, hours of mystical sensual depths that dissolved in tenderness the most acrid clots of sorrow, hours of complete happiness that abolished time and the entire world, a long sip at the wellsprings of Oblivion! And then I would see you again Manuelita: keeping watch pale and distant: your simple soul closed in your simple weapons.

I know Manuelita: you were looking for the great rival, I know: you looked for her in my weary eyes that never revealed anything. But now you must know if you can: I had to remain faithful to my destiny: it was a restless soul I always remembered when I went out to sit on the benches in the deserted square under the racing clouds. It was for her alone that dream was sweet for me. It was for her that I would forget your small body convulsing in the grip of the pillow, your small dangerous body all adorable with slenderness and strength. And yet I swear to you Manuelita I loved you I love you and I will always love you more than any other woman . . . of the two worlds.

Pampa

Quiere Usted Mate? uno spagnolo mi profferse a bassa voce, quasi a non turbare il profondo silenzio della Pampa.—Le tende si allungavano a pochi passi da dove noi seduti in circolo in silenzio guardavamo a tratti furtivamente le strane costellazioni che doravano l'ignoto della prateria notturna.—Un mistero grandioso e veemente ci faceva fluire con refrigerio di fresca vena profonda il nostro sangue nelle vene:—che noi assaporavamo con voluttà misteriosa—come nella coppa del silenzio purissimo e stellato.

Quiere Usted Mate? Ricevetti il vaso e succhiai la calda bevanda.

Gettato sull'erba vergine, in faccia alle strane costellazioni io mi andavo abbandonando tutto ai misteriosi giuochi dei loro arabeschi, cullato deliziosamente dai rumori attutiti del bivacco. I miei pensieri fluttuavano: si susseguivano i miei ricordi: che deliziosamente sembravano sommergersi per riapparire a tratti lucidamente trasumanati in distanza, come per un'eco profonda e misteriosa, dentro l'infinita maestà della natura. Lentamente gradatamente io assurgevo all'illusione universale: dalle profondità del mio essere e della terra io ribattevo per le vie del cielo il cammino avventuroso degli uomini verso la felicità a traverso i secoli. Le idee brillavano della più pura luce stellare. Drammi meravigliosi, i più meravigliosi dell'anima umana palpitavano e si rispondevano a traverso le costellazioni. Una stella fluente in corsa magnifica segnava in linea gloriosa la fine di un corso di storia. Sgravata la bilancia del tempo sembrava risollevarsi lentamente oscillando:—per un meraviglioso attimo immutabilmente nel tempo e nello spazio alternandosi i destini eterni . . . Un disco livido spettrale spuntò all'orizzonte lontano profumato irraggiando riflessi gelidi d'acciaio sopra la prateria. Il teschio che si levava lentamente era l'insegna formidabile di un esercito che lanciava torme di cavalieri colle lancie in resta acutissime lucenti: gli indiani morti e vivi si lanciavano alla riconquista del loro dominio di libertà in lancio fulmineo. Le erbe piegavano in gemito leggero al vento del loro passaggio. La commozione del silenzio intenso era prodigiosa.

Che cosa fuggiva sulla mia testa? Fuggivano le nuvole e le stelle, fuggivano: mentre che dalla Pampa nera scossa che sfuggiva a tratti nella selvaggia nera corsa del vento ora più forte ora più fievole ora come un lontano fragore ferreo: a tratti alla malinconia più profonda dell'errante un richiamo: . . . dalle criniere dell'erbe scosse come alla malinconia più

Pampas

¿Quiere Usted Mate? a Spaniard offered me in a whisper, almost as not to disturb the deep silence of the Pampas.—The tents stretched a few steps from where we sat silently in a circle and from time to time we would glance at the strange constellations that tinged the unknown of the nocturnal grassland with gold.—A magnificent vehement mystery made the blood flow in our veins with the cool freshness of a deep fresh vein:— which we savored with mysterious wantonness—as in the cup of the purest starry silence.

¿Quiere Usted mate? I received the pot and took a sip of the warm drink. Stretched on the virgin grass, facing the strange constellations, I was gradually giving in to the mysterious play of their arabesques, delightfully rocked by the muffled noises of the camp. My thoughts wavered: my memories drifted by in quick succession: that delightfully seemed to submerge and reappear in the distance now and then lucidly beyond the human, as if through a deep mysterious echo, within the infinite majesty of nature. Slowly gradually I was rising to the universal illusion: from the depths of my being and of the earth, across the paths of the sky I followed mankind's adventurous journey toward happiness through the centuries. Ideas shone with the purest starlight. Wonderful dramas, the most wonderful of the human soul pulsated and echoed across the constellations. A star flowing in magnificent flight marked with a glorious line the end of a course of history. Unburdened the scale of time seemed to spring up again swaying slowly:—for a wonderful instant the eternal destinies alternating immutably in time and space . . . A livid spectral disk appeared on the distant fragrant horizon radiating icy glimmers of steel onto the grassland. The skull that was slowly rising was the formidable standard of an army that hurled throngs of horsemen with their lances couched, sharppointed and gleaming: the Indians dead and alive charged forward in lightning charge to reconquer their dominion of freedom. The grasses bent in a light wail at the wind of their passage. The emotion of the intense silence was prodigious.

What was fleeing above my head? The clouds and the stars were fleeing, they were fleeing: while from the shaken black Pampas that fled now and then in the savage sweep of the wind at times stronger at times fainter at times like a distant iron roar: now and then a call went to the deepest melancholy of the wanderer: . . . from the manes of the shaken grasses as

profonda dell'eterno errante per la Pampa riscossa come un richiamo che fuggiva lugubre.

Ero sul treno in corsa: disteso sul vagone sulla mia testa fuggivano le stelle e i soffi del deserto in un fragore ferreo: incontro le ondulazioni come di dorsi di belve in agguato: selvaggia, nera, corsa dai venti la Pampa che mi correva incontro per prendermi nel suo mistero: che la corsa penetrava, penetrava con la velocità di un cataclisma: dove un atomo lottava nel turbine assordante nel lugubre fracasso della corrente irresistibile.

Dov'ero? Io ero in piedi: Io ero in piedi: sulla pampa nella corsa dei venti, in piedi sulla pampa che mi volava incontro: per prendermi nel suo mistero! Un nuovo sole mi avrebbe salutato al mattino! Io correvo tra le tribù indiane? Od era la morte? Od era la vita? E mai, mi parve che mai quel treno non avrebbe dovuto arrestarsi: nel mentre che il rumore lugubre delle ferramenta ne commentava incomprensibilmente il destino. Poi la stanchezza nel gelo della notte, la calma. Lo stendersi sul piatto di ferro, il concentrarsi nelle strane costellazioni fuggenti tra lievi veli argentei: e tutta la mia vita tanto simile a quella corsa cieca fantastica infrenabile che mi tornava alla mente in flutti amari e veementi.

La luna illuminava ora tutta la Pampa deserta e uguale in un silenzio profondo. Solo a tratti nuvole scherzanti un po' colla luna, ombre improvvise correnti per la prateria e ancora una chiarità immensa e strana nel gran silenzio.

La luce delle stelle ora impassibili era più misteriosa sulla terra infinitamente deserta: una più vasta patria il destino ci aveva dato: un più dolce calor naturale era nel mistero della terra selvaggia e buona. Ora assopito io seguivo degli echi di un'emozione meravigliosa, echi di vibrazioni sempre più lontane: fin che pure cogli echi l'emozione meravigliosa si spense. E allora fu che nel mio intorpidimento finale io sentii con delizia l'uomo nuovo nascere: l'uomo nascere riconciliato colla natura ineffabilmente dolce e terribile: deliziosamente e orgogliosamente succhi vitali nascere alle profondità dell'essere: fluire dalle profondità della terra: il cielo come la terra in alto, misterioso, puro, deserto dall'ombra, infinito.

Mi ero alzato. Sotto le stelle impassibili, sulla terra infinitamente deserta e misteriosa, dalla sua tenda l'uomo libero tendeva le braccia al cielo infinito non deturpato dall'ombra di Nessun Dio.

if to the deepest melancholy of the eternal wanderer across the shaken Pampas rose a call that fled mournfully.

I was on the speeding train: stretched out on the car the stars above and the gusts from the desert were fleeing in an iron roar above my head: the undulations coming toward us like the backs of beasts in ambush: savage, black, swept by winds the Pampas racing toward me to take me into their mystery: that the rushing train was penetrating, penetrating with the speed of a cataclysm: where an atom struggled in the deafening whirlwind in the mournful din of the irresistible current.

Where was I? I was standing: I was standing: on the pampas in the rushing winds, standing on the pampas that were flying toward me: to take me into their mystery! A new sun would greet me in the morning! Was I speeding among the Indian tribes? Or was it death? Or was it life? And never, it seemed to me the train would never stop: while the mournful clanking commented incomprehensibly on its destiny. Then the weariness in the cold of the night, the calm. Stretching out on the iron flooring, concentrating on the strange constellation fleeing among light silver veils: and my whole life so similar to that blind fantastic irresistible rush coming back in bitter vehement streams.

The moon now lighted the whole Pampas, deserted and even, in a deep silence. Only some clouds playing with the moon now and then, sudden shadows scurrying across the grassland and still a strange immense brightness in the great silence.

The light of the now impassive stars was more mysterious on the infinitely deserted earth: a vaster homeland had destiny given us: a sweeter natural warmth was in the mystery of the savage good earth. Now I was drowsily following the echoes of a wonderful emotion, echoes of ever more distant vibrations: until the wonderful emotion died out along with the echoes. And it was then that in my final torpor I felt with delight the new man being born: man being born reconciled with nature, ineffably sweet and frightening: delightfully and proudly vital juices being born to the depths of being: flowing from the depths of the earth: the sky like the earth high above, mysterious, pure, deserted of shadows, infinite.

I had stood up. Under the impassive stars, on the earth infinitely deserted and mysterious, from his tent free man extended his arms toward the infinite sky not defiled by the shadow of Any God.

Buenos Aires

Il bastimento avanza lentamente
Nel grigio del mattino tra la nebbia
Sull'acqua gialla d'un mare fluviale
Appare la città grigia e velata.
Si entra in un porto strano. Gli emigranti
Impazzano e inferocian accalcandosi
Nell'aspra ebbrezza d'imminente lotta.
Da un gruppo d'italiani ch'è vestito
In un modo ridicolo alla moda
Bonearense si gettano arance
Ai paesani stralunati e urlanti.
Un ragazzo dal porto leggerissimo
Prole di libertà, pronto allo slancio
Li guarda colle mani nella fascia
Variopinta ed accenna ad un saluto.
Ma ringhiano feroci gli italiani.

Buenos Aires

The ship advances slowly
Through the gray morning fog
On the yellow water of a fluvial sea
The gray veiled city appears.
We enter a strange port. The emigrants
Go wild, grow fierce, jostling
In the bitter thrill of an imminent struggle.
A group of Italians dressed
Ridiculously in Buenos Aires
Style throw oranges
At their bewildered, shouting countrymen.
From the port a light-limbed boy
Son of freedom ready to spring
Watches them with his hands tucked in a multicolored
Sash and makes as if to greet them.
But the Italians snarl back savagely.

→ Alfredo Bufano (1895–1950)

Alfredo Bufano was born in Apulia on August 21, 1895, and died in San Rafael, in the province of Mendoza at the foot of the Andes, on October 31, 1950. Bufano never wanted to reveal the name of his Italian birthplace because he wanted to be an Argentine poet in every sense of the word. He claimed to have been born in Guaymallén, in Mendoza, and only in a few rare poems does he refer vaguely to his true origins elsewhere. Nonetheless, his interest in the language and literature of his motherland is clearly reflected in some of his writings, such as in the essay "Misticos italianos de la Edad Media" (Italian Mystics of the Middle Ages). His translation into Spanish of the "Lauda donna del paradiso o Pianto della Madonna" (Lady of Heaven, or, The Lament of the Virgin) by Jacopone da Todi is exemplary. For ten years he wore the Franciscan habit because his mother vowed to have him do so if he survived a very severe illness. While working as a shoeshine boy and later in a bookstore in Buenos Aires, he discovered his poetic vocation and went on to publish his first book of poetry, *El viajero indeciso* (*The Undecided Traveler*), in 1917.

Bufano was a contributor to well-known journals such as *Caras y Caretas* and *Mundo Argentino*. He married Ada Giusti and had five children. Upon returning to San Rafael, he was given a position as a road inspector in 1923; later, he was appointed professor of Spanish, literature, and geography at the Escuela Normal. His poetic and literary production is contained in some thirty books. Among them are *Poemas de provincia* (*Provincial Poems*, 1922), *Tierra de huarpes* (*Land of the Huarpes*, 1926), *Poemas de la nieve* (*Snow Poems*, 1928), *Valle de la soledad* (*Valley of Solitude*, 1930), *Romancero* (*Ballad*, 1932), *Infancia bajo la luna* (*Childhood Under the Moon*, 1940), and *Mendoza la de mi canto* (*Mendoza of My Song*, 1943). His poetry is essentially descriptive and praises nature. Master of a remarkable rhythmic ability, Bufano made use of all the lyrical devices of Spanish poetry, in particular the couplet. He requested burial in the Villa 25 de Mayo, just a few miles from San Rafael, under a rough stone with the inscription "Poet, sower, and settler."[2]

Égloga

da *El viajero indeciso*

En estos melancólicos crepúsculos,
cuando la soledad, hecha un anillo
de suave cielo azul, me envuelve el alma,
pláceme hablar con estas gentes recias
de violento perfil y ojos serenos,
claros a fuerza de mirar las nubes,
dolor y gloria de sus vidas rústicas.
—"¿Cómo van esas viñas, don Giuseppe?"
—"*Fin ora, bene; l'uva è già al suo punto,
e la raccoglieremo in questi giorni,
se Iddio lo permette.*"
El rostro firme
se aclara todo con el pensamiento
de la cosecha opima. Hay en sus ojos
una dulzura inusitada y honda
cuando mira a lo lejos los viñedos
inmóviles y grávidos.
—"¿Y el precio, don Giuseppe?"
El ceño arruga
y dice en su sonora lengua itálica:
—"*Ho lavorato assai, signor Bufano!
Quindi, vedrò che tutte le fatiche
sian premiate.*"
—"¡Muy bien hecho, amigo!
¡No en vano usted se pasa aquí los años
en dura lucha con la tierra!"
—"*È vero!*"
Y vuelve a contemplar la viña ubérrima
como si fuera una mujer querida.
Brilla el lucero sobre las montañas,
y hay en los aires un frescor de pámpano.

Idyll

from *The Indecisive Traveler*

In these melancholy crepuscules,
when solitude, forming a ring
of gentle blue sky, envelops my soul,
I find pleasure in speaking with these robust folk
with violent profiles and serene eyes,
whose clarity comes from watching clouds pass by,
the pain and glory of their rustic lives.
—"How are the vines doing, don Giuseppe?"
—*"Fin ora, bene; l'uva è già al suo punto,*
e la raccoglieremo in questi giorni,
se Iddio lo permette."[3]
His firm visage
brightens up with the thought
of the excellent crop. In his eyes there is
a sweetness deep and rare
when he looks into the distance at
the immobile and laden vineyards.
—"And the price, don Giuseppe?"
His frown wrinkles
and he says in his rich italic tongue:
—*"Ho lavorato assai, signor Bufano!*
Quindi, vedrò che tutte le fatiche
sian premiate."[4]
—"Very well done, friend!
It is not in vain that you pass your years here
struggling with the land!"
—*"È vero!"*[5]
And he returns to contemplating the abundant vine
as if it were a beloved woman.
A star glistens above the mountains,
and the fresh scent of pompano fills the air.

El Viajero

Dove son? dove fui? che m'addolora?
Leopardi

da *Valle de la soledad*

Dove son? E dove fui? Se pregunta el viajero,
¿desde qué mundos vengo, y hacia qué mundos voy?
Una voz le responde: ¡prosigue tu sendero,
peregrino, prosigue, mañana igual qué hoy!
Dove son? dove fui? El viajero repite
absorta la mirada en el pálido azul;
otra voz a lo lejos: qué el viajero medite,
sin hacer las preguntas del hebreo Saúl.
Los caminos se abren como sierpes de plata
tenuemente alumbrados por un alba escarlata
y el viajero repite su tenaz obsesión:
Dove son? dove fui? entre heroico y sumiso,
y contestan las voces al viajero indeciso
como un eco siniestro: *Dove fui! dove son!*

The Traveler

Dove son? dove fui? che m'addolora?
Leopardi

from *The Valley of Solitude*

Dove son? E dove fui?[6] The traveler asks himself,
From what worlds have I come, and to which worlds do I go?
A voice replies to him: continue along your path,
pilgrim, continue on, tomorrow is the same as today!
Dove son? dove fui? Repeats the traveler
his glance captivated by the pallid blue;
another voice in the distance: may the traveler meditate,
without posing the same questions as the Hebrew Saul.
The paths open up like silver serpents
faintly lit by a scarlet sunrise
and the traveler repeats his tenacious obsession:
Dove son? dove fui? between heroic and submissive,
and the voices answer the indecisive traveler
like a sinister echo: *Dove fui! dove son!*

⤳ Severino Di Giovanni (1901–1931)

Severino Di Giovanni was born in Chieti on March 17, 1901, and died before a firing squad in Buenos Aires on January 31, 1931. He had hoped to become a schoolteacher but was unable to finish his studies. Still, he was able to teach in Italy until the fascist government forced him to emigrate in 1923, when he went to Argentina and earned a living by selling flowers in Ituzaingó, a town west of Buenos Aires. He later married, fathered four children, and began to work as a typographer in Morón. He read Nietzsche and the other great philosophers of freedom, socialists or anarchists like Proudhon, Bakunin, Reclus, Kropotkin, Malatesta, and Stirner, and promoted, through his journal *Culmine*, individual anarchism and a head-on struggle against fascism. At the time of Sacco and Vanzetti, he worked with all his might for the campaign to free the two anarchists. What he writes in the union newspapers, anarchist publications (*Antorcha, Avvenire, La Protesta della Fora, Federación Obrera de la República Argentina*) and his own paper alerts the Argentinian police and the Italian embassy, as well as the US embassy in Buenos Aires.

After several robberies and assassination attempts, he became the most wanted anarchist in the country. He then met the American Josefina Scarfò, nicknamed "Fina," a sixteen-year-old young woman and sister of the Scarfò brothers, also anarchists. He asked them to help him find an apartment where he could hide. They offered him a room in their own home. Love between Fina and Severino flared up and was documented in letters they wrote to one another in their native languages. In one of his, Severino wrote: "Before I lived my hours like Tantalus, and now, today, in the eternal today that binds us, I experience, without ever being satisfied, all the harmonious love sentiments dear to Shelley and George Sand." On August 19, 1928, he wrote, "I would like to express myself in your idiom, to sing each moment of my life the sweet songs of my soul, to convey to you the throbbing of my heart, the delicate forms of my thought that shall never give *finis* to its elegy." Both the letters and the poems that Severino wrote to Fina were seized by the federal police of Buenos Aires and kept for more than sixty years before they were given back to Fina in 1999.

Di Giovanni believed that poetry, literature, singing, music and art happen when certain individuals emerge, those "who throw their soul into the burning and tumultuous battle that people sustain in order to redeem and better themselves." He believed that "the artist is someone whose heart beats with the rest of humanity, who interprets the needs and the aspirations of the people, collects their sufferings and their hopes." Contemporary views of Di Giovanni see in his transparent ideology not only a militant artist, but also a "militant of poetry and human sensibility." Oscar D'Angelo states that "in many of the writings of Severino Di Giovanni, beneath his political assertions lies a fine poetic prose. He is a passionate anarchist, violent and headstrong, very intelligent, capable of expressing the most profound sentiments with incisive and beautiful metaphors." The following two poems from his newspaper, *Culmine*, can attest to his poetic stature.[7]

Urlìo Notturno

da *Culmine*

Finita la festa di luce, quel crepuscolo ebbro di rosso se ne andava
lontano nelle profonde voragini del suo impero.
Il sole folle.
Se ne andava, lontano, lontano.
E con esso la festa che mi aveva riscaldato di entusiasmi e di promesse.
E nell'ebbrezza del suo rosso, gli mandai il mio ultimo addio con lo
sguardo, mentre con trionfi ingressava nell'ampia voragine di fuoco.

Se n'è andato!
Oh voracità non mai sazia di nostalgia!
Oh disperazione infinita di tanta munificenza sfuggita!
Oh strazio immenso di amore che stringi in attimi e ad attimi lasci!
Lasci bramosi di te, ardenti nel desiderio del tuo soggiorno fugace.
E così insoddisfatto e assetato mi abbandoni nella sera con il solo
ricordo dell'aria infocata che soffoca col profumo opprimente.
Ma anche il tuo profumo lentamente svanisce, mentre profondo e
maestoso viene la notte. E sento con la sua venuta al luccichio d'un
infinito stuolo di lucciole fosforee, mille canti che giungono al mio
orecchio come mille urli. E si accentuano, sibilano, stormiscono,
sbattono crepitando in urli maggiori e in musica notturna.
Urlìo notturno e per la mia nostalgia vorace e disperata l'eterna musica
notturna.
Musica notturna!
Pianto del creato e riso scrosciante di venti gementi!
Oh quanta febbre arde nel tuo immenso oscuro!
Oh quanta gioia fai godere nel tuo dolore di silenzi!
Oh musica notturna!
Urlìo delle tenebre!

Al calore soffocante della festa solare della mia gioventù di flussioni, a
questa notte succeduta fra il fresco dell'aria mossa e la rugiada che
imperlava di umide goccioline l'erba, mi dava il sollievo ristoratore e
con slancio cantai la mia canzone.

Nocturnal Howl

from *Summit*

Having completed its fest of lights, that drunk red crepuscule went far
away into the profound abyss of its empire.
The mad sun.
It went away, far, far.
And with it the fest that had warmed me with enthusiasm and promises.
And in the drunken state of its redness, I sent it one last goodbye with
a glance, as it entered triumphantly into the ample abyss of fire.

It went away!
Oh voracity never sated of nostalgia!
Oh infinite desperation of so much escaped generosity!
Oh immense torment of love that you grip for moments and in
moments let go!
Leave them longing for you, in ardent desire of your fleeting sojourn.
And so unsatisfied and thirsty you abandon me in the evening with the
lone memory of the red-hot air that suffocates with oppressive scent.
But even your scent vanishes slowly, as night arrives profound and
majestic. And I can sense its arrival from the twinkling of an infinite
crowd of phosphorescent fireflies, a thousand songs that reach my
ear like a thousand howls. And they intensify, hiss, rustle, flap about
crackling in greater howls and nocturnal music.
Nocturnal howl and for my voracious and desperate nostalgia the
eternal nocturnal music.
Nocturnal music!
Cry of creation and thunderous laughter of groaning winds!
Oh how much fever burns in your immense obscurity!
Oh how much joy you pass on in your pain of silences!
Oh nocturnal music!
Howl of the darkness!

In the suffocating heat of the solar fest of my turbulent youth, on this
night that took place between the freshness of stirring air and the
dew that beaded the grass with damp little drops, it gave me
refreshing relief and with enthusiasm I sang my song.

Canzone libera, che univasi alla musica degli urli delle tenebre.

Cantai:

Oh notte, di misteri, di consolazioni e di silenzio che mi pesi dentro
del mio spirito.

Il tuo pesare come un corpo di bella fanciulla, che si afferma,
s'immedesima e lascia un'infinita dimenticanza.

E il mio spirito di te sente il dolore, che poi mi trapassa nelle carni.

E pesa.

Come corpo di bella fanciulla.

E mi dai voluttuosamente il possesso di te.

Oh notte di misteri!

Oh notte di silenzi, senza la luna pallida e luci di stelle.

Ma solo.

Oh mia notte oscura, solo, senza chiari e nel tuo possesso mi dai
dolcezze e tormenti.

Con momenti di desideri lievi come un'aureola!

E con la mia canzone cantavano anch'essi i segreti e misteriosi cantori
della notte!

E la loro canzone era l'eco di un coro melodioso che invogliava
maggiormente il mio canto.

Coro di urli, battiti e crepitii di rami schiantati e scrosciati dal vento,
artefice del canto eterno, che mestamente nel dolore mi erano
compagni.

Cantiamo ancora e mescoliamo le mie lagrime di contento, alle vostre
linfe succose di dolore che ormai la vasta notte è nostra, come
nostro è il velo nero che adorna le nostre bare aspettanti la lieta
resurrezione.

Resurrezione di vita!

Lieti di così immenso possesso il nostro tormentoso dolore si
tramutava celere in dolcezze infinite.

E il possesso grandioso della notte che tramutava il tormento in
dolcezza, mi cancellava la nostalgia che ruggiva nel petto e spegneva
la sete della disperazione.

Alle forze arcane di cori eterni, rimasi ad essi come alla notte, e mi
esultai con essi, amando le tenebrose compagne che mi donavano il
vigore di nuove conquiste.

Free song that bound itself to the music of the howls of darkness.
I sang:
Oh night of mysteries, of consolation and silence, within me you
weigh down upon my spirit.
You weigh down like the body of a beautiful girl that asserts itself,
makes itself one and leaves behind a forgotten infinity.
And my spirit that feels your pain that passes right through to my
flesh.
It weighs down.
Like the body of a beautiful girl.
And voluptuously you give me possession of you.
Oh night of mysteries!
Oh night of silences, without pallor of moon or starlight.
But alone.
Oh obscure night of mine, alone, with no moonlight and in your grasp
you give me sweetness and torment.
With moments of soft wishes like a halo!

And along with my song so too sang the secret and mysterious singers
of the night!
And their song was the echo of a melodious chorus that encouraged
even more my song.
Chorus of howls, throbs and cracklings of branches torn off and
crashed down by the wind, author of the eternal song, sadly they
were my companions in pain.
We still sing and mix together my tears of happiness with your juicy
saps of pain, for by now the vast night is ours, as is ours the black
veil that adorns our coffins awaiting the happy resurrection.
Resurrection of life!
Happy to control something so immense our tormenting pain turned
quickly into infinite sweetness.

And the grandiose control of the night that turned torment into
sweetness rid me of the nostalgia that roared within my breast and
extinguished my desperate thirst.
With those arcane forces of eternal choruses, I stayed with them as
with the night, and I rejoiced with them in adoration of the
mysterious companions who granted me the vigor of new
conquests.

Esultante, scordai tutto e quando il sole volle riprendermi col suo albeggiare d'oro mi dispersi nel grembo interminabile del novello sogno conquistato e non volli più vedere le sue danze di raggi e di luci.

While rejoicing I forgot everything, and when the sun returned to consume me with its golden dawn I lost myself in the interminable womb of my newly conquered dream and no longer wanted to see its dances of rays and lights.

Inno alla dynamite
(Frammento)

Gino Lucetti,[8] nome bandiera, fiaccola agitata, eroismo incitante, anima di ribellione, anima dinamitarda, anima nostra, anima anarchica! . . .

Nostro, nostro, nostro!

Ci hai dato tutto, vita, febbre, azione, dinamite!

Vita, perché essa deve essere tale, goduta, aspirata, bevuta fino all'amaro, a sorsi di cicuta e fiele, a sorsi di odio e di amore; l'odio al liberticida e l'amore alla

libertà. Libertà, che è la vita stessa.

Febbre, febbre e delirio, pazzia, pur che si infranga l'idolo! Febbre e spasimo, ferocia, pur che s'annienti la fiera! Febbre d'esaltazione, di distruzione, pur che sia salva la specie umana! La specie degli umani ribelli!

Azione, che fa temere, impallidire, tremare, spaventare, fuggire dal panico, ma che come fulmine raggiunge, annichilisce! Azione, poesia del maschio, frutto di femmina, suprema divinizzazione dell'uomo. Azione: ribellione!

Dinamite, potenza del diseredato, potenza della miseria, potenza della fame, potenza del tormento. Dinamite, pallore del tiranno! Dinamite, squarciatrice dei riempiti vampiri! Dinamite nostra arma, arma anarchica, forte voce che lacera i timpani più incartapecoriti!

Tu meriti il nostro più fiorito pensiero, tu meriti di essere colto in un giardino d'elevazione spirituale in bocciolo e poi lasciata aprire come rosa nel cuore della tirannide.

Hymn to Dynamite
(Fragment)

Gino Lucetti,[9] flag name, agitated torch, inciting heroism, soul of
rebellion, soul of dynamite, soul of ours, anarchist soul! . . .
Ours, ours, ours!
You gave us everything, life, fever, action, dynamite!
Life, because that's how it has to be, enjoyed, inhaled, drunk until
bitter, in sips of hemlock and bile, in sips of hatred and love; hatred
to liberticide and love to liberty. Liberty, which is life itself.
Fever, fever and delirium, madness, provided it smashes the idol!
Fever and spasm, ferocity, provided it annihilates the beast! Fever of
exaltation, of destruction, provided it saves the human species! The
species of rebellious humans!
Action that makes one fear, turn pale, tremble, become frightened, flee
from panic, but that like lightning reaches out, annihilates! Action,
masculine poetry, feminine fruit, supreme divination of man.
Action: rebellion!
Dynamite, power of the deprived, power of misery, power of hunger,
power of torment. Dynamite, pallor of the tyrant! Dynamite,
slayer of
filled vampires! Dynamite our weapon, anarchic weapon, strong voice
that lacerates the most shriveled eardrums!
You deserve our most blossomed thought, you deserve to be placed in
a garden of spiritual elevation as a bud left to open like a rose in the
heart of tyranny.

⇢ *J. Rodolfo Wilcock (1919–1978)*

J. Rodolfo Wilcock was born in Buenos Aires of an English father and an Italian-Swiss mother on April 17, 1919, and died in Lubriano (Velletri) on March 17, 1978. Known as one of the finer Argentinian poets, he was inspired by the English romantics and composed six volumes of poetry: *Libro de poemas y canciones* (*Book of Poems and Songs*, 1940), *Ensayos de poesía lírica* (*Essays of Lyric Poetry*, 1946), *Persecuciones del las musas menores* (*Pursuits of the Minor Muses*, 1945), *Paseo sentimental* (*Sentimental Walk*, 1945), *Los hermosos días* (*The Beautiful Days*, 1946), and *Sexto* (*Sixth*, 1953).[10] His various stages of life granted him a number of different profiles, including math student, telephone solicitor, prizewinning poet, salaried hermit in the desert, translator, adversary of and contributor to the cultural enterprise, simple professor, and casual traveler. As a literary figure, he frequented the circle of Borges, Bioy Casares, and Silvina Ocampo.

In 1967, Wilcock wrote about his experience as a member of the Borges circle in the following terms: "These three names, these three people were the constellation and the trinity from whose gravitational field in a special way I drew that light tendency noticeable in my life and in my works to rise above, albeit in a modest way, the grey level of my origins." Borges represented the total genius, idle and lazy; Bioy Casares represented active intelligence; and Silvina Ocampo was the sybil and the sorceress who reminded both of them, in her actions and words, of the strangeness and mystery of the universe. "Unknowing spectator of such a show, I was forever fascinated by it and preserve the indescribable memory of one who had the mystical happiness of seeing and hearing the play of lights and sounds that makes up a certain divine trinity."

Wilcock migrated to Italy in 1958 and settled in Rome, where he decided "to change language and readership . . . and began to write in a sort of Italian." Roberto Calasso, one of the few Italian critics interested in Wilcock's work, has said: "He knew, as very few do, not to depend on anyone or on the world. When he began to write in Italian he succeeded quickly in transmitting to the language that quality typical of his gesture, of his demeanor. Thus his Italian is like a little tropical island, laden with ancient thick vegetation, caught in the current of a river infected by industrial waste, flowing in a lean and haughty land. On that little island, very few, until now, have tried to set foot." Giorgio Luti has noted that Wilcock was a poet of "fine crepuscular sensibility, a narrator who showed an eclectic capacity which was inclined to blend an exasperated realism with fantastic tonalities, irony, cruelty, a sense of surprise and an erudite taste, to the point of being clearly eccentric."

Vivere è percorrere il mondo

da *Luoghi comuni*

Vivere è percorrere il mondo
attraversando ponti di fumo;
quando si è giunti dall'altra parte
che importa se i ponti precipitano
Per arrivare in qualche luogo
bisogna trovare un passaggio
e non fa niente se scesi dalla vettura
si scopre che questa era un miraggio.

To Live Is to Traverse the World

from *Common Places*

To live is to traverse the world
crossing over bridges of smoke;
when you reach the other side
what does it matter if the bridges fall.
To arrive in some place
you must find a ride,
and it's no big deal to get out of the car
and discover it was just a mirage.

A mio figlio

da *I tre stati*

Abbi fiducia nella vita
e non nelle ideologie;
non ascoltare i missionari
di quest'illusione o quell'altra.
Ricorda che c'è una sola cosa
affermativa, l'invenzione;
il sistema invece è caratteristico
della mancanza d'immaginazione.
Ricorda che tutto accade
a caso e che niente dura,
il che non ti vieta di fare
un disegno sul vetro appannato,
né di cantare qualche nota
semplice quando sei contento;
può darsi che sia un bel disegno,
che la canzone sia bella:
ma questo non ha certo importanza,
basta che piacciano a te.
Un giorno morrai; non fa niente,
poiché saranno gli altri ad accorgersene.

To My Son

from *The Three States*

Have faith in life
and not in ideologies;
don't listen to missionaries
of this or that illusion.
Remember that there's only one affirmative
thing, invention;
yet characteristic of the system is
a lack of imagination.
Remember that everything happens
by chance and that nothing lasts,
which does not forbid you from making
a drawing on misted glass,
nor from singing some simple
notes when you're happy;
it might be that the drawing is beautiful,
might be that the song is beautiful:
but this is of course not important,
that they are pleasing to you is enough.
One day you will die; it's nothing,
since it will be the others who will notice.

Undici ministri giocano al calcio

da *I tre stati*

Undici ministri giocano al calcio
con gli undici ministri dell'altra squadra:
vecchi ostinati, giocano malissimo,
ma nel pallone è il sorcio della storia.
Su scalini che salgono alle nuvole
si agitano dimentiche le nazioni:
dentro il pallone voltola la loro sorte.
Gli spettatori intanto copulano, partoriscono,
riversano bambini lungo i gradini,
ma i ventidue vecchi giocano a pallone
con le stampelle o seduti in poltrone,
fra le urla e le esplosioni e i bradisismi.
Un gatto immenso dirige il loro gioco,
di quando in quando leccandosi la pelliccia
pronto a balzare sul topo del pallone.

Eleven Ministers Playing Soccer

from *The Three States*

Eleven ministers are playing soccer
with the eleven ministers of the other team:
stubborn old men, they play so poorly,
but within the ball is the mouse of history.
On steps that climb up to the clouds
they stir about oblivious of nations:
inside the ball tumbles their destiny.
In the meantime the spectators copulate, give birth,
dump babies all along the curbs,
but the twenty-two old men kick the ball
with crutches or sitting in armchairs,
amid the screams and explosions and bradyseisms.
An immense cat conducts their game,
from time to time licking its fur
ready to pounce on the mouse in the ball.

Il mendicante

da *Poesie inedite*

Vicino a Roma, sulla Via Appia
un mendicante si lagnava:

"Mi hanno scacciato dalla città,
e da solo non posso tornare."

Le automobili passavano
ma nessuna si fermava.

"Se mi offrissero un aiuto
li vestirei di velluto."

Era sul ciglio della strada
ma non poteva camminare.

"Se mi portassero in ospedale
li farei tutti industriali."

Passò la guardia stradale
e gli ordinò di spostarsi.

"Voi cercate una donna bella,
io so dove abita Elena."

Passò un prete e lo benedì
e aggiunse qualcosa in latino.

"Se mi date da mangiare
vi farò vedere il mare."

Ormai si era fatto sera
e l'uomo si accasciò sull'erba.

"Se avessi i gioielli che ho dato
non mi avrebbero abbandonato."

Pover'uomo, non sapeva
che il mare non esisteva,

The Beggar

from *Unpublished Poems*

Near Rome, along the Via Appia
a beggar was griping:

"They chased me away from the city,
and I can't go back alone."

Cars were passing by
but not one of them stopped.

"If they were to offer me help
I'd clothe them in velvet."

He was at the edge of the road
but could not walk.

"If they were to bring me to the hospital
I'd make them all industrialists."

A street guard passed by
and told him to move.

"You're looking for a beautiful woman,
I know where Elena lives."

A priest passed by and blessed him
and added something in Latin.

"If you feed me
I'll show you the sea."

Evening had come by now
and the man collapsed on the grass.

"Had I still those jewels I gave
they wouldn't have abandoned me."

Poor man, he did not know
that the sea did not exist,

né i gioielli, né il velluto;
era vissuto un minuto
e chissà che aveva sognato
in quel minuto sprecato.

nor jewels, nor velvet;
he had lived a minute
and who knows what he had dreamed
in that wasted minute.

Ma io mi sciolgo davanti a uno snack-bar ...

da *Italienisches Liederbuch*

Ma io mi sciolgo davanti a uno snack-bar
se solo so che ci sei dentro tu,
e ho fatto verniciare d'oro il telefono
perché una volta mi hai chiamato tu.
Perciò ho deciso di regalarti gli Oceani,
fuori si intende dalle acque territoriali,
l'Atlantico, il Pacifico, l'Indiano,
e insieme a queste ingenti masse d'acqua
salata l'Artico e i Mari del Sud
con tutte le isole nuove disabitate,
che da lontano sembrano così verdi
per quanto, immagino, saranno piene di vipere.

But I'll Break Down in Tears Before a Snack Bar . . .

from *Italian Songbook*

But I'll break down in tears before a snack bar
if only I know that you're inside,
and I had my telephone painted gold
because you called me one time.
So I decided to gift you the Oceans,
not including of course territorial waters,
the Atlantic, the Pacific, the Indian,
and with these enormous masses of salted
water the Arctic and the South Seas
with all the new uninhabited islands,
that seen from afar seem to be so green
in so far as, I imagine, they are full of vipers.

Eh no, voi paladini, che state a fare

Eh no, voi paladini, che state a fare
e personaggi veloci della storia
che vi perdete la cima della scala
e non rendete onore a chi la onora?
Soltanto gli Hohenstaufen dovranno farlo?
Venite a Roma, cavalieri d'Artù,
prodi di Orlando, mussulmani rabbiosi,
voi tutti che viaggiate sempre a cavallo,
re, masnadieri, paggi, granmaestri,
se intasate la strada non fa niente,
mongoli di Samarcanda, vandali sozzi,
crociati del Baltico, mòravi, sciiti,
e voi conquistatori delle Indie,
predoni di Bahrein e di Macao,
a mezzanotte voglio vedervi tutti
fare le corse intorno al Colosseo,
fare un torneo, o quel che preferite,
per far vedere come era rozzo il mondo
finché non è calata questa luce
che più mi abbaglia quanto più mi rischiara,
questa improbabile mutazione umana,
questa fonte energetica inesauribile,
questa gnosi, o sophia, o trascendenza,
questa persona fragile e sicura
che abita purtroppo così lontano.

Hey No, You Knights, What Are You Doing

Hey no, you knights, what are you doing
and swift characters of history
who've strayed from the stairway's summit
and no longer honor those who honor it?
Should only the Hohenstaufen do so?
Come to Rome, knights of Arthur,
brave men of Orlando, raging Muslims,
all of you riding always on horseback,
kings, scoundrels, pages, grandmasters,
it doesn't matter if you block up the street,
Mongols of Samarkand, filthy vandals,
Baltic crusaders, Moravians, Shiites,
and you conquerors of the Indies,
marauders from Bahrein and Macao,
at midnight I want to see you all
racing around the Colosseum,
have a tournament, or whatever you prefer,
to show how coarse the world was
before this light came down
that deludes me as much as it makes me brighter,
this improbable human mutation,
this inexhaustible font of energy,
this gnosis, or wisdom, or transcendence,
this fragile and certain person
who lives unfortunately so far away.

✈ Antonio Aliberti (1938–2000)

Antonio Aliberti was born in Barcellona Pozzo di Gotto (Messina, Italy) on December 15, 1938, and died in Buenos Aires on July 29, 2000. He had arrived in Buenos Aires on November 1, 1951.

Poet, essayist, literary critic, and freelance journalist, Aliberti wrote nearly twenty books of poetry in Spanish. In Italian, he wrote only one: *Nessun maggior dolor* (*No Greater Sorrow*), published by Ediciones La Luna Que in Buenos Aires in 1998.[11] He also edited the first complete collection in Spanish of Dino Campana's *Canti orfici* (1986). Many influences are present in Aliberti's poetry, from the neocrepuscular to the romantic and the realistic. Aliberti learned Italian in Argentina, and it was in Buenos Aires that he began to love the literature of Italy. As Aliberti himself stated: "In these poems there is the heart-rending story of a severed man who witnessed his own uncertainty, yet was able to be integrated into Argentinian life and was able to undertake the career of a writer, translator and literary critic sustained entirely by Argentinian, Latin American and Italian literature. It is not a new story, it is indeed the old story of the emigrant who is that little boy leaning on the rails of a ship: he knows and does not know, but perceives." Aliberti observed that his life took shape between two Souths: "My love is double, but I carry within me that child who died back in Barcellona in Sicily at age twelve. Beyond this, there is also the mark of a race tossed about that assails me and finds its settlement in Argentina. This, the destiny of a little man from the South."

Partenza

da *Nessun maggior dolore*

Cerca cerca . . .
Il mare è rosso
il cielo verde
la fiamma s'infiamma . . .
Chi ha perduto questo spillo di sole?
Io no
non ho perduto niente
nemmeno la nave:
il guscio di noce
partì
all'ora spaccata
Poi quell'uomo dal grosso coltello
aprì la ferita tra me e la sponda
Io stavo affacciato
non capivo niente
guardavo la gente che faceva addio
Alzai la mano
ma non capivo
Addio! Addio!—feci pur'io—
Oh Dio!

Departure

from *No Greater Sorrow*

Search, search . . .
The sea is red
the sky green
the flame inflames . . .
Who lost this sliver of sunlight?
Not me
I've lost nothing
not even the ship:
the cockleshell
departed
at the hour on the dot
Then that man with the huge knife
opened the wound between me and the shore
I was looking out at it
but understood nothing
I was watching the people as they said *addio*
I raised my hand
but did not understand
Addio! Addio!—so I said too—
Oh Dio!

Radici

Nessun maggior dolore
che spargere
le proprie ceneri per il mondo
se mondo non è l'impercettibile
sussulto dell'erba che cresce
con il fruscio dolce dell'infanzia.
Abbandonare
un certo modo di vivere e di morire
portando le fattezze di ognuno
per luoghi in cui le fattezze
non hanno lo specchio dove riflettersi
e vanno mute
smarrite come agnelli che non trovano le madri
e si allevano soltanto di crepe
in mezzo all'erba amara della solitudine.

Nessun maggior dolore
che crescere all'insaputa
la primigenia radice sola e sconsolata.
Tra due sponde
Ormai è chiusa la strada del ritorno
il morto giovinetto piange nella bara
il vecchio da lontano l'accarezza:
ma non avverrà l'incontro
è tempo d'ignominia
il mare è una beffa alla speranza.
Intanto uno e l'altro
si guardano dicendo:
"E t'amo, t'amo"—e si disperano.
Il sangue
Il sangue mio
l'ho abbandonato un giorno
in una strada del Sud
dietro il cancello.
Dall'altro Sud del mondo
a sparlare di me lo sento.

Roots

No greater sorrow
than to scatter
one's own ashes throughout the world
if the world is not the imperceptible
twitch of the grass that grows
with the sweet rustle of childhood.
To abandon
a certain manner of living and dying
carrying the features of each
through places where the features
have no mirror in which to reflect themselves
and go muted
lost like lambs that can't find their mothers
and they are brought up only on the cracks
amid the bitter grass of solitude.

No greater sorrow
than to grow without knowing
the initial, lonely and disconsolate root.
Between two shores
By now the way back is closed off
the dead young boy weeps in the coffin
the old man caresses him from afar:
but the encounter will not take place
it's the time of ignominy
the sea is a mockery of hope.
Meanwhile one and the other
look to each other and say:
"And I love you, I love you," and they despair.
The blood
My blood
I abandoned it one day
in a street in the South
behind the gate.
In the other South of the world
I can hear it badmouthing me.

Ed ha ragione.
Ormai diffida.
Poeta argentino
No ho mai abbandonata la Sicilia:
un giorno "mi portarono per mano."
Mai cercata l'avventura
volevo restare con i sassi del quartiere
in quella villetta
che c'insegnava a fischiare
le opere dei più grandi creatori.
Quello era il mio albero.
Invece sono diventato un poeta argentino.
Ma nessuno ci crede.
Le mie radici sono rimaste in mare:
saranno ancora naufraghe
in uno sterminare d'acque senza pace.

And it's right.
By now it's distrustful.
Argentine poet
I never abandoned Sicily:
one day "they brought me away by the hand."
Never having sought adventure
I wanted to stay with the stones of my neighborhood
in that little villa
that taught us to heckle
the works of the greatest creators.
That was my tree.
Instead I became an Argentine poet.
But no one believes it.
My roots have remained in the sea:
they shall stay there shipwrecked
in destructive waters with no peace.

NOTES

1. Dino Campana, *Canti Orfici* (Marradi: Tipografia Ravagli, 1914); *Canti Orfici*, ed. Enrico Falqui (Florence: Vallecchi, 1941); for the English translation of Campana's collected works, see Dino Campana, *Orphic Songs*, trans. Luigi Bonaffini (Boca Raton, Fla.: Bordighera Press, 2003). Other works include Dino Campana, *Inediti*, ed. Enrico Falqui (Florence: Vallecchi 1942); *Opere e contributi*, ed. Enrico Falqui (Florence: Vallecchi, 1973); *Carteggio con Sibilla Aleramo*, ed. Niccolò Gallo, 2 vols. (Florence: Vallecchi, 1973); *Le mie lettere sono fatte per essere bruciate*, ed. Gabriel Cacho Millet (Fiesole: Quaderni della Fondazione Primo Conti-All'Insegna del Pesce d'Oro, 1978); *Souvenir d'un pendu. Carteggio 1910–1931 con documenti inediti e rari*, ed. Gabriel Cacho Millet (Naples: Edizioni Scientifiche Italiane, 1985); *Taccuini*, ed. Fiorenza Ceragioli (Pisa: Scuola Normale Superiore, 1990); and *Sperso per il mondo. Autografi sparsi 1906–1918*, ed. Gabriel Cacho Millet (Florence: Leo S. Olschki, 2000); Carlo Pariani, Vite non romanzate di Dino Campana scrittore e di Evaristo Boncinelli scultore (Florence: Vallecchi, 1938) (reprinted as Carlo Pariani, *Vita non romanzata di Dino Campana scrittore*, ed. C. Ortesta [Milan: Guanda, 1978], then ed. T. Gianotti [Florence: Ponte alle Grazie, 1994]); Gabriel Cacho Millet, *Dino Campana fuorilegge* (Palermo: Novecento, 1985); Sibilla Aleramo and Dino Campana, *Un viaggio chiamato amore: Lettere*, ed. Bruna Conti (Rome: Editori Riuniti, 1987).

2. See María Angelica Cicherro de Pellegrino, *Alfredo R. Bufano, hombre y poeta* (Buenos Aires: Tinglado, 1945); Francisco Luis Bernárdez, "Bufano," *Clarin*, December 4, 1969; Luis Ricardo Casnati, "Bufano, el canto con sangre," *Mendoza*, November 2, 1980; Angel Bustelo, *Alfredo R. Bufano, el montañés que vio el mar* (Mendoza: La Tarde, 1981); Alfredo Bufano, *Poesías completas*, 3 vols., ed. Gloria Videla de Rivero (Buenos Aires: Ediciones Culturales Argentinas, 1983); Gabriel Cacho Millet, *El último Borges* (Madrid: Biblioteca Nueva, 2004).

3. "Thus far, well; the grapes are at their prime, / and we'll harvest them in the coming days, / if God permits."

4. "I have worked so much, Mr. Bufano! / So I will see that all of my toil / is rewarded."

5. "It's true!"

6. The epigram reads, "Where am I? Where have I been? What pains me?"

7. See Severino Di Giovanni, *Culmine* (Buenos Aires: Rivista anarchica, 1925–1931). See also Osvaldo Bayer, ed., *Severino Di Giovanni, el idealista de la violencia* (Buenos Aires: Galena, 1970; Buenos Aires: Planeta, 1998); Severino Di Giovanni, *Il pensiero e l'azione* (Florence: Gratis, 1993); and Maria Luisa Magagnoli, *Un caffè molto dolce* (Turin: Bollatti Boringhieri, 1996).

8. Gino Lucetti (1900–1943), antifascista, anarchico italiano, nato ad Avenza (Carrara). Giovanissimo, emigrò in Francia. L'11 settembre 1926, al Piazzale di Porta Pia, a Roma, lancia una bomba contro la macchina del Duce Benito Mussolini. L'artefatto rimbalza sull'automobile ed esplode a terra. Al commissariato dichiarò che non era rientrato dalla Francia "con un mazzo di fiori per Mussolini. . . . Ero intenzionato di servirmi anche della rivoltella qualora non avessi ottenuto il mio scopo con la bomba." L'autore del terzo attentato a Mussolini diventa "un nome bandiera" degli anarchici, come lo ricorda Di Giovanni nell'*Inno alla dinamite*. Un Tribunale speciale lo condannò a trent'anni di carcere. Liberato l'11 settembre 1943 dagli anglo-americani, sette giorni più tardi muore

a Ischia durante un bombardamento nazista. Vd. Riccardo Lucetti, *Gino Lucetti: l'attentato contro il Duce (11 settembre 1926)*, Cooperativa Tipolitografica Editrice, Carrara 2000.

9. Gino Lucetti (1900–43), an Italian antifascist and anarchist, was born in Avenza (Carrara). He emigrated to France very young. On September 11, 1926, in the square of Porta Pia in Rome, he threw a bomb against the car of Il Duce, Benito Mussolini. The device bounced off the car and exploded on the ground. At the police station he declared that he had not come back from France "with a bouquet of flowers for Mussolini. . . . I intended to use even the revolver in case I did not obtain my objective with the bomb." The author of the third attempt on Mussolini's life became a "standard bearer" for the anarchists, as Di Giovanni remembers Lucetti in the "Hymn to Dinamite." A special tribunal condemned him to thirty years in prison. Freed by the Allies on September 11, 1943, he died seven days later in Ischia during a German bombardment. See Riccardo Lucetti, *Gino Lucetti, l'attentato contro il Duce, 11 settembre 1926* (Carrara: Cooperativa Tipoligrafica Editrice, 2000).

10. In 1980, Adelphi of Milan printed all the poetic works of Wilcock in Italian, along with a selection of his Spanish verses translated into Italian, with the title *Poesie* (*Poems*). The verses contained in this anthology come from *Luoghi comuni* (*Common Places*) (Milan: Il Saggiatore, 1961); *I tre stati* (*The Three States*), a collection containing some poems published in *Intelligenza 2* (1963); and *Italienisches Liederbuch* (*Italian Songbook*) (Milan: Rizzoli, 1974).

11. Among Aliberti's works in Spanish are *El hombre y su cáliz* (*The Man and His Chalice*) (Buenos Aires: Grupo Arlt, 1973); *Cuestión de piel* (*A Question of Skin*) (Buenos Aires: Grupo Arlt, 1978); *Lejanas hogueras* (*Distant Bonfires*) (Buenos Aires: Anagrama, 1981); *Cuartos contiguos* (*Adjacent Rooms*) (Buenos Aires: Epsilon Editora, 1986); *Todos recordaron a Casandra* (*Everyone Remembered Cassandra*) (Buenos Aires: Editorial Plus Ultra, 1995); and *Incierta vocación* (*Uncertain Vocation*) (Buenos Aires: Editorial Plus Ultra, 1995).

Australia

Australia

GAETANO RANDO

Some sporadic examples aside, such as the poems of Raffaello Carboni in the mid-1800s and of Pietro Baracchi at the beginning of the 1900s, the writing of Italian Australian poetry can be historically categorized in two distinct, albeit discontinuous, periods—1922–40 and after 1947—that coincide with the substantial migration of Italians to Australia, and the aftermath of this migration. Texts produced in the first period appeared extensively in the Italian Australian press. For the most part, with the exception of Giliberto's *Frutto consolatore and Raggi d'idealismo (poesie, poemetti e dramma)* and Bisietta's *Fiore di Ghibli* and *Orme*, poetry in volume form began to appear systematically only at the end of the 1940s, a period that marks the beginning of mass Italian migration to Australia (three hundred and fifty thousand people between 1947 and 1972). Between 1947 and 2003, thirty-seven first-generation poets published eighty-five volumes of poetry: seventy-one in Italian (including some poetry in dialect); five in English; eight in Italian/English; and one in Italian, English, and French. Six second-generation poets have published fifteen volumes of poetry in English. Poetry by two hundred or so other writers has appeared in anthologies, journals, magazines, and newspapers (published both in Australia and Italy) as well as in eight anthologies dedicated exclusively to Italian Australian poetry, and a number of anthologies containing "mixed" genres.[1] There is also a considerable corpus of unpublished material. Numerous studies on Italian Australian poetry by first-generation poets have been produced,[2] and Rando La Cava has examined the oral dialect poetry of the *Eoliani.*

This pattern can be explained in part by the substantial increase of Italians in Australia (8,000 in 1921; 33,000 in 1947; and close to 300,000 in 1971), in part by the different sociodemographic parameters that marked the post-1947 Italian migration to Australia, and in part by the changes that the postwar migration phenomenon brought to Australian society,

77

culture and identity, changing it from a remote outpost of the British Empire to a semi-independent pluriethnic nation in the Asia Pacific region. Post-1947 Italian migration to Australia has been characterized by increased educational levels and a more varied socioeconomic base, compared to the prewar period. It included Italian middle-class intellectuals and professionally qualified persons who decided to leave what appeared to be a hopeless postwar environment for a land of new hope, Australia, where the somewhat slow and delayed acceptance of non-Angloceltic languages and cultures by some segments of Australian society was creating a more encouraging atmosphere for "ethnic" cultural expression.

The bulk of postwar Italian Australian poetry by first-generation writers is written in Italian. Some 30 percent of texts are produced in English and about 17 percent in dialect, with a substantial minority of authors writing texts in two out of the three possible combinations. While language choice is often determined by functional and contextual parameters, there is nevertheless a substantial overlap of thematic patterns across the three areas of language use. Characteristic and distinctive thematic patterns found in Italian Australian poetry include perceptions of the transition into a new world and a new life with its successes and failures, the migrant's reaction to and relationship with Australia, his/her fascination with the natural environment (bush and outback) so different from the one s/he left behind, the Australian cityscape and the people that are found there, and the comparison between the old land and the new, in some cases viewed from the perspective of nostalgia for one's native land.

The most prominent first-generation Italian Australian poets are Luigi Strano, Enoe Di Stefano, Mariano Coreno, and Lino Concas. The quantitative and qualitative parameters of their published writings represent not only continuity in terms of the historical and contemporary aspects of the Italian Australian migration experience, but also subjective expressions of personal sentiments relating to the meaning of life, love, nature, and human relationships. Such "universal" themes are, of course, also found in the works of other poets, such as Valerio Borghese's brief expressions of existential introspection, which recall the early poetry of Giuseppe Ungaretti and the "*frammenti poetici*" of Giovanni Boine and Scipio Slataper, as well as the introspective subjectivity found in the more discursive prose poetry of Walter Cerquetti and Paolo Totaro. Totaro's poetry in particular allows us to journey with him into the deepest recesses of his soul and to experience the spiritual anguish of the existential condition.

While these "universal" themes constitute a constant feature of the corpus, there is initially, especially in texts written between the 1940s and the 1980s, a particular emphasis on the explicit expression of the migration experience. Part of this is the tendency to look back to one's native land with nostalgia. The long distance in time and space that separates the migrant from his/her native land can in some writers create the desire to contemplate places, persons, and things left behind, the memories of their youth, the impossibility of expressing family affection. The poems of Giovanni Calabrò and Domenico Marasco, for example, many written in Calabrian, contain marked elements of nostalgia. The separation from his Calabria creates in Giovanni Calabrò "na piaga funda nta lu cori / e mai cchiù la pozzu risanari. / Quandu partia i tia eru figghiolu / e pirdia lu to suli e u to splinduri" (such a wound in my heart / that it can never be healed. / When I left you I was a young lad / and I lost your sun and your splendor). So much so that even after over forty years in Australia, "Nel pensare a te un desio dolce m'apprende / e del verdeggiante bosco sento il richiamo" (When I think of you it is with sweet desire / and I feel the call of your verdant forests). Domenico Marasco finds that he cannot accept the new land because of the pain and nostalgia he feels for his Calabria. Leonardo Castellana declares his attachment to Sicily with "nel calor del sole / nel profumo degli aranci. / Figlio della tua terra / So io" (in the warmth of your sun / the fragrance of your oranges / Son of your land / am I), and Pietro Mercuri (from Palermo) feels that pride in his origins can constitute both a defense against and compensation for the many problems and acts of racism he has had to endure during his time in Australia, declaring that "quannu è calpistatu / lu senzo nostru umanu / putemu gridari forti / IU SUGNU SICILIANU" (when our human dignity / is trampled upon / we can shout at the top of our voices / I am sicilian). For Pino Boiano, nostalgia for Naples is equated with longing for his mother—"Vurria lassà st'Australia / e 'a casa mia turnà, / addò aspettasse mammema / come a tant'anne fa" (I'd like to leave Australia / and go back to my home / where my mother waits for me / like so many years ago), while Giuseppe Ceres realises that nostalgia prevents him from feeling that he belongs to the new land: "Intravedi la terra lontana / La patria che ami . . . / Capisco ora perché / dopo tant'anni / ancor non prendi / la cittadinanza / australiana . . . / Tu non cambierai / sarai sempre soltanto / un vero italiano" (You see far away / the fatherland you love . . . / I now understand why / after so many years / you still don't take up / Australian / citizenship . . . / You will not change / you will always be only / a true

Italian). The sad memory of the poet's native Istria, lost but not forgotten, is evoked by Renata Spadoni, while Anna Maria Guidi, in a poem written in the Roman dialect, nostalgically recalls Sunday walks with her mother at Il Pincio.

But nostalgia and the pain of separation are not the only sentiments evoked by looking back on past lives in now-distant places. Domenico Marasco's collection contains a number of poems that describe daily life in his home town and his people, the natural beauty of his native Calabria, and the cultural glories of its ancient past, which are in dramatic contrast with its current state of degradation, brought about by exploitative "foreign" governments. Pino Sollazzo looks back not with nostalgia but with a critical appraisal of the political and social conditions endemic in southern Italy, Calabria in particular, that have forced millions of its inhabitants to emigrate because of systemic violence and injustice, and articulates the existential anguish that this phenomenon has created. The south is a land where "Non si può passare più nei campi . . . terre / abbandonate come i nostri vecchi" (You can no longer walk over the pastures . . . land / abandoned like our old people), and where "la bandiera della speranza ha i / colori / delle vane promesse" (the banner of hope has the / colors / of empty promises).

In *Dalla baia di Melbourne ai lidi natii* (*From the Bay of Melbourne to the Native Shores*), Corrado Bianchi reflectively compares the new land with the old, places separated by time and space but ideally linked by the medium of the sea that creates an appraisal between past and present in the evaluation of his Australian experience. Like Bianchi, many other writers have engaged in a similar process of appraisal of the new country.

Italian migrants who came to Australia from the late 1940s on settled in coastal urban areas or in areas relatively close to these. This is the environment that forms the basis of the work of most Italian Australian writers, although a few have ventured beyond these confines to the bush and the outback. Renata Spadoni's "Kirribilli His Domain" presents glimpses of nature (a kookaburra, a jacaranda tree) in an urban area near Sydney's city center that seems to exclude the migrant's presence despite her attempt to find meaning in the environment ("Now suddenly he stops / to preen to stare / at me / as if to say / what you are searching for / in here / is vain / you know quite well that this is / My Domain!"). Anna Maria Guidi writes of the hard humid summer, where relief from Sydney's furnacelike skyscrapers is only obtained by brief glimpses of the blue Pacific, which trigger a longing for the Tyrrhenian Sea. Despite his nostalgia,

Domenico Marasco finds that Melbourne is a flowering metropolis with expansive smiling suburbs, while for Walter Cerquetti, Goosberry Hill, which reminds him of his faraway Umbria, is an oasis amidst the chaos of the city, a "Fuga dal tuono / dei tunnel, dalle raffiche dei / traffic lights, dal vigili all'erta. / Ora salgo tra i pini pionieri, l'anima / cangia come la faccia d'una moneta. / M'avvolge il regno dell'eucaliptus. / Di vedetta è l'opossum. / Dalla preistoria, / frusciando, l'iguana di rame s'affaccia" (Refuge from the noise / of the tunnels, from the battery of / traffic lights, from the vigilant traffic police. / Among the pioneer pines, my soul / changes like the flip side of a coin. / I am immersed in the kingdom of the eucalyptus. / The opossum its sentry. / The copper iguana steps out of prehistory). Rita La Cava finds that Wollongong is a place "sinuosamente adagiata / tra il Keira e l'oceano / a riposare"(meanderingly spread out / between Keira and the sea / resting), where "Un volo di gabbiani / arabesca il cielo blu. / L'onda stanca spumeggia / infrangendosi / sulla roccia / erosa dal tempo. / Nel tempo che passa / per noi / tra noi" (A flight of seagulls / arabesques the blue sky. / The tired wave froths / breaking / on the rock / worn by time. / The time that passes / for us / among us). The sea is also a defining element for Port Macquarie, "un angolo / di mondo / dove l'onda / eterna / si scaglia spumeggiando / contro la roccia / immobile / che aspetta i / colpi / per cedere al / mare poco a poco / come noi / cediamo / agli anni!" (a corner / of the world / where the wave / eternal / breaks foamingly / against the rock / immobile / that awaits / the onslaught / to surrender to the / sea little by little / like we / surrender / to the advancing years!).

The inversion in the seasons that occurs in Australia is a further source of thoughts and sentiments inspired by the environment. For Maria Valli, "La primavera in Australia / E' la peggiore delle stagioni: / Appassisce le rose / E spoglia i jacaranda / Dei fiori violette . . . / Solo le nuvole, amiche del sereno, / Lascian dappertutto matigni fatati / E all'improvviso ci s'illude / Che il cuore non è morto" (Spring in Australia / is the worst season. / It withers roses / and strips the jacaranda / of its violet flowers . . . / Only the clouds, friends of calm weather, / their magic awakening / And suddenly you hope against hope / that your heart is not dead). In April showers Walter Cerquetti finds liberation "Dall'afa pesante del febbraio australe / Dal semitorrido marzo che taglia / Le gambe, pensieri e idee," that ". . . risveglia le menti, allevia / Lo spirito ansioso di dire, d'agire" (From the heavy humidity of an austral February / from semitorrid March that cuts / legs, thoughts and ideas . . . [April showers] awaken minds, bring relief / to spirits eager to talk, to act). Australian seasons are for Gennaro Cozzi "mezz'anno corto" (half a year too short), since in January, "'nvece d'esse tutto 'nfredolito, / la callaccia te stenne mezzo morto" (instead of being all shivering and cold, / heat and humidity make you feel half dead), and even after many years in Australia, "ancora è strano / passa' er Natale ar mare e Pasqua in serra" (it still feels strange / to spend Christmas at the seaside and Easter in the hothouse).

The bush and the desert present an environment so new and different from the landscape of their past that some Italian Australian poets tend to use metaphors and concepts that reflect their European experience. Australian nature uncontaminated by the presence of the white man is for Raffaele Scappatura a "Verde tesoro, la chioma oscillante delle foreste, / dove il Baobab patriarcale domina sovrano / accanto al Jarrah incorruttibile e al possente Kingkarri / con le sue guglie di cattedrale gotica" (The oscillating foliage of the forest is a green treasure / where the patriachal Baobab reigns supreme / beside the incorruptible Jarrah and the powerful Kingkarri / with spires like a gothic cathedral), while for Emilio Gabbrielli the tree-shaped bushes that appear on the journey back from Uluru are almost like cypresses. For a few, however, the bush and the outback are places of existential and metaphysical significance that can potentially provide meaning to the redefinition of life and identity. This is particularly the case in the poetry of Luigi Strano, Giovanni Andreoni, and Giuseppe Abiuso.

For Abiuso, the "true" heart of Australia is to be found in the Northern Territory, an area where very few Italians have emigrated but which for Abiuso holds a special fascination, and in the sugarcane fields of North Queensland, an area that experienced substantial Italian migration between the end of the 1800s and the mid-1900s, thanks to its attractive economic potential. Contrary to Gaetano De Luca's idyllic description of life and work in the sugarcane areas ("I tagliatori della canna"), Abiuso's poetry speaks of the harsh realities of the difficult environmental and socioeconomic conditions faced by canefield workers and their subsequent existentialist angst. Tropical heat, privations, and hard work result in the worker shedding "submerged tears" during his brief nightly rest ("I dubbi della notte alla canna da zucchero"), finding relief only at the pub that "ci dava birra e sogni / mentre la notte cupa ci portava / misteri e profondi sospiri" (gave us beer and dreams / while the gloomy night brought us / mysteries and profound sighs), or in sex that "al sabato sera, in città, / compravamo ciecamente" (on Saturday nights in the city / we would blindly buy). Despite all this, the worker who has left the canefields misses the life, the sun, the wide open spaces: "Se solo potessi tornare / al fuoco della canna. / Ritroverei allora la vita" (If only I could return / to the fire of the canefields. / I would find life again).

The poets' reflections on and reactions to Australia also embrace the social landscape through their views and judgments on Australian society, one whose values are not necessarily accepted in their entirety, portraying in some cases the sense of an insurmountable barrier between migrants and Australians.

Much of Rocco Petrolo's poetry, written predominantly in English, presents a sometimes ironic discourse on Australia and a critical commentary on the customs and attitudes of a society that lacks a humanitarian dimension and is characterized by implicit manifestations of racism. Pino Sollazzo displays mixed feelings, in that the host society is in some aspects accepting and welcoming, but does not exclude discrimination and exploitation, while for Domenico Marasco, even at Christmas time Australians display cold hearts despite the hot weather, are hostile when the non–English-speaking migrant goes from factory to factory looking for work, and behave like animals in the pubs. At a more abstract level, Franco Bottaz questions "Perché sei così ricca / di sole / così avara / d'amore?" (Why are you so rich / in sun / so miserly / in love?), and Cristiana Maria Sebastiani comments that "Qui l'amore ... / Forse mai nato / è un aborto illuso / questo anglosassone ventre / sotterrato" (Here love ... / Perhaps never born / is an aborted illusion / buried / in this Anglo-Saxon womb). Giuseppe Drago has spent many years in reaching an understanding of his Australian experience: "Or riconosco il frutto che mi hai dato, / ma per mangiarlo son diventato vecchio / perché prendesti da me ciò che ti ho portato" (Now I understand the fruits you have given me, / but in eating them I have become old / because you took from me what I brought you), while Anna Maria Guidi finds in her experience a contrast between the fear of the passing of time bringing bitter disenchantments and a prism of hope that does not fade, consoled by the discovery of the marvelous poetic expression of the natural landscape. Emilio Gabbrielli's view of Australian society is, on the other hand, enthusiastically positive in that it presents the premises for a potential union between Australians and migrants in its "friendly face of tolerance." For Maria Valli, Australia is a country that defends and respects the integrity of humankind both in the natural and the social environment.

The existential and spiritual dimensions of the migrant experience constitute yet another characterizing thematic element in Italian Australian poetry. Raffaele Scappatura's poem "Emigranti" is, like part of Paolo Totaro's poetry, a hymn to the brotherhood of "men of every race and color," anonymous heroes united by "the same earthly adventure" as they sail the seas to find work in a foreign land, where they create "fragments of recent history, cathedrals, skyscrapers, schools." These migrants are forced to leave their native land, driven by stark hunger: "cercando Americhe lontane, / paradisi giocati sulla nostra pelle. / E ci inghiottì il gorgo / d'un angoscia muta, / sfaldate le nostre famiglie" (searching for faraway Americas, / paradises paid for with our lives. / And the whirlpool of a muted angst / swallowed us, / our families disintegrated). Agostino Gaeta and Pietro Mercurio write of how migrants have faced suffering and adverse circumstances in the attempt to create a place for themselves in their adopted land through sacrifices and hard work, while Pietro Tedeschi and Domenico Marasco deal with the monotony of work in manufacturing industries, the dirty and dangerous jobs that are the lot of CALD migrants who have to pay their way in "altra terra in mezzo a genti strane / che a noi di benvenuti non ne dà" (another land amidst strange peoples / who do not welcome us).

As well as the explicit articulation of the diaspora and the migrant condition, a substantial number of works deal with "universal" themes not explicitly linked to the migration experience that explore feelings, relationships, questions of life and philosophy. These can be found together with the more explicit "migration" themes in a number of the poets discussed above, such as Luigi Strano, Lino Concas, Mariano Coreno, Enoe Di Stefano, Walter Cerquetti, Paolo Totaro, Pino Sollazzo, Rocco Petrolo, Cristiana Maria Sebastiani, and Pino Bosi. In Bosi's case there is a tendency to concentrate on explicit migration themes in his Italian poetry, while his poetry written in English deals with matters of a more "universal" nature. Other poets have chosen to concentrate on "universal" rather than migration themes. The poetry of Carla Fiumara explores with rare sensitivity solitude, unrequited love, desperation, and hell on earth, negative aspects of the human condition, comforted by faith and her relationship with her children. Franco Paisio writes mainly on time, space, love, and truth, although in his work there is also some reference to his native land and to the sense of belonging to Australia. These themes become more predominant in work published from the beginning of the 1990s by Flavia Coassin, Emilio Lo Iudice, Corrado Bianchi, Giovanna Li Volti

Guzzardi, Lidia Valerio-Dell'Oso's poems in Italian and English, and Caterina Spanò Papalia's poetry in Italian, English, and French.

Flavia Coassin deals with the search for self, communication and non-communication in relationships between men and women, sexual experience, and the need to find her own space in a male-dominated environment ("'Veramente io son socialista' / dico—per farlo pensare / ma anche del resto / per buttar giù anch'io / una carta" ("Actually I'm a socialist" / I say—to make him think / and anyway also / to play / some cards of my own). Part of Rita La Cava's poetry articulates the search for liberation from the more mundane aspects of life. Relationships with family members are featured in the poems of Lidia Valerio-Dell'Oso, Caterina Spanò Papalia, Rita La Cava, and Pino Boiano. Valerio Borghese articulates fragments of existential introspection on "questo mio vivere / che continua senza scopo" (this life of mine / that continues without purpose), and on the passing of time that takes away his "piccolo mondo / pieno di sogni e fantasia" (little world / full of dreams and fantasies). Paolo Totaro contemplates serenity, and Lidia Valerio-Dell'Oso hope and solitude. Rocco Petrolo applies the traditional wisdom of the southern Italian peasant to reflect on society; the mysteries of life; becoming old ("Se allo specchio / vedo un decrepito, / non dico nulla, / non faccio strepito; / mi viene invece / gran voglia di cantare: / La vita è bella / tira a campare . . ." [If in the mirror / I see a decrepit old man / I don't say anything / I don't scream out; / instead I get / the urge to sing: / Life is beautiful / keep on living]); and on his literary vocation.

Although characterized by the discourse of diaspora, the poetry produced by first-generation Italian Australian writers presents a substantial variety of themes, contents, and concepts, as well as diverse styles and means of expression that present an often complex mix of gravitas, poignancy, irony, and humor. Migration and more general life experiences are in many ways seen as two interrelated aspects of the individual's search for the meaning of the journey of life. For some writers, the passage to a new world and a new life is seen as an acceptable realization of a richer and fuller life. For others, however, the long crossing did not live up to its promise. The dream did not become reality, and nostalgia triggers a sense of not belonging either to the past or to the present, a metaphysical wandering that cannot be fully resolved. While some poetry deals with the social realities of the diaspora, most provides perceptions of the thoughts and feelings that constitute the inner life of the migrant, the constant and ever-shifting appraisal of two different worlds and two different cultures in an attempt to demythologize and remythologize past and present in the light of new experiences.

BIBLIOGRAPHY

Abiuso, G. "Cuore d'Australia." In *Voci nostre. Antologia italo-australiana di novelle, commedie, poesie e ricordi, scritta da emigrati italo-australiani*, ed. G. Abiuso, M. Giglio, and V. Borghese, 151–157. Melbourne: Tusculum, 1979.

A.L.I.A.S., ed. *Antologia A.L.I.A.S. 1996–1997: Antologia del quarto premio letterario internationale: poesia e narrativa*. Avondale Heights, Victoria: A.L.I.A.S., 1997.

Barbalace, G. *L'attesa. Poesie*. Empoli: Ibiskos Editrice, 2001.

Bianchi, C. *Raccolta di poesie*. Brunswick: Insegna, 1996.

———. *Dalla baia di Melbourne ai lidi natii: Seconda raccolta di poesie*. Brunswick: Insegna, 2001.

Bisietta [pseud. of G. Fontanella]. *Fiore di Ghibli*. Milan: Gastaldi, 1943.

———. *Orme*. Milan: Gastaldi, 1943.

Bosi, Pino. *I'll Say Good Morning*. Sydney: Kurunda, 1973.

———. *Thirteen Continents and a Rocket / Magi Lost*. Sydney: Kurunda, 1988.

Calabrò, G. *Il focolare*. Sydney: Southern Cross Press, 1987.

Cincotta, V., ed. *Italo-Australian Poetry in the '80s II*. Wollongong: Department of Modern Languages, University of Wollongong, 1989.

Concas, L. *Poesie Volume 1. Brandelli d'anima. Ballata di vento. Uomo a metà. L'altro uomo*. Redhill South: Elgua Media Editrice, 1988.

———. *Poesie Volume 2. Mallee. Muggil. L'uomo del silenzio. Cobar*. Redhill South: Elgua Media Editrice, 1988.

Crupi, P. *Sommario di storia della letteratura calabrese per insegnanti di lingua italiana all'estero. Profili*. Bivongi: International AM Edizioni, 2002.

Di Stefano, E. *L'itinerario*. Petersham: Southern Cross Press, 1997.

Fiumara, C. *Richiami*. Sydney: Tip. Fabreschi, 1962.

Genovesi, P., ed. *Compagni di viaggio*. Carlton: CIS Publishers, 1991.

Giliberto, G. *Frutto consolatore*. Sydney: Privately published, 1929.

———. *Raggi d'idealismo (poesie, poemetti e dramma)*. Sydney: Tip. Tomalin, 1939.

Guzzardi, G. *Isola azzurra*. Bulleen: IQ 100 Plus, 1990.

———. *Volerò: Poesie*. Avondale Heights, Victoria: A.L.I.A.S., 2002.

Lo Iudice, E. *Feelings*. West Brunswick: Insegna Publishers, 1994.

Marasco, D. *Ricordi di un emigrante*. Decollatura: Grafica Reventino S.n.f. Editrice, 1980.

Niscioli, P. "Migrant Writing and Beyond: The Voices of Four Italian-Australian Poets—Lino Concas, Mariano Coreno, Enoe Di Stefano and Luigi Strano." MA thesis, The Flinders University of South Australia, 1996.

O'Connor, D. "Il peso della lontananza nell'opera di Enoe Di Stefano." Paper presented at the AISLLI Conference, Belgium, 2003.

O'Connor, M., ed. *Two Centuries of Australian Poetry*. Melbourne: Oxford University Press, 1991.

Paisio, F. *Poesie del quaderno blu*. Bologna: SIA, 1961.

———. *Col gusto della morte sulle labbra*. Padova: Rebellato, 1963.

Papalia, C. S. *Unfolded Memories of True Feelings.* Kelmscott: Privately published, 1992.

Petrolo, Rocco. *The Shadows of the Mystery.* Warrawong: Privately published, 1986.

Polizzi, U., ed. *"Antologia" A.L.I.A.S: Poesia e prosa.* Melbourne: A.L.I.A.S., 1994.

———. *Antologia A.L.I.A.S. 1995: Poesia, prosa, teatro.* Keilor: A.L.I.A.S., 1995.

Rando, G., ed. *Italian Writers in Australia: Essays and Texts.* Wollongong: Department of European Languages, University of Wollongong, 1983.

———. *Italo-Australian Poetry in the '80s.* Wollongong: Department of European Languages, University of Wollongong, 1986.

Rando, G., and G. Andreoni, eds. "Le relazioni tra l'Italia, l'Australia e la Nuova Zelanda." *Il Veltro* 27 (April–June 1973): 2–3.

Rando La Cava, R. "Alcuni aspetti della tradizione orale eoliana: Fatti e misfatti raccolti presso eoliani emigrati in Australia e residenti nelle città di Melbourne, Sydney e Wollongong." BA honors thesis, Department of European Languages, University of Wollongong, 1983.

Savoca, C. "Italo-Australian Poetry: A Study of Selected Poets." In Rando, *Italian Writers in Australia: Essays and Texts*, 81–102.

Sebastiani, Cristiana Maria. *L'approdo (Ashore).* Marrickville: Southwood Press, 1884.

———. *Fragilità.* Guerra: Perugia, 1894.

Sollazzo, P. *Jenco.* Rome: Gabrieli, 1983.

Valerio-Dell'Oso, L. *Un angolo della mia penna.* Melbourne: Privately published, 1996.

Valli, M. *Poesie australiane /Australian Poems.* St Lucia: University of Queensland Press, 1972.

Luigi Strano (b. 1913)

Luigi Strano was born at Castellace di Oppido Mamertina in 1913 and emigrated to Sydney in 1929, where, over the years, he achieved a secure and respected socioeconomic position. However, Strano did not aspire to live by bread alone, and through his literary activity has earned recognition as one of the leading Italian Australian first-generation poets, having published twenty volumes of poetry and two volumes of memoirs. He received an honorary master of arts degree from the University of Wollongong for his literary and cultural activities.

Shortly after his arrival in Australia, Strano learned English, Latin, Greek, and German, and, using the pseudonym "Lino Gras(s)uti," began to publish poetry in Italian Australian newspapers. Initially his texts (sonnets, *canzoni,* and ballads) were written in literary Italian and closely modeled on the Italian classical literary canon. Throughout the 1930s, stylistic and thematic changes led him to progressively adopt a more "modern" approach, and to write not only in Italian but also in English, Calabrian, and Latin.

Luigi Strano has developed as a poet without regrets or nostalgia, one who is able to assimilate and adapt not only traditional and modern Italian poetry, but also English and Anglo-Australian poetry, to achieve his own brand of free and profound literary communication. His poetry explores a wide and varied range of themes expressed with rare unembellished sincerity. These themes include everyday realities as well as the existential aspects of the diaspora, the poet's relationship with his native land and his adopted country, nature, Australian society, and Italian migrants' reactions and attitudes towards Australians. But Strano's poetry also embraces more "universal" themes about life, love, and philosophy. Life is seen as a rocky road that leads to a succession of painful and joyous experiences, but that still needs to be lived to the full and at the highest level of one's humanity, since *"è tutto ciò che abbiamo"* (it's the only thing we have).

Feelings and attitudes towards his native land expressed in poems such as "Castellace" and "La mia terra" are complex and not without contradiction. They range from the denunciation of the hate and violence endemic in his home town to the realization that the place and its meaning can never be forgotten, even though returning there can be a mixed experience of sadness and joy.

Equally complex are feelings and attitudes toward his adopted country. The Australian natural setting can present cruel and tragic aspects, but the wide open spaces, the welcoming landscape, the untainted sky, and the primordial bush can often provide a setting for serene contemplation, a sense of peace and stability, a place for thought and philosophy. Less inviting and encouraging is Australia's social landscape, characterized by a degrading materialism that leaves little scope for the expression of difference, and relegates to the fringe those (migrants, aborigines) who cannot or do not wish to assimilate. "U Pappu a l'Australia," written in Calabrian, is a strikingly realistic and emblematic depiction of the existential anguish of elderly parents brought to Australia by their children for the sake of family reunion.

Personal relationships constitute another dominant and constant theme in Strano's work, with poems like "A Phyllis H.," "A Fortunato La Rosa," "Eros," and "Linda." The theme predominates in the volume *Elvira* (2002), published after the death of his sister, which expresses the memories, the feelings, the reflections, the places, the good and the bad times of a long life spent together.

For many years now, Luigi Strano has been living in retirement at Mt. Wilson in the Blue Mountains, an area that is in some ways reminiscent of his native Aspromonte. He continues to write poetry and read his favorite authors. Among his books are *Inquietudine* (1964), *Di qui ci son passato anch'io* (1984), *Carmi scelti* (1986), *Le vecchie rughe dell'anima* (1996), and *Rocciosa è la vita. Memorie* (1999).

La mia terra

da *Italian Writers in Australia*

Il paese natio non si scorda,
anche quando non c'è alcuna
ragione d'amarlo . . .
ma io porto con me,
la gioia e il dolore
della mia terra.

Ancora ho negli orecchi
la nenia delle cornamuse,
il campano delle capre
lungo il letto dei fiumi,
la sonagliera delle mule
sulla strada incavata nei monti,
l'oscena facezia del mulattiere,
la bestemmia a denti stretti
del manovale che maledice la terra . . .

I limpidi orizzonti
vedo chiudendo gli occhi
col fumo dell'Etna e dello Stromboli

la madonnina al bivio
con le offerte di fiori appassiti,
la pineta di Garibaldi,
il mare d'Ulisse . . .

Amo il paese che m'ospita,
ma chi può sopprimere
le visioni del dormi-veglia?

My Land

from *Italian Writers in Australia*

You can't forget your hometown,
even when there is no reason
to love it . . .
but I carry within me
the joy and pain
of my country.

I still hear the mourning sound
of the bagpipes,
the heavy bells of the goats
along the riverbeds,
the mule's bells
along the road carved out of the mountains,
the dirty joke of the mule driver,
the curse uttered through a tight mouth
of the laborer who curses his land, . . .

If I close my eyes
I see the limpid horizons
with the smoke of Etna and of Stromboli

The little Madonna at the crossroads
with the offer of wilted flowers,
the pine grove of Garibaldi
the sea of Ulysses . . .

I love the country where I live
but who can suppress
the visions of dreamtime?

Forse non tutto è stato invano

Il falchetto
vibra su la valle . . .
uno sciame
di piccoli uccelli
si rifugia
spaurito nel bosco . . .
anch'io entro nel bosco
seguito da Bruno,
che corre, s'arresta
s'addossa a me
sull'orlo del precipizio,
quasi apprensivo
della stranezza del luogo.
Sull'estremo orizzonte
la città
della mia
gioventù tormentata;
dalle sue mille e mille
fabbriche esala
fumi e vapori nell'aria . . .
niente più m'obbliga
o induce
a rifar quelle strade . . .
forse
non tutto è stato
invano . . .
né fu in tutto come
fluisce nel pensiero . . .
ma affondando
gli occhi sul verde,
inoltrandomi
sempre più nell'ignoto
mastico
un'erbetta amara . . .

Perhaps All Was Not in Vain

A little falcon
hovers over the valley
and a flock of birds
hides in fear in the nearby wood.
I too enter the wood
followed by Bruno
who stops and leans against me
next to the edge of a cliff
apprehensive for the strangeness of the place.
Far away on the horizon
the city of my tormented youth.
From the thousands of factories
exhales smoke and vapor in the air.
Nothing obliges me
or pushes me to tread this road again
perhaps not all was in vain
nor was it all exactly
as it flows in the mind
but sinking my eyes upon the green
penetrating deeper into the unknown
the grass feels bitter to the taste.

Homecoming

da *Italo-Australian Poetry in the 80's*

Ritorno al paese desolato
dei miei giovani anni,
ricordando ancor le punture
dei ricci di castagne
per le scarpe rotte . . .
Non cerco
le facce di trenta
e sette anni fa;
non vengo a ostentare
ciò che non ho mai posseduto . . .
se mai,
vengo a portare un tributo
di affetto
ad una vecchia zia,
nelle cui mani
feci i primi passi.
L'uomo, con le sue macchine,
ha di certo sbandito
le pecore e i pastori
dai nostri monti,
e tra gli elci e le querce,
non incontri il porcaro,
come allora
come ai tempi d'Omero . . .
Ritorno, al paese desolato
dei miei giovani anni,
ricordando ancora le punture
dei ricci di castagne
per le scarpe rotte . . .

Homecoming

from *Italo-Australian Poetry in the 80's*

I return to the desolate town
of my youthful years,
remembering the pricking
of the chestnut husks
through my broken shoes . . .
I am not looking for
the faces of thirty-seven years ago;
I do not come to show off
what I have never had . . .
if anything
I come to pay a tribute
of affection
to an old aunt
in whose hands
I took my first steps.
Man, with his machines,
has certainly cast out
the sheep and the shepherds
from our mountains
and among the ilexes and the oaks
you no longer meet the swineherd
as before
at the times of Homer . . .
I return to the desolate town
of my youthful years
still remembering the pricking
of the chestnut husks
through my broken shoes . . .

Sabato dopopranzo

Da dietro le tendine
sbiadite e sdrucite,
una donna senza grazia
si scarica del suo risentimento,
lo versa come un secchio
d'acqua sporca
sopra il suo uomo
stolido ed ebbro
che risponde
con improperi . . .
È sabato dopopranzo.
Tu ti aggiri senza meta
per questi luoghi sordidi,
evitando qualche ubriaco
dagli occhi screziati di sangue
e donne, donne, donne . . .
insidiose, litigiose, discinte;
dal sorriso sguaito,
dai capelli attorcigliati
agli uncini,
con la sigaretta
tra le labbra smunte,
in attesa, in preparazione
agli svaghi di questa sera . . .
È sabato dopopranzo.
Una voce fessa e concitata
alla radio,
anticipa i cavalli
al traguardo . . .
e tutto sa di birra e di fumo
di falsa festività:
degradazione, desolazione, tristezza . . .

Saturday Afternoon

Behind the faded, torn curtains
a woman without grace
dumps her resentment
upon her stolid, drunken man
like a pail of filthy water;
he answers back
with curses of his own . . .
It's Saturday afternoon.
You wander aimlessly
around these sordid places
avoiding drunks
with bloodshot eyes
and women, women, women . . .
insidious, litigious, undressed,
with vulgar smiles
with hair twisted
around hooks
with cigarettes hanging
from their colorless lips,
waiting, preparing
for the orgies of the coming night.
It's Saturday afternoon.
A broken excited voice
on the radio
prognosticates
The horses on the finish line . . .
And everything smells of beer and smoke,
of false festivities:
degradation, desolation, sadness.

Bush fire

da Le relazioni tra l'Italia, l'Australia e la Nuova Zelanda

Ci arriva solo il fumo
e la calura
degli arsi eucalipti
abbarbicati alle rocce.
I nudi tronchi
dalle gran macchie nere,
muti testimoni
d' altri incendi.
Oh è dura
qui l'esistenza
anche per gli alberi . . .
Fin dove l'occhio
arriva
desolazione e sfacelo . . .
Il sole
gran palla fuoco,
brucia
negli occhi,
ti arroventa 1a faccia.
Non senti
che un batter di fronda,
su l'erba che avvampa;
non vedi
che un rettile
dalle rudi scaglie
color delle rocce
e impassibile
come le rocce,
sta fermo
e neppure ti guarda.

Bush Fire

from *Le relazioni tra l'Italia, l'Australia e la Nuova Zelanda*

Only the smoke arrives here
and the heat
of the burned-out eucalyptus trees,
growing out of the rocks.
The naked trunks
with great black spots,
mute eyewitnesses
of other fires.
Oh life is hard here
even for trees . . .
as far as the eye can go
only desolation, destruction . . .
the sun
a great ball of fire
burns
in your eyes
it burns your face.
You hear only
the beating of a branch
on the burning grass;
you only see
a reptile
with hard scales
the color of rocks
impassible like the rocks
that stands still
and does not even look at you.

U Pappu a l'Australia

da *Inquietudine*

'Mmavissi 'rrumputu l'anchi
quandu partia di jani!
lu 'mmorzu d'ortu
e lu pertusu i casa l'avia,
chi mi mancava u pani?
'cca simu comu
non si canusci nenti,
non sai mancu chi 'ttinnu,
lu patri non è patri,
non c'è 'chiu religioni;
ti manca di rispettu
chiddu chi s'avi e fari . . .
simu comu i nimali,
parlandu cu crianza,
peju di li maiali;
si campa pe la panza! . . .
li fiji miei, li viditi?
si sparanu pe lupi,
pari ca s'annu e spartiri
la fascia di lu duca.
a mia ancora mi tennu
nommi parlanu i genti,
ma sapiti? mi tennu
comu 'ddoluri i panza! . . .
'mmavissi 'rrumputu l'anchi
quandu partia di jani! . . .

Il nonno in Australia—Avrei dovuto rompermi l'anca / quando me ne andai di lì! / Una manciata di terreno / e un buco di casa ce l'avevo, / che mi mancava il pane? / Qui siamo come / se non si conosce niente, / non sai neanche chi hai, / il padre non è padre, / non c'è più religione; / ti manca di rispetto / chi non è ancora nato / siamo come animali / con rispetto parlando, / peggio dei maiali; / si vive per la pancia! / i miei figli, li vedete? / Sembrano lupi / come se devono dividersi / il terreno del duca. / A me ancora mi tengono / rispetto quando parla la gente, / ma sapete? Mi tengono / come dolori di pancia! / Mi fossi rotto l'anca quando me ne andai di lì! . . .

Granddad in Australia

from *Uneasiness*

I should have broken my hip
before leaving my place.
I had a piece of land
a roof above my head,
I sure didn't lack bread.
Here we're all messed up.
We don't know anything.
We don't know what we have:
a father is not a father
there's no religion here
even those yet to be born
don't have any respect
we're like the animals,
speaking respectfully,
we're worse than swines;
we live to fill our bellies.
You see my children here
They're wolves to one another.
It's as if they have to share
The duke's field.
They still put up with me
People don't talk to me
but if you must know
they consider me a pain in the proverbial . . .
I should have broken my hip
before leaving my place.

Non più compianti

da *Carmi scelti*

Non più
compianti,
non più rimpianti,
la vita
è tutta piena di sorprese;

Per ogni fiore
che secca,
sboccia
un fiore novello;
per ogni avello,
vagisce una nuova culla . . .
a che
guardar nel triste
cuore de l'uomo
e ne la mente gretta,
quando
per ogni vetta
solo la vista
per goder ti giova?
e di tutto far prova,
finché i ginocchi
son forti
e mai fino alla morte
dire "che vale?" o "che
giova?"

No More Complaints

from *Selected Poems*

No more complaints,
no more regrets,
life is ever full of surprises.

For every flower that dies
a new flower blooms;
in every hearth
a new crib wails.
Why look
inside the sad heart of man
and in his uncouth mind
when from every hilltop
the view alone allows enjoyment?
And try everything
until your knees are strong
and never say until death
"What's the use?"
or "Why bother?"

Di qui ci son passato anch'io

da *Di qui ci son passato anch'io*

Perché
o per chi
io abbia scritto
non lo so neanch'io.
Quando m'inoltro nel bosco
per facilitare
il ritorno,
qui raggruppo dei sassi
rompo un virgulto
do dell'accetta su un tronco . . .
In questa
escursione
senza ritorno,
a volte scarabocchio
una frase una nota su un libro
raggruppo parole su un foglio . . .
forse per cercar di capire
la realtà del momento,
forse soltanto per dire
"questo è un sentiero
battuto, di qui
ci son passato anch'io"

I Too Have Passed Through This Place

from *I Too Have Passed through This Place*

Why
or for whom
I have written
I don't know myself.
When I enter a forest,
to make returning easier
I make a pile of rocks
or break a branch
or strike a tree trunk with my ax . . .
in this
excursion
without return,
sometimes I scribble
a phrase, a note on a sheet of paper . . .
perhaps to try to understand
the reality of the moment,
perhaps only to say:
"This is a traveled path.
I too have passed through this place."

→ Enoe Di Stefano (b. 1921)

Enoe Raffaelli Di Stefano was born in Rovereto in 1921 and emigrated to Sydney in 1949, having obtained a primary teaching diploma. She became a well-known personality in the Italian Australian community through her work with the Italian language newspaper *La Fiamma,* as a broadcaster for community radio programs, and as a driving force in the promotion of Italian language classes for second-generation Italian Australian children. Her artistic aspirations found expression in painting as well as in the production of poetry and prose, and have gained her recognition as one of the leading first-generation Italian Australian poets.

While Di Stefano's narrative presents an investigation of the diaspora experience based on sociocultural parameters and with generally positive outcomes, her poetry is a detailed, sensitively expressed lyric diary that presents a complex and not always positive comparison of the ambience, the traditions, the temporal and natural spaces of her native land and of her adopted country. From nostalgia for her native land to appraisal of the new country, her first two volumes, *Terra australis* (1970) and *Voci di lontananza* (1978), express feelings and reflections triggered by the experiences of the migrant: the temporal dislocation of the physical and the metaphysical journey that marks the transition from Italy to Australia; the strange and different material and spiritual facets of the new country; the memory of premigration places and experiences.

In her next two volumes, *Mio e non mio* (1985) and *Se rimarrà qualcosa . . .* (1988), Di Stefano explores the concept that as the time spent in Australia has weakened her ties with her native land; the new country, despite its positive aspects, does not fully satisfy all the migrant's spiritual aspirations. Although she no longer feels that she can entirely belong to Italy, Di Stefano realizes that she has not achieved acceptance of the new country. She has, however, realized an appreciation of the material security Australia has to offer, and of its natural beauty, even though there are instances of doubt. The silence that descends with sunset in the eucalyptus forest creates an environment of doubtful happiness, and limited joy is also to be found in the celebration of an Australian Easter, through the uneasiness provoked by the inversion of the seasons and the different practices that mark the celebration, which to some extent are a mixture of old and new traditions. These thoughts and feelings are intermingled with memories of her native Trentino and the periodic emotional visits back to Italy to see again places that she holds dear.

In *L'itinerario* (1997), Di Stefano reflects on the outcomes of a life spent between two worlds. The memory of her Italian past is now distant in time, and it is no longer possible to contemplate alternatives that might have been, despite lingering reservations in her relationship with Australia.

Compared to Strano's poetry, themes that relate to the collective aspects of the diaspora are less evident in Di Stefano. The poem "Lucia," however, can be read as emblematic of the situation of aged Italian Australians forced to end their lives in a nursing home in a foreign land, while "Discorso vuoto" subtly criticizes the panegyric speech inevitably delivered whenever an Italian politician is sent on a lavishly funded trip to Australia to visit the Italian Australian community.

Enoe Di Stefano's poetic journey is ultimately an optimistic one, doubts and nostalgia notwithstanding, and her integrated contemplation of life and the migration experience indicates a large measure of acceptance of her adopted land, as well as the achievement of an equilibrium between past and present. It is a journey that "*anche se rimane quasi sempre autobiografico . . . è la stessa (strada migratoria) che è stata intrapresa da milioni di italiani che hanno lasciato il proprio paese*" ("even if it is always autobiographically based . . . it is the same migratory path followed by millions of Italians who have left their country").

Non mi piace . . .

da *Se rimarrà qualcosa*

Non mi piace il pavone,
Onorevole che fa la ruota
perché non si legga
il vuoto dei suoi occhi.

Non mi piace il maiale
arricchito d'astuzia
e di lavoro altrui
che muove la pancia
per farsi notare.

Non mi piace la cagna,
Politica infida e lorda
che mentre lecca
cerca dove affondare i denti.

O la volpe di quel prete,
primo in processione
e se non avesse il colletto
finirebbe ultimo in coda.

E nemmeno il merciaio
che truffa col sorriso
o il guidatore
che mi butta fuori strada
per provare la sua perizia.

Tant'altro non mi piace . . .

Ma se colgo una rosa
mi riempio il petto di profumo
e dico grazie a Dio
per qualche cosa.

I Don't Like It . . .

from *If Anything Will Be Left*

I don't like the peacock,
his Honor who spreads his tail
so that the emptiness in his eyes
cannot be read.

I don't like the pig
endowed with shrewdness
and with others' work
who moves his belly
to be noticed.

I don't like the bitch,
treacherous, and filthy politician
who, while licking,
looks for a place to sink her teeth.

Nor that fox of a priest,
first in the procession,
and if he had no collar
would end up tail-end last.

And not even the merchant
who cheats with a smile
nor the driver
who pushes me off the road
to prove his ability.

So much more I don't like . . .

But if I pick a rose
my breast fills up with fragrance
and I say thanks to God
for something good at last.

Il ruscello

Nel silenzio del bosco
un ruscello alpestre
d'acqua pura
scende, salta rimbalza,
s'illumina di sole
e poi s'oscura
al capriccio del vento.

Dall'orlo del castagno
assorta guardo
quel flusso mutevole.

Dov'è finito il rosario
di perle, or or sgranato
nell'urto col sasso inaspettato?
Dov'è sparita la vena
a treccia attorcigliata,
la bolla, la schiuma
che un attimo è durata ?

E penso ai giorni perduti
alle scorse stagioni
alla vita che fugge
sulla china del tempo
senza tregua o ragione,
né cenno di conforto o di pietà
ai miei occhi umidi di pianto
inatti ad accettar l'addio . . .

E già il ruscello alpestre
d'acqua pura
si perde in un sussulto
nell'anonimo spazio
del fiume che l'ingoia.

The Brook

In the silence of the woods
an alpine brook
of pure water
flows down, springs and leaps,
brightens up with the sun
then darkens
at the whim of wind.

From the edge of the chestnut tree
pensively I look
at the mutable flow.
What happened to the rosary
of pearls, just now unstrung
in its crash with a sudden stone?
Where did the rush
of water disappear, twisted in a braid,
the bubble, the foam
that lasted for a moment?

And I think of the lost days
the seasons gone
life fleeting
on the slopes of time
without a break or reason,
nor a sign of comfort or piety
for my eyes moist with tears
unused to accept the farewell . . .

And already the alpine brook
of pure water
with a jolt is lost
in the anonymous space
of the river that swallows it.

Autunno romano

da *Voci di lontananza*

Roma, Stazione Termini.
Bruma di crepuscolo
e odore di castagne
arrostite in piazza
dentro innumerevoli bracieri.

I bracieri sono lucciole bluastre
nel brusio di formicaio umano.
"Come si chiamano?" domanda Gregory.
"Ah, tu non conosci le caldarroste?"

Tu vieni dall'estate d'Australia,
abbronzato, vestito leggero.
Conosci la spiaggia infinita
l'onda possente d'oceano
e il silenzio degli eucalipti.

Non sai i castagneti e gli ulivi,
non sai il rumore di foglie
di vigne ammucchiate
pei sentieri di campagna . . .
Le scarpe di tua madre,
nell'infanzia lantana dei ricordi,
erano sporche di terra e di fogliame
e il dito usciva svelto,
dal guanto rotto,
a staccare la buccia rovente.

Due lame di fuoco, a ponente,
scendono tra le guglie orgogliose
che domani vedrai.
Ma le caldarroste ? . . .
Compriamole, ti piaceranno.
Scoprirai un mistero nuovo
e l'arco della diversità
sarà rimpicciolito.

Roman Fall

from *Voices from Afar*

Rome, Termini station.
Mist of dusk
and smell of chestnuts
roasted in the square
on countless braziers.
The braziers are bluish fireflies
in the hubbub of a human anthill.
"What is their name?" Gregory asks.
"Ah, you don't know roast chestnuts?"
You come from the Australian Summer,
suntanned, lightly dressed.
You know the infinite beaches
the powerful ocean wave
and the silence of the eucalyptus.
You don't know chestnut groves and olive trees,
you don't know the noise produced by leaves
in clustered vineyards
along the country paths . . .
Your mother's shoes,
in the faraway childhood of your memories,
were soiled with dirt and foliage
and her finger quickly came out
from the ripped glove
to remove the scorching peel.
In the west, two blades of fire
come down among the proud steeples
you will see tomorrow.
What about the roast chestnuts? . . .
Let's buy them, you will like them.
You will discover a new mystery
and the arch of difference
will become smaller.

Lingua madre

La scala al vecchio ufficio
più ripida e più' stretta
mi sembra nel salire.
Dietro quell'uscio
trovo il mio patire,
e chi di parole che parevano
vane ed eran sacre
solo nel mio ardire.
Al muro d'una società
ancorata ai pregiudizi
scagliavo la sfida
con passione di missionaria:
"l'Italiano per i nostri figli . . ."

Dopo quindici anni
le scalfitture sono brecce
nel muro anglosassone
e la lingua madre
ha spazio per vivere
e andare lontano.

Quando esco dal portone,
e il sole improvviso m'acceca,
penso, immodesta e giuliva,
che la battaglia è vinta.
I fantasmi hanno trovato pace.

Mother Tongue

The stairs to the old office
steeper and narrower
appear to me while I climb.
Behind that door
I find my suffering,
echoes of words that appeared
vain but were sacred
only in my daring.
Against the wall of a society
anchored to its prejudices
I threw my challenge
with the passion of a missionary:
"Italian language for our children . . ."
Fifteen years later
the breaches are gaps
in the Anglo-Saxon wall
and my mother tongue
has its space to live
and to go far.
When I go out of the door,
and suddenly the sun blinds me,
I think—conceited and merry—
that my battle is won.
My ghosts have found peace.

Mio e non mio

Non continuerò ad aggrapparmi
ai noti scogli
che mi respingono taglienti.
Non m'ostinerò a trattenere
tra le dita
la rena rubatami dall'onda del tempo.

Sempre meno, ad ogni incontro,
io t'appartengo, o tu a me, luogo natio
e strazio mi da questo pensiero.

Il lungo travaglio
di ciò che è mio e non mio
terminerà?
A te ritorno, terra adottiva,
cercando dopo tanti anni
una risposta . . .

Non è ancor tempo.
Forse, vegliarda, ti raggiungerò
traguardo del mio e non mio
e sarò paca.

luglio 1979

Mine and Not Mine

I will not continue to hang on
the known rocks
that sharply reject me.
I will not persist in holding
with my fingers
the sand stolen by the wave of time.

Less and less at every encounter
I belong to you or you to me,
my native land,
and I anguish at the thought.

Will it end,
the long struggle
of what is mine or not?
To you I come back, my adoptive land,
after so many years,
looking for an answer . . .
It is not yet the time.
Perhaps, once old, I will reach
the goal of what is mine and not
and I will be serene.

July 1979

Australia

Ti voglio bene, Australia,
anche s'è un bene limitato
con riserve.
Tu non mi chiedi molto
in pace conviviamo
ché l'una l'altra serve.

Io non t'appartengo interamente,
questo è il male,
che se potessi esser figlia vera
tu madre saresti uguale.

La prima madre amo sempre
non so se n'ho diritto.
Tu sei stata paziente e generosa
ed hai retribuito l'amarezza
mutandola in forza ed agiatezza.

E finalmente siam venute
amiche l'una dell'altra rispettosa
e t'ho accettata serenamente
chè siamo parte della stessa cosa.

La strada è stata lunga,
ma un giorno tu m'avrai,
figlia adottata eternamente
quando nel tuo pietoso grembo
le mie povere spoglie accoglierai.

Australia

I love you, Australia,
even if it's a love with limits,
with reservations.
You don't ask much of me—
we live together in peace
since one serves the other.

I don't belong to you entirely,
that's the problem,
for if I could be a true daughter to you
you would be an equally true mother.

I still love my first mother
though I don't know if I have the right.
You have been patient and generous
and have rewarded bitterness,
changing it to strength and affluence.

So we finally became friends,
respecting each other,
and I have accepted you serenely,
for we are part of the same thing.

The road has been long,
but one day you will have me,
adopted daughter in entirety,
when you will gather my remains
in your compassionate womb.

Discorso vuoto

Il discorso
dotto ed elegante
del Senatore venuto dall'Italia
risuona ardente
nel Club della città.

"Siamo fieri di voi,
lo debbo dire,
di quanto guadagnato
in terra straniera.
Vi siete fatti onore,
meritato prestigio e rispetto . . ."

"Bravo!" gridan le voci
d'un pubblico sedotto
da tanta adulazione.

Ma Senatore,
le sue parole vuote,
adatte su misura
ad un pubblico ingenuo
e domani già scordate,
permetta che Le chieda a cosa servono?
Ha mai capito
per un breve istante
cosa significa
essere emigrante?

Speech without Meaning

The learned and elegant
speech
of the senator
come from Italy
resounds impressively
in the city club.

"I must say
we're proud of you,
of what you have achieved
in a foreign land.
You have distinguished yourselves,
merited prestiege and respect . . ."

"Bravo!" shout the voices
of an audience seduced
by so much adulation.

But senator,
may I ask what is the use of
your empty words,
made to measure
for a naive audience
and tomorrow already forgotten?
Have you ever understood
even for a brief instant
what it means
to be a migrant?
And can you even begin to imagine
how much the success
being praised today
has really cost us?

→ Pietro Tedeschi (1925–1998)

Pietro Tedeschi was born in Reggio Emilia in 1925. He migrated to Australia in 1952 after a period of employment at the Officine Reggiane as a turner and fitter. He then began his working career in Australia as an unskilled laborer at the Port Kembla steelworks, although his skills and qualifications were subsequently put to use by the Italian Australian company EPT. However, Tedeschi did not only aspire to a weekly wage increased by overtime from double shifts. An avid reader, he developed an interest in writing, and in the mid-1960s he sent regular articles on local Italo-Australian sporting events to *La Fiamma*, subsequently publishing commentaries on political and social issues as well as a few short stories in the same newspaper. His retirement in 1982 gave him greater freedom to dedicate his time to the creation of metal sculptures, as well as to writing poetry and narrative.

A writer of markedly populist origins, Tedeschi has written two autobiographically based novels, *Senza camicia* and *53B*, that relate the pre- and post-migration experiences of a blue-collar worker from Reggio Emilia who moves to Port Kembla, dealing not only with personal dilemmas but also with some of the political issues of the migration process seen from a left-wing perspective. In some of his other narrative and in much of his poetry, Tedeschi writes, often from an ironic, critical perspective, of the migrant worker's experience, of the problems faced in coming to terms with a new and usually unwelcoming workplace environment, and of the exploitation of workers by Italian Australian employers.

Many of Tedeschi's poems relate to workplace experiences of the 1950s and 1960s, when newly arrived Italian migrants found themselves at the bottom of the industrial pecking order. These poems deal with, among other things, the monotony of work, the infernal atmosphere of the steelworks (reminiscent of Dante's *Inferno*) where underpaid non-English-speaking-background migrant workers were condemned to dangerous and dirty jobs and lived lives severely limited by the requirements of an exploitative industrial process. A number of the poems in *Le rime e le prose del Maligno* (1997) evoke the image of an Italian Australian construction company, "Italpi," whose executives are ex-fascists who have migrated to Australia, and who resort to various stratagems in order to secure high earnings for the company. In charging for contracted work they add the names of nonexistent workers; they favor the hiring of workers who are "sempliciotti / pronti e ligi a tal dovere" (simpleminded / ready and loyal to their duty); and unquestioningly accept difficult working conditions as well as low rates of pay.

Tedeschi's poetry, however, is not only about the migrant worker. In *Le rime e le prose del Maligno* and in *I camminanti quasi poesia di Pietro Tedeschi* (1998), there is an appreciation of the Australian natural setting, despite the odd, though significantly disappointing, discovery that its beautiful flowers have no perfume, a condemnation of modern society for the damage it is causing the environment, and the contemplation of ideal feminine beauty from a sculptural point of view.

The uniqueness of his poetry nevertheless lies in the way he has managed to give voice from the "inside" to a common aspect of the Italian diaspora and to articulate the experience of a class that has by and large not been able to articulate what the transition from a largely rural Italian context to the industrial environment of Australia has meant.

Pietro Tedeschi died in Wollongong in 1998.

Emigranti

da *I camminanti quasi poesia*

Fatti siamo di terra d'aria e di mare
e come l'onde rimodelliam le rive
quell'onde che nel lor venire e andare
lascian granelli nuovi e cose vive

Emigrants

from *The Walkers' Almost Poetry*

Made of ocean earth and air
like waves we remodel the seashore
coming and going always leaving
new grains of sand, things that are living

Hostel '58

Stanzone anonimo, impersonale
dalle pareti nude imbrattate solo
di graffiti e degl'incubi
d'altri esseri di ieri.

Volgere di sguardo atono
al soffitto grigio e rugginoso,
dal giaciglio freddo e grugnoso mentre
il respiro da altri giacigli
freddi, accompagna il giro vizioso
dei pensieri.

Riandare alla giornata trascorsa
tra il lezzo del fumo o del sudore
nero; tra frastuoni e boati
e nel calore immane per cercare
su colline di ferro, nei torrenti di lava
e lungo le rive del fiume di parole
incomprensibili, il ciuffo d'erba verde.

Membra stanche, dolenti di fatica
e di solitudine, che s'allungano
tra coperte impregnate di umori inutili
e di lacrime passate, per cercare
tepori infantili
e quei prati lasciati di viole.

Occhi che si socchiudono
nell'oblioso sogno notturno
... se la stanchezza vuole.

Hostel '58

Big anonymous room, impersonal—
stains on the naked walls,
graffiti and the nightmares
of previous boarders.

Looking blankly
at the gray crumbling ceiling
to the cold creaking bunks
while the cold breaths
of the cot dwellers
keep time with the vicious churning
of my thoughts

Going back to the day just gone,
through smoke and black
sweat, noises, immense heat
to the iron hills and the lava streams, searching
the banks of rivers of incomprehensible
words for a single tuft of grass.

Limbs weary, worn, aching
from work and loneliness,
stretched under sheets damp
from wasted tears of the past, searching
for childhood warmth
and those lavender fields left behind.

Eyes closing
in forgetful nightly sleep—if only
weariness will let them.

Fiore Australiano

Nella foresta d'eucalipti
sull'erto pendio
pria d'affrontar
la china del ritorno
ho colto un fiore
tra le rocce gialle
Era stupendo!
Son rimasto affascinato.
L'ho colto nell'impulso
del momento, il cuor
più che la mente
m'ha dettato il gesto.
Poi nel cavo delle mani
al viso l'ho accostato
per assorbir l'essenza
della sua bellezza.
Che delusione!
Non era profumato.

Australian Flower

In the eucalyptus forest
on the steep slope
before undertaking
the climb back down
I found a flower
among the yellow stones.
What a beauty.
It held me amazed
and I picked it
on an impulse of my heart
more than my mind.
In the hollow of my hands
I brought it to my face
to breathe in the essence
of its beauty.
What disappointment!
There wasn't any fragrance.

. . . E domani?

Cerchiam di giustificare
le nostre debolezze
nel nome di quel Moloc
creato da le allucinazioni
della febbre consumistica.

Viviamo in quest'opulenza
di giornata,
svaligiando i forzieri della terra,
come gl'antichi ladri di tombe,
ammorbando l'aria
con le nostre presunzioni
di dei immortali,
coprendo anche 'il sole
mentre i nostri figli
ci guardano esterrefatti
con una domanda disperata
negli occhi:
. . . e domani?

And Tomorrow?

We've tried to justify
our weaknesses
in the name of Moloch,
offspring of the hallucinations
of our consumer fever.

We live in the luxury
of the here and now
rummaging through the earth's safeholds
like looters of ancient tombs,
infecting the air
with our presumption
of godlike immortality,
covering even the sun
while our terrified children watch us,
a desperate question
in their eyes
                    . . . and tomorrow?

Ideale

Ho plasmato forme nell'argilla
mutevole del pensiero
T'ho scolpita poi reale nel
desiderio.
T'ho dato un volto di Madonna, un seno
caldo ed accogliente. T'ho dato un corpo
morbido e sensuale
di Venere pagana. Volevo
la donna perfetta
ho creato la statua perfetta,
che dell'alto piedistallo
degli ideali, dove l'ho posta, mi guarda
senza vedermi.

Vorrei accarezzarti, scuoterti, stringerti
baciarti con passione, penetrarti:
vorrei vederti piangere, sorridere di gioia
di mestizia, arrossir di piacere
di pudore. Vorrei che il petto tuo
si sollevasse d'ansia e d'emozioni
e che il ventre liscio e piatto
s'inturgidisse di vita nuova.
Vorrei che fosti viva!
Ma i tuoi occhi, i tuo costato
sono di marmo
duro, freddo. Il tuo cuore
non palpita, non tremano
le membra quando ti stringo a me . . .
E allor che vale? . . .
            Una furia devastatrice m'assale:
La statua giace a terra, spezzata
informe.
Ora non sei più tu. Ora sei frammenti
che serviranno per costruirne
un'altra migliore.

The Ideal

I molded forms
from the changeable clay of thought
and sculpted you real
in the shape of my desire,
gave you the face of a Madonna
and a Madonna's
warm and welcoming breast,
and the body, subtle and sensual,
of a pagan Venus. I wanted
the perfect woman, created
the perfect statue,
who, from a high pedestal
of ideals where I placed her
looks down
without seeing me.

I want to caress you, shake you, press you to me,
kiss you passionately, enter you.
I want to see you cry, smile with joy
and sorrow, blush with pleasure
and shame. I want your breast
to rise with grief and passion
and your belly, smooth and flat,
to swell with new life.
I want you alive.

But your eyes and your flanks
are marble
hard and cold. Your heart
doesn't throb. Your limbs
don't tremble when I press you to me.
So what's the use.

I fly into a rage.

The statue lies shattered on the floor,
formless.
You are no longer you—just fragments
that will come in handy
for building a better one.

Lamento dei Fanti
(visto da sinistra)

da *Le rime e le prose del Maligno*

Manovali o col mestiere
"contrattor" siam batezzati
ma pe'l capo del cantiere
siamo un branco d'imbranati

> *Questa ditta che in effetti*
> ha un suo campo organizzato
> c'ha baracche con i letti
> per lo scapolo scasato.

La cucina con la mensa
i garages di lamiera
c'è la zona di decenza
e c'è il pal con la bandiera

> Poi c'è il luogo di ritrovo
> per la "truppa", e'l magazzino
> C'è un'ufficio tutto nuovo
> mentre il cuoco vende 'il vino

Dove il tempo ti appartiene
è nel letto, ch'è privato
ma c'è il capo che poi viene
anche se non è invitato

> C'è un'urgenza giù'n cantiere
> c'è quel forno ch'è scoppiato
> lui ti sveglia a fa' il dovere
> pur se mezzo addormentato

Anche quando non lavori
e t'en vai pe'i cazzi tuoi
devi al capo certi onori
altrimenti sono guai.

Foot Soldiers' Lament
(Seen from the left)

from *The Poetry and Prose of the Evil One*

Skilled or unskilled workers,
they baptize us "contractors,"
but to the site boss
we're a bunch of bunglers

> *This company has a camp*
> and keeps it organized—
> barracks with bunk beds
> for men without homes or wives,

outbuildings made of tin
a kitchen and a mess hall
and there's an outhouse, too,
and a flag on a pole.

> Then there's the recreatation hall
> for the "troops" and the equipment,
> and there's a new office
> while the cook sells wine.

The place where time is yours
is in your bunk. That's private.
But the boss can come there too
even if he's not invited.

> If there's a crisis at the site
> or a furnace has split open,
> he'll slap you awake to get to work
> with your head still half-asleep.

Even when you're off the roster
and you're doing your own thing,
the boss must get his due
or else you're in deep shit.

L'atmosfera che si respira
è di un campo militare
ma se vuoi beccar 'na lira
qui la burba devi fare.

A military air
is the air you breathe in camp,
but to barely earn a lira
you've got to be like a recruit.

→ Anna Maria Guidi (1926–1994)

Anna Maria Kahan Guidi was born in Rome in 1926, where she obtained a diploma in English language and literature at the British Institute before migrating to Sydney in 1954. Her time in Australia was characterized by a variety of commercial and professional occupations, which did not, however, exclude the production of literary texts. She has written and translated poems in Italian and English, and her poetry, which includes some texts written in Romanesco, has been widely published in anthologies, magazines, and journals in Italy, India, America, and Australia.

Guidi's poetry focuses on the places where she has lived or visited, and reveals a particular sensitivity in linking the contemplation of the landscape and the environment with the personal meaning it holds for the poet.

In looking back to the Roman setting and experiences of her premigration youth from the standpoint of her diasporic situation, she uses Romanesco, a choice significant to her theme. These poems, which contain stylistic elements that are to some extent modeled on the tradition of the Roman dialect poet Giuseppe Gioacchino Belli, present the lightly nostalgic memory of the now distant *passeggiate* at the Pincio in the company of her mother in "C'era 'na vorta . . .," while "Giorno de piova," dedicated to her father, evokes the thoughts brought on by a passing shower that briefly disrupts the routine of the life of the *borgata* where she lived, without, however, upsetting a fundamental optimism in facing the events that life may bring. In the English version of the former poem, the Roman setting and her mother's presence are somewhat less evident. Vastly different is Guidi's perception of the city of Venice, smothered in mist and characterized by "palazzi / improbabili, semisommersi" (improbable semi-submerged buildings) and "vetri / soffiati, colorati, avvolti nel mistero / di vecchi merletti" (blown colored glass / wrapped in the mystery /

of old lace), which combine to form an "onirica penombra dell'inconscio" (oneiric shadow of the subconscious).

By contrast with Venice, which contains past meaning, the Sydney cityscape featured in "I muri, il vento" has significance for the present, with its sea and sunlight bringing spiritual relief and hope for the future, despite the oppressive summer humidity and furnacelike heat and the briefly nostalgic recall of the Tyrrhenian Sea. Guidi's Australian experience is, however, one that presents mixed feelings, containing both the fear of passing time that carries bitter disappointments as well as ongoing hope deriving from the realization that permanent settlement carries with it a sense of belonging. It is an experience that contains among its positive aspects the discovery of the marvelous poetic essence of Australia's natural environment, represented by a kaleidoscope of visual images and sensations perceived by the writer in long-familiar places (the urban coastal strip) or in places she has visited (the Great Barrier Reef, the desert). One of the images presented in this poem, "l'arida maestà di Uluru" (the arid majesty of Uluru), uses the Aboriginal name of this sacred site known to the white colonizers as Ayers Rock. This image is elaborated in another poem, "Ayers Rock," which describes not only the grandeur of the monolith's landscape, but also the sense of fear that it inspires in the uninitiated casual visitor.

Like Enoe Di Stefano, Anna Maria Guidi develops in her poetry a sense of the relationship with the place to which she has migrated, yet aspects of the diaspora are much less evident, as is the need to overcome the dislocation brought about by the migration experience.

Anna Maria Guidi died in Sydney in 1994.

From Australia with Fear

da *Italo-Australian Poetry in the 80's*

dietro la siepe
incombe la paura
e c'è come una fretta
di smentire il presente
perché s'affretti
a mutare in passato

dietro il muro
degli anni, trincerato
ogni sentire s'ammorbidisce
nel favoloso "ieri."

Affanni
noti ed ignoti
scardinati pensieri
rissanti risonanti
approdano a una riva
d'immagine miniate
in lontananza.

Non più soggetto ormai
ma oggetto
porzionato frammentato
nel prisma di speranza che non cede.

Si può accettare tutto
se ridotto.
Il vuoto tradimento. Disillusioni
amare. Un non-amore

E un chicco solo di gioia assaporare
ingigantito, grande,
perché "passato"

From Australia with Fear

from *Italo-Australian Poetry in the 80's*

behind the hedge
fear looms
almost in a hurry
to deny the present
so that it will hasten
to change into the past

behind the wall
of the years, entrenched
all feelings soften
into a fabulous "yesterday."

Worries
known and unknown
unhinged thoughts
—scuffling sounding—
land on a shore of illuminated
images
in the distance.

No longer subject now
but an object
portioned fragmented
in a prism of unrelenting hope.

Everything can be accepted
if reduced.
The empty betrayal. Bitter
delusions. An unlove

And one grain of joy alone to savor
magnified, large,
because "past"

La poesia australiana

...e ti dicono poi
Scrivi di poesia Australiana.

Ma allora il kukaburra che si sveglia
e comincia a ridere
di contentezza, tra i rami dell'eucalipto
che ricamano un solerte merletto
sullo sfondo dell'alba di giada
e quarzo rosa
appena finita la notte,
non è poesia Australiana?

Il caleidoscopio del corallo
che si dondola pigro
nel cristallo dell'acqua che sciaborda
sotto la tua barca senza fondo,
mentre le isole fulgono
tutt'intorno
e sulle rocce
i pellicani stendono le ali ad asciugare
nel caldo del nuovo giorno...
È poesia Australiana.

I gabbiani
accovacciati nella sabbia
al tramonto
dopo una sontuosa cena di molluschi,
mentre la nera e bianca gazza
e il currawong
stridono nel cielo che si oscura
e si chiamano
disperatamente,
per non perdersi nella notte che avanza...
Non è questa forse la poesia
Australiana?

E tra le albe e i tramonti
d'una costiera amena

Australian Poetry

. . . and then they tell you
Write about Australian poetry.

But then the kookaburra waking up
and laughing
with joy, between the eucalyptus branches
embroidering an industrious lace
on the background of a dawn of jade and
pink quartz
as soon as night is over
isn't this Australian poetry?

The coral kaleidoscope
lazily swaying
in the crystal water lapping
under your bottomless boat,
while the islands shimmer
all around
and on the rocks
pelicans spread their wings to dry
in the warmth of a new day . . .
Is Australian poetry.

Seagulls
sitting on the sand
at sunset
after a lavish dinner of shellfish,
while the black and white razorbill
and the currawong
squeak in the darkening sky
and call each other
desperate,
not to lose each other in the approaching night . . .
Isn't this perhaps
Australian poetry?

And between the dawns and sunsets
of a charming coast

che conosco da anni,
vive uno sfondo antico,
intraveduto ignoto,
sorvolato qualche volta . . .
La terra rossa dell'interno,
l'arida maestà di Uluru
assorta
nella magia ininterrotta da secoli,
formicolante
di una gente esoterica
innocente
irrimediabilmente posseduta
di spiriti prepossenti
che sanno della storia
accaduta
nei perduti millenni
di questa Terra arcana . . .

Eccola dunque, viva,
la poesia Australiana.

I have known for years,
an ancient backdrop lives, glimpsed
unknown, overlooked at times . . .
The red earth inland,
the arid majesty of Uluru
absorbed
into a magic uninterrupted for centuries,
crawling
with esoteric people
innocent
irreparably possessed
by possessing spirits
who know about the history
that happened
in the lost millennia
in this arcane Land . . .

Then here it is, alive,
Australian poetry.

I muri, il vento

Dura estate vischiosa
di Sydney

Grattacieli spossati
immolati alla fornace
della città

Tra muro e muro
uno scintillio d'azzurro
pacifico
una vela o tante

Intanto,
mancano folate di vento
secco
squarci di tele
di vecchie vele rosse
che solcano il Tirreno

Pensieri pigri di sole
e il senso
di un lungo domani.

The Walls, the Wind

Hard sticky summer
in Sydney

Worn-out skyscrapers
sacrificed to the furnace
of the city

Between walls
a twinkling of blue
Pacific
one sail or many

Meanwhile,
there lack the gusts of dry wind
rents in the cloths
of old red sails
cleaving the Tyrrhenian Sea

Thoughts made lazy by the sun
and the sense
of a long tomorrow.

Ayers Rock

Cupe grotte
risonanti
di amuleti nascosti
dipinte di arcane folgori
in calceviva e sangue

Animistici anfratti riverberanti
urli d'aquile impervie
e cantano il mistero
di epoche lacrimate
in cumuli segreti d'ossa
sbiancate puntate a morte
nell'innocenza
del gioioso ritorno
ai tempo-sogno
del primo giorno del mondo

Ayers Rock

Dark caves
resounding
with hidden amulets
painted with arcane bolts of lightning
in quicklime and blood

Animistic recesses
reverberating
cries of impenetrable eagles
singing the mystery
of mourned times
in secret mounds
of whitened bones
pointed to death
in the innocence
of a joyful return
to the dreamtime
of the first day of the world

C'era 'na vorta . . .

A mi' madre

". . . Signo' come sei bella!
Che posso cammina' co' te, signora? . . ."
Era quer gioco nostro
de le passeggiate ar Pincio . . .
e così camminavo
pe' li viali d'estate
co' te che illuminasti
tutti li giorni miei
e me guidasti
pe' tutte le staggioni
da quanno m'aricordo che so' nata . . .

Certe matine
de primavera nova
tu te svejavi all'arba
e poi corevi
ne la cammera mia
e me dicevi
"Svejete che c'è er sole,
guarda fora!
Chi sta a letto a quest'ora?" . . .
E io m'arzavo
de malavoja, ch'ero regazzina
(e pigra pure),
e poi guardavo
giù ner cortile, dove 'na dozzina
de piccioni beccavano
e l'aurora
cominciava a spunta' gialla e aranciona
Com'era bella quela luce de primavera
Mo' che se n'è annata
solo un ricordo
come un viale oscuro
dove me perdo sola, abbandonata
m'arimane. E se puro cerco d'arichoama'

Once Upon a Time

To my mother

"...Madame you are so beautiful!
Can I walk with you, Madame?..."

It was our game
during our walks at the Pincio...
so I walked
along the summer roads
with you brightening
all my days
and guiding me
through all the seasons
I can remember since I was born...

Some mornings
of new spring
you would wake up at dawn
and then run
into my room
and tell me
"Wake up, the sun is up,
look outside!
Who stays in bed at this time?"...
And I would get up
unwillingly, because I was young
(and lazy too),
and I would look
down into the courtyard, where a dozen
pigeons were pecking
and dawn
beginning to break
all yellow and orange

How beautiful that spring light was
Now that it's gone
only a remembrance
like a dark road

co la memoria
tempi che so' passati,
m'aritrovo sbattuta contro a un muro,
l'occhi cecati da 'na benda nera
come 'na condannata.

A mia madre—"... Signora come sei bella! / Posso camminare con te, signora? ..." / Era quel
nostro gioco / delle passeggiate al Pincio ... / e così camminavo / per i viali d'estate / con te
che illuminasti / tutti i giorni miei giorni / e mi guidasti / per tutte le stagioni / da quando mi
ricordo che sono nata ... / / Alcune mattine / di una nuova primavera / tu ti svegliavi all'alba
/ e poi correvi / nella mia camera / e mi dicevi / "Svegliati che c'è il sole, / guarda fuori! / Chi
sta a letto a quest'ora? ..." / E io m'alzavo / di malavoglia, ch'ero ragazzina / (e anche pigra) /
e poi guardavo / giù nel cortile dove una dozzina / di piccioni beccavano / e l'aurora /
cominciava a spuntare gialla e arancione / com'era bella quella luce di primavera / or ache se
n'è andata / solo un ricordo / come un viale oscuro / dove mi perdo sola, abbandonata / mi
rimane. E se pure cerco di ricreare nella memoria / tempi che sono passati, / mi ritrovo
sbattuta contro un muro, / gli occhi cecati da una benda nera / come una condannata.

where I am lost alone, abandoned
remains for me. And even if
I try to recall in my memory
times that are past,
I find myself banged against a wall,
my eyes blinded by a black patch
like someone sentenced to death.

⇒ Lino Concas (b. 1930)

Lino Concas was born in Gonnosfanadigia in 1930 and, after having obtained a degree in philosophy, emigrated to Melbourne in 1963, where he became a secondary-school teacher of Italian. He began writing poetry at the age of fifteen, and his subsequent production of poetic texts has placed him among the leading first-generation Italian Australian poets.

His first volume, *Brandelli d'anima* (1965), is a collection of his early poems about love, solititude, alienation, religious vocation, the need for life and for purification. It also introduces the theme of migration, which is then elaborated in Concas's second volume of poetry, *Ballata di vento* (1977), which focuses on the sense of isolation and exile resulting from migration to Australia, seen as a forever-foreign land, given the impossibility of assimilation. These ideas are developed in the subsequent two volumes, *Uomo a metà* (1981) and *L'altro uomo: Poesie 1981–1983* (1988), in which the native land is revisited and reassessed not only from the point of view of an exile's nostalgia, but from the critical perspective of the social and existential conditions that have forced the poet to leave. Australia, while still a foreign land, is seen as a little less alien and alienating since it has begun to accept some aspects of the Italian migrant presence.

These four volumes, reprinted in the first volume of the 1998 collection *Poesie*, constitute the first phase of Concas's poetic journey, while his subsequent poetry, published in *Poesie 2: Mallee. Muggil. L'uomo del silenzio. Cobar* (1998), is a metaphysical investigation that explores possible points of equilibrium between Australia and his native Sardinia.

Malee, the Aboriginal word for the scrub that periodically explodes in the flames of the bushfire, is also "the expression of feelings . . . of something that burns inside [me]." This collection juxtaposes the contrasting realities of Sardinians and Aborigines, both groups that live "on the fringes of the modern world," both having been subject to invasion and exploitation and then forgotten. In the search for connections between places and times that appear so very different, but that can contain significant common meanings, *Muggil* explores the links between the "primitiveness" of the Australian Aboriginal and the Sardinian shepherd whose traditions have been obliterated by modern society. The comparison between Australia, which has now become the poet's land too, and his place of origin is the macrotheme of *L'uomo del silenzio*. This collection explores the possibility of conciliation between the two worlds by juxtaposing an Australian present with a Sardinian past that is still very much alive both in memory and in the contemplation of a possible return. *L'uomo del silenzio* also explores and reappraises the physical and metaphysical rites of passage from the old land to the new; Australia's history, society, and urban landscape; and the meaning of the world of the Aborigine, which has almost disappeared, but which has left significant traces for those who desire to seek them. The merging of Australia and Sardinia is continued in the final section of the volume, *Cobar,* an Aboriginal word meaning "red earth," which is also the name of an opal mining settlement in the Australian outback. Christmas in Australia has now become *"felice senza neve"* (happy without snow) because of the manifestations of both "ethnic" and Angloceltic traditions, while the landscapes of the poet's native Sardinia and his adopted country merge in an ideal unity, a merging that is also seen to occur in some aspects of the two cultural traditions.

Lino Concas's poetry is the expression of an intensely lived internal life in which the diaspora is an important overriding element, where the discovery of hope and love in the adopted land alleviates existential anguish, and where the Sardinian shepherd and the Australian Aboriginal meet and recognize each other in a universal bond of suffering, love, hope, and redemption. Like Luigi Strano for Calabria and the Australian bush, Concas has created a link between the desolate mountains of his native Sardinia and the red deserts of Australia, reaching an ideal though a not uncritical fusion between the two worlds.

Lino Concas lives in retirement in Melbourne, where he continues to write.

Siccità

da *Brandelli d'anima*

Ho bisogno d'acqua
e piove sangue
nelle mie zolle arse.
Non basta a spegnere
la mia sete
il sudore degli uomini stanchi,
né, la schiuma degli armenti assetati.
Ho bisogno d'acqua
nel pane fatto di grano,
nelle fontane asciutte
nei ruscelli,
nelle sorgive vene dei colli.
Nella spiga ingiallita
già trema la fame.
Ho bisogno d'acqua
nella casa, nei fiori,
nelle erbe, negli occhi
piangenti dei bimbi.
Ho bisogno d'acqua nell'Altare
ove anche tu, Signore,
sei fatto di pane e di acqua.
L'acqua può lavare il mio sangue.
Mi sento già nel covone di morte.

Drought

from *Tatters of the Soul*

I need water
and it rains blood on my parched turf.
The sweat of tired men
is not enough to quench my thirst,
nor the lather of thirsty herds.
I need water
in the bread made of wheat,
in the dry fountains,
in the brooks,
in the hills' springs.
In the yellowed spike of corn
already trembling with hunger.
I need water
in the house, in the flowers,
in the grass, in the weeping
eyes of the children.
I need water on the altar
where you, Lord,
are made of bread and water.
Water can wash my blood.
I already feel in death's bundle.

In terra straniera

Mesta una preghiera
di ombrose valli silenti,
di querce nodose,
di pini robusti
dritti su ispide rocce
scende mescolata
alle fonti e al sangue
degli armenti avviati
in fila alla morte.
Il canguro a fine giornata
chiuse ha le braccia
in croce dopo svelti salti
in circo aperto al sole.
Anch'io nudo mi trovo
la sera, fra le ombre,
aggrappato ad una roccia
e sale la preghiera
e il mio grido
come volo d'ali
tra sentieri smarrito
in terra straniera.

In Foreign Land

A sad prayer
from silent shadowy valleys,
gnarled oaks,
sturdy pines
upright on bristly rocks
falls mixed
to fountains and to the blood
of herds started
on the line to death.
The kangaroo at day's end
has its arms closed in a cross
after quick jumps
in an open circus to the sun.
I also find myself naked
in the evening, among the shadows,
clinging to a rock
and the prayer rises
and my cry
like a flight of wings
lost among paths
in foreign land.

Hanno rubato la mia terra

Hanno rubato la mia terra. Chi la possiede?
Non è più mia
da quando il pastore
ha lasciato le pecore
e nel maggese l'aratro
con un orizzonte secco di erbe.

Riempio ora
la mia giornata di sassi,
ora che il serpe
ha sconfitto il malocchio
e attorno ai nuraghi
un baccanale di prostitute
approdate agli scogli.

Le janas[3] hanno serrato le porte,
la loro isola venduta
le soffoca in un disperato silenzio.

Anch'io cerco altrove una nuova terra
che somigli alla mia
ricca di sole
e verde di pensieri.

Due mondi si odiano,
il fucile spara
mascherato di vendetta.
La morte è in agguato
su tutte le strade,
sulle fronde dolenti dei sugheri
scorticati come tronchi di uomo ucciso.

La processione si snoda,
il santo ciondola
tra il sì e il no.
Suonano le campane,
"sas launeddas"[4] accompagnano il voto.
Il miracolo della civiltà continua,

They Have Stolen My Land

They have stolen my land.
Who owns it?
It isn't mine anymore
from when the shepherd
has left the sheep
and in the fallow land the plow
with a dry horizon of grasses.

I fill now
my day with rocks
now that the snake
has defeated the evil eye
and around the Nuraghi
a Bacchanalian orgy of prostitutes
has landed on the rocks.

The *janas*⁵ have locked the doors,
their sold island
suffocates them in desperate silence.

I too look elsewhere for a new land
that is similar to mine
rich with sun
and green with thoughts.

Two worlds hate each other,
the gun fires
masked with vendetta.
Death is in ambush
on all the roads,
on the sad branches of cork trees
skinned like trunks
of slain men.

The procession unfolds
the saint dangles
between yes and no.
The bells ring,

danza di musica pop
con al collo merletti di corallo.

Ho scelto un'altra strada,
qui altri pastori sono venuti con me,
derubati anch'essi,
curvi su un messaggio
che tarda a venire.
Non disperate!
Non fuggite!
Il vostro lavoro
già esalta
questa mia nuova terra.

Il mondo si allarga
su un cuore che batte. Sperate!
Basta volere, basta amare.

"*sas launeddas*"[6] accompany the vow.
The miracle of civilization continues,
dance of pop music
with coral lace at the neck.

I have chosen another road,
here other shepherds
came with me,
these also robbed,
bent on a message
that is late coming.
Don't despair!
Don't flee!
Your work
already exalts
this new land of mine.

The world extends
on a heart that beats.
Have hope!
It's enough to want, enough to love.

La danza degli spiriti

da *Mallee: Qualcosa che Brucia*

I sughereti,
la chiesetta rustica,
il campo,
poi l'acqua
con la voce
delle montagne
e di altre valli.

Si aggiungono
altri suoni,
altre voci,
un pascolo dolce
di verde e di cristallo
specchio di cielo
e di fanciulle vestite
con i colori a festa.

Danzano,
ridono,
cantano
muovendosi a cerchio
in una nudità di grazia
che la fisarmonica accompagna.
Spiriti fecondatrici
della mia terra antica.

The Dance of the Spirits

from *Mallee: Something That Burns*

The orchards of cork trees,
the little country church,
the field,
then the water
with the voice
of the mountains
and of the other valleys.

Other sounds
are added,
other voices,
a sweet meadow
of green and crystal
mirror of sky
and of girls dressed up
in festive colors.

They dance,
laugh,
sing
moving in a circle
in a graceful simplicity
as the accordion plays.
Fertilizing spirits
of my ancient land.

Melbourne

da *Poesie volume 2*

Popolo di nuovi spiriti,
città delle nostre patrie,
dai solchi la tua prima
infanzia alla terra,
dai pascoli i tuoi primi
occhi alla luce.
Battezzata
con giardini di sole,
stravagante e composta
parli cento lingue,
hai monumenti e grattacieli
fabbriche e camini ruttanti.
Privilegi i canti d'Europa
come torma
di fatiche e di speranza
e la musica di
un ballo gitano come armonia
delle tue native foreste.
Tu che nascondi
i miei crepuscoli ai sogni
e mi dai le voci
pulsanti di passione
accogli questa volontà
acerba di amare
come profetica certezza
che le tue spighe
sono i nostri corpi,
le tue case
tele animate di luce
dove fiorisce il sangue
della mia vecchia terra.
Tu sei la mia casa,
la casa di tante case,

Melbourne

from *Poetry Volume 2*

People of new spirits,
city of our old lands,
from the furrows your first
infancy to the earth,
from meadows your first
eyes to the light.
Baptized
with sun gardens,
extravagant and composed
you speak a hundred languages,
you have monuments and skyscrapers
factories and belching chimneys.
You favor the songs of Europe
like a multitude
of hard work and hopes
and the music of a gypsy dance
like the harmony of your native forests.
You that hide
my sunsets in dreams
and give me voices
pulsating with passion
welcome this determination
bitter from loving
as prophetic certainty
that your ears of corn
are our bodies,
your houses
canvasses animated by light
where blood flourishes
from my old land.
You are my home,
the home of so many homes,

il nostro nome,
la forza dei nostri spiriti
in cieli aperti
e monti sofferti di grido.

our name,
the force of our spirits
in open skies
and shouting suffering mountains.

Noi i Kanakas

da *L'uomo del silenzio*

Fossa calda di silenzio,
figura di uomini,
occhi neri e polmoni bucati.
Noi i Kanakas[7]
quelli che tu non vedi,
cui pensi tra colline
di sole e venti di canne.
Camminare con chi?
Se anch'io non ci sono
come l'acqua di un fiume
e la corrente di uno scoglio.
Siamo e non siamo
senza mai trovarci,
foglie di steppe e di resina,
di salici e prati
in sedili vuoti
con gente che non conversa,
spezzati di parole
e mangiati di ombra.
Ritornerò un giorno
nella mia casa,
riaccenderò il camino
che il vento ha spento,
ritroverò tovaglie e bicchieri
e il mio vecchio pane
in una stanza accesa di sole.
Sentirò la mia voce
e le mie parole,
rivedrò la faccia delle montagne
e qualcosa che non è morto
anche sotto la povertà della terra,

We Kanakas

from *The Silent Man*

Hot pit of silence,
shadow of men,
black eyes and punctured lungs.
We Kanakas[8]
those you don't see,
whom you think about in the hills
of sun and reed winds.
Walking with whom?
If I too am not there
as the water of a river
and the current of a reef.
We are and we aren't
without ever finding ourselves,
leaves of steppes and resin,
willow trees and meadows
in empty seats
with people that don't converse,
broken by words
and eaten by shadows.
I will return one day
to my house,
I will relight the fireplace
the wind has put out,
I will find again tablecloths and glasses
and my old bread
in a room lit up by sun.
I will hear my voice
and my words,
I will see again the face of the mountains
and something not dead
also under the land's poverty,

la neve e il sole,
i covoni rossi di grano,
il mattino che nasce
e la gente che passa.

the snow and the sun,
the red sheaves of wheat,
the morning that's born
and the people that pass by.

→ Paolo Totaro (b. 1933)

Paolo Totaro, born in Naples in 1933, has been living in Australia since 1963 as a result of the diaspora of corporate executives who promoted Italian industry abroad in the wake of Italy's economic miracle. His considerable managerial skills and his wide cultural interests—he has university degrees in law and music—led him to accept an offer to create the Community Arts Board of the Australia Council in 1975. From 1977 to 1989, he was foundation chair of the Ethnic Affairs Commission of New South Wales, and in that role pioneered many fundamental multicultural initiatives. He subsequently held other appointments in positions involving constitutional and legal reform, was for a time visiting professor at the University of Western Sydney and pro-vice chancellor and member of council at the University of Technology Sydney. A busy schedule that also includes journalism and television appearances and an interest in science has not prevented him from the practices of chamber music and writing. His short story, *Storia patria*, won the 1993 edition of the *Premio Letterario 2 Giugno*.

Paolo Totaro writes both in Italian and English and was the first, and is still one of the very few, writers to depict the soundtrack of Australia's multicultural work environment, rich in linguistic dislocations. His over one hundred poems are, however, largely unpublished, although a number of his poems have appeared in magazines and anthologies, as well as in the volume *Paolo poesie* (1981). The themes enunciated in his poetry range from the unforgettable childhood traumas of war, to the dilemma of whether to follow music or other paths, to the expressive tension and a search for possible equilibriums between Catholic and Marxist, humanistic and scientific, Italian and Australian cultures.

His early poetry expresses the rebellion of a young intellectual toward the elitist culture of his place of origin ("Il comizio," 1959). His later Australian poems express the challenge of the awareness that participation in the culture of his adopted country leads to contributing to its transformation. There are explicit references to the diaspora, although they are by and large veiled by the need not to indulge in nostalgia. The migration experience is thus perceived as the courageous translocation from one society to another, representing constant dynamic change, a linguistic melting pot, with its challenge of not overlooking the reciprocal recognition of the continuity and dignity of each individual person.

In this context, Totaro's plurilinguistic lyric experimentation, more unique than rare in Italian Australian poetry, is particularly interesting, and displays a rare sensitivity towards the human condition of the migrant. Many of these poems written in a mix of languages relate to salient aspects of the presence of non-English-speaking-background first-generation migrants in Australia, who account for about 12 percent of its population. Poems like "Port Kembla," composed in 1977, express the theme of the "nonmeaning" of life in the punishing environment of the blast furnaces at the steelworks, and present interesting parallels with the later poems of Pietro Tedeschi. In "6 p.m. Cleaners," plurilingualism becomes the symbol of the brotherhood between workers from Italy, Spain, and Latin America, a brotherhood that in "Homer: fish shops" is extended also to Greeks. Further references to Australian pluriculturalism are found in "Lydia Nausicaa: In Memoriam," a moving elegy for a young friend.

Paolo Totaro's themes include his relationship with the environment in which he lives and the people that are important in his life: his Jesuit teachers, his parents, his wife, his children. Enchanting Pittwater, on the coast north of Sydney and surrounded by an immense national park, on whose shores Totaro lives ("Linee diritte"), constitutes an idealized oasis of peace in sharp contrast with the hectic and alienating environment of New South Wales politics. Pittwater, where the calm dawn sea is later disturbed by the midday trade winds, represents a serenity that perhaps mirrors a conscience disturbed by the tension between a wistful aspiration to interior peace and the reality of social conflict. The difficulty of saying things that really count is perhaps another way of expressing that active participation in the culture of the adopted country is a no less wistful aspiration than past participation in the culture of the country of origin.

The old, the new, the exotic, the familiar, and the stress of constant travel are the themes of "Sono passato anche per la Guinea," written in 1960, when Totaro traveled the world on behalf of Fiat. Addressing his faraway parents, he invites them to come to Sydney to see his new life. He recalls with yearning the sound of his mother's footsteps when in the dead of night she would get up to make the coffee that would send her back to sleep, and the image of his father, and his abandoned land in Puglia with its wine, olives, and wheat, another lifetime ago. The exotic totems brought from New Guinea become "two obscure Christs" that share space on the walls of his Sydney home with two other familiar totems brought from Naples, the miniature portrait of a baroness aunt and the "mute" square of a Sacred Heart.

"Il Comizio" is a *passeggiata* in the ancient historical center of the city of Naples and a metaphor of the passage from Benedetto Croce's neoidealistic philosophy, studied by many students in the Italian south at the time, toward Gramsci and Togliatti's brand of Marxism. The poet, then twenty and a student at the Conservatorium, and his friends talk about the fact that Naples presents very few opportunities, and that they would soon have to leave, perhaps for the most distant corner of the world, which with prophetic perspicacity is identified as Australia.

Paolo Totaro continues to work on his writing and remains deeply committed to social reform.

Prima Ballata Cavalcanti: Le parole

Perch'io non spero di tornar già mai,
Ballatetta, in Campania,
Va tu leggiera a dire:
C'è guerra fra la madre
Lingua e la seconda,
In Australia e col dialetto.

Tu chiederai soccorso a quei sonori
Modi di dire e di cantilenare:
Ma guarda che ho bisogno di parole
Dolci alla voce, e di molto valore:
Parole cui affidare quel pensare
Che a Napoli formato
E risciaquato in Arno
Ora torto in inglese
Non riesce a volare,
Nè a cantare in poesia.

Tu digli, Ballatetta, le parole
Si travian qui e spesso ci abbandona
Speranza di poter significare
Quel che si vuole, e non sol che si deve
O che si teme o che vien dato a dire.
E con l'inglese è duro:
Non tornan quelle tronche
Parole e quelle acca
Che bisogna aspirare.

Deh vaga Ballatetta, quando torni
Col tuo carico ricco di parole
Antiche e nuove, e di modi di dire
E d'inflessioni, in un battibaleno
Voglio che tu li meni nell'arteria
Più vicina a quel centro
Definito da Broca
Del parlare . . .

First Ballad Cavalcanti: Words

As I don't hope to ever return,
Little Ballad, to Campania,
Go lightly and say:
It's war between the mother tongue
And the second, in Australia
Against dialect.

You will ask help of those sonorous
Idioms and ways of singing:
But take care that I need words
Sweet to the voice and very meaningful;
Words to which I can entrust the thought,
Formed in Naples,
Rinsed in the Arno River,
Now turned to English,
Which does not take flight
Nor sing in poetry.

Tell him that here the words
Are often misleading and that
We lose hope of expressing what we want
To say, and not only what we must or what
We fear, or what we're supposed to say.
And with English it is hard,
The words don't make the count
Then there's that H
We have to aspirate.

Say, little Ballad,
When you return
With your load
Of new and ancient words
And idiomatic sayings and inflections
I want you to take them
To the nearest artery
Of speech defined by Broca

                    . . . Oooh che grande
Tempesta: ecco ritorna
Il timbro musicale,

La voce è sbigottita: ricompare
Felice, chill'acciento che 'mme pare
Che sta parlanne 'Ntuone 'o marenare.
"Ué Ballatè, m'e fatte allicriare ! "
Risponne, questa volta, Ballatetta:
"Questa vostra servente,
Mentre che era assente
A comperar per voi
Tutte queste parole,
V'ha preso pure questo."

E m'inietta un solvente
Che dritto nella mente scioglie tutto
Lo qual che disattiva la memoria
Liberando nel vuoto laceranti
Rintocchi che credevo imprigionati.

Ed il battito dell'anima riprende
Dove aligeri stracci
Di passato lontano
Orbitano il domani.
"Per la misericordia:
Riprendi ogni parola
Che mi hai donato! Chiudi,
Grido, chiudi il passato!"

Scompare tutto. Anche Ballatetta
È andata, con le scarpe di cartone
E le pupille cieche della memoria,
Tinnulante tarlo che non deve più
Cricchiare . . .
                    . . . Oh forgetta
forgetta le parole
E questa fenza che da tanta parte
Delle colonne e i simulacri.
E il carro.

Oh what great storm,
Behold the musical tone returns

The voice is stunned.
Felice has returned
With that accent of his
That reminds me of a Tony the sailor.
"Hey, little Ballad, you really made my day."
Answer this time:
"This your servant
while out shopping for you
has brought you this as well."
And she injects a solvent
In my brain that there dissolves
All that disables the memory
Freeing rending bell peels
That I had deemed enchained.

And the beating of the soul resumes
Where winged rags
From a distant past
Orbit tomorrow.
"For mercy's sake
Take back every word
You've given me.
Shut off the past," I scream.

Everything disappears. Even the little Ballad.
She has gone away
with her shoes made of cardboard
and the blind pupils of memory,
a lightly ringing moth
that must no longer make a sound."

Oh, forgetta
Forgetta the words
And the fence which is part of much
Of the columns and the sacred images
And the car

1. Collector
Skein, jejeune, dewsilky kine:
joyous overflow of Joyce;
driftwood snakes
and a wing of Samothracia
smoothed by incessant washing
of waves on sand;
yarda, spaghettibar, il carro.

They are all archived
with companionway doors
and seawrecked rudders.

We collect junkwords
from books, our beach and passing
conversations of people not quite
speaking English, who zabil[9]
their own razgavòr[10]
che forgettano
their own linguamadre

2. Linee diritte: Straight lines
Scure bande di terra
sottolineate dal brulichio bianco
di barche minutamente ancorate.
In alto, larghe onde di eucalipti
intrecciano dita di rosa in riccioli
di nuvole.

"'O rododactyylos eos[11]
precede d'estate qui in Australia
il vento di nordovest
che fra un'ora
scompiglierà il mare
e le linee ora dritte
saranno, per il resto del giorno,
incertamente increspate."

3. Surging tide at dusk : marea crescente al tramonto
Il progresso è prevedibile
per osservatori ostinati

1. Collector

Skein, jejeune, dewsilky kine:
joyous overflow of Joyce;
driftwood snakes
and a wing of Samothracia
smoothed by incessant washing
of waves on sand;
yarda, spaghettibar, il carro.

They are all archived
with companionway doors
and seawrecked rudders.

We collect junkwords
from books, our beach and passing
conversations of people not quite
speaking English, who zabil[16]
their own razgavòr
che forgettano
their own linguamadre

2. Linee diritte: Straight Lines

Dark strips of earth
underlined by a white shimmering
of closely anchored boats.
up high, wide waves of Eucalyptus trees
interlace rosy fingers into curls of clouds.

"O rododactylylos eos"[17]
here in Australia precedes in summer
the northwest wind
that within an hour
will stir up the sea
and the lines that were straight
will remain uncertainly rough
for the rest of the day.

3. Surging tide at dusk: marea crescente al tramonto

Progress is predictable
for obstinate observers

di quel fronte ambiguo
dove mare è spiaggia
e spiaggia, mare:
tà parà thàlattan.[12]

Impronte di tallone generano pozze;
dune di sabbia riccioli di schiuma;
la linea maginot azzurra
dei soldier crabs si ritira
e poi s'insabbia;
minutaglia di foglie triturate
galleggia indifferente al nuovo.

Inquisitivi riflessi sorgono
su per le palafitte incrostate:
arenaria ambrarancione
liquefa vibrazioni grigie
e, come tramonto annega in notte,
ci si immagina quel nero: mare.

4. Aspettare una vela
Aspettare una vela
seduti alla punta del molo
dopo avere cercato
l'orizzonte migliore:
a livello dell' acqua
si anticipa meglio un incrinatura viola
sulla tavola vuota della baia.

E come si vede una linea assai tenue,
l'unica perpendicolare
dopo ore di calma allunata,
occhi erranti
senza pace
ora si tendono attenti
assorbono ogni goccia di luce:
ecco !
la forma familiare.

of the ambiguous front
where sea is beach
and beach sea:
tà parà thàlattan.[18]

Heel prints generate pools;
sand dunes curling foam;
the blue maginot line
of soldier crabs moves back
and is submerged by sand;
what's left of shredded leaves
floats indifferently again.

Inquisitive reflections rise
upon the encrusted wood piles:
amber-orange arenaria
liquefies gray vibrations
and, as sunset drowns in the night,
we can imagine that blackness: sea.

4. Waiting for a Sail
Waiting for a sail
sitting at the edge of the pier
after looking for the best horizon:
at water level
one can best foresee a violet creasing
on the empty table of the bay.

And as you see a very faint line
the only perpendicular one
after hours of moonlight calm,
searching eyes
without peace
now focus attentively
absorb every drop of light:
behold!
the familiar shape.

Il colore no:
quello verrà col sole.

5. Child drawings

Rude men roll grey barrels
over long jetties
with piercing noises of words and metal .
Barges with extended slides
go and come, loaded
with more of that colorless cargo.
You, little child,
didn't seem to be looking
but now, solitary as you draw
the day's walk,
all the harshness has blossomed
into flowers and heart-shaped petals.

6. Voci

Voices fly low,
scivolano sull' acqua
a bit uncertain,
like black cormorans that wonder
whether or not to land.

Sunday is for fishing
in tinnies hired from Church Point:
"Did you catch qualcosa?"
"Tira!" "Dai!"
"Gar nicht!" "Helfen!"[13]
"Tò psàri !" "Tò capèllo!"[14]
"Opàsnii!" "Nicevò!"[15]

Not the color!
that will come with the sun.

5. Child drawings

Rude men roll grey barrels
over long jetties
with piercing noises of words and metal.
Barges with extended slides
go and come, loaded
with more of that colorless cargo.
You, little child,
didn't seem to be looking
but now, solitary as you draw
the day's walk,
all the harshness has blossomed
into flowers and heart-shaped petals.

6. Voices

Voices fly low,
glide over the water
a bit uncertain,
like black cormorants that wonder
whether or not to land.

Sunday is for fishing
in tinnies hired from Church Point:
"Did you catch qualcosa?"[19]
"Tira!" "Dai!"[20]
"Gar nicht!" "Helfen!"[21]
"Tò psàri!" "Tò capèllo!"[22]
"Opàsnii!" "Nicevò!"[23]

Homer: fish shops

Telemacos

Con Karanges
fish and more fish shops

antica ecclesia orthodoxa
di Wollongong
colle pitture y madonne
negras ebony

la mia coscienza
si confounds

tell me Jimmy Joyce
qual' è quis est
il greco?

L' English Ghetto: Gardeners

L' uccelli aves et birds
que da Pymble
stormano sui trees
they know saben conoscono
solo motti inglesi

words
more words
more more words

ma but
al sabbato ammatina
especially al weekend
entiendono
palabras
e parole

delle terre nuestras

Port Kembla

Extremadura
coke havens
altiforni hornos
de fundicion
aqui la vita è breve
meaningless
non ha significado

hermanos o calor
red-hot-white
blanco fierro
c' è ancora l'hope
y l'esperanza

da l'Estremadura
tu veinistyou came
frade meu
brothero
español ancora
and yet
el pianto mio
my cry
si confounds se mixa
col tuo

6 p.m. Cleaners

cuando quando
when

l'office
is closed

e l'executivo
todo all tutto
va home

then
entonces allora
quattro four or five
poveri devils
pobre diablos

umildemente

escoban
vacuumclearanno
l'oficio

Chester Hill: Refugee School

Vietnam est fini
et tu almond-eyed
est ici
among strangers?

hardly so si tu veux
love avoir qui t'enseigne-teach
la langue English
with les dessins from Peanuts

et tu ? de Beirut

la guerre est fini
pour tous parents

poor orphans
of us all
pauvre infelicitè
de notre
madnesse

→ *Pino Bosi (b. 1933)*

Born in Tolmino in 1933, Pino Bosi emigrated to Australia in 1951, and after initially working in manual occupations, began a long-term journalistic career, initially with *La Fiamma* in 1955 and subsequently with other Italian Australian and Anglo-Australian newspapers and magazines. Over the years he became a well-known personality in the Sydney Italian Australian community, not only as a journalist in the print and electronic media but also as master of ceremonies at numerous community functions.

A prolific writer—he has published novels, short stories, collections of poetry, biographies, and essays—Bosi had experienced during his school years "a sense of physical pleasure in discovering the meaning of words . . . that had a form all of their own" that went hand in hand with an aptitude for writing poetry, fiction, and other genres. This aptitude, together with the realization that the stories published in Italian Australian newspapers in the 1950s originated exclusively in Italy, led him to write in Italian a series of humorous stories based on the reality of the Italian Australian diaspora, which appeared in *La Fiamma* in the 1950s during one of the peak periods of Italian migration. As the author explained in a lecture delivered at the University of Wollongong in 1986, his intention was to produce "original prose . . . created here . . . so that people could understand local realities." Writing as a way of expressing the migrant experience is also applied to a substantial part of his poetry written in Italian, gathered in *Mi sono scocciato* (1968), although it is far less evident in his poetry written in English, gathered in *I'll Say Good Morning* (1973) and *Thirteen Continents and a Rocket/Magi Lost* (1988), which is more about expressing feelings, affects, and philosophical and existentialist questions.

Bosi is one of relatively few poets who have dealt with the humorous aspects of the Italian Australian diaspora, and he is one of the very few to systematically use in some of his texts the Australian variety of Italian in poems such as "'O Bisinisse" and "Astrocultura." The latter poem is an Italian Australian version of Dante's *Divine Comedy* written, of course, in terza rima, which begins: "Nel mezzo del camin della marchetta / mi ritrovai stoppato da un polisse / giusto alle luci rosse di una stretta. / "Ehi, draiva!" quello subito mi disse / "Tu stai luccando per un accidente / oppure stai pensando ai tuoi bisnisse?" (Midway in the journey to the market / I found myself stopped by a policeman / at the red traffic light in a street. / "Hey driver!" he immediately said to me / "Are you looking for an accident / or are you thinking about your business?"). Bosi, however, does not deal only with the more immediate and direct aspects of the Italian Australian experience. Other poems present themes related to aspects of Australian history and culture, such as the rewriting in Italian of the Anglo-Australian canonical texts *Waltzing Matilda* and *Botany Bay: Versione italiana*. Yet others are fanciful diversions of the course of Australian history, such as the discovery of Australia by the Italians, which would lead to a situation where "a Canberra invece / di Hawk e i suoi picciotti / ci saremmo trovati / o il Craxi o l'Andreotti / . . . Ma ai fatti del passato / non si può chiedere grazia / e noi ci accontentiamo / della nostra . . . disgrazia" (In Canberra / instead of Hawk and his underlings / we would have found / Craxi o Andreotti / . . . But past happenings / do not bring dispensation / and we have to accept / our misfortune).

Bosi's Italian poetry dealing with the diaspora can thus be seen as an attempt not only to make sense of the migration and settlement experience, but also to dwell on its humorous and less negative aspects in the search for the establishment of an Italian Australian cultural space.

Pino Bosi lives in Melbourne, where he continues his activity as a writer.

Austrocultura

da *Italian Writers in Australia: Essays and Texts*

Nel mezzo del cammin della marchetta
mi ritrovai stoppato da un polisse
giusto alle luci rosse di una stretta.

"Ehi, draiva!" quello subito mi disse
"Tu stai luccando per un accidente
oppure stai pensando ai tuoi bisnisse?"

Guardando quel gran figlio di sergente
gli dissi: "Non aver nessuna fia
che io non cerco di chillar la gente!

Piuttosto è tutta colpa di Maria
che mi ha mandato a prender veggetabile
per noi, per sua sorella e per la zia.

Ma io, che c'ho la mente un poco labile,
ho forghettato cosa ho da baiare
per questo che draivavo un poco instabile.

Ma tu non mi vorrai mica bucare
che sono figlio di una madre etnica
e l'inglese non so manco spiccare?"

Lui disse: "Non usar la vecchia tecnica
di far l'ebreo per fottere il cristiano
in base alla cultura plurietnica.

Parca il tuo carro e poi, licenza in mano;
la legge non ammetta l'ignoranza.
C'avete rotto a tutti il deretano

con la multi-del-cacchio culturetnica.
A questo punto caccia fuor la grana
o ti mando in galera a far vacanza."

Australian Culture

from *Italian Writers in Australia: Essays and Texts*

Midway in the journey to the market
I found myself stopped by a policeman
just at the red light of a street.

"Hey driver" he said to me immediately
"You're looking to cause an accident
or you are thinking about your business?"

As I looked at that big son of a sergeant
I told him: "You need not be afraid
I not going to kill the people here.

It's really Mary's fault for sending me
to buy the vegetables
for us, her sister and her aunt.

But since my memory is somewhat feeble
and I forgot what I was sent to get
that's why my driving was a bit unstable.

But you don't really want to book me
As I am the son of an ethnic mother
and I can't even speak English."

He said: "Don't use with me the old technique
to play the Jew so as to screw the Christian
playing the card of multiethnic culture!

Park your car and have your license handy;
the law does not allow for ignorance
as an excuse. You've busted all our balls.

Leaving aside the multiethnic culture crap,
either you pay in cash immediately,
or I'll send you to jail on a vacation."

Fu così che per poco in Giorge Stretta
non mi trovai ai polsi le manette.
Ma io, scappando dentro alla market,
col cul feci al polisse una trombetta!"

That's how I almost found myself handcuffed
right there on George Street,
but then as I fled to the market,
for the cop I turned my ass into a trumpet.

Botany Bay: Versione italiana

Su brindiamo augurando
salute agli autori
del progetto di legge
che vuol buttar fuori
tutti i ladri, ruffiani,
imbroglioni e altri rei
per fondar 1a colonia di Botany Bei.

Con arte o mestiere non
comprano il pane,
anzi sfruttan la gente
nel modo più infame;
han le mani bucate,
bevon fino alle sei
dall'alba e son degni
di Botany Bei.

Ed i profittatori
che sol hanno in mente
di spremere il sangue
alla povera gente?
Costosa è la carne
fagioli e pisei ...
e allora mandiamoli
a Botany Bei.

Le puttane, i lenoni,
son bastardi anche loro
che mangion e bevon
col nostro lavoro.
Niente paga o pensione
per quei cicisbei ...
che vadano a nozze
a Botany Bei!

Se piazza pulita
poi far si volesse
dovremmo cacciar

Botany Bay

Let's drink to the good health
of the authors of the law
that wants to throw out
all thieves, and ruffians
con men, of felons an array
to found the colony
of Botany Bay.

With art and know-how
they buy no bread,
they exploit the people
in the most infamous way;
their hands are a sieve
they drink until six
from the dawning of day
and they are worthy
of Botany Bay.

What about the profiteers
who have only one goal
to squeeze the blood out of the poor?
for meat peas and beans
too dear you have to pay
so let's send them
to Botany Bay.

Whores and pimps
are bastards as well
they eat and they drink
on the work that we do
give those worthless parasites
neither pension nor pay . . .
let them have their reward
at Botany Bay.

If we really wanted
to clean out the place
we should throw out

gli esattori di tasse.
E chi sopra agli altri
va a caccia di nei
si guadagni il suo pane
a Botany Bei.

Ce ne sono a migliaia
in galera e in prigione
ma quelli al di fuori
son più d'un milione
che imbrogliano, ammazzan,
deruban gli dei . . .
Mandiamoli tutti
a Botany Bei.

Se tra voi c'è persona
rimasta un po' offesa
si palpi la parte
rimasta più lesa
e segue un consiglio,
glielo dedico a Lei:
la vada a curarsela
a . . . Botany Bei.

all tax collectors.
And those who spend time
scrutinizing all others
for something to say
let them earn their keep
at Botany Bay.

There are thousands of them
in prisons and jails
but those who are out
are more than a million
and they cheat and they kill
despoiling the gods . . .
Let's send them all
to Botany Bay.

If among you there's someone
who's offended by this
let him touch the part
that was most injured
and do what I say
go get it cured
at . . . Botany Bay.

'O bisinisse

Io stavo di bordo
da un vecchio gringrossa
che s'era arricchito
rompendosi l'ossa.[24]
Per fare moneta
un giorno mi disse
ci vuole costanza
ci vuol bisinisse.
Se stai tutto il giorno
a bere nel pabbo
non hai mai la ciansa
di farti nababbo.
Se invece hai 'na giobba
e mangi formaggio
ti fai prima i semi
e dopo il cottaggio.
Dimentica ghelle
dimentica il carro
cammina e lavora
e ingoia catarro.
Fin quando la lacca
non nocca alla dora
tu tira bestemmie
ma intanto lavora.
Non prender tichette
della lotteria
il veig e l'overtaime
tu mettili via.
E nel tuo uichende
in sta terra bastarda
pulisci giardini
e ramazza la iarda.
Quantunque snobbato
raccogli moneta
finché verrà il giorno

The Business

I lived as a boarder
with an old greengrocer
who had gotten rich
by breaking his bones.
To make some good money,
he told me one day,
you need to be constant,
you need a good business.
By staying in pubs
and drinking all day
you don't stand a chance
to become a tycoon.
But if you've a job
and you eat plain cheese,
you start by buying a semi-detached house
and then get a cottage.
Forget about girls.
Forget about cars.
Just walk and then work
and swallow your phlegm.
Until some good luck
comes to knock at your door,
just spit out your curses
and continue to work.
Don't go buying tickets
from the lottery ever.
And just put away
your wage and overtime.
And during the weekend
in this horrible land,
go out and clean gardens
and sweep out the yard.
Although you'll be snobbed
you will collect dough
until the day comes

che giungi alla meta.
Sarai rispettato
persin dai polisse
dai preti e dai frati
se tieni bisinisse!

when you reach your goal.
You will be respected
even by the police
by priests and by monks
if you have a business.

Ma lo sa il gabbiano
Che se alle tre
Non mi presento dal direttore di banca
Domani farò brutta figura?
E che ne sa il sole
Che ho litigato con mia moglie?

from *I'll Say Good Morning*

But does the seagull know
That if at three o'clock
I don't appear before the bank director
I will look pretty bad tomorrow?
And what does the sun care
That I had a fight with my wife?

Dio.
Dio, Dio, Dio, Dio
Parola con la quale
Faccio una rete
E cerco di raccogliere Il senso dell'universo
E della mia anima.
E invece poi ti capita
Qualche volta
Di toglierti un paio di scarpe strette
E ti pare
Di aver scoperto tutto!

God
God, God, God, God
A word with which
I create a net
And try to gather the sense of the universe
And of my soul.
On the other hand, however,
It happens sometimes
That you take off a pair of tight shoes
And you think
You've discovered everything!

Sensazioni

da *Italo-Australian Poetry in the 80's*

Non farle male
quando l'accarezzerai la prima volta.
La sua pelle è così chiara.
Le tue mani
sono così ruvide.
Non farle male.

Ma tu pensi che un vecchio
che rastrella foglie secche
d'autunno
e ne fa tanti mucchietti
ai lati della strada
sia una cosa da niente?
Ma scherzi?
Non senti l'odore degli anni
che scivolano tra i denti sgangherati del rastrello
e quelli che invece si intoppano
e si lasciano ammucchiare
come i ricordi?

Feelings

from *Italo-Australian Poetry in the 80's*

Don't hurt her
when you caress her for the first time.
Her skin's so light
your hands
are so rough.
Don't hurt her.

But you think that an old man
who rakes dead leaves
in the fall
making many small mounds
on the side of the road
is a thing of little importance?
Are you joking?
Don't you smell the odor of his years
that slip through the broken teeth of his rake
and those that bunch up
and allow themselves to grow into mounds
like memories.

Immagini

Pioggia amica
pioggia antica
che si ricorda
di tanto tempo fa . . .

Si ricorda ancora
come piovere scrosciante
quando deve lavare
sporcizia e peccati
per me
per lei per lui
e per loro
finché tutto diventa più chiaro
perfino il grigio domenicale della noia.

Ma sa anche giocare
la pioggia
come fosse una bambina . . .
a fa correre la goccia lungo il filo
finché smette di scivolare
fermata da un pensiero
e cade rincorsa da un'altra goccia
che si ferma e cade
rincorsa da un'altra goccia
che corre
e cade
corre
e cade
goccia
a goccia
scivolando senza sbalzi
liscia e liquida
finché si ferma
si gonfia
e cade
giù
una

Images

Friendly rain
ancient rain
that we recall
from a long time ago . . .

We still remember it
like the thundering rain
when it has to wash away
dirt and sins
for me
for her for him
and for them
until everything becomes clearer
even the Sunday gray of boredom.

But rain knows also how to play
like a little girl . . .
and she makes each drop run along the line
until il stops slipping
arrested by a thought
and falls chased by another drop
that stops and falls
pursued by another drop
that runs
and falls
drop
by drop
sliding down without bumps
smooth and liquid
until it stops
swells
and falls
down
one
by one
one
by one

ad
una
una
ad
una
una
ad
una
giù
giù
giù . . .
Ogni città
ha il suo angolo sporcaccione
dove pare che il vento
c'abbia gusto a raccoglier tutto
come per far vedere alla gente
che la loro civiltà
produce soprattutto
plastica e carta straccia.
E allora i cani
per non essere da meno
ci vanno in fila indiana
per lasciarci anche il loro.

C'era un albero straniero
tra i quattro eucalipti stradali
che ogni anno perdeva le foglie
e faceva il morto
per farti sentire un po' triste
e volergli più bene.

one by one
Down
down
down . . .

Every city
has its filthy quarter
where the wind seems to enjoy
gathering everything
as though to show the people
that their civilization
produces mainly plastic and rubbish.
So the dogs
not to be outdone
form a line
to leave their own.

There was once a foreign tree
amid the four eucalyptus trees on the road
that lost its leaves every year
and played dead
to make you feel a little sad
and love it a little more.

⇢ Giovanni Andreoni (b. 1935)

Born in Grosseto in 1935, Giovanni Andreoni emigrated to Australia in 1962 after having obtained a degree in political science. He was attracted to Australia by a spirit of adventure and the freedom of its wide-open spaces, and he quickly found his niche in its universities as a lecturer in Italian language and literature. His university teaching and research has not, however, kept him from writing novels, short stories, and poetry.

Although more widely known for his prose writings, his poetry is nevertheless a more intense reiteration of the theme (also present in some of his narratives) of the bush and the desert seen as the "true" face of Australia, as places containing arcane mysteries despite the geophysical aridity of the desert. He is one of the very few first-generation Italian Australian poets to focus on these themes, which, to some extent, albeit more intensely, reflect similar concepts found in the poetry of Luigi Strano and Giuseppe Abiuso. For Giovanni Andreoni, Australia's natural environment, with its bushfires and droughts, can be extremely harsh both physically and spiritually, but it can also hold the key to the fundamental and basic mysteries of human existence. In these latter aspects it can lead to the formation of a new and more fundamentally true identity through the achievement (if possible) of a sense of mystical union with the Australian bush and the Australian desert, since these are places where it is potentially possible to make a distinct break with the past and rediscover one's true self.

Conceptually complex and emblematic of the potential spiritual union between humans and nature, Andreoni's poetry, particularly that written during his first years in Australia, has significant similarities with Anglo-Australian poetry written on identical themes. In "Nella croce del sud," the constellation of the Southern Cross, a distinctive feature of the Australian skies at night, is a symbol for spiritual light, and the desert dawn is represented as the bringer of a new and vital force, while the red earth characteristic of the Australian desert is described in its symbolic elemental aspects.

In later developments, more evident in Andreoni's prose than in his poetry, the sense of enchantment and newness brought by the discovery of intensely primordial environments and concepts is attenuated by the idea that the bush and the desert can potentially become alien places that refuse to reveal their secrets to the migrant, rejecting him though paradoxically holding him prisoner.

Having retired from his university position some years ago, Giovanni Andreoni now lives in rural northern New South Wales.

All'alba saprai

da *Le relazioni tra l'Italia, l'Australia e la Nuova Zelanda*

All'alba saprai
la pietra
impastata alla carne
la carne
impastata alla terra
la terra impastata col sangue.
Il vento
tra gli alberi verdi
la forza
tra i monti di pietra
il giallo
nel caldo del sole
l'amore.

Aspettali all'alba
coperto
di polvere e sudore
verranno
col sole del giorno
fatti di terra e calore.

At Dawn You Will Know

At dawn you will know
stone
mixed with flesh
flesh
mixed with earth
earth
mixed with blood.
The wind
in the green trees
the force
between mountains of rock.
The yellow
in the heat of the sun.
Love.

Expect them at dawn
covered
with dust and sweat.
They will come
with the day's sun
formed from heat and earth.

Nella Croce del Sud

Nella Croce del Sud
è piantato l'albero di luce
tra i lamenti vestiti di nero
dei bianchi cockatoos.

Chi fuggì morendo
dal canguro ucciso
per non mangiare carne
di violenza intrisa
si liberò dal sangue
lassù.

Chi preferì morire
a uccidere giace lassù
tra i lamenti vestiti di nero
dei bianchi cockatoos.

In the Southern Cross

In the Southern Cross
the tree of light is planted
where the cries of white cockatoos
are clothed in mourning.

Whoever dying fled
from the slaughtered kangaroo
so as not to eat meat
that was kneaded in violence
freed himself from blood
down under.

Whoever died
rather than kill will lie
where the cries of white cockatoos
are clothed in mourning.

Terra rossa bruciata

Terra rossa bruciata
alberi bianchi
pietra rosa di quarzo.

Terra negli occhi
caldo nel sangue
fuoco nelle mani.

Fantasmi di notte bianchi
pietre
dure e sigure.

Terra rossa bruciata
alberi bianchi
pietra rosa di quarzo.

Terra
cosparsa di silenzio.

Scorched Red Earth

Scorched red earth
white trees
rose quartz stone.

Earth in the eyes
warmth in the blood
fire in the hands.

Ghosts of white nights
stones
hard and knowing.

Scorched red earth
white trees
rose quartz stone.

Earth
sprinkled with silence.

→ Mariano Coreno (b. 1939)

Born in Coreno Ausonio in 1939, Mariano Coreno migrated to Melbourne in 1956. There he has been engaged in various occupations, never losing sight of his activities as a writer and his deep commitment to social issues. He is one of the leading first-generation Italian Australian poets, and in the fifty years that he has been writing poetry, he has published eight volumes, while his work has also appeared widely in newspapers, journals, and anthologies in both Australia and Italy. He is one of five writers from the provinces of Frosinone and Latina to be included in the 2002 anthology *Il Carrubo e l'oceano*, edited by Francesco di Nicola.

Coreno's first four volumes of poetry, *Gioia straziata* (1962), *Pianto d'amore* (1963), *Ricordanze* (1964), and *Sotto la luna* (1965), are characterized by a Leopardian sentimental pessimism and present reflections on love, death, the meaning of life, anguish, and the passing of time. The early volumes are dominated by a search for an unfindable equilibrium, a vain attempt to find answers to the enigmas posed by life and to resolve its uncertainties. This sense of uncertainty is emphasized in the collection *Pianto d'amore*, which focuses on the concept of love, symbolized through the figure of Silvia as either a lost love or one for which the poet is searching who, if found, could present a possible solution to the enigmas of life. Everything in life "E' tutto amaro / come voci di aborigeni / persi nel tempo" (Is all bitter / like the voices of Aboriginals / lost in time), while the ever-evasive figure of Silvia represents potential hope and resolution: "Ascolta. Senza di te / la sera finisce qui. / Ascolta, Silvia bella . . ." (Listen. Without you / the evening ends here. / Listen, beautiful Silvia . . .).

Pianto d'amore also marks the initial introduction of images with Australian referents, but it is not until *Vento al sole* (1968) that Australian themes and a discourse on the existential condition of the migrant become predominant. *Yellow Sun* (1980) is a collection of Coreno's English poetry (including some Italian poems from the preceding volumes rewritten in English) and is in large measure the result of the substantial encouragement given to Coreno by leading Anglo-Australian poet Judith Wright. It is also in this volume that Coreno's social themes begin to emerge.

In the development of Coreno's poetry, Australia is initially a place without even illusions, since it represents spiritual marginalization, isolation, and a life experience that is melancholic, destructive, and fatal. This theme begins to take shape in "Emigrato" and is then developed in "Australia," where there is some hint of the possibility of acceptance even though, in the final analysis, the diasporic condition is no less anguishing that the experience of love since, for Coreno, migration represents exile. Forced to live far from his native land, it is only in the idealized memory of a pre-emigration past that it is possible to find some inkling of happiness, of "lacrime di ricordi, / di gioia smarrita" (the tears of memory / of lost joy), even though the reality of life in the native land was one of endless suffering, a life without hope that offered poverty as its only element of merriment.

The humble migrant who exchanges his "sudore / nella pazienza del giorno / per un futuro sicuro / . . . nella soggezione delle strade straniere" (sweat / in the patience of the day / for a secure future / . . . among the uneasiness of foreign roads) has to confront a land that cannot offer a sense of belonging nor spiritual satisfaction: "Lavoro tante ore al giorno / che quando sono libero / mi sento smarrito, / incapace di muovere un dito. / Eppure, / mi chiamano, quasi con disprezzo, / 'nuovo australiano'" (I work so many hours a day / that when I am free / I feel lost, / unable to move a finger. / Yet, / they call me, almost despisingly, / "new Australian"). In contrast to the concepts expressed in Luigi Strano's poetry, even the attempt to seek a reconciliation with the new land and its society remains unrequited in an environment that marginalizes people (Aborigines, non-English-speaking-background migrants) who are perceived as people who do not belong.

Mariano Coreno's poetry is thus marked by an existentialist experience characterized to a large extent by an anguish caused by the realization that migration has brought neither fortune nor happiness but "la stessa luna / e la stessa disperazione" (the same moon / and the same desperation). However, in his latest poetry, social issues are highlighted and elements of optimism are introduced through the gradual and suffered acceptance of the new land and the contemplation of nature, despite a pervasive and persistent feeling of being excluded from a full participation in life ("passano sulla loro strada / bellissime ragazze: / impossibili da afferrare / come sulle foglie / all'imbrunire / il sole che tramonta" [they go along their way / these beautiful girls / impossible to catch / like the setting sun / on the leaves / as dusk advances]).

Mariano Coreno's most recent poems are gathered in *Stelle passanti* (2001). He lives in Melbourne, continuing his intensive activity in writing and other cultural interests.

Australia

da *Vento al sole*

Australia
giovane terra sorridente
dalle acque circondata;
mi ascolti?
Ho spezzato il mio cuore
per saperti, per conoscere
il sangue delle tue vene,
per attingere nuove rose
dai giardini della tua poesia.
Sai, questo esilio volontario
adesso è cara fusione
tra passato e presente,
tra realtà e sogno,
tra erba e polvere.
Con l'andare del tempo
qualcosa in me s'è spento
e poi è risorto a farmi luce
nel crepuscolo della sera.
L'integrazione
si scopre a poco a poco
come le parole
di un grande amore,
Australia del mio cuore.

Australia

from *Wind in the Sun*

Australia,
smiling young country
surrounded by water;
are you listening to me?
Getting to know you
broke my heart, to know
the blood in your veins
and reach new roses
in the gardens of your poetry.
You know, my voluntary exile
is now a welding
of past and present,
reality and dream,
grass and dust.
As the time passed
something in me went out
but is back, relit
in the evening twilight.
Integration
came slowly at first,
like the words
of a great love,
Australia of my heart.

Emigrato

da *Ricordanze*

Emigrato io sono
e vivo di nostalgia,
di ricordi lontani.
Il verso nasce dal cuore,
dal sangue
ed è dolce conforto
al mio affanno.
L'Australia m'abbandona
al nuovo stato
e mi spezza gli odori della vita,
mi condanna la lingua al sale.
Ricordanza è croce dell'emigrato,
fuga di ombre
e chicco di lacrima.

Emigrant

from *Remembrances*

An emigrant am I
and I live on nostalgia
and far-off memories.
Poetry is born in my heart
and in my blood
and gives sweet comfort
to my grief.
Australia abandons me
to the new state
and breaks the fragrances of life.
Memory is the emigrant's cross,
a fleeing shadow,
a grain of tear.

Questi giorni che ora consumo

Questi giorni che ora consumo .
sotto il cielo del profondo Sud
Domani saranno polvere nel vento.

Eppure, io vivo ed amo
da bravo cristiano
il popolo australiano . . .

Australia è terra di sole,
di deserti e di boschi,
di aborigeni condannati a vivere
ai margini della società.

Lontani orizzonti spezzati
dal vento che spinge la luna
verso quei posti dove la fortuna
si perde nei ruscelli belli
o meno belli
secondo gli occhi del visitatore.

Questi giorni che ora consumo
domani saranno tutti consumati
nella polvere del crudele vento.

These Days That I Am Now Wasting

These days that I am now wasting
under the sun of the deep south
tomorrow will be dust in the wind.

And yet I live and love
as well as a man can
the Australian people . . .

Australia is a land of sun
of deserts and bush,
of Aborigines condemned
to live at the margins of society.

Far-off horizons broken
by the wind that pushes the moon
into places where good luck drowns
in beautiful streams
or not so beautiful
as the eye of the visitor judges.

These days I am now wasting
tomorrow will be wasted
in the dust of the cruel wind.

Vie delle Colline

Sotto questi alberi
cresciuti contro i palazzi
con tenace pazienza,
passano sulla loro strada
bellissime ragazze:
impossibili da afferrare
come sulle foglie
all'imbrunire
il sole che tramonta.

Paths in the Hills

Underneath these trees
that push up stubbornly
against the castles,
beautiful young women
walk their ways,
no easier to grasp
than in the sunburnt leaves, the sun
as it goes down.

La Notte

da Pianto d'amore

La notte non cambia
il volto delle cose
anche se il cielo
è pieno di stelle lucenti.
La notte costringe la nonna
a spegnere la luce
nella vasta cucina,
a spegnere la fiamma nel camino,
ad accettare
il dono della cenere.
La notte
ispira i grilli canterini,
gli amanti che cercano l'ombra,
che accordano
il passo all'avventura.
La notte è popolata di fantasmi,
di ombre,
di povera gente
che tenta di dormire
al riparo di un tetto.
La notte ci raduna
e ci benedice con la sua dolce luna.

Night

from *Love's Lament*

Night doesn't change
the face of things
even if the sky
is full of stars.
Night compels Grandmother
to put out the light
in the vast kitchen
and put out the fire in the fireplace
and accept
the gift of ashes.
Night
inspires a chorus of crickets
and lovers looking for the shadows
that lead them to adventure.
Night is peopled with ghosts
with shadows,
with poor people
looking for a roof
to lie down under.
Night gathers us
and blesses us with its sweet moon.

Ritorno

Dopo tanti anni
ritorno alla mia campagna,
al mio tenero verde,
alla mia vecchia casa
di pietra e di calce
solitaria
sotto il cielo sereno
amico delle rondini.
Dopo tanti anni
ritorno ragazzino
e mi rivedo
aggrappato alla gonna di mia madre
per chiederle una fetta di pane.
Ritorno
anche se per breve tempo
tra queste pietre, tra questi ciottoli,
dopo aver sudato su terre lontane,
a strascicare l'antica pena,
eterna fatica, tribolata luce
di speranza, d'amore e di risurrezione.

Return

After all these years
I come back to my country
to my green lands
and my old stone house
all by itself
a friend to the swallows
under the clear sky.
After all these years
I become again a little boy
and see myself again
clinging to my mother's skirts
pestering her for a slice of bread.
I come back home
if only for a little while
among these stones and pebbles
after sweating in a far-off country,
dragging the old sorrow,
the never-ending weariness,
the agonizing light of hope
for love and resurrection.

Che Sarà

da *La lunga traversata*

Che sarà
di noi italo-australiani
se un giorno
gli australiani
ci manderanno a casa?

Saremo allora
eroi senza Patria;
genitori senza famiglia;
lavoratori senza casa

Saremo allora
traditi e traditori,
umiliati da servi e da padroni.

Che Sarà?

from *The Long Crossing*

What will happen
to us Italo-Australians
if one day
the Australians
send us packing?

Then we will be
heroes without a country,
fathers without families,
workers without homes.

Then we will be
traitors and betrayed,
despised by slaves and masters.

Sono andato all'estero

Sono andato all'estero
per trovare fortuna.

Ma ho trovato
la stessa luna
e la stessa disperazione.

I Went Abroad

I went abroad
to seek my fortune

but only found
the same moon
and the same despair.

→Alberto Avolio (b. 1949)

Alberto Avolio was born in Fagnano Castello in 1949 and emigrated to Australia with his family in 1955, where he subsequently chose to follow an academic calling. He is currently associate professor in the graduate school of biomedical engineering at the University of New South Wales. As well as his professional activity, a long-term interest in Italian Australian connections and culture has led him to take on roles such as the New South Wales secretary of the Association for Research between Italy and Australia (ARIA-NSW), performer in the folk musical group Vento del sud, participant in the Italo-Australian Writers Association, writer of an account of the migration experience of the Faganesi who settled in Mareeba (North Queensland), and writer of literary texts.

Whereas the production of 1B poets (writers born in Italy who migrated to Australia at a young age) and second-generation Italian Australian poets is almost exclusively in English, Avolio is one of the very few Italian Australian poets educated in Australia, if not born in Australia, to write predominantly in Italian and in some cases dialect. The themes of his poetry deal with individual and group identity, the premigration past, the transition from the old world to the new, and the family members who are the protagonists of this transition.

A number of Avolio's poems espress the existential aspects of migration seen from the perspective of the 1B generation. "Atto di richiamo" articulates the hopeful wait for the visa to migrate to Australia and the sense of relief when it arrives: "chissà quale santo fu / ad intervenire / giusto in tempo / ci sarà qualcuno che ci vuole bene" (who knows what saint it was / to intervene / just in time / there must be someone who likes us). "In Australia col monopattino" describes the attempt by the young child, temporarily left behind when his father leaves to spearhead the family's migration to a distant and unknown Australia, to accompany his father in fantasy, and "I ricordi del passato" evokes the memory of the Calabrian dialect, the language of the past, and the consequences of the transition to the use of Italian.

Avolio's poetry also reflects on personal experiences in Australia. "Il pianto del Kookaburra," written in 1988 when the problem of Aboriginal deaths in custody had become a burning political and social issue, explores thoughts and perceptions of the time when the author, newly arrived in Australia, played with Aboriginal boys in the rivers of the tobacco plantations of North Queensland.

Alberto Avolio lives in Sydney, where he continues his commitment to Italian Australian connections.

L'atto di richiamo

da *Italo-Australian Poetry in the 80's*

Un'espressione che si capisce poco bene
un momento di speranza
un attimo di dolore
un futuro indeciso
una vita che continua
Un richiamo
come un ritorno
ad un luogo già conosciuto
nell'interno di un sogno
che giunge l'alba e scompare

Si aspetta
si attende
si prega
si riceve
si risponde

Ecco la grazia è fatta
chissà quale santo fu
ad intervenire
giusto in tempo
ci sarà qualcuno che ci vuol bene

Ti devo molto
per l'atto di richiamo
la scorsa chiamata fu altrove
e mi sento vero fortunato
ad essere così richiamato

Intendiamoci bene
poso i piedi per la prima volta
in questo paese strano
dove senza saper come
mi trovo nell'atto di richiamo

Application for Sponsorship

from *Italo-Australian Poetry in the 80's*

An expression that is little understood
a moment's hope
a second of pain
an undecided future
a life that goes on

A call
like a return
to a place already known
inside a dream
that reaches the dawn and disappears

One waits
one expects
one prays
one receives
one responds

There, the wish has been granted
who knows which saint it was
intervening
just in time
there must be someone who loves us

I owe you a lot
for the sponsorship
the last call was elsewhere
and I feel truly lucky
to be called in such a way

Let's understand each other well
I stand on my feet for the first time
in this strange country
where without knowing how
I find myself sponsored.

I ricordi del passato . . .

Le prime parole son state dette
veramente in dialetto
"Sì daveru m'a rricuordu
cumi fussa statu l'atro juornu"

Ma poi con lo sviluppo in avanti
ci siamo istruiti tutti quanti
"Però certi cosi ti rimananu
sembri cumi t'a' 'mbarati"

Alle volte nella lingua così perfetta
non si arriva alla parola adatta
"Na vota mancu i genti inalfabeti
avijenu guaj'i ssa manera"

E il vuoto si riempie
con cambiamenti e sfumature
"Ma chiri primi paruleddri
ti fannu vidi u munnu i natru culuri"

I ricordi del passato—Le prime parole sono state dette / veramente in dialetto / "Sì, mi ricordo veramente / come se fosse stato ieri" / / Ma poi con lo sviluppo in avanti / ci siamo istruiti tutti quanti / "Però certe cose ti restano / sempre come le hai imparate" / / Alle volte nella lingua così perfetta / non si arriva alla parola adatta / "Una volta neanche gli analfabeti / avevano problemi di questo tipo" / / E il vuoto si riempie / Con cambiamenti e sfumature / "Ma quelle prime parolette / ti fanno vedere il mondo di un altro colore"

Memories of the Past

The first words were really
spoken in dialect
"Yes, true, I remember it
as if it were yesterday"

But then with progress
everybody got educated
"But certain things stay with you
the way you learned them"

At times such a perfect language
can't give you the right word
"Once upon a time not even illiterates
had this kind of trouble"

And the emptiness fills
with changes and nuances
"But those first little words
make you see the world in different colors"

In Australia col monopattino

Un giorno come tutti gli altri
ci alziamo la mattina
aspettiamo il lattaio
arriva l'avviso
tutto a posto

E' una vettura di noleggio
che arriva alla porta
il bagaglio
una semplice valigia
legata con la vecchia cinghia
portata una volta da un garibaldino

La partenza l'indomani
come quella da soldato
no
questa volta oltre mare
verso il Sud
all'incontro della Croce
come quella del Calvario
chissà

Papà vengo anch'io
no bambino mio
non c'è più posto
nella valigia il tempo sarà breve
qualche anno solo
ma ascolta
lì non ci sarà neanche la neve

Arrivederci
quando arrivi scrivi
magari una piccola cartolina
per natale
noi facciamo il presepio
come sempre
le figurine di creta gialla
i fischietti di canna secca

In Australia with the Push Scooter

A day like any other
we get up in the morning
wait for the milkman
the notice arrives
everything is in place

It's a rental car
that arrives at the door
the luggage
a simple suitcase
tied with the old strap
once carried by a Garibaldian

The departure tomorrow morning
like that of a soldier
no
this time overseas
towards the South
at the meeting of the Cross
as that of Calvary
who knows

Papà I'll come too
no my child
there isn't room in the suitcase
the time will be short
only a year or so
but listen
there won't even be snow there

'Bye
when you arrive write
even a small postcard
for Christmas
we'll make the Crib
like always
the figurines of yellow clay
the dry reed whistles

Ma io voglio andare
ecco tuo cugino
ti porta lui in Australia
su monta
non ci vuole tanto
con un semplice monopattino
verso il vecchio camposanto

But I want to go
there is your cousin
he'll take you to Australia
get on
it won't take too long
with a simple push scooter
toward the old cemetery

Il pianto del kookaburra

da *Nuovo Paese*

Ti ricordavo da ragazzo
nuotavamo insieme nei fiumi
con una destrezza naturale
acchiappavi i pesci con le mani
ti guardavo da lontano
ti parlavo da vicino
cercavo di capire le radici
del tuo passato distaccato
ove nacquero le origini
dell'umanità australiana

I tuoi occhi fulminanti
sono colmi di tristezza
ma le sbornie quotidiane
ti fanno dimenticare l'amarezza
di un mondo che non riconosce
la tua vera unicità
come testimone
di questa specie dominante
di ciò ch'esiste sulla terra

L'altra sera nel paese
ti trovarono sotto l'albero
con la bottiglia in mano
tu parlavi con le stelle
vedendo i tuoi antenati
in cammino
verso il pianto del kookaburra

Il tuo letto fu spostato
per scopare via il problema
e ti svegliasti dietro le sbarre
di un carcere senza pena
e la radio stamattina
racconta ancora di un'altra vittima

The Cry of the Kookaburra

from *New Country*

I remember you as a boy
when we swam together in the rivers
and with a natural ability
you caught fish in your hands
I watched you from a distance
I talked to you up close
I tried understanding the roots
of your separated past
where the origins of Australian
humanity were born

Your flashing eyes
are full of sorrow
but the daily drunkenness
makes you forget the bitterness
of a world that doesn't recognize
your true uniqueness
as witness
of this dominant species
which exists on the earth

The other evening in town
they found you under the tree
bottle in hand
you talked to the stars
seeing your ancestors
on the road
following the cry of the kookaburra

Your bed was moved
in order to sweep away the problem
and you woke up behind the bars
of a pitiless jail
and the radio this morning
tells of yet another victim

una morte in detenzione
senza ragione o spiegazione

La vergogna la sentiamo
ma per capire bene
bisogna ritornare nel fiume
e nuotare come prima
insieme

a death in detention
without reason or explanation

Yes, we feel ashamed
but to fully understand
it's necessary to return to the river
and swim as before
together

→ Oral Dialect Poetry

Although a substantial number of Italian migrants to Australia came from a linguistic and cultural background significantly linked to dialect and an oral literary tradition, it would appear that there has been minimal continuity of the practice of the production of extempore dialect poetry in the Italian Australian context.

A telling example of this state of affairs can be found among immigrants from the Isole Eolie (Aeolian Islands). In a research project undertaken among the Aeolian community in Sydney, Wollongong, and Melbourne, about 9 percent of respondents were able to recall and recite some oral dialect texts.[25] Once asked, these respondents were quite willing to recite the texts they knew, although it appears that such requests were few and far between, as though leaving the social structure that had supported the production of oral dialect literature had brought about a substantial lack of interest in its maintenance, since it was no longer part of the immigrant's everyday reality, even though it could continue as part of the personal memory of the place of origin. This loss of traditional oral literature can also be linked to the relegation of the dialect to restricted domains in the Australian setting.

Among the oral poetry remembered by the respondents, there were a few texts related to the massive diaspora experienced by Aeolian society since the mid-nineteenth century. Along with some poems and short oral narratives that dealt with migration in general terms (and in a few instances migration to America), one poem, "Cum'o pisci ammucchi all'amu," which seemed to have enjoyed substantial popularity in the late 1940s to early 1950s, describes in ironic tones how the *Eoliani* who were in the main skilled fishermen experienced deskilling when emigrating to Australia in the vain hope of finding sudden riches. Among the Aeolian community in Perth, Onofrio Tesoriero was noted in the 1960s for his ability to "invent" poetry related to personal experiences and observations. One such piece, "Doppu tant'anni chi giru lu munnu," reflects on some of the strange things he has had to come to terms with as a result of his Australian experience. Another example can be found in Sydney's Sicilian community, where in the 1970s Filippo Ragusa was known for his recitation of poems such as "Lìmmina bella mia tu mi criscisti," which reflects on his relationship with his hometown Limina, in the province of Messina.

These examples tend to suggest that the production of oral dialect pieces occurred somewhat sporadically during the first phase of postwar Italian migration to Australia, but that these performances have tended to fade away over time. Although one of the many casualties of the diaspora, it is nevertheless an interesting example of the way in which traditional cultural forms have been used to articulate the migration experience.

Cum'o pisci ammucchi all'amu
'chiappi l'attu di richiamu!
E ti cridi ch'i sterlini,
Sunnu carti di latrini.
Va all'Australia,
Va all'Australia!
Va a 'llustrari pumi e pira
Da mattina 'nfina a sira.

Come il pesce abbocca l'amo / afferra l'atto di richiamo! / E tu credi che le sterline, / Sono carta igenica. / Va in Australia, / Va in Australia! / Va a lustrare mele e pere / Dalla mattina fino alla sera.[26]

Like the fish bites on the hook
Grab your entry visa!
And you believe that pound notes
Are like toilet paper.
Go to Australia,
Go to Australia!
Go to polish apples and pears
From morning until night.

Doppu tant'anni chi giru lu munnu
fortuna nun m'ha fattu riccu e tunnu;
scarsu di sordi, sì, ma riccu di sennu.
Ma pir mantiniri d'Onofriu Tesorieru lu cuntegnu,
aiu fattu diffirenti comu tutti quanti l'autri fannu.
Viegnu d'unni d'està si vesti di pannu,
d'unni dicembri è 'stà e giugnu inviernu,
d'unni di l'anuri poccu cuntu fannu,
d'unni poccu progressu fannu la genti di sennu,
e l'ignuranti gran furtuna fannu.
Ma chisti sugnu cibbi di puallària,
e diffirenti di l'Australia.

Dopo tanti anni che giro per il mondo / la fortuna non mi ha fatto nè ricco nè rotondo; / scarso di soldi, sì, ma ricco di senno. / Ma per mantenere il contegno di Onofrio Tesoriero, / ho fatto diversamente da tutti gli altri. / Vengo da dove d'estate si porta il cappotto, / dove dicembre è estate e giugno inverno, / dove l'onore è tenuto in poco conto, / dove persone assennate poco progresso fanno, / e gli ignoranti fanno gran fortuna. / Ma questi sono semi per gli uccelli, / e diversi dall'Australia.

After many years traveling the world
fortune has not made me rich and round;
not much money, sure, but rich in sense.
But to maintain the dignity of Onofrio Tesoriero,
I've acted differently from everyone else.
I come from where in summer you dress in warm clothing,
where December is summer and June winter,
where honor is held in low regard,
where sensible people make little progress.
But these are all fanciful tales,
and different from Australia.

Lìmmina bella mia tu mi criscisti
e a statu di raggiuni mi purtasti.
Chiànciri tanti voti mi vidisti
però siddisfazzioni minni dasti.
La sula cosa sturta ca facisti
ca all'estiru mi campu mi mannasti.
Su veramenti cosi storti chisti
ca io invicchiai e tu ti ruinasti.
Comu abbitanti un po' diminuisti
però comu paisi ti llargasti.

Bella Limina tu mi ha cresciuto / fino all'età della ragione. / Tante volte mi hai visto piangere / eppure soddisfazioni me ne hai date. / Solo una cosa storta hai fatto / per campare mi hai mandato all'estero. / Queste sono cose davvero storte / che io sono invecchiato e tu sei rovinata. / Quanto ad abitanti sei un po' diminuita / però come paese si ingrandita.

My beautiful Limina you saw me grow up
and took me to the state of reason.
Many were the times you saw me cry
yet you gave me much satisfaction.
The only wrong thing that you did
was to send me abroad to earn my living.
And these were very wrong things
'cause I grew old and you went into decline.
The number of inhabitants became a little less
but as a town you expanded.

1. In the last category, see G. Abiuso, M. Giglio, and V. Borghese, eds., *Voci nostre: Antologia italo-australiana di novelle, commedie, poesie e ricordi, scritta da emigrati italo-australiani* (Melbourne: Tusculum, 1979); G. Rando, ed., *Italian Writers in Australia: Essays and Texts* (Wollongong: Department of European Languages, University of Wollongong, 1983); U. Polizzi, ed., *Antologia A.L.I.A.S.: Poesia e prosa* (Melbourne: A.L.I.A.S., 1994), *Antologia A.L.I.A.S. 1995: Poesia, prosa, teatro* (Keilor: A.L.I.A.S., 1995), and *Antologia A.L.I.A.S. 1996–1997: Antologia del quarto premio letterario internationale: poesia e narrativa* (Avondale Heights, Victoria: A.L.I.A.S., 1997).

2. See C. Savoca, "Italo-Australian Poetry: A Study of Selected Poets," in *Italian Writers in Australia: Essays and Texts*, ed. G. Rando, 81–102 (Wollongong: Department of European Languages, University of Wollongong, 1983); and P. Niscioli, "Migrant Writing and Beyond: The Voices of Four Italian-Australian Poets—Lino Concas, Mariano Coreno, Enoe Di Stefano and Luigi Strano" (MA thesis, The Flinders University of South Australia, 1996).

3. *Janas*: piccole fate.

4. Strumento musicale sardo.

5. *Janas*: Little fairies.

6. A Sardinian musical instrument.

7. *Kanakas*: i neri delle isole del Pacifico ingaggiati per il taglio della canna.

8. *Kanakas*: Melanesians hired to cut sugar cane on Australian plantations.

9. *zabil*: Parlano (russo).

10. *razgavòr*: Conversazione (russo).

11. Aurora dalle dita di rosa (greco).

12. Ciò che è lungo il bordo del mare (greco).

13. Niente, aiuto (tedesco).

14. Pesce, cappello (tedesco).

15. Pericoloso, niente (russo).

16. *zabil*: "They speak" (Russian).

17. Rosy-fingered dawn (Greek).

18. The strand along the sea (Greek).

19. Something (Italian).

20. Pull; move (Italian).

21. Nothing at all; help (German).

22. The fish; the hat (Greek).

23. Dangerous; nothing (Russian).

24. Note that Bosi plays on Italianizing English words to obtain comic effect. He is making a parody of the assimilation of Australian English lexical items of Italian that occurs among the Italian / dialect spoken by Italian Australians. Thus *bordo* is boarding, *greengrossa* is greengrocer, *moneta* is money, *pabbo* is pub, *ciansa* is chance, *giobba* is job, *bisnisse* is business, and so on.

25. See R. Rando La Cava, "Alcuni aspetti della tradizione orale eoliana: Fatti e misfatti raccolti presso eoliani emigrati in Australia e residenti nelle città di Melbourne, Sydney e Wollongong" (BA honors thesis, Department of European Languages, University of Wollongong, 1983).

26. Translations into standard Italian by Joseph Perricone.

Belgium

Belgium

SERGE VANVOLSEM

Writing about Italian emigration literature in Belgium is at once easy and difficult. It is easy because of the evident presence of both Italian writers and writers of Italian origin, because of their products, the published literary works. It is difficult because of the lack of a rigorous theoretical framework within which to establish what is meant by the term *literature*,[1] how to distinguish between immigrants and nonimmigrants; the mix of languages used and generational issues also present complications. Even chronological boundaries are not precise, given that one may speak of Italian *presences* from the fourteenth century on, though Italian writers had yet to make a strong showing in the area's written record then. This presentation will thus be limited to the so-called historical migration, the one that was ratified in 1946 between the two countries, bringing thousands of Italian workers into the coal mines of Belgium and raising, in just a few decades, the number of Italians from about thirty-five thousand in the 1940s to more than three hundred thousand at the end of the 1970s.[2]

The linguistic aspect is important because for subsequent generations, competency in Italian diminished, and consequently the literature of emigration is less and less Italian. Many texts were written in one of the two Belgian national languages, French or Flemish, as writers were adhering more and more to the French or Flemish literatures of Belgium. The linguistic situation, however, is even more complex because one must also consider those who wrote in dialect. Poetry in Sicilian, for instance, is well documented. There are also those who wrote in several languages. Roman Firmani, for example, author of a 1981 novel in Italian, *L'ultima valle* (*The Last Valley*), also published, in 1989, *Andren, L'ultimo gnomo, Zadnji skrat* (*The Last Gnome*). This is a bilingual story in Italian and Slovene, the language of the valleys of the Natisone area in Friuli, where the author is from. There is also the case of the minstrel Robert Stieltjies, who has a Flemish name but was born in Calabria, and whose mother is

Calabrian and a poet in her own right. He spent his youth in Calabria before emigrating to seek work in Belgium, a country he subsequently left for Congo, and then went on to Kenya, Argentina and Brazil, only to return to Italy at the end. He has published poems in Italian and in Calabrian, and has written short stories in five languages. The language that an author refers to may also be fictitious: Ugo Crespini, born in Belgium from Apulian parents, in 1982 wrote *Gustavson*, a detective story in French, which was presented as a translation from Sardinian.

One can thus appreciate how crucial the linguistic issue is in this literature. Many texts are translated and, contrary to what happens in the case of classical literature, it is the authors themselves who translate their own works or publish bilingual texts with some poems written directly in Italian, others in French, as is the case of Gianni Montagna in his *I mesi e le stagioni* (*The Months and the Seasons*) in 1978. There are even texts in three languages, for instance Rosario Sollami's 1982 volume *Elementi. Poesie per il tempo di migrare* (*Elements: Poems for the Time of Migration*). Teresa D'Intino, a poet from Abruzzo who arrived in Belgium in 1958, testifies that she does not remember in what language her initial inspiration came to her and speaks in terms of a primary source or "mother" inspiration that begets twins: "The influx of inspiration during the translation creates a model identical to the original, the two languages, being complementary, enrich one another. What you do not find in one language after a brief reflection, you will find in the other, perhaps capturing your thought even better in the other language; the outcome is that, with this system, the poetry is more substantial."[3] These forms of literary bilingualism reflect directly the existential situation of the emigrant, who in fact lives, speaks and thinks, and frequently mixes up, two or more languages. Such situations reflect also the particular laceration of the immigrants who, especially in cases where they live not too far from Italy, do not want to abandon it completely and write in hopes of reaching that audience as well.[4] Those who write in the language of the host country are not read in Italy and are known only in limited circles since, among members of the first generation, knowledge of the host country's language is limited and the channels of distribution are not developed. Writing in Italian, the circulation among speakers of Italian is easier, but one remains excluded from the rest of Belgium's French- and Flemish-speaking communities. In order to be read in Italy, it seems more effective to choose an Italian editor, but it is not easy to break into big publishing houses, making it necessary to work with small regional publishers who do not have a large distribution network.

Migration literature in Belgium as a social phenomenon, as a reflection of a collective consciousness, comes about somewhat late with respect to the migration waves themselves. The migrant worker is involved first of all in the struggle for survival. As the community becomes established, however, the time for individual reflection and collective awareness also comes, and these establish the premises for artistic creation. To leave and start from scratch is a traumatic experience, and this tumult is a stimulus for writing because the very act of narration is part of the catharsis: Writing is a necessity born of the need to pass on memories so that "the children's children" will know. Migration literature would look very different if authors who had published only one book were to be eliminated from representation. In many cases once the verses are written down, the fruit of an emotional outlet, the poetic vein seems to be depleted or at least temporarily blocked.[5] It is not surprising that the collective awareness happened precisely in the span of the great sociocultural movement of 1968, which counts also for the workers' world. Twenty years after the bilateral agreements of 1946, the Italian community in Belgium had firmly settled, and its integration in the country was excellent. Only the cultural threshold had not received the appropriate attention. Except for the works of Gianni Montagna, who perhaps should not be considered a real emigration author, and the isolated autobiographical novel *La legion du sous-sol* (*The Underground Legion*) by Eugenio Mattiato, in 1959,[6] a greater number of literary works were written after the 1960s. This period began immediately with a decade of abundant productivity, a veritable literary boom.

This initial flowering is linked directly to the initiatives of the Movimento Arte e Cultura (Art and Culture Movement, MAC), created at the end of 1968 by a few writers, among whom the best known were Francesco Tessarolo and Franco Caporossi, who was then chancellor at the Italian consulate in Liege.[7] Thanks to Tessarolo, who was well integrated into the French-speaking world, contacts were facilitated with French and Belgian writers as well. MAC succeeded also in establishing a literary weekly, *Sole d'Italia* (*Sun of Italy*), that carried a section that would accept poems, reviews, and short stories written by immigrants. Movimento Arte e Cultura played an important role in publishing and disseminating works by immigrants.

What have these nearly forty years of migration literature achieved? To answer with just numbers, it means between fifty and seventy authors who have produced over one hundred and fifty works in print.[8] During the first decades a certain balance persisted between French and Italian texts, but since the 1980s the production in French dominates. Very soon, the language learned in school becomes also the main instrument of communication, practical as well as literary. In this phase of migration literary production, poetry is the main genre practiced but it is difficult to contrast prose and poetry according to traditional standards, as the prose tends to read much like narrative poetry. In migration literature, "verse is at times a powerful narrative instrument, it is not used merely for expressive purposes. Narration in verse is often preferred because verse provides a relatively simpler structure with respect to prose and is more incisive and captivating, a sort of tracing that the still inexpert pen executes more readily."[9]

The topics treated by Belgian migration literature are various but can be organized along two axes: the migration experience and the classical themes of universal literature. This last kind can stand for the negation, either conscious or unconscious, of migration, or for overcoming it. For Belgium, however, these topics are not static compartments; rather they are communicating vessels which intersect both chronologically and also among the authors. The first trend, as Frank Lentricchia defined it in the 1970s, constitutes "a report and meditation on first-generation experience, usually from a perspective of second-generation representation."[10] We find in it the traditional array of nostalgias: the goodbye, the departure, the voyage, the distance, the birthplace, the parents (the mother), the hopes, and the harshness of work (the black world of the mine, called inevitably *mina*). A special note is sounded by nature (the green of the Ardennes, the fog of Flanders) along with the meteorological conditions of this country, which is described as grey and rainy, everywhere darkened by the dust of the coal ("the rain falls slowly / on the rooftops / and on the sidewalks / against the panes of the windows / infinitely time flows," by Teresa D'Intino; "Skies of dust / and of dust the air. / Rooftops / dust plated / dust on the walls / on the streets. / Trees and flowers / soaked with dust / dust on clothing. / Skin covered with dust / thin / invisible / and within / within the body / dust still," by Walter Vacca), all in contrast with the sun, the warmth and the blue of the sea in Italy. Even the difficult (impossible?) return or reintegration inspires writing, either because with the passing of time comes retirement and sometimes people return to their town of origin, or because people attempt to re-emigrate to their country of origin ("I, pilgrim anew, / tourist in my fatherland, / look upon the great mountain / with watery eyes / and I dream of riding over it," by Giovanni Brigando; or again, "I've returned to you, / My birthplace / and wonder solitary / through the streets / I no longer know you / Everything is changed / In you alone still is the same / the color of the sky / and the murmur of the sea," by Cosima Marchese). Such topics typical of migration literature alternate with those of universal classical literature: life and death, love, religion, nature, poetry, and often also with the larger problems of today's society, such as war, solitude among the masses, indifference, intolerance, racism, and specific historical matters such as the events in Sarajevo or the fall of the Berlin wall. A few names that emerge in this group are Gianni Montagna, in Italian, and Francis Tessa, Anita Nardon, and Carino Bucciarelli, who have always published in French.

The nonmigration themes in poetry as well as in prose constitute the more interesting development of Italian literature in Belgium today, since they underscore the passage from a literature of migration to *literature* pure and simple. Whatever definition one wishes to give to *migration literature*, the mere fact of adding an adjective means that it is always considered a second-rate literature, the literature of a specific minority group. It is always a restriction, as when we speak of *colonial literature* or of *women's literature*, a procedure that may be useful to protect or promote the specific kind, but it is nonetheless a passing stage. Migration literature is obviously an important resource for history and an irreplaceable testimonial of the facts relative to migration and to the material and psychological existence of its protagonists in the world. However, if it is to be remembered in the history of literature, it must be regarded and appreciated for its specifically literary quality as well. Authors such as Montagna, Tessa, and Malinconi, among others, now belong to the sphere of pure *literature*.

BIBLIOGRAPHY

Bortolini, M. "La production littéraire des Italiens de Belgique depuis 1945." In *Littératures des Immigrations, Un espace littéraire émergent*, ed. C. Bonn, 1:65–78. Paris: L'Harmattan, 1995.
Botti, M. *Dentro alla valigia una penna . . . Approccio alla letteratura italiana d'emigrazione*. Padua: Libreria Padovana Editrice, 1999.

Cieters, I. *Il movimento arte e cultura*. Louvain: Louvain University Press, 1992.

De Jonghe, S. *Dall'idea all'opera. Genesi e ricezione della letteratura dell'emigrazione italiana*, Louvain: Louvain University Press, 1994.

Loriggio, F., ed. *Social Pluralism and Literary History: The Literature of the Italian Emigration*. Toronto: Guernica, 1996.

Morelli, A., ed. *Rital-Littérature. Antologie de la littérature des italiens de Belgique*. Mons: Ed. du Cerisier, 1996.

Portoghese, D. "Le roman de la deuxième génération d'écrivains italo-belges: Thilde Barboni, Carmelina Carracillo et Nicole Malinconi." Thesis, Università degli Studi di Bari, 2004.

Vanvolsem, S. "La letteratura italiana in Belgio: Tre lingue, tre culture e più generazioni." In *La letteratura dell'emigrazione. Gli scrittori di lingua italiana nel mondo*, ed. J.-J. Marchand, 81–94. Turin: Edizioni della Fondazione G. Agnelli, 1991.

———. "Il codice linguistico della letteratura dell'emigrazione." In *Gli spazi della diversità*, ed. S. Vanvolsem et al., 2:557–572. Louvain: Louvain University Press, 1995.

———. "Nouvelles directions de recherche en sociolinguistique de l'immigration italienne." In *Passions italiennes, pour André Sempoux*, ed. S. Vanvolsem, 59–77. Brussels: Van Balberghe, 2000.

———. "L'italiano dell'immigrazione 'alta.'" In *Italia linguistica anno mille. Italia linguistica anno duemila*, ed. N. Maraschio et al., 391–399. Rome: Bulzoni, 2003.

———. "Lingua ed educazione scolastica tra la collettività di origine italiana in Belgio." *Studi Emigrazione/Migration Studies* 42, no. 160 (2005): 867–893.

———. "Un andirivieni tra Francia, Lussemburgo e Belgio: Ritorno a Salicia." In *Paroles et images de l'immigration*. Luxembourg: Université du Luxembourg, 2005.

⤳ *Giovanni (Gianni) Montagna (1905–1991)*

Giovanni (Gianni) Montagna was born in 1905 in Borni, a town on the Po River area near Pavia where he spent the first years of his life and received his elementary education. His was an ordinary life, as narrated in *Sulla via Emilia (On the Emilian Way*, 1984), a collection of heavily biographical short stories. In it the author states: "Beginning with the sixth year of my life, all children's existence was regulated by a bell which, with its ringing that reached far and wide in the silence of the roads back then, gathered and dispersed them two times a day in swarms screaming through the streets. During the summer months it was quiet, as the kids were on break, running around in the fields and climbing up hills." What singled out Montagna from the other children was an insatiable desire to read, and although books were few in his house, he read everything that came his way. After completing elementary school, he enrolled in a technical institute in Pavia and received a diploma in business in 1923. However, his real passion was literature and, consequently, he also got a diploma in classics in 1925, then began courses in the Department of Literature in Bologna. He finished there in 1929 with a dissertation, published in 1933, on Cecco Angiolieri's poetry.[11] The satirical vein would prove fundamental for the poetic works of Montagna.

Armed with a degree in education, he began to work for the MAE and was finally able to develop what would be his true vocation: being an ambassador of the Italian language and culture. It marked the beginning of a long career as a teacher that carried him through most of Europe: Zara in 1930, Barcelona in 1933 (where he witnessed the dramatic political events of that country), Athens in 1935, Paris in 1936, and Sofia in 1937, where he settled until 1943, when he returned to Italy to teach in Milan and then in Genoa, but especially to join the resistance movement. In 1950 he landed in Brussels, where he lived practically until his death, save for a brief interval spent in Italy after 1957, when his foreign ministry job ended. He continued to teach in Brussels and, in 1952, the year after the publication of his first book of poems, *Ormeggi*, was sent as lecturer to the University of Leuven. In 1962 he accepted a position as Italian teacher in an institute of higher learning in Mons, but in 1966 he returned to the capital and worked at a school for translators and interpreters that had recently been founded by the city of Brussels. He stayed there until his retirement in 1977.

Settling in Belgium after so many years of nomadic behavior also granted him the time to write. These were thus years of intense activity. His first collections of poetry came out, some of which were written in French, followed by some of his first stories recounting tales of childhood and youth and of his time spent in different countries. His contacts with various colleagues in Leuven and agreeable collaboration with various journals in Italy and in Belgium, especially the one with the Romanists from Leuven, *Les Lettres Romanes* (*The Roman Letters*), developed a new aspect of Montagna's vast activity: the role of cultural mediator between the two countries. Montagna not only taught Italian and translation, he was also a translator-poet of great talent who tirelessly translated Italian poetry for the Belgian public. He also introduced French poetry to Italian readers and often had his translations printed in elegant bilingual publications. In 1958 he even published an anthology, *Un secolo di poesia belga* (*A Century of Belgian Poetry*), a work with a valuable introductory essay that presents to the public around one hundred Francophone Belgian poets, many of whom had become his friends.

The poetic vein that is most congenial to Montagna is the lyrical, and along with it, the satirical. In this style he published four volumes. This is the best of his poetry, in which he points out the hypocrisies of the world around him,[12] but he does not hesitate to adopt the same tone regarding himself. This initial spiritual testimony, *Testamento* (*Testament*), appeared in 1974: "All that I know to give you / I will serve in a rondeau for you. He returned to this theme in 1978 with *Codicilli* (*Codex*): "Three years ago I wrote a testament / thinking I was near my departure. / Alas, they were a hurried bequest / I was only in the November of my life. / Now that of December I am well on the way / . . . still being healthy in mind, / I am taken again by the desire / to try it all over again, / to tack on with three pins to the previous writings / these long codices / without witnesses nor lawyers." With a wink to Petrarch's *nugae*, Gianni Montagna presents these poems as little things of no importance: "Here now just out of the oven / Ariosto's satires to you are given. / They are good gossip, in old style / made while in an armchair I lie. / They do not need praise / with no problem, with ease / you can throw them in the basket / hurrying them along to their casket" (from *Divertimenti e favole* [*Amusements and Stories*], 1970).[13]

The literary works of Gianni Montagna have all been published in Italy. This is not by chance, because he is and wanted to be a part of Italian literature. For him, the category *literature of emigration* was not of great significance. It is not even a genre that he mentions in his writings.[14] Living abroad only gave him more freedom and independence with respect to traditional canons, an autonomy that he held very dear: "I do not have a mind for bows; / especially now that I am ready to gather the sails. / Let me go on living as I grew up, / looking on remaining alone."[15] For Montagna, literature does not need adjectives, and for this reason he never belonged to a literary movement: "I know nothing of schools or circles; / do not ask me how I write: / I like my narrow streets / and I write because I am alive. // The old nimble verses / often smile to me. / I love simple things: / I am extraordinarily lazy. // With simple lines / that others throw out / with cloth not so fine / I weave poetry, why not?"[16]

Le rive dell'Entella

da *Ormeggi*

Non so come oggi siano le rive dell'Entella.
Le rivedo con gli occhi d'un'età che fu bella.
L'età che scopre ovunque casi straordinari,
che viaggia col Baedeker di Verne e di Salgari,
che fabbrica con poco i più strani paesi
e fa d'un torrentello un Nilo o lo Zambesi;
che solo vede, intorno, tentazione d'inviti
e stupisce del nuovo ed ha fede nei miti.
Oggi,—ma quanti anni!—che distrutto è l'incanto,
da un cantuccio del cuore è salito il rimpianto.
E' venuto improvviso, fantasma non chiamato,
lungo un filo di tempo che pensavo tagliato.
E non riaffiora un mondo, ma un frammento, una stella;
si precisa un'immagine: le rive dell'Entella.
Un po' di verde, i colli, un corso d'acque chiare
e molto sole, molto, e la luce del mare,
tentennano le biade, docili ad ogni vento,
grige come le volpi, grige come l'argento.
Ci fornivano i lacci per le cacce più strane:
caimani le lucertole e leoni le rane;
eran le cavallette od un modesto topo
le fiere più temibili, sui bordi del Limpopo.
La sponda di Lavagna di fronte a noi s'offriva.
due passi appena: ignoto un mondo ci si apriva.
Di là si nascondevano avventure eccitanti:
tigri della Malesia, cannibali, briganti.
Un mondo inverosimile; ma un mondo ripulito,
col trionfo del giusto e il malvagio punito.
Poi, come declinando il sol nel mar si perde,
ciascuno dalla foce cercava il raggio verde.
Del futuro sognato aruspici curiosi,
scrutavano presagi nei segni luminosi.

Si levava, con l'ombra, la prima fresca brezza,
scorreva il primo fremito per l'acqua, una carezza.
Ma il brivido improvviso ci spennava le ali;
si tornava alla terra, rifatti collegiali.

The Banks of the Entella

from *Dockings*

Today I don't know
the banks of the Entella.
I see them again with
eyes of a lovely age.
The age that discovers everywhere
amazing graces,
that travels with the Baedeker
of Verne and Salgari,
that devises from nothing
the most exotic lands
and transforms a trickle into
the Nile or the Zambese,
that sees only, all around
the temptation of calls—
and is still amazed and
has faith in myths,
old and new.
Today—so many years have passed!—
now that the magic has flown
from a corner of the heart
a certain remorse emerges,
coming suddenly like
an unsummoned ghost
along a wisp of time
I had thought spent.
So a world does not
blossom again, only
a fragment,
a star:
the image sharpens:
banks of the Entella
splashed by green,
the hills,
a coursing of clear waters

and so much sun
and the light of the sea
and the harvest sways
yielding to each wind,
gray like foxes,
gray like silver.
It granted us the interweavings
of the strangest hunts:
caymans, lizards and lions, frogs;
locusts or a rat or two,
the wildest beasts on the shores
of the Limpopo.
Or the banks of
the Lavagna facing us
with only two ways out:
an arcane world opened to us . . .
There were concealed awe-filled
adventures: Malaysian tigers,
cannibals, brigands, an impossible world, but purified
by the victory of the just
and the castigation of evil.
Then, as the sun set into the sea,
every estuary sought
the green ray.
Looking toward a future of dreams
the intent auspices scrutinized
omens in the luminous signs.
And there wafted,
with the shadows,
the first cool breeze,
the first quiver of water
rising like a caress.
But
the sudden shudder
plucked our wings
and we fell
back to earth though
still conspirators.

Crepuscolo nordico

da *Testamento*

Immobile è la sera, come vela
che rinunci a tessere il suo viaggio
in mare senza vento.

Un tenero alitare di vapori
sale dai prati e indugia,
condannato all'altezza degli steli:
incenso che il rifiuto umilia al suolo.

Il cielo sgombero è spazio vuoto: il nulla.
Non isola di nube e non un'alla
che vi sfrecci all'approdo.

Il languore d'attesa è un'agonia
di desiderio tale
che farà luminosa anche la notte

E la morte sarà come una vita.

Nordic Twilight

from *Testament*

The evening is still
like a sail
that refuses to unfurl
on its voyage across
a windless sea.

A sweet breath of vapors
rises from the meadows,
lingers
condemned at the height
of the stelae:
incense whose rejection
humiliates the threshold.

The flushed sky is
empty space:
the void . . .
No isle
of clouds, no wing
darting over the dock.

The languor of waiting
is like dying
of such desire
that could make
the night beam.

And death will be
like a life.

Novembre

da *I mesi e le stagioni*

Novembre. Nella nebbia stagna un suono di corno:
sogni cani latranti per la cieca brughiera
e nel silenzio, invece, un anemico giorno
entra a vele ammainate al porto della sera.

E' il tuo Novembre: ammaina. Sulla via del ritorno
cadono i venti, tacciono il canto e la preghiera.
Non è il tardivo approdo incitante scogliera;
un paludoso greto t'attende, ultimo scorno.

Oh, riva solitaria cui attraccano mute
le algose carene dal sale logorate!
Velieri che drizzarono le loro prore acute

nei tenaci sargassi, in acque disperate,
vanno all'indegna fine delle cose perdute,
ché non una scoprirono delle terre sognate.

November

from *Months and Seasons*

November. In the fog a sound
of a horn stagnates:
dreams barking dogs across
the blind heath and
in the silence
an anemic day
sweeps in with the furled sails
toward the evening port.

It's your November, it furls.
On the road of its return
the winds drop, the song
and the prayer are silent.
It's not the late landing
spurring reef—only a swampy
bed awaits you, as one last
mockery.

So, lonely shores where
there land
the slimy keels
eroded by the salt!
Clippers that align their sharp prows

in the clinging Sargasso,
in desperate waters,
launch toward the base end
of things lost for good,
not one ever discovered
in those dreamed paradises.

→ *Franco Caporossi (b. 1930)*

Had Franco Caporossi been born during the Renaissance, he would have to be introduced as a polygraphic writer, since, in addition to a vast literary production, he is the author of numerous essays and studies on a variety of topics, including local histories, culture, labor relations, and social surveys. On top of his works that are presented here, Caporossi has works for the theater circulating in a limited number of photocopies, some of which have been presented frequently. For a more complete list see the recent publication by the author, *Summer Tales.*

Caporossi was born in Segni, near Rome, in 1930. He learned at a young age the roadways of migration when, in 1934, his father, a surveyor working for the Land Headquarters, was sent to Bengasi, in Libya. There the child lived happily in a home that "seemed like a palace, in comparison to the small house in Carpineto Romano. The city, the climate, the nearby shore and the friends formed a truly happy mosaic."[17] Upon returning to Italy, he continued his studies, first in a college of the Italian Fascist Youth, afterward at the Technical Institute of Anagni, where he earned a diploma and, in 1952, the qualification for practicing his profession. After completing his military service, he emigrated, in 1956, to Belgium, where an acquaintance of his father had promised to find him a position in a mine of the Vallonia (in Ressaix, near La Louvière). He was not a typical emigrant: He descended down into the wells, but his background allowed him early on to join the social service of the mine workers, charged with the task of welcoming and assisting the new emigrants. In 1958, the embassy employed him as delegate of the miners of the area of Liège and, a few years later, as the winner of the MAE job posting, he became a clerk of the court. In 1974 he left Belgium, and his career in the foreign office took him to Conakry, then to Madrid, Tehran, and Bengasi. In the meantime, he was also sent on missions to Africa (Cairo, Addis Ababa, Dar es

Salaam), Asia (Peking, Bangkok), and Central America (Haiti, Santo Domingo). In 1996, he retired with the title of head clerk.

During the nearly twenty years he spent in Belgium, young Caporossi developed his artistic talent and discovered his exceptional gift as a promoter of culture. He was active in the organization Amitiés Belgo-Italiennes, and in 1968 he founded the Movimento de Arte e Cultura (MAC) for the promotion of immigrant Italian culture through meetings, exhibits, conferences, and competitions. Initially, the Movimento had a vast organization, with district sections on literature, sculpture, painting, and photography, to mention only a few. During those same years, Caporossi was cofounder of the biennial Italian Writers of the Benelux prize, which encouraged for a decade the cultural activities of Italians and helped spread their literary works through the publication of anthologies and prize winning works.

For many years Caporossi had also been writing poetry, the earliest sonnets going back to 1948, which he began to publish at first timidly through mimeographed copies and subsequently in elegant collections in print. These are simple poems of a youthful romantic tone, but they also reveal the author's gift for metaphor and rhyme. His themes include places, large life events—life / death, love, nature, nostalgia—but he also focuses on current issues. Emigration became a topic for him even before he actually left his hometown. "This energy is useless, / like the river's / nobody captures it / and is lost at sea. / Is lost in the streets, / it ages in anxiety. / I too will have to leave, / cross over the mountains: / should I be cursing / or forgive everyone." These poems have a signature, a date and a locality, a practice typical of Caporossi, which enables the reconstruction of the poetic evolution of this writer and tireless functionary of the Foreign Affairs Office.

The theme of emigration, with its difficult living experiences, is important throughout his early writings. "After so much studying," he writes in 1956, soon after arriving in Belgium, "I am a laborer in a coal mine. / This is not the sense my father / gave to his long sacrifices, / it is not what my mother prayed for, / it is also not what I hoped / while I was becoming a man. / My diploma is folded in my pocket, / They want my muscles! / ... If I were alone I would lament my lot, / but we are so many. / What will be left of us, what will become / of these bodies offered without distinction, / human guinea pigs / through no faults of ours.[18] Emigrants are always present in Caporossi's prose works, in which he recounts the testimonials of emigrants he knew the world over. The more "Belgian" collections are *I cieli del nord* (*The Northern Skies*, 1974), when he left Belgium to go back to Guinea, and *La voce del pensiero* (*The Voice of Thought*, 1982). In these poems he describes Belgian landscapes, the climate (Rain! / this grey sky knows nothing else), nature and human relationships, along with dynamism and grace (This countryside relaxes / quickly it becomes your friend).[19]

Subsequent stays abroad were not so long, but leave other marks on his later poetry: sedimentations of other places, other encounters, other human experiences. His native land also finds more and more a place in his "foreign verses," since Caporossi is also the poet of his mountains, of places like Carpineto Romano, Segni, Supino, and Gavignano, mentioned alongside so many other exotic ones like Marrakesh, Zanzibar, Dar es Salaam, and Guadalajara. As Gianclaudio Macchiarella writes in the preface to the collection *Despues* (*Afterward*), living "seems to have given daring and consistency to Caporossi's poetic form, in constructing verses and in choosing imagery. Yet the delicate touch typical of this poet's production is always present, a distinctive trait of his works."[20] Franco Caporossi is thus a "poet of movement, of travels in the world . . . almost a special envoy in the troubled areas of Italian laborers abroad," but "even in leaving his home, he never forgets his own land of origin, his own 'region,' the people and the countryside. The topics that Caporossi prefers above all others, while highlighting the values of the conscience, are the inner landscape, reflections on life, encounters with other people, and, above all, with his own self."[21]

E di questo mare uggioso,
rugato da onde aggressive,
resta una schiuma bianca:
d'ira sembra ribollire.
E il vento che le spinge, urla:
il cielo che le copre è grigio;
le nubi invischiate all'orizzonte,
sono lunghi lamenti.
Guarda impassibile la terra
dalle sue gialle dune,
con la pelle imbevuta di nebbie,
venata da lunghi canali
che le portano il sangue.
E . . . aspetta ancora l'estate
quando è già autunno,
e lavata da pioggia che cade . . .
lente novene sussurra
in attesa del sole.

from *The Northern Skies*

Of this gloomy sea
a white foam remains,
wrinkled by aggressive waves,
it seems to boil with rage.
And the wind that pushes them, howls;
the sky covering them is grey:
the entangled clouds on the horizon,
are long laments.
The earth looks on impassively,
from her yellow dunes,
with her skin soaked in fog,
veined with elongated canals
bringing her blood.
And . . . she still waits for summer,
when it's already fall,
and bathed by the falling rain
she whispers slow novenas
expecting the sun.

Stavelot 1972

da *La voce del pensiero*

Siamo venuti
nei boschi profumati
per udire il mormorìo dell'Amblève
e ritessere
nei telai della quiete
pensieri
ramificati
di immagini e illusioni.
Siamo venuti
nel cuore delle Ardenne
per riudire la voce del tempo.
Qui d'Apollinaire
il suono di poesie d'amore!
Siamo venuti
con i corpi stanchi
tre le alte erbe di luglio
a riempire le mani di terra,
a stordirci di aria immacolata
che fermenta palpiti e carezze
nel respiro dell'estate.

Stavelot, 1972

from *The Voice of Thought*

We have reached
the fragrant woods
to hear the murmur of the Amblève
and weave once more
ramified thoughts
of images and illusions
in quiet looms.
We have reached
the heart of the Ardennes
to hear the voice of time once again.
The sound of Apollinaire's
love poems here!
We have come
with weary bodies
among the high grass of July
to fill our hands with earth,
be stunned by immaculate air
fermenting throbs and caresses
in the breath of summer.

da *Nell'arco del sole*

È l'ora in cui la notte
sembra tutto concedere,
perché diventa profonda
di dolore o di gioia.
È l'ora del silenzio . . .
complici le illusioni
vanno sospirando insonni.
Come un maestro invisibile
il vento accorda l'intimità
con i ritmi del tempo
che ci carica di anni
senza chiedere perdono.
È l'ora in cui le stelle
passeggiano innocenti
e la luna diventa sovrana
di uno splendido cielo.
È l'ora in cui il vuoto
diventa un'immagine chiara
e vive con intimo piacere
una vacanza felice.

It's the hour in which the night
seems to promise everything
since it deepens
in despair and joy.
It's the hour of silence
illusions are accomplices,
sighing insomniacs.
Like an invisible Maestro
the wind tunes intimacy
with the rhythms of time
burdening us with years
without seeking forgiveness.
It's the hour in which the stars
stroll innocently
and the moon becomes sovereign
of a splendid sky.
It's the hour in which emptiness
becomes a clear image
living a happy vacation
of intimate pleasure.

Anni e anni persi al mercato della vita,
acquistando essenza di gioia,
valigie piene di dolore,
sacchi di speranze e delusioni:
Anni e anni venduti nei negozi del destino,
come merce pregiata
al prezzo dell'usato,
che poi passa di moda:
mai custodita!
Vita che ci passi accanto
calzando le nostre stesse scarpe,
poggiando il capo sui nostri guanciali:
scrivi dentro di noi le parole
di una vocazione ricorrente
che tenga a guinzaglio il tempo:
mai veramente libera!
Solo meramente eterna.

from *The Color of the Sky*

Years and years lost in the market of life,
purchasing essence of joy,
suitcases full of pain,
bags of hopes and disappointments.
Years and years sold in shops of destiny,
like valuable merchandise
for used prices
which then go out of style,
never guarded!
Life that passes us by,
wearing our own shoes,
leaning its head on our pillows,
inside us you write words
of a recurring vocation
keeping time on a leash
never really free
merely eternal.

L'indomabile bisogno di vivere
echeggia nello spazio acceso di luce,
gonfia i polmoni di gridi di speranza
e porta i desideri sui pascoli del Mondo.
Ci sono campi che sembrano infiniti,
oltre l'orizzonte fuggono silenti:
verdi poi gialli, lentamente grigi . . .
come i nostri giorni transitano
dannati a diventare oscurità.
C'è un grande e limpido specchio su di noi
dove l'immagine dei giorni e delle notti
si alterna con puntuale distacco,
indifferente ai ritmi scontati
dell'inarrestabile macchina del tempo.
E nella forza nascosta del destino
placida, poderosa, roteante
si svolge la bobina del futuro
e al ritmo che si avvolge
è già il passato.

The untamable need to live
echoes in the space charged with light,
swells lungs with cries of hope
and brings desires to the pastures of the world.
There are seemingly infinite fields
that silently flee beyond the horizon
green then yellow gradually grey
just as our days transit
damned to become obscurity.
There is a great and limpid mirror upon us
where the image of our days and nights
alternates with punctual detachment
indifferent to the expiated rhythms
of the unstoppable machine of time.
And in the hidden force of destiny
placid, powerful, rolling
the spool of the future turns
and at such a rhythm
that it's already past.

1. The only *History of Italian Literature* that treats this particular problem is the one edited by Enrico Malato (Salerno, 1995–2005). Ermanno Paccagnini dedicates an entire chapter of *Italian Literature Outside of Italy* (2002), to Italian literature and minority literature, using the term *writing* rather than *literature*, and making a distinction between "Italophone writing outside of Italy," such as in Malta, what was formerly Yugoslavia, and Switzerland, and "Italophone writing of the Italian migration."

2. This omits publications from the Renaissance period, such as *La descrizione di tutti i Paesi Bassi* (*The Description of the Low Countries*) (Antwerp, 1576) or *L'ora di ricreazione* (*The Recreation Hour*) by Guicciardini (Antwerp, 1568), as well as other more recent ones such as *Le Vecchie romanze spagnole, recreate in italiano* (*The Old Spanish Romances Translated in Italian*) by Giovanni Berchet, or the famous political treatise *Del primato morale e civile degli italiani* (*The Moral and Civil Primacy of Italians*) by Vincenzo Gioberti (Brussels, 1843).

3. Teresa D'Intino is the author of three collections of bilingual poems: *Terra mia* (*Land of Mine*) 1981; *Il passato e la promessa* (*The Past and the Promise*) 1991; and *Petali e armonie* (*Petals and Harmonies*) 1994.

4. D'Intino, during a meeting on Italian literature by emigrants at the Italian Cultural Institute of Brussels in 1993, reproached the director, saying that Italy did very little to promote poetry written in Italian outside of Italy. She shouted: "But I do not want to be just studied; I want to be read in Italy before I die."

5. I know several authors with just one book who continue to appear at readings, perhaps to present their old verses and state that they would like to go back to writing: "Oh, poetry, what a passion, I should find the time to write." I do not think that it is really a question of time. What is missing is an equally profound and traumatic experience: Memory alone is no longer able to arouse emotions strong enough to write about.

6. Montagna, however, always published his books in Italy, and Mattiato belongs to the second generation, even though his book appeared so early. His father arrived in Belgium in 1922, and Mattiato joined him in 1924 to work in the mines when he turned fourteen. *La légion du sous-sol* (*The Legion Below the Ground*) documents life in the mines, but it is also a manual full of advice on safety, the product in fact of the long experience of the author. The poet Carlo Masoni can be placed in the same group, born in Belgium in 1921: His father stayed on in Belgium after World War I and his mother is Belgian. His first collection of poetry came out in 1947. He does not treat migration; his themes are nature, the Ardennes, the area where he was born, God, humanity; he wrote nearly ten books of poetry as well as some short stories. In 1995 he published a mystery novel, *Les signaux inutiles* (*The Useless Signs*).

7. Francesco Tessarolo (pen name Francis Tessa) was born in Rossano Veneto in 1935 and joined his parents in Belgium in 1952, after completing his schooling in the seminary in Vicenza. Tessa has written over thirty books of poetry and won several literary prizes. His first novel, *Les enfants polenta* (*The Polenta Children*), published in 1966, is an autobiography and was published in Italian with the title *I ragazzi polenta*. Tessarolo is a demanding and critical writer. In creating the Movimento Arte e Cultura, he envisioned a small group of people of a very high artistic caliber. Initially he accepted an offer to be the director of the poetry section, but he later withdrew from the group because of its popular choices, which he termed *populist* (*populisme*). In a general assembly on "Cul-

ture: Everyone's Action," MAC revealed early on its interest to be inclusive, rather than address just a few select people.

8. While waiting for more rigorous criteria and the rigorous judgment of time, always inexorable, numbers tell very little. A bibliography lists usually only collections, not the publication of individual poems in journals. Who is the better poet, one who published regularly in journals, or someone who prints a small collection on his or her own?

9. Serge Vanvolsem "Il codice linguistico della letteratura dell'emigrazione," in *Gli spazi della diversità*, ed. S. Vanvolsem et al. (Leuven: Leuven University Press), 2:572.

10. Cited in F. Loriggio, ed., *Social Pluralism and Literary History: The Literature of the Italian Emigration* (Toronto: Guernica, 1996), 191.

11. Giovanni Montagna, *La poesia di Cecco Angiolieri* (*The Poetry of Cecco Angiolieri*) (Pavia: Istituto Pavese di Arti Grafiche, 1933).

12. Here he criticizes English usages such as *italfring, italfringle,* and *italfringlese* with ironic phonetic adaptations. "With this pedigree you'll find cleared / the road to success in the good world: / it will be opened for you the cafè sossaiti, / the new elite of a class sans sussi, / that vegetates in 'naits,' to spite those / who advise dancing on the volcano / or on the platform of the guillotine" (*Testamento* [Padua: Rebellato, 1974], 39). In the *Ariostesche* (Padua: Rebellato, 1972), he writes a long poem on *L'italfring* (29–35).

13. *Codicilli* (Quarto d'Altino: Rebellato, 1978), 23. In *Divertimenti e favole* (*Pastimes and Fables*) (Padua: Rebellato, 1970) he writes, "Heart of flower / Reader, my sonnets / are like handkerchiefs, / they are sold by the dozen" (7).

14. For a complete list of Montagna's works, see E. Hoppe, "Gianni Montagna: l'uomo, lo studioso, il poeta," in *Studi in onore di Giovanni Montagna per il suo 80E compleanno*, ed. D. Gardella et al. (Leuven: Leuven University Press, 1985), 179–189.

15. "De vacuo dolio," in *Ariostesche*, 57. Montagna puts "*raccogliere le sarte*" (fold the sails) in italics because he remembers Dante's "When I realized I reached that part / of my life where each one should / lower the sails and fold them" (*Inferno* XXVII). Montagna's poetry is full of similar references to Italian classics.

16. From *Ormeggi* (*Dockings*) (Milan: Gastaldi, 1951), cited in Hoppe, "Gianni Montagna," 181–182.

17. F. Caporossi, *Un uomo, una famiglia. Cronistoria della vita di Andrea Caporossi* (*A Man, A Family: A Chronological History of the Life of Andrea Caporossi*) (Rome: Edizioni CIAS, 1985), 26.

18. "Realtà," in *Singhiozzi poetici* (Liège: Ed. M.A.C., 1971, 1991), 4.

19. *I cieli del nord* (*The Northern Skies*) (Liège: Ed. M.A.C., 1974), 12 and 11, respectively.

20. *Despues* (*Afterward*) (Rome: Ed. Associazione Artisti Lepini/CIAS, 1981–84), 3.

21. Elio Filippo Accrocca in the preface to *Il colore del cielo, Dove passano le rondini* (*The Color of the Sky, Where the Swallows Pass*) (Gavignano: Associazione Artisti Lepini, 1995), 3.

Brazil

Brazil

ANDREA LOMBARDI

Brazil, truly ineffable: here, literature and culture are filled with a scent of old and new, a result of late and arbitrary rereadings. Halfway between anthropophagy and irony, Brazil portrays itself as a mixture of delicacy and modesty, even in its most popular stereotypes, all represented with overly elaborate, theatrical freshness.

Ezra Pound's famous command to "make it new" still rings true here, as it does for the Americas in general and for Brazil in particular, as confirmed by Claude Lévi-Strauss's acute observations. What Brazil does not display, however, in contrast with the Italian tradition, is a regard for the oppressive weight of the past that the Italian tradition has to reaffirm regularly and occasionally relegates it to petty positions. At once strength and weakness, this historical absence is also contradicted by thousands of histories, including that of the natives—who are, in fact, completely dispossessed. Nonetheless, Brazil's fascinating cultural milieu and multiethnicity, though more problematic than some would suggest, provide very fertile ground for discussion and debate of contemporary social issues.

Fragments of Italo-Brazilian literature are offered here in their necessarily decentralized center, since there is no longer a center for an Italian Brazilian writer. The examples presented here show complementary elements of multilingual complexities and universal tendencies.

Yet how can only three poets represent the entire macrocosm of Italian culture in Brazil—that is to say, of Italian Brazilian culture?

It must be a daring and arbitrary selection to be sure, invariably the result of objective limitations. Nonetheless—and this is a very important element here—the wide range of possibilities is noticeably smaller than the vastness of Italian immigration to Brazil would suggest; according to as yet unverified statistics, traces of Italian heritage are found here and there in small and irregular patches all over the country, all nine million square kilometers of it, in a kaleidoscope of cities with picturesque names (almost tongue-twisters), some of them undoubtedly suggesting Italian origins: São Paulo, Nova Trento, Nova Venezia, Cascavél, Pindamon-hangaba, Itaquaquecetuba; in the states of Rio Grande do Sul and Santa Catarina, and also in Espírito Santo and Bahia; even in the impenetrable and exotic Amazonia, in the distant Pará and Mato Grosso, in all parts of this territory-dictionary.

Limiting the count to those who read and speak Italian fluently, the numbers drop considerably, aided by the allure of Brazil's melting pot and by an irremediable, incomprehensible couldn't-care-less attitude on the part of Italians that makes us think about a repressed experience. A multiplicity of languages could be heard in Brazilian cities at the turn of the twentieth century, and the Italian language was sustained by a number of publications regularly printed in Italian, which then dwindled due to the famous bans enacted during World War II, a time in which Brazil and Italy opposed one another, with even a small Brazilian military presence on the Italian peninsula. Since then, there has been a revival: Italian, as target language and language connect directly to affection, starts working as bridge between Brazilian and Italian communities and traditions, although with no fruitful prospects. This has resulted in an expanded use of Italian in journalistic and quotidian spheres, and the study of Italian has increased. Such developments stimulate indeed a more productive debate on issues such as heritage and linguistic mixtures and repression.

The choice of just three poets to represent the Italian Brazilian cultural sphere is as symbolic as it is subjective. One, Ermanno Minuto, speaks the Ligurian dialect; another, Marco Lucchesi is a speaker of Italian, though he is also multilingual and now elected in the prestigious Acadêmia Brasileira de Letras; the third, Vera Lúcia de Oliveira, also a professor, mastered the ability to write in both languages as needed. Multilingual by choice and vocation, these three poets represent and present a plural universe in their writing that leaves behind the idea of a fatherland as cultural identity, that leaves behind a tradition distinctly conservative, one that confines to a narrow and closed pattern the freedom obtained in the field of writing, in the realm of the word. A word that should be replaced—and perhaps these days it has already been overcome—by the use of a literature that is ironic, authentic, and open, result of a new and musical elaboration: homeland/motherland, documented in the songs of Caetano Veloso, a Brazilian singer and composer who is also an interesting ambassador of Brazilian culture.

Ermanno Minuto, from Savona, although Brazilian by custom and dialect, is a writer who possesses a vitality in his dialect expression that joins images of external landscape to inner tonalities of *"saudade,"* a nostalgia that is no longer just Italian or Ligurian. Marco Lucchesi, Brazilian by birth, is a professor, essayist, and translator, and he expresses himself in a number of distant and, for Brazil, exotic languages such as Russian, Arabic, and German. And last, there is Vera Lúcia de Oliveira, who writes about the pain of uprooting and resettling through variations on the themes of nostalgia and solitude. Her melancholy runs through her writing and arrives at new shores, a moving inspiration that carries its own solutions.

❧ Ermanno Minuto (b. 1929)

Ermanno Minuto was born in Savona on August 5, 1929, and holds a degree in business. He worked in the Italsider complex, an industrial plant that no longer exists, and toured the world as an envoy to Iran, Libya, and, finally, Brazil, where he settled in 1987. For Minuto, the need to write is as old as the age of reason, but for various reasons, such as his shyness and lack of time, he began to write only after his retirement. His first attempt consisted in writing, in dialect, the many memories that swarmed in his mind. He is a sort of *repentista*, a kind of improviser according to a custom of the northern part of Brazil. His writing was influenced by his reading of the classics of the nineteenth century, such as Leopardi, Carducci, and Pascoli. He collected his dialect poetry in a volume called *A cantia di ravatti* (*The Storage Room of Old Things*, 2002). He writes in dialect because that is the language in which he thinks when reflecting on his friends and events from his youth. *Il gusto aspro delle more ed altri racconti* (*The Bitter Taste of Berries and Other Stories*, 2005) is his only prose work.

In a letter to me, Ermanno Minuto has explained,

The motifs and the feelings present in my writing are after the fruit of my memories. I always thought that the *saudade* (nostalgia) that comes over someone like me who lived in different places so distant from each other is a two-way feeling. Such "*saudade*" as the consequence of a feeling felt for two different lands is the main element that lies at the source of my writings in prose and poetry. It is like a thread that continues to connect me to both lands. From Brazil I take the broad views of the vast horizons, the innate happiness of its inhabitants overburdened by heavy problems, the contrast between the grandiose breadth of the avenues and of the buildings of its metropolis against the humiliating poverty of the *favelas*, where large groups of people are forced to live in spite of everything. From Italy I take nourishment from the lost world of my childhood, the games played in the streets, the snowy Christmases which showed few surprises under the trees, and my experiences as an adolescent during the war, the fear and the hunger. These are all things found among the trinkets that make up the collection *Cantia di Ravatti*. I run constantly from one world to the other where, for me, nothing is without a soul. All things small and large—be they squares, streets, trees, fields or dwellings—are testimony of life, of life-giving essences.

A stae trupicäle

da *A cantia di ravatti*

Cum'u fa cädu! U su u brûxa u fiattu.
I raggi cazan zû cume de prie,
e, anche standu all'umbra, u sulu imbattu
u fa strenze e parpële cume gioxie.

I colibrì çercan ûn pösatoiu
tra e ramme basse di erbi ciû umbrusi.
Anchêu u xöa sulu l' avultöiu,
i ätri öxelli se ne stan sitti e ascusi.

U mundu, in-te l' äia rarefaeta
u pä, 'na futugrafia un pö sfucâ.
A cuae de fä quarcösa a se ne andaeta.
Se fa fatiga anche a respiâ.

Estate tropicale—Come fa caldo! Il sole accende il fiato. / I raggi cadono giù come pietre / e, anche stando all' ombra, il solo riflesso / fa stringere le palpebre come persiane. / I colibrì cercano ove posarsi / tra i rami bassi degli alberi più ombrosi. / Oggi vola solo l'avvoltoio, / gli altri uccelli restano zitti e ascosi. / Il mondo, nell' aria rarefatta, / sembra una fotografia un po' sfocata. / La voglia di far qualcosa se n'è andata. / Si fa fatica anche a respirarare.

Tropical Summer

from *The Storage Room of Old Things*

It's so hot. The sun cuts your breath off.
The sunrays pelt down like stones.
Even in the shade, the rays bore through
the eyelids like they're coming through Venetian blinds.

The hummingbirds are searching
for places among the lowest branches of the shadiest trees.
Today, the only thing flying is the vulture.
The other birds are still and hidden.

In the rarified air, the world
looks like a slightly out-of-focus picture.
The desire to do something is gone.
Even to breathe is a labor.

Futugrafia (Mëzugiurnu de stae a-u tropicu)

Nu gh'e 'na bäva d'äia, ûn cädu infernäle
u schissa tûtte e cöse de 'stu mundu
in-te 'n'atmusfera immobile e irrëale,
in-te 'n silensiu magicu e prufundu.

E sciue dell'ibiscus, che impan l'estae,
pendan da-e ramme, in te l'äia ch'a stagna,
ferme cume se ghe fuisan inciuae.
Ogni tantu u passa in-sce a campagna

u reciammu sulitäiu de 'n garbé.
U su desfa l' asfältu, u brûxa e spiagge,
u batte a piccu in-sce i teiti e in-sce i parmé,

poi u straciungia zû, rasente a-e miagge,
e u furma, tûttu lungu i marciapë,
strisce d'umbra streite cume picagge.

Fotografia (Mezzogiorno d'estate ai tropici)—Non c'e una bava d'aria, un caldo infernale / schiaccia tutte le cose di questo mondo / in un'atmosfera immobile ed irreale, / in un silenzio magico e profondo. / I fiori di ibiscus, che riempiono l'estate, / pendono dai rami, nell'aria immobile, / fermi come se fossero inchiodati. / Ogni tanto passa sulla campagna / il richiamo solitario dell'oriolo. / Il sole disfa l'asfalto e brucia le spiagge, / batte a picco sui tetti e sulle palme, / poi strapiomba giù, rasenta i muri, / e forma, tutto lungo i marciapiedi, / strisce d'ombra strette come nastri.

Photograph (Midday Summer in the Tropics)

There was no movement of air, an infernal heat
crushing down on every thing in this world,
in an atmosphere that was immobile, and unreal,
in a silence that was magical, and profound.

The hibiscus flowers that fill the summer
hang from limbs in the unmoving air
are closed up tight, as if they have been bound and gagged.

Every so often, the solitary call
of an oriole floats over the countryside.
The sun melts the asphalt. On the beaches, it scorches the sand.

It beats down the peaks of the roofs. The tops of the palm trees.
Then free-falls, brushing against the walls.
Along the whole length of the sidewalk, it spreads
into bands of shade
as tight as any closed blossom.

Malincunia

L'è 'na seia ciûvusa e u cazze da-u çë,
mesc-ciâ cun l'aegua, anche a malincunia.
Leggere cume tocchi de papë
e nivue grixe se rûbattan via.

Ma u ventu, che u sciûscia da punente,
u nu riesce a spassâ tûtta 'sta cappa.
Rassegnou, cu 'n fremitu imputente,
u giurnu u mêue in-te 'n çë de ciappa.

L'äia fûmusa a se tinze de ametista,
lentu u passa ûn sciammu de marsêu.
U mundu, scuu francu, u se rattrista

e u pä ch'u fasse u sapin cume 'n figgiêu.
Quest' aegua finn-a a me apann-a a vista
e a cazze, freida, drita in-sce u mae chêu.

Malinconia—È una sera piovosa e cade dal cielo, / mescolata alla pioggia, la malinconia. / Leggeri come pezzi di carta / le nuvole grigie ruzzolano via. / Ma il vento, che soffia da ponente, / non riesce a spazzare tutta la cappa. / Rassegnato, con un fremito impotente, / il giorno muore in un cielo che pare d'ardesia. / L'aria fumosa si tinge d'ametista, / lento passa un volo di pavoncelle. / il mondo, bagnato fradicio, è triste / e sembra faccia il broncio come un bambino. / Questa pioggia sottile, mi appanna la vista / e cade, fredda e dritta, sul mio cuore.

Melancholia

A tinge of melancholia is also raining
with the rainy evening.
The clouds roll away,
light as pieces of paper.
But the wind, that renewing west wind,
cannot break up the whole mantle.
Resigned, with an impotent shudder,
the day dies in a sky that is slate.
The smoky air is tinted with amethyst;
a flock of northern lapwings passes by slowly.
The world, mired in a mudhole, is sad;
it seems like a boy in a sulk.
This subtle rain clouds my eyes,
and falls, cold, straight, into my heart.

Natäle 1960–Natäle 1987

Oua che vivu squaexi a fin du mundu
possu rivive ûn mûggiu de Natäli.
U nu l'è difficile perchè, in fundu,
a ben pensâ-ghe sun staeti tutti uguäli.

Giurni che u se fa tinta d'ëse ricchi,
che u se fa e u se riçeive di regalli,
e tutti quanti, au mä cume in-sce i bricchi,
se cumpurtemmu cume pappagalli.

Quand'ëa figgiêu spetäva u Natäle
che u duveiva ëse uguäle pe tutti
(Ma u mae u l'ëa ûn po mènu uguäle).
Gh' ëan guaera e miseia, ëan tempi brûtti.

Ma mi restäva piggiou dall'invexendu
da gente che a pareiva vegnî matta.
E u mae zeneivu u l'ëa n' èrbu stûpendu, e ëa feliçe cun u mae trenin
de latta.

Quandu, poi, sun introu in te l'ingranaggiu,
ch'u maxinn-a e cöse e i sentimenti,
ho capiu ch'u l'è tûttu un mûntaggiu,
tûtta 'na finta pe parei cuntenti.

Natale 1960–Natale 1987—Ora che vivo quasi in fondo al mondo / posso rivivere moltissimi Natali. / E non è difficile, perché, in fondo, / a ben pensare son stati tutti uguali. / Giorni che si fa finta d'essere ricchi, / che si fanno e si ricevono regali, / e tutti quanti, al mare come ai monti, / ci comportiamo come pappagalli. / Quand'ero bambino aspettavo il Natale / che doveva essere uguale per tutti / (Ma il mio era sempre un po' meno uguale). / C' erano guerra e miseria, erano tempi brutti. / Ma io restavo preso dalla confusione / della gente che pareva diventar matta. / E il mio ginepro era un albero stupendo, / ed ero felice col trenino di latta. / Quando, poi, sono entrato nell'ingranaggio, / che macina le cose ed i sentimenti, / ho capito che era tutto un montaggio, / tutta una finta per sembrare contenti

Christmas 1960–Christmas 1987

Now that I'm living almost at the end of the world
I can relive a whole bunch of Christmases.
It's not difficult to do. Because if you think hard
about them all, all your Christmases are the same—

days you pretended to be rich,
gift-giving, gift-receiving—
and all the rest that goes along with it—from sea to shining sea,
copy cats, parroting each other. Monkey-see-monkey-do.

When I was a boy, I used to wait and wait for Christmas,
which was supposed to equal for everyone.
(But mine was always slightly less equal.)

War and hard times. Difficult years.
Although I was protected from all that chaos
by people always poised at the edge of insanity.

And my juniper tree was a fabulous tree
and I happy with my tin toy train.

When, later on, once I was a good cog in the grind
that chews up and spits out all objects and emotions,
I understood it's just a montage—
the whole business a pretence for seeming content.

Nustalgia? . . . scî però . . .

Quandu a vitta a m'ha scuriu distante
cuscî luntan da Sann-a e da-u mae niu
e, pe 'n destin curiusu e stravagante,
ho lasciou tûttu e tûtti e sun partiu,

ho preparou cun cûa e mae valixe,
e, cunsigliou da çerte vuxi arcäne,
insème a vestì, scarpe e camixe,
g'ho missu 'na brancâ cöse sträne.

I ricordi de schêua e da Villetta,
de quelli attimi de feliçitae
che ho vixûu quand'ëa 'na balletta
cun i cumpagni de zêugu e de rapae.

Me sun purtou dere u cantu de 'n gallu
ch 'u me desciäva prestu de matin,
e i riflessi de 'n tramuntu giallu
ch 'u inçendiäva e Ninfe e i Capuçin.

Me sun purtou derë l' oudu da taera
bagnâ da 'n impruvvisu lavasun,
i ricordi tristi de 'n guaera,
l'oudu du pestu e du minestrun.

Nostalgia? . . . Sì peró . . .—Quando la vita mi ha cacciato distante, / così lontano da Savona e dal mio nido / e, per un destino curioso e stravagante, / ho lasciato tutto e tutti e son partito, / ho preparato con cura le valigie, / e, consigliato da certe voci arcane, / insieme ai vestiti, le scarpe e le camicie, / vi ho messo una manciata di cose strane. / I ricordi di scuola e della Viletta, / e di quegli attimi di felicità / che ho vissuto quand'ero bimbetto / con i compagni di gioco e delle rape. / Ho portato con me il canto del gallo / che mi svegliava presto Ia mattina, / e i riflessi di un tramonto giallo / che incendiava le "Ninfe e i .. Cappuccini". / Mi son portato l'odore della terra / bagnata da un acquazzone improvviso, / i ricordi tristi della guerra, / l'odore dei "pesto" e del minestrone.

Nostalgia. Yes. Up to a Point.

When life has hunted me far,
so far from Savona and my little nest
and, because of an odd and bizarre destiny,
I left everybody and everything behind,

I packed my bags carefully,
and advised by certain mysterious voices,
along with suits, shoes and shirts,
and a handful of strange things.

Memories of school days and Viletta,
and the flashes of happiness
that I had a young boy
with friends playing and beets.

I carried with me the rooster's crowing
that woke me up early in the morning,
and the glinting of the yellow sunrise
that illuminated the Ninfe and the Cappuccini.

I carried with me the smell of the earth
soaked in a sudden downpour,
the sad memories of the war,
the odor of minestrone and pesto.

Tramuntu

U gh'è ûnn' du giumu ch'a pä faeta apposta
pe indûe a gente a riflette e a raxunâ;
a truvâ pe ogni dumanda 'na risposta,
a tiâ i remi in barca e stâ a pensâ.

A l'è l'ua sûbitu prima du tramuntu,
quando a lûxe a cangia de culure
e ri ti pêu tiâ zû u rendicuntu
d'ogni têu gioia, d' ogni têu dulure.

L'umbra a se slunga finn-a a-l'orizunte,
in çe a prima stélla a fa l' êuggettu.
U su u va a cacciâ-se derë a 'n munte
e tûtte e cöse se tinzan de viulettu.

Pe l'äia u passa u sun de 'na campann-a
che u se perde luntan inseme a-u ventu.
A matassa di ricordi e se dipann-a
e ti ti pêu cuntâ-te in-te 'n mumentu

tûtta a têu vitta cume 'na vëgia foa.
Ûnn-a cadenn-a de giumi brûtti e belli.
U chêu u se quëta e u pensieru u xöa
derë a 'n sciammu neigru de strunelli.

Tramonto—C'è un'ora dei giorno che pare fatta apposta / per indurre la gente a riflettere e a ragionare / per trovare una risposta ad ogni domanda, / per tirare i remi in barca e starsene a pensare. / È l'ora che precede il tramonto, / quando la luce cambia di colore / e si può fare un bilancio / d'ogni gioia e di ogni dolore. / L'ombra si allunga fino all'orizzonte, / in cielo la prima stella fa / l'occhiolino. / Il sole va a cacciarsi dietro un monte / e tutte le cose si tingono di violetto. / Per l'aria passa il suono di una campana / che si perde lontano insieme al vento. / La matassa dei ricordi si dipana / e tu puoi raccontarti in un momento / tutta la tua vita come una vecchia fiaba. / Una catena di giorni brutti e belli. / Il cuore si acquieta ed il pensiero vola / dietro ad uno stormo di storni neri.

Sunset

It's an hour of the day that seems to exist
just to get people to reflect and consider,
to search for an answer to each and every question,
to pull the oars back into the rowboat and sit there and think.

It's that hour before the sunset,
when the light changes color
and you can make a balance
of each and every joy and sorrow.

The shadow is growing toward the horizon,
in the sky, the first star is winking.
The sun is chasing itself behind a hill
and everything is tinted in violet.

The sound of a bell comes through the air,
then loses itself along with the wind.
The skein of memories untangles
and in one instant you can tell yourself

all your lousy moments as if it was one big tall tale.
A litany of ugly and glorious days.
The heart is hushed. Thought disperses
on the tail of a flock of black starlings.

U vëgiu mainä

U l'äva e brasse pinn-e de tatuaggi,
a faccia magra, chêutta da-u su e da sä.
I êuggi pin de memöie di sêu viaggi,
u chêu pin de ricordi du sêu mä.

U l'äva navigou in-sce i barchi a veia,
prima che e nävi andessan a vapure;
u se ricurdäva ancun de quella seia
ch'u l'ëa rivou a vedde Singapure.

U l'ëa naufragou due votte e u l'ëa scampou;
e a-u Santuariu u gh'ëa ûn quadrettu
che u musträva cume u s'ëa sarvou.
Oua, de sutta l'äa de 'n gran berettu,

u se ne stäva de ue a miâ distante,
a spiâ u mä cun l' êuggiu attentu
squaexi u speresse de vedde pe 'n istante
rivâ u sêu brigantin cun e veie a-u ventu.

E, quärche votta, 'na lacrima, cian cian,
a strisciäva lungu e rûghe ciû prufunde.
U l'ëa u ricordu de 'n amu luntan
o a nustalgia da mûxica de unde?

Il vecchio marinaio—Aveva le braccia piene di tatuaggi, / la faccia magra cotta dal sole e dal sale. / Gli occhi pieni delle memorie dei suoi viaggi, / il cuore pieno dei ricordi del suo mare. / Aveva navigato sui velieri, / prima che ci fossero le navi a vapore; / si ricordava ancora di quella sera / ch'era arrivato a vedere Singapore. / Era scampato a due naufragi; / e al Santuario c'era un quadretto / che mostrava come s' era salvato. / Ora, da sotto la tesa di un gran berretto, / restava delle ore a guardare lontano, / a spiare il mare con occhi attenti / quasi sperasse di vedere per un istante / arrivare il suo brigantino con le vele al vento. / E, alle volte, una lacrima pian piano, / strisciava lungo le rughe più profonde. / Era il ricordo di un amore lontano / o la nostalgia della musica delle onde?

The Old Fisherman

His arms were covered with tattoos,
his face was baked by sun and salt.
Eyes filled with memories of his journeys,
and he had a heart filled with memories of his sea.

He had navigated on barks with masts,
before steam engines were invented;
he recalled that evening
he arrived in Singapore.

He had survived two shipwrecks;
and at the Sanctuary there was a plaque
telling how he had been saved.
From under the brim of a big cap,

he'd remain for hours looking into the distance,
on the lookout at the sea, with those alert eyes—
almost as if he hoped to see his brigantine with its sails
arrive with the wind at any moment.

And, occasionally, a tear, one, two,
would roll down the deepest furrow.
Was it the memory of a far off love
or the nostalgia of the wave's music?

→ Vera Lúcia de Oliveira (b. 1958)

Vera Lúcia de Oliveira was born in Candido Mota in 1958. She is professor of Portuguese and Brazilian literatures in the Department of Foreign Languages and Literatures at the University of Lecce. She is the author of many works on contemporary writers published in Italian and foreign journals. She has taught in Brazil as well and has published a number of books, including *Pedaços/Pezzi* (*Pieces*) in 1992, *Tempo de doer/Tempo di soffrire* (*Time of Suffering*) in 1998, *La guarigione* (*The Recovery*) in 2000, *Uccelli convulsi* (*Convulsive Birds*) in 2001, and *No coração da boca/Nel cuore della parola* (*In the Heart of the Word*) in 2003. A collection of her poems was published as *Il denso delle cose. Antologia poetica* (*The Density of Things: An Anthology*).

She is the recipient of two important national awards for poetry—the Spiaggia di Velluto prize and the Gino Perrone prize. She also won the Osilo Literary Prize (Mediterranean section, Sassari, 2000) for her poetry in Portuguese.

Terzo mondo del cielo

da *Il denso delle cose: Antologia poetica*

nel terzo mondo
del cielo
vanno piccole anime
calpestate
vanno bambini
il cui dolore divora l'infanzia

e gli ubriachi del nulla
lavoratori del proprio lutto
affamati di poesia
e pane

ombre
lì si stendono
in attesa delle trombe
del giudizio

Third Universe of the Sky

from *The Density of Things: An Anthology*

The Third Universe
of the Sky
is where small trampled
souls go
children
whose sorrows are devoured infancy

and worthless drunks
toilers of their own struggle
starved of poetry
and bread

shadows
stretched out
waiting for the trumpet
of judgment

Lo stagno e il mare

per Gladys

Non è in mare che depongo le reti,
non è àncora
il denso del mare
Il mare non progetta il gesso delle urne,
il mare lacera le cicatrici
corrode gli aghi
Non conosce indugio il mare
Non è stato guardando il mare che ho imparato a ritagliare le parole
nel silenzio duro della casa,
scavando in città
le malattie dello stagno,
sognando cimiteri più piccoli per frenare l'evasione
delle cose
del sangue
Crepe che le grondaie affondavano
e il suolo cullava come una cosa che si deve gonfiare,
che deve per destino assorbire la palude
Per questo dinnanzi al mare sto come chi ha paura
come chi ingoia in fretta i rattoppi i sassi
gli stiletti che il mare nel suo movimento corrode.

Stagnant Pond and the Sea

for Gladys

It isn't in the sea where I drop the nets
the depths of the sea
is not an anchor
the sea doesn't bother with making plaster urns
the sea lacerates scars
it corrodes needles
The sea knows nothing about hesitation.
The sea hasn't sat there noticing that I have relearned to cut out words
in the house's hard silence,
excavating diseases
in the stagnant ponds of the city
dreaming the tiniest cemeteries in order to staunch the escape
of the blood-things
Crevices that sank the drainpipes
and that the ground cradles like something to be inflated
that the swamp is destined to absorb.
That's why I stand before the sea like someone afraid
like someone swallowing the patches the stones
the daggers which the sea corrodes with its movement.

Gli dei

il cielo è popolato da Dei
(a nostra immagine e somiglianza)

i vinti optano per un Dio minore
che abita negli scantinati del cielo
i ricchi
per un Dio che viaggia in prima classe
e ignora i mutilati

gli Dei sono sempre in guerra ma chi
vince è il Dio dei vincitori

The Gods

the sky is populated by Gods
(in our own likeness and resemblance)

the defeated opt for a lesser God
who lives in the basement of the sky
the rich
choose a God who travels in first class
and ignores the mutilated

the Gods are always at war but whoever wins
is the God of the victors

L'utero

da *Geografie d'ombra*

In ottobre tutti i colori mi esiliano,
le foglie che calpesto mi corrodono
Sono nata in un paese che non cambia quasi
volto
Si impara la morte in un paese perpetuo?
La vecchiaia è una lezione
            quotidiana
Le foglie che calpesto
mi perforano
Ammalarsi è sognare l'utero

The Uterus

from *Geographies of Shadow*

In October all the colors exile me,
the colors I trample eat away at me.
I was born in a country that almost never changes
in appearance
Can one learn death in a perpetual country?
Old age is an
        everyday lesson

The leaves I trample
perforate me
Becoming ill is to dream of the uterus.

Pezzi

sono frantumata silenzi escono dalla bocca
tenui
stavo disegnando
parole
ho perso il modo di destarmi
sono in tanti pezzi
da essere quasi infinita

Pieces

I am in shatters
from my mouth silences escape
tenuous
I had been tracing
words
I lost the way of rousing myself
I'm in so many pieces
it seems almost infinite.

Poesia per Manoel de Barros

da *Tempo de doer*

strappo le vene della carta e prendo
il tuo muschio
il tuo vischio di lumaca il tuo occhio di occhio
il tuo corpo
avviluppato in ventre
di chiocciola

strappo
striscio sull'erba
graffio sussulti
scivolo su virgole
assorbo limo
e lacrima
di animale
in attesa
che il dolore galoppi le acque senza travolgere

Poem for Manoel de Barros

from *Time of Suffering*

I tear out the veins of the paper and I pull up
your moss
your slug trap the eye of your eye
your body
tangled in the stomach
of a snail

I rip out
I slither in the grass
I scratch slashes
I slide above commas
I absorb slime
and animal
tears
while waiting
for sorrow to gallop off with the waters without carrying it all away.[1]

Scrivere

da *La carne quando è sola*

liscia carne
carne di occhi
carne di foglie
vive
carte di mani fragili
carne di carta
carne di segno
carne di sogno che dico (non dico)
quasi uscisse l'anima
dal dito

To Write

from *When the Flesh Is Lonely*

smooth flesh
flesh of eyes
flesh of leaves
living
papers of fragile hands
flesh of paper
flesh of sign
flesh of dream I tell (I don't tell)
the soul almost escapes
through the fingers

ho messo dentro la terra un lettino
era autunno lasciavo le foglie
ammucchiarsi soffici su suolo
facevo come un lenzuolo dorato
che si stendeva avvolgeva le orecchie
dentro la culla non so chi avevo
messo a dormire qualcuno c'era
piangeva a dirotto mai che avessi
potuto vedere il suo volto

I put a little bed in the earth
it was autumn I let the leaves
pile up soft on the ground
I made a sort of golden sheet
that expanded wrapped the ears
inside the cradle I do not know whom I had
put to sleep somebody was there
was crying non-stop never was
I able to see its face

dicevi la poesia è un lampo
la vedi ti acceca questo è il bello
e il brutto che la vorresti sempre
che vorresti quella vita vista
non quella che bisogna vivere
in attesa

You used to say poetry is a flash
You see it it blinds you that's the beauty
and the foul is that you'd want it always
you'd want that life seen
not the one that we have to live
while waiting

giungi in un soffio di voce
giungi in mezzo alla notte
nel cigolare del vento
giungi come le zampe felpate
degli animali feriti
che non si danno pace

you arrive with a breath of voice
you arrive in the middle of the night
in the groaning of the wind
you come like the stealthy claws
of wounded animals
that can't find peace

se nella casa vorranno entrare le piante
c'è posto anche per loro
potranno crescere sugli angoli fino
alle finestre e poi girare i loro rami
sopra le porte e fare della casa
una piccola foresta

if plants want to enter in the house
there is also room for them
they can grow in the corners up to
the windows and then twist their branches
over the doors and turn the house
into a little forest

⇀ Marco Lucchesi (b. 1963)

Marco Lucchesi was born in Rio de Janeiro in 1963 and is a professor at the Federal University of Rio de Janeiro. A history professor, he published his poetry collection *Sphera* in 2004. Later books include *Lucca dentro: Poesie* (*Lucca Inside: Poems*) and a volume of collected poems. He was a finalist for the Jabuti Prize, the most prestigious of literary prizes in Brazil, in 2002. He has edited a number of classics, such as Tasso's *Jerusalem Delivered* and the poetry of Leopardi, and he has translated numerous works from Italian (Eco's *The Island of the Day Before* and *Bandolino*, Vico's *New Science*), as well as from German and Russian. He is the recipient of several awards and prizes, the most important being the special prize of the Order of the Star of Italian Solidarity of the President of the Italian Republic, which he received in 2005. His book of poetry *Poesie* (*Poetry*) was translated into Armenian and Persian. His poems have appeared in Denmark, Germany, Italy, and Portugal.

Esilio

da *Poesie*

da quando
sei passata
al nero
varco
del sonno

(follore
di frale
destino)
provo

una
strana
quiete

sazio
di quel nulla
che m'agghiada

Exile

from *Poems*

Since you
went
through the black
passage
of sleep

(folly
of frail
destiny)
I experience

a strange
quietness

sated
by that nothingness
which pierces me

Svela il tuo

Svela il tuo
volto di nebbia
una lontanìa
di rondini al tramonto

reggono le tue
mani quelle
di un naufrago
spossato di sé

Fitta di foschi
presagi, cerchi
la terra lontana,
di seme
e di sogni cosparsa

eppur non sai
che il cerchio
delle rondini
segue sempre più basso

non sai
che la tempesta
non consente di toccare il porto

non sai
che tutto è sogno e che siam soli

Unveil Your Own

Unveil your own
face of mist
a distance
of swallows at sunset

support your worn-out
shipwrecked hands

Dense with gloomy omens, you seek
a distant land
strewn with seed
and dreams

and yet you don't know
that the circle of swallows
follows ever more low

you don't know
that the storm
doesn't allow us to touch port

you don't know
that all is a dream and that we are
alone

Ghimel

da *Poemas reunidos*

A parte de
uma parte

em muitas
se reparte

tal como
o sol poente

nos raios
derradeiros

e assim
a dor que sentes

é apenas
uma parte

da parte
de outro mal . . .

tão nobre
como a tua

a dor de
teu irmão

tão nobre
quanto a dele

a dor que aflige
a Deus

(o rosto
dessa dor
embrionária)

e assim
já não conheces
mais limites

Ghimel

from *Collected Poems*

The part of
a part
into many
is divided

just as
the lingering

rays
of the setting sun

and likewise
the pain you feel

is merely
a part

of the part
of another illness

just as worthy
as yours

the pain of
your brother

just as worthy
as another

the suffering
afflicting God

(face
of embryonic
suffering)

and thus
you know
no more limits

que o Todo
é apenas parte

de nova contraparte
saudoso de outro mal

since All
is simply a part

of a new counterpart
longing for another illness

Limite

da *Lucca dentro: Poesie*

Siamo
sospesi
da
un sol
richiamo
da
un sol
disio

tu di là
dal tempo

e me
naufrago
ancora

e senza porto

siamo
sospesi

da
un sol
richiamo

da
un sol
disio

da una scontrosa gioia
smentita all'infinito

Limit

from *Lucca Inside: Poems*

We are
suspended

by
one
call only

by one
desire
only

you beyond
time

and me
shipwrecked
still
and without port

we are
suspended
by one
call only

by one
desire
only

by an ill-tempered joy
infinitely denied

Marinaio

Also fuhr das Schiff allein aus, und sein
Kapitän war das grosse braune Kruzifix.
Kasimir Edschmid
o Cristo
      crocefisso
      capitano

o tu pietoso
      ulisse
      di maremma

riportami
      a quei liti
      sì lontani

Sailor

And so the ship went out alone,
and its captain was the great brown crucifix.
Kasimir Edschmid
oh Christ
> crucified
> captain

oh compassionate
> Ulysses
> of the marshes

bring me back
to those shores
so far away

Yvy Marae'y

A te
vorrei
tornare

o patria
sì
lontana

vi
sono
appena
due
cammini da
percorrere:

l'arida
morte

o il canto
prosciugato

appena
due
cammini
per riedere

alla
perduta
patria . . .

sia il
timore
men
saggio
della
scelta

che ti
riporti ai

Yvy Marae'y

I'd like to return to you

oh country
so far away
there are

barely two roads to take:

arid death

or a dry song

barely two roads to return

to the lost country

may the fear be less wise than the choice

which will carry you to boundless skies

not arid death

but the dry song

where harmonious
sauces

of rough torrents

run
the waters
of the Paraguaçu

cieli
sconfinati

non l' arida
morte

ma il canto
prosciugato

ove salse
di armonie

e mosse
dai torrenti

corrono
le acque
del Paraguaçu[2]

NOTES

1. Manoel de Barros, born in 1917, is the great poet of the Pantanal, the huge expanse in Mato Grosso of Brazil that was submerged by the flooding of the Paraguay River into a boundless freshwater sea.

2. "Place where no evil exists," from the Guaraní language.

Canada

Canada

JOSEPH PIVATO

When did Italian Canadian writing begin? The first Italians to reach the shores of what is now Canada were explorers. Giovanni Caboto landed here in 1497 and was the first to write about what he saw. But since Caboto, later called John Cabot, was sailing for the king of England, Henry VII, he probably wrote his words in Latin, rather than in Italian or English. In 1524 another Italian explorer, Giovanni Da Verrazzano, sailed for King Francis I of France and charted the east coast of North America, naming part of it Nuova Gallia or Nouvelle France. Da Verrazzano was probably the first to write down the words *New France*, thus naming the new territories of Canada in terms of European geography. Da Verrazzano wrote a long report in Latin on his voyage of discovery for King Francis I, *Codex de Cellere*, which still exists in libraries in the Vatican, Florence, and New York. Hostile natives killed Da Verrazzano in 1528. Among his crewmembers was Jacques Cartier, who continued these French explorations on his own later voyages.

When we use the term *Italian* for these centuries of European history, we must remember that the people living on the Italian peninsula did not comprise a unified nation like the France, England, or Spain of the time, but instead lived as a collection of city states, principalities, papal states and territories often occupied by foreign powers like the Spanish, the French, and the Germans. Giovanni Caboto was a Venetian navigator. Venice had been an independent republic for several hundred years. Caboto was born in Genoa like Colombo, but his family moved to Venice. Like Amerigo Vespucci, Giovanni Da Verrazzano was from Florence.

The first Italian visitor to Canada who wrote about his experiences in Italian for an Italian audience was Francesco Giuseppe Bressani, a Jesuit missionary who worked in New France.

Sections of his long 1653 work, *Breve Relatione*, demonstrate Bressani's conscious effort to look at Canada and its indigenous people from an

Italian perspective and with terms of reference that are Italian rather than French.

There were many Italian explorers and soldiers with the French in North America. In 1682 Enrico Tonti assisted Robert de La Salle to explore the Mississippi. In 1759 Francesco Carlo Burlamacchi was a general in the army of Montcalm during the battle of Quebec. There were Italian soldiers in the de Meuron Regiment and the Watteville Regiment, who settled in Canada in 1816. Did any of these people write back to relatives and friends in Italy about their experiences in Canada? Descendants of these soldiers included Monsignor Paolo Bruchesi, bishop of Montreal (1897–1939), and Quebec historian Jean Bruchesi.

There were several Italian writers living in Canada, but their works did not constitute a conscious literature. Most were individual works produced by isolated writers who did not see themselves as creators of a new literature, but as Italian writers in exile, or as travelers, or as writers in Canada who adopted the new language. In 1885 A. A. Nobile published *An Anonymous Letter/Una lettera anonima*, a novel with English and Italian facing pages. Anna Parken Moroni published *Emigrante. Quattro anni in Canada* in 1896. Writers like Nobile and Moroni were visitors to Canada, as was the inventor Marconi. Most of the 1920s poetry of Liborio Lattoni and Francesco Gualtieri has disappeared. In 1946, journalist Mario Duliani published *Città senza donne*, an account of his experience in an internment camp during World War II. Duliani wrote a 1959 book review of Elena Albani's Italian novel, *Canada, mia seconda patria*—the only extant evidence that there was a spark of an Italian writing community in Montreal. In the 1950s, Italian-language papers did flourish in both Toronto and Montreal, but there was little literary activity in these weekly periodicals. When Antonio Spada published his 1969 social history, *The Italians in Canada*, he included a few pages on writers. Among the authors he described briefly are Mario Duliani, Elena Albani, John Robert Colombo, Jean Bruchesi, Guglielmo Vangelisti, and a few birds of passage like Giose Rimanelli.

ANOTHER GENERATION

In the 1960s and 1970s, the sons and daughters of the great post-war immigration from Italy started to attend universities in Canada. This is also the period of the great awakening in Canadian nationalism reflected in English-Canadian literature. This spirit influenced young Italian Canadian writers, promoting cultural identity and diversity in Canada. In Quebec, the 1960s was the time of the Quiet Revolution, and here too Italians became conscious of the search for cultural identity. For the first time a large group of university-educated young people provided the critical mass to create a community of writers, artists, filmmakers, musicians, and academics.

This was also the time when historian Robert Harney began to publish his articles on the immigration of Italians to Canada, and thus fostered more research in the social history of ethnicity. Harney's pioneering work encouraged a whole generation of young scholars to study the history of Italian settlement in Canada. These researchers included Franc Sturino, Bruno Ramirez, John Zucchi, Roberto Perin, Gabriele Scardellato, and Franca Iacovetta, people who often worked with writers on conferences and publications devoted to the study of the Italian Canadian community. One such historic event was an international conference called "Writing the Italian Immigrant Experience in Canada," held in Rome in May 1984 at the Canadian Academic Centre in Italy. The conference organizer, Roberto Perin, and Franc Sturino later edited a collection of papers from this meeting, *Arrangiarsi: The Italian Immigration Experience in Canada* (1991).

Italian Canadian literature began in about 1975 with Pier Giorgio Di Cicco, the first writer to realize that the possibility for a distinct body of literature did exist in Canada. As an editor for the Ontario literary magazine *Books in Canada*, Di Cicco became aware of a number of young writers of Italian background who were just then beginning to publish in literary magazines and with small presses. There were writers working in English, in Italian, and in French. Though they used different languages, they all reflected the sensibilities of their Italian background and encouraged one another. This spirit of self-awareness made many writers and readers conscious of the Italian language and of the writers and journalists who published in Italian.

Di Cicco published the anthology *Roman Candles* (1978) in Toronto. The experience of publishing was both exciting and shocking. The Italian Canadian writers in the anthology were happy with the reception of this first collection of Italian Canadian poetry in English, but we were shocked as well by the realization that we had discovered a literature about ourselves, and the great responsibility that this entailed. This is where Italian Canadian literature begins: with a self-conscious realization about our writing. Di Cicco clearly articulates this self-awareness in the introduction to *Roman Candles*:

> In searching for contributors, I found isolated gestures by isolated poets, isolated mainly by the condition of nationalism prevalent in Canada in the last ten years. However pluralistic the landscape seemed to be to sociologists, the sheer force of Canadianism had been enough to intimidate all but the older "unofficial-language" writers. Some of the contributors I had already been aware of through their publishing efforts, but most came as a surprise; and finally, all involved were surprised by the anthology itself. It put a stop to the aforementioned isolationism. (9)

Many of the seventeen poets included in *Roman Candles* (1978) soon published their own books of poems. Caroline Morgan Di Giovanni edited *Italian Canadian Voices* (1984), the first anthology of this writing that tried to represent it as a body of literature. Here Italian-language writers were translated into English. There were other anthologies in the 1980s and 1990s that collected works from groups of writers: *La poesia italiana nel Quebec*, edited by Tonino Caticchio; *Quetes. Textes d'auteurs italo-quebecois*, edited by Fulvio Caccia and Antonio D'Alfonso; *A Furlan Harvest*, edited by Dore Michelut (1993); *Pillars of Lace*, edited by Marisa De Francheschi (1989); *Curaggia: Writing by Women of Italian Descent*, edited by Nzula Angelita Ciatu et al.; and *Our Grandmothers, Ourselves*, edited by Gina Valle.

The Anthology of Italian-Canadian Writing, which I edited in 1998, is in this tradition of service to the diverse communities of Canada: the English, the French, the Italian Canadian, and others. In this context of service, we must also mention Antonio D'Alfonso's founding of Guernica Editions, which has published writers working in English, French, and Italian, and has promoted translations between and among these languages.

These previous anthologies are evidence of the growth of groups of writers who became aware of their ethnic identity. In 1986 one group of writers in Vancouver, Dino Minni, Genni Gunn, and Anna Foschi, organized the first national conference of Italian Canadian writers. By the end of this historic meeting, the Association of Italian-Canadian Writers was founded to promote the work of these writers and continue to foster a sense of community across the country. The many Italian-language writers scattered across the country were encouraged and supported by those writing in English and French, the official languages of Canada.

Soon Italian Canadian writing was making an impact on the national literature of Canada. We had two winners of the Governor General's Awards, Nino Ricci for English Fiction with *Lives of the Saints* in 1990, and Fulvio Caccia for French poetry with *Aknos* in 1994. Several of the other authors also won literary awards: Mary di Michele, Marco Micone, and Antonino Mazza.

Many of these Italian Canadian writers, who were once invisible or forgotten, are now the subjects of literary studies and theses in universities in Canada and Italy. There are now many critical articles on some of these writers in literary journals. Some books devoted to the works of these writers include *Contrasts: Comparative Essays on Italian-Canadian Writing* (1985 and 1990), edited by J. Pivato; *Echo: Essays on Other Literatures* (1994), by J. Pivato; *Social Pluralism and Literary History*, edited by Francesco Loriggio in 1996; *In Italics*, by Antonio D'Alfonso in 1996; Marino Tuzi's *The Power of Allegiances* in 1997; *Devils in Paradise* (1997), by Pasquale Verdicchio; and *The Dynamics of Cultural Exchange* (2002), edited by Licia Canton.

REDISCOVERING ROOTS

One of the significant effects of all this writing in English and French was the rediscovery of our Italian roots in the works of Italian-language authors. There are many Italian-language writers in Canada, both past and present, who had been forgotten. I will try to mention the work of as many as possible in the rest of this brief introduction. I do not pretend to include all of them here since there are some who have never come to my attention or whose work has gone missing, such as the poetry books of Francesco Gualtieri. I would include in such a list the 1958 book *Biglietto di terza*, by Giose Rimanelli, even though he only stayed in Canada a short time.

One of the senior writers is Camillo Menchini in Montreal, who produced many books of history, including *Giovanni Caboto scopritore del Canada* in 1974, *Giovanni da Verrazzano e la Nuova Francia* in 1977, and *Francesco Giuseppe Bressani, primo missionario italiano in Canada* in 1980.

The first attempt at a complete history of Italians in Canada is Guglielmo Vangelisti's *Gli Italiani in Canada* in 1956. In Toronto, historian Luigi Pautasso published *Il Santo cappuccino di Toronto* in 1990.

One of the most common genres is the memoir or personal history of the immigrant experience. Giuseppe Ricci's 1981 *L'orfano di padre* is a personal account of his life beginning in 1907, and continuing through his immigration to Canada, where he lived from 1927 to 1944. Another autobiography is *La dottoressa di Cappadocia*, by Toronto doctor Matilde Torres in1982. In Ottawa, in 1984, Anello Castrucci put his life story in a novel-like narrative with *I miei lontani pascoli*. In Montreal, Aldo Gioseffini produced *L'amarezza della sconfitta*, a mixture of personal memoir and political commentary. He also helped Andrea Masci publish his 1996 *Diario di un povero soldato*.

In the 1988 narrative by Dino Fruchi, *Il prezzo del benessere*, we have real-life experiences disguised in the form of a novel. In this tradition of realism and social criticism, we have the novels of Giuseppe Ierfino, *L'orfano di Cassino* in 1990, and *Il cammino dell'emigrante* in 1992. In Montreal in 1984, Ermanno La Riccia brought out a collection of short stories about the experiences of immigrants caught between Italy and Canada, *Terra mia*. Guelph's Gianni Bartocci has produced a number of books that deal with his years in New Zealand; however, his North American short stories are in a 1980 literary collection called *La riabilitazione di Galileo*. Another world traveler is Camillo Carli, who wrote the novel *La giornata di Fabio*. The editor of *Vice Versa* magazine, Lamberto Tassinari, produced *Durante la partenza* in 1985. In the genre of children's fiction, we have Elettra Bedon's *Ma l'estate verra ancora* in 1985.

The other genre that is often chosen by Italian writers in Canada is social commentary. One of the earliest works in this vein, the 1962 *Non dateci lenticchie* by Ottorino Bressan, makes pointed criticism of social conditions in Canada. As a journalist, Gianni Grohovaz practiced this tradition of social critique. Benito Framarin examines personal morality with *I cattivi pensieri di Don Smarto* in 1986. The trials and tribulations of working at a private Italian school in Toronto are captured in Giuseppe Ranieri's 1996 book, *Intervista Professore*. Stories of Italian pioneers in British Columbia were collected by Giovanni Bitelli and Anna Foschi in the 1985 anthology *Emigrante*. This environment of Italian writing and publishing encouraged some to produce poetry.

The books of Italian poetry are not as numerous as those of prose, but I will mention a few that have struck me as interesting. One of the earliest is *Tristezza*, published in 1961 by Baldassare Savona, who later returned to Italy. Typical of his poems is this one, called "In Canada," translated by J. Pivato:

Furon quattro anni,
quattr'anni di gran pene.
quattr'anni lunghi penosi e tormentosi,
in questo selvo Canada e la gente,
s'ignorante, incolta e materiale,
pesava sempre piu su le mie spalle:
con quello, loro fare si barbarico,
e con l'ipocrisia loro maestra.

It's been four years
Four years of hard labor
Four long years of trouble and torment
In this wild Canada and the people
So ignorant, uncultured and materialistic
Weighed more and more on my shoulders
With their very barbaric ways,
And with hypocrisy their teacher.

It is not clear here if Savona is criticizing English-speaking Canadians, Italian immigrants in Canada, or both. The poem also captures in an unvarnished way the snobbery and sense of superiority sometimes found among the better-educated immigrants from Europe.

In contrast to Savona's negative attitude are the many books of poems that try to explore the honest feelings of newcomers to the New World. Montreal has the most active group of writers, beginning with Tonino Caticchio, who wrote poems in the Roman dialect—*Rugantino* in 1982, *La storia de Roma* in 1981, *La scoperta der Canada* in 1980—and edited the 1983 bilingual anthology *La poesia italiana nel Quebec*. Among the younger writers included in this Quebec anthology is Giovanni di Lullo, who produced *Il fuoco della pira* in 1976, and the trilingual Filippo Salvatore, author of *Tufo e gramigna* (1977). Lisa Carducci also writes in French, but one of her best books is her Italian work *L'ultima fede* (1990). One of the senior poets of the Montreal group is Corrado Mastropasqua, who collected his Neapolitan poems in *Ibrido. Poesie 1949–1986* (1988).

Toronto has a variety of writers. The modest little 1976 collection by the late Vito Papa, *Poesie del carpentiere*, includes a poem in Calabrian dialect. Luigi Romeo has one book of poems from 1963, *Battesimo*. Roberto Pisapia collected his Neapolitan poems in *Tiempo ca nun tornero* in 1977. Domenica Giambagno's 1976 collection, *Risveglio e Trionfo*, is self-published, as are several of the other volumes noted in this paragraph. Vittoria Ruma Conte simply calls her 1977 book *Raccolta di poesie*. Antonio Filippo Corea's first collection, *I passi* in 1981, is all in Italian, but his second book, *Per non finire* in 1986, includes many Calabrian poems. Using the pen name Bepo Frangel, in 1977 Father Ermanno Bulfon published *Un friul vivut in Canada*, a collection of his poems in the Friulian dialect. In Montreal, Doris Vorano published the unique *Puisis e Riflessions in* 1983. The work of five Friulan women was collected in 1993 in *A Furlan Harvest*, edited by Dore Michelut and featuring the Friulan poems of Rina Del Nin Cralli. In Ernesto Carbonelli's 1990 volume *Fieno secco*, each Italian poem has an Italian commentary.

In Burlington, Anthony M. Buzzelli produced *The Immigrant's Prayer*, a 1994 bilingual collection of short poems. Windsor's Maria Agnese Letizia in D'Agnillo published 172 poems in *Cento poesie molisane ... plus* in 1992. In Hamilton, Franco De Santis produced *Sotto Vento* in 1990 and *L'impronta del tempo* in 1991. In Sarnia, Anthony Barbato published his bilingual collection of poems, *Acque chiare, Clear Waters* in 1989.

We do not often think of western Canada as a space for Italian-language writing, yet for decades the paper *L'Eco d'Italia* has appeared in Vancouver and promoted Italian writers and artists. One of these prolific authors is Romano Perticarini, who has published five books of poetry, all with the English translation on facing pages. A few of them are *Quelli della fionda* (1981), *Il mio quaderno di Novembre* (1983), and *Via Diaz* (1989). Carlo Toselli produced two trilingual collections of his Italian poetry by including both English and French translations: *Lo specchio di peltro* (1993) and *La fanciulla di terracotta* (1996). In Edmonton, Silvano Zamaro published *Autostrada per la luna* (1987), while in Winnipeg, Carmine Coppola published *Poesie per Giulia* (1996).

One of the early pioneers of western Canada was Giorgio Pocaterra, who arrived in Alberta in 1904 and began to establish the Buffalo Head Ranch in the Kananaskis Valley near the Rocky Mountains west of Calgary. The Rocky Mountains reminded Pocaterra of the Italian Alps near his birthplace of Rocchette. Though fluent in Italian and some Indian languages, he chose to write in English, always inspired by the landscape of Kananskis country:

> Majestic mountains
> And foaming waterfalls
> Enfolded softly
> By mystic moods!

From all of these poets I have selected eight for this anthology. I hope readers will find them interesting.

BIBLIOGRAPHY

Ardizzi, Maria. *Conversations with My Son / Conversazione col figlio*. Toronto: Roma Publishing, 1985.
Canton, Licia, ed. *The Dynamics of Cultural Exchange*. Montreal: Cusmano, 2002.
Carducci, Lisa. *L'ultima fede*. Poggibonsi: Lalli Editore, 1990.
Costa, Giovanni. *Impressioni in terre amiche*. Quebec: Les Ateliers Graphiques, 1989.
De Franceschi, Marisa, ed. *Pillars of Lace: An Anthology of Italian-Canadian Women Writers*. Toronto: Guernica, 1989.
Di Cicco, Pier Giorgio, ed. *Roman Candles*. Toronto: Hounslow Press, 1978.
Di Giovanni, Caroline, ed. *Italian Canadian Voices: An Anthology of Poetry and Prose (1946–1983)*. Oakville: Mosaic Press, 1984.
Grohovaz, Gianni. *Per ricordar le cose che ricordo*. Toronto: Casa Editrice Dufferin, 1974.
Loriggio, Francesco, ed. *L'altra storia: Antologia della letteratura italo-canadese*. Vibo Valentia: Monteleone, 1998.
Mastropasqua, Corrado. *Ibrido: Poesie 1949–1986*. Montreal: Guernica Editions, 1988.
Michelut, Dore, ed. *A Furlan Harvest*. Montreal: Trois Editions, 1993.
Perin, Roberto, and Franc Sturino, eds. *Arrangiarsi: The Italian Immigration Experience in Canada*. Montreal: Guernica Editions, 1991.
Perticarini, Romano. *Quelli della fionda / The Slingshot Kids*. Vancouver: Azzi Publishing, 1981.
Pivato, J. *Contrasts: Comparative Essays on Italian-Canadian Writing*. Montreal: Guernica Editions, 1991.
———. *Echo: Essays on Other Literatures*. Toronto: Guernica Editions, 1994.
———, ed. *The Anthology of Italian-Canadian Writing*. Toronto: Guernica Editions, 1998.
Salvatore, Filippo. *Tufo e gramigna*. Montreal: Edizioni Simposium, 1977.
Verdicchio, Pasquale. *Devils in Paradise*. Toronto: Guernica Editions, 1997.
Zamaro, Silvano. *Autostrada per la luna*. Montreal: Guernica Editions, 1987.

→ Gianni Grohovaz (b. 1926)

One of the early writers from the 1950s period of Italian Canadian writing was Gianni Grohovaz, a journalist and poet who came to Canada as a displaced person and began to work on railway construction in northern Ontario. Grohovaz was born in 1926 in Fiume, a city in Istria, a northeastern region of Italy that became part of the Yugoslavian Republic of Croatia after World War II. Grohovaz and many other Italians of Istria were left without a country. His early experiences in Canada are captured in his posthumously published autobiographical narrative, *Strada Bianca* (1989).

In the Toronto area, Grohovaz is best known as a journalist who wrote for many Italian-language papers. In 1953 he participated in the founding of *Corriere Canadese*, the major Italian paper in Canada. He was also active as a broadcaster and his social and political commentary are collected in *E con rispetto parlando e al microfono Gianni Grohovaz*. His book *To Friuli from Canada with Love* chronicles Canadian aid to towns in Friuli after the 1976 earthquake.

For Italian Canadian writers, Gianni Grohovaz is best known for his Italian poetry collected in two slim volumes. In his first collection, *Per ricordar le cose che ricordo* (1974), we find poems in Fiuman dialect. His second collection is *Parole, parole a granelli di sabbia* (1980). His poems also appeared in many newspapers and magazines, and are included in the anthologies *Italian Canadian Voices* (1984) and *The Anthology of Italian-Canadian Writing* (1998).

Io ti ripago: Italia senza core

da *Per ricordar le cose che ricordo*

Io ti ripago Italia "boteghera,"
pavida, rinunciatrice e "calabraghe"
che senza arrossire di vergogna
hai ceduto la mia terra a Tito.
L'Istria bella, italiana e mia
è diventata oggetto di baratto . . .

Due volte son partito via in esilio,
due volte ho dovuto pagar caro
il mio amore per l'Istria e per l'Italia.
. . . per questa Matrigna che al Governo
fa a pezzi lo Stival finquando, ahinoi!
dell'Italia di Vittorio del '18
non rimarrà che una ciabatta rotta!
Vergogna!
Ma ti ripago, Matrigna senza core
perché impunita non rimanga nella Storia
la Tua doppia faccia, impenitente!
Se gli Slavi han ricevuto per regalo
la Zona B e la mia Terra amata,
anch'io voglio donar loro qualcosa!

Tanto, mio Nonno non riposa;
per l'insulto si rigira nella fossa:
ha sofferto per nulla e non ha pace . . .
Sul Carso, sul Piave e a Caporetto,
a Santa Gorizia, sui monti e giu' in trincea
quel ch'Egli ha fatto per unir l'Italia
non conta più nulla. Anzi è un delitto!

Guarda Matrigna quel che io faccio:
con la Medaglia d'oro (che ormai è 'no scherzo)
e con la Croce del Cavalierato,
che per mio Nonno volean dir tutto,
più della vita stessa perché ingannato

I Repay You: Heartless Italy

from *To Remember the Things I Remember*

I pay you back, "shopkeeping" Italy,
gutless, relinquishing "pants-dropper"
who without turning red in the face
gave away my land to Tito.
My beauteous Italian Istria
became just a bartering tool . . .

Two times I left in exile,
two times I had to pay dearly
my love for Istria and for Italy
   . . . for that Mother-in-law, that
boot destroyed by its politicians
until, sadly, King Victor's Italy
of 1918 will be just a tattered
slipper! For shame!

But I will repay you, heartless Mother-in-law,
so that your double face will not remain
unpunished by unforgiving history!
If the Slavs obtained as a gift
Zone B and my beloved Land,
I too want to leave them something!

Besides, my Grandfather is not at rest:
he turns in his grave at the insult;
he uselessly suffered and has no peace . . .
On the Carso, along the Piave, at Caporetto
in Santa Gorizia, in the mountains and
in trenches, whatever he did to unify Italy
is worth less than nothing, indeed it's a crime!

Mother-in-law, watch now what I do:
with the Gold Medal (that now is a joke)
and with the Cross of Honor
that meant everything to my grandfather,
meant more than life itself because, duped,

pensava che Tu eri sincera, Italia d'oggi:
li faccio una risata,
amara se vuoi, ma una risata . . .

Delle sue glorie, mio Nonno volontario,
mi fece erede, e gli fui grato
perché credevo in Te, anch'io t'amavo
come solo un'Istriano lo sa fare . . .
Ora?
Non t'odio, perché anche questo è un sentimento;
non t'amo perché hai giocato il tradimento!
La Tua infingardia me la lego al dito
e, Nonno perdonami,
le Tue medaglie le regalo a Tito!

he believed you were sincere, present-day Italy:
I give you my full-bellied laughter,
bitter if you will, but a great laugh . . .
With gratitude I inherited the glories
of my volunteer grandfather
since I believed in You, I also loved You
as only one from Istria can do.
Now?
I do not hate you, because even that is a feeling;
I do not love you because of your betrayal!
I wrap your slothfulness around my finger
and, forgive me grandfather,
Your medals I will give to Tito!

Primavera

L'aria profumava
de scarpete de Madona.
La bruta strada che portava
a la ceseta sul confin,
(passado el scovazon de Valscurigne,)
sembrava una Via Crucis:
da una parte i campi coverti de verdura e
latte vecie che gnanca el tempo
riussiva a inruzinir,
da l'altra quela prigion
de anime in pena
dimenticade dal mondo
solo perché le ragionava a modo suo . . .
La rete del confin
dixeva molto.
Un sopra l'atro i sassi,
messi da man ignota,
ed un porton de rovere
con una croxe in zima,
jera el fortin
del mondo de Ocidente,
e el serbo mustacion
che dal'altra parte de la rete
faceva la guardia per l'Oriente
se domandava: perché mai
tanta gente vegniva in questo posto
per ascoltar parlar el Padre Andrea . . .

Spring

The air was scented
by Lady's Slippers.
The rough road leading
to the church by the border
(past the dump by Valscurigne)
seemed like The Way of the Cross:
on one side large fields of vegetables
and old tin cans not even the years
had succeeded in rusting,
on the other, a prison that
housed souls in pain,
ignored by the world only
because of what they thought . . .
The border fence
said a lot.
One stone on top of the other,
laid there by unknown hands,
and an oaken door
with a crucifix on top,
it was the small fortress
of the western world,
and the mustachioed Serb
who on the other side of the fence
guarded the Orient
asked himself: Why did so many
come here to hear Father Andrea . . .

Dolor de padre

El 29 febraio 1972 a Downsview, mentre tua me dreate te cambia a le panuzze ti non ti gavevi ancora mille giorni de vita. Go lassà de guardar la television per guardarte, a ti e tua madre, e dentro al cuor me go sentì morir . . .

Go visto sangue
vegnirte zo dal peto nudo,
sgorgar da un buso largo come un dito:
una patrona ga lassada el segno
su la tua carne
E come de bestia ferida.
go senti' el fiato rauco
che rantolava sui tuoi polmoni
gonfi ormai de tute le miserie.
Te vedo, la in zinocio
davanti a quela spada
che te fa s-ciavo del tuo fradel Caino
e in quel momento, credime
go odiado el mondo
Go pianto, Nini mio
perche' picio come ti xe . . .,
già adesso xe marcà sul libro nero
el tuo destin de omo: Un Abele, come tanti . . .

Pain of the Father

February 29 at Downsview, while your mother changed your clothes, you still were not a thousand days old. I stopped watching the TV to look at you and your mother, and I felt death in my heart . . .

I saw blood
flowing along the naked breast
spurt from a hole as big as the thumb:
A lady boss left the seal
there on your flesh.
And like a wounded beast
I heard the feeble rattle
gurgling in your lungs
that spilled over with your sorrows.
I see you, on your knee
facing the sword
that enslaved you to your brother Cain
and in that instant, believe me
I hated the world.
Go slowly, my Nini
because small as you are . . .
already your destiny as man
is written on the black book:
An Abel, like so many . . .

Ciudi la porta che xe giro d'aria . . .

Quando me meto a scriver queste robe
non lassario mai più
cascar la pena,
eco perche' difizile xe ciuder
quest'umile pensiero a Fiume mia . . .

Ritornaremo ancora nel Quarnero?
Non xe soltanto una speranza magra
ma la certeza de chi crede sempre
che tuto quel che noi butemo in aria
deve tornar per forza su la tera.

Se qualchedun me dà del grande iluso
mi ghe rispondo grazie per l'elogio:
tireme via sti diexe schei de sogno . . .
cossa me resta ancora da la vita?

(Quando la naja stava tramontando,
e "DEMOGHELA" se cantava in coro
i Alpin se caparava una VI-DUE
co i abiti borghesi in valigeta.
In quele strazze jera la speranza
poder salvar la pele e ritornar.)
Se pur tremila miglia ne separa
dal nostro Fogoler de Valscurigne
xe pronte le valige . . . caso mai
dovessimo tornar a casa nostra.

Fiume ne aspeta, passarà anca i guai
e tornaremo indrio ma senza gloria,
perché l'apuntamento con la storia
xe l'ilusion che ne fa star in piedi . . .

Close the Door, There Is a Draught . . .

When I start to write these things
I would never again
put down the pen,
that's why it's hard to conclude
these humble thoughts for my Fiume . . .

Will we go back again to the Quarnero?
It's not only a flimsy hope
but the certainty of one who believes
that whatever is blown up in the air
must eventually fall back to the ground.

If someone accuses me of grand illusions
I thank him for the compliment:
empty my pocket change of dreams
. . . what is there left to live for?
(When army life was almost done,
and together we sang "LET'S POUND THEM," the Alpine troops
    bartered for
a V-2 and street clothes in a suitcase.
In those rags hid all the hopes
of saving one's skin and return.)

Although three thousand miles separate
us from our hearth of Valscurigne
the suitcases are ready . . . just
in case we can come back home.

Fiume awaits us, these troubles will pass
and we will return but without glory
because this appointment with history
is the illusion that keeps us standing . . .

→ Corrado Mastropasqua (1929–2009)

Corrado Mastropasqua was born in Cimitile, Naples, in 1929. He studied medicine at *l'Università di Napoli* and became an MD in 1953. He was a doctor in the Italian navy until 1961, when he emigrated to Canada. From 1967 until he retired, he specialized in anesthesiology at Santa Cabrini Hospital in Montreal. In 1974 he cofounded an Italian theater group, *Le Maschere di Montreal*, and participated as an actor and director for many years. He was active in poetry readings, radio and TV cultural programs, and newspapers. Many of his poems are written in Neapolitan dialect and often allude to the music, customs, and folklore of the Campania region. His first book of poems, '*Na lacrema e 'na risa,* was published in Naples in 1969. His poems have appeared in many newspapers and magazines. Guernica Editions published a bilingual collection of his poems, *Ibrido* (1988), with Italian and English on facing pages. He died in Montreal in 2009.

Canto doloroso

da *Ibrido*

Freddo e immobile sul duro
marmo giaci padre mio!

Gli occhi chiusi per sempre,
le tante rughe, dolori
di tutta una vita, fermi
rappresi sul dolce viso
la tua anima fanciulla
lasciò il corpo di quercia,
già non sei più fra noi
non senti le teatrali
alte grida dei parenti
non avverti lo sgomento
muto di noi figlioli.

Ricordo a Forio d'Ischia
—ancora non era il molo—
barche lente portavano
a riva i passeggeri,
noi piccoli con la madre
facevamo a gara a chi
prima scorgesse il bianco
tuo capo da lontano
e quando ti si avvistava
di gioia mai più provata
tumultuavano i cuori.

Ricordo il tuo muto dolore
quando dal paese
per essere a noi vicino
ti trapiantasti in città,
fra gente ammodo eri solo
ogni giorno più schivo
intristivi come fiera
ingabbiata dalla civiltà;

Sorrowful Song

from *Hybrid*

My father, on hard marble
you lie motionless and cold.

Your eyes are closed forever,
so many lines, the sorrows
of your whole life, now still,
curdled on your dear face,
your youthful soul departs
your oaklike body, already
you are no longer with us,
you do not hear the showy
cries of your relatives,
you do not heed your children's
silent grief and fear.

I remember Forio d'Ischia
—we hadn't reached the pier—
the slow boats that were bringing
passengers to the shore,
we little ones with our mother
were vying to see who
would be the first to see
your white head from the distance
and when we spotted you
our hearts shook with a joy
they never knew again.

I remember your silent sorrow
when you left the countryside
and settled in the city
just to be near us,
alone and shy with others
and more withdrawn each day,
you withered like a wild beast
caged by civilization,

a volte tornavi al paese
ma sempre ti riportava
la tua famiglia in gabbia.

Ti ricordo all'ospedale
sul bianco letto di morte
con lo sguardo di nebbia
con le spaurite colombe
delle mani chiedermi
il perché di tanto soffrire.
Un rantolo ostinato
ti scandiva nella gola
l'inutile agonia
io mi torcevo le mani
disperato in silenzio.

you left the city sometimes
but always would come back
to your family in the cage.

I remember the hospital,
on the white bed of your death
the misty look on your face
the scared doves of your hands
begging me for the reason
for so much suffering.
An obstinate death rattle
beat a rhythm in your throat
of useless agony
while I wrung my heads
in silent desperation.

Noi quelli di fuori

Per Bruno e Coco

Noi quelli di fuori
costretti all'esodo
da una società marcia
vi abbiamo lasciato
una terra verde da custodire
la ritroviamo bruttata di cemento.

Noi cafoni del sud.
abbiamo appreso alieni
idiomi per sopravvivere
ma con i figli giochiamo
a tressette e parliamo
il nostro melodioso dialetto.

Noi quelli di fuori
nel deserto americano restiamo
caparbiamente abbarbicati
al laghetto-miraggio
della cultura dei nostri padri
anche se deteriore o folcloristica.

Noi cafoni del sud
con dita di ghiaccio pazienti
raggranelliamo ogni giorno
il gruzzolo-speranza
per ritornare in patria
a sognare e morire.

We Folks from Foreign Parts

For Bruno and Coco

We folks from foreign parts
forced to emigrate
by a putrid society
there we left behind
a green land that we tended
we find it again disfigured by cement.

We yokels from the south
have picked up alien
idioms to survive
but we play *tresette*
with our children and we talk
to each other in our melodious dialect.

We folks from foreign parts
are clinging stubbornly
in the American desert
to the mirage oasis
of the culture of our fathers
even as it corrodes or turns to folklore.

We yokels from the south
with fingers like icicles
patiently scrape together
each day our hoard of hope
to go back to our homeland
to dream and then to die.

Santo Donato

Calcinato dal sole agostano
scompariva quasi il tratturo
nella nebbia di terriccio
del trepestio lento dei buoi,
andavamo uccelli di passo
con cicaleccio dissacrante
la meridiana pausa dei campi,
dalle verdi fogliate alabarde
si levava improvviso
il campanile di Santo Donato;
il sagrato un fazzoletto
con fette d'anguria sul muricciolo,
il santuario uno stanzone
disadorno dal piancito
di terra battuta,
fumante una dozzina di candele
nell'angolo stava
il santo saraceno.
Fuori il sole dardeggiava
i suoi strali di fuoco
nelle gole riarse
e due soldi costava il paradiso
due soldi per sparare
la pallina liberatrice
di gioia fresca-spumante
dal verde della bottiglietta.
A sera si tornava a casa
stanchi di felicità
impastati di sole e terriccio
con la certezza avvenire
di altre fiere di Santo Donato.

Santo Donato

Calcined by the August sun
the sheep track all but disappeared
in the loamy haze made by
the slow trampling of the oxen,
birds of passage, we passed,
desecrating with shrill chatter
the midday rest of the fields;
amid the leafy green halberds
the bell tower of Santo Donato
rose up suddenly;
the churchyard a handkerchief
with melon slices on the low wall,
the sanctuary a greenhouse
disadorned by the pavement
over the battered earth,
the Saracen saint
stood in the corner
smoking a dozen candles.
Outside the sun shot
its fiery arrows
into parched throats
and paradise cost a few cents,
a few cents to fire
the liberating cartridge
of cold sparkling joy
from the green of the little bottle.
In the evening we went home,
wearied with happiness,
kneaded with sun and loam,
knowing there'd be other shows,
new exhibits of Santo Donato.

Civiltà contadina

Dopo anni vi ho rivisti
nipoti contadini
le cui radici affondano
nella terra di boscofangone
ho rivisto il padre vostro
dal volto tagliato nel tufo
eppur dolce negli occhi
ho mangiato con voi
lo stesso pane di una volta
bevuto lo steso vino del contado
sull'aia della masseria.
A Napoli-terremoto
a Milano-nebbia
non rinnegate la nostra
contadineria
fregiatevi di essa
come di titolo nobiliare
fatene una bandiera
per gli uomini sani.
Quei pochi che restano.

Country Civility

For Manlio d.p.

I've seen you again after years
my country nieces and nephews
whose roots grow deep
in the woodmire earth
I've seen your father again
with his face carved out of tufa
but sweet-eyed nonetheless
I've eaten with you
the same bread as long ago
I've drunk the same country wine
on the farm's threshing floor.
In the earthquake of Naples
In the haze of Milan
you never surrender your
countrified air
you flaunt it like a ribbon
of noble rank
you make it a banner
for right-minded men.
Those few who remain.

Epilogo

Il presente di ape operaia
monotona fatica
con sogni sterili e guizzi
di farfalla senza ali,
il futuro prospettiva
di lamentazioni
e farfugliamenti senili,
immergersi vale
nello sgocciolio d'innumeri ore
dalla memoria raccolte
in bagno spumoso di passato;
il padre mi traeva per mano
alla pace dei camaldoli
—mistero di raccoglimento –
poi a scurrilità di avvinazzati
in trattoria di campagna,
la ragazza puttana
un attimo intravista
in bagliore di anche
desiderata allo spasimo,
l'approdo dei figlioli bambini
al porto delle mie braccia
in un mare odisseo
azzurro d'innocenza
affannoso d'occulti perigli.
La morte mi recherà sulle braccia
recisi i fiori di tanto
incantesimo di vita
io le sorriderò placato.

Epilogue

The present of the worker bee
monotonous toil
with sterile dreams and flittings
of a wingless butterfly,
the future a prospect
of lamentations
and senile mutterings,
its farewell a plunge
into the last drop of countless hours
of memory collected
in the foamy bath of the past;
my father drew me by the hand
to the peace of the Camaldoli
—a mystery of concentration—
then to the scurrility of the drunks
in a country inn,
the young whore
glimpsed for an instant
in the dazzle of stirring
the pang of desire,
the landing of the little children
in the port of my arms
on an Odyssean sea
bright blue with innocence
troubled with hidden perils.
Death will summon me to his arms
all the flowers of so much
enchantment of life will be cut
I'll smile at them content.

→ Maria J. Ardizzi (b. 1931)

Maria J. Ardizzi was born Maria De Dominicis in 1931 in Leognano, in the Italian province of Teramo. After she finished her studies in Rome, she moved to Toronto, Canada, with her husband in 1954. For many years she was involved with the Italian community in several cultural activities, especially the printing of books and other materials. She has been writing fiction in Italian for many years and has published short stories and articles in many newspapers and magazines. Her first novel, *Made in Italy* (1982), won the Ontario Arts Prize and was published in an English translation with the same title. Both the English and Italian editions were widely distributed, in part due to Ardizzi's links to many community networks. This first novel deals with the memories of an old physically paralyzed woman as she reconstructs the story of her immigration to Canada and the difficulties of adjusting to life in North America, the death of her husband and children, and finally her confinement to a wheelchair. The physical handicap becomes a metaphor for the condition of the immigrant woman.

Ardizzi's second Italian novel, *Il sapore agro della mia terra* (1984), was followed by *La buona America* (1987). This cycle of immigration novels was completed with *Tra le colline e di là dal mare* (1990). While all the novels are concerned with telling the story of immigration in a realistic fashion, the later books tend to use the Italian language in a more poetic style. It is as if Ardizzi, with each successive volume, was freeing herself of the burden of chronicling the immigrant experience and could focus more attention on using the Italian language in a way that was authentic to the experience in Canada.

She published *Conversazione col figlio* (1985), a bilingual collection of her poems dedicated to her son, Paolo, who died of leukemia at twenty years old. The poems are lyrical meditations on relationships, love, and loss. In 1999 Guernica Editions republished the English version of *Made in Italy,* which is an indication of the book's value and popularity. The following year they published *Women and Lovers,* an English translation of Ardizzi's novel, unpublished in Italian, *Donne e amanti.*

All of Ardizzi's novels were originally issued by Toma Publishing in Toronto. Her work has been included in the anthologies *Italian Canadian Voices, Pillars of Lace, L'altra storia,* and *The Anthology of Italian-Canadian Writing.* Literary criticism on her work can be found in Joseph Pivato's *Contrasts: Comparative Essays on Italian-Canadian Writing* and *Echo: Essays on Other Literature* (1994), as well as Marino Tuzi's *The Power of Allegiances* (1997).

Conversazione col figlio

da *Conversazione col figlio*

I

Abbiamo camminato insieme, dal principio,
su questo scoglio;
siamo adesso sull'orlo, a decifrare il baratro,
il cuore svuotato come una noce,
il sapore del frutto cancellato.
La vita!
Un incanto intravisto
e il tempo che già comincia a non essere più.
Sei ad una tappa forzata,
ma non sei stanco
non hai sete
e il sole è alto a mezzogiorno.
La straniera ti ghermì a tradimento;
sbalordì il tuo occhio fanciullo,
fiume di gioia impaziente di giungere al mare.
Guardavi nella lontananza degli anni,
giù . . . giù . . .
dove si adagia la stanchezza dell'uomo.
Era febbraio:
e sognavi solo primavera.

II

Porgesti il braccio alla siringa,
offristi tutte le tue vene,
fili tenui, fragilissimi, impreparati.
La nausea. Il vomito. La bocca in fiamme.
Interrogavi i miei occhi.
Volevi credere.
"Ce la farò!" sussurravi stringendo i denti.
E mentre L-Asparaginase e Vincristine
ti violentavano fino alla radice,
in te nasceva l'Uomo:
ragazzo trasformato in uomo

Conversation with My Son

from *Conversation with My Son*

I

We have walked together from the beginning
on this rock.
We are on the edge now, trying to make sense of the abyss,
the heart emptied, like a walnut shell,
the flavor of the meat no longer there.
Life!
An incantation flitting quickly by
and time already coming to an end.
You are forced to run,
yet are neither tired nor thirsty
and the sun is at high noon.
The stranger grabbed you from behind;
she astounded your youthful eyes,
river of joy impatient to reach the sea.
You looked out into the distance
far . . . far off . . .
to where the weariness of man finds rest.
It was February:
you dreamed only of spring.

II

You offered your arm to the needle,
surrendering all your veins,
slender threads, so fragile and unseasoned.
Nausea. Vomiting. Your mouth aflame.
You searched into my eyes, wanting to believe.
"I'll make it!" you murmured through clenched teeth.
And while the L-Asparaginase and the Vincristine
ravaged you to the core,
the man within you was blossoming:
a child become a man
in the time it takes the sun to cross the sky.
Alone,

nel tempo che il sole impiega a traversare il cielo.
Solo,
nel campo seminato di morti, senza un gemito,
senza un ripensamento a proseguire,
rivendicavi millenni di dolore,
innumeri steli tagliati all'aurora.
Parlavamo,
ma ti sentivo già eco.

III
Dalla finestra del quinto piano
frugavamo sui tetti, nelle vie,
tra la neve di marzo che faceva tutto eguale:
l'umanità pareva placata,
le cose come restituite a se stesse.
"Non c'è nulla, laggiù," avrei voluto dire.
"Laggiù,
è solo questione di tempo."
"E grave, Ma'!" dicesti sottovoce. E poi:
"La settimana scorsa andavo a scuola."
Ebbi un brivido.
"Ce la farai," dissi, ma non udisti;
continuavi a frugare laggiù,
come a raccogliere una briciola di sogno.
Poi dicesti, sciogliendo l'amarezza:
"Se non è fastidio . . .
vorrei il mangiare da casa . . .
"Qualunque cosa. Vuoi il brodo, domani?"
"Mi piacerebbe, se non è fastidio . . ."
"Non dire sciocchezze!"
"Avrai bisogno di un thermos . . ."
"Ce l'ho già."
"È marzo," dicesti dopo un po'.
"La neve scioglierà presto."
Le tue parole vaghe, trasparenti,
scivolarono sui miei pensieri più pesanti della pietra.
"A che pensi, Ma'?" chiedesti trepidante.
"Alla neve di marzo che domani non ci sarà più," dissi,
guardando dall'altra parte.

amid the field sown with the dead,
without a whimper,
unhesitant in forging on,
you redeemed thousands of years of sorrow,
countless shoots cut down at break of day.
We spoke,
but you were already an echo.

III

From the fifth-floor window
we gazed out over the rooftops, onto the streets,
over the snow of March:
humanity seemed at peace from there,
as though creation had regained its pristine self.
"There's nothing down there," I wanted to shout.
"Down there,
it's only a matter of time."
"It's serious, mom!" you said under your breath.
Then:
"Last week I was going to school."
I shuddered.
"You'll pull through," I said, but you weren't listening;
you kept searching for something down there,
as though trying to capture a shard of some dream.
Then, all bitterness gone:
"If it's not too much trouble . . .
I'd like home-cooked meals . . .
"Anything. Would you like some broth for tomorrow?"
"I'd like that, if it's not a bother . . ."
"Don't be silly!"
"You'll need a thermos bottle . . ."
"I already have one."
"It's March," you said after a while.
"The snow will melt soon."
Your veiled words, so crystal clear,
Weighed on my thoughts more heavily than stone.
"What are you thinking, Mom?" you asked hesitantly.
"The March snow will be gone tomorrow," I said,
looking away.

IV

Nella stanza silenziosa,
plaga isolata intrisa delle lacrime inghiottite da altri
che vi erano passati prima di te, apristi gli occhi.
"Non lo so." sussurrasti,
come a voler capire l'insensato gioco del nascere e del morire,
il castigo a chi non ha colpa. "Che cosa non sai?"
"Non so più nulla . . .
Ho strani sogni . . .
Sogno i morti nella guerra . . ."
"È per i films che hai visti . . ."
"Sogno persone che soffrono . . . Che vuol dire?"
Cercasti al di là dei vetri un cielo che non c'era;
dicesti, in un soffio:
"Sento la mancanza di casa mia . . ."
"Vuoi mangiare, un poco?"
"No."
"Ti ho portato il tuo brodo preferito . . ."
"No."
"Vuoi una pera?"
"Una pera . . . sì . . ."
Volesti la luce spenta, la porta chiusa.
Le ombre invasero la stanza,
il silenzio divenne solido.
Che cosa c'era nella tua mente,
non lo so.
Nella mia,
l'angoscia dell'attesa e il rancore . . .
il ricordo di un Dio immaginato.
Sentivo la tua stessa nausea,
ma per un'altra cosa.

IV

In the silent room,
lonely sanctuary filled with the tears of those
who had preceded you, you opened your eyes.
"I don't know..." you murmured,
as though trying to fathom this foolish game
of dying and being born,
the punishment the innocent must bear.
"What don't you know?"
"I don't know anything any more...
I have strange dreams...
I dream of those who died in war..."
"It's from the movies you've seen..."
"I dream of people suffering... What does it mean?"
You sought a sky that wasn't there beyond the pane;
and in a whisper:
"I miss being at home..."
"Would you like to eat something?"
"No."
"I brought your favorite soup..."
"No."
"Would you like a pear?"
"A pear... OK..."
You insisted on having the light off, the door shut.
Shadows rushed into the room,
you could almost reach out and touch the stillness.
What was on your mind just then
I do not know.
In me
seethed a lingering bitterness,
the memory of an imagined God.
I felt the nausea with you,
but for another reason.

→ Romano Perticarini (b. 1934)

Romano Perticarini was born in Fermo, in the Le Marche region of Italy, in 1934. He was trained at the local Istituto Technico Industriale, worked in Italy for some years, and then moved to Vancouver, Canada, in 1967. He began to publish poems in Italian newspapers and magazines and still does to this day. He describes himself as a natural poet who is driven to write all the time. His first book of poems, *Quelli della fionda / The Sling-shot Kids* (1981), is a bilingual collection that deals with his youth, emigration, and nostalgia. His second collection, *Il mio quaderno di Novembre / From My November Record Book* (1983), is also bilingual and examines various aspects of life in Canada for an Italian immigrant: family relations, memories, work, and nature along the Pacific coast. Perticarini has won several literary prizes: Premio la Città di Pompeii, Premio Amicizia, the Bressani Prize, and the AICW Prize.

Perticarini writes regularly for the Italian papers *L'Eco d'Italia* and *Il Cittadino Canadese*. Guernica Editions published *Via Diaz* (1989), again a bilingual collection of occasional poems that deal with a wide variety of topics. Perticarini in 2001 published *I ragazzi di ieri / Yesterday's Children*, a bilingual collection with English translations by fellow poet Pasquale Verdicchio. In 2004 he published *One of You*. His poems have been included in the anthologies *Italian Canadian Voices* (1984) and *The Anthology of Italian-Canadian Writing* (1998).

Birilli

Fanciulli di borgata
dall'occhio vispo
noi eravamo,
guasti di fame e pidocchi.
E nei miseri pranzi,
sopra dischiodate tavole
imbandite d'illusioni:
il duro pane di mais
—umile farina—che spacca
palati infantili.
Pallidi birilli noi
nudi nell'aria, o dietro
finestre di carta
a succhiar pollici.

Gridi di mamme
dagl'aridi seni
a lutto vestite
su usci intrisi d'orina,
con esili mani tese
a bocche sorridenti
ad orecchie sorde.
Luridi birilli loro
che oltre la miseria
al par d'un lazzaretto
passano beffardi.
Il tempo cancella ferite.

Vedo in fondo al borgo
una casa d'argilla e pula,
la sola a testimoniar miseria:
vi nacque un uomo
che ancora mastica mais,
che ha avuto la neve
dei rigidi inverni sui piedi,

from *The Slingshot Kids*

Skittles

Children of the outskirts
With flashing eyes
We were ridden with hunger,
We were plagued with parasites.
Those scanty meals
On age-corroded tabletops
Laden with illusions,
And cornbread of humble flour
Would scrape infantile palates.
We pale skittles
Would play naked in the air,
Would suck thumbs
Behind paneless windows.

Mothers of arid breast
And feeble hand
Would stand in mourning garb
On urine-drenched thresholds
Beckoning calls—
To our smiling lips
And deaf ears.
Dirty skittles we were
Mockingly passing through
Lazaret misery.
Time heals all wounds.

I see below the outskirts
A house of clay and hulls,
All alone exuding
Destitution.
A man was born there,
Who still recalls
The bitter taste of cornbread,
Who has known chilblain cold
Of snow on exposed feet,

sulle gracili ossa,
il sole sulle spalle, sul viso,
le pulci che lo stanavano
da sotto bianche lenzuola
lavate di lisciva.

I miei, nelle loro tombe
riposano, stanchi d'ingiustizie,
per aver cercato più di me
che Dio guardasse chi aveva
un cuore di carne.

On frail bones.
Who had known scorching sun
On his shoulders,
On his parched face.
Parasites would flush him out
From white bed sheets
Washed with pungent lye.

My dear ones are resting—
In tombs,
Wearied of injustice,
Their souls seeking
More than I
That God will bestow compassion
On those with hearts of flesh.

Ricchezza di un sogno

Quella brocca
portata d'inverno,
nella tiepida primavera,
nel grigio autunno,
d'estate, ogni giorno,
sulla testa bianca,
questa notte ho sognato
e la mia sete ha spento.

Quella vecchia madia
dove accorto custodivo
le mie poche molliche
era aperta e generosa,
i fornelli accesi,
la tavola imbandita,
questa notte ho sognato
e la mia fame ha placato.

Ieri
che ogni passo ricorda
nei giorni di sole,
di neve o di primavera,
l'immacolata ventola
delle piume d'oca,
mai che avesse azzardato
vento sui carboni,
nuova la stagnata,
vecchia la mia fame,
appena cheta la sete.

Quell'acqua di fonte
oggi impetuosa
scorre nel petto,
e mi avventura per il mondo.
Ma dispero di trovare
negli angoli più remoti,
una madia aperta,

Preciousness of a Dream

That water jug
Daily toted
On snowy head
Through tepid springtimes,
Summers and slate autumns.
Tonight I dreamed of it,
And my thirst is spent.

That old kitchen cupboard
Where I used to keep
My scarce crumbs
Yet always open
And generous, nevertheless.
The burning range,
The laid-out table.
Tonight I dreamed of it all,
And my hunger is placated.

Yesterday:
Each of my steps
In days of sun, of snow
Or springtime—
I recall . . .
The immaculate fire-fan
Of goose feathers
That never dared
Fanning the coals—
And the cauldron that was as new
As my hunger was old,
And my seldom-sated thirst.
Today:
That old spring water
Impetuously flowing
In my veins
Spurs me around
The world.
Yet, I despair of finding

un fornello acceso,
un'acqua di sorgente,
un giorno da Uomo!

Solo sognando,
stringo l'immensa ricchezza
d'un pane e un po' d'acqua:
come un antico carcerato.

—Even in the remotest places—
That open cupboard,
That burning range
That spring water.
A man's day!
Only through my dreams
Can I clutch to myself
—Like an ancient captive—
That bit of bread
And water . . .
Its preciousness.

L'altra spiaggia

L'onda che usurpava
il mio castello
di sabbia e di conchiglie,
che piena era la spiaggia
del lido di Fermo
dov'io correvo serena
non è quest'onda di piombo
dove i corvi in riva saziano
—senza gracchiare—la fame.
Dove l'onda percuote
con violenza le rocce,
dove il gabbiano gridando
assale vorace i resti
        Là
ai piedi di quel mare,
rimescolavo sulla riva
la sabbia d'oro cocente
che la mia pelle
avida accaparrava.
Riusurpare il mio castello
vorrei da te, onda di ieri,
che affannavi il respiro
di chi t'abbracciava felice
nuotando allegramente.
        Ma

The Other Shore

Those waves were usurping
My castle made of sand
And clamshells
Borne so generously
By the beach of Fermo.
There I would run
—Serenely
These leaden waves,
A contrast,
Where the silent raven
Satiates its hunger
Along the shore—
Where the waves violently
Pound against rocks,
Where the screeching gulls
Voraciously assault
Meager remnants.
Back there,
At the foot of the sea
I was blending along the shore
With golden burning sand,
Which my skin avidly hoarded.
I wish I could repossess
My castle from you,
O wave of yesterday.
You would shorten the breath
Of those who embraced you
With happiness.
Treading your waters joyously.
Instead,
Here, this new sea,
Where a violated
Indian canoe
Rests against rocky shore.
I am of those days,
Of the wave, high,

di questo mare ho i giorni:
e una canoa indiana
sta violentata sugli scogli.
E l'onda è alta, e fredda,

Cold and hostile.
I fear them,
As I walk aimlessly upon shores,
Amongst these rocks
Never will be given me
Man's castle to build
Never will I be allowed
The illusion of dreams.

Emigrante

Trascinati d'antichi pesi
nel baratro dell'ingiustizia,
stiamo sulle bocche
delle piste pronti allo scatto,
e sulle bocche dei "ramarri"
pronti all'agonia.

Figli d'antica madre
che nelle doglie più sofferte
ha voluto partorire
migliori uomini, e ladri.
e noi con i primi esuli,
stanchi d'un pane nero,
stanchi di correre, di cercare,
e nelle piatte città d'acciaio
ci lasciammo vincere, esiliare.

Nelle chiese dell'infanzia
ancora il Cristo muove
la pietà dell'uomo
che sta su pietre assolate,
su cave brecciose, di granito,
sul teatro del dolore,
sulle screpolate vene
della dura terra.
E nelle sere stantie
ingoiar insalate acerbe,
e vino per annegare mattini
d'erbe cotte, di pani duri.

Ha scolpito profondo l'aratro
sulle giovani gote
arabescate di sudore,
invecchiate anzitempo
e chi nella speranza vinse
le distanze, l'incerta meta:
lentamente muore di ricordi.

Immigrant

Trailed by ancient burdens
In the abysses of injustice—
We stand as at the starting
Line of the dirt track,
Ready to go—
As ready as we are for agony
At the cunning ones' word.
Sons of primal mother
Who with most suffered delivery
Produced her best sons,
And her thieves . . . and us,
Among the first migrants.
Wearied of black bread,
Wearied of running, tired of seeking,
By the numbing steel cities
We let ourselves be convinced into exile.
In the churches of infancy
Christ is still reaching out
To the pity of man
Living on sun-scorched stones,
In granite fragmented pits,
On the parched veins
Of toughened soil
—Theater of sorrow—
To gulp down, on monotonous
Sundowns, crude salads—
And wine to drown
Dawns of mushy vegetables
And hard bread.
Deeply has the plough sculptured
Precociously aged
Sweat-arabesqued
Young cheeks—and those that
In hope conquered
Distance and uncertain goals
Are slowly dying of memories

—Una farfalla all'ultimo volo—
Riposavano le fresche acque
sul palmo della mano
come in devota preghiera,
e l'acqua svaniva, così i giorni.
Sono anch'io uno di voi
ho contato mucchi di sabbia,
molliche di pane, giorni amari.
Il mio volo d'ape
dall'alba al tramonto, e quando
le monete d'oro delle piante
ad una ad una caddero:
si sollevarono le ancore e
soffiò il vento le mie vele.

Un asilo nuovo—fiore di terra –
ma il tarlo della fatica
da sempre nelle mani.
Le mia ricchezza giace
in quelle antiche cave,
nei digiunati mattini,
nelle sere ubriache di stanchezza.

—A butterfly's last flight—
Like cool water collected
In prayer-grasped hands,
The days were seeping away.
I too am of your own
I have counted mounds of sand,
Breadcrumbs, bitter days
My beeline from
Sunup to sundown
—When the gilded trophies
Fell shallowly
One by one,
The anchors lifted
And the wind blew

Swiftly through my sails.
A new haven—earthly flower—
But always in these hands
The woodworm of labor.
My true wealth resides
In those ancient caves,
In fasting, empty mornings,
And in evenings
Inebriated by exhaustion.

Bella Vancouver

Sulle rive del Pacifico:
lungo le sponde del Fraser,
adagiata sul fianco dei monti
l'immensa città si distende,
come un'amante pulita, che sa
d'essere bella, bella Vancouver.

Un gregge in cielo cammina
son lane bianche, grigie e pigre,
e sull'invisibile rete s'adunano
lasciando spicchi d'azzurro,
dove si specchiano le mie pupille.

Sei tu pennello bizzarro
che dipingi il cielo turchino,
di bianco di rosso corallo,
di luce, di stelle d'argento.
Mia tavolozza, mio cielo.

L'insuperabile scalpello di Dio
ha scolpito montagne rocciose:
file d'immobili cammelli adorni
di laghi profondi, di valli.
Mio cuore, prigioniero felice
di questo paradiso che mi veste.

Basta tacere, chiudere gli occhi
per naufragare sul tuo giardino
mia bellissima Vancouver.

Vancouver the Beautiful

On the fringe of the Pacific
Abreast the Fraser's banks
Reclined on the mountain's slopes,
Calmly stretched you are,
Like a tender lover
Aware of your beauty—beautiful Vancouver—

Flocks gliding along the sky
Of woolly clouds, white grey and slate,
Gathering against an invisible net
To donate scattered pearls of blue
To mirror my eyes.

Whimsical brush
To tease that blue
With white, coral red,
Pure light and sultry stars—
A master's palette, my sky.

God's supreme chisel
Carving rocky mountains
Into frozen rows of camel's humps,
Blue lakes and deep valleys.
My heart—contented prisoner—
Wrapped in your solace.

To just close my eyes—
In silence to burrow
In your magic—it's easy,
My beautiful Vancouver.

⤳ Giovanni Costa (b. 1940)

Giovanni Costa was born in Vizzini, Sicily, in 1940. His early education took place in Italy. He emigrated to the United States in 1962 and taught Italian and French until 1965, then again from 1970 to 1979. From 1965 to 1970 he was at Concordia University in Montreal, where he established the Italian program. Since 1979, he has been teaching Italian at Laval University in Quebec City. He earned a PhD in French Literature from the Université de Montreal. Costa has published many academic papers in Italian and French.

Costa's first collection of poems, *Impressioni in terre amiche* (1989), is only in Italian, while his second volume, *Parlami di stele, Fammi sognare* (1994), is bilingual with English translations on facing pages. His third collection, *Alternanze Alternances Alterations* (1999) is in three languages: Italian, French, and English. This trilingual format also appeared in *Al di là dell'orizzonte* (2004).

As the title of the first collection suggests, these poems are impressionistic, and capture a vivid and concrete sensuality with a simplicity not often found in the poetry published in Italy in the last three decades. Costa's region of origin is that of Giovanni Verga, perhaps accounting for certain spiritual influences. The second book, *Parlami*, features echoes of Ungaretti and Palazzeschi. In addition to Italian literature, Costa's major influence is that of the Canadian environment. Costa is a constant traveler and we visit China, Japan, and Thailand in *Alternanze*. As Sandro Briosi has observed, in his introduction to *Parlami*, of Costa's use of language: "Probably his living away from Italy for a long period of time has helped Giovanni Costa both to maintain, in relation to the language of poetry, a detachment from all that has happened since the end of the 1950s, and to measure his need to express himself directly on the masters who wrote at the beginning of the century."

Giovanni Costa's poetry has been included in *The Anthology of Italian-Canadian Writing* (1998).

Un silenzio di parole

da Impressioni di terre amiche

Il soffio d'una corda di chitarra
t'accompagna,
o dicitrice amena,
singhiozzando
un'aria d'habanera
e tu rivivi Montale
nelle pupille
del tuo sguardo ispirato;
e Quasimodo affiora
con la sua dolce
terra di dolori.
Un silenzio chiaro di parole
s'apre nei tuoi occhi
pensosi
come un'aria di luce
ove tu sposi
l'ombra del pensiero nascosto
al sentimento.
Non dire più parole;
taci, o veggente,
rilassa le tue braccia
e il poema diventa verso dopo verso
un cielo di ricordi
dove leggi la voce
come un gesto di pace.

A Silence of Words

from *Impressions of Friendly Lands*

The breath of a guitar
string
accompanies you,
charming reciter,
sighing
a habanera aria
and you revive Montale
in the pupils
of your inspired look;
and Quasimodo flowers
with his sweet
lands of sorrows.
A clear silence of words
opens in your pensive
eyes
like an aria of light
where you wed
the shadow of hidden thought
to sentiment.
No more words spoken;
silent, seer,
you relax your arms
and verse after verse
the poem becomes
a heaven of memories
where you read aloud
like an act of peace.

In quest'ora d'ombra

L'uscita
in quest'ora d'ombra non c'è.
Sono in guerra
contro me stesso,
contro tutti.
Il passato
porta al presente;
ed il futuro?
Quasimodo, dammi
l'ala della tua parola
fatta di voci d'ambra
ove la luce vi trafigga
una speranza
d'uscita.
In questa carta di silenzio
si trastulla un'esistenza;
prestami la tua voce
per estrarvi una forma
di verde
ove si posi
una farfalla non di desideri
ma di libertà,
perché l'esule viva,
ad ora ad ora,
un angolo di luce
e non di croci di pensieri
in un cerchio di morte.

In This Shadowy Hour

In this
shadowy hour there's no
escape.
I am at war
with myself,
with everyone.
The past
leads into the present;
and the future?
Quasimodo, give me
the wing of your word
made of amber voices
where the light transfixes
a hope
of escape.
On this page of silence
an existence plays with itself;
lend me your voice
to draw from it a model
of green
where there alights
a butterfly not of desires
but of freedom,
because the exile lives,
hour after hour,
in a corner of light,
not of crosses of thought
in a circle of death.

L'odore della mia terra

Il silenzio di questa sera
mi accarezza.
Aro il tempo
d'ogni stagione
e l'odore della mia terra
mi attacca.
Terra nera, bruna, bianca,
zolla ciascuna di memorie.
Stacco un episodio
alla mia vita
e lo getto nel solco
a maturarvi
ore di giovinezza
nella mia terra.

The Smell of My Land

This evening's silence
caresses me.
I plow the time
of every season
and the smell of my land
clings to me.
Black, brown, white land,
each clump a memory.
I pull out an incident
from my life
and cast it into the furrow
to ripen there
times of youthfulness
in my land.

La ragazza di Parc Forillon

e i suoi capelli
neri
come le zolle
della Gaspesia,
un mare di capelli,
cresposi,
selvaggi,
aguzzi scogli
della sua terra.
A volte malinconica
come un gabbiano
bianco in attesa;
aperta
come l'orizzonte
vasto
del San Lorenzo.
Ha scelto la città, ma
solitaria capinera
ha la voglia del bosco.

The Girl at Parc Forillon

and her hair
black
as the earth
of Gaspé,
a sea of hair,
ridged,
wild,
sharp rocks
of her land.
Sad sometimes
as a waiting
white seagull;
open
as the vast
horizon
of the Saint Lawrence.
She's chosen the city, but,
a solitary blackcap,
she craves the forest.

Omaggio a Quebec

Oggi
un veto grigio di bruma
riflessa
sul profilo di Quebec
mi dava
vividi sensi
sciolti in parole
di silenzio.
Questa mattina
ho riscoperto
la città sinuosa
accanto al suo fiume
largo quanto un sogno.
Stradette sonnolenti del mattino
colorate di case
e di alberghi
d'altro tempo.
Vi entrammo e d'improvviso
ci affacciammo al passato
senza saperlo.
Fra le molte vie anguste:
Sainte-Ursule, Sainte-Anne,
due gioielli;
e Porta Saint-Jean
che t'investe
come una madre
e t'apre il grembo
dei suoi figli
abbracciati col tempo
nel presente.
Ne uscimmo
lungo il viale Champlain
e fu un disco d'oro inatteso
di ponente
che si attaccò
ai miei occhi,

Homage to Quebec

Today
a gray veil of reflected
fog
over the outline of Quebec
gave me
vivid sensations
released in words
of silence.
This morning
I rediscovered
the winding city
beside its river
as wide as a dream.
Drowsy alleys of the morning
colored with houses
and inns
from another time.
We went inside and all at once
we were standing in the past
without knowing it.
Among the many narrow streets:
Sainte-Ursule, Sainte-Anne,
two jewels;
and Porte Saint-Jean
that accosts you
like a mother
and opens its bosom
to its children
encircled with time
in the present.
We came out
along the Boulevard Champlain
and an unexpected golden disk
in the west
attached itself
to my eyes,

stanchi di gioia,
e vi tracciò, ultimo segno,
una pennellata di bagliori
stesa in brividi
di acque eterne
del San Lorenzo.
La mia donna e d'un altro.

Carta di silenzio,
vorrei gridarti, stasera,
il mio nodo di tristezza.
Andammo al film;
sentivo il calore, morbido,
della sua mano
appoggiata alla mia;
le stringevo le dita,
e assaporavo, solo per attimi,
i sensi inquieti.
Poi ci lasciammo:
la mia donna è d'un altro.
Angoscia di lasciarsi
così,
senza almeno un caffè:
ella nell'ombra della paura.
Serata senza ragione.
Si arriva
all'indomani
per singhiozzi di tempo
dopo una notte senza voce.
Consumarsi così;
ed io, solo,
nell'aria d'una speranza,
resto.

wearied with joy,
and outlined, a final sign,
a brushstroke of gleams
spread out in shimmers
of the infinite waters
of the Saint Lawrence.
My woman is someone else's.

Page of silence,
I'd like to cry out my knot
of sadness to you this evening.
We went to a movie;
I felt the tender heat
of her hand
resting in mine;
I squeezed her fingers,
and savored, just for moments,
my restless senses.
Then we parted:
my woman is someone else's.
The anguish of separating
like this,
without even a coffee:
she in the shadow of fear.
Evening with no rights.
You come
to the next day
through the sobbing of time
after a voiceless night.
Wasting away like this;
and I stay
in an air of hope,
alone.

→ Lisa Carducci (b. 1943)

Lisa Carducci was born in Montreal, Canada, in 1943. She attended French schools, earned a degree in education, and taught French for many years. She has been writing since she was sixteen years old in a variety of genres: poems, short stories, novellas, and essays. She has published in both French and Italian, with work appearing in Canada and in Italy. Her other pursuits include painting, theater, and broadcasting. For many years she contributed articles to *Il Cittadino Canadese*, the Italian-language paper in Montreal, and has continued to do so even after moving to China in 1993.

Her first book of Italian poems, *L'ultima fede* (1990), was followed by *Paesaggi e quadri* (1991), *Vorrei* (1991), and *Viaggiando* (1993). The 1997 book *Stagioni d'amore* is a novel. Carducci has won several Italian prizes: the Premio Letterario San Giulio, Premio LaTorre, and Premio Unione Italiani all'Estero. Her Italian poetry is characterized by a simple use of language but a wide range of subjects from immigration and relationships to world travel.

Her first French book was fiction, *Nouvelles en couleurs* (1985). The 1986 *Prix Jeux Floraux* was awarded to her poetry collection *Les héliotropes*. Her other fiction works include *Affaire classée* in 1992 and *A l'encre de Chine* in 1994. In 2002 she published a bilingual French-Italian collection of poems, *Pays inconnu / Paese sconosciuto*.

Verano

da *L'ultima fede*

uscire da roma dalla porta di dietro
direzione verano
camminare
tacere, camminare
comprare un mazzetto di anemoni
verano: perché?
chi m'insegnerà
saggezza e raccoglimento?
questo viale, sì
rallentare la mia frenesia
fermarmi
ascoltare

l'atto di vivere
ulisse
è viaggio senza ritorno
perché questa tomba?
perché ti ho chiamato ulisse?
chi sei?

dalla terra nasce la pace
riflettere sull'umana condizione
5 novembre 1983

un dono mi sarà concesso
fuori del tempo
regni si creano
o si ricreano
fermarmi
imparare ad accettare
questo tuo sguardo
mi convince dell'esistenza delle stelle
da ulisse ti riceverò
nel fuoco di mezzo-dì
a ulisse del verano

Verano

from *The Final Faith*

going out of Rome through the back door
direction verano
walking
in silence, walking
buying a small bunch of anemones
verano: why?
Who will teach me
wisdom and meditation?
This avenue, yes
slowing down my frenzy
stopping
listening

the act of living
ulysses
is a voyage without return
why this grave?
Why did I call you ulysses?
Who are you?

From the earth peace is born
reflecting on the human condition
November 5, 1983

a gift will be granted to me
outside time
kingdoms are created
or recreated
stopping
learning to accept
this look of yours
convinces me of the existence of the stars
from ulysses I will receive you
in the midday fire
to ulysses of verano

prometto di accoglierti
cinque novembre ottantatré
dal Campo di pace
ritorno con un mazzetto di anemoni
Incandescenza dei giorni
come oggetti candidi
privilegio della trasparenza
turbolenti immagini
attraverso specchi senza stagno
la poesia denuda i nostri sensi
trasmuta l'illusione
tra i sortilegi
il pellegrinaggio si compie
verso la memoria essenziale
non siamo più che emozioni
che nominiamo appena con pena
musica di fiamme e di effervescenze
tu sei io sono l'ieri e il domani l'istante
in uno spasmo creatore

I promise to welcome you
November 5, '83
from the field of peace
I return with a small bunch of anemones
Incandescence of the days
like candid objects
privilege of transparency
turbulent images
through tinless mirrors
poetry bares our senses
transmutes illusion
among sorceries
the pilgrimage is done
toward essential memory
we are nothing but emotions
that we barely name in pain
music of flames and effervescences
you are I am yesterday tomorrow the instant
in a creating spasm

Assenza

Un pugnale di ghiaccio ha strappato il mio petto
Non c'eri
Il sole ha naufragato ai confini della notte
Non c'eri
Quando una vana ferita ha distrutto il mio essere
Non c'eri
Ora
Vorresti saper se respiro ancora

Togli il tuo viso che veda la tua maschera!
Togli il tuo sorriso che contempli la tua smorfia
Davanti a questa vischiosa limaccia
Che sopravvive alla propria morte!

Absence

A dagger of ice has shred my chest
You were not there
The sun has shipwrecked at the edges of night
You were not there
When a vain wound destroyed my being
You were not there
Now
I would like to know if I am still breathing

Take off your face so I can see your mask!
Take off your smile so I can contemplate your grimace
Before this slimy snail
That survives its own death!

Chinook

Quando lo chinook avrà riscaldato il tuo cuore d'uomo
E sciolto come cera il tuo orgoglio
Quando il tuo dolore avrà domato la solitudine
E spaccato lo scudo delle paure
Tornerai
So che mi senti
Quando mi restituirai la mia vita
Rubata per proteggerla da te
Quando mi concederai il diritto
Di scommettere sul numero scelto
Tornerai
Sai che ti aspetto
Quando comprenderai che muoio
Dal non respirarti più
Quando avrai meno male
E che la piaga si sarà chiusa
Fra un mese fra un anno
Tornerai
In un giardino
Su una panchina
I tuoi occhi guardano il vuoto
E il vuoto te lo rende
La disperazione veglia
Non ascoltare le sirene
Fa' come se non avessi niente
Dentro
Niente nel cuore
Nemmeno un cuore
Non deve saper
La disperazione
Che sei preda facile
Con questo buco nel tuo amore
Questa ferita alla tua speranza
Quest'orribile confusione
Nel tuo essere
Sorridi

Chinook

When the Chinook has warmed your heart of man
And melted your pride like wax
When your pride has tamed solitude
And split the shield of fears
You will come back
I know you can hear me
When you will give me back my life
Stolen to protect it from you
When you will grant me the right
To bet on the chosen number
You will come back
You know I'm waiting for you
When you will understand that I'm dying
From not breathing you anymore
When you will have less pain
And the wound has closed
In a month a year
You will come back
In a garden
On a bench
Your eyes look at the emptiness
And the emptiness looks back at you
Desperation keeps watch
Don't listen to the sirens
Act as if you had nothing
Inside
Nothing in the heart
Not even a heart
Desperation must not know
You're easy prey
With this hole in your love
This wound in your hope
This horrible confusion
In your being
Smile
Act as if you had nothing

Fa' come se non avessi niente
Da piangere
Nemmeno lacrime
Come se non avessi male
Sorridi
Come se fossi seduto
Per caso semplicemente
Su una panchina
In un giardino

Per scriverti avrò
Nastri di scintille
Campanine di capre
Magici tamburelli
Per scriverti avrò
Penne d'argento
Ali di gabbiani
Come vele spiegate
Per scriverti avrò
Fiocchi di sole
Labbra di nettare
Mani d'ambrosia
Per scriverti avrò
Occhi stella

To cry for
Not even tears
As if you had no pain
Smile
As if you were seated
By chance simply
On a bench
In a garden

To write to you I will have
Ribbons of sparks
Goat bells
Magical tambourines
To write to you I will have
Silver feathers
Seagull wings
Like unfurled sails
To write to you I will have
Sun flakes
Nectar lips
Ambrosia hands
To write to you I will have
Star eyes

→ Filippo Salvatore (b. 1948)

Filippo Salvatore was born in Guglionesi, in the Molise region of Italy, in 1948, and emigrated to Montreal in 1964. He has degrees from McGill University and a PhD from Harvard, and he now teaches Italian literature at Concordia University in Montreal. In the province of Quebec there are some bilingual writers, but Salvatore is a trilingual writer, as evidenced by his many books in Italian, French, and English: *Tufo e gramigna* (1977), *Suns of Darkness* (1980), *La fresque de Mussolini* (1985), *Le fascisme et les italiens à Montreal* (1995), *Scienza ed umanità* (1996), *Tra Molise e Canada* (1994), and *Le cinéma de Paul Tana, parcours critiques* (1997), the last with Anna Gural-Migdal.

Fillippo Salvatore has also published many academic articles on cinema and Italian and Italian Canadian literature, including his important literary essay "The Italian Writer of Quebec: Language, Culture and Politics." His poems are written in Italian, his first language and the one that best captures his feelings. The subject of his poems is the immigrant experience in Montreal, but in the historical context of French Canada and a rapidly changing Italy. Salvatore spends part of every year in Italy. His poems have been included in the anthologies *Italian-Canadian Voices* (1984) and *The Anthology of Italian-Canadian Writing* (1998).

Nonnò

da *Tufo e gramigna*

Bambino sei ripartito
come e dove sei nato, nonnò.

Un'aquila d'acciaio,
serie DC8, voli transatlantici
diretti, sotto una sua rombante
penna di prese, tra le nuvole ti cullò,
col ronzio dei motori
una ninna nanna ti cantò
ed al risveglio ti adagiò
presso l'acquedotto diroccato
di non ricordo quale imperatore.

L'eterno bambino in te
che amava la malandata
bicocca, di fichi avviluppata,
sul colle di tufo sgarrato
il vecchio uomo convinse
a riprendere il volo.
Per riabbracciare tua madre
i figli ti spinse a lasciare
arcigna e povera madre,
pur sempre amata però.

Bambino sei ripartito
come e dove sei nato, nonnò.
E quando tornasti la lingua faceva
sempre *yè, yè*, invece di *sì, sì,*
e Ricuccio ti sfotteva.
il verso ti rifaceva *yè, yè*
e ti domandava se anche tu
i Beatles avevi ascoltato laggiù.

Grandpa

from *Tufo and Weed*

A child you have left again
The way and where you were born
grandpa.

A steel eagle,
DC8 series, direct transatlantic
flights, took you under its
roaring feathers, it cradled you
amid the clouds,
with the buzzing of engines
it sang you a lullaby
and when you awakened it laid you down
near the crumbled aqueduct
of an emperor I can't remember.

The eternal child in you,
who loved the dilapidated hovel
enveloped in fig trees,
convinced the old man
to fly again.
He drove you to leave your children
so you could embrace your mother again,
your poor grim mother,
but always beloved.

A child you have left again
the way and where you were born
grandpa.
And when you came back your tongue went
always *yeah yeah*, instead of *yes yes*,
and Ricuccio made fun of you,
he mimicked your *yeah yeah*
and asked you if you too
had listened to the Beatles down there.

Tu amatore di pace, vecchio soldato,
con un sorriso gli occhi hai chiuso
(m'hanno fatto sapere per iscritto)
e non—figli—ma—mammà—usci
col rantolo dalla gola.
E delle galline il coccodè
spaventate dal grido allarmato
della tua devota compagna
il tuo più pomposo requiem fu.

E bambino felice riposi
dietro il canneto ed i cipressi
una schioppettata lontano dal fico
davanti alla tua adorata bicocca.

Bambino sei ripartito
come e dove sei nato, nonnò.

Cambridge, 14 gennaio 1972

You lover of peace, old soldier,
closed your eyes with a smile
(so they informed me in writing)
and not—children—but—mama—came out
with the death rattle.
And the clucking of chickens
frightened by the alarmed scream
of your devoted woman
was your most pompous requiem.

And happy child you rest
behind the canebrake and the cypress trees
a gunshot far from the fig tree
before your adored hovel.

A child you have left again
the way and where you were born
grandpa.

Cambridge, January 14, 1972

Gente mia

Gente, gente mia,
gente a me più cara
dell'anima stessa mia.

Gente che avete il viso rozzo,
donne grassotte che vestite sempre di scuro,
uomini che avete i pantaloni sporchi
e rattoppati ed i calli alle mani,
giovani inconsci, carne da macello negli immensi
sweat-shops cittadini,
giovani che v'accontentate della stretta
di un altro corpo giovane e di baci il sabato
giovani dai facili piaceri e volubili emozioni,
vecchi che vi riunite in gruppetti nei giorni
di sole nel parco e giocate a scopa bisticciandovi
in dialetto come vecchi monelli aspettando
rassegnati la morte:
donne, uomini, giovani e vecchi
voi siete tutti gente
tutta gente mia.

Io vi guardo vivere tutti i giorni,
quando vi asciugate il sudore o quando
vi soffiate sulle mani intirizzite;
quando uscite di casa ancora col sapore
del caffè in bocca o quando
parlate del cibo che v'aspetta tornando
la sera a casa in autobus.
Io vi vedo arrivare,
lavorare, odiare, amare,
imparare la nostra nuova vita;
ascolto le vostre lamentele a vostra insaputa,
sedendo con l'orecchio teso perché
parlate sempre a voce bassa.
Odio le vostre meschinità,
ammiro il vostro coraggio
adoro la vostra tenacia.

My People

People, my people,
people dearer to me
than my own soul.

People with a rough face,
chubby women always dressed in black,
men with dirty patched-up pants
and calloused hands,
thoughtless youth, fodder
for the immense urban sweatshops,
youth who are satisfied
with squeezing another young body
and kisses on Saturdays
youth with your easy pleasures and inconstant emotions,
old men gathering in small groups
on sunny days in the park to play *scopa*
and quarrel in dialect like old brats waiting
for death in resignation.
Women, men, young and old people,
you are all people
my people.

I watch you live every day,
when you wipe your sweat or when
you blow on your numb hands;
when you leave the house still
with the taste of coffee in your mouth
or when you talk about the food
waiting for you when you get back
home in the evening on the bus.
I see you arrive,
work, hate, love,
learn our new life.
I listen to your complaints without your knowing,
sitting with my ears pricked up
because you always talk in a low voice.
I hate your pettiness,

Mi commuovo da sciocco sentimentale
se sento che avete ricevuto una lettera da lontano
e dice che la nonna è ancora malata
e già stanno mietendo il grano,
se sento che t'è nato un bel bimbo maschio
e vedo la tua pupilla di giovane padre brillare
se sento che l'ami per la prima volta tanto,
tanto, è un bel giovane e gli piace lavorare.

Sono le vostre, le nostre piccole gioie
affanni, debolezze, qualità
che amo ed odio tanto
gente, gente mia,
gente a me più cara
dell'anima stessa mia.

I admire your courage
I adore your tenacity.

I am moved like a silly sentimentalist
if I hear you received a letter from far away
and it says that grandma is still sick
and they're harvesting the wheat already,
if I hear that a handsome male child was born to you
and I see your young father's eyes sparkle
if I hear that you love him so much for the first time,
he's a handsome young man and likes to work.

These are your, my small joys,
worries, weaknesses, qualities
I love and hate so much
people, my people,
people dearer to me
than my own soul.

A Giovanni Caboto 1

Giovanni, non ho avuto bisogno
di coraggio, come te,
non mi sono imbarcato
verso l'ignoto su un vascello
insicuro, non ho dovuto combattere
contro la forza delle ondate,
non ho sofferto la fame,
non ho guardato la morte in faccia.

Ho viaggiato comodamente
con un DC8 dell'Alitalia,
ho volato sulle onde perigliose,
ho chiuso gli occhi,
ho sonnecchiato per qualche ora
e sono arrivato
nella terra dei miei sogni.

Non c'è voluto molto, sai,
non c'è voluto niente.
E per partire
sono bastate alcune male annate,
un atto di richiamo, un visto.
Non c'è voluto molto
per farmi alzare le braccia;
è la disperazione che m'ha fatto
sormontare l'amore della mia terra
e le ultime indecisioni

Di pane ne ho in abbondanza.
di acqua calda pure,
ma non ho scoperto l'Eldorado
che cercavo.
Ho scoperto invece occhiate sprezzanti,
una natura ostile, un vuoto
incolmabile nell'anima,
ho scoperto cosa vuol dire essere emigrante.

E non c'è voluto molto, sai,
non c'è voluto niente.

To John Cabot 1

John, I didn't need
courage, like you,
I didn't set sail
for the unknown on an unsafe
vessel, I didn't have to fight
against the strength of the waves,
I didn't suffer hunger,
I didn't look death in the face.

I traveled comfortably
on an Alitalia DC8,
I flew over the perilous waves,
I shut my eyes,
I napped for a few hours
and I arrived
in the land of my dreams.

It didn't take much, you know,
it took nothing.
And to make me leave
a few bad years were enough,
an *atto di richiamo*, a visa.
It didn't take much
to make me raise my arms.
It was desperation that made me
put aside the love of my land
and the last indecisions.

I have bread in abundance,
warm water too,
but I didn't discover the Eldorado
I sought.
Instead I discovered scornful glances,
a hostile nature, an unfillable
emptiness in my soul,
I discovered what it means to be an emigrant.

It didn't take much, you know,
it took nothing.

A Giovanni Caboto 2

Giovanni ti hanno eretto
un monumento, ma ti hanno cambiato nome:
qui ti chiamano *John*.
E tu li scruti dall'alto del tuo podio
di pietra con un sogghigno
appena percettibile sulle tue
labbra bronzee.
Dove guardi? Verso il vecchio
o il nuovo mondo?
Non mi rispondi, certo,
rimani là, impalato ad Atwater
e continui a scrutare lontano.
Quanti erano gli italiani
imbarcatisi con te?
Oggi ne siamo tanti, tanti
e la maggior parte di noi è giovane,
è giovane ed ambiziosa, come te,
giovane ed ha dovuto emigrare, come te,
rifarsi una vita altrove, come te.
Sullo scoglio brullo, battuto
dalle ondate, tu primo piantasti.
accanto allo Jack regio, il leone
di San Marco; oggi sventola il tricolore
accanto alla foglia d'acero
in cima ai grattacieli costruiti
in questa terra di gelo
da tanti tuoi compatriotti.
Ascolta quanti di essi uscendo
dal metro ben imbacuccati
parlano di dollari e di case da comprare
e si strofinano il naso
aspettando impazienti il 79 al capolinea.
Sono pochi quelli che ti conoscono, sai,
nel vederti impassibile,
con un mantello di ghiaccio sulle spalle,

To John Cabot 2

Giovanni, they erected
a monument to you, but they changed your name:
here they call you *John*.
And you peer down at them from your podium
of stone with a barely
perceptible sneer on your
bronze lips.
Where are you looking at? Toward the old
or new world?
You don't answer me, of course,
you just stand there at Atwater,
and keep on peering far away.
How many Italians
set sail with you?
Today we are so many, so many,
and most of us are young,
young and ambitious, like you,
to build a new life elsewhere, like you.
On the bare reef, struck
by the waves, you first planted
St. Mark's lion next to the royal Jack.
Today the tricolor waves
next to the maple leaf
on top of the skyscrapers built
in this land of ice
by so many of your compatriots.
Listen to them as they come out of the subway
all wrapped up speaking of dollars and houses to buy
and rub their noses
waiting impatiently for the 79 at the terminus.
Those who know you are few, you know,
seeing you impassive,
with a cape of ice on your shoulders,
and oblivious to the frenzied movement
and the blinding lights of this rush hour.

ed incurante del movimento frenetico
e dei bagliori accecanti di questo rush-hour.

Ed io, fermatomi ai tuoi piedi a parlarti,
mi sento gelare la punta degli orecchi
dopo uno spintone ricevuto da un vecchio
ubriacone che biascica fra i denti
e la bocca puzzolente di whisky, *muzì*.

And I, stopping at your feet to talk to you,
feel the tips of my ears getting numb
after getting shoved by an old
drunkard who mumbles between his teeth
and a mouth reeking of whisky, *muzì.*

Poesia a Giovanni Caboto 3

Giovanni, t'ho rivisto
un fresco mattino di giugno:
avevi la tua posa di sempre
un sole giallognolo faceva
da contrappunto cromatico
alle tua membra bronzee
ti conferiva un'aureola irreale.
Una cppia di piccioni ti saltellava
sulle spalle, ti rivelava di certo
i suoi segreti d'amore, ma tu restavi
impassibile ai loro gorgheggi,
sapevi che erano illusioni e
continuavi a scrutare lontano.

Fermatomi a guardarti da vicino
ero il solo a fare compagnia al vecchio
alcolizzato disteso ai tuoi piedi
sulla panchina verde scolorita.
Una patina incolore impastava
le sue cerulee labbra, una bottiglia
senza tappo, vuota, gli era accanto
sulla ghiaia bianca.

Gente esce ad ondate dal metro
ad Atwater, guarda corre,
perde l'autobus, impreca.
É lunedì, una giornata come tante
altre m'aspetta.

M'ero fermato per parlarti, Giovanni,
ma non ci sono riuscito; tu sei statua
tra gerani rossi appena piantati
ed alberi avviluppati
di un nuovo mantello pisello, simbolo.
La vita della tua memoria
m'è eterea come questo sole
di primo mattino, quanto la mia lucidità.

Poem to John Cabot 3

John, I saw you again
on a cool morning in June.
You were in your usual pose
a yellowish sun was
a chromatic counterpoint
to your bronze limbs
it lent you an unreal glow.
A couple of pigeons were hopping
on your shoulders, they were no doubt
telling you their love secrets, but you remained
indifferent to their warbling,
you knew they were illusions
and kept on peering far away.

Stopping to look at you up close,
I was the only company
for the old drunkard at your feet
on the faded green bench.
A colorless glaze covered
his bluish lips, a capless
bottle, empty, lay by his side
on the white gravel.

People come out in waves from the subway
at Atwater, they look, run,
miss the bus, curse.
It's Monday, a day like so many others
awaits me.

I had stopped to talk to you, John,
but I couldn't do it. You are a statue
among freshly planted
red geraniums and trees wrapped
in a new pea green mantle, a symbol.
The life of your memory
is ethereal to me like this
early morning sun, like my lucidity.

Mi sento la pella d'oca,
ad un alito più intenso di brezza
che mi gonfia la camicia;
la gente continua ad uscire a frotte,
mi scuote, m'ingorga, mi trascina.

Montreal, 20 giugno 1971

I get goose pimples
when a stronger breeze
bulges my shirt.
People keep on streaming out,
they push me, envelop me, pull me along.

Montreal, June 20, 1971

→ *Silvano Zamaro* (b. 1949)

Silvano Zamaro was born in Cormons, Gorizia, Italy, in 1949. After training as a draftsman, he moved to Edmonton, Canada, in 1976. He completed an MA in Italian literature at the University of Alberta in 1988. His Italian poems have appeared in Canadian, American, and Italian publications. His poetry has won a number of literary prizes, including Il Leone di Muggia in Trieste in 1976, and Il Premio Nardi in Venice in 1985.

His collection of Italian poems, *Autostrada per la luna* (1987), won the Bressani Prize for Poetry in Vancouver in 1988. The lines in the poems demonstrate the influence of Italian literature, popular culture, and the Friulano folklore of Zamaro's region of origin. Some poems could be used as lyrics for folksongs. Many poems evidence a sense of irony as well, something often found in the work of Italian immigrants who came to North America after the great migration following World War II. His work is included in the anthology *L'altra storia* (1998).

Refrain 2

da *Autostrada per la luna*

Laggiù
tra le ore dell'Artico
lunghe come il sole
bianche come il mare
piene di rimpianti
secche come polvere di stelle
i resti di un bacio, di una vela, di un occhio ebreo,
guardano immobili senza voltarsi
parole di caccia, pellicce di foca.
Dietro la chiesa di tutti i santi
nel vicolo cieco
coperte di fumo
due canoe sottobanco giocano a carte,
come a riflettere navi salpate
puntando sul fante dal cuore smarrito.

Refrain 2

from *Highway of the Moon*

Down below
amid the Arctic hours
long as the sun
white as the sea
filled with regrets
dry as the dust of stars
the remains of a kiss, of a sail,
of a Jewish eye,
they gaze immobile without turning round
words of the hunt, sealskin stoles.
Behind All Saints Church
in the blind alley
two canoes covered
in smoke under the counter are playing cards,
as reflecting ships that have set sail
set their courses for the lost jack of hearts.

Indian Summer

Questi giorni corti sulle labbra
parlano di uccelli migratori
vedono il sorgere del sole
tra i grattacieli della città
sotto le nuvole indaco
mentre finisce l'estate indiana.

Questi giorni corti sulle labbra
ogni mattina più corti
più bui
mi si addormentano davanti
con la tazza del caffè in mano
prima di svenarmi con la lama di ogni giorno.

Ottobre 1978

Indian Summer

These days brief on the lips
speak of migratory birds
they watch the sun as it comes up
between the city's skyscrapers
under the indigo clouds
as Indian summer comes to an end.

These days brief on the lips
every morning briefer
darker
lull me into early sleep
with a coffee cup in my hand
before they bleed me with the blade of every day.

October 1978

For Earth and Heaven

Ho mangiato le cervella di bufalo
per sentirmi vero tra i grattacieli
per vedermi correre sonnambulo lungo la settima strada,
e ho raccolto gerani nei quartieri di Harlem
dai davanzali colorati di Ma' Josephine.

Ho giocato con Marcus, il figlio del droghiere,
a stappare bottiglie di coca-cola coi denti
fino a sentirci uomini bevendo;
ho rivisto Mirage giù all'angolo,
vendeva giornali come ogni sera
ma non mi ha salutato,
e pensare che solo una settimana fa
le ho prestato diecimila dollari
e un bacio senza cuore.

Ho conosciuto un pittore alla casa del lavoro,
dice che è Italiano ma ha gli occhi a mandorla
e dipinge svelto
bianco su nero;
ho mangiato i crostini di zia Emeritt
nascosto dietro a un natale appannato
e ho graffiato i vetri della finestra
per non ricordare di essere zingaro maledetto
sperduto tra gli uomini.

Ho conosciuto la famiglia della porta accanto
esquimesi dell' est,
mangiano soltanto pesce
e ti buttano sempre fumo negli occhi;
il padre, senza una mano,
dice che è stata una balena
anche perché sono in pochi a sapere
che è sempre stato contrabbandiere di pelli di orso, di foca
e di gin.

For Earth and Heaven

I have eaten the brains of a buffalo
to make myself feel real among the skyscrapers
to see myself running along Seventh Avenue in my sleep,
and I have picked geraniums in Harlem
from windowsills colored by Madame Josephine.

I have played with Marcus, the grocer's son,
opening Coca-Cola bottles with our teeth
to make ourselves feel like men drinking;
I have seen Mirage again down at the corner,
she was selling newspapers just like every evening
but she didn't say hello to me,
and to think that it was only a week ago
that I advanced her ten thousand dollars
and a kiss with no heart in it.

I have known a painter in his studio,
he says he's Italian but he has almond eyes
and he paints quickly
white over black;
I have eaten Aunt Emeritt's toast
hidden behind a misted-over Christmas
and I have scratched the window glass
so as not to remember being an accursed gypsy
uneasy among men.

I have known the family next door to me
Eastern Eskimos,
they eat only fish
and they always throw smoke in your eyes;
the father, who's missing a hand,
says that it was a whale
especially since I learn a short time later
that he's always been a smuggler of bearskins, of sealskins
and gin.

Ho visto i padri del Siam contare le gocce di pioggia
in inverno
e aspettare la notte
e far riposare gli occhi dalla luce divina.

I have seen the fathers of Thailand counting raindrops
in the winter
and waiting for night
and making their eyes grow sleepy with divine light.

26mo piano

Giorno dopo giorno
a scrivere poesie
davanti a ventose mattine
appoggiato al parapetto
del balcone piano ventisei

Sei arrivata sbattendo le ali
come falena smarrita
con fogli di domande
su dove dorme il sole
nelle notti d'estate

Poi il tuo naso rotto dalla coca
i tuoi starnuti di traverso
le tue ossa insaponate
le tue innocenti cazzate
le tue pupille annacquate
Giorno dopo giorno
a parlare su cuscini cinesi
a cercare aria sul balcone
sperando in un giudizio abbagliante
su poesie da abortire

Eri più giovane allora
lo ero anch'io
a fissare, distesi, il soffitto
a nascondere il cervello seccato
nella sera irriverente.

Febbraio 1979

Twenty-Sixth Floor

Day after day
writing poetry
facing windy mornings
leaning on the railing
of the twenty-sixth-floor balcony

You arrived flapping your wings
like a lost bewildered moth
with pages of questions
about where the sun sleeps
on summer nights

Then your nose worn from cocaine
your sideways sneezes
your soapy bones
your innocent bullshit
your diluted pupils

Day after day
talking on Chinese pillows
looking for air on the balcony
relying on a dazzling judgment
about which poems to abort

You were younger then
and so was I
staring, stretched out, at the ceiling
concealing our withered brains
in the irreverent evening.

February 1979

Portrait d'une émigrante

La torre di Babele sulle rive del San Lorenzo
splende di insipidi amori
di camicie comperate da cent'anni
di scemenze ripetute mille volte.
Tu dolce
con quel volto di nebbia
con quello sguardo malfermo
con quelle labbra più bambine di Gesù,
tu dolce
continui la storia dei limoni
lontana secoli dalla Trinacria
e un occhio di lupara ti passa la gola
e non ti lascia piangere
se non sul filo del telefono

Portrait of an Emigrant Woman

The Tower of Babel on the banks of the Saint Lawrence
shines with insipid amours
with sheets that were bought a hundred years ago
with idiocies repeated a thousand times.
You tender
with that misty face
with that insecure look
with those lips more infantlike than Jesus's,
you tenderly
go on telling the story of the lemons
centuries away from Trinacria
and the eye of a sawed-off shotgun passes over your throat
and doesn't let you cry
if not on the telephone wire

E le regine

Pa àgne Luzie

E le regine
sui troni di birra sedute
avanzavano nel buio
nelle notti estive
sui carri merci fuori città
tra sconosciuti stranieri
a bere umido vino.
Professavo assiomi
cantavo ricorrenze mai celebrate,
e giovani preti blasfemi
mi toglievano l'anima di bocca
con pretesti di fasulli cristi,
di braccia meschine
di inumane ossa inumate,
e cancellavo lo sguardo dal mio passaporto
svendevo fotografie nelle taverne
tra gioiose cameriere in topless
dietro le unghie rifatte dell'oste,
e la mia regina la segnavo io a dito
sperando di sognare
toccandole gli occhi.

Edmonton 1977

And the Queens

For àgne Luzie

And the queens
seated on thrones of beer
come forward in darkness
on summer nights
on freight cars outside the city
amid unknown foreigners
to drink watery wine.
I professed axioms
I sang never-celebrated anniversaries,
and young blaspheming priests
took the soul out of my mouth
with the pretexts of bogus Christs,
of the shabby arms
of inhuman bones interred,
and I wiped the look off the face of my passport
I sold photos for a song in taverns
amid merry topless waitresses
behind the host's redone nails,
and I pointed to my queen there
hoping to dream
touching her eyes.

Edmonton 1977

Croatia and Slovenia

Croatia and Slovenia

ELIS DEGHENGHI OLUJIĆ

Istria, a peninsula in southeastern Europe that juts into the Adriatic Sea between the Gulf of Trieste to the west and the Kvarner to the east, is today divided between Croatia and Slovenia. Here, as well as in Rijeka/Fiume (Croatia) and, in small numbers, Dalmatia and Slavonia, lives a small community of Italians. Data from the most recent census, taken in Croatia in 2001 and in Slovenia in 2002, shows that the residents of Italian nationality—in the sense of ethnic identity, not to be confused with citizenship—are nearly thirty thousand in the first republic and less than three thousand in the second.

The young states of Croatia and Slovenia came into being in the 1990s, following the disintegration of Yugoslavia. The Italians of Croatia and Slovenia constitute the Italian national community and have as their representative unit the Italian Union (Unione Italiana), which has made coexistence the cornerstone of its politics. The representatives of the Italian national community constitute a native ethnic group and live alongside the larger Croatian and Slovene populations. Many more Italians, however, live in Istria, some scattered along the coastal area of the peninsula and some in the hinterland, as well as in Rijeka/Fiume, in an area of permanent mixture of various cultures, a multicultural and multiethnic social context marked currently by a transitional process toward democracy.

The pages that follow are exclusively about the literary activity, poetic in particular, of those Italians who, at the time of the exodus that has affected Istria, Rijeka/Fiume, and Dalmatia in the period immediately following World War II, have not left their land of origin. They do not deal with the rich and significant production both in poetry and in prose preceding World War II. Thus the present discussion will focus on the production of Italian literature that developed in Istria and in Rijeka/Fiume after World War II, from the time that the greater part of the territory passed over to Yugoslavia down to the present.

The literary and artistic production of Italians from Croatia and Slovenia is particularly intense in Istria and Rijeka/Fiume, where the Italian national community, although numerically contained, can list a considerable number of artists and literary figures that make that community rather distinctive. In spite of the consistent exodus of Italians between 1945 and 1955, those who stayed in this region, though reduced to a minority, have shown themselves to be exceptionally faithful to their roots and to have an ability to survive, to endure, and to adapt to a political and social context that is radically changed. Facing frustrating conditions and political inferiority, and with the representation of only a few intellectuals and writers—such as Osvaldo Ramous, Lucifero Martini, and Domenico Cernecca—those who remained have been able to restore their ties to their Italic roots.

In a climate of demographic collapse, ideological change, and dangerous polemics with Italy over the Trieste crisis at the end of the 1950s, within the triangle outlined by Koper/Capodistria (Slovenia), Pula/Pola (Croatia), and Rijeka/Fiume, the literature of Istria and Rijeka/Fiume had its beginnings, now merited with giving concrete literary and artistic citizenship to the Istro-Kvarnerian world. This literary output wisely took into account the suggestions of Italian national literature in a spirit of fertile harmony, along with the new political and social reality of the area in which it developed. It has clearly defined thematic and stylistic attributes. This literature is an expression of the need, on the part of Italians who continued to live in Istria and Rijeka/Fiume after World War II—detached from the Italian state, placed in a new political and social reality alongside the numerically larger Croatian and Slovene populations—to maintain a national and cultural identity through the practice of the written word.

In Istria as well as in Rijeka/Fiume, the cultural and literary production immediately following World War II was an autonomous and integral project carried out by a few intellectuals from the partisan groups, such as Eros Sequi and Lucifero Martini, who were later joined by a few more young men from Italy at the end of the 1940s—Sergio Turconi, Giacomo Scotti, and, later yet, Alessandro Damiani. These figures brought a breath of vitality and rallied the energy of the few intellectuals in the area to safeguard Italian identity and initiate a project of rebirth of Italian culture. Their activity gravitated first toward vital institutions such as the Dramma Italiano (Italian Drama); newspapers and journals such as the daily *La Voce del Popolo* (*The Voice of the People*), whose first issue bears the date 1944; the biweekly *Panorama* that began its publication in 1952; and *La Battana*, a cultural quarterly founded in Rijeka/Fiume in 1964. The literature in Istria and Kvarner that came into being at the end of the 1940s and the beginning of the 1950s, initially ideologically engaged, quickly furnished the region with fertile soil for a regrowth of poetic and prose production, in Italian as well as in the local dialects of Istria and its environs.

According to an assertion generally accepted by Bruno Maier, the main expert on the literary production of Italians in Istria and Rijeka/Fiume, the origins of the literature from Istria and Kvarner can be traced back to the underground journals published during the war. The text that both chronologically and ideally stands as the archetype for the subsequent literary production is the poem "Ho visto . . ." (I saw . . .) by Eros Sequi, which revisits the atrocities of the war and restates the reasons for the struggle for freedom. The poem, the first "public document of poetic activity of the Italian ethnic group" worthy of artistic and documentary value, according to Sergio Turconi (*La poesia degli italiani dell'Istria e di Fiume*), was published in April 1945 in *Nostro Giornale* (*Our Newspaper*), an underground publication. In this poem, Sequi assumes the identity of the politically committed poet engaged in expressing lyrically the atrocities of war, in describing and denouncing its horrors, in recounting the drama of a people that faces with dignity its own tragedy. The inevitable emotional involvement of the poet as protagonist does not relegate to a secondary plane the collective drama of war. The poem is a clear example of how major historical contingencies demand and sustain the poet's awareness, and of how poetry is frequently a life experience, a psychological and emotional condition, before it is an intellectual exercise.

The first poetic expressions, born in the enthusiastic climate that characterized the period immediately after the war, assumed the poetic forms of politically committed verses, common currency at the time of all European literature. The certainty of a 'better tomorrow' in that precise historical context was a widespread sentiment shared the world over; the triumph of "true" democracy and the advent of a "new world" were a common dream. The models from whom the poets from Istria and Kvarner drew much inspiration were Brecht, Èluard, Gatto, and Russian authors, along with the Yugoslavian partisans whose poetry was beginning to be known through translations. The poetry of Istria and Kvarner made use of the tones and forms of realist poetry spreading in Italy at the time as well. Such works found inspiration in the poetics of political commitment, which proposed the exaltation of the collective community, and looked at the literature circulating in Italy inspired by the pages of Elio Vittorini's *Politecnico*. The literary value of these works, whose prevalent character was that of testimonials, was minimized because of the need to stay in tune with the political ideas, which inhibited creativity, even though they might have been exalting emotionally. As Lucifero Martini, one of the pioneers of the literature from this area, observed in 1985, during the war and the years immediately following, "history essentially jumped atop the horse of literature, bestriding the saddle and spurring it on to what one then saw as a gallop, whereas looking at it today makes it seem, from a primarily literary perspective, just a trot." Poetry, which is usually the expression of the self and subjectivity, began to use words, themes, and expressions that normally belong to other types of discourse, such as history and politics, thus losing its efficacy, particularly with respect to its literary value. There are historical moments, as the World War II period proved to be in Istria and Kvarner, in which poetry is expected to open up to themes that are collective in nature, to historical problems, to current issues, with the hope of having a real influence on society on the scale of changing it and rendering it more human, instead of addressing the problems of the individuals themselves, of their emotions and private worlds.

Adherence to neorealist poetics did not produce works of any particular artistic worth, but it did enhance in the poets from Istria and Kvarner a taste for reality and an attraction to plain language that would lead them to refuse the lure of daring and exaggerated stylistic experimentation. When, in 1963, Giacomo Scotti's collection of poetry was published in the volume *Is the Devil Dark?*, characterized by a posthermetic quality veined by expressionism and surrealism, as well as hints of crepuscular and futurist motifs, in Italy, the posthermetic mode had been overcome along with neorealism by the revisions of the neo-experimentalists of *Officina*, first, and subsequently by the disturbances of the neo-avant-garde. The delay with which twentieth-century poetics reached the writers of Istria and Kvarner was due to the long-lived realist manner, on the one hand, and on the other to the cultural isolation, during those years, of the Italian national community. Giacomo Scotti, along with Sequi, Turconi, Martini, and Damiani, belongs to the group of intellectuals that arrived in Istria and Kvarner after World War II from outside the national confines. Their arrival was a positive event for the literary life of the Italian national community, which at that crucial time of its history was facing the risk of extinction. They filled, at least in part, the losses caused by the exodus, gave life to and maintained many cultural initiatives, and contributed to a certain extent to the continuity of the literary activity of Italians in Istria and in Rijeka/Fiume.

A real turning point in the literary history of Istria and Rijeka/Fiume occurred in the 1960s, when cultural life and literary activity intensified. In 1963, the Circle of Poets, Literati, and Artists was formed, and in October of 1964 the cultural and literary journal *La Battana* was founded, an instrument of cultural growth and a forum for the promotion of new literary and cultural initiatives. The journal was a vehicle that brought the creative works of Istria and Rijeka/Fiume beyond their national boundaries. In 1964 began also the work of the People's University of Trieste (Università Popolare di Trieste), appointed by the Italian Ministry of Foreign Affairs to be the interlocutor of the Union of Italians of Istria and Rijeka/Fiume, which became the Italian Union in 1991. In 1967, the art and culture competition Istria Nobilissima (Noblest Istria) was launched. With time, this competition allowed the plurality of experiences of the authors from Istria and Rijeka/Fiume to emerge through the publication of anthologies compiling award-winning works, this being one of the principle ways for the Italian national community to reach the public and, at the same time, document its own vitality. Whereas the first period of the poetic production of Istria and Rijeka/Fiume, except for Ramous's work, was marked by realism, during the second period, which dates from around 1964 to 1974, writers opened themselves up to a vision of the world in which there no longer is any place for a single perspective; they displayed a steady, growing interest in private, personal worlds, as well as in analyses of the existential condition of humanity. There was a growing awareness that human beings do not only fulfill a public role, nor are their activities commensurate only to the social realm, but rather they possess also an internal dimension. The poet as subject and as interpreter of life returned full force—the poet and interpreter who, through his or her personal experience in the world and in individual existence, finds modes of inspiration and sufficiently common themes through which to communicate with others. Thus the poetry focusing on the collective *us* diminished rapidly in favor of poetry focusing on the *I*. The poetic language also changed to accommodate these new needs by eliminating many of the dramatic elements of the versification and of the exclamatory and hortatory emphasis indispensable to admonitory *us* literature. Verses became short and dense with meaning, analogy and hermetic metaphor made a comeback, and pauses and blank spaces became in vogue. In short, the experience accumulated through the poetic expression of the twentieth century was brought to fruition.

In the field of poetry, in addition to the already mentioned Ramous, Sequi, Martini, and Scotti, other names were added, such as Alessandro Damiani, Mario Schiavato, Umberto Matteoni, Mario Cocchietto, Claudio Ugussi, and Anita Forlani, to whom two more women poets with strong personality and sensibility can be added, Adelia Biasiol and Loredana Bogliun. In their poetry, these authors returned to the elementary, basic questions of human existence, the meaning of life, the questions that arise from a life of solitude, unachieved dreams, and powerlessness. Theirs is a poetics of sorrowful introspection reminiscent of posthermetic experience.

In the works of the area of Istria and Rijeka/Fiume, dialect poetry occupies a very respectable place, especially when the dialect becomes a language of art, as in the case of Zanini's work and Bogliun's, and frees itself from all provincial references, falsely familiar or popular. It is true poetry that needs to be judged with the same measures as poetry in Italian. The vernacular poet is connected to a different culture, rooted in concrete objects, in precise references to places, in the *pietas* for the vulnerability of all that lives and vanishes. Dialects privilege a direct relationship with the world and solidarity with the world of one's own origins, since dialect poetry evokes the myth of the intimate and homogenous community. Dialect poets of Istria and Rijeka/Fiume discovered in dialect the hidden, interior codes cherished also by poets who write in Italian. Dialect is also something extra with respect to the standard language: it is the mother tongue. Dialect represents the myth of the original being in the world of childhood and everything that evokes it: the sea, the olive trees, the dry walls that traverse the countryside of Istria, the vineyards, the red earth.

At the beginning of the 1960s, when Eligio Zanini published his first collection of poems in the dialect of Istria, dialect poetry began to thrive in that region. Zanini's Istrian dialect, in its variant from Rovinj/Rovigno (Croatia), overcame for the first time the narrow boundaries of folklore without foregoing the anthropological and geographical social ambit of the historical area in which it came into being. It became the poetry of a language capable of cosmic suggestiveness that speaks in general about humanity, of its existential condition, of its life and the forces that govern it, of the rhythms that organize it. Through dialect poetry, Zanini allowed the dialect of Istria to try its hand at poetry as a language connected, even more than the "standard" language, to personal and biological origins, to collective events. The result is a cross-section of a world well defined in time and space. The poet's obstinate fidelity to this world and to its value system seems like the testimonial of a hermit of a lost Eden.

The availability, in 1968, of *Panorama*, the bimonthly journal directed by Lucifero Martini, and the publication in the journal *La Battana* of poetry by poets who were then beginning to write verses, alongside the presentation of new names for the art and culture competition Istria Nobilissima, became important milestones toward the renewal of the literature from Istria and Kvarner. Young writers who were replacing the founders in the "historical project," like Alessandro Damiani, would define the renewal of an original Italian culture in Istria and Rijeka/Fiume, enjoying greater freedom from those ideological constructs that had impeded the expression of the generation of intellectuals immediately following World War II. The founders suffered the drama of the exodus, the anxiety of the loss of population, and the sense of need ensuing from territorial degradation. The children who grew up in a different cultural and historical climate thus developed their own self-awareness and sensibility deserving of the label "Istrian-ness." Born and raised with at least two languages (Italian and Croatian or Italian and Slovenian, to which must be added one of the local dialects) and two cultures, the youth of Istria and Kvarner (re)discovered their native reality and took joy in their diversity without ostentation; in intimate terms, they affirmed their identity and acted as bridges between cultures, a function that is pertinent to the entire Italian community. In writing verses, they usually preferred poetic forms that, free of obstacles, offered greater space for imagination and sentimental expression. Ugo Vesselizza, Maurizio Tremul, Roberto Dobran, and Laura Marchig proposed new topics and experimented with new forms, believing that poetry is first of all representation of an inner being, a willingness to tell about oneself and look critically at oneself in order to bring about an intellectual synergy that encourages the formation of a collective spirituality. The fragmentary and fluid nature of reality engaged these young poets, bringing them inventive and imaginative tension leading to anticonformist themes, often clearly provocative and profane. To these young poets one can add Gianna Dallemulle Ausenak and Ester Sardoz Barlessi, who came to writing verses especially through their participation in "Istria Nobilissima." Other dialect poets include Lidia Delton from Vodnjan/Dignano (Croatia), the place of her constant source of elegiac inspiration, and Romina Floris, author of poems in the dialect of Bale/Valle (Croatia), a little town in the Istrian hinterland full of stones and red earth. For both of these poets, the choice of dialect, which is better than the standard language to express the emotional pathos of the self-representation of their community, is motivated by a search for identity, by the need to descend to the depths of their origins in order to raise something firm against the disintegration of the surrounding world, to convey a personal mythology of town and childhood, of landscapes and the rustic people who inhabit them. They identify in the peasant culture a universally positive set of values that are gradually disappearing and that instead deserve to be saved from the devastation of time. In their works, both authors give importance to the topos, the place where their great grandparents, grandparents, and their own parents worked and operated, modifying the surroundings according to their desires, their mentalities, and their needs.

The cultural world of Istria and Rijeka/Fiume is in continuous evolution. New trends have been developing since the last decade of the twentieth century, with a rich and varied poetic landscape. New voices in this panorama include Vlada Acquavita, Marco Apollonio, Libero Benussi, Vlado Benussi, Sandro Cergna, Marianna Jelicich, Mirella Malusà, Mauro Sambi, and Giuseppe Trani. This list could go on and, to be complete, it would have to include many more writers as well.

Omissions are inevitable, yet it is hoped that this introduction makes clear the creative vivacity of poets from this area since World War II, a creativity that is never monotonous or monolithic, rather varied both formally, with respect to the rhythms and tones of the representative verses, as well as thematically, with respect to the inner worlds of the poets and their common historical experiences marked by strong local traits. Languages, traditions, customs and lifestyles are appropriately territorial and are invariably strong shapers of individuals.

In all its complexity, the literature from Istria and Rijeka/Fiume is a work in progress, an ever-growing, lively cultural reality that captures the identity of the Italian national community in all its multiple expressions: its origins, its history, its consistency and perspectives. The historical role of this literature from Istria and Rijeka/Fiume, so deeply connected to the multiethnic reality of Istria that exists in direct contact with the Slovene and Croatian cultural universe, is to act as a bridge between different worlds destined to know one another, to understand, communicate, even challenge one another, in order to ascertain their values in a context of availability and free exchange. The future challenge of this area will be collaboration among ethnic groups and the appreciation of their respective specificities, which together form the composite Istrian cultural heritage.

Works of narrative prose, poetry, criticism, essays, and history published by Italians in this region would amount to a well-furnished library. Many of these volumes were published by prestigious publishing houses in Italy (Sellerio, Feltrinelli, Ibiskus, Campanotto, Hefti Edizioni, Scheiwiller), and many also by EDIT in Rijeka/Fiume, the publishing house of Italians living in Croatia and Slovenia, founded in 1952, which has collected, "in the place of its origin," documents manifesting the rich and vivacious journalistic tradition in Italian begun in this area in 1807 with the *Foglio periodico istriano* (*Istrian Periodical*). Many volumes are published by the Centro di Ricerche Storiche di Rovigno (The Center for Historical Research of Rovinj/Rovigno), founded in 1968, which houses, preserves and maintains the historical records of the Italian national community; by the Società di Studi e Ricerche Pietas Iulia (Society for Study and Research Pietas Iulia), founded in 1995; by the recent Società di Studi Storici e Geografici di Pirano (Society for the Historical and Geographical Studies of Piran/Pirano [Slovenia]), founded in 2005; and by the Centro per l'Informatica, la Programmazione e l'Orientamento dei Quadri (CIPO) (Center for Computer Science, Planning, and Guidance of the Sectors). Writers and poets of the Istrian peninsula are regularly translated into Croatian, while their literary works are also featured in literary journals such as *Književna Rijeka* (*Fiume Letteraria / Literary Fiume*), published by the Rijeka/Fiume chapter of the Association of Croatian Writers.

Italians of Croatia and Slovenia, though numbering around thirty thousand people, were able to preserve and promote Italian traditions in the area they have inhabited historically, overcoming the considerable division caused by the traumatic experience of World War II. Through their wealth of cultural activity in an ambience of coexistence and collaboration with the more numerous Croatian and Slovene populations, the Italians residing in the Istrian region and in Rijeka/Fiume contributed to the fostering of a cultural and literary exchange that has enriched the culture of all the people sharing this land for centuries. Lacking factories, businesses, and agencies of labor promotion, the Italians of Croatia and Slovenia attained recognition through their cultural promotion after World War II, in an attempt to maintain their identity by giving expression to the age-old civilization of which they are legitimate heirs. Italian artists and intellectuals of Istria and Rijeka/Fiume have understood that culture in today's world must be pluralistic and that, for a minority group, culture is the rigorous instrument through which its intellectual freedom can be asserted.

For a more complete understanding of the development of the literature of the Italian national community of Croatia and Slovenia, and in order to read the works of authors from that area, it is advisable to consult the volumes of the cultural journal *La Battana* (Rijeka/Fiume, EDIT), founded in 1964; the volumes that collect works that won awards through Istria Nobilissima (Unione Italiana-Università Popolare di Trieste); and the volumes of the series Biblioteca Istriana (Unione Italiana-Università Popolare di Trieste).

BIBLIOGRAPHY

Bergnach, Laura, ed. *L'Istria come risorsa per nuove convivenze*. Gorizia: ISIG, 1995.

Bogliun Debeljuh, Loredana. *L'identità etnica. Gli italiani dell'area istro-quarnerina*. Trieste-Rovigno: Centro di Ricerche Storiche di Rovigno, 1995.

Colummi, C., L. Ferrari, G. Nassisi, and G. Trani. *Storia di un esodo. Istria 1945–1956*. Trieste: Istituto Regionale per La Storia del Movimento di Liberazione nel Friuli-Venezia Giulia, 1980.

Damiani, Alessandro. *La cultura degli italiani dell'Istria e di Fiume*. Trieste-Rovigno: Centro di Ricerche Storiche di Rovigno, 1997.

Deghenghi Olujić, Elis. *La forza della fragilità. La scrittura femminile nell'area istro-quarnerina: aspetti, sviluppi critici e prospettive*. Fiume: EDIT, 2004.

———. *Per molti versi*. Fiume: EDIT, 1998.

Deghenghi Olujić, Elis, and Miran Košuta, eds. *Versi diversi. Poeti di due minoranze/Drugačni verzi. Pesniki dveh manjšin*. Koper/Capodistria: Edizioni Unione Italiana, 2006.

Giuricin, Gianni. *L'Istria è lontana. Un esodo senza storia*. Trieste: Italo Svevo, 1981.

Glavinić, Vera. "La letteratura degli italiani in Jugoslavia nel quotidiano *La Voce del Popolo*." *La Battana* 80 (1986): 91–96.

———. "Quarant'anni di attività letteraria del Gruppo Nazionale Italiano, in Il Gruppo Nazionale Italiano in Istria e a Fiume oggi." In *Una cultura per l'Europa*, ed. Giorgio Padovan and Ulderico Bernardi, 67–78. Ravenna: Longo Editore, 1991.

Maier, Bruno. "La letteratura istro-quarnerina del dopoguerra." In *La letteratura italiana dell'Istria dalle origini al Novecento*, 113–124. Trieste: IRCI, 1996.

Martini, Lucifero. "Storia e letteratura nel secondo dopoguerra—History and Literature after the Second World War." *La Battana* 75 (1985).

Mazzieri, Gianna. *La "Voce" di una minoranza*. Torino: La Rosa Editrice, 1998.

Miglia, Guido. *L'Istria una quercia*. Trieste: Edizioni Circolo di cultura Istria, 1994.

Milani, Kruljac Nelida. *La comunità italiana in Istria e a Fiume fra diglossia e bilinguismo*. Trieste-Rovigno: Centro di Ricerche Storiche di Rovigno; 1990.

Molinari, Fulvio. *L'Istria contesa. La guerra, le foibe, l'esodo*. Milan: Mursia, 1996.

Pellizzer, Antonio. *Voci nostre*. Fiume: EDIT, 1993.

Pupo, Raoul. *Tra Italia e Jugoslavia. Saggi sulla questione di Trieste*. Udine: Del Bianco, 1991.

Salimbeni, Fulvio, ed. *Istria. Storia di una regione di frontiera*. Brescia: Editrice Morcelliana, 1994.

Tomizza, Fulvio. *Alle spalle di Trieste*. Milan: Bompiani, 1995.

Tommassini, Stefano. *L'Istria dei miracoli. Viaggio in una terra di mezzo*. Milan: Il Saggiatore, 2005.

Turconi, Sergio. "Una tarda stagione del neorealismo: La letteratura degli Italiani in Istria." *La Battana* 83 (1987): 89–96.

———. "La poesia degli italiani dell'Istria e di Fiume." *La Battana* 38 (1976): 68–108.

→ Osvaldo Ramous (1905–1981)

The last of six children, Ramous was born in the low-income neighborhood named Cittavecchia in Rijeka/Fiume (Croatia), the same city where the famous exiles and writers Franco Vegliani and Enrico Morovich were born. He spent his childhood and youth in the Istrian territory that, perhaps more than any other European city, was greatly affected by the changing course of history in the last century. After earning his teaching certificate, Ramous studied music for a few years at the City School of Music, dedicating himself to the violin and the piano. His passion for music left a deep mark in his poetry. He became interested in literature and poetry at a young age and contributed works to various journals, including *Delta*, edited by Giani Stuparich, in which Ramous published his first works in 1923. After a long silence, the publisher EDIT printed his first collection of poetry, entitled *Vento sullo stagno* (*Wind Over the Pond*, 1953). After 1947, in the wake of the Peace Treaty signed in Paris and the exodus of the Italian component of the Istrian population, Ramous opted to continue to live in his native city, now considered foreign. In 1946 Ramous was given the directorship of the Dramma Italiano di Fiume (Fiume Italian Drama), the theater company of the Italian national community, where he worked as artistic director until 1961, the year he retired. Thereafter, his literary activity increased considerably. Among his works published after 1960 are *Pianto vegetale* (*Vegetable Tears*, 1960), *Il vino della notte* (*Night's Wine*, 1964), *Risveglio di Medea* (*Medea's Awakening*, 1967), *Realtà dell'assurdo* (*Reality of the Absurd*, 1973), *Pietà delle cose* (*Pity for Things*, 1977), and, posthumously, *Viaggio quotidiano* (*Daily Voyage*, 1982). Ramous also wrote several novels: *I gabbiani sul tetto* (*The Seagulls on the Rooftops*, 1964) and *Serenata alla morte* (*Death's Serenade*, 1965). In addition to having produced numerous theatrical representations, Ramous has contributed works to several journals, including *La Fiera Letteraria, Il*

Caffè, L'Europa Letteraria, Il Dramma, Musical America, and *La Revue Théatrale* of Paris.

Ramous's poetry features two interlocking themes: life's precarious fleetingness, and time that conquers all things in its inevitable march. Alessandro Damiani has defined Ramous's poetry as "an insistent variation on a theme." Ramous's poetic evolution concerns his stylistic modulation over time. In his lyrics, the poet tells of the human condition and reflects on doubts, hopes, and illusions, all the while expressing his trust in a better future, although pessimistic traits punctuate his thoughts on the loss of loved ones, aging, and the persistence of evil in the world. Ramous, the man and the poet, questions what will forever remain without answers: How can we come to know the truth? Ramous's search is a perennial analysis of his own identity. His verse relies on musicality, and does not reject the symbolist tradition, nor does it shun erudite references. Ramous found strength in the reality of his own city, in his membership in the Italian national community whose destiny he shared in one of the most troubled moments of its history. Ramous, who prided himself on declaring that he was a citizen of the world, lived through the drama of feeling an outsider in his own native city, uprooted while living in a space that was his by birth. His sentiment amounts to a common paradigm of modernity: to feel connected to one's own local world while aspiring to a universal dimension.

Cristallo

da *Nel canneto*

Grumo di solida luce racchiusa
in simmetrica forma, cristallo.
L'iridato mattino in te dorme
dei secoli;
e miri, occhio fermo, il trascorrere
vertiginoso del sole.

Crystal

from *In the Canebrake*

A mass of solid light trapped
In symmetric shape, crystal.
The iris-like morning sleeps
for centuries within you;
and you fix, unmoving eye,
the giddy passing of the sun.

Nessuno ascolterà

Nessuno ascolterà più la dolente
preghiera, e ai sospiri degli afflitti
risponderà soltanto il verso
pettegolo e insolente della risacca.
Non vi è più tormentosa solitudine
di quella assediata dagli echi.

No One Will Listen

No one will listen to the mournful
prayer, and to the sighs of the sufferers
the only answer will be the insolent
tittle-tattle of the backwash.
The most tormenting solitude
is the one surrounded by echoes.

Tremano luci sui monti

da *Vento sullo stagno*

Tremano luci sui monti
al vento di prima sera.
Nella sua voce leggera
c'è il murmure delle fonti.

Scompigliano i suoi capelli
le raffiche vespertine.
Sulle plaghe turchine
le nubi vanno a brandelli.

I rami hanno un palpito umano,
un brivido appena distinto;
e da quel palpito avvinto,
nel suo mistero silvano

ritorna ad immergersi il senso
dell'essere. Sopra le alture
s'agitano figure
che vanno nell'immenso.

Lights Flicker on the Mountains

from *Wind Over the Pond*

Lights flicker on the mountains
in the early evening wind.
In its weightless voice
is the murmur of the springs.

The afternoon breezes
ruffle her hair.
In the turquoise skies
the clouds are breaking up.

Branches show a human beat,
a shiver barely seen;
embraced by that palpitation
in its sylvan mystery

the sense of being submerges
again. Above the heights
there are figures shaking
who move in the immensity.

Di quel mercato rumoroso

Di quel mercato rumoroso
non m'è rimasto
che un vago suono di zufolo.
Oleandri fioriti
sotto un balcone aperto,
e la pioggia
una nube iridata.

Se ritorno fanciullo
per pochi istanti,
scrollo il peso che mi rattrista
e varco il regno della fantasia
con passo ondulato di donnola.

Di quel mercato rumoroso
mi son rimasti anche due occhi lucenti
ed un volto di bimba
coronato da un fazzoletto scarlatto.
Altro non mi appartiene.

Così leggero, ritorno fanciullo,
al suono dello zufolo
ammaliatore.

Of That Noisy Market

Of that noisy market
I have nothing left
but the faint note of a pipe.
Flowering oleanders
beneath an open balcony,
and the rain
is a rainbow-colored cloud.

If I become a child again
for a few moments
I shake off the weight that saddens me
and enter the realm of fantasy
with the wavy step of a weasel.

Of that noisy market
I've also kept two shiny eyes
and the face of a girl
wrapped in a scarlet scarf.
Nothing else belongs to me.

Thus light, I become a child again
at the sound of the pipe
that enchants me.

Le chitarre assordanti

da Pianto vegetale

Le chitarre assordanti dei mattini
e l'arpa solitaria,
nascosta dal verde,
che spruzza
gocce di suoni sul ventre
del pomeriggio estivo;
e l'organo che si perde,
sulla scia dei propri echi,
con le canne alte, nel buio:
di queste musiche è colma
e pur sempre vogliosa
la mia caducità.

The Deafening Guitars

from *Vegetable Tears*

The deafening guitars of the mornings
and the solitary harp
hidden by the green
that sprinkles
drops of sound on the belly
of a summer afternoon;
and the pipe that fades
on the traces of its own echoes
with the tall pipes, in the dark:
of such music
my transience is filled
although always wanting.

Di là dai vetri

da *Risveglio di Medea*

Di là dai vetri un passero
infreddolito
mi ricorda che siamo a dicembre.
Batte l'onda, gonfiata
dallo scirocco,
sulla roccia ai cui piedi
giocavo, bambino, con le conchiglie.

Le conchiglie di allora
stanno oggi affondate nella rena
e assorbono col tempo
il loro destino di fossili.

E qui si affaccia l'inverno,
ma il destino è ancora mutevole,
e ancora una volta il brillìo
di un albero inargentato
segna il varco di un anno.

Beyond the Window Panes

from *The Awakening of Medea*

Beyond the window panes
a sparrow
nearly frozen
reminds me it is December.
The wave is pounding, swelled
by the south wind,
on the rock at whose base
I played, as a child, with the seashells.

The shells of those years
are now buried in the sand
and with time soak up
their fate as fossils.

Here winter approaches,
but fate is still mutable,
and one more time the flashes
of a silvery tree
marks the passing of the year.

→ Lucifero Martini (1916–2001)

Born in Florence in 1916 of parents from Pula/Pola (Croatia), Lucifero Martini is considered one of the pioneers of Italian literature from Istria. He enrolled in the Department of Economics at the University of Trieste and worked in a bank, but discovered soon enough that the life of a banker did not suit him. In 1941 he was drafted into the army and, in 1943, as an officer, he took part in the reprisals of Cefalonia, which resulted in a few months of imprisonment. During the following October, he joined the partisans, and at this time he began to write. In the 1950s he settled in Rijeka/Fiume and worked for the daily *La Voce del Popolo*, eventually as the editor of the cultural page. From 1970 on he was the editor-in-chief of *Panorama*. In collaboration with Eros Sequi and Sergio Turconi, he founded the journal *La Battana*, and for decades he was promoter of the cultural assemblies organized by the headquarters of the journal, which played a key role in encouraging knowledge and cultural exchange between the two Adriatic coasts. He remained committed to the promotion of the Italian national community through journalism and literature and any other means available.

In his numerous works of prose and poetry as well as in his plays, Martini depicted the Istrian reality in its evolution. In his literary activity he brought together with great dedication the historical dimension of literature, tying it with the inner world. In his poetry especially, Martini documents the process that the engaged intellectual follows moving between the two opposite poles of dreams and action, contested by individualism and social awareness. For Martini, like Vittorini, the poet cannot live apart from the historical and social context; his model of the writer is someone working for a better society, who realizes before all others the ills that affect it. Without forfeiting an individual and personal dimension and its complex relationship with social reality, Martini inserts in his poetry the political and ethical vision of his generation, creating verses of ideological tension. Biographical elements in his works are not only a focus on the individual world, but also a search for what is common. In his poetry, the medium is never considered less important than the commitment to the self and to life. Martini's poetry shows clearly that he is concerned with the craft of writing verse, since the intimate problems of poetry are related to technique and to issues of poetic language. The broad free verse of his poetry is the premise that allows his subjectivity to flow according to its inner rhythms. In his pieces surface some of the situations that have left a mark on his life; melancholy runs through his poetry like an invisible thread, a sorrowful melancholy dominated by the resignation to a changed world, to the falling down of youthful idealism for which he had fought. But in his poetry there are also symptoms of renewal, a desire to forget the past in order to look at the future and move toward a world of peace and serenity.

The trauma of the exodus is an inexhaustible source of poetic expression. Often present in his poetry is the theme of departure through an abandonment of the city Rijeka/Fiume, which is intimately connected to his own life through his father, who did leave, while the poet stayed. War is another theme at the center of Martini's poetry, through memories that surface throughout his works. There are no resentments for the enemy of old. Rather, what is expressed is a need for a brotherhood that unites all people by recognizing their common suffering and the need to overcome all past hatreds.

Lucifero Martini was awarded numerous national and international prizes. He contributed to numerous journals and newspapers: *La fiera letteraria, Bianco e nero, Paese sera, Uomini e libri,* and *L'Unità.* He is the author of many narrative works and plays. His most important poetic works are: *Il segno del mare (The Sign of the Sea,* 1971); *La bora spegne il fuoco (The Bora Puts Out the Fire,* 1973); *Aroma d'alga (Algae Aroma,* 1974); *Vento sul mare (Wind over the Sea,* 1975); *Nuvole in cielo (Clouds in the Sky,* 1975); *L'erba non è ancora verde (The Grass Is Not Green Yet,* 1978); *Versi in corsia (Verses on a Highway Lane,* 1981); *Somiglianze (Resemblances,* 1982); *Colloquio con la città (Dialogue with the City,* 1987); *Tempo nostro (Our Time,* 1987); *Schegge di tempo (Shards of Time,* 1990); *Versi de sbando (Stray Verses,* 2001). His works have been translated into Serbian, Croatian, Spanish, French, and English.

Colloquio

da *Il segno del mare*

Tra me e il mare continuo colloquio,
non lo guastano queste onde ed il soffio della bora,
e questi corpi distesi sulla sabbia, perduti.
Va il mare tra Omiš e Brač e sussulta e soffre,
ed io lo ascolto e tra i pini raccolgo la sua voce.
Talvolta mi coglie il silenzio, la barca si muove senza peso,
l'isola è distrutta dalla lontananza, nella foschia leggiera.
Un grido echeggia sulla spiaggia immobile:
stupore di bimbo dinanzi ad antica conchiglia.
Ed il tempo si arresta, nel mattino di giugno,
come uno spillo che ha fermato il corpo di velluto
di una farfalla dalle ali piene di colori.

Conversation

from *The Sign of the Sea*

Between me and the sea a continuous conversation,
not ruined by these waves and the blowing north wind
and these bodies stretched out on the sand, lost.
The sea flows between Omiš and Brač, agitated and suffering,
and I hear it and gather its voice from between the pines.
At times silence finds me, the boat moves without weight,
the isle is undone by the distance, in the light fog.
A scream echoes on the motionless beach:
a child's surprise in front of an ageless shell.
And time stands still, on this morning in June,
like a pin that has stilled the velvet body
of a butterfly whose wings are pregnant with colors.

Istria

Sono dentro i miei occhi
le notti solcate da stelle
come grumi di sangue nelle vene.
La bora macera
la rossa campagna
ed è frusta in cielo
per l'uccello migratore.
Stagioni d'incauta giovinezza
nei ritratti dei padri.
In bocca l'erba del mare
ha il gusto del tempo.

Istria

They are in my eyes
the nights traced with stars
like blood clots in the veins.
The north wind chews up
the red fields
and is a whip in the sky
to the migrating bird.
Seasons of reckless youth
in the portraits of the fathers.
To the mouth the sea grass
has the flavor of time.

I tuoi capelli neri

da *Aroma d'alga*

Nei tuoi capelli neri
aroma d'alga
mi strugge.
Fresca di riso
e candida di sole
ti specchi nei miei occhi
inteneriti.
Muto il tempo ammonisce:
il naufragio
ci allontana dalle sponde
aspre di resina
e la fiamma convulsa si spegne
negli ultimi guizzi.
Il domani ci attende
con i suoi disperati silenzi.

Your Black Hair

from *Aroma of Algae*

In your black hair
the perfume of algae
destroys me.
With a fresh smile
and whitened by the sun
you mirror yourself in my
softened eyes.
Mute time admonishes:
the shipwreck
pushes us far from the shores
pungent with resin
and the fitful flame burns out
with one last sputter.
Tomorrow awaits us
with its desperate silences.

Sono cresciuto con il mare
onda dopo onda
e ho parlato con la bora
in taciti sussurri.
Con passo d'uomo
ho percorso millenni
di inquietanti sospetti
e ho incontrato ombre
su strade infinite
di inutili glorie.
Ora aspetto che le stelle
sbiadiscano sull'orizzonte.

from *Shreds of Time*

I grew up with the sea
wave after wave
and I have spoken with the north wind
in mute whispers.
With human steps
I have traversed millennia
of troubling suspicions
and encountered shadows
on infinite roads
with useless stories.
Now I wait for the stars
to fade on the horizon.

da *Versi de sbando*

Xe le robe semplici
che fa bela la vita:
tirar fora de la scarsela
fregole de pan
per darle ai colombi,
scoltar per radio una canzon
in una lingua
che no xe la tua
e andar lontan con ela,
vardar sul molo l'omo
che buta la togna.
Sperando de ciapar qualcosa.
Tanti no i capissi
cossa ti son
ma ti ti senti de esser uno
e non de sparir
nel niente.

Sono le cose semplici—a fare bella la vita: / estrarre dalla tasca / briciole di pane / per darle ai colombi, / ascoltare alla radio una canzone / in una lingua / che non è la tua / e andare lontano con essa / guardare sul molo l'uomo / che butta la lenza. / Sperando di prendere qualcosa. / Tanti non capiscono / cosa sei / ma tu ti senti di essere uno / e non di scomparire / nel nulla.

It's the simple things
that make life beautiful:
take out from the pocket
some bread crumbs
to feed the pigeons,
hear a song on the radio
in a language
that is not your own
and go far away with it,
watch the man on the pier
flip the fishing pole.
Hoping to catch something.
Many don't understand
what you are
but you know to be one
and you won't disappear
into nothing.

Xe cressuda la luna
E la se rampiga
Sui teti de Citavecia
che no i xe
come i iera.
Tuto xe diverso
e anche el fritolin
xe diventado bar.
La luna impigrissi
sul porto.
Solo el mar
nissun lo ga potudo
cambiar.

La luna è cresciuta—e si arrampica / sui tetti della Cìttavecchia / che non sono / come erano. / Tutto è diverso / e anche la bettolina / è diventata bar. / La luna s'impigrisce / sul porto. / Solo il mare / nessuno l'ha potuto / cambiare.

The moon has grown
and climbs above
the rooftops of the Old City
that are no longer
as they once were.
Everything has changed
and even the hole-in-the-wall
has become a big bar:
the moon turns lazy
over the port.
Only the sea
no one has been able
to change.

→ Eligio Zanini (1927–1993)

There is an interesting tradition of dialect poetry in the Istrian literary context. Some of the best poetry written by the members of the Italian national community is in Istrian. Eligio Zanini, from Rovinj/Rovigno (Croatia), was the first to have had an awareness, in the beginning of the 1960s, of the artistic possibilities of the "*istrioto,*" the "*favalà,*" which, as Zanini saw it, could have poetic effects.

Zanini's artistic world finds inspiration in his native Rovinj/Rovigno, dominated by the bell tower with the statue of Saint Eufemia at the top. His dialect poetry is the largest collection in that language and is of particular importance in the conservation of a cultural value intimately tied to the life of the Italian community of this small town. In his poetry, Zanini speaks of fishermen, boats, the sea, the sky, and the wind in authentic dialect verses full of power and light, modeled after a specific, at once particular and universal human existence.

At the start of his poetic career, Zanini was not influenced by any particular poetic school because of the isolation in which Istria existed during World War II, when the political relationship between Italy and Yugoslavia was tense and cultural contacts were almost nonexistent. From the beginning, therefore, Zanini did not have any influence and developed his style independently. The first collection that Zanini published was *Buléistro* (*Ashes*, 1966). In 1968 and 1970, in the anthology that published the prizewinning works of Istria Nobilissima, appeared *Mar quito e alanbastro* (*Quiet Alabaster Sea*) and *Tiera viecia stara* (*Very Old Land*). The collection *Favalando cul cucal Filéipo in stu canton da paradéisu* (*Conversations with the Seagull Philip in the Corner of Paradise*) is from 1979 and was translated into Croatian in 1983 in the series Istria kroz stoljeća (Istria Through the Centuries). This collection, stylistically and metrically coherent, is equivalent to a true *canzoniere*. *Sul sico de la Muorto Sagonda* (*On the Shoal of Segunda*) was published in 1990, while his last collections were printed in 1993 as a posthumous publication titled *Cun la prua al vento* (*With the Prow to the Wind*). Zanini also published an autobiographical novel, *Martin Muma,* in 1996 in the journal *La Battana.* In it, he talks about his childhood and adolescence and refers to the tragic years of his political involvement and the ensuing disillusionment, a story common to many Italians in Istria in the postwar period.

The most frequent themes treated in Zanini's poetry are the splendor of uncontaminated nature and the relationship between the individual and nature. In his intimate dialogue with nature, Zanini gives the sea a privileged spot and captures its most familiar aspects. In the vastness of the sea, the poet recognizes a part of himself and of his own voice; writing about the sea allows him to confront the world and to assert his independence from a reality that does not satisfy him. The charisma that the sea-father exercises on Zanini-son is great because of the severity of its rule; in his poetry the sea loses its mysterious contours and becomes the only reality that can suggest models of living or is seen as deserving complete respect. Whether at night, immersed in a boundless abyss of darkness, or during the day, splashed by the sun under a silent sky, the sea that dances, heals, kills and speaks with its salty words is, for Zanini, the unchallenged owner of humanity, an omnipotent sovereign, at times terrible, at times benevolent. Zanini's poetry is a sea poem, the song of an expert "fisherman" who interprets the perfect and anarchic order of nature and longs for the ideal of a clean, honest, and orderly living. His enduring conviction is that he must defend, from the corrosion of time and social conventions, a sentimental, ethical, and psychological heritage, as well as the humble ideals of Franciscan poverty and the force of existential contemplation.

El cucal Filéipo

da *Favalando cul cucal Filéipo in stu canton de paradéisu*

In sta zurnada da maltenpo
a ma suven ca lasù 'n Siruoco
xi 'óun cucal fra tanti,
saruò 'l martéin de l'ano passà,
ca ogni giuorno a ma spieta.

Sul sico da Cunvarsari
o su quil de la Taronda,
su la fóusa da Gustéigna
o su quila del Purier
el xi senpro préima da méi.

El xi biel, nito e grando;
dóuto 'l santo giuorno
el x'in lavur cun li satuléine
contro vento e curantéia
par stame rente, par vidame meo.

I ga favielo e dóuto 'l capéisso,
a sa vido ch'el patéisso
parchì a ga manca la paruola
e cui uciti el ma conta, a mèi ch'i siè,
cossa ca xi la fan.

Cu i lu ciamo Filéipo
za 'l sa liva par ciapà 'l pissito,
uciando par divierse méie,
ca nu séio 'óun cuncurente
pióun svielto d'ingurgaghe 'l bucon.

Suovi xi i ribunséini,
li dunzalite e li maréincule,
féin ch'el sul va a li basse,
féin ca sassio e cuntento
el pol sbulà par li suove.

Philip the Seagull

from *Conversations with the Seagull Philip in the Corner of Paradise*

On this day of bad weather
I recall that in the southeast wind
there is one of many seagulls,
maybe the seagull of the past year,
which waits each day for me.

On the sandbar of Conversari
or on that of Taronda,
on the ditch of Gustigna
or on the one of the Porer
he is there always before me.

He is lovely, big and clean;
the whole blessed day
he works with his legs
against wind and current
to stay close to me,
to see me better.

I talk, he understands everything,
maybe it hurts him
to be without speech,
telling me with his eyes, since I know,
what hunger is.

When I call him Philip
he flies off to catch a small fish,
scanning the sky for many miles
to make sure a stronger competitor
will not steal his morsel.

His are the pale sardines, scallops, and trout
until the sun goes down
then happy and full-bellied
he flies off wherever he wishes.

E méi, in quila sira,
i turno cun bai pissi
e cul racuordo d'óuna bona cunpanéia.

Il gabbiano Filippo—In questa giornata di maltempo / mi ricordo che laggiù a Scirocco / c'è un gabbiano fra i tanti, / forse sarà il gabbianino dell'anno scorso, / che ogni giorno mi aspetta. / Sulla secca di Conversari / o su quella della Taronda ,/ sulla fossa di Gustigna / o su quella del Porer / è sempre prima di me. / È bello, pulito e grande; / tutto il santo giorno / è al lavoro con le zampette / contro vento e corrente / per starmi vicino, per vedermi meglio. / Gli parlo e tutto egli comprende, / si vede che soffre / perché gli manca la parola / e con gli occhietti racconta, proprio a me che lo so, / che cos'è la fame. / Quando lo chiamo Filippo / già si alza al volo per prendere il pesciolino, / scrutando se nel raggio di diverse miglia / non ci sia un concorrente / più agile di lui ad inghiottirgli il boccone. / Suoi sono i fragolini pallidi, / le donzellette e le marincole, / fino a che il sole va al basso, / fino a che sazio e contento / può volare per le sue. / E io, in quella sera, / ritorno con bei pesci / e con il ricordo di una buona compagnia.

And on that evening
I return with good, fresh fish
and remember his good company.

Zura da méi li stile

Zura da méi li stile
in sta nuoto frida
da caléigo rasente,
ca scondo i signi a traguardo
da dout'i sichi fondi.

Sbusinava la bora
in sti giuorni passadi;
tiera véia pian pian,
cume ch'i fago adiesso,
a ma tuchiva ramaname
spatando bunassa
e bona, c'almieno uò restà
zura da méi li stile.

Sopra di me le stelle—Sopra di me le stelle / in questa notte fredda / di nebbia radente, / che nasconde i segni a traguardo / di tutte le secche profonde. / Soffiava forte la bora / durante i giorni trascorsi; / lungo la costa, / come faccio adesso, / ero costretto a navigare lentamente / aspettando bonaccia / e grazie che sono rimaste, almeno, / sopra di me le stelle.

Above Me the Stars

Above me the stars
in this frigid night
with low-lying fog
hiding the docking posts
of every deep shoal.

The north wind blew strong
these past few days;
along the coast,
as I do now,
I was forced to sail slowly
waiting for gentle breezes,
and thank God that
over my head at least
hung the stars.

Cucal cume teî

da *Tiera vecia stara*

Cucal, cume teî
vagulo punteîn bianco,
alto int'el sil
nigaro da ragan;
cucal, cume teî
lisera vila in sbul
feîn a pil del'onda
ciara da maistral.
    Cucal, cun teî
    sul scuio virgino:
    largo dali pulvare,
    largo dal paltan;
    cucal, cun teî
    in sirca del bucon:
    feîn ch'i verno li ale bianche,
    feîn ch'i verno i uóci vierti.
Cucal, meî e teî
ancura in sbul,
    parchi la nostra carno magra
        sà da pisculoûn.

Gabbiano, come te—Gabbiano, come te / penzolante puntino bianco, / alto nel cielo / nero per l'uragano; / gabbiano, come te / leggera vela in volo / sino alla cresta dell'onda / chiara per il maestrale. / Gabbiano, con te / sullo scoglio vergine: / lontano dalla polvere, / lontano dal fango; / gabbiano, con te / in cerca del boccone: / sino a che abbiamo le ali bianche, / sino a che abbiamo gli occhi aperti. / Gabbiano, io e te / ancora in volo, / perché la nostra carne magra / ha l'acre sapore di pesce.

Seagull, Like You

from *Very Old Land*

Seagull, like you
swaying white dot,
high in the sky
darkened by the storm;
seagull, like you
thin sail in flight
up to the crest of the wave
made clear by the northwest wind.
      Seagull, with you
      on the virgin reef
      far from the dust,
      far from the mud;
      seagull, with you
      in search of a morsel:
      as long as we have white wings,
      as long as we have open eyes.
Seagull, you and I
still in flight,
      because our lean flesh
           is acrid-tasting like fish.

Sensa pas

da *Mar quito e alanbastro*

Aque del mar
cun vui sensa pas,
parchì i altri na spenzo;
na spenzo i venti,
la lóuna e li stile;
el sul cunpagno na scalda,
la sissa tramuntána na giássa.

Drento da nui mai pas,
parchì i altri na smagna;
na smagna el pióun grando,
ca divuóra 'l péicio
e la féin da dóuti dui,
el sabion da ponte pastade,
ca sufaghia i fiuri dei capui.

Aque del mar, geri
in óun atimo da lissiér
in vui i ma iè véisto.

Senza pace—Acque del mare / con voi senza pace, / perché gli altri ci spingono; / ci spingono i venti, / la luna e le stelle; / il sole ugualmente ci riscalda, / la stessa tramontana ci raffredda. / Dentro di noi mai pace, / perché gli altri ci tormentano; / ci tormenta il più grande, / che divora il piccolo / e la fine di tutti e due, / la sabbia di sporgenze rocciose battute, / che soffoca i fiori delle alghe. / Acque del mare, ieri in un attimo di bonaccia mi sono visto in voi.

Without Peace

from *Quiet Alabaster Sea*

Waters of the sea
at your side without peace,
because the others push us;
the winds, the moon
and the stars push us;
the sun equally warms us,
the same north wind chills us.

Inside us there is never peace
because the others torment us;
the biggest one torments us
who devours the smallest
and the end of them both,
the sand from rocky spurs flattened
that chokes flowers and algae.

La miéa batana

Du tuóle farmade
cun quatro ciuódi e
óun uócio da viro sul fondo:
óun móussulo, óun móussulo véivo.
Bona, cun granda passiensa
dundulandusse la ma spiéta
par purtame fora.
Fora dal grumasso
da case e da panseri:
pel mar, pei scui a favalà
da cor cun pissi e datuli,
cui sul quito al tramonto,
culi stile, ca tramando da frido,
li ma muóstra la cal . . .
Turnà al miéo dóuro grumasso
la ma spieta, da nuo, bona
cun granda passiensa dundulandusse.

La mia battana—Due tavole fissate / con quattro chiodi e / un occhio di vetro sul fondo: / un mussulo, un mussulo vivo. / Buona, con grande pazienza, / dondolandosi mi attende / per portarmi al largo. / Fuori dall'agglomerato / di case e di pensieri: / per il mare, per gli scogli a conversare / di cuore con pesci e datteri, / col sole calmo al tramonto / e con le stelle, che tremolando dal freddo, / mi indicano la via. / Ritornato alla mia dura vita, / nuovamente mi attende buona, / con grande pazienza, dondolandosi.

My Flat Boat

Two boards held together
by four nails and
a glass eye on its bottom:
an ark, a live ark.
Good, with great patience,
swaying, it waits for me
to take me to sea.
Beyond the chaos
of houses and thoughts:
upon the sea, on reefs to talk
heart-to-heart with fish and mussels,
with the sun calm at sunset
and with the stars that shiver with cold
showing me the way.
Returned to my rough living,
again she waits for me gently,
with great patience, while swaying.

Cóuguli

Ali Ponte,
fora deli aque muórte,
el mar ráia
zura da núi
giuórno e nuóto.
Nel bianco rabisso
na stramanía
par la cuguliéra,
óun contro l'altro
e dóuti contro li gruóte;
da nui, pin pian;
fa lóustro sabion.
Giuórno e nuóto,
el mar dóuti
na stramanía
e sensa riequie
a sa stramanía
anche lóu.

Cogoli—Alle Punte, / fuori dalle acque morte, / il mare urla / su di noi / giorno e notte. / Nella bianca furia / ci sbatte / per la cogolera, / uno contro l'altro / e tutti contro le rocce; / di noi lentamente / fa lucida sabbia. / Giorno e notte, / il mare tutti / ci tormenta / e senza requie / tormenta / anche se stesso.

Break Walls

At Le Punte,
beyond the still waters,
the sea screams
at us
day and night.
In its white fury
It pounds us
along the break wall,
one against the other
and everyone against the rocks;
slowly it makes us
shiny sand.
day and night
the sea torments
us all
and without rest
it also flails itself.

→ Alessandro Damiani (b. 1928)

Alessandro Damiani was born in Sant'Andrea Jonio, Calabria. He arrived in Croatia in 1948 with the young workers' groups. His main occupation was journalism, first in Rome, where he was a dedicated film critic, and later in Rijeka/Fiume (Croatia), where he was the editor for the publisher EDIT of the magazine *Panorama* and the daily newspaper *La Voce del Popolo* (*The Voice of the People*). An intellectual of deep and broad interests focused on interpreting his own sentiments as well as those of his times, wrought with divisions and contradictions, Alessandro Damiani has been for decades a careful witness and severe judge, engaged in searching out and affirming authentic human and moral values. His rich artistic output in prose, poetry, and drama is wedded to an intense production as a critic and essayist. His newspaper articles made available in *La Voce del Popolo* and *Panorama* constitute a wealth of intellectual energy and ethical tension, enough to delineate on their own the lasting emblem of an authentic culture.

An eclectic writer, an uneasy and "heretical" protagonist of all the stages of cultural and political debate in the Istrian peninsula since World War II, Damiani has published the novels *Ed ebbero la luna* (*They Did Get the Moon*, 1989) and *La torre del borgo* (*The Tower of the Town*, 1995); the plays *Ipotesi* (*Hypothesis*, 1968), *Non di solo pane* (*Not by Bread Alone*, 1976), and *Aporie* (*Uncertainties*, 1979); essays such as *Restare a Itaca* (*Remaining in Ithaca*, 1978) and the collection of essays *La cultura degli Italiani dell'Istria e di Fiume* (*The Culture of Italians from Istria and Fiume*, 1997). His works of poetry include *Le ali del tempo* (*The Wings of Time*, 1967), *Appunti romani* (*Roman Notes*, 1967), *Motivi istriani* (*Istrian Motifs*, 1968), *Se questa è poesia* (*If This is a Poem*, 1981), *Satire ed epicedi* (*Satire and Elegy*, 1982), *Idilli ed epigrammi* (*Idylls and Epigrams*, 1983), *Illudere parvenze di vita* (*To Delude Life Appearances*, 1986), *Dal ponto* (*From Pontus*, 1998), *Note di viaggio* (*Travel Notes*, 2001, in bilingual edition,

Italian/Croatian), and *Trittico* (*Triptych*, 2005, in bilingual edition, Italian/Croatian).

In his poetry, Damiani pursues paths that lead to universal themes such as time, eternity, history, suffering, destiny, and wounds caused by life, which allow poetry to blossom, and without which there can be neither wisdom nor authentic greatness. He talks about delusions and regrets, the ancient eternal questions that remain unanswered because there is perhaps no answer: death as obsession and liberation; bitterness for degradation and the impoverishment of civilized societies; inner mortification to the point of judiciousness and maturity which allow one to look back and accept, with calm serenity, even the fissures of time and death itself in an ultimate understanding of life. Damiani's verses carry the signs of many passions, uncertainties and existential preoccupations brought under control by will alone. In fact, the author succeeds in channeling the palpitations of feelings into forms of refined classicism and expresses them in a dignified, well-behaved, and rigorous poetry, a musical poetry, marked by a magisterial sense of meter and syntactical measure. With his poetry, the author enacts the poetics theorized in his *Epicedi*, where poetry is defined as the ethereal connection between the urgency of sounds and the thoughtful clarity of ideas. By virtue of his formal control, Damiani's verses fulfill their communicative function, the very role that is essential for poetry to survive. It is necessary to safeguard a sacrificial ritual in poetry in which both the poet and the reader are officiates. This ancestral complicity has always existed between poet and reader, whereby the poet is the protector of great myths and great truths, and at the same time s/he succeeds in sharing them with the reader. Aware of the function of the poet and of poetry, Damiani dominates the cultural models abundantly present in his works, from Virgil to Horace, Dante, Petrarch, Foscolo, Leopardi, Carducci, D'Annunzio, and Montale, whom he channels according to his lyrical needs and transmits on a level suited to the average reader. Inner demons that Damiani contends with become, therefore, the reader's own. The prose-like verses of Damiani's poetry should not be disappointing, since behind them there is a well-conceived metrical and rhythmical architecture rooted in a classical model.

For Damiani, the only salvation possible is noninvolvement, the choice of a voluntary exile and almost a rejection of life itself and the consequent solitary decline toward death, toward nothingness, which is the ultimate substance of history. Still, there is a fundamental civic and intellectual honesty in the troubled existence of this author, who reveals in his most recent collection of poetry his own shortsightedness and disillusion-ments, admitting the failure of some of his convictions: "I have always cared for / the beginning of roads / that you don't know where they could lead. / Now I no longer venture / on paths lost in the fields / silent and thoughts in turmoil" (*Trittico/Triptych*).

Although Damiani's poetry expresses all aspects of a vanishing moral world that is becoming almost incomprehensible in the setting of a new inhumanity, a world of infernal people, disoriented in exasperated pursuits of vain objectives, it is also hospitable, deep enough to give solace to lost readers looking to it for comfort when everything else fails. Damiani, like his beloved Leopardi, would like to harbor and promote at least one ultimate utopian vision, that of allowing art and poetry to keep alive at least the most vital illusions about life. Poetry cannot solve anything, but it can console; it does not give final answers to universal questions, but it safeguards jealously the right to question.

Damiani is an integral part of the Istrian literary tradition in Italian, albeit a somewhat anomalous member because of his acute and complex intellectual personality, reared with refined aesthetic tastes on the best of the classical tradition.

Che senso ha oggi

da *Se questa è poesia*

Che senso ha, oggi,
scrivere poesie?
Gioco vano di parole
di suoni e simboli,
gioco più vano
d'illusioni e rimpianti
che la realtà ignora
e l'animo, colmo
d'assuefatti dolori,
riassorbe a fatica.

Non ha più vita
la metafora
né colori le immagini,
dacché la gioia fanciulla
e il pianto
non sgorgano
come acqua di fonte
dal cuore dell'uomo.

Che senso ha oggi
illudere
parvenze di vita?

What Does It Mean Today?

from *If This Is Poetry*

What does it mean today,
writing poetry?
Vain game of words,
sounds, symbols,
vainest game of
illusions and remorses
that knows not reality,
that the mind, full of the usual pains,
hardly integrates.

The metaphor is
now defunct.
There are no more colors
or images since
the youthful joy and lament
no longer gush
like waters from fountains,
from human hearts.

Today what does it mean
to feign we're alive?

Terra di poggi e doline
di scogli
ove i pini lambiscono l'acque
di orti tra i sassi,
Istria cinta di isole
che il monte guarda sereno!
  Ai tuoi riposi io torno
  e non è fuga dal mondo
  né rifugio nel mito
  meno antico della vicenda
  racchiusa
  nella tua rude saggezza.
Amore di pace mi chiama
oltre i presenti rumori
simili a refoli
quando la bora corre le alture
rivestendo
di luce i tuoi aspetti.

Earth of rises and dips
of reefs where
the pines lap the waters
of orchards among the rocks,
Istria girded by isles
the serene mountain overlooks . . .
        I return to your resting places,
        it's not a flight from the world
        nor refuge in the myth
        less ancient than the trials
        imbuing your bitter wisdom.
Love of peace calls me
beyond these noises
deafening like gales
when the bora sweeps the heights
redressing with light
all your nuances.

Ho curato fino allo spasimo
l'armonia del verso
e il rigore del pensiero.
Ora più non m'illude il
sorriso delle Muse
—retaggio letterario—
né mi tormenta l'ansia
per l'uscita del tunnel.
Mi sono accasciato
ricoperto della mia solitudine
in attesa che il tempo
sfumi gli aspetti,
dissolva i pensieri.

from *Travel Notes*

I've edited to the point of shuddering
the harmony of my lines and
the precision of my thoughts.
Now I have no more
illusions when
the Muses smile.
That old literary baggage
and the angst of leaving tunnels
no longer torments me.
I collapsed wrapped
in my solitude
waiting for time to nuance
the subtleties
and to dissolve thoughts.

Nessuno mi accusi,
nessuno mi condanni.
Delle mie colpe
sono stato già io
giudice severo
e inflessibile carceriere.
Quando avrò scontato la pena
non dovrò spettegolare
sui miei trascorsi
con alcuno.
Neppure con Dio.

Let no one accuse me,
let no one condemn me.
I've been the sternest judge
of my worst faults.
And my cruelest jailor.
When I'll have done my time,
I won't have to squeal
about my years spent with anyone.
Not even with God.

Quando il giorno riposa
nella quiete dei lunghi meriggi
avulsi, sgombri
dalla fatica di vivere,
e il tempo che pure scorre
sembra immobile
—distesa di acque non turbate
dal capriccio dei venti—
anch'io trovo pace
con me assiduo
come un cane a cuccia
che le mosche non molestano,
e mi abbandono, mi perdo,
assaporo l'ignara
beatitudine della morte.

When the day rests
in the dead of long noons
ripped clean
from the fatigue of living
and time flows but
seems immobile—
stretch of waters untroubled
by caprices of wind—
I also find peace
with myself and stretch out
like a dog in its house
where flies cannot intrude
and I let myself go,
get lost tasting
the arcane
beatitude of Death.

Nel ricordo di Ramous

da Satire ed epicedi

Ci siamo ritrovati, i pochi
amici rimasti, su a Tersatto
tra i viali dei cipressi. Rade
nubi e terse per la recente
pioggia si sfilacciavano al sole
di marzo, sotto i nostri passi
la ghiaia aveva un suono
di favella antica. E tra le voci
sommesse, le orazioni, i discorsi
d'addio c'era nell'aria un non so
che lieve, sereno, quasi giulivo
come ai brevi saluti per un
viaggio di sospirate vacanze.
Ma io che non inseguo più
mondi di fiaba, sentivo la tua
partenza solutrice d'interminabili
indugi e, forse, già approdo
in un porto di quiete; mentre
noi si resta—e il confessarlo
è duro—a vaneggiare al sole.

In Memory of Ramous

from *Satires and Elegies*

We met again, the few
friends, still friends,
up there in Tersatto
on the cypress boulevards.
Sparse clouds, brief
in the recent rain
unraveled in the sun
of March, beneath our feet
the pebbles resounded
with ancient tales.
Amid the voices,
subdued, the prayers, the goodbyes,
hung in the air, ineffable,
so light, serene,
almost joyful
like fleeting wishes
of long-dreamed voyages.
But I who no longer pursue fairytale worlds
still felt your ultimate
departure after
endless hesitations
and, perhaps, I've docked
in a safe port—while we stay—
and, to be honest, I'd say
it's hard to wander in the sun.

⇥ Giacomo Scotti (b. 1928)

Throughout more than fifty years of activity, Giacomo Scotti has written in a variety of genres—narrative, prose, poetry, essays—and published numerous works in Italian and Croatian, including translations and journalistic works. He is the recipient of several literary prizes, including one of the most prestigious, the Umberto Saba—Writers Without Frontiers, and the Premio Internazionale Calabria in 2005.

Giacomo Scotti was born in Saviano, near Naples. After World War II, he moved to Istria, where he was a journalist for *La Voce del Popolo* (*The Voice of the People*). Scotti writes about his double exile, from his native land and from his adopted residence, but this experience has been an occasion for enrichment and personal growth. He has always felt himself to be a son of two countries to which he was especially attached. In his poetry he treats the painful conflicts of living between two different and distant worlds.

Scotti published his first collections in the beginning of the 1960s. Since then he added several collections, of which the best known are *Se il diavolo è nero* (*If the Devil Is Black*, 1963), *Un altro mare un altro giorno* (*Another Sea Another Day*, 1968), *Ghe voio ben al mar* (*I Care for the Sea*, 1971), *Bandiere di salvezza* (*Flag of Salvation*, 1976), *Nell'umile occhio dell'uomo* (*In the Humble Eye of Man*, 1978), *Colore d'arancio* (*The Color Orange*, 1981), *Il cuore della vita* (*The Heart of Existence*, 1992), *Soffrendo per la Croazia* (*Suffering for Croatia*, 1993), *In viaggio, la vita* (*Traveling, Life*, 1994), *Cercando fiumi segreti* (*Looking for Secret Rivers*, 2000), *La luna, il gallo e altre poesie per i più giovani* (*The Moon, the Rooster and Other Poems for Younger People*, 2002), and *La memoria di pietra e altre poesie* (*Stone Memories and Other Poems*, 2004). A selection of his best poetry, which for the most part was translated into Croatian, was published in a bilingual Italian-Croatian anthology entitled *Appunti per una biografia* (*Notes for a Biography*, 2001).

Scotti's poetic production has evolved from an initial neorealist style to delve into inner experience without neglecting altogether issues of a social nature. Scotti treats a broad spectrum of topics in his poetry: living between two worlds, the war in Yugoslavia, the seascapes of Istria, the loss of his son, and the instability of earthly things. After the early realistic verses, comparable to Scotellaro's and to Edgar Lee Masters's, Scotti responded to the influences of other twentieth-century masters such as Quasimodo and Montale. The evolution of his work, not so drastic over the years, follows his life experiences and the constant effort to make his verse adhere to life. The result is a poetry that communicates directly to the reader, an honest and sincere account of experience. There are no impenetrable verses, just a poetic voice that reaches out in establishing a dialogue with a possible other. In a shipwrecked world of values sunk by the desire for power and money, Scotti finds hope again in seeing a rebirth of noble human sentiments as those that inspire the nomads of peace to continue to travel the most troubled roads of the world. His poetic trajectory is marked by simple sentiments, feelings expressed in a language that is accessible, but respects the aesthetic and metaphorical components of original poetry. Scotti goes beyond obscure verbal abstractions and searches for a dignified poetic language that brings the personal element to a universal and elegiac level. This results in a poetry expressing suffering and anxiety, full of humanity and respectful of reality.

A true child of two worlds, Scotti has been working to maintain the memory of Italian culture since World War II, after the passage of Istria to the former Yugoslavia and the consequent exodus of the majority of people of Italian language and culture. In 1969, Scotti wrote poems in dialect that he did not publish until later. In the note that precedes these poems Scotti writes: "The author of poems not meant for mere leisure reading desires to communicate with the public." In these words, Scotti expresses his trust in poetry. It is important to have faith in one's convictions, in the justice of one's beliefs. The polyvalent and plentiful work of Scotti is a testimonial to his belief in the value of the written word.

Il vento e il faro

da *Quasi favole (versi per l'infanzia)*

Soffiava vigoroso il vento.
Il faro sovrastava il porto
simile a un monumento.
Era mosso, agitato il mare.
Al largo un bastimento
rischiava di affondare.
Il vento, urlando forte,
minacciava di spargere
rovina e morte.
Rispose allora il faro:
"Ed io spargo la luce e porto in salvo
la barca e il marinaro!"
Seguendo quella luce,
la nave si salvò. Spuntò l'aurora,
se ne scappò la bora.

The Wind and the Lighthouse

from *Almost Fairy Tales (Poems for Childhood)*

The wind blew with rage
the lighthouse overlooked the port
like a monument.
The sea was restless, agitated.
A ship offshore
was in danger of sinking.
Blowing angrily, the wind
threatened to sow
destruction and death.
So the lighthouse answered:
"And I give off light and bring home
the boat and the sailor safely!"
Following that light
the ship was saved. Morning came,
the north wind blew off.

Io sono la mia casa finché vivo

da *Gli ultimi miracoli*

Questa casa che ascolta
i venti e il mare,
e sa di me la pena di resistere,
sempre è pregna di odori
di letto, di cucina,
delle mie donne
che vanno e vengono
con sogni nei capelli.
Questa casa mi invoca,
e insegue ogni mio gesto
che scende
sulla parola.
E qui, nella casa sospesa
su venti e mare,
la parola dilata ogni creatura,
e cresce, si scompone,
si compone di me.
Io sono questa casa finché vivo.

I Am My House as Long as I Live

from *The Final Miracles*

This house that listens
to the winds and the sea,
and knows the pain of my resisting,
is always filled with the smells
of beds, of kitchen,
of my women
who come and go
with dreams in their hair.
This house calls me
and follows my every move
that drips
on the word.
And here, in the house suspended
on the winds and the sea,
the word enlarges each creature
and grows, unravels itself,
remakes itself with me.
I am that house as long as I live.

Il pane

da *Ogni giorno da capo*

II pane sulla tavola
mi ricorda la faccia di mio padre,
quel suo colore di grano,
quella grinzosa ruvida crosta
da fatica segnata.

Quando prendo quel pane
ricordo la croce che vi segnava mio padre
prima di spartirlo ai figli a tavola.

Quando tocco quel pane
mio padre diventa figlio,
lo benedico, lo bacio.
Nutrendomi del pane, nuovamente
mio padre è padre.

The Bread

from *Every Day from Scratch*

The bread on the table
reminds me of my father's face,
with its color of wheat,
that wrinkled rough crust
marked by tiredness.

When I handle that bread
I recall the sign of the cross my father made
before passing it around the table to his sons.

When I take that bread
my father becomes my son,
I bless him, I kiss him.
Eating the bread, my father
is father again.

Paesaggio interno

da Le rose il marcio il sangue

Irritante paesaggio interno
dell'uomo che spegne
il televisore:
disgregazione è il minimo.
Troppi segnali incerti,
notizie vaghe, sintomi
dispersi, segni
di un tempo deluso.
Le vendette sono improbabili.
Manca il coraggio
di piantare un fiore
sull'arida landa devastata
da frasi indecifrabili
sottintesi, mezze-parole
i venti del nostro tempo
deluso.
Né ci garantisce la sicurezza
il gregge che siamo
di reciproci sconosciuti.
Non c'è coraggio che vinca
il destino di vivere.

Inner Landscape

from *Roses Rot Blood*

Irking inner landscape
of the man who turns off
the television:
disintegration at the very least.
Too many unsure signals,
vague news, diffused
symptoms, signs
of a deluded time.
Improbable revenges.
Absent the courage
to plant a flower
on the desolate land destroyed
by incomprehensible phrases
misunderstandings, half-words
the winds of our deluded
time.
Nor is safety a guarantee
to the herd that we are
composed of reciprocal strangers.
There is no courage that conquers
the destiny of living.

Sulla strada, la vita bambini e vecchi

Leggeri come farfalle, hanno stelle negli occhi
e il volo nelle mani.
Sono bambine e bambini che passano
rapidi e avventurosi
accanto a donne e uomini lenti.
Ma sono sempre gli stessi uomini, le stesse donne:
quelli di ieri, nei giorni splendenti,
questi, il loro domani.

Bello scoprire nel vecchio il ricordo di un fiore,
saggio scoprire nel bimbo una ruga, segno di dolore.
Al passo del tempo, non dei passi loro,
li accompagna l'armonia della futura morte.
I bambini non ci pensano ed hanno gli occhi d'oro,
i vecchi lo sanno ed hanno il cuore forte.

On the Road, Life, Children, and Old People

Light as butterflies, they have stars in their eyes
and flight in their hands.
They're girls and boys who pass by
quickly and full of adventure
next to slow women and men.
But they are always the same men, the same women:
those of yesterday, in days full of light,
and these, their tomorrow.

In the old it's lovely to discover the memory of a flower,
wise to discover a wrinkle on a child's face, the sign of grief.
To the footsteps of time, not to their footsteps,
the harmony of future death accompanies them.
The children don't think about it and have golden eyes,
the old know it and have a strong heart.

→ *Mario Schiavato (b. 1931)*

In 1943, Mario Schiavato moved with his family from Quinto di Treviso, where he was born, to Vodnjan/Dignano d'Istria (Croatia). He is one of the most significant and original voices in Italian from this region. In 1948 he moved again to Rijeka/Fiume to work for the publisher EDIT. In his voluminous literary production, Schiavato dedicates all his intellectual resources to his major interests—Istria and Dignano, and his love for mountains. He has traveled widely and, in his diaries and works of prose, he records his experiences and adventures as a mountain climber in Africa, in the Himalayas, in Argentina, and in Ecuador. His narratives also focus on the plight of the peasants and the history of the Istrian peninsula. He has written for the theater and dedicated some of his time to writing for children.

It is only since the 1980s that Schiavato turned to writing poetry, and he has compiled diverse collections in which he seeks solace from daily disillusionment. Some of the titles of his vast production include *Istrian Poems* (*Poesie istriane*, 1993), *Time's Voracity* (*La voracità del tempo*, 1997) and *A Different Country* (*Un paese diverso*, 2003). Some of these poems are dedicated to Schiavato's pilgrimages as explorer and mountain climber. In this activity Schiavato celebrates a refulgent and pristine nature. However, he realizes that the problems of daily existence never abandon him, not even in the most secluded and distant places of the world. His travels are thus dotted with an appearance of penitence and a mystical searching for the self. Whatever the destination of his travels, be they exotic or alpine lands or the Istrian peninsula, the goal for Schiavato is the same, the investigation of an existential condition. Schiavato never insists on his inner and personal life, referring to it only fleetingly: his main objective is the descriptions of the countrysides, places, and lands that he visits.

Schiavato's more recent works, *Time's Voracity* or *Vague Bewilderment* (*Indefiniti smarrimenti*, 2000), reveal a more pessimistic vein. Unlike the earlier lyrics, composed of idyllic verses celebrating his love for mountains and dales, his more recent poetry has grown dark as uneasiness, concern, and doubt begin to surface. The natural rhythms of the seasons have been replaced by artificial ones, by the cycles of an industrial and electronic society that have given rise to a time that is truly "voracious." Its passing destroys everything, devours people and things. Schiavato's attitude, which has further narrowed the gap between writing and living, is ruled by the awareness of his own powerlessness. His most recent production is dominated by the drama of chaos and of change. Ever more disillusioned and embittered, Schiavato focuses on the theme of death, his own and that of a civilization, the rural and peasant one, that he cares about the most. Schiavato's poetry, however, remains sober and controlled.

The motto "I write, therefore I am" can help capture the spirit of Schiavato's intention in his writings as well as those of many other writers of the Istrian area. It is not just a question of translating into words one's inner world, of capturing in artistic and literary terms a given message. The question is to affirm one's own identity and the persistence of entire cultural communities, to ensure the memory and the survival of the values of people and of the lands they inhabit.

Carso

da *La voracità del tempo*

Non c'è il sole
eppure lo respiro
e lo sento appiattirsi e covare
su queste pietre bianche
dove il sudore
ha il sale di secoli.
Nessuno riuscirà a cancellare
le nostre impronte giganti
anche se ormai siamo ombre
rintanate negli antichi covi.
Lo sciacquio del mare
ha dolcezza di lacrime.
Poter essere gabbiano
per raccogliere la luce
che conforta gli orizzonti.

Carso

from *The Voracity of Time*

There is no sun
yet I breathe it
and I hear it flatten out and nest
on these white stones
where the sweat
wears the salt of centuries.
No one will be able to cancel
our giant footprints
even though we are only shadows
nestled in ancient dens.
The surf of the sea
has the sweetness of tears.
Oh to become a seagull
so as to catch the light
that comforts the horizons.

Estate

Rotea la pupilla del sole
sopra i maggesi combusti:
nella vampa i tralci
sono ali ferite
e il frinire delle cicale
acuto tormento.
Nel vuoto dell'orizzonte torrido
un asino impastoiato raglia
rassegnata disperazione.
Eppure la pace s'allarga
mentre giaccio supino,
le braccia spalancate,
nell'ombra raccolta del tiglio:
ho ritrovato gli odori buoni
della selvatica innocenza
e volo alto
come allodola ebbra di luce.

Summer

The pupil of the sun turns
above the burning fallow lands:
in the fire the vine shoots
are wounded wings
and the buzzing of the cicadas
is a sharp torment.
In the void of the torrid horizon
a tethered donkey brays
in resigned desperation.
However, the peace spreads out
as I lie spread out
with splayed arms
in the gathering shade of the lime tree:
I have rediscovered the clean aromas
of wild innocence
and I fly high
as the skylark drunk with light.

Odore di salvia

da *Un paese diverso*

Odore di salvia, di mirto e ginepro
porta il vento che passa, asciutto.
Lo stridere delle cicale è fermo
come la luce accecante
che fa spietati i colori dell'estate:
mi assale il ricordo delle fughe
verso il mondo regale delle onde,
i seni selvatici e misteriosi
delle calette nascoste dai fichi,
i prati turchesi dei fondali
dove i raggi del sole
si spezzavano come lame.
In quell'orizzonte c'era
tutto quello che ho perduto,
ieri figlio di re, oggi soltanto
mendicante a porte straniere.
Potessi avere una conchiglia,
accostarla all'orecchio e fingere
che il mormorio del suo vuoto
sia il discorso di quel mare
dove portavamo a lavare le pecore:
io e Biagio. Tutti e due figli di re.
Con castelli di nuvole bianche
che si spandevano nel cielo.

The Smell of Sage

from *A Different Place*

The smell of sage, myrtle, and juniper
carried by the dry passing wind.
The screeching of the cicadas has stopped
as the blinding light
given off by the colors of summer:
I am overcome by the thoughts of flights
toward the regal world of the waves,
The wild and mysterious breasts
of trellises hidden by figs,
The turquoise fields of the sea bottom
where the sun's rays
are shattered like blades.
In that horizon were
all the things I have lost,
yesterday as a king's son, today
only begging at strangers' doors.
Could I possess a seashell,
draw it to my ear and make believe
that the sound of its emptiness
was the chatter of that sea
where we took the sheep to be washed:
Biagio and I. Both sons of a king.
With castles of white clouds
spreading out in the sky.

Due di noi

da *Zaino in spalla*

Due di noi, diversi:
l'uno crine, denti di lupo
e cuore tenero come d'agnello,
l'altro sorriso dolce
di putto d'altare.
La grande città
non li ha tarati.
Sono arrivati in terra kirghisa
con pieni gli occhi
di Grigne incantate
e il cuore colmo
di aria paesana, pulita.
Si sono disfatti di tutto
per fare amicizie che certo
domani non conteranno.
Dovevo imparare
la loro umiltà.

Two of Us

from *Pack on Shoulders*

Two of us, different:
one with wild hair, a wolf's teeth
and the soft heart of a lamb,
the other with a smile sweet
as a choir boy's.
The big city
didn't corrupt them.
They arrived in Kirghizia
with eyes filled
by enchanted fairies
and hearts overflowing
with clean country air.
They let everything go
to make friends that surely
won't matter tomorrow.
I needed to learn
their humility.

Indugiano i passi

da *Questa terra era*

Indugiano i passi
accanto ai pruni dai frutti asprigni
dove un dì mi fermai
a saziare la fame:
nell'abbaglio del meriggio,
inseguivo ramarri di velluto
lungo le masiere
fatte di ossa grige
e gridavo con le rondini
della chiesa sulla collina
lo sgomento di sapermi uomo.
Potessi così inseguire
e gridare ancora
gli affanni maturi
nel baluginare estatico
del sole al tramonto.

Steps That Hesitate

from This Land Was

Steps that hesitate
wear the prune trees with bitter fruits
where I stopped one day
to satisfy my hunger:
in the glaring afternoon
I chased velvety lizards
along the fences
made of gray bones
and screamed with the swallows
by the church on the hill
the discontent of being a man.
Could I still chase like then
and yell out again
my grown-up worries
in the ecstatic flickering
of the setting sun.

La terra trasuda

da *Ribellioni e abbandoni*

La terra trasuda
rugiada sul trifoglio,
una civetta piange
sopra la casa vuota
senza cune che dondolano
senza braci che scoppiano.
Eppure mio padre ride
dalla cornice rotta
e mia madre ha gli occhi
dolci di sempre.
Ascolto stordito
il tempo che passa
e infilo ricordi
sul refe già corto.

The Land Sweats

from *Rebellions and Retreats*

The land sweats
dew on the clover,
an owl cries
above the empty house
without swaying cribs
without smacking kisses.
Still my father laughs
from the broken picture frame
and my mother shows
her everlasting sweet eyes.
Stunned I listen
to time passing
and weave memories
on the already short thread.

→ Ester Sardoz Barlessi (b. 1936)

Ester Sardoz Barlessi was born in 1936 in Pula/Pola (Croatia). She is faithful to the historical events of that city, whose local language she uses,
alternating it with Italian in her prose as well as in her poetry. Her first
publication was a series of poems in the dialect of Pola, which appeared
in *La Voce del Popolo* in 1984. With her very first publications, the author
put her pen at the service of her native community to keep alive its traditions, to narrate its unhappy history, and to keep alive in the citizens
of Pola the memory of their complex roots. In her many works in prose
and in verse, such as *E in mezzo un fiume* (*And Between a River*, 1997),
Paure e speranze (*Fears and Hopes*, 1987), *Viaggio su una nuvola* (*Voyage on
a Cloud*, 1988), *Così di sera* (*Thus in the Evening*, 1989), and *Fra l'anima e
la storia* (*Between the Soul and History*, 1999), Barlessi revisits the past and
reviews the present in order to reconstruct a world while keeping the level
of poetic discourse high. Her poetry privileges melancholy and the sentiment of suffering as she recomposes the Istrians' difficult struggle for survival, a foundational struggle for a civilization she views as cordial,
humane, and honest.

Barlessi adheres to dialect for its malleable and elastic qualities and for
its utility as an instrument having the same dignity as the national language. In her lyrical dialect poetry, she conserves the memory of a human
reality where tears and blandishments, errors and regrets blend through
necessary human communion. In clear and firm verses, Barlessi treats
themes such as friendship and the memories of youth.

The main topic of many poems is the sad moment of the exodus of the
Italian population from Istria, which was particularly heavy after the end
of World War II. In these verses from *Gente istriana* (*Istrian People*), Barlessi captures the drama of Italian families at a time when a decision had
to be made about their destiny: "Per orgolio, per la lingua / o per ideal /
chi se ga trovà de qua / e chi de là de la baricada / ma tuti ga a le spale /

una famiglia sbregada" (For pride, for the language / or for ideals / some found themselves here / others over the other side of the barricade / but everyone has behind / a broken-up family). In their simplicity, these verses transmit all the tragedy experienced by the Italian community in those decisive days and pass on the trauma that left many wounds still open. In spite of the trials that life puts people through, the road must be followed to the end since "tuto dura un momento / po cala l'ombra" (all lasts but a moment / then the shadow descends). The poet turns then to the future, "Ogi me go infasado el colo / per no' voltarme indrio" (Today I drew in my neck / to avoid turning back), lines that also confirm that in dialect there is an immediate expressiveness that Italian may not have. Dialect is the language of the depths with strong evocative and imaginative powers that inspire in writers and in readers a wide sphere of associations. For Barlessi, dialect has evocative and imaginative powers, is a sweet and musical language with a rich flow of rhymes and rhythms, and represents art that both acknowledges cultural specificity and breaks with tradition.

In her lyrical production, Barlessi treats also the landscape of the Istrian peninsula, drawn with the ability of an impressionist painter, into which she pours all her anxieties and suffering, finding energy and strength therein. In these poems prevail the adjectives that capture the specificity of the Istrian universe, its splendid seascapes, and the atmosphere of its fields. The Istria that Barlessi describes is not a mythical and idyllic place; it is rather the representation of a real world that has maintained its Arcadian beauty, its pristine aspects, because it is still free of the consumer society that cheapens all things. The nature that lives in these poems is impervious to the actions of humanity; nothing can change the authentic face of a land whose very nature conditions the character and customs of its inhabitants.

Tra anni

da *Viaggio su una nuvola*

Tra anni, quando
i figli dei nostri figli
studieranno di quel tragico
maggio russo,
ancora serpeggerà tra le radici
veleno di morte
e ancora spunteranno
nei campi e negli ospedali
i fiori di Cernobyl
e si intrecceranno ghirlande
dall'amaro profumo
per ornare la lapide
del mondo nucleare.

Years Hence

from *Voyage on a Cloud*

Years hence when
the children of our children
study that tragic
Russian May, still
among the roots
there will snake
poison of death
and the flowers of Chernobyl
will bloom in
the fields and hospitals
and garlands will intertwine
with bitter scent
to decorate the tombstone
of the nuclear world.

Terra mia

Nell'ansia di amare
questa mia tormentata terra
ho scordato i suoi conflitti,
gli odi, le lotte,
paga solo di respirare
il suo sudore,
la sua zolla rossa
dissodata con fatica
e l'odor di timo e di mentuccia
che timidi s'affaccian
tra le pietre
che quivi abbondan
come altrove il grano.

My Land

In the angst of loving
this, my tortured earth,
I've forgotten its
wars, battles, hates—
at peace only breathing
its sweat, its red
clods of earth,
plowed with fatigue,
and the aromas of
thyme and mint that rise
in their timidity
among the stones
rife here
like the grain
everywhere else.

Sera a Verudela

da *Per molti versi*

Co el sol se tocia
in mar
a Punta Verudela
e a l'orizonte sbrissa
una vela bianca
in alto, sora i pini,
pigra passa
la caressa del vento.
Sona alora un'orchestra
de strani strumenti:
taca i grili
le graie rispondi.
Canta l'aqua che sbati
sui sassi
con sento rumori
che nassi
che mori
rinassi più forti de prima
e de novo i mori in sordina
sul stanco bordesar
de vece batanele.
Sui pini, le grote
e le grespe del'onda
passa legero un brivido
che par voler fermar el tempo.

Evening in Verudella

from *In Many a Verse*

When the sun sets in the sea
at Verudella Point
and across the horizon a white sail sluices up over the pines, lazy,
    the caress of wind passes.
Then an orchestra of
strange instruments plays.
The crickets resound,
the bushes re-echo,
the water sings by
striking the rocks
with choirs of noises
that are born,
that die,
to be born again
stronger than ever,
then die again mute
under the weary tacking
of the old dinghy.

Above the pines, the grottoes
and the crests of waves
a slight shudder passes
as if it wants to stop time . . .

Tuto dura un momento
po' cala l'ombra
e l'aria vien violeta
in un colpo de man
e se impissa una lanterna.
Lontan.

Sera a Verudella—Quando il sole tramonta / in mare / a Punta Verudella / e all'orizzonte
scivola / una vela bianca / in alto sopra i pini / pigra passa / la carezza del vento. / Suona allora
un'orchestra / di strani strumenti: / attaccano i grilli / i cespugli rispondono. / Canta l'acqua
che sbatte / sui sassi / con cento rumori / che nascono / che muoiono / rinascono più forti di
prima / e di nuovo muoiono in sordina / sullo stanco bordeggiare / delle vecchie battane. / Sui
pini, le grotte / e le crespe dell'onda / passa leggero un brivido / che sembra voler fermare il
tempo. / Tutto dura un istante / poi cala l'ombra / e l'aria diventa violetta / d'improvviso / e si
accende una lanterna. / Lontano.

All lasts an instant,
then the shadows drop
and suddenly the air
goes violet, lit
like a far-off lantern.

L'odor dela tera

A la matina co' se alsa
el sol
nissuna tera al mondo
no' ga l'odor dela mia tera
bagnada dela piova
de la note.
Xe un odor
dolse e palpabile
che te va su pel naso
e par che el te imbriaghi
come el mosto de novembre
co' opaco el boi
in te le bote
stivade in te le cantine.

Xe l'odor de la cuna
De la radise dei moreri
e dei olivi.
Xe l'odor de l'Istria.

L'odore della terra—Al mattino quando si alza / il sole / nessuna terra al mondo / ha l'odore della mia terra / bagnata dalla pioggia / della notte. / È un odore / dolce e palpabile / che va su per il naso / e sembra ubriacarti / come il mosto novembrino / che opaco ribolle / nei tini / allineati nelle cantine. / È l'odore della culla. / Delle radici dei gelsi / e degli ulivi. / È l'odore dell'Istria.

Smell of Earth

Mornings when the sun
rises
no land on earth
smells like mine,
so bathed by the rains
of night.
It's a smell so
sweet and palpable
that it rises through the nose as if making you drunk
like November ferment
that in the dark of vats
ages row by row.
That smell is like the cradle's,
the mulberry's and the olive trees'.
The smell of Istria.

Voio vardar in avanti

Ogi me go infassado el colo
per no' voltarme indrio
perché no' voio veder
la mia ombra per tera
né quel che iero . . .
Voio veder bianchi ricami
su le rame del mandoler
e del serieser fioridi
e sentir
su l'onda del vento
un scampanelar de argento
e el rider dei fioi
sul sitolo.
Ogi voio vardar in avanti.

Voglio guardare in avanti—Oggi ho infossato il collo / per non voltarmi / e non vedere / la mia ombra per terra / né quello che ero . . . / Voglio vedere bianchi ricami / sui rami del mandorlo / e del ciliegio in fiore / e sentire / sull'onda del vento / uno scampanellio d'argento / e le risate dei bambini / sull'altalena. / Oggi voglio guardare in avanti.

I Want to Look Ahead

Today I sunk my neck
so as not to turn around,
not see my shadow on the ground
or what I was . . .
I want to see white
lace patterns on
the branches of almond
and cherry trees in bloom
and feel on waves of wind
a tinkling of silver and
the laughter of children
on their seesaw rides.
Today I want
to look ahead.

→ Vlada Acquavita (1947–2009)

Not at all circumscribed by the local, regional culture, Vlada Acquavita's poetry has surfaced suddenly and with authority in the poetic microcosm of the Istrian peninsula. She occupies a relevant position in the contemporary literature of the Italian national community. She was born in Koper/Capodistria (Slovenia), but has always lived and worked in Buje/Buie d'Istria, Croatia. Among the cities that occupy a significant place in her experience are Zagreb/Zagabria in Croatia, where she earned her university degree in French language and literature, and Trieste, where she attended the Advanced School of Modern Languages for Translators and Interpreters. Vlada Acquavita has invested a great deal of time and dedication to her cultural education, being an avid reader and a careful researcher, activities that stimulated her travels to France and Italy and allowed her to visit several historical libraries such as the Laurenziana, the Vatican, and the Marciana, where she deepened her understanding of the medieval world that feeds her poetry. Working primarily in isolation and keeping her distance from local literary circles, Vlada Acquavita set out on a course of self-discovery, an undertaking that has taken her on a journey in search of herself and the magical dimensions of the Istrian terrain. The first stage of this journey is in the collection *La rosa selvaggia e altri canti eleusini* (*The Wild Rose and Other Elysian Songs*, 1997). As Acquavita explains in an interview with Luciano Dobrilovic, "The book is the fruit of a process of individuation, of the search for the self according to Jung's definition, an inner journey that I call 'psicosofia' to distinguish it from the narrow meaning of psychoanalysis." *Psicosofia*, Vlada explains further, is not a doctrine. Rather, it is a demanding literary undertaking of inner renewal that recreates harmony between the soul and wisdom.

In this first collection, the poetic discourse is grounded in a balance of myth, ritual, language, and countryside. However, the use of myth in

Acquavita is not a sign of the postmodern or a symptom of calligraphic writing. Myth, acquired through Pavese's mediation, is pure poetic language, an alternative language replacing rational discourse, a total metaphor through which it is possible to express amazement before the magic of nature, which represents the root of Acquavita's poetry. Through this amazement, the poet frees herself of the usual, habitual modes of perception in order to enter a dimension that allows her to withdraw from the horizontal flow of time and history, and to then open up to the vertical dimension of time in which Ingeborg Bachmann and Emily Dickinson had already seen the possibility of poetry. In the poems of this first collection, divided into seven sections, the landscape of the soul blends perfectly with the geographic one, the Istrian landscape that is part of the poet.

Vlada's private temple is a space in the shade of an ancient oak tree, at the top of a hill. From that secluded spot begins Acquavita's journey of contemplating nature in order to discover signs of the divine. To reach the top of the hill one must follow a pathway. On the sides of the paths grow the thorny bushes of the wild rose. This collection of poems ends with the composition *Il congedo* (*The Departure*). Pagan thought takes its leave from the wild rose, related to the mystical rose of the Middle Ages.

Acquavita's poetic discourse grows in the next work, *Herbarium mysticum. Clausole medievali* (*Herbarium Mysticum: Medieval Clauses*, 2000). For this collection, Acquavita received a prize from Istria Nobilissima. Because of its frequent references to the Middle Ages, an epoch of blood and of roses, *Herbarium mysticum* is replete with refinements, cultural and literary, and a bit elitist, requiring a careful reader accustomed to meditation. Acquavita's poetry aims at a personal interpretation of the world and defies gossip and hearsay. Her drive for introspection has as its objective the discovery of the fundamental values of being and of life. She fulfills her aim in solitude, bent over those fascinating medieval herb books, anonymous and eternal, in which she discovers feeble streaks of poetry that she approaches with a nearly religious sense, searching out the word that can save—a cathartic, noble expression.

In an age of diminishing religiosity, the poet cultivates a poetry that is an itinerary toward a complete, total meaning of life, which brings one back to the great experiences of philosophy and religion. A frequenter of museums and exhibits, an explorer of herbal lore and bestiaries, an admirer of tapestries and a solitary visitor of the ancient towns and castles of Istria, Acquavita suggests a daring hypothesis: the poetic conception of the world is akin to scientific or philosophical visions of existence. Her refined poetry is studded with narrative inserts, notes and commentaries useful for the understanding of a past so different from the contemporary world.

Acquavita's creative world is inhabited primarily by female beings, nuns and oblates who, in the tradition of the troubadours, offer ecstatic words of love to the Highest as though to a lover. In her Istrian fantasies, Acquavita brings back to life the great medieval mystics, Saint Catherine of Siena and Saint Theresa of Avila; in Istrian mode the *lais* of Marie de France come to life again, placed in a setting of ruined castles abandoned in the Istrian landscape that inspire the imagination of the poet. An expert in French culture and literature, and well acquainted with writers such as Claudel, Péguy, Mallarmé, Bernanos, Gide, and Valéry, Acquavita naturally finds references in the medieval Provençal lyrical tradition and the courtly love tradition that surface in her own texts.

The heart of her lyrics reveals an ethical conception based on love of Wisdom, which one obtains after a long and gradual voyage into the self, undertaken with humility. Of a reserved character, unwilling to make public appearances, the poet lives in a symbiotic relationship with poetry. Her ideal is a poetry founded on contemplation and a search for truth, a poetry in which the invisible becomes visible, where the idea becomes an image. The lines "L'invisible non ama il clamore, / diffida dall'imitazione" (The invisible does not appreciate noise, / does not trust imitation), from "La visita," may be taken as an expression of her poetic ideal.

La rosa di Sant'Eliseo

da *Herbarium mysticum. Clausole medievali*

INCIPIT

Là—all'ombra della chiesa di Sant'Eliseo—
    in un'aureola di vigneti
        è la mia casa (4 passi per 8).
Fra le silenziose pareti
    l'umile giaciglio
        lo *scanno nero e scabro*
           un asse per scrittoio—
    la pergamena alla finestra.
Nella cassapanca
    il vestito di panno vermiglio
        un fermaglio
    quattro anelli di stagno
    il velo
        una borsa di coniglio.
Imbevuta di amarezza
        contemplo le vigne
    recito le Ore
        copio i versi leonini—
maledico il mio esilio.
Sulla via lastricata
    —alla prima e al vespro—
        lo zoccolìo dell'asino
           il passo del contadino
    —a tratti—
        il belato delle greggi
           il grugnito dei maiali spazzini.
Nel viluppo della notte—
        il mattutino e le laudi.
Parca la mia mensa—
    minestra di lardo
        (aringhe e fichi nei giorni di magro)

The Rose of Saint Eliseo

from *Herbarium Mysticum: Medieval Clauses*

INCIPIT

There—under the shadow of the church of Saint Eliseo—
in a halo of vineyards
is my house (4 steps by 8).
Among the silent walls
the humble bunk
the *black and rough stool*
a board for a desk—
the parchment at the window.
In the seat
the suit of vermilion cloth
a clasp
four tin rings
the veil
a rabbit bag.
Saturated with bitterness
I contemplate the vineyards
I recite the Book of Hours
I copy the leonine verses—
I curse my exile.
On the paved road
—early and at evening
the donkey's hoof
the peasant's step
every now and then—
the bleating of the herds
the grunt of the scavenging pig
In the tangle of night—
Matins and the Lauds.
My meal is frugal
lard soup
herrings and figs in lean days)

Vlada Acquavita   647

pane
fresca acqua.
Tra le vigne
—dimentica delle proprie radici—
una rosa avvizzita.

bread
        fresh water
             Among the vineyards
             —forgetting its own roots—
             a withered rose.

Frammenti del codice gigliato

Con dolcezza soavissima
mi abbandono alla tua pen(n)a.
Non sei solo.
Come immagine rimandata dallo specchio
che nulla di sé
e tutto dall'essere in cui è
(diventando sua immagine)
riceve,
      anch'io (anima nuda)
      legata sono a te.

Fragments of the Lilied Codex

AD CHARTARIUM
With the most delicate sweetness
I give in to your pain (pen).
You aren't alone.
Like an image sent back from the mirror
that receives nothing of itself
and all from the being in which it is
(becoming its image),
    I'm also (naked heart)
    tied to you.

La visita

da *La rosa selvaggia e altri canti eleusini*

La mia camera
è una stanza quasi spoglia—
un tavolo, una sedia, un letto,
qualche libro appena.

Eppure il divino
—fra tutte le stanze riccamente addobbate
piene di tavole imbandite e di festosi inviti—
per la sua breve visita terrena
ha scelto la mia.

L'invisibile non ama il clamore,
diffida dall'imitazione.

Forse ha visto la mia anima nuda,
ha udito il battito di un cuore puro.

Io sono la dormiente.

I pochi versi
che qui offro
di conforto possano essere—
a molti.

The Visit

from *The Wild Rose and Other Eleusinian Songs*

My room
is a room almost bare—a
table, chair, a bed,
scarcely some books.

And yet the divine
—among all the rooms richly decorated
full of lavish tables and festive invitations—
has chosen mine
for its short earthly visit.

The invisible doesn't love uproar,
distrusts imitation.

Perhaps it has seen my naked soul,
has heard the beat of a pure heart.

I am the sleeper.

The few verses
that I offer here
may be of comfort—
to many.

Melancholía

Conosco l'arte che sa trasformare
la cupa malinconia
in una gioia quasi perfetta.

Quando la bile tinge di nero l'incauto pensiero,
silenzioso l'istinto mi prende per mano e
—via via dall'afflizione e dal pianto—
lungo il sentiero dei cervi
mi conduce alla luminosa radura
dove rigoglioso cresce l'elleboro.

Con i fiori della pianta che purga la bile
intreccio una delicata corona—
la poso sul triste capo reclino.

Ed ecco—magia bizzarra—
si dissolve la nera malinconia
e riappare il sole d'oro.

Gaio nasce il sorriso
quando nel buio sprofonda il dolore.

Melancholy

I know the art that knows how to transform
the dismal melancholy
into an almost perfect joy.

When bile blackens the careless thought,
instinct silently takes me by the hand and
away from torments and tears—
along the deer's path
leads me to the luminous clearing
where lushly grows the buttercup.

With the plant's flowers that purge the bile
I weave a delicate crown—
I place it on a sad bowed head.

And there—bizarre magic—
the black melancholy dissolves
and the golden sun reappears.

A joyful smile is born
while in the dark the pain sinks.

Mitopoiesi

Ho giocato con la luce
e con le tenebre.

Sulla mia pelle ho sentito
il vento gelido dell'Ade—
la Bellezza rarefatta delle praterie divine
mi è amica.

Ho lottato con la mia ombra
e nell'istante in cui mi sono arresa
—sconfitta—ho vinto.

A lungo ho cercato la misura.

Ora l'universo è dentro di me.
Mito vivente—
POESIA.

Mythopoeia

I played with the light
and with the darkness.

On my skin I felt
the frozen wind of Hades—
the rarefied beauty of the divine meadowlands
is my friend.

I struggled with my shadow
and in the instant in which I surrendered
—defeated—I won.

At last I found the beat.

Now the universe is inside of me.
Living myth
—POETRY.

⇢ Adelia Biasiol (1950–2000)

Born in Vodnjan/Dignano d'Istria (Croatia), Adelia Biasiol devoted her-self to poetry at a very young age. Her earliest works were published in 1968 in the slender volume *Primi voli* (*First Flights*). She was singled out for the first time in 1972 through the art and culture competition Istria Nobilissima, from which she subsequently obtained prizes and honorable mentions. Year after year her poems, which experience had rendered more mature and more intense, were published at regular intervals also beyond the confines of Istria and were translated into Slovene, Croatian, Macedonian, and Serbian in various journals, drawing attention for their maturity, for the earnestness that led the author to accept the responsibil-ities of the poet, for her new poetic language, and for the readiness and courage with which she dealt with themes still considered taboo, related in particular to the feminine world.

Biasiol's most intense creative period was 1970 to 1980, a time in which she engaged herself in a fruitful formal search through a process of lin-guistic refinement. During this decade, her content also broadened to accommodate newer and more mature experiences. Love and life themes, which were present since her earliest adolescent experiences, and social topics accrued, as well as an increased sensibility for the great and small things of this world. In the poems of Biasiol one finds the life and works of men and women—women especially—who climb the slopes of life alongside us, the women of the world of Istria, which becomes a metaphor for the rest of the world. Biasiol thus puts herself in the geographic and social frame of the land dearest to her, the Istria of fishermen, workers, peasants, and, above all, mothers. Anchored in this picture, Biasiol's poetic discourse proceeds gradually from external observations to reflec-tions about what joins us to the earth, to life, to other humans, and about what lies within and beyond life, within ourselves and others. Her dis-course is focused completely on eternal, existential worries. Sensitive and delicate, not always happy to be alive, yet clutched to life like ivy, Biasiol engages the reader at times with warmth and humanity, at other times in a bitter tone as she reveals hidden passions. Biasiol's expressive language is modern. She is meditative and firmly grounded in the reality and suffering of people, a poet who pours into her poems the gentleness and fullness of feelings.

Looking at the whole of her poetry, it is clear that Biasiol's work goes beyond initial inspiration, and that her concept of poetry is that of a means to allow both personal sentiment and collective experience to have a voice. When her poetry came into being during the early 1970s, it appeared from the start mature, different, new, even daring, and it was held as a turning point in the still brief and dense history of Italian literature in the Istrian area. Biasiol's poetry stood out because of its form and content at a time when women's literature still lacked a certain freedom of expression. Biasiol is a being of intimate feelings, anxieties and dismay, which she expresses with surprising sincerity. Hers are principally love poems in which, with a diffused sensuality and in a fluid and harmonious language, the poet declares a burning desire to give, even when that includes giving her own self. She conceives love as a moment of life magically suspended, in which the exclusively feminine psychological and sentimental dimensions find satisfaction. The joy, for instance, of becoming a mother finds expression as a very strong and intense union with creation, with the water, the earth, the sky. To have a child means to give oneself a future, to touch with one's own fingers the possibility of living forever. A child, something living and earthly, is a being to rock on the waves, to raise under the blue sky and atop the red terrain of Istria, but it is especially a supreme gift of love, as she shows in *Infinito vivere/Infinite Living*.

Shy by nature, Biasiol lived her short life intentionally secluded, "behind the gray armor / of a suit / the thread of corals the only color" ("Donna in tailleur" [Woman in a Suit]). Adelia Biasiol never blasted out the words of her poetic discourse. On the contrary, hers can be considered a subdued voice, as the title of her posthumous collection, containing all her works, quite clearly attests: *Una voce sommessa* (*A Subdued Voice*, 2004).

A mio padre

da *Una voce sommessa*

Noi che abbiamo conosciuta la terra
siamo nati secoli fa
dentro al passo dell'uomo.

Noi che siamo cresciuti accanto alla fatica
degli uomini e dei buoi e l'abbiamo vista
premere incidere urgere sollevare

ci muoviamo dovunque in continuo
come se fosse terra tirato dorso
lucida perla.

To My Father

from *A Subdued Voice*

We who have known the earth
were born centuries ago
inside of man's step.

We who grew up near the hard work
of men and oxen and have seen it
pushing etching urging rising

we move everywhere continually
as if it were earth taut back
shiny pearl.

Infinito vivere

Quale gioia
avere un figlio.
Avrò un figlio
ripeto a me sola
che sola più non sono.
Sarà nostro amore
ed io lo donerò
alla culla dell'acque
e tu l'avvolgerai
al color mattone della terra
e il cielo
non più cielo sarà
ma infinito vivere.
Quale dono amore
per mai dimenticare
chi ci ha sorpresi
non più bambini.
Chi ci ha visti pur sempre
gocce
e granelli
nell'infinito vivere.

Infinite Life

What joy
having a son.
I will have a son
I repeat to myself alone
that alone I will no longer be.
He will be our love
and I will give him
to the cradle of water
and you will wrap him
in the brick color of the land
and the sky
will no longer be sky
but infinite life.
What a gift love
to never forget
who surprised us
no longer babies.
Who always has seen us
drops
and grains
in infinite life.

Tutto mi dice

Sopraggiunge il mare
a regalarmi il suo umore.
Tutto mi dice-lascia fare
il ragno che fila la sua tela
il culmo che porta alta la sua spiga
i mandorli che a marzo
son schiacciante brivido e bellezza.

Scorro in rivoli di resina
tra pensieri e linfa.

Il guizzo di uno scoiattolo divampa nell'aria
e l'incendia.
Come cenere si posa il mio tempo
Sull'altrui davanzale.

Everything Tells Me

The sea arrives
and gives me its mood.
Everything tells me—leave alone
the spider that spins its web
the stem that carries high its ear
the almonds that in March
are crushing shudder and beauty.

I pour in rivulets of resin
among thoughts and sap.

The dart of a squirrel flashes in the air
and sets it on fire.
Like ashes my time rests
on someone's windowsill.

Cuore di pesce

Il mio mondo è fatto
di strette calli
dove oltre feritoie
si allarga il respiro del mare.
Prima e poi solo cielo
prima e poi
è nell'azzurro che la mia pupilla
si vuole tuffare
mentre cespi di callio e vitalba
oltre i dorsi dell'asparago
stuzzicano l'occhio nel suo angolo.
Le percorro così queste calli
così come le formiche
e incurante cicala per i fuochi dell'estate
ardo mediterranea
nelle strettoie del ghetto.
Per questo sono cuore di pesce
che esplode nelle bocche dell'oceano.

Fish Heart

My world is made of narrow streets
where beyond embrasures
the breath of the sea expands.
Before and then only sky
before and then
it is in the blue that my pupil
wants to dive
while tufts of galium and calemis
beyond the backs of the asparagus
poke the eye in its corner.
This is how I cross these streets
like an ant
and indifferent cicada for the fires of summer
I burn Mediterranean
in the narrow passages of the ghetto.
This is why I am the fish heart
that explodes in the mouths of the ocean.

Mia madre

Mia madre
mi viene incontro
portando un gran fascio di fiori
e li porta
sfidando il tempo, la calura
la fretta dei passanti . . .
mia madre mi riporta sempre
ciò che la vita mi toglie
e sempre allo stesso modo
leggera, leggera,
mia madre
che è più forte di me
più saggia di me
mi riaccosta in silenzio
a quella vita
che lei stessa m'ha donato
e che io stessa stavo lì per lì
per buttare via.

My Mother

My mother
comes to meet me
carrying a big bundle of flowers
and brings them
defying time, the heat
the rush of passers-by . . .
my mother always brings me back
what life takes away from me
and always in the same way
lightly, lightly
my mother
who is stronger than me
wiser than me
reconciling me in silence
to that life
that she herself gave me
and that I myself came very close
to throwing away.

Notte a Dignano

Com'è in pace il mio paese
i grilli incrociano canti tra le case
e nelle stalle un assonnato chiocciar
tra sasso e trave
i mariti dormono accanto alle mogli
i figli davvero esistono
i vecchi ancora in quiete muoiono
è lontano il fragore dell'onda
di tanto in tanto un motore romba.
Nel cortile di casa mia
i passeri dormono sui rami del susino
l'edera s'avviluppa nel campo dei gerani vermigli
un tralcio di vite selvatica
tenta la luna e nascono lucciole
tra i ciuffi di parietaria e gramigna.
Per questo grande amore
che mi allenta il gomito
quando da donna vado per le vie del mondo
ho un cesto di bacche e piene serenate
da infilar tra sosta e cammino.

Night in Dignano

How peaceful is my town
the crickets' songs intersect among the houses
and in the stalls a sleepy clucking
between stone and beam
husbands sleep next to their wives
and children really exist
old folks still die in their sleep
the roar of the waves is distant
from time to time a motor rumbles by.
In the courtyard of my house
sparrows sleep on the branches of plum trees
ivy folds in the field of scarlet geraniums
a wild vine branch
tempts the moon and the fireflies are born
among the tufts of meadowland and weeds.
For this great love
that relaxes my elbow
when as a woman I go by the ways of the world
I have a basket of berries and full serenades
to thread among the stop and go.

→ Loredana Bogliun (b. 1955)

An old prejudice, still maintained by a few skeptics but completely rejected by experts, that considers dialect poetry inferior and provincial, secondary to poetry in the official Italian language, has been definitively reversed by the poems of Loredana Bogliun. Her works in the "istrioto" dialect have crossed the Italian border and found outstanding admirers such as Franco Loi and Andrea Zanzotto. She has also won praise from critics such as Franco Brevini, who included Bogliun among the poets in dialect of the twentieth century in his anthology *Le parole perdute. Dialetti e poesia nel nostro secolo* (*The Lost Words: Dialects and Poetry in Our Century*, 1990).

Loredana Bogliun was born in Pula/Pola (Croatia) in 1955. She earned a degree in psychology from the University of Ljubljana in Slovenia, where she also earned a PhD in social psychology. She now teaches sociology in the Department of Literature and Philosophy at the University of Pula/Pola.

Since her first publication in 1973, which appeared in the journal *La Battana*, she has been using, in addition to Italian, the dialect from Dignano, as her first collection of poems, *Dignano Poems* (1973), shows. Loredana Bogliun's use of dialect is different from that of some other dialect poets. For her, dialect is no longer the language of reality, but a vehicle that establishes a different rapport with reality and is capable of exploring the identity of the self, the many aspects of the world, and of memory. She does not pursue populist ideas or recreated settings. She aims for a metaphorical use of dialect that goes beyond the territorial. Her poetry cannot be simply labeled "dialect poetry," because it goes beyond the confines of local themes. The universal character of her poetry is due to the fact that dialect is cleared of its local, closed coordinates and is addressed to everyone. Bogliun's poetry does not just describe people and places of the dialect she uses; it goes beyond the local character and opens itself up to the world.

Loredana Bogliun is well represented in international journals. Her best known books are *Mazere/Gromače/Muri a secco* (*Dry Walls*, 1993); *La peicia/La piccola* (*The Little One*, 1996); and *Soun la poiana/Sulla poiana* (*About the Buzzard*, 2000). The first book is in a trilingual edition with an introduction by Tonko Maroević, an Italianist and art historian who translated the book into Croatian with Mate Maras. The second collection is an elegant edition with the drawings of Giorgio Celiberti, featuring a preface by Andrea Zanzotto and a note by Franco Loi. The most recent book was edited by Michelangelo Camilliti and presented by Franco Loi, who describes the verses as light, melodic, and sinuous like the rustling of leaves or a whisper, yet assertive, full of passion.

Bogliun is a careful observer of nature, the orphic suggestions of the trees and animals mixed with all the mute noises of the earth, the rustles, the silent human passions captured through personal stories and those of an entire town. Dignano is the mirror of pain, tears and also of childhood happiness. It is a voyage full of excitement from the past and a movement toward a maternal civilization. In her poetry, marked by the harsh and soft sounds of the language of Istria, is revealed the epiphany of the absolute, its silent prints disseminated all along dry walls, the pathways that run through the fields of Istria, its flower beds, its sea, its countryside. Bogliun has been able to capture these signs as presences that reveal life in a landscape that is the mirror of the soul.

The world of Dignano is at the center of Bogliun's poetry for both biological and poetic reasons. There is a necessary physical relationship between poetry and geography. The place of origin is a tableau of human forces, familiar and friendly, that sustain the poet with their vitality and love. The birthplace is the life cell of the poetic self in which the parental network is connected vertically and horizontally—a place where the original self sees itself reflected in the faces, the streets, the stones, and the air. But the town of origin is also the place where past and present merge. Its dialect is the connection with the mysterious lower world of the magic land of Istria. The idea of the birthplace supports Bogliun's poetic search for life in the origin of words themselves.

Given today's crises of local speech, it is legitimate to ask what might become of dialect poetry. Cesare Cases has written that "dialect is not an instrument for the regression to childhood or to express popular common places. Dialect is not a tool to stress regional distinctions which are always defeatist; nor should it be used to invent artificial cultural purity." What will resist the test of time, then, will be poetry, the poetry of those writers like Bogliun, who found in dialect the most apt instrument to express the universality and completeness of the world.

Deignan meio peicio

da *Soun la poiana*

Veive le ierte tien soun le piere ingroumade
de la tera, sigoure cumo la forsa del me curaio.

Douto me varda par ste contrade.
Deignan meio peicio sconto in tal simiteiro.

A ſi sigouro ouna fourbeissia drento
ch'a spita a mori inseina comandaghe al furesto.
Ma pour a visso valisto spalancà Santa Catareina.
In sta me contrada nissoun santo fa comedia.
Vudia me par anca l'anema co vidi al colmo in sfessa.

Sto piurà ch'a me salta fora
zi cumo vento ch'a me sparneissa
mei me ingroumi
i ſarè a respirà la louna
ch'a gila la me par de cumpaneia.

Dignano mio piccolo—Vivi gli stipiti tengono su le pietre raccolte / dalla terra, sicure come la forza del mio coraggio. / Tutto mi guarda per queste contrade. / Dignano mio piccolo nascosto nel cimitero. / C'è sicuramente una furbizia dentro / che attende di morire senza comandare al forestiero. / Eppure avrebbe valso spalancare Santa Caterina. / In questa mia contrada nessun santo si muove. / Vuota mi sembra anche l'anima quando vedo il tetto far fessure. / Questo pianto che mi salta fuori / e come vento che mi disperde / io mi raccolgo / andrò a respirare la luna / che lei mi sembra di compagnia.

Dignano My Little One

from *On the Plain*

Living transepts support the stones collected
from the earth, sure as the strength of my courage.
Everything watches me in these neighbourhoods.
Dignano my little one hidden in the graveyard.
There's surely an inner cunning
waiting to die without bossing around the stranger.
Still it would have been worth it to open up wide St. Catherine.
In my neighbourhood no saint moves about.
Even my soul seems empty when I see cracks in the roof.
This crying that pours out
is like a wind dispersing me.
I will gather myself again
so as to inhale the moon
that seems to promise good company.

Liſiera

I soin ſeida a navigà in tal acqua,
ſuta al mar vula ch'a longa ſi l'onda
me speci drento la paſ ch'a me favela.

In tal acqua cumo in tal aria
i vaghi a oci spalancadi, liſiera.

No ſi fadeiga, l'amur me mena.

Anca drento la louna
  al mar ſi liſiero e grando.

I ſarè a coucalo par la festa dei lumeini

  gnente da inguantà

  cumo squaiadi
  reido e se romena
  culuri de cultreina

tei cumo de oro cuntenteissa meia,
ciapite forto drento al ciaro

ch'a ſi in cultoura l'anema nostra ſogatolona.

Leggera—Sono andata a navigare nell'acqua, / sotto il mare dove lunga è l'onda / mi specchio dentro la pace che mi racconta. / Nell'acqua come nell'aria / vado a occhi spalancati, leggera. / Non è fatica, l'amore mi porta. / Anche dentro la luna / il mare è leggero e grande. / Andrò a sbirciarlo per la festa delle lucciole / niente da afferrare / come dissolti / ridono e scherzano / colori di coltrina / tu come d'oro felicità mia, / tieniti forte dentro al chiaro / che è in coltura l'anima nostra giocherellona.

Lightweight

I went to sail on the water,
beneath the sea where the wave is long
I mirror myself in the peace that tells of myself.

In water as in the air
I go lightly, with eyes wide open.

The love that moves me is not a burden.

Even inside of the moon
      the sea is light and large.

I will give it a peep at the feast of the lightning bugs

      when there's nothing to grab

      as the tints on a curtain
      laughing and playing
      completely dissolved

and you my happiness as if made of gold
hold on tightly to the light

since our playful soul is sprouting.

Vecio eistrian

da *La peicia*

Iè cugnusoudo in tra i monti
oun vecio ch'a iò la pele doura.
El iò ſuta i oci ouna reiga
ch'a par ouna fisoura,
el iò le man grande e la muier peicia.

In tai varti ghe criso l'aio—
ch'a douta piena la dresa peica—
El ghe reido a la miſeria grama
in tala so fursa al so castel de paia
pien de ouna fata ch'a sparagna al dano.
In tala so squara veivo al busco,
                    l'anemal ch'a raia
e seito, a peindulon, el se cumpagna a caſa.

Vecchio istriano—Ho conosciuto tra i monti / un vecchio dalla pelle dura. / Sotto gli occhi ha una riga / che sembra una fessura, / ha le mani grandi e la moglie piccola. / Negli orti gli cresce l'aglio / tutta piena la treccia pende / Ride alla povera miseria / nella sua forza il suo castello di paglia / pieno di una fata che risparmia il danno. / Nella sua dimensione vive il bosco, / l'animale che raglia / e silenzioso, pendolando, si accompagna a casa.

Old Man from Istria

from *The Little One*

In the mountains I got to know
an old man with tough skin.
Under his eyes there is a line
that looks like a fissure,
his hands are huge his wife is tiny.
Garlic grows in his fields
full rows entangled that dangle.
Laughing at his own poverty
his strength is a castle of straw
filled by a fairy that limits the loss.
On the spot is the forest,
a braying beast
that silently swaying takes him home.

La piera

in tala campagna
ſ'gionfa la piera
la speta
al so samer ch'a reiva
cu la recia ſgaia

mai sti oci iera ſbarlombadi,
gnanca in tra le piere de la stalita,
vula ch'a la bora pasa la caniſela
e l'anema scalda la magnadura
de sto anemal seito,
e cousei el reiva
da la stalita a la caſita
fato cumo par scoltà ste piere,
insembro par dase l'anda

ſi bela sta meia caſita
cu al samer la varda incantado.

La pietra—dentro alla campagna / gonfia la pietra / aspetta / il suo asino che sta arrivando / con l'orecchio attento / questi occhi mai sono stati assonnati, / neanche tra le pietre della stalletta, / dove la bora passa la stradina / e l'anima scalda la mangiatoia / di quest'animale silenzioso, / e così arriva dalla stalletta alla casetta di campagna / fatto per ascoltare queste pietre, / insieme per darsi portamento / è bella questa mia casetta di campagna / quando l'asino la guarda incantato.

The Stone

under the fields
the stone swells
waiting for
the donkey that's coming
with ears wide open

these eyes have never been sleepy,
not even inside the stones of the barn,
where the north wind blows by the side road
and the spirit warms the feeding troth
of this silent beast,
and so it moves from barn to farm house
born only to listen to stones,
to share the comings and goings

my farm house is so lovely
when the donkey admires it, enchanted.

Me paro la madona

Co le caſe se diſgourba a pian a pian
mei se ch'a piura douto Dignan.
Ancui ghe vidi sulo la ruveina
i se ch'a mai el turnarò quil de preima.
Oun amur cu fineiso lasa sempro
sta disperasion ch'a ſlangueiso

e la nostra tera ſi douta drento la maſera,
al formenton impiantà cumo omini de pana,
cu la radeiga soia, al cavel ingarisà

a ſi me paro ch'a favela, la me tera
imbastardeida s'ciavuneiſada,

ſi la me campagna ingraiada.

Me paro scanteina al se iò fato vidurno:

al cavo par aria, se poſa cumo calado,
in sirca d'al nouvolo ch'a vignarò ſbrombolando.

virdo e ſalo in tra le veide,
al so cameinà iò impinei la boto.

    Me paro la madona.
        Parchì no ſi viro ch'a sulo
            le fimene iò lagrema santa.

Mio padre la madonna—Quando le case si sfasciano giorno per giorno / so che piange tutto Dignano. / Oggi vedo dentro la sua rovina / e so che mai tornerà come prima. / Un amore che finisce / lascia questa disperazione che langue / e la nostra terra sta tutta dentro il muricciolo di campagna, / il frumento piantato come uomini di pannocchia, / con la radice, il capello sgualcito / è mio padre che parla, la mia terra / imbastardita fatta schiavona, / la mia campagna cespugliosa. / Mio padre traballa, si è fatto gerbido: / il capo in aria, si posa come afflosciato, / in cerca della nuvola che arriverà rotolando. / Verde e giallo tra i vitigni, / il suo camminare ha riempito la botte. / Mio padre la madonna. / Perché non è vero che solo / le femmine hanno lacrima santa.

My Father the Madonna

When the houses collapse day by day
I know that the whole of Dignano is crying.
Today I look at its ruins
and know it will never return as before.
A love that comes to the end
leaves such languishing desperation

and all our land is inside this brief country wall,
with the wheat standing like scarecrows
with its roots and frayed hat

it's my father who's talking, my earth
bastardized and enslaved,

my countryside filled with bushes.

My father wavers, he is a wasteland:

his head in the air hangs like a rag,
looking for a cloud that should be rolling in.

Green and yellow among the vineyards
his footsteps have filled up the barrel.

    My father the Madonna.
        Because it's not true that only
            the women shed holy tears.

La caſa d'al monto

da Mazere/Gromače/Muri a secco

In seima al monto ouna caſa. Vudia.

Vudia zi sta caſa soun al monto
ch'a la se diſgourba a pian a pian
cul vento ch'a ghe favela in tala pansa vudia
ſburtandose drento par sercala, magnala douta.

Al ghe fa frido ai mouri ſbiadeidi de fiuri
ch'a se rampiga in feila cumo par ricamo
soun par la reiga de le scale sfasade.

Spousa de ſento ch'a no se sento pioun.
Soun al monto no ſi pioun gnanca ledan
de la vaca, al gal ch'a te ciama bunura.
Scuverto al couso d'al porco. Silensio.

Sulo sta caſa. Fata par veivi e par lavurà.
Restada la ſi anca despoi de la deſgrasia
a fa bela l'ombra, a vardase la cuchera.

Meio monto, pais de l'Eistria ch'a no iò memoria

I soin restada, crisouda par descuverſi le maſere
par no piurà anca se i vidi secase le fighere
Straca i me fermarè in ta l'ombra de ogno caſa

vula ch'a bagula ſgourle e sempro fourbe le mediſime
furmeighe ch'a magari le geira cumo ch'a vuravo i altri

The Mountain Home

from *The Dry Wall*

On top of the mountain a house. Empty.

Empty this house on the mountain,
it slowly crumbles.
The wind howls inside its gutted out belly
pushing deeper to search and destroy it.

Cold walls with faded flowers
climbing in rows to embroider
the fallen stairs.

The smell of people no longer there.
On the mountain not even the cow dung
or the morning call of the rooster.
Even the pigpen is roofless. Silence.

Only this house. Built for living and working it remained
even after the mishap to make shade, to enjoy the chestnut tree.

My mountain, Istrian place without memory
I remained, grown so as to clean up countryside walls
without crying, although I see fig tree dying out.
Exhausted I will rest in the shade of each house
where the same silly but always sly aunts hang around
maybe like others would like to do
yet they can always find in the dirt some crumb
a boiled seed, all that is needed to eat and survive.

ma sempro le cata soun sta tera, ouna meigula
oun gran ʃbruvà, quil ch'a basta par veivi e par magnà.

La casa del monte—In cima al monte una casa. Vuota. / Vuota e questa casa sul monte / che si rovina lentamente / col vento che le parla nella pancia vuota / spingendosi dentro per cercarla, mangiarla tutta. / Fa freddo ai muri sbiaditi di fiori / che si arrampicano in fila come per ricamo / su per la riga delle scale sfasciate. / Puzza di gente che non si sente più. / Sul monte non c'e neanche il letame / della vacca, il gallo che ti chiama buonora. / Scoperta anche la stalletta del porco. Silenzio. / Solo questa casa. Fatta per vivere e per lavorare. / È rimasta anche dopo la disgrazia / a fare bella l'ombra, a guardarsi il noce. / Mio monte, paese dell'Istria che non ha memoria / Sono rimasta, cresciuta per ripulire i muriccioli di campagna / per non piangere, anche se vedo seccarsi i fichi / Stanca mi fermerò all'ombra di ogni casa / dove bagolano grulle e sempre furbe le stesse / formiche che magari girano come vorrebbero gli altri / ma trovano sempre su questa terra, una briciola / un chicco bollito appena, quello che basta per vivere e per mangiare.

→ Laura Marchig (b. 1962)

Laura Marchig was born in Rijeka/Fiume (Croatia) in 1962. She is part of the generation of young poets that was instrumental in the renewal of Istrian poetry during the 1980s. Laura Marchig began writing when still very young and has received a number of prizes for her several collections of poems. She studied at the University of Florence and wrote her dissertation on Enrico Morovich, a writer from Fiume. Laura Marchig is now director of the National Croatian Italian Drama Theater, called Ivan de Zajc, a prestigious theatrical company. She is also the chief editor of the literary journal *La Battana*. In 1988 she won first prize in the competition Istria Nobilissima with the collection *Raccontare uomini* (*Narrating Men*), where the style was meditative and colloquial; since then, her more recent collections have become experimental, lexically and stylistically fragmented. The most striking aspect of her work is the humorous selection of words. This gives the impression that the real world is given life through words that transform it into sounds, into simple musicality. The language becomes the protagonist of her poetry and captures all shades of chaotic and transgressive moments.

Laura Marchig's poems are written in free verse, and capture biological rhythms while avoiding metrical constraints of punctuation and organization of words on the page. For her, poetic language must comply with the movements of life, imitating life and also reproducing it through the play of a court jester. The poem "Ma Dio" (But God) is one example among many: "Ma Dio è troppo grande / dice Spinoza / trabordante / da noi e dal di fuori / operante e statico / inconosciuto / imbabelato, babelante / ampante /ahi che mi struggo / e mi prostro / prostrata fino al pollice / al mignolo del piede / iante ierante mamma / prova a definirlo / niente" (But God is too great / says Spinoza / spilling over / from within us and outside / active and static / not known / won by the Babel / muttering Babel / spreading / how I consume myself / and kneel down / bent down to my thumb / my little toes / hieratic old mother / try to define it / nothing). The result is a vital poetry, at times ironic and disrespectful. At the same time she does not scorn tradition, since she does make use of rhyme and pays attention frequently to the melodious flow of the lines. A few poems evolve from a tense relationship with reality, a traumatic vision of existence. Other themes that surface in her writing are the search for an identity and the reconciliation of her femininity with the writing of poetry.

Another collection of poems, *Lilith*, published on the occasion of a photography exhibit for Palestinian children by the city of Siena in 1998, is written in dialect. The choice of dialect is not a rejection of the "standard" Italian language; rather it is a further search for her multiple identities, an attempt to absorb her ancient, maternal culture. Her dialect is contemporary, accessible, and reflects contemporary reality, unlike the dialect verses of Egidio Milinovich (1903–1981), whose verses in dialect reflect a more archaic diction. The dialect of Fiume, where Marchig was born and where she lives, has its base in the dialect of the Veneto region, with the addition of the cultural assimilation and influx of cultures that are inherent to a very active seaport such as Fiume. Laura Marchig is particularly interested in the exploration of feminine identity in her poetry through pieces that reveal her exuberant creativity. She reflects on the physicality of time, of places, and of objects. There is a vein of ironic narcissism in her poetry also marked by a sensuous association of ideas and sentiments. Her poems alternate between protests and denials, rejections and celebrations, in an attempt to assert a different concept of the feminine self, a testimonial to the pleasures of facing and praising life as a woman and of being a woman.

Canto di una rosa rossa

da *Dall'oro allo zolfo*

Nei prati profumati delle pergamene
tu nasci
le silenziose spighe odi frusciare
al vento della sera.
Mostri il velluto e la falce
dei tuoi mille visi
come il diamante lubrico che s'ammanta
di casta luce, del suo sguardo terribile.
Così il raggio lunare ti scopre
graziosamente piegata
nella sarabanda delle fiaccole.
Timida ospite
amara e dolce tu spunti odorosa
tra le colline delle parole
nelle elegie dei poeti.

Song of a Red Rose

from *From the Gold to the Sulfur*

In perfumed meadows of parchments
you are born
the silent sprigs you hear rustle
in the wind of the evening.
You show the velvet and the sickle
of your thousand faces
as the lewd diamond enveloped
by the chaste light, its terrible look.
So the lunar light discovers you
gracefully bowed
in the dance of the torches.
Timid guest
bitter and sweet you appear fragrantly
among the hills of words
in the elegies of poets.

Marea

S'alza e s'abbassa il mare
dolce marea
ed anche l'onda
è tutto un rimestare
d'acqua che si schiuma
per abbracciar la Luna.

Tide

The sea rises and falls
sweet tide
and the wave also
all tossed about
water that froths
to embrace the Moon.

Solo un piccolo coso

I'm just a poor thing.
Sono solo un piccolo coso
un povero piccolo coso.
La notte dormo,
il lauro sui vetri della finestra
batte garbato:
ecco i rumori della mia piccola stanza.
I tramonti in autunno
bellissimi
il monte, il mare
cremisi, porporini
gli oh! e gli ah! dei miei
piccoli, piccoli sospiri
appannano i vetri
e delicato è il mio verso
così originale, perché da sempre
si sa
son fantasia.
Di giorno mangio
unghie, dolci, indifferentemente.
Se la boccuccia tingo
è per sentirmi bella.
Piacerò? Son contenta.
Ed è curioso,
io mi sento grande
grande e infuocata
fin da quando son nata
infuocata
e sono solo un piccolo coso
senza piangerci su
la piccolina
niente di più.
Mentre il fuoco osservo
ed anche il fuoco che mi vede sacro
alberga in menti
che io fingo di non vedere

I'm Only a Small Thing

I'm just a poor thing.
I'm only a little thing
a small, poor thing.
At night I sleep,
the laurel beats gently
on the panes of the window:
These are the noises of my small room.
The sunsets in autumn
very beautiful
the mountain, the sea
crimson, purple
my oohs and ahs!
small, small sighs
mist the panes
and delicate is my verse
so original, because always
one knows
I'm fantasy.
During the day I eat
nails, sweets, indifferently.
If the dainty mouth I dye
it is for feeling beautiful.
Will I be attractive? I am content.
And it's curious,
I feel great
great and inflamed
from when I was born
excited
and I am only a little thing
without crying about it
the little one
nothing more.
While I observe the fire
and also the fire that sees me sacred
dwells in minds
that I pretend not to see

(so di odiare maledettamente)
ed anche il fuoco che mi sfiora sacro
senza bruciare
passa e sorride
ironicamente.

(I know I hate damnably)
and also the fire that grazes me sacred
without burning
passes and smiles
ironically.

La luna nera

E adesso
qualcossa me zuca:
ciamila aria bianca
per i brazi
una siringa de nebia
ne le rece
cussì el zervel se insempia.

Sbriso ancora una volta drento i muri
su la mia testa nera
ridi una luce stanca.
Mi son un vento
che sufia soto tera
che se rodola nel mar
per i bechi de la piera dura.
Tra i sassi increspadi de fiori
trovo una natura
tremenda e inamorada
e incantada dai colori
come anche mi dai odori atìrada
del tuo corpo, ancora.

El colar de aria che se stringi
come dei diti sti denti consola.
Oltre l'aurora
mi son una joza
de acqua,
dal tuo profumo profumada
bevo un miel che no taca.
"Lilith vien, vien qua su!"
Xe viola e rosa la arpa de una vose
e la me parla pian
de robe misteriose

The Black Moon

And now
something pulls me:
by the arms
call it white air
the fog's syringe
in the ears
so the brain grows dull.

I still slide inside the walls
on my black head
laughs a tired light.
I am a wind
that blows underground
that rolls along the sea
on the edges of the hard rock.
Among the stones rippling with flowers
I find a nature
fearsome and loving
and enchanted by colors
as I too am attracted by the scent
of your body, still.

The collar of air contracting
these teeth console like fingers.
Beyond the dawn
I am a drop
of water
scented by your scent
I drink a honey that is not sticky.
"Lilith come, come up here!"
The harp of a voice is violet and pink
and it whispers to me

el mistero del ciel e de la tera.
Mi son una miniera
alta, no go sostanza, la speranza
xe verità che incontra l'altra parte.

La luna nera—E adesso / qualche cosa mi tira: / chiamala aria bianca / per le braccia / una siringa di nebbia nelle orecchie / così il cervello s'istupidisce. / Scivolo ancora una volta dentro i muri / sulla mia testa nera / ride una luce stanca. / Io sono un vento / che soffia sotto terra / che si rotola nel mare / per i becchi della pietra dura. / Tra i sassi increspati di fiori / trovo una natura / tremenda e / innamorata / e incantata dai colori / così come anch'io sono attirata dagli odori / del tuo corpo, ancora. / Il collare di aria che si stringe / come delle dita questi denti consolano. / Oltre l'aurora io sono una goccia / d'acqua, / dal tuo profumo profumata / bevo un miele che non appiccica. / "Lilith vieni, vieni qua su!" / È' viola e rosa l'arpa di una voce / e mi parla piano / di cose misteriose / il mistero del cielo e della terra. / Io sono una miniera / alta, non ho sostanza, la speranza / è la verità che incontra l'altra parte.

of mysterious things
the mystery of heaven and earth.
I am a deep mine, I have no substance, hope
is the truth that meets the other side.

Mare slava

'Sti coli giali de tera che ciapa
piziga i oci come
zize gagliarde.
A ti te lo domando mare slava
che ti sburti in alto i sorisi de late
quale xe el mio sguardo originale
varado dal peto col primo respiro?
Fra i mii maestri ti la più bestiale:
che dai odori tui te go imparado
el naso pien de miel e de cipola.

Su la strada de fughe, de le scelte
vedo arpioni de lagrime e medaglie
tuti che me zuca
conceti e comozioni.
Ma se straparme provo de 'sta tera
resta striche de pele e sangue amaro.
Lechime alora le feride, insegna
a rispetar la piera, el oro, el zolfo
e la maniera de intuir la quieta
doglia che scava e che ne fa contente.

Madre slava—Questi colli gialli di terra che acchiappa / pizzicano gli occhi / come tette gagliarde. / Lo domando a te madre slava / che spingi in alto i sorrisi di latte / qual è il mio sguardo originale / varato dal petto con il primo respiro? / Fra i miei maestri tu la più bestiale: che ti ho imparato dai tuoi odori / il naso pieno di miele e di cipolla. / Sulla strada di fughe, delle scelte / vedo arpioni di lacrime e medaglie / tutti che mi tirano / concetti e commozioni. / Ma se provo a strapparmi da questa terra / rimangono strisce di pelle e sangue amaro. / Leccami allora queste ferite, insegna / a rispettare la pietra, l'oro, lo zolfo / e la maniera d'intuire la quieta / doglia che scava e che ci fa contente.

Slavic Mother

These hills yellow with grasping earth
pinch the eyes
like hearty teats.
I ask you Slavic mother
who pushes up milky smiles,
which is my original look
heaved from my chest with my first breath?
Among my teachers you are the most brutal:
From you I learned by your smells
my nose full of honey and onion.

I see harpoons of tears and medals
fleeing on the road, from choices
that pull me
concepts and emotions.
But if I try to tear myself from this earth
strips of flesh and bitter blood remain.
Lick then these wounds, teach me
to respect stone, gold, sulfur
and the way to sense the quiet
pain that digs and makes us content.

Ripudiada

L'architetura del mio corpo tuta
xe una voluta gotica, 'n elisse
e me piego in sto afano
un urlo de la boca rosso scuro
come 'na ombra spanta, silenziosa.
Un incendio de strade
sui montìsei, tra i boschi disturbadi
la frenesia che frisi
oltre 'l color de perla de la pele.
Nel cellofan che brila
sti mii giorni xe onde che se maza
su le grote spacandose e no i strila.

Ripudiata—L'architettura del mio corpo tutta / è una voluta gotica, un'ellisse / e mi piego in
questo affanno / un urlo dalla bocca rosso scuro / come un'ombra versata, silenziosa. / Un
incendio di strade / sui monticelli, tra i boschi disturbati / la frenesia che frigge / oltre il colore
di perla della pelle. / Nel cellofan che brilla / questi miei giorni sono onde che si ammazzano /
sulle rocce spaccandosi e non strillano.

Repudiated

My body's whole architecture,
is a gothic spiral, an ellipse
and I bend into this sorrow
a dark red shout from the mouth
like a spreading shadow, silent.
A blaze of streets
on the hills, among the troubled woods
the frenzy that sizzles
beyond the pearl color of the skin.

Through shiny cellophane
my days are waves that crash themselves
on rocks breaking without screaming.

→ Maurizio Tremul (b. 1962)

Maurizio Tremul was born in 1962 in Bertocchi, near Koper/Capodistria in Slovenia. He belongs to the group of young intellectuals of the Italian national community who were responsible for the renewal of the cultural scenario in the 1970s and 1980s on the Istrian Peninsula. Tremul is currently the president of the Italian Union Assembly (Assemblea dell'Unione Italiana), which represents the Italians of Croatia and Slovenia.

Tremul was very young when he discovered his vocation for poetry. His first work, *Amore come vita* (*Love as Life*), which won first prize in the competition Istria Nobilissima, goes back to 1979. In this first collection of poetry, Tremul exhibits a dramatic, emotional, and solitary temperament. In *Amore come vita* he composes a youthful, existential treatise which reflects the worries of the generation of the 1980s. The most productive decade for Tremul goes from 1979 to 1990. In 1982 he won first prize in the youth category of Istria Nobilissima. *Vento in controluce* (*Wind in Cross Light*) shows Tremul's interest in exploring a more modern and experimental language, making use of free forms and irregular lines that avoid traditional syllabic organization. This poetry is spurred on by the natural need to express oneself and is tied to the very source of sentiments. Some verses are written following the manner of the futurists, where punctuation is eliminated. The isolated word at times occupies the entire verse, often reduced further to a few syllables in order to achieve the desired expressive intensity. The pauses and the blank spaces often achieve a suggestive intensity. In the early 1980s, experimenting with stylistic elements, Tremul participated in a process to renew Italian poetry on the Istrian peninsula which, until then, had been mindful of traditional poetic diction. For this reason his work was hailed as one of the highest expressions of the new generation of poets. Tremul's poetic profile is further defined by the later collection of poetry, *Frammenti per una crisi* (*Fragments for a Crisis*), which won the first prize at Istria Nobilissima in

1985. He won again in 1987 for *Volo di donna dedicato a Susi* (*Flight of a Woman Dedicated to Susi*). A third collection, *Rifrazioni* (*Refractions*), was published in 1986. These collections constitute the most significant work by Tremul and are noteworthy for the fine-tuned use of poetic language at once modern and sophisticated. Perhaps the more impressive group of poems is found in *Rifrazioni,* where the poet tells of his desire to blend intimately with the elements and with nature in order to flee from the constricting vice of a civilization focused on industrialization. In some ways this collection calls to mind the hermetic canon because of its synthetic and essential diction. Images of landscapes and nature are combined with nostalgic references to people and events that have long vanished. All this is couched in poems that make the most of single words, dense with daring analogies and unusual associations. Tremul's poetry is not sentimental evocation; rather, it is a poetry of memory, of things lost, of people and situations that are reminiscent of an existential condition. Nature plays a prominent role in Tremul's poetry. The poet fuses his sentiments and personality with nature in a sort of mystical symbiosis where the self blends with nature in a life-giving exchange.

Tremul's latest work, given the first prize by Istria Nobilissima in 1990, *Un tempo che precede quale segreto dopo* (*A Time Preceding a Certain Secret*), examines further the rift that exists between the self and the contemporary world, often presented as hostile. Images in this last work do not blend in harmony but are characterized by breaks that suggest a rhythmic tension, the other side of a meditation marked by solitude.

Tremul is also the author of several works of prose that complement his poetry and tell of his experiences in a direct, communicative language in which the self reveals its anxieties, reflections, hopes, and desires. The dominating motif of works like *Chimerici sogni di un adolescente* (*The Chimera Dreams of an Adolescent,* 1980) or *Quadricromia* (*Four-Colored Composition,* 1988) is a human and existential concern and a need to reach deep within the world of the self.

da *Rifrazioni (Refractions)*

la terra era argilla
e l'argilla era campo
disidratai l'esistenza erbosa
(allora le mie briglie
eran sciolte)
e per non solcare
carsici visi
tolsi il respiro
alla zizzania,
il silenzio brado
del seminato era
il suono della terra
tra le dita
al ricordo sfilacciato

tra viti ondose
di bassi filari
il nonno era pulce
su quel palmo di mano
e l'argilla bagnata
si modellava compatta
in animali rimossi
d'assimilare giocando

la mano era argilla
e argilla era campo,
nell'amenità indifferente
del frumento era la vetta
                    Istria

la terra era argilla
noi s'era alberi
senza fusto
fibre
foglie
senza frutto

from *Refractions*

the earth was clay
the clay was field
I dehydrated the grassy being
(then my reins
were loosened)
and so not to plow
ancient hill visages
I held my breath
against my will
the unbroken silence
of the sown field was
the sound of earth
between fingers
in memory of fragments

among ripping vines
of low rows of trees
grandfather was a flea
on that palm
and the wet clay
could be shaped as
animals to be
by playing

the hand was clay
the clay was field
in the stony amenity
of the wheat that was
pinnacle
            Istria

the earth was clay
we were trees
without trunks
fiber
leaves
without fruit

respirammo carbonio
e idrogeno argilloso

il sole era terra

tacemmo i
mormorii linfatici
e i canti clorofilliaci

fummo campo
e il campo era terra
la terra era argilla
e l'argilla riempì
il nostro umano
infinito disforico
   Istria

we breathed carbon monoxide
and clay hydrogen

the sun was earth

we silenced the
lymphatic murmurings
and the chlorophyllic chants

we were field
and the field was earth
the earth was clay
and the clay filled
our human
                    infinite
dysphasia
        Istria

Memento

da *Per molti versi*

lo scalpiccio dei tacchi
a ferro di cavallo sulle labbra
gole pizzicate
lingue nervose,
ho scalato vergini scoscese
dove l'oceano ammara
e il fuoco a spire affluma
per arrivare alla vergogna
d'una terra crocifissa

fin troppi eroi e puttane
abbiamo avuto
in memoria del popolo tradito

Memento

from *In Many a Verse*

the click-clack of heels
horse hooves on the lips
strummed throats
tense tongues . . .
I've scaled virgin scarps
where the ocean laps
and the coiling fire
                rushes in
arriving to shame
a crucified earth

so far we
betrayed people
have had to recall
too many heroes and whores

A Susi

da *Volo di donna dedicato a Susi*

tra le mani
mi sei sbocciata
una notte di maggio
e con le labbra
(delicati)
quei petali ho baciato
nel luogo più
caldo di me,
fiore ti ho cresciuta
ed il mio sangue
(sereno)
l'animo ti nutrì

il tuo polline
hai disteso
sulla mia pena d'esistere
e la solitudine
hai colmato
con il tuo profumo

in un soffio d'aria
volare via,
chissà se per ritornare
una mattina di rugiada
il prodigio che sei
     o non saprò
     mai la vita
     che tu sola
     mi potevi donare
te ne sei andata
con il caldo d'agosto
che brucia i miei occhi
continui a sbocciare
come di primavera
quel fiore
che non volli strappare

To Susi

from *Flight of a Woman Dedicated to Susi*

in my hands
you bloomed—
                    for me—
one May night—
and with my lips
I kissed your exquisite
petals in that warmest
place of mine—
I raised you as a flower
and my blood—
                    so serene—
nurtured your being

you spread your pollen
over my pain of existing
and filled my solitude
with your fragrance

in a wisp of air
to fly away—
never to return?—
that dew-laden morning

the prodigy that is you
(perhaps I'll never know
the life you alone
granted me)—
                    you left
in the August heat
that still burns my eyes—
and yet now
                    you keep blooming
like the spring flower
I refused to uproot

Partenze III

abbiamo vagato
sopra una scorza
di desiderio
senza rotta
nei meandri
dell'amore
per un istante
dilatato

ci sviò
l'approdo sicuro
di una baia

di riprendere l'oceano
avemmo paura:
se il vento
non avesse più
ingravidato la vela
partorito il
nostro viaggio?

osare era dovuto
ma tu sei
scesa prima

perché da navigatore
non riconobbi
la stella polare

Departures III

we have drifted upon
a bark of desire
without course
in the meandering

                     of love

for an instant

                     dilated

we were deviated
by the safe mooring
in a bay

to face the ocean again
we were afraid:
what if the wind
would not swell again
the sail to rebirth our journey?
to dare was our duty
but you disembarked first

because as navigator
I did not recognize
the North Star

Un tempo che precede quale segreto dopo

da *Un tempo che precede quale segreto dopo*

Voci spente
in riva alla fuga
e naufragi d'aria
nel tempo che precede
quale segreto dopo

Naufragi d'aria

attimi di sincerità
fissati con lo spillo
nella perdita lunare:
serici veli all'antartide
abbandonati in
un biancore . . .

innati sul palmo delle
intenzioni mummificano
sui fogli strappati
alla castità

immemori sequenze
murano la finestra,
la stanza cieca
accoglie flussi di
musica salina:
gorgheggio di note
in notti stellate.

a pensarne la
muffa parietale
il sangue
resta

la corrente trascina
un tronco d'albero
nelle rapide
(pulsioni si fanno

A Time Preceding a Certain Secret

from *A Time Preceding a Certain Secret*

Thereafter, muffled voices
on shore, in flight
and shipwrecked of air
in the time that proceeds
whatever secret to come

Shipwrecks of air

instants of sincerity
fixed with the pin
in the lunar loss:
silken Antarctic veils
abandoned in that
swathe of white

innate on the palm of
intentions they mummify
on strafed leaves
in chastity's name

oblivious sequences
wall up the window

the blind room
welcomes flows
of saline music:
gurgle of notes
on starlit nights

I think about it
               and still
the parietal mildew clings
in my blood

the current sweeps
a tree trunk
through the rapids

spruzzi di tumulti
incontrollabili)

il tronco s'incaglia
affonda e riemerge
(come un cadavere
gonfio di rancore)

un cercatore d'oro
trova un chiodo
nella melma del canale putrido
lo fissa arrugginito sulla quercia

ci appenderà gli abiti
dopo essersi lavato
se la baia
fosse una scultura marmorea
e diamanti cesellati a mano,
un sasso qualsiasi
(abortito dal mare)
sarebbe un'opera d'arte

arsi mari da scontare
per ogni lacrima d'intensità
nell'incavo della verità
nel sommerso pensiero
inspira disagio a pieni polmoni
intima (tesa) condizione
ma sarà facile—istrione
vomitare minime
falsità saline

il gratuito è firmare
una cambiale in bianco
che domani mi soffocherà

discriminare
tra il fuoco e la fiamma
è salire
lungo fori di collisione

(pulses become
splashed of tumults
beyond control)

the trunk sticks, sinks
and resurfaces
(like a corpse swollen
with rancor)

a prospector for gold
finds a nail
in the slime of the
                    stinking canal
and sticks its rustiness
in the oak
it will hang our clothes
recently washed
if the bay were
a marble sculpture
and hand-cut marble
or any stone
(aborted by the sea)—
it would be a work of art

scorched seas to discount
for every tear from depths—
the sockets of truth—
in the sunken thought
it inspires full-blown *angst*
intimate (taut) existence—
but, it will be easy:
                    ham actor
for you to spew
saline hype

the free ride is to sign
a blank check
that tomorrow
will choke me

aprire ali d'ombrello
ribellioni abbaglianti
alle stelline d'alluminio
violate poi spente

m'abbandono remissivo
ai mentali
indelebili giochi
diffusi a spasimo—estranei
all'effimero vincente

vorrei rigare il tuo volto
di benzina
e accenderlo di follia

il torpore ci aggroviglia
la lenza attorno agli occhi,
il piede nello stagno
affonda

to distinguish between
the fire and the flame
means rising along
plazas where all collides

to open umbrella wings
dazzling rebellions
against aluminum stars
violated then spent

I yield spent
to the mind blown
and indelible games
diffused in spasms—

                    aloof
to the ephemeral victor

I'd love to rut your face
with gasoline—and
light it with glee

the torpor entangles
the fishing lines of our eyes,
the foot in the pond
sinks

→ Roberto Dobran (b. 1963)

Roberto Dobran was born in Pula/Pola (Croatia), a city that he left after the tragic events in Yugoslavia. He was a journalist there and opted to move to Gorizia, Italy, after spending some time in Lujbljana in Slovenia. His life choices bring him to living on the margins, committed to a rebellious self-isolation in a rehabilitation center for handicapped people and drug addicts, a scene that finds reflection in his works. His first poems from the 1980s appeared in the journal *Panorama*, edited by Lucifero Martini. A collection of these poems was published in 2001, followed by another collection in 2003: *Implosioni* (*Implosions*) and *Esodi* (*Departures*). More recent, yet not complete, is the collection *Patacca globale* (*Global Plaque*). These poems were put on a Web site and readers have been invited to offer comments that the poet promises to take into consideration. Poetry, it seems, has difficulty competing with other types of media and therefore needs special venues to reach the public.

Dobran's poems were written in the 1980s and 1990s, but his first collections did not appear until after 2000. Among the authors Dobran read in his youth and was influenced by are Vladimir Mayakovsky, Allen Ginsberg, and Nazim Hikmet. But Dobran's principle source of inspiration comes from his direct observation of the world expressed according to his own original style and diction. As Apollinaire states, since the poet is free in every way, s/he can also claim the freedom to choose the forms that best suit his or her own way to communicate. Thus Dobran often makes use of graphic and visual elements to ponder, reflect and express the significance of the existential experience. The poet takes advantage of typographical techniques that call to mind a good number of poems with a visual component, from illuminated manuscripts to Mallarmé's "Coup des Dés," a poem that appears as a sort of architectural structure. Exemplary is, for instance, the poem "Nullità granellina" (Grainy Nothing) from the section "L'io divisible" (The Divisible I), which appears fragmented as so many pieces of a shattered mirror. Words seem to take the shape of a wound that zigzags on the page. Lacking pauses, the poem is read nonstop in long breaths, but it must be seen on the page in order to be understood, since the arrangement of the words is important. The poet seems to suggest that we are small particles, nothings, instants. With a strong dose of irony, the poet reminds himself that he is but a grain of that nothing. Poetry for Dobran is not for consolation, but a way to take into consideration, objectively if possible, some of life's commonplaces. In the poem "Dualismo perenne" (Perennial Dualism), the poet proceeds along the divide between life and death along which, as in a suspended condition, human beings are stalled, focused on looking as far ahead as possible, eternally nostalgic and agitated by expectations, worn out by the continuous strife between life and death. In other sections of the collection *Codice del caos* (*The Code of Chaos*), Dobran adopts instead a narrative style punctuated by flights of diction, inspired by the vital force of life.

More recently, in 2003, Dobran's expressive opus received a new addition with the publication of *Esodi* (*Departures*) in a Croatian bilingual text. This collection is complemented by an introduction by Nelida Milani and a concluding essay by Srda Orbanić, who prepared the translation in Croatian with the assistance of by Teana Tomažin. In these poems, all preceded by rubrics that call to mind medieval treatises, the poet reflects on his preoccupations and questions of an ethical nature, sharing the deep concerns that trouble his spiritual world. The diction in these poems seems traditional, characterized by a regular syntax and familiar vocabulary, marked by an evident musicality. The main theme is the contrast between the public self that conflicts with a painful social reality, exemplified by the lack of ideals, both cultural and civic, of the end of the millennium. Dobran's special position as a person both different and maladjusted, who chose a voluntary exile that is nonetheless painful, gives him the possibility to explore fully the condition of physical and cultural displacement, a frequently visited literary topic. Suspended between the nostalgia of what does not exist and expectation of what may exist but is not materializing and may in fact never be, Dobran engages in intellectual and moral existential individualism. Istria, the lost Eden that attracts and enchants, has a fortifying quality. The native land surfaces in Dobran's poetry with vital force veiled by a tint of nostalgia, as in the poem "Del viaggio" (About the Voyage): "Attraverso anch'io / luoghi che m'affascinano, godo / però soltanto se poggio / i piedi nudi su scogli calcarei / per sentirne la compostezza, / per saggiarne la concretezza: per / ricondurmi fra i vivi" (I too pass through / places that fascinate, I enjoy / however, only if I place / my bare feet on the calcareous rocks / in order to feel the consistency, / in order to test their reality: in order to / bring myself back among the living).

Se

da *Implosioni*

Se il nesso non percepisco,
se l'inizio
                    non vedo
(se c'è)
                    e la fine
e se il luogo dove cammino
si chiama Forse, allora
subito tremo.

If

from *Implosions*

If I don't perceive the connection
if the beginning
        I don't see
(if it's there)
        and the end
and if the place where I walk
is called Maybe, then
I suddenly tremble.

non so
        ma credo di non avertelo ancora
mai detto, un po' per timidezza e un po'
per un certo senso di colpa inesplicabile,
di chi sa di non aver meritato
l'amore, il sentimento consensuale

non so, a volte mi esalta il desiderio
di fuggire, irrequieto, di sentirmi
mancare. Non da te, ma da questa aspra
esistenza.

I don't know
        but I don't believe I've ever
said it to you, a little from shyness and a little
from a certain sense of inexplicable guilt,
from one who knows he didn't merit love, the
feeling of mutual consent

I don't know, at times the desire to flee
excites me, restless, feeling myself missed.
Not by you, but by this harsh
existence.

Mille Acque Mille Fiumi

Mille acque mille fiumi,
mille. In questo modo,
così la vita se ne va
con il roteare dell'universo.

Io, il Niente,
e l'universo a sembianza
del Tutto, come Nulla
fosse.

Thousand Waters Thousand Streams

Thousand waters thousand streams,
thousands. In this way,
so goes life
with the rotating of the universe.

I, Nothingness,
the universe in the image
of All, as if it were
Nothing.

Dualismo perenne

Instancabile e frenetico
pulsare della vita. Un batter
di palpebra e i defunti non si
faranno aspettare. Nondimeno
urla l'istinto nell'adesione dei corpi:
si schiude il creato! L'amore impone
e smuove l'ombra della morte.

Dualismo perenne.

In questa larga consolazione
o inganno strutturale, viviamo
un simile estremo.

Perennial Dualism

Untiring and frenetic
pulsing of life. A beating
of eyelids and the dead
aren't waiting. Nevertheless
the instinct in the adhesion of bodies shouts:
Creation opens! Love imposes
and moves the shadow of death.

Perennial dualism.

In this long consolation
or structural deception, we live
a similar extreme.

Se vuoi cercarmi, sono qui.
Troverai il corpo
ancora tutto intero e l'anima
gittata di qualche migliaio
d'anni luce. Di te
in attesa.

If you want to find me, I am here.
You will find my body
still whole and my mind
within range of a few thousand
light years. Waiting for you.

Nullità granellina

Un istante
        infinitesimale
             siamo
                   rispetto
al trascorrere del tempo
               inarrestabile
secolare
        millenario
              plurimillenario
                 eterno
inestinguibile, e coscienti
                 della
nostra nullità
        granellina
e dell'esistenza
        che sulla
             sabbia
abbiamo scritta—mi diletto
             a rimembrarmelo,
a modo di poesia
             nell'illusione
d'una chimerica
             immortalità

Grainlike Nothingness

An infinitesimal
          instant
             we are
                  in relation
to the passing of time
             unstoppable
over centuries
          millennial
             multimillennial
                    eternal
inextinguishable, and conscious
                   of
our grainlike
            nothingness
and of the existence
          that on the
          sand
we have written—I delight
            in remembering it,
a kind of poetry
            in the illusion
of a daydream
          immortality

→ *Marianna Jelicich (b. 1976)*

Marianna Jelicich was born in Koper/Capodistria in Slovenia. She lives and works in Buje/Buie d'Istria in Croatia. She is a graduate of the University of Trieste and is one of the youngest poet members of the Italian national community. Alessandro Villa edited her first collection, *Eterea* (*Ethereal*), which came out in 1999 through the Youth Poetry Center of Triuggio in Italy. Other works appeared in the journal *La Battana*, and some were included in Romanian translation in the journal *Semne* in Bucharest. She is the recipient of several important prizes for her poetry.

The affiliation with the Youth Poetry Center, directed by Alessandro Villa in Triuggio, has been the most important formative experience for Jelicich, who put the advice of her mentor to good use, as demonstrated by her second book of poetry, *Scenari possibili* (*Possible Scenarios*). In this collection the style is less concise; her poetic word becomes an instrument that embodies her emotions and thoughts. Inversions, repetitions of the words in different contexts, and omissions of punctuation marks are some of the characteristics of her poetry. The dominant theme of her works centers on waiting for something that never occurs, but this theme is presented in different ways in her various works. Although she is particularly attentive to word choice, Jelicich proceeds from a perception that language is the means and not the end of poetry. Her poetic evolution does not end with the search for poetic words; rather, she is concerned with expressing her deep feelings and with translating into words the visionary images of her mind. Exemplary is the poem "Immane" (Extraordinary), which seems to deal with the immersion in the subconscious. The first four verses create a temporal suspension that precedes a voyage beyond time and space. The sinking of the ship alludes to a temporary suspension of the ordinary state of her conscience. Silence as the premise to some other event, an experience that transcends the real, is a frequent practice in her poetry. Silence reinforces the time of waiting, heightens the anxiety and the desire to live more intensely each moment of her life.

Marianna Jelicich's poetic discourse is amplified in the brief lyrical composition "Arriva un tempo" (A Time Comes), published in *La Battana* in 2001. This prose passage is rich with captivating images that reiterate the intimate motifs that dot her poetry. The introductory passage is as follows: "A time comes when the streets are infested with rain and mud and the overflowing rivers raise the sea and you drown in the streets of any city whatsoever, slumbering and silent. The slow and rhythmic steps of a funeral march where you accompany your own self without garlands are the silly smile of having you next to me. Beneath the gravel crackles the present time, livid like a sleepless night."

Immane

da *Alba prima*

Lunghe le sere estive
Più lunghe al tramonto
Quand'anche le ombre
Non sono più simili.

Allora mi persi
In un gelido mare,
Immenso di scogli immensi
E profondo di onde brune.

E la voce udivo
La voce, di passanti
Forestieri, marinai
Con vele disciolte.

A picco andava la
Nave: il sole celeste
Immane, nei miei pensieri
Onnipresente sera estiva.

Immense

from *First Dawn*

Summer evenings are long,
Longer at sunset
When even the shadows
Are never the same.

Then I lose myself
In a frozen sea
Sunk in boundless reefs
And brown waves.

And I would hear the voice,
The voice of wayfarers,
Strangers, sailors
With unfurled sails.

The ship would plunge into the sea:
The sun on high, so grand,
In my thoughts, omnipresent
Summer evening.

Il tempo tuo verrà

da Scenari possibili (Possible Scenarios)

Quando il silenzio avrà cancellato
le nostre presenze
—rondini d'inverno—

verrà il tempo.

Niente
—tra un passo
e l'altro—
per tornare dove c'eravamo lasciati
funamboli
senza rete.

Quando verrà il tempo
mi troverai
all'altro capo
della tua solitudine.

Your Time Will Come

from *Possible Scenarios*

When silence will hush
our presences—
swallows of winter—

time will come.

Nothing—
between one step
and another—
to return where
we left each other:
tightrope walkers
without net.

When the time will come
you'll find me
at the other pole
of your solitude.

Istante

Vedo su di me
il tempo
andato
altrove

l'acqua
scorrere
lentamente
cadere.

Perché tanto aspettare?

E sono fradicia
grondante
ansimante

finalmente
tua

un istante.

Instant

I see on my skin
time . . .
passed
elsewhere . . .

water
passing
lapping
to fade . . .

Why wait so long?

And I'm soaked
dripping
panting

finally
yours

an instant . . .

Preludio d'inverno

Si trascinano nuvole
—processionarie caotiche—
nel preludio d'inverno

—frenesia a mani legate—

Brusio del nulla
si espande
ancorato al volto tuo
imperturbabile.

Un arabesco
scolpito in cielo

l'amore.

Winter Prelude

Clouds sweep by—
chaotic moths
in the winter prelude

—frenzy with tied hands—

buzz of the void
extends
anchored to your
imperturbable look . . .

An arabesque sculpted
in the sky . . .

Love . . .

L'autunno mite

Distendimi
su di te
come un autunno mite—

lieve
sarò
purpurea la pioggia.

Il crepuscolo
saprà di fresia
—dolce come sei—

. . . scivolare
sugli specchi
con le mani
sulle ombre nel respiro
di noi due . . .

Mild Autumn

Spread me
upon you
like a mild autumn—

soft
I will be
mauve like the rain.

The twilight
will taste of freesia—
sweet like you—

. . . to slide
across mirrors
with hands
on the shadows of breath . . .

France

France

LAURA TOPPAN

Italian emigration literature of the twentieth century, with the exception of works by Giuseppe Ungaretti, does not boast of a rich production in France. This can be attributed to the geographic proximity and the cultural and linguistic closeness of the two countries, which accounts also for the dearth of works in French or of bilingual texts like Ungaretti's. The disproportionate ratio between the relevant Italian presence in France with respect to quantity, duration, and variety, and the scarcity of literary works it produced is the research objective of centers such as the Cedei (Centre des Études et de Documentation sur l'Emigration Italienne), directed by Pierre Milza, and the Circe (Centre Interdisciplinaire de Recherche sur l'Émigration), chaired by Jean-Charles Vegliante, who finds in the literary works of Italian emigrants a valuable testimony of their unique *"sentimento del tempo"* (awareness of their times).[1]

For many years, the Italian language in France was considered a "weak," peripheral language. In the 1978 novel *Il paese in esilio* (*The Exiled Country*) by Maria Brandon-Albini, for instance, the Arrivabente family invents the association of the *"gégé,"* which stands for *"génies gênés"* (people of Italian origin, characterized by elements of awkwardness and wretchedness). On the other hand, France was able to lend a helping hand to some literary works such as *Fontamara*, by Ignazio Silone, which was published in Italian in 1934, and to some marginalized writers, such as Emmanuel Carnevali, who published his *A Hurried Man* with Contact Editions in 1925.

Up until the 1970s, French culture was heavily self-centered, and when looking beyond itself to foreign cultures, it focused mostly on English, German, or Russian spheres. As such, its interest in literature from beyond the Alps was sparse, certain exceptions being Dante; eighteenth-century writers such as Leopardi, Vico, Fogazzaro, and D'Annunzio; and the reception of authors such as Ruzante, Svevo, and Ugo Betti, who were discovered in France before they were in Italy.

But the situation changed radically in the 1980s, when all things Italian became fashionable, due in part to more frequent cultural exchanges and in part to European projects favoring modern Italian literature, much of which had not been readily available in translation in previous years. Regarding contemporary poetry, many translators sought to convey a dialogue between the two nations, whose geographic proximity further complicated the relationship between their languages and literatures. The oft-cited expression "*presque même*" (nearly the same) is a poetic category full of ambiguities that makes the literature from beyond the Alps near and distant at the same time. And the solitary and indefatigable work of professors and critics such as Jean-Charles Vegliante and François Livi, along with poet-translators such as Bernard Simeone and Philippe Renard, have resulted in translations of Vittorio Sereni, Mario Luzi, Giorgio Caproni, Valerio Magrelli, Giuseppe Raboni, Alda Merini, and Patrizia Valduga, to cite only a few. Clearly, these translators' aim has been to fill a space that remained empty for a long time.[2]

A summary can be drawn, though short of being complete, of writers who emigrated to France in the course of the twentieth century for political, ideological, and work-related reasons. The gallery will consist of portraits of poets, particularly those of the most recent generation, who reside in the capital and for research purposes travel frequently to both sides of the Alps. An important feature of their activity is that they write in Italian, in dialect, and in French, and that they translate their own works. The portrait is useful in presenting the course of contemporary Italian poetry in France with the aim of providing testimonials of the lives of men and women who, following Ungaretti's vein, wrote about their personal concerns as well as public ones, of exile and political commitment, of Italian history and of their observations of the world.

Luigi Campolonghi (1876–1944) is the first figure with whom to start this gallery. He arrived in France in the 1920s and became president of the Italian League of Human Rights by writing an essay in French, entitled *Avec l'Italie—Oui! Avec le Fascisme—Non!* (*With Italy—Yes! With Fascism—No!*), on Franco-Italian and fascist relations. In 1933, he published in Italian a collection of poems entitled *Esilio* (*Exile*). Written between 1920 and 1930 while traveling through France by train, the book is organized in seven sections: "Le Tombe," "La Strada," "Ritorni," "Canti civili," "Ora grigia," "Notturni," and "Idillio Guascone (The Tombs, The Road, Returns, Civic Songs, Gray Hour, Nocturnes, and Gascoigne Idyll). One of the best collections of Campolonghi, *Exile* shows a technically accomplished poet with experimental verses in sonnet, "contrast," "canzo," and epigram forms. All the poems deal with the political theme of exile, as expressed in "Il volto dell'esule": "Lord, allow me to see again my / country absolved from this unjust punishment, / the humble borough in the midst of thick woods / wood by the murmur of the river." The poems in *Exile* also treat death, in lines like "Death also is the last proud wave / of a tempest that, in its wild running / toward the unconquered avenging cliffs, / gathers all the anger of the sea." These verses are woven with reminiscences of the classical Italian lyrical tradition from Dante, Leopardi, Foscolo, and Carducci, yet they are not without French inspiration as well, namely from Victor Hugo and Verlaine.

Another significant Italian voice present in France was that of Beniamino Joppolo, born in Patti in 1906, in the province of Messina, in the eastern part of Sicily, which was replete with symbolist and futurist beginnings. He belongs to a generation of Sicilian artists who left their land of origin attracted by the promises and cultural stimuli of the cultural capitals of Italy and Europe, and who nonetheless remained tied to their island origins through blood and their memories. In the case of Joppolo, the European capital was Paris, where he moved in 1954 and where he died in 1963. A fervent antifascist who was politically committed, in the 1930s he was arrested and sent to confinement in the province of Potenza. He was a poet and novelist, author of short stories, painter, art critic, and, above all, a playwright. He uses diverse expressive codes, often mixing them together, a sign of his experimentalism aiming to "express a religious and philosophical faith in the destiny of man," according to the author's own definition of his work. The travels of this unusual islander, which coincide with his intellectual voyage, include, as stopovers, Florence, Milan, and Paris, all centers of surrealist art and of the poetic and avant-garde theater. Joppolo's debut dates back to 1929, with his first collection of poems, entitled *I canti dei sensi e dell'idea* (*Songs of the Senses and of Thought*), an early title that already describes the nature of much of his creative output. This search was first stimulated by futurist examples and by the cultural ambiance of Messina during the reconstruction years, a vitally active scene with avant-garde and utopian interests. In 1984, the publisher of Patti, Pungitopo, published the collection *Scandinavia*, in which a voyage to the North Pole ("a frontier past which / a lime region / liquefied and kneaded with the sun / is a white night / with a yellow tint"), becomes immediately a voyage to the outer limits, a voyage into a dizzying universe. The landing on the island ("placed in the center / of

the universe with just suns / skies airs and colors / beyond imagination")
assumes, for a moment, the traits of his native land ("the island / where
you'll get your nourishment / of warmth and will be perfumed / soft and
alive like / white milky / orange blossom") before flourishing with flashes
of symbolism ("Oh flight / . . . / toward that mysterious island / totally
new in the center / of the universe oh night / oh white night!"), conveying
the tension between the two poles of this poetry, the abstract flights of
utopia and the warm, pulsating signs of existence.

Emotionally bound to Joppolo's Sicily is the Milanese Maria Brandon-
Albini, who left Mussolini's Italy in 1936 to find asylum in France, where
she collaborated with the antifascist daily *La Voce degli Italiani* (*The Voice
of the Italians*). During World War II, she was totally engaged in the
Resistance movement, and during the reconstruction she taught in vari-
ous universities in France (Toulouse, Poitiers, Tours). From 1950 to 1984,
she was one of the most active supporters of the Dante Alighieri Society
for the promotion of Italian language and literature throughout the world.
Perfectly bilingual, Brandon-Albini has written numerous essays in
French about the southern Italian countryside, especially the islands of
Sicily and Sardinia. She is also the author of several novels in Italian—
Ragazze inquiete (*Restless Girls*), 1935; *Terra nera* (*Black Earth*), 1937; *I pro-
letari del Buon Dio: Cronaca del sud* (*The Proletarians of God: Chronicle of
the South*), 1958; and *Cala l'inferno* (*Inferno Descends*), 1971—in which
most of the settings feature a historical and political background. She promoted the French reception of certain Sicilian authors and their works,
such as Vittorini's collection of short stories *Piccola borghesia* (*Petite Bour-
geoisie*, 1948), and the poet Ignazio Buttitta, whose dialect collection *Lu
pani si chiama pani* (*The Name of Bread is Bread*, 1953) she translated in an
edition prefaced by Carlo Levi and illustrated by Renato Guttuso.
Buttitta's poetry, which Levi describes as "essentially a sacred drama and
epic tale," draws its inspiration from the thirteenth century, from Jacopone da Todi and Cecco Angiolieri. It becomes the expression of an
entire people, as in, for example, *La morte di Turiddu Carnevali* or
Lamenti d'una matri, about the massacre in Portella della Ginestra in
1947, which Maria Brandon-Albini renders in French in a mannerly and
refined style:

Fils! Pourquoi t'as-t-on tué,
quel mal as-tu fait,
je lui disais:

tu étais une colombe
de sucre et de miel.

Partout où tu entreras
je te suivrai;
s'il y a le feu
je m'y jetterai
s'il y a des épines
elles seront pour moi
et s'il y a des larmes
mon coeur les boira.

My son! Why have they killed you,
what wrong have you done,
I'd say to him:
you were a dove
of sugar and honey.

Everywhere you go
I will follow you;
if there is fire
I will throw myself on it
if there are thorns
they will be for me
and if there'll be tears
my heart will drink them.

Nella Nobili is another woman writer, in addition to Maria Brandon-Albini, this time from Bologna and of the same generation as Luciana Frezza. Nella Nobili died prematurely. Her first collection of poetry, *Poesie 1948*, was published in Italy in 1949. Other poems appeared separately in journals such as *La Fiera Letteraria*, where the "Ballata della città" (Ballad of the City) was published:

Quando nacque la città
era tutta terra
e tenera erba.
Poi vennero le strade, le case, le cattedrali
e sui fiumi che attraversavano la città
s'inarcarono ponti leggiadri. . . .

Nella dolce stagione, sotto il sole nuovo
l'uomo ama e vorrebbe amare—
mille campane d'argento suonano a festa nelle sue vene . . .
sente l'anima sfuggirgli dalle mani.

When the city was made
it was all earth
and new grass.
Then came the roads, the houses, the cathedrals
and on the rivers that cross the city
beautiful bridges arch over. . . .
In the mild season, under the new sun
man loves and wishes to love—
a thousand silver bells ring festive in his veins . . .
he feels his soul run out of his hands.[3]

After a brief stay in Rome, Nella Nobili emigrated to France in 1953. The daughter of very poor workers, she sold milk, was an apprentice in a ceramics factory, a worker in a box factory, a glass blower, and, in her spare time, studied German in order to read Rilke in the original. Around the middle of the 1970s she began to write verses in French, continuing her earlier themes, and in 1978 she published *La jeune fille à l'usine* (*La ragazza in fabrica*, or *The Factory Girl*), dealing with her childhood, stolen by the factory: "De l'extérieur à l'intérieur il n'y a qu'un pas / un arrache-ment / des lambeaux de ciel d'odeurs de brins d'herbes d'escargot / collés aux semelles aux poignets aux cheveux / du sommeil tiède des endoloris" (From the outer to the inner is but a step / a jerk / strips of sky scents of blades of snail grass / stuck to the soles to the wrists to the hair / of the tepid slumber of the knees in pain). Nobili's poetry is a perfect example of migration between two languages. Her last collection of poetry, *Poèmes de deuil* (*Poems of Mourning*), was published in 1980 by Stern, in Paris, and her other poems were published in 1986 in the journal *Les Langues Néo-latines*.

Another poet is Mirella Muià who, after a period in France, returned to live in Calabria, where she restores icons. She is totally bilingual and writes and translates in Italian and in French, both prose and poetry. The 1986 collection entitled *Tela/Toile* (*Woven Cloth*), which she translated herself, is a narrative poem woven around the myth of the woman in waiting and of male wanderings, which is a myth both ancient and universal, but nowhere are these myths so rooted as in the Mediterranean world: "innalzerà i numi di pietra / attorno a un ceppo d'ulivo / nessuna nave sarà ancorata mai / come la sua casa / e se la sposa vuole / . . . lascerà il ramo più alto / slanciarsi fino al soffitto" (He will raise high the stone gods / around the trunk of an olive tree / no ship will ever be anchored / as his house / and if the bride wishes it / . . . he will leave the highest branch / thrusting up to the roof). *Empedocle* (*Empedocles*), a 1997 book-length narrative poem, was written in French in 1997. In it, a sandal left behind on the edge of a crater in Sicily turns into an object symbolic of disillusioned sincerity reaffirmed before the world's brutality, a sign of abandonment as well as a sign of the highest commitment among people.

Maria Venezia, like Mirella Muià, is also a bilingual poet who writes in Italian and translates her own work into French. She returned to Italy after a long period spent in France. Her published collections of poetry, like *Vocalità e scherzi* (*Vocality and Scherzi*, 1986), are composed around the image of the labyrinth of Borges as a sign of the search for a thread of life:

Prendi un labirinto
e ritorcilo
inventa nuove strade
incroci
intrecci tortuosi
annoda e sconvolgi
le linee dello spazio
in tutte le possibili combinazioni
frangi il tempo
dividi
separa
scomponi,
riaggrega
collega
combina
che resta?
La camera del faraone
è un'assenza
posta al centro del tempo e dello spazio.

Take a labyrinth
and twist it again
invent new roads
crossroads
tortuous crossways
tie knots and disarrange
the lives of space
in all the possible combinations
smash up time
divide
separate
take apart,
rearrange everything
connect
combine
what is left?
The Pharaoh's room
is an absence
placed at the center of time and space.[4]

Among the poets of the younger generation, Andrea Inglese's voice, from Turin, is one of the more significant ones. He lives between Milan and Paris, where he teaches. He writes in Italian, and his collections worthy of mention here are *Prove d'inconsistenza* (*Proofs of Inconsistencies,* 1998), *Inventari* (*Inventories,* 2001), and *Bilico* (*Precarious Position,* 2004). The topics treated by Inglese are generally of a sociopolitical character, as in the collection *Inventari,* which takes its cue from a photograph of the great demonstration against the World Trade Organization of November 1999 in Seattle: "Carni da squalo al palo della Cuccagna . . . // Carni elementari che hanno / innocuo, in sè, il germe umano nudo / e crudo / prima del pomo cognitivo . . . // Carni d'incommensurabile felicità / non tornate, state pure dove siete" (Meat for sharks on the pole of plenty . . . // Elementary meats that have / innocuous in them the human germ plain / and simple / before the apple of / Flesh of incredible happiness / do not come back, stay where you are). In the collection *Bilico* (*Precarious Position*), on the other hand, the poet treats the human condition as existing on a thread, in an intermediate state between instability and the fall. Such a condition is reflected in a style showing a provisional control threatened in its very becoming. Inglese uses both lyrical and nonlyrical tones, not to pit one against the other, rather to relate the two tones in a dialogue, as in *Inventario dei giovani II* (*Inventory of Youth II*): "In tossiche faccende presi, spesi, e laboriose / sopravvivenze alcoliche / e chini / Nella perpendicolare di aghi in capillari rari, i crampi nei visi, / lo sfascio soffice del corpo" (In toxic situations caught, spent, and laborious / alcoholic survivals / and closed / in perpendicular of needles in rare capillaries, cramps in their faces, / the soft breakdown of the body).

The poetic voice of Francesco Forlani, on the other hand, is altogether different from that of Andrea Inglese. Forlani's poetry is that of a minstrel, an entertainer. Born in Caserta, Forlani grew up in Naples, a city with which he has maintained a close relationship. He moved to France around 1990 and writes in Italian and French as well as in Neapolitan dialect. From 1995 to 2000, he was artistic director of the multicultural journal *Paso doble,* and since 2001 he has been the director of the journal *South.* He has written a collection of short stories entitled *Metromorphoses,* dealing with the topic of "becoming, that is to say, how a writer finds himself vis-à-vis the thorny principle of reality." His most important contribution has probably been the book *Poétiquettes,* compositions written in Neapolitan dialect with Italo-French insertions on computer-generated images or photographs. This book is a kind of family portrait of friends and historical characters focusing on the theme of existence and political involvement. With Inglese, Forlani contributes to E-dizioni, the publishing house directed by the poet Biagio Cepollaro.

To complete this mosaic of tesserae that are difficult to keep together because of their simultaneously centralized (in the French capital) and scattered cultural milieu, we should mention the French collections *Aiguilles* (*Needles,* 1999) and *Plan secant* (*Intersecting Plane,* 2001), by Emanuela Burgazzoli, an Italian who lived in Paris and now lives in Switzerland. It is interesting to note how the choice of language changes according to situations and moments. For some poets, the adopted language is completely integrated, while for others it is only the language of migration. For others still it is the dialect that emerges from the depths of creativity like an eruption of forsaken, or perhaps forgotten, linguistic inspiration (as in the case of Andrea Genovese), while only a few choose Italian as their lone expressive possibility, clear of any combination with other tongues or dialects (as in the case of Gian Carlo Pizzi).

Brandon-Albini, M. *Radioscopie de la culture italienne*. Paris: Entente, 1983.

Denyl, L. *La poésie italienne de nos jours*. Paris: Éditions Littéraires Artistiques Nouvelles, 1952.

Fido, F. "Gli scrittori italiani in Francia e nel mondo di lingua inglese." In *L'Italia fuori d'Italia*, 299–321. Rome: Salerno Editrice, 2003.

Vegliante, J. C. "La presenza italiana in Francia oggi." *Affari Sociali Internazionali* XV, no. 3 (1987): 77–87.

———. "Italiani trasparenti: la letteratura d'emigrazione in Francia fra impostura e dimenticanza." In *La letteratura dell'emigrazione. Gli scrittori di lingua italiana nel mondo*, 61–80. Turin: Edizioni della Fondazione Agnelli, 1991.

———. "La réception de la poésie italienne au XXe siècle: une illustration du malentendu italo-français." In *La traduction-migration*. Paris: L'Harmattan, 2000.

→ Andrea Genovese (b. 1937)

Andrea Genovese was born in Messina in 1937 in the neighborhood known as Giostra, one of the poorest in the Sicilian city, where he lived until the age of twenty-three. For his native city, Andrea Genovese always harbored conflicting feelings of attraction and repulsion. Although Messina is on the sea and Punta Faro, one of the three extremities of the island, is only five miles away, Genovese always experienced the Mediterranean Sea in his youth as a mythical and unreachable place. Genovese crossed the Strait of Messina, with all its Greek myths—Scylla and Charybdis, the sirens—for the first time when he was seven years old, in the midst of a storm, mistaking it for the Arno River, where he had played as a child during the war when his family had relocated, as refugees, to Tuscany in Santa Croce sull'Arno. Only six months after he returned to Messina, he learned the local dialect, which, for him, was a sociological accomplishment and a necessity in order to avoid the insults of the neighborhood children who jeered him because of his Tuscan accent: "He speaks 'talian," they would say to him in their tongue. A place full of insults and vulgar behavior, it was also a microcosm where solidarity prevailed. It is here where Genovese began to write poetry in an attempt to escape from a miserable ambience.

In 1960 he decided to move to Milan, where he published his first poem in the journal *Prove*, edited by Nino Palumbo, and in 1964 his first collection was published, *Odissea minima* (*Essential Odyssey*). He began his collaboration with journals such as *Il ponte* and started to frequent literary circles while he worked for the post office. He became a member of the Communist Party and began to participate actively in union struggles without, however, becoming fully integrated in intellectual circles, which seemed hostile to him because of his proletarian origins. In 1976 he published the collection *Sexantropus and other Prehistoric Poems*, some of which were dedicated to a basket maker with whom he had fallen in love when he was a high school student. These compositions, which seem to have a Greek tone, are somewhat archaic, but also show a natural disposition for musicality and linguistic density. The following year he published *Bestidiario* (*Beast Diary*) for Scheiwiller. These poems are almost all written in unrhymed hendecasyllables in a provocative tone, as is usually the case for Genovese, who looks for an internal order through form to oppose, I believe, the outward chaos of his personal and literary life.

In 1979 he published *Un trenino per David* (*A Little Train for David*), dedicated to his son, and in 1981 he moved to Lyon, where he began to write poems in French, translate Italian poets (such as Luzi, Sereni, and Quasimodo) and edit a bilingual anthology of Sicilian poets. In 1982 he published *Lyonlamer*, a title that plays with the words *il mare* (the sea) and *amaro/a* (bitter). The collection contains thirty-two poems dealing with his third country, which only has two words of the original language (one is Sicilian, the other Milanese) to define the cathedral of Lyon: *matrici* and *Domm*, residence and welcome. The collection *Mitosi* (*Mitosis*), from 1983, has poems dealing with the city of Milan, such as "Città di transito": "Città di transito / di mezzo . . . dove / comincia o finisce / il labirinto l'anamnesi / il transfert / il sonnolento viaggio / al centro del dipinto?" (City of transit / in the middle . . . where / begins or ends / the labyrinth the anamnesis / the transfer / the sleepy voyage / to the center of the painting?). These poems also deal with Messina, as in "Lo stretto": "Lo stretto / questa gabbia / di non risolti miti // da un capo all'altro / il triangolo s'inscrive dentro al cerchio / e l'azzurro punta / al connubio nel tricorno // trina / è la lama / che ci squarta" (The strait / this cage / of non / resolved myths // from one end to the other / the triangle is inscribed / within the circle / and the blue points / to the marriage in the tree corners // embroidery / is the blade / that cuts us in quarters). The title of "Erinni" shows the frequent return to myths that underscores the Greek roots (in addition to the Latin and Arabic-Hispanic roots) of the poet: "Erinni / che colo / scirocco / frequenta // ingoia / nuvole / il sole / drago // ronzando / la sua / lingua" (Furies / that only / sirocco / visits // swallows / clouds / the son / dragon // buzzing / his language). In 1985 Genovese published *Nugae delle quattro stagioni* (*Tidbits of the Four Seasons*), where the first three sections represent the first three cities of the poet ("Primavera Manzoniana [Manzoni's Spring], "La ghiotta (dell') estate" [The Glutton of the Summer], and "La pigrizia autunnale [Autumn's Laziness]). The fourth one, "Le Dispute In/Ernali" ("Disputes In/Ernali"), which has words in Sicilian and verses in French, has cosmic ambitions: "Storia del passaggio / dell'astro / sulla superficie del Mostro / violenza di civilissimi cocci d'impas / sibili civiltà / maniacali spinte all'oltraggio / cette traînée est d'une blancheur délirante" (Story of the passage / of the star / on the surface of the Monster / violence of very civilized shards of impasse / hissing civilizations / maniacal pushed to outrage / such a row is of a delirious whiteness).

In 1986, Genovese also had to deal with the loss of his wife. During this difficult time, the dialect from Messina arose within him and helped him compose verses almost extemporaneously. So it is that he composed the collection *Ri/stritti/zzi, mummuriati in lingua giustrota* (for which he won the Vann'Antò prize). Its title is made up of *ristrettezze* (shortages), *rarefazioni* (rarefactions) and *frontiera dello stretto* (frontier of the strait). The book is composed of aphorisms, imprecations, short sayings, epiphanies, and memories in the very narrow dialect of the Giostra di Messina neighborhood. These verses were produced spontaneously in French as well (for example, the expression *mettri a pinzari* is an ironic duplication of the French *maître à penser*—thinking specialist). As Giuseppe Cavarra describes in his introduction to Andrea Genovese's 1993 collection, *Tinnirizzi*, the dialect emerges as a "safety valve," as "a kind of lava flow which gives rise, in just a few days, to some one hundred poems" (9). These texts "come out spontaneously, almost automatically, with a psychological recovery of childhood."

The poet returned to the use of dialect with the collection *Tinirizzi* (*Tenderness*, 1993), which includes some forty poems in pure dialect according to Pancrazi's definition of *pure dialect*: poetry that asks dialect only for "the expression and the sound" and the capacity to give life through the imagination to experiences of the same ambiance, human and urban, to which they belong. Gradually, as the poet descends within the dialect, the patterns that are his very own, his aggressive nature comes out—polemical, ironic, dissatisfied, and restless. In his verses, the past reappears together with gestures and words already taken as symbols of an eternal condition of life. "A poetry of place to the point that it becomes a denunciation": so it is defined by Giuseppe Cavarra in his preface to the collection, "where the representative efficacy, beyond the syntactical and lexical construction, lies in the choral sentiment of the neighborhood and in the objective narration to express the light and shadows of all that passes under the sight of man." Genovese gives voice and dignity to a poor, peripheral language, just as he does to the community that speaks it. He coaxes it, shakes it, provokes it to make it respond to his own expressive needs: "Cu è ci cchiù di tia / si mèrita na puisia / risu duratu / di gghjotta succusa / piramidi di nòbbili fattura / geroglifica scrittura / arancina sapurusa / chi càudda càudda nni scungiuri / di patria storia / peni e-dduluri? / Cu rispettu di mànciu / e-ssenza bbòria" (Who more than you / deserves a poem / golden smile / of succulent glutton / pyramid of noble build / hieroglyphic writing / tasty *arancino* / that very warm denies / pain and suffering / of paternal history? I devour you with respect / and without airs).

In addition to dialect and Italian, French is the third language of the poet, which, in the collection *Les nonnes d'Europe* (*The Nuns of Europe*, 1986), reveals the secrets of his cosmopolitan soul, of his love and resentment for old Europe. Behind the veil of a voyage in the crevices of history, mythology and geography, the poet embarks on a road covered with linguistic and metaphysical traps that begin in Africa and reach up to Scandinavia, passing through the mixture of his Sicilian roots. The city on the Bosporus Strait returns also in the French verses, with "*portus et porta Siciliae*" (port and gate of Sicily) for the Romans, "*Zanclès*" (scythes) for the Greeks, mother and stepmother, sharp blade and enigma, crossroads and point of escape. Within the poet, a sense of separation remains strong, a notion of division that the place represents: "Questa fessura / questo sfregio / che è in me" (This opening / this wound / that is in me), he writes in *Idylles de Messine* (*Idylls of Messina*, 1987).

During the 1980s Genovese took on prose narratives with the publication of two novels, *Mezzaluna con falcone e martello* (*Half Moon with Falcon and Hammer*, 1983) and *L'arcipelago lontano* (*The Distant Archipelago*, 1986), and then, in the 1990s, he began to dedicate himself completely to the writing of plays. This very productive period of playwriting lasted until 2000, when he returned to prose writing and, less frequently, poetry. He is currently writing a narrative trilogy in which he aims to trace his own "human comedy" tied to political objectives, starting with his own family history during the war years. Genovese possesses a very strong southern identity. Through the evocation of a microcosm in a neighborhood of Messina (an unfortunate city because, after being destroyed by an earthquake in 1908, it became the most bombarded Italian city during World War II), he testifies for the history of an entire island, indeed an entire country. Genovese's prose possesses a rhythm much like verse, a clear indication that he is foremost a poet.

La colonna nemica

da *Sexantropus e altre poesie preistoriche*

sciame dorato
lingotti di luce
in vortice
signori di quali
tempeste
inchiodate l'azzurro
in occhi naufragati?

dove s'avventa la sonda
quest'atto
di superbia
a scandagliare pianeti
mai tempi mai concentrici
punti imprigiona

la lama affonda
in quanto di carne
ormai ci resta

e al di là
di questa piazza
dove per pochi
compromessi
s'ammira il gran
disco del sole sradicato
con argani dal cielo
strisciano serpenti
su un vasto fronte
lastricato
ci vengono incontro
sul loro ventre duro
pieno d'ostia

The Enemy Column

from *Sexantropus and Other Prehistoric Poems*

Golden swarm
ingots of light
swirling
Lords of what
tempests
nailed the blue
in foundering eyes?

Where the probe hurls itself
This act of pride
To scan planets
Never imprisons
times never concentric points

The blade
Sinks in whatever flesh is left us
And beyond
This square
Where for a few
Compromises
You can admire
The great disc of the sun
Unhinged from the sky with cranes
Snakes slither
On a vast stone-paved front
They come toward us
On their hard bellies
Full of host.

La cestista

9. Tiepide ancora le sere
di quel primo autunno
fiorivano d'un tratto
sopra i tetti, qualche
stella s'accendeva odorosa,
tremavano per aria
infantili richiami.

Nella palestra era
una quiete satura
di rumore lontano, di tonfi
a terra del pallone,
di vocio muliebre subito
zittito dall'allenatore.

Sbiadiva al nuovo colore
la tua figura d'anfora
guizzante sullo sfondo
cinereo della collina.
Ansavo: un dolore lieve
dapprima; poi il lampeggiare
del neon mi dava come
una puntura di spina.

The Basketball Player

9. Still-mild evenings suddenly
Bloomed upon the roofs
That early autumn, a few
Stars spread their scent
Children's calls
trembled in the air
In the gym the silence
Was full of distant noises
Of balls thumping the ground,
of female voices
quickly hushed by the coach

Your amphora-shaped figure
Dashing against

The ash gray background of the hill
Faded in the new color.
I was breathing hard.
A light pain at first,
Then the intermittent neon light
Felt like
the prick of a thorn.

L'incostanza del mare

da Mitosi

Esplode il mare.
Il mare si fa duna
nuvola gabbiano.
Viaggio.

Accostare le voci
i piani glissanti
le uova covate nella mente
la maliziosa pera galleggiante.

La gelatinosa materia si contrae.

Si riduce il mare
oltre i margini dell'arbirtrio.

Agonizza il mare
sopra asciutte terre.

Carcasse di navi
ardono al sole
milioni di arche da diporto.

E questo lupo di mare
con figlie incestuose
è prosciugato sul punto di salpare.

The Sea's Inconstancy

from *Mitosis*

The sea explodes.
The sea becomes dune
Cloud sea gull.
Journey.
To bring voices close
The sliding planes
The eggs incubated in the mind
The sly floating pear.
The gelatinous substance contracts.
The sea is reduced
beyond the margins of the will.

The sea agonizes
Over dried-up lands.

Carcasses of ships
Burn in the sun
A million arches to play with.

And this sea wolf
With incestuous daughters
Is drained when he's about to sail.

Missa cantata

da *Ri/stritti/zzi*

Quant'è beddra Missina
quannu gghiovi!
L'acqua sciddrica
pi strati e cantuneri
i ciumiceddri si iettunu
nte fogni comu picciridduzzi
a mmari ntall'estati

Sutta l'umbrellu naturali
da furesta comunali
a cavaddru
di cavaddruzzi arditi
turnianu amàzzuni minnìfuri
minnefora chi so zziti

Supr'e terrazzi
càntunu a gloria
nuvulazzi scuri
chi rrisìstunu cu ffidi
o martiriu du ventu
santa Missina
pi lavari e livàriti
u piccatu origginali

Na fimmineddra
nta n'agnuni
isa a vistuzza
participannu coscinziuosa
a stu lavacru univessali

Messa cantata—Com'è bella Messina / quando piove! / L'acqua scivola / giù per le strade e gli
angoli / i rigagnoli si buttano / nelle fogne come bambini / quando giocano d'estate al mare /
/ Sotto l'ombrello naturale / della foresta comunale / a cavallo / temerari cavalieri /
volteggiano seni nudi / amazzoni seni nudi con i fidanzati / / Sulle terrazze / grosse nubi
oscure / resistono con fede costante / il martirio del vento / cantano i loro gloria / per lavare e
togliere il peccato originale / / Una vecchietta / in un angolo / si alza la gonna / e partecipa
fedelmente / a questo lavacro universale

Choral Mass

from *Re/stri/tions*

How beautiful Messina is
When it rains!
The water slides
Down streets and corners
The rivulets fall down
The sewers like children
Playing at the beach in summer

Beneath the natural umbrella
Of the town forest
Riding
Daring little horses
Revolve bare breasted amazons
Bare breasted amazons with their betrothed

On the terraces
Great dark clouds
Resisting with great faith
The martyrdom of the wind
Sing their glorias
To wash away and to remove
The original sin

A little old woman
In the corner
Lifts her skirt
And conscientiously takes part
In this universal washing.

Missa spugghiata

E gghiovi
gghiovi paru paru.
Sì cca mmenz'u linzola
pi davveru o sì nu pinzeru
du pinzeru? Stu paisaggiu
è ffatatu picchì è scrittu
o picchì l'haiu davanti
nto quatru da finestra?
Di quali liuni
m'haiu a ffidari?
Pi si spàttiri troppu
e stari a tutti i patti
puru u Signuruzzu
fici big-bang.

Forsi è nta testa
chi mmi gghiovi
e mmi gghiuvìa trent'anni fa
o mill'anni chi nni sacciu.
O è dumani chi gghiovi
e chi trent'anni ancora gghioviravi?
Ghiuvissi mill'anni nte linzola
e allargassi stu nidu
e stu buschittu!

M'arrìzzunu i canni
sentu a to mani chi ffuria
ma c'è u nvennu arreti a ttia
c'è sta città unni nascìa
chiddra unni fici finta i vìviri
chiddra unni murìa
ci sunnu 'n saccu i facci canuscenti
ch'oramai mi scàppunu da menti

Undressed Mass

And it rains
It pours continuously.
Are you here between the sheets
Really or a thought of a thought?
This landscape is charmed
Because it's written
Or because I see it before
The frame of the window?
Which lion am I
To trust?
To share too much
And to remain faithful to all pacts
Even the Lord
Went big-bang.

Perhaps it's raining
In my head
And it rained there thirty years ago
Or a thousand years ago what do I know.
Or maybe it's going to rain tomorrow
Or it will rain for thirty years more
May it rain a thousand years in the sheets
And may it widen this nest
And this forest
I get the chills
I feel your hand searching
But you have winter behind you
There is this city where I was born
Where I made believe I lived
Where I died
There are so many faces of acquaintances
Who are already fading from my mind

ci sunnu lingui chi parrai
e cchi mmi sunnu indifferenti

mentri chi gghiovi
e gghiovi paru paru

Messa spogliata—E piove / una pioggia costante. / sei qui fra le lenzuola / veramente o sei pensiero / di un pensiero? Questo paesaggio / è magico perché è scritto / o perché ce l'hai davanti / nel riquadro della finestra? / Di quali leoni / mi devo fidare? / per spartire troppo / e stare ad ogni patto / anche il signore / ha fatto big-bang. / / Forse è nella testa / che piove / e pioveva trent'anni fa / o mille anni che ne so. / O è domani che piove / e che pioverà ancora fra trent'anni? / Che piova mille anni nelle lenzuola / e allarghi questo nido / e questo boschetto. / / Mi si agghiacciano le carni / sento le tue mani che infuriano / ma l'inverno ti sta alle spalle / questa città dove sono nato / quella dove feci finta di nascere / quella in cui sono morto / ci sono tanti visi di conoscenti / che ormai mi sfuggono dalla mente / ci sono lingue che ho parlato / e che ora mi sono indifferenti / / Nel frattempo piove / e piove costantemente

There are languages that I spoke
And that are now indifferent to me

Meanwhile it's raining,
pouring continuously.

N' autru sonnu

Brisci. U celu
spalanca
a so buccazza
e a racineddra di stiddri
si mmucca
Brisci. U mari
s'arrispigghia
e a rina nta spiaggia
cci sbadigghia

Brisci supra
i macerii i fora
e chiddri dintra

Brisci comu na vota
e comu sempri

Beddra iunnata
U tirrimotu
mu nzunnai

Un altro sogno—Comincia. Il cielo / spalanca / la bocca / e divora / i grappoli di stelle /
Cominicia. Il mare / si sveglia / e la sabbia sulla spiaggia / vi sbadiglia / / Comincia sopra / le
rovine fuori / e quelle dentro / / Comincia come una volta / e come sempre / / Bella giornata
/ ho sognato / il terremoto

Another Dream

It starts. The sky
Opens up
Its wide mouth
And devours
The grape bunches of stars

It starts. The sea
Awakens
And the sand on the beach
Yawns at it
It starts upon
The ruins outside
And inside
It starts like once
And like always

Beautiful day
I dreamed of
The earthquake

da *Tinnirizzi*

Ntâ scinnuta chi-ppotta â piscaria
n' abbireddru si mmùccia nta na gnuni
pi-nnon mustrari i fogghji mpennuluni

U mari é-ccammu
na bbacchjceddra si ggiria
a-ffozza i remi senza gran valìa

Sutta a sta calura puru i casi
sùdunu comu cristiani
e-cci cadi u ntònucu muffutu

Unni vai chi vaddi
cu st'occhi i pisciceddru scaffidutu
chi non sapi comu jìnchiri a junnata?

A Calabbria pari na bbalena ddrummintata

Nella discesa che porta alla pescheria / un alberello si nasconde in un angolo / per non
mostrare le foglie penzoloni / / Il mare è calmo / una barchetta si muove / spinta da remi
senza tanta forza / / Sotto questa calma anche le case / sudano come persone / e l'intonaco
ammuffito cade / / Dove vai tu che giri / con questi occhi di piccolo pesce maleodorante /
che non sa come riempire la giornata? / / La Calabria sembra una balena addormentata

from *Tenderness*

In the street that leads down to the fish market
A little tree is hiding in a corner
So as not to show its limp-hanging leaves

the sea is calm
A little boat moves round
Pushed by oars without much strength

Beneath this heat wave even the houses
Sweat like people
And their moldy sidewalls crumble

Where are you going what are you looking at
With your eyes like a stinking little fish
Who doesn't know how to fill up his day?

Calabria looks like a sleeping whale.

→ Giancarlo Pizzi (b. 1950)

Giancarlo Pizzi's early poetry is attuned to meteorological changes (rain, sun, inner rhythms of days and seasons) and tends to reflect on melancholy, meditation, and dreams. In these verses, one detects echoes of Russian poetry (Pasternak, in particular) and Spanish poetry (Alberti and early Lorca), as well as some influence from the Iberian surrealists, who were much more carnal and less intellectual than their French counterparts. One finds also, in Pizzi's works, an underlying presence of Pavese in his manner of employing symbolic realism and landscape details (fog, frost, gloom). Pizzi grew up around Novara and, after a brief period of his life when dream and poetry were experienced as escapist flights from reality, he settled in Milan, where he got a university degree in philosophy and committed himself to political and union activism, first with leftist revolutionaries and then with Workers' Autonomy.

In 1968, Pizzi experienced a break between poetry and politics, between the work of art and engagement. This phase lasted until 1977, when he recommenced writing verses, these dedicated to a woman. Herein he expresses the idea that the only space for intimate writing is that which is bound to impossible, unreachable loves. Then, at the end of the 1970s, he withdrew, or perhaps fled, from the period's repression, from mafia denunciations, and from what he saw as an inability for leftist movements to remain unified.

In February 1982, Pizzi exiled himself voluntarily and went to Mexico, where he remained until September 1983, a year that also inaugurated a new period of poetry for him. Having learned Spanish, he wrote works to explode, without any plan, aiming to introduce a form of poetry of meditation on defeat. At this point, his understanding of Joseph Roth was crucial, along with his postwar spin-off inspiration, the breakdown of the generations he had survived, and their loss of a sense of direction. So the theme of exile became a meditation on revolution, a thematic choice to bring history to a metaphysical level. Pizzi's poetry thus took on a certain prophetic tone in its melancholy, like that of the wandering Jew recalling his diaspora.

In 1983, Pizzi returned to Europe and chose to live in Paris. But his French exile signaled for him a loss of intensity and an incapacity to integrate, compounded by a long period of a bedridden illness. Then, back on his feet, he put together all the poems he had written during his wanderings and, in 1999, published his first book, *Rémanence de l'oubli*. This volume represents a return for him to poetry as a daily, formal exercise, where its calligraphic, virtually ideographic ancient forms merge. The collection is a kind of diary where dates of poems have deep meanings, in so far as they relate to the moments of composition. In these poems, one hears the influences of Celan, of Rilke's *Duino Elegies*, of Trakl's *coloratura*, and of Anna Akhmatova.

Pizzi's poetry is ontological, dealing with death, life, and nothingness. It all hinges, often violently, on the fundamental question, "To be or not to be?" which is then tinged with meteorological nuances. An understanding of the twelfth-century Persian poet Omar Khayyam can help one to grasp the subtleties and essence of Pizzi's poetry; here's an English rendering of Bausani's 1965 Italian translation of Khayyam's *Quartine*: "We come pure from nothingness / and we leave impure / we come here happy / and we depart sad / a fire lights in our hearts / water in our eyes / we cast our life on winds / and then earth took us in." From the presence of fire, water, earth, and air, everything is born. Departing from that point, Pizzi avails himself of a natural rhythm. His poetic tension is created via an interplay of images, not concepts, as is a recurrent tendency in contemporary poetry, because the poet is convinced that one cannot get caught up in a purely dialectical game of intellectual signs. If so, the result is not so much a poetry of sterility as it is a celebration of data.

Pizzi's choice to write in Italian is twofold. He chooses not to write in French because he does not regard it as his language, and he eschews his dialect due to his conviction that to write in dialect is to write in a "quasi-language," like Venetian or others even more marginalized, such as Istrian or Friulian.

After the publication of *L'altra riva* (*The Other Shore*, 2003) and *Fino all'ultimo settembre* (*Until Last September*, 2004), Pizzi's more recent compositions, *Raggrumato sangue* (*Clotted Blood*, 2009), evokes ancient Greek poetry and diction as a testimony to his knowledge of classical history and the Gospels (the *archē-neo-logos* of Saint John). Pizzi's poetry, at once deeply personal, politically engaged, and persistent in its religious exploration, is, in essence, a reflection of a most controversial period of Italian history and an existential probing into the meaning of life.

Recordant

da *Rémanence de l'oubli*
Ad Andreas Baader e Ulrike Meinhof

Cessiamo di far galleggiare i corpi
di Rosa Luxembourg e di Karl Liebknecht
semi-affondati nell'onda scura, nelle nebbie
notturne!
Dal dover essere affiorano su pallide campagne
dove li lascia ogni mattina senza detriti
un fiume periodico,
i capelli sciolti nella chiara luce dalle dita della morte,
dai tenaci legami dell'erba d'autunno.
Qui non si esce sbattendo la porta,
non serve delicatezza e memoria,
non basta alzare la voce:
da questi corpi siamo chiamati
alla solitudine della storia.
In essa totalmente disfatti
con stupore ancora accostano la sostanza della vita.
Per sempre. Oltre il cadere dei soli
e l'estinguersi del significato.
Arriva all'oblio la memoria.
Siamo stati—in altri corpi e in altri nomi.
Questa greve coscienza dell'esistere—quando affondano nella notte
i vecchi parapetti d'Europa.

                                                    5 Maggio 1978

Recordant

from *Remains of Oblivion*
to Andreas Baader and Ulrike Meinhof

Let's stop floating the corpses
of Rosa Luxembourg and Karl Liebknecht
virtually sunk in the dark wave,
in the nocturnal fog!
From the duty to be they surface
in the pale fields where
every morning without silt
a recurrent river leaves those bodies
with hair flowing
in the clear light
loosed by the fingers of death
by the clinging of
the autumn grass.
Here you don't leave
slamming the door,
tact and memory are useless,
it's not enough to raise your voice:
by these bodies we are called
to face the solitude of history.
Here totally undone
with amazement they approach
the substance of life.
Forever. Beyond the fall these suns
and the extinguishing of meaning.
Memory reaches oblivion.
We have been—in other bodies with other names.
This grave awareness of existing—when the old parapets of Europe
sink into the night.

May 5, 1978

A Toni Negri

Perché molte cose ancora dovranno accadere,
continuamente accadono
scambio di capitale e lavoro.

Molte cose ancora dovranno accadere
prima della fine,
quando l'oro non sarà più convertibile,
quando il tempo non sarà più utile,
quando ci parleremo con lingue diverse,
quando il Palazzo d'Inverno
sarà coperto da muschio irrimediabile,
quando la catastrofe non sarà venuta
e nessun Angelo suonerà la tromba
e non si leverà un sole nuovo.

Allora, dispersi
ai quattro angoli della terra,
costruiremo nel vuoto.

13 Novembre 1979

To Toni Negri

Because many things still
must happen,
the exchange of capital and labor
happens continually.

Many things still must happen
before the end,
when gold will no longer
be convertible.
When time will no longer
be useful,
when we will speak to each other
in different languages,
when the Winter Palace will be
covered by unscrapeable moss,
when the catastrophe
will not have happened
and no Angel will sound a trumpet
and a new sun will not rise.

Then, dispersed to
the four corners of the earth,
we will construct in the void

November 13, 1979

Rileggendo Rilke

da *Fino all'ultimo settembre*

Non dire mai addio prima del tempo,
non è questione di stile.
Le cose alle tue spalle ancora durano.
Le bacche rosse come in quegli altri inverni
sui rovi giallogrigi—non avere fretta che cada la neve.
Così anche tu dura,
anche quando è passata la voglia.
Non distaccarti, non cercare
il tuo essere puro.
Stare, anche se non vale più la pena.
Tu sai questa ostinazione,
tu sai: il seme deve morire.
Non anticipare l'ultima primavera,
non si può dire addio alla vita,
in anticipo per non morire.
Tu non devi essere fuori
ma sempre immerso nel continuo ciclo
accettare l'andarsene via di qui
e il venirci,
secondo il suo tempo.

Villareggia, 22 dicembre
Cinisello Balsamo, 26 dicembre
Lazise, 29 dicembre
2002

Rereading Rilke

from *Until the Last September*

Don't ever say goodbye
before the time is ripe—it's not a matter of style.
Things behind you still abide.
The red berries like those
of other winters
among the yellow-gray brambles—don't rush to await the snowfall.
So you also last
even after the will is gone.
Don't withdraw, don't seek
your pure being.
Stay even if it's
not worth it anymore.
You know of this stubbornness,
you know: the seed must die.
Don't look ahead to
the last spring,
you can't bid adieu to life
in advance so you won't die.
You must not be detached
but always immersed
in the continuous cycle
to accept leaving this place
and coming to it
all within its time.

Villareggia, December 22
Cinisello Balsamo, December 26
Lazise, December 29
2002

A mio padre

da *L'altra riva*

Mi fosti dato.
Dono di ciò che mi ha preceduto,
antecedente nascita
di un destino che devo ripercorrere.
Così anche il fiore del ciliegio a ogni primavera,
così prova il giallo della forsizia
a ripetere ciò che è stato
ancora un altro anno.

Non cercare risposta, tu,
alle parole del padre,
perché deve restare interrotto
il racconto che ti fece,
perché ogni primavera deve tornare a splendere
il giallo della forsizia contro il muro scrostato.

Mi fosti dato.
Dopo di me solo il giallo.

15 Aprile 2002

To My Father

from *The Other Shore*

You were given me.
A gift of what preceded me,
antecedent birth of a destiny
I must retraverse.
Like the cherry tree flower
every spring, the yellow
of the forsythia feels just so
when repeating what's been
one more year.

Listen, don't ask for answers
to the words of the father
since the story he told you
must never be interrupted,
since every spring
the yellow of the forsythia
must shine again
against the flaking wall.

You were given me.
After me there is
only yellow

April 15, 2002

Il lago lontano

L'inverno circonda di silenzio
le rive del lago. Giunchi
si piegano e il vento
ritorna a gemere
nell'erba gialla.
Un tempo pensavo
che questo fosse l'oblio.
Ora so che tutto è memoria
e conosco il segreto
dell'erba piegata dal vento.

Mexico, 3 Febbraio 1982

The Distant Lake

With silence
winter girds
the shore of the lake.
Reeds
bend and the wind
moans once again in
the yellow grass.
Once I thought this
was oblivion.
Now I know all
is memory
and I sense the secret
of the grass
bent by the wind.

Mexico, February 3, 1982

NOTES

1.   In the years following World War II, the first expression of the common identity assumed by the Italo-French community as an emblem of their collective entity was the novel *Les Ritals*, by François Cavanna, published in 1978, the year in which Italian immigration into France was at its lowest. The novel offers a full vision of childhood and was well received by the Italo-French community, who saw themselves reflected in it in spite of the negative connotation of the title (*ritals* is made up from the word *ricain*, meaning buddy and bandit, and the French word *italien*), using a word that came into being in the 1970s to replace the older and more offensive *macaroni*. In 1981, *L'anniversaire de Thomas* came out, produced by the Italo-French community of Villerupt in Lorraine (the home of the yearly Festival of Italian Cinema), a film that deals with the work of Italian immigrants in the steel and iron mines, which today are closed.

2.   Translations of twentieth-century Italian poetry continue through the work of Jean-Yves Masson (for Mussapi, Luzi, Caproni), Jean Michel Gardair and Philippe di Meo (for Pasolini and Zanzotto), Christophe Mileschi (for Campana), and Isabel Violante (for Sanguineti).

3.   English translations by Joseph Perricone.

4.   Translated by Joseph Perricone. The translations from dialect into standard Italian that follow in the text are also by Joseph Perricone.

Germany

Germany

CARMINE CHIELLINO

Intercultural literature in Germany was born and developed in a highly politicized sociocultural environment without any postcolonial influence, unlike the postcolonial impact felt in other European countries, such as France, Holland, and Great Britain. Forty years after the birth of intercultural literature, Gianni Bertagnoli's report *Arriverderci, Deutschland!* (*Goodbye, Germany!*) came out in 1964. From the foundation of the Federal Republic of Germany to today, intercultural literature was born and has developed within a process of the general renewal of German literature.

This rebirth was begun by the literary movement Gruppe 47 with its promotion of a renewed humanization of the German language after the nationalist orgies of the Nazi regime. The literature of Gruppe 47 was followed by productions by members of the Workers' Literature of Gruppe 61. After the student movement came the explosion of women's literature, which sharpened the expressive potential of the German language. Women's literature has placed at the center of its aesthetic project the first-person plural pronoun, not only as a literary metaphor of a homogeneous literary class, but as a grouping of a minority, defined genetically, that connects various social classes.

Following the collective *we* of women's literature, other groups appeared that included minorities reflecting a cross-section of the population. Among these were the *we* of the *letteratura degli immigrati* (immigrant literature), which did not go past the initial phase and lasted at best until the 1980s. In fact, immigrant literature came into being with a transversal *we* that was intended to connect it to the other ethnic and cultural minorities that arrived in Germany from 1955 onward. It aimed at including workers' literature and women's literature. However, it proved to be short-lived. After the initial phase of the collective anthologies, the participants distanced themselves from immigrant literature, which was perceived to treat a limited palette of themes.

In order to complete the general picture of the German literature of the second half of the twentieth century, one needs to mention the literature of socialist realism, which also had its base in a specific social class and was thus limited in its possibilities. Intercultural literature in Germany was and still is one the five literary movements that has contributed and still contributes to ensure a future to literature in German, which seriously risked remaining trapped in the ethnocentric, autoreferential, and monocultural literature typical of the twentieth century almost everywhere in Europe.

Within a literary scene so vast and complex, the literature of writers of Italian cultural origin made a small but decisive contribution. Writers such as Franco Biondi, Gino Chiellino, and Fruttuoso Piccolo have personally contributed to the creation of an intercultural literature in German. Others, like Giuseppe Giambusso, Marisa Fenoglio, Cesare De Marchi, Silvia De Natali, Lisa Mazzi, Piero Salabè, Franco Sepe, and Salvatore A. Sanna, with their works written in Italian, have contributed to the intercultural development of the Italian language which, in Italy, is finding it difficult to open itself up to an intercultural future. It seems, however, that this resistance should begin to change; Italian is the language of one of the founding nations of the European Union, which should furnish the language with more openness, and Italy is now a country of immigration for people from non-European countries.

In spite of their unmistakable aesthetic and thematic differences, this group of authors has worked and continues to work for a two-pronged aesthetic project. On one hand, writers who use German introduce into the German language of their works the cultural-historical memory of their characters, a memory that is typically based on the Italian language. Writers who use Italian introduce into the language of their works a non-Italian quotidian reality, which is the quotidian reality of protagonists who live in a German world. Both of these procedures bring to their respective languages an intercultural dimension.

Considering that German literature is very rich in works set in Italy, one could conclude that those writing in German have an advantage over those who write in Italian, since there is not a great tradition of works set in Germany. Readers of works by Italians living in Germany are not numerous, and they may not keep in mind that intercultural works are born of a rupture with the pact that is the foundation of every national literature. The pact, that is, that stems from every national writer assuming that protagonists and readers share the same memory corresponding to the language of a work, that the mother tongue of a work's protagonists is also that of its readers.

In the case of intercultural works, none of this can happen because protagonists and readers share only the memory of the language being used to write the work: Italian or German. The monocultural reader, whether Italian or German, remains excluded from that part of the memory that protagonists pour into their own language. Access to this memory is obtainable only for those readers who, going through the language in which the work is written, succeed in reaching the cultural memory of the protagonists of a narrative work, or the lyrical self in the case of a collection of poems.

The language of works set in Italy or in Germany is monocultural, since they present their reality to an Italian or German reader. Generally, the protagonists of such works are characters in search of experiences in unknown cultural spaces who try to explain otherness to themselves, that is to say to the reader excluded from this experience.

Intercultural works, on the other hand, address readers capable of reading at once the written language and the intercultural complexity of the historical and cultural memory of the protagonist, who comes from a different linguistic background from theirs. In that case, readers do not need a language to have the otherness explained since, if anything, they are looking for a language that will capture the intercultural authenticity in which they are living. The intercultural reader plays an active role in testing the intercultural reliability of the novel or of the poem.

⇥ Salvatore A. Sanna (b. 1934)

Salvatore A. Sanna was born in Oristano, in Sardinia, in 1934 and has been living in Germany since 1958. Currently residing in Frankfurt, he is the cofounder and president of the Deutsch-Italienische-Vereinigung (German-Italian Union). Since 1979, he has been the editor of the journal *Italienisch*, which he founded. He has been writing poetry since 1966. His books include *Fünfzehn Jahre Augenblicke* (1978), *Wacholderblüten* (1984), *Löwen-Maul* (1988), *Feste* (1991), *La fortezza dell' aria* (1995), and *Fra le due sponde/Zwischen zwei Ufern* (2004).

Sanna, with his four collections of poetry written in Italian and published in bilingual editions, occupies a unique position. Sanna's poetry comes about as an aesthetic project within the national literature in the wake of Montale's poetry. Two basic characteristics link Sanna's poetry to Montale's: first, the relationship of the self with nature and with urban landscapes, and second, the constant dialogue between the self and the second-person *you*. To these instances can be added the careful selection of words, at times almost archaic, which the author uses to create his poems. Sanna knows that, on one hand, he is within the traditions of twentieth-century Italian poetry; on the other hand, he has defended his autonomous position by defining his poetry as an example of decentralized literature, a literature that evolves far away from the center and therefore in complete autonomy. Besides being decentralized culturally, Sanna's four collections are decentralized with respect to their content; however, they have unity through a noticeable continuity with their aesthetic models. Sanna's poetry is not marked by the social engagement that distinguishes the literature of the founding group of Italian writers in Germany. Nonetheless, it would be inexact to think that Sanna's poetry develops in a sort of empty space devoid of Italian characteristics within the society of a metropolis such as Frankfurt. His collections abound with poems in which encounters play a dominant role because of the landscapes (Sardinian, German, French, Swiss, and European in general), and also because the encounters take place between personae and addressees from different cultures. Sanna's Italian had to be open to the cultural differences of the experiences of his poetic persona in order to avoid being faulted for fidelity to the models of metropolitan poetry, to which he owes so much but from which he maintains, at the same time, a degree of autonomy.

da *Fra le due sponde*

I

Mi scopro a mettere
i ricordi ormai pallidi
in grandi valigie
dentro scatoloni di cartone
per portarli con me
su una costa ricca d'azzurro
perché vivano ancora
Se un giorno ti metterai
sulle loro tracce
li ritroverai, purificati
dalle acque del fiume,
sulla via in ascesa del Capo

from *Between Two Shores*

I
I discover myself placing
paling memories
in big suitcases
inside large cardboard boxes
to take them with me
on a coast rich with blue
so they may live again
If one day you'll follow
their tracks
you'll find them again, purified
by the waters of the river,
on the ascending life of the Cape

II

È un retaggio antico
che si rinnova diffuso
per chi corre ancora
verso il traguardo
Messaggio che ci passiamo
di mano in mano
come una staffetta
in gara. Se il tuo compagno
di corsa non lo trasmette
e il tuo braccio vanamente
rimane in attesa
allora si fa il dolore acuto

II

It's an ancient heritage
that renews itself widely
for those still running
toward the finish line
Message that we pass
from hand to hand
like a relay team
in a race. If your
teammate does not convey it
and your arm remains
waiting in vain
then the pain becomes sharp

III

Erano i frutti ancora
verdastri dell'orto
presso lo stagno
che mio padre tagliava
a fette per te. Forse
vedevi in lui il tuo
scomparso nelle falde
di un tempo barbarico
Discreta ne seguivi il rito
nell'attesa infantile
del gusto inconsueto
Si creava un accordo
per memorie invisibili
e con fierezza ostentavi
a noi del nucleo
la tua appartenenza

III

The fruits in the orchard
near the pond
that my father cut
into slices for you
were still greenish. In him
maybe you saw your own
who had disappeared in the folds
of a barbaric time.
Discreetly you followed the rite
in the childish expectation
of the unusual taste.
Invisible memories
created harmony
and proudly you showed
to us of the family
that you also belonged

IV

I ricordi balzano fuori
dal fondo dalla terra
come le talpe in primavera
Tanti i piccoli cumuli
nel terreno che sente
allentarsi la morsa del freddo
È come un'esplosione vitale
che eccita i pensieri
e li esorta alla chiarezza
Ma niente è ancora possibile
e le immagini disgregate
rientrano

IV

Memories jump out
from the bottom of the earth
like moles in spring
So many small heaps
in the ground that feels loosening
the grip of the cold
It's like a vital explosion
that excites thoughts
and spurs them to clarity
But nothing is still possible
and the disintegrated images
come back in

V

Tutte le mattine all'albeggiare
nei mesi che annunciano
l'estate ci giungeva
dalle fronde della piazza
un messaggio canoro
impertinente qualche volta
certamente un tenore
robusto fra gli uccelli
Fossi stato Melampo
ne avrei compreso il senso
Il suo infausto avvertimento

V

Every morning at dawn
in the months that announce
summer a musical message reached us
from the leaves of the square
impertinent at times
no doubt a robust
tenor among the birds
Had I been Melampus
I would have understood its meaning
its dire warning

VI

Il San Rocco sul pianerottolo
di casa incuteva paura
a chi saliva le scale impreparato
così grande e improvviso
Ma il cagnetto ne addolciva
l'impressione, spiegava
il senso del bastone pellegrino

C'era un sole vibrante
sulla pianura ondulata della March
e tu camminando lungo il fiume
ripassavi con me la tua infanzia
Ecco in lontananza la cappella
bizantina sull'altura
la Wutzelburg del Signor von Teufenbach
dove aleggia lo spirito del santo

Un vinello bianco
seduti a dei tavoli
di legno accumunò
tutti nella conoscenza

VI

The Saint Rocco on the landing
of the house aroused fear
in anyone climbing the stairs unprepared
so big and sudden
But the puppy softened its impression,
it explained the meaning of the pilgrim's staff

There was a vibrant sun
on the wavy plain of the March
and you walking along the river
went over your childhood with me
There in the distance was the Byzantine
chapel on the rise
the Wutzelburg of Mister von Teufenbach
where the spirit of the saint lingered

A nice white wine
as we sat at wooden
tables united
all in the knowledge

→ Marcella Continanza (b. 1940)

Marcella Continanza was born in Roccanova, near Potenza, in 1940 and has been living in Germany since 1986, now in Frankfurt. She has been writing in Italian since the 1960s, prose as well as poetry. She is founder and editor of the journal *Vietato Fumare: Tutto cinema e dintorni*. Marcella Continanza is also founder and editor of the publication *Clic! Donne 2000*, and she is the inspiration for the group *Donne e Poesia*, which promotes the creative writing of Italian women in Germany.

Marcella Continanza continues to write in Italian and continues to astonish her readers with a vast diversity of topics. Her first work, entitled *Piume d'angeli* (1996), is dedicated to fifty angels among whom the author will look, in vain, for the guardian angel or the angel of death. The presence of these two angels in the collection introduces a certain degree of awkwardness, as the atmosphere dominating the collection seems to be quite distant from the religious ambience these angels might make one expect, in that the book incorporates certain positive, serenity-bearing spirits such as the angels of happiness, laughter, beauty, kisses, memory, and friendship. Perhaps more than angels, these figures represent moments of daily life that the writer would like to regain in order to infuse them with a human element. In the second collection, titled *Rosas Nocturnas/Rose notturne*, published in a bilingual edition in Santiago de Cuba in 1999, the regions and cities of the poetic self are contrasted: Naples continues to represent a known and reassuring world, while Frankfurt is presented as unknown and alien. In the third collection, *Passo a due voci* (*Passage with Two Voices*, 2002), erotic themes dominate, though they are not the only themes of the collection. *Passo a due voci* is a monologue in three parts that evokes the drama of the protagonist's emancipation. The erotic outburst of the first part is followed by the abandonment of the lover in the second part. The third part concludes the reconciliation of the protagonist with herself. The poem "La ragazza dai capelli di medusa" (The Girl with the Medusa Hair) is part of the author's recent unpublished work.

La ragazza dai capelli di Medusa

Quando arrivò
la ragazza dai capelli di Medusa
avvertii l'inganno.
Era Aracne che tesseva
tesseva una tela:
una camicia affatturata.
Non so
se tu l'abbia mai indossata:
so solo
che è vuoto il tuo posto
a tavola
e la solitudine
mi si posa sul capo
come corona regale.

Forse, fu per gelosia
che l'invitasti a bere
sali, ho del buon vino
ero fuori
per incontri di lavoro.
Forse, fu per solitudine
le sere d'inverno
nella metropoli sono tristi;
ero ai concerti
Bach Beethoven
Juliette Greco Leonard Cohen.
Non fu per gioco
o per avventura
che ti impigliasti in lei

Lei correva
correva per la tua strada
Io, al crocevia
della tua anima

mele avvelenate
affatturate.

The Girl with Gorgon Hair

When the girl with Gorgon hair
arrived
I felt the deceit.
It was Arachne weaving
weaving a cloth:
a charmed shirt.
I don't know
if you ever wore it:
I only know
that your place is empty
at the table
and loneliness
sits on my head
like a royal crown.

Maybe it was out of jealousy
that you invited her for a drink
come up, I have some good wine
I was away
on business.
Maybe, it was out of loneliness
winter nights
in the city are sad;
I was at concerts
Bach Beethoven
Juliette Greco Leonard Cohen.
It wasn't for fun
or for adventure
that you got tangled in her

She ran
and ran along your way
I, at the crossroads
of your soul

poisoned charmed
apples.

Ridevi. Spingesti il motore
a 180
ero al tuo fianco
ti sentivi potente.
Lei fu un gioco maligno
di seduzione degli dei.
Ti parlava da ladra
come da ladra
era entrata nella nostra vita.

Ho da fare. Avevi fiato corto
al telefono. Ci risentiamo.
Mordevo i dubbi
della paura
già contando l'attesa

Quando la incontravo
altera mi guardava.
Sapevo che era venuta a sottrarmi
il bene più prezioso
e ad annegarmi il cuore.
Ma il dio fu pietoso
e mi donò dei versi

I versi erano il sole
il mare il vento
lo sguardo delle cose
e degli uomini
e- divenni strada.

Ti lasciai
nel pozzo segreto
della tua anima
e non mi accorsi
che era senz'acqua

Ti lasciai
ma non ti tradii;
fui la Penelope dei versi
mentre i proci aspettavano

You laughed. You pushed the engine
to 180
I was by your side
you felt powerful.
She was a wicked game
of seduction by the gods.
She spoke to you like a thief
and as a thief
she had come into our life.

I am busy. You were out of breath
on the phone. I'll talk to you later.
I bit the doubts
of fear
counting the wait already

When I met her
she looked at me proudly.
I knew she had come to take away from me
my most precious possession
and to drown my heart.
But god was pitiful
and gave me some verses

The verses were the sun
the sea the wind
the gaze of things
and men
and I became a road.

I left you
in the secret well
of your soul
without realizing
it had no water.

I left you but did not betray you;
I was the Penelope of verses
while the proci waited

Sette paia di scarpe ho consumato
Sette anni di lacrime ho versato
Sette mari del mondo ho attraversato

Ora la tua voce è
inqueta, tenera, a volte
dolorosa nel chiedermi
ricordi? ricordi?

Cadeva la neve, cadeva
e ovattava ogni cosa
non i tuoi passi lungo il viale
non il fischio sulle scale

Perché Aracne ordi l'inganno
rimane oscuro;
mentre rimane chiaro
il giorno dell'incontro

Nel bosco mi chiamasti
riconosco la voce
viene dal passato
e fu sposalizio d'anime

noi due invecchieremo insieme

Una sera
è venuta a salutarmi
la ragazza dai capelli di Medusa.
Partiva. Per quale direzione?
Riprendeva la sua strada
rimani, non ho più paura
io e lui invecchieremo insieme
Era triste. Abbuiata.
Non si è voltata indietro.

Ho chiuso la porta piano
e gli occhi

cade la neve, cade
sento
il tuo fischio sulle scale . . .

I used up seven pairs of shoes
I shed seven years of tears
I crossed the world's seven seas

Now your voice is
Restless, tender, at times
full of sorrow when asking me
remember? remember?

The snow was falling, it fell
and muffled all things
not your steps along the walk
not the whistle on the stairs

Why Arachne plotted the deceit
remains a mystery;
while the day of the encounter
is still clear

In the woods you called me
I recognize the voice
it comes from the past
and it was a marriage of souls
The two of us shall grow old together

One night
the girl with Gorgon hair
came to say goodbye to me.
She was leaving. For which destination?
She was on her way again
stay, I am no longer afraid
he and I shall grow old together
She was sad. Gloomy.
She did not look back.

I softly closed the door
and my eyes

the snow falls, it falls
I hear
its whistle on the stairs . . .

→ Gino Chiellino (b. 1946)

Gino Chiellino was born in 1946 in Carlopoli, in Calabria, and has been living in Augsburg, Germany, since 1970. Since 1973 he has written poetry primarily in German. He is professor of comparative literature at the University of Augsburg and has been working for more than a decade on a project regarding a possible science of intercultural literatures.

Chiellino began writing poetry in 1973, composing directly in German. His first work, *Mein fremder Alltag* (*Il mio quotidiano straniero, My Foreign Newspaper*, 1984), is a collection of occasional poems documenting the birth of writing without a historical-cultural memory. Thus Chiellino does in poetry what Franco Biondi had done for prose. The poems of *Mein fremder Alltag* deal with the daily life of a self foreign to the language in which the work is written. The self comes in contact with German as a language that is being spoken to him, but which does not leave him any room to express, in that language, that which he is not. The collection ends with the poem "Der deutsche Pass" ("Il passaporto Tedesco" [The German Passport]), which addresses the rejection of a model of integration of the "melting pot" type, which forces one to become a different person. Such a rejection, after thirty years of writing, appears as an aesthetic model in the sense that the rejection of the German passport, of the norm, of accepting existing monocultural models and aesthetic projects, has allowed Chiellino to get to the point of writing intercultural literature in the German language. In other words, he was able to integrate into the language of his poetry the historical and cultural memory accumulated in his other two languages: Calabrian and Italian. *Mein fremder Alltag* was followed by the publication of *Sehnsucht nach Sprache* (*Voglia di lingue, Desiring Languages*, 1987) and *Sich die Fremde nehmen* (*Togliersi/ Prendersi la diversità, Get Rid of/Acquire Diversity*, 1992), with which Chiellino focuses on the *Fremde* topic, convinced that it could be overcome through a patient analysis of the strata that constitute it. A step toward overcoming the difference is the awareness that by immigrating, one goes through a condition of estrangement and cultural growth and at the same time becomes a carrier of diversity for the society into which one immigrates. Only through the intuition of the double function of *Fremde* can one succeed in coexisting with it and avoid being determined by it. With the collection *Landschaften aus Menschen und Tagen* (*Paesaggi di uomini e giorni, Landscapes of Men and Days*), published in 2010, Gino Chiellino attempts an erotic type of writing as the last resort for one who writes in a language different from his own, according to what Vladimir Nabokov maintained. The following cycle of poems, written in Italian, evidences the point of transition between the two parts of the work, in a sense the very driving force of the collection.

Canto 1

Nel cielo
lavato dai pensieri
con i colori di Gjelosh
già sull'orizzonte
attendo la tua voce
per iniziare l'alba

Canto 1

In the thought-washed
sky
with Gjelosh colors
on the horizon already
I wait for your voice
to begin dawn

Canto 2

Sappimi
                  sereno
nel tuo pensiero
                      e lontano
nell'invidia degli occhi
a cui è dato vederti

Canto 2

Know me
    to be peaceful
in your thoughts
    and far
in the envy of the eyes
privileged by your sight

Canto 3

A questa vita fuori
ho rubato
cinque giorni
e le tue notti
per ricominciare
a vivere

Canto 3

From this life outside
I stole
five days
and your nights
to start
living again

Canto 4

Se gli occhi non
ti raggiungono
ed io affido la voce
a rumori
che negano il mio volto
ti cerco in me
e ti trovo tra le parole
che mi rimettono la memoria

Canto 4

If my eyes can't
reach you
and I lend over my voice
to noises
that conceal my face
I seek you inside me
and find you among the words
that return my memory

Canto 5

Adesso che
gli amanti al mare
ti sanno
e vicini ti cercano
per la città deserta
nel vuoto delle stanze
guidato dalle tue risa
da lontano
ti inseguo

Canto 5

Now that
lovers believe you
to be at the beach
and seek you close by
through the deserted town
in the emptiness of rooms
guided by your laughter
from far away
I chase you

Canto 6

Ho messo l'anima
a sventolare alla finestra
di questo mattino
in blu secco
uscito dalle tue mani
in una notte di nebbie
filigranate tra le betulle

Canto 6

I poured my soul
to wave outside the window
of this morning
in dry blue
coming out of your hands
in a night of fogs
watermarked through the silver birches

Canto 7

Questa vita fuori
dolce avversaria del mio esilio
spinge i sensi al noto
ti ha scorta a me non diversa
e generosa nel corpo
questa vita fuori
non vive
dove il ricordo ti insegue

Canto 7

This life outside
sweet adversary of my exile
leads the senses to the known
it has perceived you to be not unlike me
and generous in the body
this life outside
can't live
where memory chases you

Canto 8

Terreno ed umano
mi sento mentre
ti allontani e ritorni
al mio corpo
la tua mano mi scorre
sulla schiena
tracciando mari e continenti
e mi affido
all'oscillare della tua immagine
che scivola leggera sui pensieri

Canto 8

Earthly and human
I feel while
you walk away and return
to my body
your hand runs
down my back
tracing seas and continents
and I abandon myself
to the swaying of your image
lightly skimming over thoughts

Canto 9

Il corpo
mi si allontana
nei pomeriggi sottovoce
tra sguardi di donne in amore
si avvicina alla tua assenza
e la svela in una lingua
dove sa che non sei

Canto 9

The body
goes far from me
in whispered afternoons
among glances of women in love
it draws near to your absence
and it reveals it in a language
where it knows you are not

Canto 10

mi porto dentro
il ricordo del tuo sesso
nero
di nero mi invade
il sole la stanza
del mio non vivere
e
mi scindo a pensarti
disciolta in orgasmo
e serena in occhi
che non sono i miei

Canto 10

I bring inside of me
the memory of your sex
black
it invades me with black
the sun the room
of my nonliving
and
I'm severed in the thought of you
melted in an orgasm
and peaceful in eyes
that are not mine

→ Franco Biondi (b. 1947)

Franco Biondi was born in Forlì, Romagna, in 1947 and has been living in Germany since 1965, currently in Hanau. Since 1973 he has been writing in Italian and, since the mid-1970s, also in German. His works include novels, short stories, and essays. The denial of returning or rather commuting is one of the basic themes of the literature of the Italian writers in Germany. It is to Franco Biondi's credit to have treated it in all its complexity in his Italian tale *Il ritorno di Passavanti* (*Passavanti's Return*), written in 1976, which led to the title of his first collection of short stories in German in 1982, titled *Passavantis Rückkehr*. Passavanti's return to his land of origin in Romagna does not obtain the results desired by the protagonist. The return to the community of origin is not successful for two reasons: because living outside of his community of origin has sharpened the protagonist's perception of his own dignity, which forces him to reject all suspect situations; and because the conflict that led to his initial departure becomes more acute each time the protagonist returns to his point of origin. Passavanti's decision to return to Germany is made with the awareness that his return either to Germany or to Italy will not ever turn into a permanent stay. Biondi, however, had not exhausted his study of the condition of commuting. He went beyond the tales of *Passavantis Rückkehr* and *Die Tarantel* (*La tarantola*, *The Tarantula*, 1982) with the novel *Abschied der zerschellten Jahren* (*Addio agli anni infranti*, *Goodbye to the Shattered Years*, 1984), in which the protagonist, Mamo, in spite of his generational problems and problems of integration into the work force, is committed to making sense out of his young life in Germany. In addition, Biondi wrote three other novels focusing on the development of German society from the economic boom to the end of the twentieth century: *Die unversohnlichen. Im Labyrinth der Herkunft* (*Gli inconciliabili: nel labirinto della provenienza*, *The Irreconcilable Ones: In the Labyrinth of the Origin*, 1991); *In deutschen Kuchen* (*Nelle cucine tedesche*, *In German Kitchens*,

1997); and *Der Stau* (*L'ingorgo, The Traffic Jam*, 2001). Biondi's contribution to German intercultural literature consists precisely in underscoring the multicentered nature of all national languages as a possible point of departure toward a German language open to an intercultural future. In the poems selected for this anthology from the bilingual 2005 collection, *Giri e rigiri/Laufend*, Biondi has returned to his initial theme after thirty years of writing.

I

da *Giri e rigiri*

per esempio adesso allacciata
al modulo d'espansione d'un computer
che ti piazza un piatto di lasagne surgelate
fra le fibre della dentiera
e ti schiaffa nel mezzo delle occhiaie
cinquanta teleberlusconi
mentre ti masturbi in cima ai timpani
con le canzonette di Andreotti
viaggiando ai zero all'ora sulla A1
e telefonando con qualche nemico personale
ma certo ma certo
le dittature si proliferano solo in periferia
qui regna solo l'imperativo
della totale efficienza del tempo
e chi non è d'accordo
vada altrove
dove gli spediremo i prodotti made in Italy

I

from *Round and Around*

For example now linked
to the expansion module of a PC
that places a serving of frozen lasagna
between the fibers of your dentures
and slaps fifty teleberlusconis
in the middle of the rings under your eyes
while you masturbate at the top of your eardrums
with Andreotti's jingles
traveling at zero miles per hour on the A1
while phoning some personal enemy
but of course of course
dictatorships only proliferate in suburbs
here rules only the imperative
of total efficiency of time
and those who don't agree
can go elsewhere
where we will send them products made in Italy.

II

ancora una volta
a fare giri e rigiri
e rivedere la vecchiaia di mia madre

ancora una volta
strade piazze caseggiati e vite
rigonfie di ripetizioni

respiro l'ozono di noia e indifferenza
fra aliti di gioia e di tristezza
maturando il congedo dei rigiri

ora vado a seppellirli
nella tomba di famiglia

II

once again twisting and turning
to see my mother's old age

once again
streets, piazzas, buildings and lives
filled with repetitions

I breathe the ozone of boredom and indifference
among sighs of joys and sadness
nourishing the farewell of turnings

now I go to bury them
in the family tomb

III

la luce si fa più sottile

l'aria più trasudata

lo sguardo torbido

& i capelli si colorano di grigio
& le foglie ingiallite cadono
& la scorza si scannella sempre più
& gli anelli aumentano nel tronco
& i rami si diradano
di anno in anno

sì osservandomi
l'autunno è inconfondibile
irrevocabile:

ma sui miei rami crescono
fianco a fianco tristezza e gioia
si proliferano & turgide
come su un caco
pesante di frutti carnosi
in un cielo invernale

III

the light grows dimmer

the air grows sweatier

the eyes blur

& the hair becomes gray
& the yellow leaves fall
& the crust keeps peeling off
& the rings increase in the trunk
& the branches thin out
from year to year

yes observing myself
autumn is unmistakable
irrevocable:

yet on my branches grow
side by side sadness and joy
they proliferate as juicy
as on a khaki tree
heavy with fleshy fruits
in a winter sky

IV

lastre di pietra, ghiaia, malta
impregnano la luce
di grigio, marrone arrugginito, blu metallico

tu ed io siamo
come il cardo e il dente di leone:
non ci lasciamo espellere

ci imponiamo ogni anno
e cresciamo forti e solidi
con foglie argute e fiori gialli

& luccichiamo inesorabili

IV

slabs of stone, gravel, mortar
soak the light
in gray, rusty brown, metallic blue

you and I are
like thistle and dandelion
we won't be expelled

we impose ourselves every year
and grow strong and solid
with sharp leaves and yellow flowers

& shine relentlessly

V

le stelle sfavillano messaggi inconcepibili
il sole mantiene a galla il nostro calore
la rana gracida nello stagno
e divora mosche senza remore
i pesci festeggiano nell'acquario
la sospensione della vita nuda
ed osservano ansiosi le dita
che danno e prendono
io mi scuoto
e cerco continuamente
la benevolenza dei sogni
come pure l'intensità della vita

V

stars sparkle inconceivable messages
the sun keeps our warmth afloat
the frog croaks in the pond
and devours flies with no regret
fish celebrate in the aquarium
the suspension of a naked life
and anxiously observe the fingers
giving and taking
I rouse myself
and continuously seek
the benevolence of dreams
as well as the intensity of life.

VI

mi viene ricordato:

solo per voi sarebbe
madre
a me è stata data solo in prestito

dite quel che vi pare

sento quanto l'amo
& che da me sgorga
come una sorgente antica

si esprime attraversandomi

sento come mi riempie l'esistenza
& mi ancora
al flusso della nostra vita

mi voglio dire

è un giardino
& un fiore
& le radici di mio figlio

VI

I am reminded:

for you only she would be
a mother
for me she was only borrowed

say what you like

I feel how much I love her
& that from me she pours out
like an ancient spring

she expresses herself through me

I feel how she fills my existence
& anchors me
to the flow of our lives

I want to tell myself

she is a garden
& a flower
& the roots of my son

→ Fruttuoso Piccolo (Mao) (b. 1953)

Fruttuoso Piccolo was born in the Veneto region in 1953 and has been residing in Germany, not far from Hannover, since 1972. He wrote in Italian from 1970 to 1980, at which point he began to write in German, composing poems and experimental texts such as *Tempo Gastarbeiter*. He recently resumed writing in Italian. He is the author of the catalogue *Buchstäblich* and of the collection and exhibit *Grenzüberschreitende Literatur* (Hanover, 1993).

In his first collection, *1970–1980 Dieci anni fra due mondi* (*1970–1980 Ten Years between Two Worlds*), published in 1980, Piccolo introduces himself decisively as an immigrant anarchist and writer in Italian. He overcomes isolation with his second book, *Arlecchino Gastarbeiter* (*Harlequin Guest Worker*, 1985), and makes his way in German, which will also be the language of his third collection. His strategy consists in translating his own verses and in rewriting the texts already written in Italian, resulting in a bilingual text. This also constitutes a passage from the cultural language of origin to the language of daily living. Self-translation, a practice of so many bilingual writers, allows Piccolo to test his presence in the language of daily intercourse, even though, naturally, he has accumulated his own storehouse of memories encoded in Italian. Piccolo's third collection has the variably interpretable title *Durch die Sprache ein ander(es) Ich* (*Through Language Another Self*, 1987). But it would be misleading to see in the *Sprache/lingua/language* that transforms his self (*Ich/io/I*) a sort of melting pot for the creation of Italo-German citizens. Italian writers in Germany have never assumed the model of the melting pot, neither in aesthetic terms nor in existential and judicial terms. Neither the authors themselves nor literary critics have ever posited an official type of literature known as Italo-German, not even for the new generations coming from mixed marriages of Italians and Germans. Piccolo counts primarily on intercultural solidarity in order to overcome ethnic and social conflicts that slow down the coexistence of German and minority groups. Solidarity between man and woman turns into an intercultural love of the type of "*Liebe aus der Ferne*" (love from afar); solidarity among workers becomes solidarity of minority groups in the Repubblica Federale Tedesca (RFT) in the two cycles *Echo der Wanderung* (*Echo of Migration*) and *Tempo Gastarbeiter* (*Speed of the Guest Worker*). To such forms of solidarity, Piccolo adds the solidarity among writers against the aesthetic narrowness of nationalism in the cycle *Der Nationalismus ist unfähig zur Poesie* (*Nationalism Is Incapable of Poetry*). But the dream of a society in harmony with itself is entrusted by Piccolo to the lower classes that should carry it over from the work world to civic settings to then overcome all discrimination and socioethnic orders. Piccolo remains faithful to these themes, although at first glance the texts included here might seem very distant from those of the three collections of poetry.

Infuso

di storie, geni, cristi e ombre di vino rosso.

Nell'antica Grecia, le città repubbliche erano libere.

Cedettero! In conseguenza alle guerre con la Persia.

Cedettero!

Le arti e le scienze ad Alessandro!

Egli pensò bene di sostituirle al sistema centralizzato, al dispotismo
politico, alla ricchezza.

Specchio per le allodole.

Da Roma partirono i predoni della ricchezza.

Da Roma: lo stato centralizzato, la rapina, il dominio delle classi.

Nell'Ellade non arde più la fiaccola, simbolo di tanta civiltà e di tanta
libertà.

Da Roma, l'orgia per il potere.

Da Roma l'odio, la guerra nel mondo.

Ma! Qualcuno ha capito!

In un terreno tale, fertile di sangue e odio nasce la protesta.

Nasce in Giudea. Il suo fondatore è Cristo.

Cristianesimo.

Gli uomini cercano la pace.

Cristianesimo!

Amore di "vino" per gli uomini, per tutti! Senza divisione di rango o
razza.

Amore . . . per la vittima della violenza. Cristo è un uomo del popolo.

Ai poveri Cristo, tra i poveri Cristo e gli apostoli di Cristo.

Felicità della collettività, ideale sociale, Cristo è capace di sacrificare la
sua vita.

vita. Contro gli errori della società. Uguaglianza tra i poveri, tra gli
uomini. Amore per tutti. Perdono delle offese, nessuna vendetta.
amore.

L'amore di Cristo creò disordini e proteste, creò consapevolezza fra i
poveri.

Dalla Giudea a Roma: migliaia furono le vittime delle esecuzioni,
delle persecuzioni dell'impero Romano (disturbato da questa
nuova forma di protesta).

Vittima del suo amore: Cristo muore.

Crocefisso.

Infusion

of stories, geniuses, christs and shadows of red wine
In ancient Greece, the city-republics were free.
They gave in! As a consequence of the wars with Persia.
They gave in!
The arts and sciences to Alexander!
He thought it a good idea to substitute them with a centralized
    system, political despotism, wealth.
A lark mirror.
From Rome departed the looters of wealth.
From Rome: the centralized state, plunder, the domination of the
    classes.
In Hellas the torch no longer burns, symbol of so much civilization
    and freedom.
From Rome, the orgy for power.
From Rome the hatred, the war in the world.
But! Someone has understood!
In such a ground, fertile with blood and hate, protest is born.
It is born in Judea. Its founder is Christ.
Christianity.
Men seek peace.
Christianity!
Love of "wine" for men, for everyone! Without distinction of rank or
    race.
Love . . . for the victims of violence. Christ is a man of the people.
To Christ's poor, among Christ's poor and Christ's apostles.
Happiness for all the people, social ideal, Christ is capable of
    sacrificing his life.
life. Against the mistakes of society. Equality among the poor, among
    men. Love for all. Forgiveness for offences, no revenge. love.
Christ's love created disorders and protests, it created awareness
    among the poor.
From Judea to Rome: Thousands were victims of the executions, the
    persecutions of the Roman Empire (troubled by this new form of
    protest).
Victim of his love: Christ dies.
Crucified.

Lentamente, nel tempo i suoi discepoli se ne allontanano, cercandosi
un organo di protezione. La chiesa nuova Istituzione. Da sete di
ricchezza e potere, la Chiesa dimentica, si allontana dalla dottrina di
Cristo, Nell'amore predicato da Cristo, entra la lotta
tra il bene e il male—
la luce o le tenebre.
La chiesa dimentica Cristo e le sue dottrine: parla solo di diavoli e
satani, inculca nel popolo solo il pregiudizio. Acquista potere e se
ne fa garante con i Re. Predica l'amore con la santa inquisizione. Le
torture e i roghi. Chi sei? Tu uomo, che condanni gli altri, condanni
te stesso! Sul patibolo, il prete accompagna il boia. Il Cristianesimo
si suicida, cessa di essere la religione di Cristo Crocefisso. La
metamorfosi lo trasforma in Religione di Stato. Potere al Potere.
Giustizia alla giustizia.
Schiavitù ancora.
A riscattare la schiavitù fu la rivoluzione

Slowly, in time his disciples move away from him, they look for
   protection. The Church a new institution. Thirsting for wealth and
   power, the Church forgets, moves away from Christ's doctrine, in
   the love preached by Christ enters the struggle
                    —between good and evil
                      light and darkness
The Church forgets Christ and his doctrines: it speaks only of devils
   and Satans, it instills only prejudices in the people. It gains power
   and guarantees it with kings. It preaches love with the Holy
   Inquisition. Tortures and stakes. Who are you? You man, who
   condemn others, do you condemn yourself? On the gallows, the
   priest accompanies the executioner. Christianity commits suicide, it
   stops being the religion of Christ on the Cross. The metamorphosis
   transforms him into a State Religion. Power to Power. Justice to
   justice.
Slavery still.
Slavery was rescued by the revolution

Alle tre lettere alfabetiche:

"U . . . T . . . E . . ."[1]

UTE E TU . . .

TU UTE E . . .

E TU UTE . . .

UTE TU E . . .

E UTE TU . . .

TU E UTE . . .

To the Three Letters of the Alphabet:

"U ... T ... E ..."[2]

UTE E TU ...

TU UTE E ...

E TU UTE ...

UTE TU E ...

E UTE TU ...

TU E UTE ...

Specchio, specchio cortese

dimmi:
Chi è il più fesso in questo paese?

un gast,[3] due gast, tre gast   lavoro, lavoro, lavoro, lavoro, lavoro,
una ex camera a gas . . .

un gast, due gast, tre gast   lavoro, lavoro, lavoro, lavoro, lavoro,
una ex camera a gas . . .

un gast, due gast, tre gast
una ex camera a gas . . .   lavoro, lavoro, lavoro, lavoro, lavoro

mi só stufo de sudare
me domando chi me o fá fare

mi non voglio piú emigrare
a se ora de cambiare

a se ora de fermare
stó lavoro me fá mae

so finío in ospedale
con a malattia speciae

tbc—sifiede
eroina—diossina
gastrite—neurosi

a se ora de cambiare
qua bisogna pur lottare

per non farse ammazzare . . .

un gast, due gast, tre gast   lavoro, lavoro, lavoro, lavoro, lavoro,
una ex camera a gas . . .
un gast, due gast, tre gast   lavoro, lavoro, lavoro, lavoro, lavoro,
una ex camera a gas . . .
un gast, due gast, tre gast
una ex camera a gas . . .   lavoro, lavoro, lavoro, lavoro, lavoro

Mirror, mirror on the wall

tell me:
Who in this town is the dumbest of all?

One gast,[4] two gast, three gast   work, work, work, work, work
one ex–gas chamber

One gast, two gast, three gast   work, work, work, work, work
one ex–gas chamber

One gast, two gast, three gast   work, work, work, work, work
one ex–gas chamber

I am tired of sweating
I wonder why I do it

I don't want to emigrate any more
it's time to change

it's time to end
this work that's hurting me

I ended up in the hospital
with a special sickness

tbc—syphilis
heroin—dioxin
gastritis—neurosis

it's time to change
here we have to fight

so they won't kill us . . .

One gast, two gast, three gast   work, work, work, work, work
one ex–gas chamber

One gast, two gast, three gast   work, work, work, work, work
one ex–gas chamber

One gast, two gast, three gast   work, work, work, work, work
one ex–gas chamber

Ciao.
Una volta quando tu non avevi lo specchio della verità,
mi chiamavi e mi cercavi,
io specchio delle allodole,
ti rispondevo
e sinceramente ti dicevo
come e chi era la piú bella di questo reame.
Certo
non era e non è facile
sentirsi dire
ciò che non si vuole
e tanto meno sentire
che, ciò che si desidera
è una "proiezione."
Di colei che
allo specchio cerca
in se stessa
ciò
che lo specchio
tanto meno
le può dare,
anche
se,
appunto:
Una riflessione!
D' un' immagine
che nella realtà
tanto altro è
a quella,
che si vede
e viene vista.
Io non ti conosco,
lo specchio
non posso sostituirlo . . .
tutte quelle immagini,
sono uno rispecchio
della tua immagine,
non sei tu

Hi.
Once when you didn't have the mirror of truth,
you called me and looked for me,
I lark mirror
answered you
and sincerely told you
how and who was the fairest of this kingdom.
No doubt
it wasn't and it isn't easy
to hear
what you don't want to hear
and even less to hear
that what one desires
is a "projection."
Of she who
at the mirror seeks
in herself
what
the mirror
even less
can give her,
even
if,
precisely:
A reflection!
Of an image
that is in reality
much different
from that one,
which sees itself
and is seen.
I don't know you,
I can't replace
the mirror . . .
All those images
are a mirroring
of your image,
it is not you

e tanto meno sono io
quello che hai visto.
Siamo proiezioni.
Desideri!

Certo che nel fatto, che noi ci siamo aperti in un dialogo e a volte in una lite dei sentimenti, che sconvolti e a volte contorti dal proprio destino e dalla riflessione del perché, dalla voglia, dalla nostalgia, della speranza, la realtà d'una rivoluzione, il cercare uno o una che diventa complice, essere clandestini in una storia d'amore, essere vicini a chi è lontano e sentirsi vicini anche se si è cosi lontani, e tante altre riflessioni e somme di calcoli e pensieri, sentimenti e voglie.

Che bello! C'era tanta passione!!!!!!!!!!!!!!!!!!!!!
Perché mi scrivi questi brevi sms/mail, con queste frasi di "scusa ma
   non ti voglio disturbare."

Lo sai che ho voglia di sentirti e di conoscerti più profondamente, da come fino ad ora è successo tra noi. La paura e l'incertezza hanno avuto la ragione, sul fatto di non incontrarsi. La realtà quotidiana era ed è più forte di ciò che ci potrebbe unire . . . che bello avere paura di innamorarsi, sarà masochista ma è bello essere innamorati di chi si lascia accarezzare senza farsi toccare, da chi ti bacia senza prenderti il fiato, da chi ti risucchia la mascolinità senza bagnarsi di sperma, da chi ti da il calore senza sentirsi freddi . . . Ti ho sentita spesso e tanto e ancora adesso dove tu sei ancora più lontana, ti penso e mi manchi . . . si perché la nostra storia era una storia di amicizia vera, di quelle dove ci si cerca fino al fondo, senza darsi assicurazioni e raccomandazioni e tanto meno risposte telecomandate e volute. Siamo arrivati ad un bivio, io con la sega della paura. Tu matematica, che vuole tutto, ma sempre di nascosto. Mandandoti i miei messaggi, ti raccontavo di una storia che non vorrebbe finire e tanto meno essere sostituita. Ti ho sentito molto lontana anche se il tuo andare in bici, l'ho sentito molto vicino, mi sembrava di essere i tuoi pedali e a volte il tuo manubrio . . . ti sentivo libera con i capelli al vento, libera da tutta quella storia d'amore consumatasi con il tempo . . . anche due figli, 50 anni e voglia di innamorarsi. Ma libera ti sento piú mia, di quando ti fai le storie con i carabinieri in servizio dello stato . . . penso che tu non mi hai risposto e chiamato perché il tuo italo/brasilero, ti dá, cio'che desideri e

that you saw
and even less me.
We are projections.
Desires!

No doubt in fact we opened ourselves to a dialog and at times a quarrel of emotions, overcome and twisted by our own destiny and the reflection of why, by desire, longing, hope, the reality of a revolution, seeking a man or woman who becomes an accomplice, being clandestine in a love story, being close to one who is far and feeling close even if you're so far away . . . and so many other reflections and sums of calculations and thoughts, feelings, and desires.

How nice! There was so much passion!!!!!!!!!!!!!!!!!
Why do you write me these brief SMS/e-mails, with phrases like
"Sorry but I don't want to disturb you."

You know that I want to hear you and know you more deeply, what has happened between us till now. Fear and uncertainty have had the upper hand over getting together. Everyday reality was and is stronger than what could unite us . . . how nice to be afraid to fall in love, it may be masochistic but it's nice to be in love with one who lets herself be caressed without being touched, one who kisses you without stealing your breath, one who sucks in your masculinity without getting wet with sperm, one who gives you warmth without feeling cold . . . I heard you often and so much even now where you are still farther away, I think about you and I miss you . . . yes because our story was a story of true friendship, of those where you search deep inside, without giving assurances and recommendations, let alone remote-controlled, deliberate answers. We have reached a crossroads, I with the saw of fear, you mathematical, wanting everything, but always on the sly. Sending you my messages, I was telling you a story that would like not to end, let alone be replaced. I felt you very distant even if I felt close to your riding a bike, I seemed to be your pedals and at times your handlebar . . . I felt you free with your hair in the wind, free from that whole love story consumed by time . . . even two children, fifty years old and wanting to fall in love. But free I feel you more mine than when you fool around with *carabinieri* serving the state . . . I think you didn't answer or call me because your Italo-Brazilian gives you what you want and what

che tu vuoi sentire! Credendo che tu sei quella che fa'i calcoli . . . ti decidi
sì, di fare le schede telefoniche con quelli che non ti creano rimprovero!

Oh bella! Lo sai, che quelli che ti vogliono, sono quelli che in te
   cercano la volontà di essere diversi, originali, liberi e combattivi e
   non adeguati, associati e magari sottomessi.
Nel ruolo dell'amore ti voglio forte e libera . . . e sì! Proprio lí, ti sento
   mia, tutta mia e anche se tu ti apri e ti dai ad altri, anche se, ti dai
   e ti apri, rimani con me

il vento della primavera,
quel vento che abbracciato
dalle nuvole
e da un cielo
azzurro,
intreccia
aquiloni
e fumare di aeroplani
che circondano
il mondo
e accorciano la voglia
di sentirsi coccolati
tra i colori
dell'arcobaleno
e che
danno respiro
a sogni.

I carabinieri nell'impugnare una arma di
servizio,
seviziano la sincerità
e la volontà di saper amare.

Io non ti avrò
detto di amarti
ma ti avrò scritto
per mille volte
che ogni lettera dell'alfabeto
è una storia,
una poesia
un romanzo

you want to hear! Believing you're the one who's doing the adding . . . you
decide to get telephone cards with those that don't reproach you!

> That's a good one! You know that those who want you are those that
> seek in you the will to be different, original, free and combative and
> not adequate, associated, and maybe submitted.
> In the role of love I want you strong and free . . . and yes! Right there,
> I feel you to be mine, all mine and you too open yourself and give
> yourself to others, even though you still remain with me.

The wind of spring,
that wind that embraced
by the clouds
and by a blue
sky
entwines
kites
and airplane plumes
that encircle the world
and shorten the longing
to be cuddled
amid the colors
of the rainbow
and that
give breath
to dreams.

The *carabinieri* by holding service weapons
torture sincerity
and the will to know how to love.

Maybe I didn't
tell you I loved you
but I must have written you
a thousand times
that every letter of the alphabet
is a story
a poem
a novel
a thought

un pensiero,
una dischiarizione . . .

io ti ho sognato
desiderato
e ancora
ti voglio
e ti rivoglio . . .
ma non come tu sei . . .
ma come tu diventerai . . .

allora
a quel punto
saprò
che io
e te
siamo arrivati
a quel punto.

Orgasmo

Buon giorno,
dandan,
danblu,
la vezzo signora.
Pescatrice di uomini.
Adesso ti chiamo.

Avevo già provato, ma credo che era Gloria. A proposito la ripetizione è
certamente una prova di come ti ho visto, rivisto, ripetutamente cercato, rivista e ricercata, trovata, copiata, rispedita e riscritta e riletta e rivista e ripetutamente sentita e mancata e ricercata e trovata e accoppiata e rispedita e poi
e poi risentita , riletta, ritrovata e sognata e guardata, assorbita e sperata.

Ciao sposa, quel giorno che mi rimandi una serie del tuo culo . . .
    all'ora ritroverò la voglia di partire in un viaggio senza ritorno.

Alla tua domanda: mi sento come una lampada al posto sbagliato e
    nella direzione opposta.
Ciao buchetto di vita, luce di speranza, storia d'amore.
mao

a declaration . . .
I have dreamed of you
desired you
and still
I want you
and want you again . . .
But not as you are . . .
But as you will become . . .

Then
at that point
I will know
that I
and you
have reached
that point

Orgasm

Good morning
dandan
danblu,
lady Lavezzo.

Fisher of men.
Now I call you.

I had already tried, but I think it was Gloria. By the way repetition is
certainly proof of how I saw you, saw you again, repeatedly looked for
you, saw and looked for again, found, copied, resent and rewritten and
reread and repeatedly heard and missed and sought again and coupled
and resent and then and then heard again, read again, found again and
dreamed and looked at, absorbed and hoped.

Bye bride, the day you send me a series of your ass . . . then I will find
   again the will to leave for a trip without return.
To your question: I feel like a lamp in the wrong place and in the
   opposite direction.

Bye small hole of life, light of hope, love story.
mao

→ Franco Sepe (b. 1955)

Franco Sepe was born in Fondi in 1955. He studied psychology at the University of Rome. In 1979 he moved to West Berlin with a scholarship from the National Research Council. Since 1995, he has been lecturer in Italian language and culture at the Romance Institute of the University of Potsdam.

Franco Sepe made his debut in the 1980s with two plays: *Berlinturcomedea* (1984), a one-act tragedy on the conditions of foreign women in Berlin, and *L'incontro* (1987), a comedy in three acts on two central characters of twentieth-century Italian theater. To these two pieces for the theater he added a collection of poems, *Elegiette berlinesi* (*Little Berlin Elegies*, 1987), composed at the beginning of the 1980s, which reproduce with great intensity the first experiences of the writer with a most unique city, as Berlin was before the German reunification. But it was not until 2002 that his *Autobiografia dei cinque sensi* (*Autobiography of the Five Senses*) was published. Given the author's still young age, *autobiography* must be understood in terms of a transition from senses to language. Sepe's search is an excavation in order to allow the language of his autobiography of the senses to come forth from *Körpergedächtnis*, which, in German culture, indicates the memory that collects in the body before language can organize it by abstractions, because the body has not yet developed the language skills to do so. Sepe's search unveils itself, as a language of autobiography, through contrasts and echoes and is counterposed, through continuous dialogue, with German. In *Autobiography of the Five Senses*, one finds the writer's pursuit to make the language of his youth very concrete in order to counterbalance the abstract characters of his second language. It could be said that Sepe's approach is the opposite of Vladimir Nabokov's, who wrote first his autobiography *Speak, Memory*, in order to enter into the English language. Nabokov did this so that he could inhabit the English language, in which he would write *Lolita*. The opposite road followed by Sepe may have allowed him to continue to feel the sensuality of the first language while the second language became more and more the carrier of memories and new experiences outside the first language. Although Sepe made a nearly definitive switch to prose after his second novel, *Investigazioni su un castello* (*Investigations on a Castle*, 2003), he continues to write poetry on themes compatible with those of *Elegiette berlinesi* in preparation of a second book of poems.

I

Ricordiamoci un giorno, semplicemente,
di queste due ombre
(riflesse in forma di larve) sulla porta di vetro
del Botanischer Garten; e della

                        coppia
di stalattiti fumanti nel tepore tropicale della serra:
(il tutto, magari, per la durata di un'istantanea);

(mentre fuori si trascinano i colori del parco gelato
nelle traiettorie
verticali delle betulle,
sui rami in groppa alla quercia.)

from *Little Berlin Elegies*

I

Let's remember one day, simply,
these two shadows
(reflected in the shape of a ghost on the glass door
of the Botanischer Garten; and
                              a pair
of steaming stalactites in the tropical warmth of the
greenhouse:
(all of it, probably, for the duration of a snapshot):

(while outside the colors of the frozen park drag along in the
vertical
trajectories of the birch trees,
on the branches on the back of the oak tree.)

Hai strattonato la tua caverna d'acqua

da *Elegia planetaria*
a Ion Mavilo

VI
corpicciolo decantato dentro un fermo
liquore di bonaccia.
Sfrullare nell'ovale della culla ora è per te
rinascita da un sonno stralunato
voglia di vita il morso del viscere
che si scioglie in pianto, gola protesa
verso una vena nascosta della fonte
fiato corto a catturare il fiotto
di quell'unica linfa.
Con l'impeto animale di chi ignora
sei salvo ma chissà per quanto ancora
da poltiglie liofile, dai pasti ibernati
dai geni distesi sulla lamina a temperare
al gusto il supplizio del grano.

You jerked within your cavern full of water

from *Planetary Elegy*
to *Ion Mavilo*

VI
body decanted inside a still
liquor of dead calm.
Now your thrashing in the oval of
your cradle is born of a wild dream
the will to live the bite of the viscera
bursting into tears, throat stretched
toward a hidden vein of the fountain
breath curtailed to capture the stream
of that singular lymph.
With that animal urge you're unaware of
you're safe but who knows for how long
from lyophilic slimes, from hibernated meals
from the genes stretched on the lamina to temper
according to taste the torment of the grain.

Le alture muovono un'aria di pietra

ad Antonella Anedda

XI
il picco cinto dal maestrale scosta
da sé fiocco e arpione.
Il gelo solleva le costole a dita
aperte, svelto le unisce come palpebra
battente.
Il corpo è fionda e aratro
dura vibrazione dentro il binario
sdrucciolo.
Uno scarto di fianco al balzare
del mercurio spiana la discesa
di prospero cristallo, atomi
che si tengono per mano lanciati
nel rombo del fondo valle,
gramo friggere di vetri sotto
la molatura del ghiaccio,
il legno delle mura infisso
nella pietra sepolcrale.
Devastazioni di un rotolo
di neve.
Bianco iridato e perpetuo
a soffondere di sé
uomini e cose.

The heights move an air of stone

to Antonella Anedda

XI

the peak encircled by the northwest wind
pushes hook and grapple from itself.
The ice lifts the ribs of the spread
fingers, joins them swiftly as a fluttering
eyelid.
The body is a catapult and a plow
hard vibration in the slippery
track.
A sidewise swerve at the quicksilver
leaping smoothes the slope
of flourishing crystal, atoms
holding on by hand hurled
into the deep valley's roar,
wretched screeching of glass beneath
the grinding of the ice,
the wood of the walls fixed
in the sepulchral stone.
The ravages of a roll
of snow.
Iridescent and perpetual white
suffusing men and things
with itself.

Dell'aria, bianco calore nel petto

XXVII
respiro senza ombra, nudità
che un raggio riveste di polvere
viva, fazzoletto dalle trasparenze
scolpite nel vento—

dell'aria a preoccupare non è lo screzio
innocente del catino ossidato, ma la nera
frode sui pinnacoli sacri alti per risplendere
l'affanno dorato dei giorni dell'ozono
il piombo della cefalea.

With the air I breathe into my chest

XXVII
a shadowless white heat, a nakedness
a ray of sunlight clothes again with live
dust, a handkerchief of transparencies
carved in the wind—

it's not the harmless speckling of the oxidized
wash basin that's worrisome about the air,
but the black fraud on the high holy pinnacles
that shines the gold breathlessness of ozone days
the splitting headache's bullet.

Non è vento amico da poterci entrare,

da farsi cullare,
il passo ha gracile di un forzato,
a scatenarlo è sufficiente
l'acredine di una nube, l'umore aspro
dell'aria che non vuole stare.

Fossi soltanto ancora forza pura
che la vela fa andare, il pallone
volare. Ma altre scoperte
ti hanno chiamato a scoprire.

Così denudi la terra avvinghiato
a tutto quanto mulinando trovi:
del denaro che s'invola
tu sei il signore.

It's not a friendly wind you can go into,

LX

that can make you sway,
with footsteps as frail as a convict's,
whose release can be brought about
by the tartness of a cloud, the sour humidity
of air that doesn't want to stay.

Would that you were still only pure force
that makes the sail go away, the balloon
fly. But they have summoned you
to make other discoveries.

And so you lay the earth bare clasping
everything that you find whirling round:
of the money that disappears
you are the master.

Un transfuga da infida chimica

XIII

da malfidata fisica altererebbe
il verso al solo pronunciarne il nome.
Forse che un verso, criptico o ermetico,
varrebbe a sigillare il raggio
e la tossina?

Già il danno è in lungo in piano
in leghe sotto il mare—e sopra
a incorniciare riva e onda.

Se il verso, è vero, la natura
non offende, potrà qualcosa
in sua difesa?

A fugitive from faithless chemistry

XIII
from suspicious physics would rearrange
the verse by only saying its name.
Perhaps because a verse, cryptic or hermetic,
would serve to block the ray
and the toxin?

The damage is already far and flat
leagues under the sea—and above
framing shore and wave.

If it's true that verse does not offend
nature, might that be something
in its defense?

→ Giuseppe Giambusso (b. 1956)

Giuseppe Giambusso was born in 1956 in Riesi, Sicily, and has been living in Germany since 1974, currently in Fröndenberg. He has been writing in Italian since 1971. He is a poet and editor of educational material for the teaching of the Italian language.

Giuseppe Giambusso is the most fluid point of contact between those authors who construct their lives outside their culture of origin and define it in terms of immigration, and those who go beyond the themes of immigration and turn their attention to other life projects.

In his two collections of poetry, *Al di là dell'orizzonte/Jenseits des Horizontes* (*Beyond the Horizon*, 1985) and *Partenze/Abfahrten* (1991), Giambusso returns to immigration in two short sections of the first collection: "*Vorrei essere popolo*" and "*Lettere in versi dalla Sicilia.*" In the other three short sections, he talks about more general topics, such as peace and militarism in "Dietro le bandiere" (Behind the Flags), love in "L'aurora" (Dawn), and ecology in "Tre seni alla luna" (Three Breasts for the Moon).

The transition from the first to the second collection is also evident from the expansion of aesthetic models. In the first collection there are predominant images, open spaces, and topics that relate to Italian poetry of the 1960s and 1970s—to that poetry, in other words, which had not yet forfeited its social function, which poet-performers such as Ignazio Buttita practiced on the same footing as Pier Paolo Pasolini. In the second collection, Giambusso adapts himself aesthetically according to nascent German intercultural impulses, committing himself to overcoming his own cultural and aesthetic horizon. Giambusso's intercultural project relates on one hand to lived experiences of a life passed outside of his own cultural origin, and on the other hand to non-Italian poets who, without renouncing their own historical and cultural memories, were able to overcome the limitations of their national literature and assert themselves as authors without boundaries.

I

da *Quando passa il ramarro*

> . . . nulla è piú inabitabile di un posto
> dove siamo stati felici.
>
> Cesare Pavese

Sulle lancette disincantate

Le tegole assolate
suggeriscono ancora
isole di muschio
imitando l'ortica delle grondaie

I muri scalcinati
sposano il dente di leone
cavalcando l'argento degli ulivi

Crono divora i figli di Rea
e Federico sfiora appena
orgasmi di lingue

I bambini corrono sempre
sul filo di sole
e le direzioni svezzano
la libertà dalla luce

Ma i tuoi baci muti
dietro le porte di porte
lasciano i vicoli
per riempire le autostrade

Già ti rincorro
sulle lancette disincantate

I

from *When the Green Lizard Passes*

> . . . nothing is more uninhabitable than a place
> where we have been happy.
>
> Cesare Pavese

On the Disenchanted Clock Hands

The sunny roof tiles
once more suggest
islands of moss
aping the nettle of the gutters

The flaking walls
embrace the dandelion
riding the silver of the olive trees

Cronus devours Rhea's sons
and Federico barely skims
orgasms of tongues

Little children run
on the edge of the sun
and their courses wean
liberty from the light.

But your silent kisses
behind the doors of gates
leave the alleyways
to fill the highways.

Already I pursue you
on the disenchanted clock hands.

II

> Io vengo dalla mia infanzia
> come da una terra ...
>
> Antoine de Saint-Exupéry

Terra di terra

Mia è la terra
e la gente che attraverso

l'ombra della meridiana
che inseguo

la luce
che bevo
a cavallo del canto
del grillo

senza fili spinati
di parole

senza fili spinati

senza fili

II

> I come from my childhood
> as from a homeland . . .

> Antoine de Saint-Exupéry

Homeland of Earth

Mine is the earth
and the people I pass

the noonday shadow
I chase after

the light
I drink
mounted on the song
of the cricket

without barbed wire
of words

without barbed wire
without wire

III

Parole in prestito

A Peppe Rindone

I
con la paranoica a vasistas
e l'aspirina nell'hinterland
di un brindisi al kitsch
allergico al diktat
e al lager dell'esistenzialismo
schizzo il mio no
su un neandertaliano din a 4

II
no al rendez-vous
delle bagasce e dei ciambellani
del nuovo ancien regime di turno
no alla kermesse delle bugie
catalizzate con la pelle del popolo elettore
intelaiata in un abat-jour

III
No come un machete
nel globo dei gaudilli
no come una scimitarra
nell'alcazar di fanfaroni
e di peones servi
dei machi della pecunia

IV
Sullo zerbino del mondo
sdogano la mente
dall'eco degli almanacchi
e dalle alchimie del bazar
con un sorbetto . . .

III

Borrowed Words

to Peppe Rindone

I

with the paranoic at the transom
and the aspirin in the hinterland
of a toast to kitsch
allergic to the diktat
and the concentration camp of existentialism
I throw my no
on a Neanderthalian din at 4:00

II

no to the rendezvous
of the whores and the chamberlains
of the new ancien régime on duty
no to the kermesse of the lies
catalyzed with the hide of a choosing people
stretched on a rack in an abat-jour

III

No like a machete
in the globe of the *caudilli*
no like a scimitar
in the alcazar of the swaggerers
and the servile peons
of the machos of money

IV

On the doormat of the world
I clear my mind
from the echo of the almanacs
and the alchemies of the bazaar
with a sorbet . . .

V
. . . in pole position
sul filo del photo finish
del big bang
del no

V

. . . in pole position
at the wire of the photo finish
of the big bang
of the no

IV

Parole in subaffitto

Abito quasi nelle parole
della tua lingua

Vi salgo e scendo
con un sacchetto di sale

Parole dure
come pietra d'ardesia
soffici come onde di colza

Parole lente
come scorrimenti veloci
che mi sorpassano
resettandomi i pensieri

Con la tua presenza
piantata negli occhi
sfondo le saracinesche
del quotidiano
e con la tua assenza in tasca
prendo l'ascensore
per circumnavigare
le mie palafitte

Nei tuoi corridoi
di congiunzioni disgiuntive
vado a prendere il caffè
dalle mie parole
che da sempre
con me
e un sacchetto di sale
abitano nelle tue

IV

Sublet Words

I practically live in the words
of your language
I rise and descend
with a bag of salt

Words hard
like slate
soft like waves of rapeseed

Words slow
like the swift flows
that overtake me
resetting my thoughts

With your presence
planted in my eyes
I pound through the portcullises
of the quotidian
and with your absence in my pocket
I take the elevator
to circumnavigate
my palafittes
In your corridors
of disjunctive conjunctions
I go to take the coffee
of my words
that since always
live with me
and a bag of salt
inside yours

V

Paesaggio del ramarro

Quando passa il ramarro
le fratte si vestono di selva
e gli srotolano davanti
tappeti di stoppie arse

Si voltano tutti
quando il ramarro passa
sulla carrozza del serpente
seminando semafori rossi

Il vento seduto sui muri
innamora i rami
e i pensieri dribblano Newton
correndo sulle stampelle

I bimbi si rincorrono
dietro il ramarro senza clic
e lo attendono
sull'amaca della notte
al capolinea dell'equazione
dove il sole non sa di essere stella
perché non conosce la notte
e la luna di essere dea
perché non conosce il ramarro

Il ramarro che passa
sulla carrozza del serpente
seminando semafori rossi

V

Landscape of the Green Lizard

When the green lizard passes by
hedges dress themselves in forest
and unroll to him in front of
carpets of burned stubble

They all turn themselves
when the green lizard passes by
on the coach of the serpent
spreading red semaphores

The wind sitting on the walls
fascinates the branches
and their notions dribble Newton
hurrying on crutches

The little children chase each other
behind the clickless lizard
and they wait for him
on the hammock in the night
the terminus of the equation
where the sun doesn't know how to be a star
because he doesn't know the night
or the moon how to be a goddess
because she doesn't know the lizard
The green lizard that passes by
on the coach of the serpent
spreading red semaphores

IV

Paesaggio del dente di sciacallo

Lo scippò al volo
da una mandibola annoiata
di sciacallo rampante
e corse
il bimbo dalle labbra arse
e dal ventre di partoriente
corse tenendolo stretto
fino alle porte del mondo
e le aprí senza bussare

Una notte di luna a credito
approdò nella metafora
dell'unica spiaggia dell'uomo
dell'uomo di quella spiaggia

Si slegò dalle scarpette della multinazionale
e si spinse nel villaggio
a sogno spento
per non disturbare la gente
stringendo nella mano
il dente di sciacallo

Una mattina di Eolo a Lipari
e di campane a vita
ce lo ritrovammo vicino di casa
della tazza del caffè

IV

Landscape of the Jackal's Tooth

He snatched it on the fly
from the weary mandible
of a rampant jackal
and the boy ran
the boy with parched lips
and a parturient belly
ran holding it tight
to the doors of the world
and opened them without knocking

One night of moonlight on credit
he came ashore in the metaphor
of the only beach of man
of the man of that beach

He freed himself from the little shoes of the multinational
and made his way into the village
by means of a dead dream
so as not to disturb the people
clutching the jackal's
tooth in his hand

One Aeolian morning on Lipari
a morning of bells for life
there we found a neighbor
of the cup of coffee

Paesaggio dei nuovi barbari

E adesso come faremo senza i barbari?

Costantino Kavafis

Chi sono quei signori distinti
con le pile miopi
nel buio dei banchi
e delle strade?

I barbari

I barbari di Kavafis?

No
i nostri

E quella ragazza coi trampoli
chi è?

Doveva essere il clone del clone
ma corre con le gambe delle sue culture
tra i grattacieli nani di Francoforte

Ma ora perché i barbari
scendono dai bulldozer?

È che la banda ha iniziato a suonare
e li attendono
nei cortili monocromatici
con le medaglie

E chi li attende?

I professori
che i barbari hanno pagato
per dare un tono scientifico
alla loro barbarie
E di che medaglie
si fregeranno?
Di sparute preposizioni
che non sono riuscite a volare

Landscape of the New Barbarians

> And what will we do now without the barbarians?
>
> Constantine Cavafy

Who are those distinguished gentlemen
with their myopic batteries
in the darkness of the benches
and the roads?

The barbarians

Cavafy's barbarians?

No
ours

And that girl on the stilts
who's she?

She must have been the clone of a clone
but she runs with the legs of her cultures
between the dwarfish skyscrapers of Frankfurt

But now why are the barbarians
getting down from the bulldozer?

It's because the band has started playing
and they're waiting for them
with medals in the monochromatic
courtyards

And who's waiting for them?

The professors
that the barbarians have paid
to give their barbarities
a scientific tone

And with what medals
are they adorned?

Ma perché stanno tutti impettiti
coi parapioggia aperti?

Credono che sia pioggia

Chiudete i parapioggia
signori barbari:
piovono lingue!

With haggard prepositions
that weren't able to fly

But why are they all stiff and straight
with open umbrellas?

They think that it's raining

Close your umbrellas
barbarian gentlemen:
it's raining languages!

⇴ Cristina Alziati (b. 1963)

Cristina Alziati was born in Milan in 1963. She is editor of the journal *Guerre & Pace* (*Wars & Peace*) and has been living in Germany for several years, at present in Berlin. Her poetry has been published in *Poesia* (*Poetry*, 1994) and in *L'ospite ingrato Conflitto/guerra/media* (*The Ungrateful Guest Conflict/War/Media*, 2003). A collection with an introduction by Franco Fortini was published in *Annuario di Poesia 1991–1992* (Poetry Yearbook, 2004).

After forty years of writing, the literature of Italian writers in Germany opened up to heterogeneous themes. This happened because other writers joined the founding group. The new writers do not necessarily rely on the context of a literary movement held together by an intercultural project and an ethnic solidarity. The latter can turn at times into blinders, and thus may prevent one from seeing the total cultural condition. The youthful creative period of Cristina Alziati, however, is a case in point of one who branches out to include other perspectives. Her experience does not unfold within the world of immigration. The writer focuses her attention on surprising events such as war in general and the return of wars in the heart of Europe, where it was thought to have been eliminated. Although it may be too soon to pass judgment, one might already assume that the literary debut of Cristina Alziati is precious due to the harmony of her language and the topics that guide her verses.

I

A un amico

da *A compimento*

È' senza accesso il luogo ove ti assenti
—perpetuo altrove, un tuo non luogo
un treno.
Non credere sia spazio
il mondo che attraversi come in treno.
Altro non trovo nel tuo sguardo
se non che non ci guarda.
Deraglia
nell'incurvarsi angusto della fronte.

Eppure come stai, Horàcio, tuo malgrado
non oltre gli anni
ma coi capelli grigi il viso
da bambino parigi l'argentina
anche se tu non resti più di un anno
anche se non ci sei ci sei.

E che vorremo dirti
ci incontreremo, a volte anche felici.
Era gridi di rondini intrecciati
stamane l'aria.
È' scambio l'alba.

I

To a Friend

from *Upon Completion*

The place you escape to has no access
—eternal elsewhere, a nonplace of yours
a train.
Do not believe it to be space
the world you cross on imaginary tracks
Nothing else do I find in your gaze
except that it's not fixed on us.
It derails
in the sharp bend of the brow

Yet how you are, Horàcio, in spite of yourself,
not beyond the years
but with gray hair a childlike face
Paris Argentina
though you won't stay longer than a year
though you're not there, you're there.

And what we'll want to say to you
we shall meet, sometimes even in joy.
The air this morning
was enlaced with cries of swallows.
Dawn is an exchange.

II

Agli amici

È stata una strage violentissima
stamane, di insetti
di erbe di rami.
Lo studente dice che ha pagato la retta perciò può lordare il cortile.
Grida la donna al bambino perché cadendo ha sporcato il vestito.
A certi che dal Marocco verrebbero a orinare nei nostri quartieri
rompono le ossa alcuni miei concittadini.
È stata mandata una ruspa
per rimuovere i detriti, per fare
defluire il fango.

Sull'asfalto lucente veloci
torneranno le auto, e incuranti
dei resti decomposti nelle fosse.
Rimarrò ancora un poco, affonderò
nella melma gli stivali, raccoglierò reperti.
Domani sarà il gelo nell'argilla.

Dunque ci incontreremo nelle case
o per le disertate piazze, e camminando
ragioneremo insieme
di belle forme fossili ostinate
fortùite crepe e organismi
superstiti o mai nati.
Nella stagione ostile si faranno
le nostre verità certe più certe.

II

To Friends

It was a violent massacre,
this morning, of insects
grasses and branches.
The student claims to have paid his rent and so he can mess up the
    courtyard.
The woman yells at her boy because he has dirtied his clothes falling.
Moroccan men suspected of urinating in our neighborhoods
are beaten by some of my fellow citizens.
A bulldozer has been sent to remove the debris, to let
the mud slide away.

On the shiny concrete fast
cars will return, and pass by
unconcerned about the remains decomposing in the graves.
I shall stay a while longer, I shall sink
my boots into the slime, I shall recover artifacts.
Tomorrow there will be frost in the clay.

Then we will meet in the houses
or in deserted piazzas, and strolling
we will talk together
of beautiful obstinate fossil shapes,
fortuitous cracks and surviving or unborn
organisms.
In the hostile season our certain truths
will become more certain.

III

Muovono bassi e pesanti
elicotteri militari del mio paese
e l'ombra con essi e oscura la terra
ai nostri piedi.
Conosco ogni giorno di questo decennio
in cui i ponti sono stati bombardati
violate le lingue del Danubio putrefatto
le generazioni all'uranio generate.
Avvolte nelle coperte tossiscono al buio.
Amici nel silenzio sono andati.
Ne intendo il disperare, intendo
che dìssipa la mente, copre
delle tenaci opere il respiro; e per esse
non negata una fede.
Mi adagio nell'ombra. Grandioso
si annuncia lo scorcio di cielo,
dell'erba che spacca l'argilla il fragore.

III

Military helicopters from my country
move low and heavy
and shadows with them and they darken the earth
under our feet.
I know each day of this decade
in which bridges were bombed
the languages of the rotten Danube violated
generations born to uranium.
Bundled in blankets they cough in the darkness.
Friends have gone into the silence.
I feel their despair, I feel
it dissolving the mind, covering
the breath of persistent works; and for these
a faith not denied.
I lie in the shadow. Magnificent
a strip of sky breaks through,
and the rumble of grass splitting the clay.

IV

Non chiedere quando. Sai
come ora esistono gli uomini fra loro.
Guarda, qualcuno è nel campo
che cura il ramo spezzato dell'ulivo.
Altra certezza non chiedere.
Dove è negata, o pare, la speranza
una sola ragione è resistere
e il frutto nel novembre.

IV

Do not ask when. You know
how men exist with each other.
Look, someone is in the field
caring for the broken olive branch.
Don't ask for more certainty.
Where hope is denied, or seems to be,
resistance and the fruit in November
have a common cause.

V

Quanto ho imparato e so non mi protegge.
Girano sul foglio insetti di recente produzione,
abbozzano un'apertura delle ali, restano.
L'ippocastano dai bianchi fiori è malato
e tutti con esso saranno estinti. È' autunno,
pesa sul respiro come buio inverno.
"Perché, se più non credi, questo canto?"

V

All I have learned and know doesn't protect me.
Recently spawned insects wander across the paper,
they attempt opening their wings, then stay.
The horse chestnut with its white flowers is sick
and all will become extinct with it. It's autumn,
it weighs on breathing as a dark winter.
"Why this song, if you believe no longer?"

⇥ Piero Salabè (b. 1970)

Piero Salabè was born in Rome in 1970 and has lived in Germany since 1995. He writes some prose, but mostly he writes poetry in Italian, German, and, sometimes, Spanish. His expertise, as both critic and translator, is in South American literature. He publishes in Italian and German journals.

Almost all the poems of Salabè's first collection of poetry, *Preparo la stanza* (*I Am Preparing the Room*, 2000), are reflections in which the protagonist deals with events, facts, and everyday experiences. The meditations of the poetic persona are used to furnish with dignity life's essential yet now seemingly valueless banalities so as to intensify them and enhance, or enhance anew, their meaning.

In his single life as a "commuter of being" who is always returning but not really going anywhere, the poetic persona attunes the actions that mark his life to a lively rhythm. Piero Salabè's excellence consists in generating a rhythmic pleasure through a system of expressions that follow each other without pause as if he were a rapper of written language—a rapper who entrusts to paper and not to the body the rhythms of daily living. This collection offers other surprises as well, such as the sudden appearance of the other language of the poet, German, as in the poem "Warm ist das Bett" (The Bed Is Warm). The intrusion of German in a text of Italian poetry could have different motives: It can be interpreted as an invitation to the cultural complexity of the collection, where Italian engages in a dialogue with another language; an invitation to understand that the European reality is so changed that no national language is capable of protecting its speakers, within the confines of their national territory, from the invasion of other sounds; an invitation to the reader to match up with the intercultural reality that has become part of everyday life; and lastly, an invitation to the reader to become an intercultural reader, one who discovers being a reader of poetry through the language in which the poems are written and thus an interlocutor of the poetic persona whose experiences in another culture are being passed on to the reader.

I

da *Preparo la stanza*

Ho chiesto ancora due giorni.
Ho fatto un piano.

Solo se il vento soffia verso
la pianura,
solo se il ramo cadrà
oltre il dosso,
solo se un animale morto
devierà la corrente
arriverò.
Ho chiesto ancora un giorno,
ho ascoltato l'acqua, le foglie
e i passi della volpe.
Ho capito che morirò
ma lo stesso ho chiesto un giorno ancora.

La materia è inerte e io getto
sassolini per svegliare il tempo.
Qualcuno mi ha detto che
la salvezza è questione di secondi
pungere adesso il mostro che ci divora.

Ho chiesto un'altra ora.
Sono sdraiato, non mi posso alzare,
il cuore della terra mi batte in testa
ma ho un piano:
chiedere un'altra mezzora.

Qualcuno mi ha detto che per me
la punizione sarà più dura
che il mio corpo dovrà vivere ancora.

Ho chiesto un'ultima volta,
ho calcolato che ce la posso fare
se nei prossimi sette minuti
l'orso si scontra con il cinghiale.

I

from *I Am Preparing the Room*

I've asked for two more days.
I've made a plan.

Only if the wind blows toward
the plain,
only if the branch falls
past the ridge,
only if a dead animal
diverts the stream
will I succeed.

I've asked for one more day,
I've listened to the water and the leaves
and the footsteps of the fox.
I've realized I'm dying
but all the same I've asked for one more day.

Matter is lifeless and I fling
pebbles to awaken time.
Someone told me that
salvation is a matter of seconds,
to sting the monster that devours us.

I've asked for another hour.
I'm lying down, I can't get up again,
the heart of earth is pounding in my brain,
but I have a plan:
I've asked for another half-hour.

Someone told me that
my punishment will be harsher
because my body has to go on living.

I've asked for one last time,
I've calculated I can manage it
if in the next seven minutes
the bear encounters the wild boar.

II

Una volta
quando cresceva l'erba in aprile
ti ritrovavi con nuove mani
e gambe più forti.
E quando in agosto
bruciavano i marciapiedi
eri già morto due volte e risorto più d'una.

Una volta
quando pioveva in novembre
chiamavi gli amici, chiamavi la gente
scrivevi nomi e tutto sembrava urgente.
E quando in gennaio le scale e i sassi
erano freddi
scendevi e ridevi,
ti sedevi e ridevi,
perché niente, in gennaio,
era più urgente.

Una volta
forse solo aprile e agosto
tornavano e novembre
si spostava.
I mesi ti possedevano
e solo chiedevi di esistere.

Adesso invece hai iniziato a contare.

II

Once
when the grass was growing in April
I found you with new hands
and stronger legs.
And when the pavements
were burning hot in August
you'd died twice and arisen more than once.

Once
when it was raining in November
you called your friends, you called the people,
you wrote their names and everything seemed urgent.
And when the stairways and the stones were cold
in January
you came down and you laughed,
you sat down and you laughed,
because nothing, in January,
was more urgent.

Once
perhaps only April and August
returned and November
moved away.
The months possessed you
and all you asked was to exist.

Now on the contrary you've started counting.

III

qui l'inverno non passa
il gelo è puro
nessuno aspetta il tempo
che cambia

il cielo è vicino
si spezzano i rami come
vetro
nella neve anche
la vita degli animali
è chiara
il silenzio sempre più
copre i campi
atterrano grati i
fiocchi
neppure la pietra
solitaria resiste

dove sono i giorni,
dove la terra?

stridono i passi che non durano
qualcuno gira e inventa strade
pensando a un'altra stella

questo freddo certo
non è passeggero

III

here winter doesn't leave
the ice is pure
no one expects the weather
to change

the sky is near
the branches break like
glass
in the snow even
the life of animals
is clear
the ever-growing silence
covers the fields
snowflakes alight
agreeably
not even the solitary
stone resists

where are the days,
where the land?

footsteps creak and disappear
someone turns and makes new roads
thinking of another star

this cold is certainly
no passerby

IV

Il risveglio è senza risposta
anche se meraviglioso
come un muro bianco di campagna.

Sei andato
l'ultima sera di Roma,
le stelle che brillavano come neon,
una certezza nel cuore
la menzogna di sempre
partire per un altrove.

Un sogno che abita dentro la terra
chiama per farti scoprire.
È il dolore che sventra le gambe,
è tutto.
Nessuno assicura che non ne puoi morire.
I giorni sono più delle tue parole.

IV

Waking brings no response
even if it's astonishing
like a white wall in the country.

You went away
the last evening in Rome,
the stars that glittered like neon,
a certainty in the heart
the lie of always
leaving for somewhere else.

A dream that dwells within the earth
summons you to uncover it.
It's the pain that guts the legs,
it's everything.
No one assures that you won't die of it.
The days are more than your words.

V

Il basilico è ignaro,
la parete senza sospetti
e anche le bottiglie non sanno
che presto qualcuno riderà
dei loro progetti.

Verrà qualcuno da lontano
sarà un vento o forse solo
una mano.

Taciturni e ostinati
erano i numeri,
troppo divisibili, troppo prevedibili,
come figure in uno specchio.

Qualcuno è venuto da lontano,
qualcuno ha chiuso i giorni e i mesi
nella sua mano.

Adesso la parete respira
come un animale addormentato,
adesso il basilico
spande un nuovo odore
e nella luce la bottiglia
accoglie un fiore.

V

The basil is unaware,
the wall without suspicions,
and even the bottles don't know
how soon someone will laugh
at their intentions.

Someone will come from another land
maybe a wind or only
a hand.

Sulky and stubborn
were the numbers,
too divisible, too foreseeable,
like figures in a mirror.

Someone has come from another land,
someone has closed the days and the months
inside his hand.

Now the wall breathes
like a sleeping animal,
now the basil
scatters a new aroma
and in the light the bottle
welcomes a flower.

NOTES

1. Ute: *Nome di donna.*
2. Ute is a woman's name.
3. *Gast* (tedesco) = *ospite* (italiano).
4. Gast is the German word for "guest."

Switzerland

Switzerland

JEAN-JACQUES MARCHAND

Literary works by Italian emigrants in Switzerland began to appear in the 1960s. The first text of this kind was published in 1961, *Io sono un cinq*, or *I Am a Cinq*, by Giampiero Montana.[1] During the first decade of Italian literature in Switzerland, only about fifteen works were published, in single volumes. Beginning with the 1970s, this trend became more widespread, and thirty-six volumes were published between 1971 and 1980. In the 1980s and 1990s came a considerable expansion, and nearly one hundred works were published in each decade.

Most of these works, written and published in single volumes by Italian emigrants to Switzerland and numbering around 250, are influenced by the emigrant experience. They are marked by the events of expatriation and exile, by the crossing of borders, and by feeling foreign psychologically, politically, and administratively. They are quite different from works by Italian migrant workers in Italy, as well as from works written by Italians who had emigrated to such places as Australia and the United States.[2]

What is striking above all in reading these works is the great variety of topics and expressive forms. This gives the lie to the common notion that an emigrant could only write about emigration.[3] These works can in fact be divided into six main thematic categories: problems of emigration, ways of life, memoirs, self-analysis and lyrical expression, psychological and adventure narratives, and contemporary social problems.[4] Obviously, these are not static categories, and the same work could at times be included in two or more of these groupings.

WRITINGS ON EMIGRATION PROBLEMS

Works that treat emigration constitute the largest category. These works, it must be added, were written primarily during the 1960s and 1970s, a period of massive migratory influx during which referenda were called to limit foreign immigration into Switzerland.[5] Whether written in verse or in prose, three moments are emphasized in these works. First comes the place that is being left behind, then the contact with the new country, and finally the new life that ensues. The first two moments are invariably treated in retrospect, even in fictional form. They appear therefore always modified by the filter of memory, bound to a mythical past narrated to oneself and to others. Oddly, the departure from the place of birth is almost never narrated. This Italo-Swiss perception of emigration is very different from that of Italian emigrants at the beginning of the twentieth century: Departure almost never has that dramatic character that associated it, according to a frequent comparison, with dying. Only two writers, Sicilians, revive this trope in their poetry. One of them is Salvatore Mazzara, who closes the poem "Espatriare" (Expatriate) with "Espatriare è quasi / morire" (To expatriate is nearly / to die). His poem "È un popolo che muore" closes on a similar note: "È un popolo che muore / l'italiano all'estero" (It is a people that dies / Italians abroad). These verses are found in the collection *Amata terra mia* (*Beloved Land of Mine*). The other poet is Saro Marretta, whose long-held interest in the relationship between emigration and literature surely informed his choice to recover this nearly vanished topos.

The themes vary according to the organization of the works. In writings of social engagement or in autobiographical ones, rebellion and protest prevail, either against work conditions in Italy or against those offered by Switzerland. In more lyrical works, situations relative to the settling period are more frequent. There is the mythical memory of the native town abandoned but frequently found again. Novels usually begin in medias res, when the protagonist has just arrived in Switzerland. In works such as *Nudi col passaporto* (*Naked with a Passport*), by Attilia Fiorenza Venturini, and Montana's *Io sono un cinq* (*I Am a Cinq*), the beginning is at the border crossing or at the station, whereas in *Stagionali e rami secchi* (*Seasonal and Dry Branches*), by Venturini, it is the first clashes with the people of Zurich relative to the anti-Italian movements of 1896 that opens the story. In collections of poetry, the more generic theme of emigration as a state of being rather than action is more prevalent. The work *Amata terra mia* by Mazzara begins with the poem "L'emigrante" (The Emigrant), which is also an invitation to return to the native land. The first work of *Fame d'amore* (*Hunger for*

Love), by Franco Aste, is entitled "Emigrare" (Emigrate) and closes with an evocation of the myth of return: "Coltiveremo la nostra vecchia terra / quella che sembrava devastazione / e la trasformeremo in un giardino dell'Eden!" (We will cultivate our ancient land / that seemed devastated / we will transform it into a garden of Eden!). In this way also ends the poem "La madre" (The Mother) in *Il diario di un emigrante* (*Diary of an Emigrant*, by Antonietta De Giorgi): "Madre terra straniera mi ritrovo / a dividere un pane amaro / per ricondurre un giorno i figli / oltre la frontiera che da te, madre, da tanto mi separa" (Mother I find myself in a foreign land / to share a bitter bread / to bring back one day my children / past the border which from you / for so long separates me). Leaving presupposes first of all a judgment of the town that has been abandoned, which usually is ambivalent, or more precisely distinct from the country, the village and Italy. The town or village associated with the world of childhood has almost always a positive connotation. But the motherland is almost always contrasted with the state, the country stepmother responsible for the emigration, for the depopulation, or even for the death, at times, of the towns. The ensuing register is at times elegiac, at times dramatic, at times imprecatory, contrasted with the idyllic register of the evocation of the native town. In Mazzara's collection, for instance, harsh words are addressed to the fatherland in contrast with a serene description, as in "Sera in paese" (Evening in the Village). Another contrast can be found between the peaceful harmony of a distant solar myth (as in Mazzara's Sicily, Montana's Versilia, or Venturini's Veneto) and the cold, dark desolation of half-abandoned towns.

The initial encounter with the country of immigration, in this case Switzerland, is a motif that is present more often in prose works than in poetry. In novels, the first clash with the Swiss reality occurs usually at the beginning of the narration for the purpose of dramatization, placing the protagonists, and thus the readers, in a moment of great intensity. Beginning a narrative with the arrival in the foreign land or with the clash with the different way of thinking is, after all, a way to conform to an old rule of dramatic action, which consists in beginning a work precisely when the antagonistic forces are about to clash. This explains why *Stagionali e rami secchi* by Venturini begins with the first scenes of anti-Italian violence in 1896; it also explains why *Io sono un cinq* by Montana begins with the protagonist's arrival at the train station in Zurich.

It is difficult to provide a broad grouping for works of lyric poetry because of the very personal content of these works. A legitimate question can also be raised regarding the specific characteristics of these works. One can wonder whether these works of poetry are different from those of other collections written in Italy or by Italians in other parts of the world. In primarily prose texts, the presence of two components is evident: On one hand is the fact of living outside of one's own country, of having a different point of view as an outsider, of having crossed permanently a border both in concrete terms as well as symbolically; on the other hand, there is the fact of having come in contact with characteristics and values possibly different from one's native place, whether it is taken as a model of a democratic and socially minded state, as Montana does, or whether it is considered a bastion of wild and egotistical capitalism, as some Marxist writers portray it. In works of poetry, such motifs are no longer explicit. Rather they constitute, in a probably sublimated way, the creative spark of many of those motifs. The most frequently recurring motif is that of solitude. From this central motif, other related themes branch off that, according to each collection, assume a more or less dominant position. These could be night and darkness; vulnerability; anguish; fear of abandonment (as is the case for Dani Severo in *Sensazioni, or Sensations*); metaphysical anguish in perceiving new and infinite dimensions (as is the case for Maddalena Perrenoud in *Poesie*, or *Poems*, and *Altre attese*, or *Other Expectations*); fear of being deprived of light and love (as in Arturo Fornaro's *Musica da camera per una stella*, or *Chamber Music for a Star*); fragility of hope (in *Oltre*, or *Beyond*, by Aniello Iennaco); loss of a metaphysical and physical presence (as in Silvana Lattmann's *Fessura*, or *Crevice*); or a sense of reification (as in Alida Airaghi's *Rose rosse rosa*, or *Red Roses Pink*).

Another great theme, a given in lyric poetry, is love. Probably as a consequence of the immigrant condition, it is never a triumphant, full, serene sentiment. It is rather always threatened by a departure, a separation in time or space. For Liotta, the meeting itself has already a casual and tragic component, as might be suggested by the title of the very first collection, *Come polline al vento* (*As Pollen in the Wind*). For Maria Antonietta Piermartini, the poems of *Ciò che resta* (*What Remains*) tell about the memory of a happy moment distant in time and space, a brief encounter in a remote area along the shore.

The theme of death, whereby the poems treat larger existential issues as well, takes on special characteristics in these works by emigrants. The death of anyone left behind in Italy is perceived as a particularly painful event, since it has occurred in a distant past without any possibility to connect it to memories, to dialogues with the dead person, and since the speaker lives in a distant place where it is not possible to lessen the pain by adding new images of daily life. Silvana Lattmann treats this theme with great frequency in the first part of *Fessura*, as well as in the second part, where it takes on a more symbolic form and is associated with the metaphor of the angel that gives the collection its title, *Angeli e morti* (*Angels and Dead People*). In the works of Dani Severo, death is an obsession, from dealing with the death of his own father in "22 maggio" (May 22), to considering his own death in "Il viaggio" (The Voyage), to that of a motorcycle rider in "L'abbandono" (The Abandonment), to that of a hippie girl in "La ballata di Jennifer" (Jennifer's Ballad), to that of those who died in war in "Laos" (Laos), or of hunger in "Bengladesh" (Bangladesh), to the death of the world itself in "Incubo" (Nightmare). Death is above all fleeting and incomprehensible, distant and near at the same time.

SHORT STORIES WITH PSYCHOLOGICAL AND ADVENTURE-BASED THEMES

Emigrant writings that distance themselves even further from personalized narratives fall under a fifth category, that of psychological and adventure-based themes. In these texts, in fact, it seems as if the themes of migratory experience—autobiographical, lyrical, or otherwise—have all but disappeared. Explicit references to such issues are either diluted or entirely absent, and attempts to locate traces of them from one story to the next will often come up empty. A certain desire to evade traditional portrayals of immigrant behavior and lifestyles, and even typical narrative modes, is abundantly clear. There are many examples one could cite to illustrate this phenomenon, but three texts in particular demonstrate it most clearly: *Quando verrete a Zug* (*When You Come to Zug*), by Fabrizio Maria Colonnelli, rather than telling a story of one who overcomes innumerable obstacles to establish himself in a new country, describes instead the life of an upstanding Swiss youth who discovers a sense of life and attains moral uplifting by helping earthquake victims in southern Italy;

L'anima quadrupede (*The Quadrupedal Soul*), by Emilio Sciotti, is a collection of stories that, awash in fantasy, lack specific geographical or temporal references; and *L'ora della mezzanotte* (*The Midnight Hour*), by Gerardo Passanante, is another work that moves loosely through temporal dimensions as it revisits the stories of such figures as Adam, Judas and Don Giovanni. In general, for authors who relocate from Italy to Italian-speaking parts of Switzerland, there is little sense of breached frontiers or living abroad as immigrants. Some other names of note include Luciano Marconi, Silvana Lattmann, and Carla Rossi Bellotto.

SHORT STORIES DEALING WITH SOCIETAL ISSUES
IN THE 1980S AND 1990S

This sixth and final category of writings includes narratives that depict the second generation of emigrant families. *Nella fossa degli orsi* (*In the Bears' Den*) and *Chaos*, for example, two works by Elio Giancotti, portray German- and French-speaking children of immigrants in Switzerland as they integrate themselves, without regard for nationality or origins, into a broader environment of foreign residents in general. From their markedly marginalized standpoint, they must confront an array of contemporary societal temptations, risks and dangers, including drugs, AIDS, and depression, all the while existing in the midst of an opulent, rather conservative Swiss environ. Under such conditions, these characters do not find themselves enriched and enlightened by their experiences as immigrant residents, nor are they able to discern clear role models and desirable values from their parents and their traditions. Rather, they feel themselves more closely aligned with their peers who, for political and ethical motives, have rebuked their parents' values and examples, resulting in a collective of weak, fragile and somewhat demoralized, or at any rate disengaged, protagonists.

The texts belonging to this literary category do not constitute a homogenous body of works, nor are they all the products of truly literary figures. Some of the figures responsible for these texts are simply people who write as opposed to veritable authors, while others are true writers and poets whose works have been critically acclaimed and printed by prestigious publishers such as Einaudi, Vallecchi, and Garzanti. Nonetheless, a common thread among all these texts is a desire to communicate, through a commingling of traditional literary forms and genres, the feelings, thoughts and desires of migrant figures who were born in Italy before passing at least part of their lives in Switzerland.

BIBLIOGRAPHY

Mäder, Rolf. 1972. "Autori italiani emigrati in Svizzera." In *Il pane degli altri*, ed. Rolf Mäder, 7–8. Bern: Francke.

Madrassi, Gabriella. 1991. "Riflessi ed immagini quotidiane nella narrativa degli emigrati in Svizzera nell'ultimo trentennio." In *La letteratura dell'emigrazione. Gli scrittori di lingua italiana nel mondo*, ed. Jean-Jacques Marchand, 39–49. Turin: Edizioni della Fondazione g. Agnelli.

Marchand, Jean-Jacques. 1988. "Quando gli immigrati italiani si fanno poeti e scrittori." In *Lingua e letteratura italiana in Svizzera*. Atti del convegno tenuto all'Università di Losanna, 21–23 May 1987, ed. Antonio Stäuble, 65–74. Bellinzona: Casagrande.

———. 1991. "La letteratura dell'emigrazione italiana in Svizzera." In *Lingua e letteratura italiana nel mondo oggi*, ed. Ignazio Baldelli and Bianca Maria Da Rif, 1:457–59. Florence: Olschki.

———. 1991. "Un'antologia ideale della letteratura dell'emigrazione di lingua italiana in Svizzera." In Marchand, *La letteratura dell'emigrazione*, 29–38.

———. 1992. "Poeti italiani in Svizzera." *Bloc Notes* 25 (1992): 7–112.

———. 1996. "Scrittori e scriventi 'emigrati' italiani in Svizzera nell'ultimo trentennio." In *Scrittori e scriventi italiani esuli ed emigrati in Svizzera dall'Otto al Novecento*, ed. Marziano Guglielminetti and Jean-Jacques Marchand, 51–116. Lausanne: Université de Lausanne.

Meyer Sabino, Giovanna. 1996. *Scrittori allo specchio. Trent'anni di testimonianze letterarie italiane in Svizzera: un approccio sociologico*. Vibo Valentia: Monteleone.

➜ Silvana Lattmann (b. 1918)

Nothing predicted in this brilliant biologist, born in Naples and educated during World War II at the University of Genoa, a poetic vein. Lattmann's career continued in the institutes of biology at the universities of Milan, Bergamo, and Rome. After her marriage to a Swiss citizen, a professor at the federal polytechnic in Zurich, she moved there in 1954. But twenty-four years passed before the appearance of her first poems in the prestigious anthology *Almanacco dello Specchio* (Mondadori, 1978). Moreover, her debut with a volume all her own happened only in 1978 with *Le storie di Ariano* (*The Stories of Ariano*), published by another renowned publisher, Nuovedizioni Vallecchi, in Florence. But a new course was already in the making, because in 1983, with the volume *Fessura* (*Crevice*), she began a more intimate poetic search, one of self-excavation and probing of the subconscious. Stimulated, encouraged, and promoted by the critic Pio Fontana, a professor of Italian literature at the University of St. Gall, she published, every two years with the publisher Casagrande of Bellinzona, a number of other collections: *Assolo per tromba in fa maggiore* (*Solo for Trumpet in F Major*, 1985); *Il viaggio* (*The Voyage*, 1987); and *La favola del poeta, della principessa, della parola e del gerundio* (*The Fable of the Poet, of the Princess, of the Word and of the Gerund*, 1989). Another development occurred in the 1990s, when Lattmann dedicated herself to the study of Eastern philosophies. This was the beginning of a long intellectual and spiritual path, as well as a deeper personal understanding. The first poetic result of this experience was the collection *Malakut* (*Malakut*), marked deeply by philosophical and initiate references. The book came out in 1996, published by Scheiwiller in Milan. The same publisher put out the volume *Incontri* (*Encounters*) in 1998, in Italian and in English, which was preceded in 1996 by *Deianira* (*Deianira*), published in 1997 by Casagrande. In 2002, *Fuoco e memoria* (*Fire and Memory*) was published by the author herself. But the Swiss period seems to be over now that Lattmann spends the greater part of the year on the island of Ischia.

Since Silvana Lattmann's poetic career began when she was sixty years old, the development of her work is long and complex. *Le storie di Ariano* (*Ariano's Stories*) tells the tragic saga of an impoverished family from southern Italy. A curse related to a wrong matrimony falls upon the first generation and on all the offspring, whose pitiful or tragic ends are described in the book. Thus not even the second generation can overcome the problems of resettling that the irresponsible behavior of the parents passed on to the children. Lattmann's poetry is not realistic, to be sure, but it is concise and allusive, and the presence of various recurring characters, the plot that can be reconstructed gradually, and a temporal dimension that spans three generations give the whole work a narrative poetic structure. Already in this collection appears the figure of the angel, which will constitute a common link among Lattmann's works. The angel is a figure of many meanings: sublimation of love and of rapport with others, unspoken sensual love, a being that becomes any carnal component in order to arrive at a mysterious dimension, all the while conserving its ornithological identity (feathers, wings).

The image of the angel becomes dominant when Lattmann's poetry shifts from third to first person in *Fessura* (*Crevice*). The title of the first section, "Il filo che mi viene Dietro" (The Thread that Follows Me), exemplifies the connection between this part and the rest of the collection. It demonstrates a way to settle matters and be done with the past through a series of precise and intense revocations. The section "Angeli e morti" (Angels and Deceased) allows her to make the transition from memories of the dead, mother and father in particular, to a life that dares not fully reveal itself. With these poems the author sublimates her aspirations through the figures of the angel, which has in these poems very marked animal traits. In the other three sections, the poetic self succeeds in relating better to others and to the world. To be sure, it is always a difficult relationship, a labyrinthine journey, a disconcerting cosmic space, but it is a reality that is gradually conquered. The culminating, deepening point is the last section, "Crevice," which is dealt with more specifically in the poem of the same title. The angel, initially just a distant dream, becomes now a guide, a mute and wounded guide, who helps the poet travel through a symbolic countryside, only to then take flight again, abandoning her to her inexorable "*fessura.*" The last piece, even though situated in a mythical childhood moment, allows a sliver of hope for a possible rescue which, once more, may come from the angel.

Il viaggio (*The Voyage*), written in 1985, is a journey reaching deep into the more recondite folds of the persona's conscience, even its subconscious. It is ultimately an initiation voyage. The journey begins with two compositions dealing with a breaking up that leads to transformations, an experience that the poet expresses with the titles "Metamorphosis I" and "Metamorphosis II." The poet provides only fragments, pieces, metaphors of this reality that the reader must decipher according to a technique similar to the Hermetic tradition. Having prepared the way from this opening section, the poems of "Apertura al viaggio" (Voyage Beginnings) prepare the reader for the great adventure. The title section, "The Voyage," is made up of one poem, fifteen pages long, that tells of a complex initiation journey, dark and anxiety ridden, but the conclusion, recalling certain Buddhist mystical experiences, is that of a bright smile that opens the vision of the "enlightened one."

These two collections, and even more the third one, *La favola del poeta, della principessa, della parola e del gerundio* (*The Fable of the Poet, of the Princess, of the Word and of the Gerund*), are the outcome of a profound cultural search that the poet completed in those years, which entailed readings of and meditations on the works of Jung (more than Freud), Simone Weil, and Western as well as Eastern mystics such as Cristina Campo and the Persian Rumi. This collection differs from the earlier ones, which documented a broad spiritual journey, in that it is more descriptive, more realistic. With this collection, Lattmann returns to prose pieces, calling them "stories" though they are actually a highly poetic prose. The pieces in this collection become more and more surreal as they proceed through testimonials of a more personal, intimate experience. They deal with typical moments and life situations. The last piece is in the form of a letter, dear to this poet. The reflections about the gerund lead to a narrative that seems inspired by Eastern sources, perhaps Persian, in which the very writing assumes an existential value and transforms both writer and reader. *Malakut*, which in Persian means "the space of the angels," is made up of four sections titled "Gabriele" (Gabriel), "Angelo custode" (Guardian Angel), "Michele" (Michael), and "Raffaele" (Raphael). This voyage also begins at the spring equinox and moves to the winter solstice, passing through the summer solstice and the winter equinox. Although the whole work is immersed in an Eastern dimension, we meet again in this collection the figure of the guiding angel. The reader is faced with a veritable initiation voyage and the language is free of the realistic or narrative elements that characterized the poems of *Voyage* and *Solo*. The references deal with Zen philosophy, which the author studied a great deal in those years. There is evidence also of influences such as Rilke, D'Annunzio, and Luzi. From the very first poem of this group that includes the works dedicated to the angel Gabriel, with whom the poet converses, the reader is out of the temporal and spatial dimension. The place is totally abstract, although marked by the reference to the spring equinox, in a moment that seems propitious for enlightenment. As important as the poems are the notes provided by the author that explain the more obscure references. The notes are written in the same high style of the poems, and provide some insight into them. The author explains, for instance, that the relationship with the angel is "the sacredness of beauty in its potential to become." Critics have noted the presence of Gide and, most of all, D'Annunzio, mainly in "Laus vitae" (Praise of Life), in these poems.

In the section called "Guardian Angel," we find a poem that attempts to reconcile a sort of crepuscular modernism of the turn of the century (as in Antonio Fogazzaro) with Eastern philosophies that deny for human beings the possibility of reaching happiness in this world (one thinks of philosophers that have influenced Mario Luzi, such as Sri Aurobindo and Krishnamurti). The essential concepts are derived, however, from Christian texts, such as the orthodox and apocryphal gospels.

More dramatic and polemical is the third section, in which the poet converses with the archangel Michael to reproach him for not saving her, for he is the angel of death but also of cosmic harmony, and thus of life. But, surprisingly, while we await the encounter with the final illumination, the last piece ends with a sudden gust of wind followed by a darkness that spreads uncertainty and anxiety.

da *Fessura*

Conosco uomini indaffarati
non hanno tempo per vivere
si muovono nel loro cerchio
mordendo l'orologio.
Un giorno col fucile
finiranno per sparare allo specchio
contro se stessi.

from *Crevice*

I know busy men
don't have time to live
they move in their circle
biting the clock.
One day with a rifle
they will end up shooting themselves
in the mirror.

Un volo di rondini ha frullato nel mio petto
ha sfrecciato dal mio cuore tagliando il cielo
per venire da te.
Ma il mio occhio come vetro trinciava il romantico
guardava le pietre in giardino aguzze
feriscono il piede
e salire sul tram non ha nuvole
ancora peggio parlare al lattaio the conta le "rappe."
E non sono i gesti di tutti i giorni
ma la pena di vedere nel tuo occhio pensieri meschini
ad uccidere il fremito
a piangere dentro con quel volo mancato.

A flight of swallows fluttered in my chest
darted from my heart cutting the sky
to come to you.
But my eye like glass slashed the romantic
he looked at the sharp stones in the garden
they injure his foot
and getting on the tram doesn't have clouds
still worse talking to the milkman that counts "the bunches."
And they aren't everyday gestures
but the pain of seeing in your eye mean thoughts
killing the shiver
crying inside with that missed flight.

Mentre parlavo, tu non hai visto
sette gabbiani, li ho contati,
si sono alzati sulla Limmat.
Dietro un fondale le case grigie.
Loro pensieri sfuggiti alle maglie del traffico
ai rumori delle auto puzzolenti.

While I talked, you didn't see
seven seagulls, I counted them,
they raised themselves above the Limmat.
Behind a backdrop of gray houses. Their
thoughts escaped from the traffic snarls
to the noises of stinking automobiles.

Sai cosa ho fatto stamattina
un gesto matto, tu diresti.
Ho gettato nel fiume sporgendomi dal ponte
una mia poesia.
Il foglietto ha volato, è cascato nell'acqua
ha galleggiato un momento
poi trascinato via non l'ho più visto.
Giungerà al mare e tu lo leggerai
oppure le parole decomposte
diventeranno aria, suoni.
Le sentirai aggrapparsi attorno a te
disfarsi
in una nuvola, in un arcobaleno.

You know what I did this morning
a mad gesture, you would say.
Leaning from the bridge I threw a poem of mine
in the river.
The slip of paper flew, and fell in the water
floated a moment
then dragged out to where I no longer saw it.
It will reach the ocean and you will read it
or the decomposed words
will become air, sounds.
You will feel them cling to you
melting
in a cloud, in a rainbow.

Prismi in fuga persi in echi lontani
sono le tue parole.
Le vocali si gonfiano nel deserto delle strade
dove i passi si fanno circospetti
in punta di piedi per non sentirsi.

Prisms in flight lost in distant echoes
are your words.
The vowels swell in the desert of the streets
where steps are circumspect
on tiptoes so as not to be heard.

Mi verrà il fegato di aceto
tutta una critica io che predico tolleranza
gli uomini uguali
e adesso
in un paese civilizzato così nel cuore dell'Europa
dove vengono i re
a depositare i tesori in banca
mi sento estranea
e il mio occhio è cattivo.

My liver will bleed vinegar
stern criticism I who preach tolerance
men are equal
and now
in a country so civilized
in the heart of Europe
where the kings come
to deposit treasures in the bank
I feel alien
and my eye is so evil.

Mi sono acciambellata al caldo di un uccello
perché il mondo è freddo
non corre filo fra sguardi
se non di consuetudine
e solo strumenti raffinati in suoni e luci
riempiono gli spazi.

I curled up to the warmth of a bird
because the world is cold
no thread runs between glances
except from habit
and only instruments refined in sounds and lights
fill up the spaces.

Isola pagana
tu spezzi il mio dio
pungono me i suoi frammenti
ossa nel mare
croci nella roccia.
Divisa in due scendo all'alba nell'acqua
trasmuto in alga.

Pagan island
you break my god
its fragments stinging me
bones in the ocean
crosses on the rock.
Divided in two I descend into in the water at dawn
transformed into algae.

Devo ancora scrivere cento poemi
e libri
uno scaffale di poesie
e dipingere mille quadri
correre con te nei prati
mangiare un gelato leccandolo al vento
per questo non posso morire.
Ma tu mi parli
i tuoi occhi incavati
legano spazi immensi al mio sguardo
con promesse senza battito di tempi
mi congeli il respiro.

I still need to write a hundred poems
and books
a bookcase of poems
and to paint a thousand pictures
to run with you in meadows
eating an ice cream licking it in the wind
for this I can't die.
But you talk in my ear
your hollowed eyes
bind immense spaces to my gaze
promises without time's beat
you freeze my breath.

Le mie ansie
uccelli dalle ali puntute che si azzuffano.
Mi feriscono paure immaginate
orbite profonde, circoli e gradi di pazzia.
Scompariscono
come nuvola che si allarga bucata dal vento
e traspare l'azzurro.

My worries
birds with sharp wings who come to blows.
Imagined fears hurt me
deep eye sockets, circles and degrees of madness.
They disappear
like a cloud pierced by the wind
and the blue shines through.

→ Leonardo Zanier (b. 1935)

In a preface to a collection of short stories by Leonardo Zanier published in 1977, Mario Rigoni Stern writes: "The freshness, the truth, the feelings never flaunted, those of the poet which he then became, his is an open testimonial, and in this fifty-year anniversary of the Resistance, it reveals an aspect of the war unknown to most, bringing to light the natural course of instincts." In the same year, Carlo Sgorlon, in the journal *Tuttolibri*, recorded similarly positive thoughts on Zanier's poetry collection *Libers . . . di scugnì là—Liberi di dovere emigrare (Free to Have to Emigrate)*, just then published by Garzanti: "Zanier knows how to say things with a robust vividness, capable of leading you directly to the heart of the problem; he knows how to give his verse a cadence both repetitive and sharp, a strong cadence possessing the quality of contrast, of the dry statement, constructed with epigrammatic, incisive, cutting modes." These two quotes provide the keys to understanding the prose and poetry of Zanier: a strong tie to his roots, manifesting itself even in the use of Friulian dialect for most of his works; emigration and social issues; the relationship between his own experience and that of his society; his ethical and political involvement; and his reflections on the issues of history and the human condition.

Leonardo Zanier was born in Carnia in 1935 in a region situated in the center of Europe between Italy, Germany, and Austria, in the area that, in the years between the end of the nineteenth and the beginning of the twentieth century, came to be known as Mitteleuropa. Of this region, of these places where he returns regularly, Zanier has the memory and the values of a simple but honest preindustrial and even pre-Christian life. He also conserves the signs of a land marked by poverty, by the bloodletting that was emigration, and by the disappearance of a communal way of life.

The first challenges of immigration concerned admission into schools and overcoming the barrier of a different language, as the author himself declared in 2003 at the "Varcar frontiere" conference at the University of Lausanne: "The entry level exam was administered in Tolmezzo which was thirty kilometers away. But it was still Carnia. The Friulian language spoken there is a little different. It becomes a sort of Friulian of the plains. I do not recall who the members of the commission were. Perhaps they were from there or from who knows where. My Italian was deemed horrendous; I earned a grade of two. This is why I spoke of dying. It was like having to do a somersault. After such a terrible landing I risked remaining illiterate, at least in Italian."

Like the majority of the inhabitants of his region, he opted to emigrate. But he possessed a better professional, cultural, and ideological preparation. After going to Morocco and French Switzerland, he moved to Zurich, where he had to face the harsh accommodations of the barracks for workers, which he rejected from the very first day in order to protect his dignity. Zurich is also a big city, long open to a commingling of great intellectual traditions. In the 1960s, the political and cultural community, besides the working class, was strong as in the times of Silone. These were years of serious struggles, but hopes came about among groups that were deeply committed to the cause of improving conditions for immigrant laborers. Zanier chose the path of trade unions and vocational training institutions for his compatriots, becoming one of the major figures of Italian unionism in Switzerland. His fidelity to Carnia and his Friulian language helped maintain his roots, while his political awareness led him to analyze more deeply, and from a Marxist perspective, the social and political history of twentieth-century Italy and Switzerland. These were the years in which his family and the birth of his son brought him to strengthen his connections with Italy, all the while making him reflect on the issues of his ties with Switzerland. He deals with all of these topics in his books *Libers di scugní là* (1964), *Che Diz us al meriti* (1979), and *Sbordadura e sanc* (1982).

By the end of the 1960s, Zanier was a union leader and an intellectual with a following. In meetings and at speeches, his gifts for debating and the clarity of his opinions, along with his practical approach to problems, were very much appreciated. He began to realize in these years that, if he wanted to reach a more diverse and larger public that would also read his books, he needed to resort to writing poetry as well as prose narratives. At first, Zanier recited his works in public places and touched them up according to the reaction of the public, especially his Friulian friends, since at this time he wrote primarily in that language. His poetry is not just a message, it represents also the language of his origins, his roots. Through the rhythm and the sound, he pursues a richer and more effective means of communication with respect to the spoken word to connect the particular with the general, the individual with the universal, the past with the present, the place where he lives with the world. Yet, in spite of this need for the receptivity of the public, Zanier's works do not resemble poetry made spontaneously for a purely personal outlet. In his poetry, rather, can be seen the clear presence of a poetic tradition committed to social issues, such as is found in Fortini, as well as other tendencies of Friulian poetry of the postwar period, in which references to Pasolini's poetry are a given. In his poetic formation, his contacts with Italian intellectuals and various others in the international and multiethnic Zurich of the last decades became particularly important. His circle included poets, linguists, sociologists from Friuli with whom he always kept in touch, and members of the academic world, in particular from the universities of Rome, Lausanne, and Zurich. As the years passed and many of his works, including earlier poems, were translated into German, Slovenian, French, English, and Arabic, his readership expanded geographically, culturally, and socially. Some of his works have been set to music and several of his works have been placed on reading lists for students and as topics for research and dissertations in Swiss and Italian universities.

Distinct as it is from the paths of other Italian emigrants in Switzerland, it is still possible to follow Zanier's poetic evolution through his works. *Libers di scugní là*, which dates back to the beginning of the 1960s, can be considered, because of its title and the themes treated in it, his book of emigration. But it can also be considered as a book of life, of a relationship with the unknown, of supernatural popular beliefs. The titles of the various sections already attest to the richness of the migration issues. In the poem "Oggi" (Today), the poet's native Carnia is remembered; in "La valigia di un emigrante" (The Suitcase of an Emigrant), the poet goes beyond the mere personal situation to describe the drama of all emigrants; in "I bambini gli credono" (The Children Believe in Him), he tackles the difficult topic of humanity's relationship with the divine; in "Una lapide vecchia di secoli" (A Tombstone Centuries Old), his present-day experience is seen from a broader historical perspective; in "Vivere per non morire" (Living to Not Die), he deals with issues of living and dying; in "Domani" (Tomorrow), he looks to a future that appears problematic. When dealing with themes of migration, Zanier avoids any nostalgic tones or pathetic modes with regard to his little place of origin, and he does not break out into epic song about the conquest of a new status in a new land. Zanier's outlook is composed of love and reason—passionate love for the land and for life, and analytical reason, which at times combine in a cry of protest and anger. The style is stark, sobriety predominates, and his compositions are frequently brief and succinct, recalling Ungaretti. In "Oggi," for example: "oggi . . . / rocce senza erba / e ruote di treno" (today . . . / rocks without grass / and wheels of the train).

Zanier's perspective broadens considerably in his poems of the 1970s, collected under the title *Che Diaz . . . us al meriti* (*May Diaz . . . Reward You*). The contrasts "stay-migrate," "die-live," "present-future," are surpassed through a much broader socioanthropological vision. Italy's and Carnia's histories are revisited critically in the light of abuses since the Counter-Reformation through the carnage of World War I. From the perspective of these historical events, the themes of roots (attachment to Carnia) and of emigration (the life of emigrants into Switzerland) tend to smooth over in evocations of ancestral traditions and happy moments of the present, such as the birth of his son in "L'hai jodût a vegní int al mont" (I Saw Him Come into the World), or an outing with friends in "Was trinken Sie gern" (What Do You Want to Drink). These poems are written in a more expressionistic style, more sarcastic. Swiss-German words are inserted into the Friulian text to indicate the progressive process of opening up to the new culture of the immigrant. Political and social analyses are interspersed in the poetic texts. Some of the poems are put to music, thus indicating a movement toward greater accessibility, an appeal to the people.

At the beginning of the 1980s, *Sboradura e sanc* (*Semen and Blood*) comes out. As the title indicates, the language is free of any overt prettiness in order to express the force of instinct and suffering. The migration issues seem overcome. Issues of identity begin to surface more clearly. The identity of the people threatened by nationalist aims is treated in this collection, as in the poem "Cjermin, Grenzstein. Mejniki" (a poem leading to a later book), which deals with identity, with lay sentiment, as well as with confounding popular superstitions and beliefs.

This trilogy spanning the 1960s through the 1980s is followed by another series of works published in the 1990s: *Il calí* (*The Rennet*, 1992), *Usmas* (*Traces*, 1994) and *Licof grant* (*Big Feast*, 1997). In *The Rennet*, a reference to the transformation of milk into cheese, it is usually the recalling of a place or people that constitutes the occasion for the poem. Their surfacing to consciousness makes the idea gel and sets it in a reflection that goes beyond the occasion itself, in the sense that Montale gave to this term. The place is always far away in time and space (the Carnia of the poet's youth, a beach in the Veneto area, a winter landscape), but the memory rises like an illumination full of meaning. The verses are brief, often harsh, with strong rhythm and paratactic syntax. Subtler are the poems included in *Usmas*. The title itself refers to the traces that wild game leaves behind to be picked up by preying animals. It suggests the very thin nature of these presences. The most characteristic piece of this group of poems is "Calicanto," in which a tree branch in bloom carried through a trip from the Ticino area spreads its scent throughout the whole train all the way to Zurich. It the sign of the persistence of the theme of travel in the collection; it also represents the possibility of change, since the voyage is cause for mirth and pleasure rather than suffering and pain. The poem acquires then a more melodic rhythm. "Axis Mundi" represents another reflection on the theme of migration: anywhere a stick is planted in the ground becomes the center of the world and gives rise to a new reality. It is the opposite treatment of migration writing where the birthplace is seen as the only place of reference. The theme of migration and of the suffering of those who leave their hometowns are seen from a different perspective, as in the poem "A Merletti Renato," which evokes in a rhythmic prose the life of a worker who witnesses with his friends the razing to the ground of the factory where they worked for so many years. In the moment when the dynamite blows up the working life of the immigrant, he is at last too old to look for another job somewhere else. The tone of the poem is hopeless, a representation of the lack of parity in the struggle between people and multinational companies and consumerism, both of which have disfigured seascapes into a heap of tin roofs among machines and caravans of campers. These poems reflect that disfigurement in the chaotic structure of the compositions and the clash of sounds, the confusion brought about by such a society. "Licof grant" is the last section of the collection of the 1990s, which is a reference to a big celebration, in particular the practice of placing on the highest part of a newly built house a tree with a bow on its branches. A theme running through these poetic compositions is the memory of work done, a serene conclusion that allows the author once again to return to the usual dear topics of his inspiration, such as the absurdity of national boundaries, his condemnation of discrimination, and respect for work well done. One of these compositions bears the title "The Movie of Memory" and is a series of short images, unrelated but rich in meaning so as to suggest the behavior of human memory. At times the discourse develops in a more logical, coherent manner, almost a rational account, only to reveal at the end the absurdity of human reason typical of Pirandello. "Confins" (Boundaries) is an example of a poem, structured as a nursery rhyme, that lists all the prejudices typical of our way of reasoning through absurd and summary oppositions.

A new period in Zanier's poetry seems to begin with *Suspice caelum* (*Readings of the Universe*), published in 1999. His style in this collection is more classical; the verses are longer, the rhythm more cadenced. The most typical example of this collection is "Sotto il pel dell'aga" (Just Below the Surface of the Water), which provided later the title of an anthology of Zanier's poetry in a German and Italian translation published in Zurich, by Limmat Verlag, in 2002. In this poem, a happy day spent by a lake is juxtaposed with a slaughter perpetrated by white cormorants just below the water's surface.

Pineda di Grau

da *Usmas: Poesie 1988–1990*

come cais
e certis capis si spostin
cu la cjasa intor
cressuda adun o robada
e rèstin tacâts
as lamiêras:
il taulin cuintra la targa
radio e puartelas viertas
a fâ marinda sul savalon
sot l'ombrena dai pins
lontans da l'âga tal mieç dal desert das lôr machinas

Pineta di Grado—come chiocciole / o certe conchiglie / si spostano / con la casa attorno / cresciuta addosso o rubata / e restano attaccati / alle lamiere: / il tavolino contro la targa / radio e sportelli aperti / a pranzare sulla sabbia / sotto l'ombra dei pini / lontani dall'acqua / in mezzo al deserto / delle loro automobili

Pine Grove of Grau

from *Traces: Poems 1988–1990*

Like snails
or some shell
they get around
wearing their house
ingrown or stolen
and remain stuck
to iron sheets:
the table against the car plates
radio and side doors wide open
dining on the sand
under the shade of pines
far from the water
in the middle of the desert
of their automobiles

Marginalia/Axis Mundi

Le monde est une immense sphère
dont le centre est partout
et la circonference nulle part

            Pascal, copiant Platone

Margjinâl ce? cui? nô?
al à un biel dì il Galilei
e aitis prima e dopo
ma la cjera a è simpi al centro
e il gno pals e la mê cjasa
insomas ognidùn
e duncja encja la Cjargna
e i Cjargnei
e lôr lengàçs

Vadè: *axis mundi*
universalis columna
ch'a sêti alta mont
o antic arbulon
pâl colona baston
ch'a tègnin su tenda o cîl
come ch'a sondi sigûr
Coglians Crostas o Talm
Zoncolan Freikofel Pâl Piçul
Germula Canin
un melâr tal bearç
il tèi dal consei
o il rovul dal judissi
pâl di cucagna
o ctuirgnâl di pastor
tegnût salt in man
e ogni tet di cjasa

Encja i Achilpa
di una tribù Arunta
australians ben prin

Marginals/World's Axis

> The world is an immense sphere
> whose center is everywhere
> and the circumference is nowhere

> Pascal, after Plato

Marginal what? Who? Us?
Galileo spoke well
and others before and after him
but Earth is always at the center
so are my town and my home
everyone indeed
so is also Carnia
and its people
and what they say

Here: world's axis
universal column
be it a tall mountain
or a big old tree
pole column stick
holding up tent or sky
like surely are
Coglians Crostis or Talm
Zoncolan Freikofel Pal Piccolo
Zermula Canino
an apple tree in the garden
the council linden
or the oak of justice
tree of plenty
or shepherd's walking stick
surely held by the hand
and every roof of the house

Even the Achilpa
of the Arunta tribe
Australians much prior

ch'a rivassin lajù
i Kennedy da Letterfrak
o i Tosons da Maranzanas
il lôr grant pâl di agaç
spostansi pas stagjons
sui lôr trois segrets
viers un nôf sît
o un âti passon
lu tegnivin dapruf
e fermansi
lu implantavin
e ator dal pal e di lôr
si ricreava il mont
si sapontava il cîl
si difiniva il centro.

Marginalia/Axis mundi—"Marginalità / asse del mondo—Il mondo è un'immensa sfera / il cui centro è ovunque circonferenza in nessun luogo" (Pascal, copiando Platone) / Marginale cosa? chi? noi? / ha un bel dire il Galilei / e altri prima e dopo / ma la terra è sempre al centro / e il mio paese e la mia casa / insomma ognuno / e dunque anche la Carnia / e i carnici / e le loro parlate // Ecco: axis mundi /universalis columna / che sia alta vetta / o grande albero antico / palo colonna bastone / che sostengono tenda o cielo / come sono di sicuro / Coglians Crostis o Talm / Zoncolan Freikofel Pal Piccolo / Zermula Canino / un melo nel giardino / il tiglio del consiglio / o la quercia del giudizio / palo di cuccagna / o bastone di pastore / tenuto salo in mano / e ogni tetto di casa // Anche gli Achilpa / della tribù Arunta / australiani da molto prima / che arrivassero laggiù / i Kennedy da Letterfrak / o i Toson da Maranzanis / il loro grande palo di acacia / spostandosi lungo le stagioni / sui loro sentieri segreti / verso un nuovo luogo / o un altro pascolo / lo tenevano vicino / e fermandosi / lo piantavano / e attorno al palo e a loro / si ricreava il mondo / si appoggiava il cielo / si definiva il centro

to the arrival there
of the Kennedys from Letterfrak
or the Toson from Maranzanis
their long acacia pole
that moved with the seasons
and when stopping
they planted it
and around the pole and themselves
the world was created again
the sky leaned upon it
the center was defined.

Portatrici carniche

sares vuê almancul sui 90
encja jê *portatrice carnica*
no si è fint cumò capît
—ma cui ch'al sa nol pant—
s'a i an mandada indevour
la pratica zà spedida
o se l'an conseada
a nencja presenaâla

sìlafe si sintiva in dirit:
Cavaliere di Vittorio Veneto
come dutas chês âtas
no sai se pai cuatri francs
ch'a varessin vût di lâ
insieme al titul
o nomo pa braura
e il puntin di vêlu

insomas veve o no puartât
cjamada come un mul:
bombas e pagnocas
tal gei fînt su *la fronte?*
ma a girava na foto
cun jê sentada
a cjaval da cana; di un canon
in postatsion tra i crets
biela nuda ridint
i braçs vierts sul mont
un flôr di fantata
e ator come corona alpins
encja lôr bacon di fantats
in tiracas e ridint
cun nissuna voja di copâ
e imò mancul di muri:

na sorta di Scalarini
in cjar e vues
ma cence vaiarots:
"jo la vuesta guera me met
ta chel puest"

Women Bearers from Carnia

Today she would be at least ninety
she also a "bearer from Carnia"
up to now it has never been understood
—and those who know won't tell—
if they ever returned to her
the formal request already mailed
or if they advised her
to not even make it

truthfully she felt it was her right:
"Knight of Vittorio Veneto"
like all the others
I don't know if for the four cents
they would have had to give her
together with the title
or only for the pride
and the scruple of having it

in short did she or didn't she carry
loaded down like a mule
bombs and bread
in a wicker backpack to the front?

There was a photo
of her straddling horselike
the barrel of a cannon
positioned among the rocks

beautiful naked smiling
arms opened to the world
a splendid young woman
with a crown of alpini[6] around her
they also in the flower of youth
wearing suspenders and smiles
with no desire to kill
and even less to die

a kind of Scalarini[7]
in flesh and bone
but not spoiled:
"I will stick your war

la pas vegnuda
a fu encja intima di un gno barba
che par grât
murint
ai lassà
un ciamp

in famea discuterin
a lunc se daiel o no:
dirits no vares vüts
no vintla sposada
ma a la fin si cunvignì
ch'a veva fat plui jê
pal so bien
che ducj I parinci
tanci ch'a erin presints
a speculâ sul testament
cussì al vares vür di resonâ
encja il guviâr!
pecjâr che la foto
no si la cjâti plui
se cualchidun la ves
ch'a me mandi
la metares sul frontespiç
dal nôf libri

Portatrici carniche—sarebbe oggi almeno sui 90 / anche lei "portatrice carnica" / non si è capito fin qui / —ma chi sa non dice— / se le hanno restituita / la pratica già spedita / o se l'hanno consigliata / a neppure presentarla // in verità si sentiva in diritto: / "Cavaliere di Vittorio Veneto" / come tutte le altre / non so se per le quattro lire / che avrebbero dovuto andare / assieme al titolo / o se solo per l'orgoglio / e il puntiglio di averlo // insomma aveva sì o no portato / caricata come un mulo / bombe e pagnotte / con la gerla fino sul fronte? / ma girava una fotografia. / con lei seduta / a cavallo della canna di un cannone / in postazione tra le rocce // bella nuda sorridènte / le braccia aperte sul mondo / uno splendore di ragazza / e attorno come corona alpini / anche loro fior di giovanotti / in bretelle e sorridenti / con nessuna voglia di ammazzare / e ancora meno di morire // una sorta di Scalarini / in carne e ossa / ma senza piagnistei: / "io la vostra guerra me la metto / in quel posto" // la pace venuta / fu anche intima di un mio zio / che per gratitudine / morendo / le lasciò un campo // in famiglia discussero / a lungo se darglielo o no: / diritti non ne avrebbe avuti / non avendola sposata / ma alla fine si convenne / che aveva fatto più lei / per il suo bene / che tutti I parenti / tanti quanti erano lì presenti / a speculare sul testamento // così avrebbe dovuto ragionare / anche il governo! // peccato che la foto / non si trovi più / se qualcuno l'avesse / me la mandi / la metterei sulla copertina / del prossimo libro

up that place"
once peace arrived
she was also my uncle's companion
who, near death
in gratitude
left her a field

in the family they argued
at length whether or not
they should give it to her:
she had no rights
as they weren't married
but in the end it was agreed
she had done more
for his well-being
than all his relatives
all those who were present
to speculate on his last will
the government should have reasoned
likewise!

too bad the photo
cannot be found
if someone has it
send it to me
I'd put it on the cover
of my next book

Libertà

da botas di camions
vegnûts da lontan
svuèdin tal lâc
novelam a milions
vivorts scodolein nadant
tai cilindros vierts
cence plui confins

sclapìgnin tai grums
provisori davoi
miârs si slontànin
spaurits ma po svuelts
podìnt tancj tòrnin adun
ingropâts e lusints
tai volùms di prin . . .

Libertà—da autobotti / venute da lontano / svuotano nel lago / novellame a milioni / vivaci
scodinzolano nuotando / nei cilindri aperti / senza più confini // tirano sassi nei mucchi /
provvisorio scompiglio / migliaia si allontanano / spauriti ma poi svelti / potendo tanti
tornano assieme / aggrovigliati e luccicanti / nei volumi di prima . . .

Freedom

From truck tanks
arrived from afar
they dump in the lake
millions of seed fish
wiggling excitedly they
swim from open cylinders
no longer confined

they throw stones at the bunch
a sudden flurry
thousands take off
afraid then quick
if they could many would return
all bunched together and shiny
to their previous containers . . .

Leonardo Zanier   1013

"Elettrificati paletti"

tai verts passons
dal Berner Oberland
tra paluts di legn
frontâts a confin
sui ôrs dai prâts
cor corint
su fi di ram
isolâts cun pipas
di bakelite rossa e zala

co las vacjas
passonant
ju trùssin
a ur peta na sorta
di scoriada
strica sot-piel
di sutil e font ghitsi
come lunc troi
di furmias

na vôlta capît
mangjin e rumiin lontan
tal mieç dal prât
e ator dal fîl
no'nd è un balìn sgarfât
cença plui bars
como invecit fares
cjaminant dì e not
cença vê pâs
na lova scierada
oltri na filiada

"Elettrificati paletti"—sui verdi pascoli / del Berner Oberland / tra paletti di legno / conficcati a confine / sugli orli dei prati / corre elettricità / su fili di rame / isolati con pipe / di bakelite rossa e gialla // quando le mucche / pascolando / li sfiorano / le attraversa una sorta / di frustata / striscia sottopelle / di sottile e profondo solletico / come un lungo sentiero / di formiche / una volta capito / mangiano e ruminano lontano / in mezzo al prato / e attorno al filo / non c'è un calpestio graffiato / senza più erba / come invece farebbe / camminando giorno e notte / senza mai pace / una lupa rinchiusa / dietro una rete.

"Electrified Poles"

On the green pastures
of the Berner Oberland
from wooden poles
marking the border
at the edge of the fields
electricity flows
along copper wires
insulated by red and
yellow Bakelite cups

when the cows
graze
they barely caress them
a sort of whiplash
runs through them
a ribbon under the skin
of thin and deep tickling
like a long trail
of ants

once they get it
they graze and chew the cud far away
in the middle of the meadow
and around the wire
there is no scratched trampling
without any grass
as instead would do
pacing day and night
without ever a rest
a she-wolf locked
behind a fence.

Arlevament II

par scrupulâ
l'inteligjença
di una scimia.
oltre i gaters
da sgjaibula
mètin. un argagn
e par vê na banana
ch'a pò usmâ
e ogni tant jodila:
no à di tirâ
ma di pocâ un baston

sôl dopo un lunc
dûr insistiût provâ:
fan disperatsion
vilias magreças
odôr ch'al si vicina
e si slontana
a impara il truc
e a riva na banana
e cussì par copâ
cristians e pajans
nus an insegnât
che invecit di pocâ
fracâ frontâ impirâ
si à di tirâ viers di sè
arc fionda balestra
oturatôr grilet

chest iêr
vuê basta
un tast come chest
dal *computer*
vadì prenotâ

Breeding II

To investigate
the intelligence of a monkey
behind the bars
of a cage
they place an instrument
and to grab a banana
if it can smell
and see every once in a while:
it cannot pull
but push a stick

only after a long
hard insistent attempt:
hunger despair diets weight loss
smell that gets nearer
and farther
it learns the trick
and the banana arrives

likewise to kill
Christians and pagans
they taught us
that instead of pushing
pressing
thrusting inserting
one must pull
toward one's self
bowstring sling
crossbow
breechblock trigger

this in the past
today is enough
a key like this

un biliet di aereo:
destinatsion orari
enter e via

Allevameto II—per indagare / l'intelligenza di una scimmia / oltre le sbarre / della gabbia /
mettono uno strumento / e per avere una banana / se può annusare / e ogni tanto vedere: /
non deve tirare / ma spingere un bastone // solo dopo un lungo / duro insistito tentare: /
fame disperazione digiuni dimagrimenti / odore che si avvicina / e si allontana / impara il
trucco / e arriva una banana // così per ammazzare / cristiani e pagani / ci hanno insegnato /
che invece di spingere / premere / conficcare infilare / si deve tirare / verso di sé / arco fronda
/ balestra / otturatore grilletto // questo ieri / oggi basta / un tasto come questo / del *computer*
/ tutt'uno che prenotare / un biglietto d'aereo: / destinazione orario / *enter* e via . . .

of the *computer*
to instantly book
an airplane ticket:
destination dates
enter and off you go . . .

⇥ *Saro Marretta (Saraccio) (b. 1940)*

Saro Marretta, also known as "Saraccio," was born in 1940 in the province of Agrigento. He completed his studies, specializing in teaching, at the end of the 1960s, then moved to Switzerland, where he taught courses in Italian language and culture at Einsiedeln. That experience, lasting one year, inspired him to write a short story in the form of a diary called "Piccoli italiani in Svizzera" (Little Italians in Switzerland), which was very successful. Nevertheless, his critical mind and the lively irony shown in his story, which in a friendly manner derides the flaws of both the emigrants and the local inhabitants, caused him to lose his job. After various activities, including promoting culture for the Italian emigrants in Bern, he went back to teaching, first in a school for interpreters in Zurich, then later presented his works at various European universities (Barcelona, Salzburg, Norwich) and earned a degree in literature at the university of Bern. From 1990 to 1996 he served as the president of the AAIS, the Italian writers' association in Switzerland. Saro Marretta is totally bilingual, having been married to a native Swiss woman. He actually uses four languages, including his native dialect from Agrigento and the dialect Bernerdeutsch, which is spoken widely in Bern in everyday life. The poems included in the collection *Agli* (*Garlics*, 1982) are in fact written in these four languages (his wife, as well as the critic and professor Rolf Mäder, assisted him with the Bernerdeutsch). He also wrote two books of tales focusing on the Italian and the Swiss realities. One of them takes place in Sicily, *Le doppie verità* (*The Double Truths*); it was published in Italian in 1989, but was actually written in the 1970s and published in a German version in Switzerland with the title *Allegro Svizzero* (*Swiss Allegro*, 1976).

In 1977, Marretta published a narrative that is still among the most important in the literature of Italian immigrants in Switzerland, *Il paese finiva alla stazione* (*The Town Ends at the Railway Station*). Beginning with the 1980s, Marretta explored a new narrative vein, the detective novel, with a book titled *Chi è l'assassino* (*Who Is the Murderer*, 1982), followed by two installments of *Pronto, commissario . . .* (*Hello, Commissioner . . .*), containing around thirty stories for students.

The topics and themes that surface in Marretta's narratives are also in different ways present in his poetry in *Agli*. In this poetic work, greater attention is given to the problem of identity. The use of the dialect from the Agrigento area is more prominent as the language of childhood. This device gives way to Marretta's revolt, which is often controlled or repressed in other works. Poems from the 1980s also accompany the initial poems written in the 1960s, but without jeopardizing the unity of the collection. The poems are marked by invocations, apostrophes, and even maledictions addressed to people who caused difficulties and suffering for those who had to emigrate. The dialogue form is also used, at times even harsh addresses aimed at those who, like the poet's own father, did not want to understand the reasoning of others. At times the poems express a desire to bring down the wall of silence that impedes outbursts or prevents dialogues. In these invocations and addresses, couched in the intensity and concreteness of popular Sicilian expressions, the human presence is noteworthy, as is the involvement of the rest of nature, animate and inanimate alike.

Gli occhiali di cuoio

da *Agli*

I
In mezzo alla casa
quattro vecchi pallidi
guardano la bara
con gli occhi spiritati
mentre un bimbo
caccia le mosche al morto
rimasto col mento mezzo storto.
Sulla strada i cavalli
cogli occhiali di cuoio
affilano le orecchie
al rancore di bue malato
di un tamburo. Buttano
pallottole fumose
di sotto la coda
zappano sul selciato
con le bave di fuori.
Schiumano i cavalloni del mare
e queste associazioni c'accompagnano
morti e mulinelli
schioccano come la frusta
del cocchiere
dietro al corteo
del Signore
chiuso nell'urna del
venerdì santo
che non si gira o si muove
perché alle feste
ha fatto l'abitudine
e le sue piaghe non odorano
più d'aceto
sanno d'abbandono
e di tempo passato.

The Leather Eyeshades

from *Garlics*

I
In the center of the house
four pale old men
stare at the casket
with spooked eyes
while the kid
fans flies from the dead
with his mouth half crooked.
On the street horses
with leather eyeshades
sharpen their ears
at the rage of a bull wounded
by a drum. They drop
smoky pellets
from under their tails
they dig at the ground
while slobbering.
Huge sea waves gallop
and these parallels accompany me
dead and swirls
snapping as a coachman's
whip
behind the procession
of our Lord
sealed in the urn
on Good Friday
that does not turn or move
because it has become
used to the holidays
and his wounds no longer smell
of vinegar
they taste of abandonment
and ages past.

II

"Potessi rivivere
il giorno della mia partenza
che mi metterei a correre
come un cattivo animale
a scornare tutti
a gettarli a mare
che non avverrebbe più
la mia partenza."
Questa canzone
che mi gira a cerchio senza tregua
bolle nel petto e da morsi
visita àntri e non trova riposo
batte col martello
la sua litania
ma da qui è lontano e resta chiusa
dentro il petto a mordere
solo "a mia."
Eppure la vita
sembra esplodere impazzita
di fronte a questo vento d'aprile
scopri donne
che si dondolano i seni
tra le margherite
con le teste sorridenti.

II

"Could I live again
the day of my departure
I would start to run
like a mean beast
goring all with my horns
catapulting them into the sea
so that my departure would
never happen."
This song endlessly
swirling in circles around me
burns in the breast and bites
digs holes and finds no rest
its litany
wounds with a hammer
but it's so far from here and remains shut
inside the breast solely
to erode "only me."
And yet life
seems to explode crazed
in front of this April wind
watching women
with bouncing tits
among marguerites
with smiling heads.

Tigri elemosinanti

I

Stanno ormai per fermarsi
le nostre campane. Le bandiere
che impazziscono fuori dalle pertiche
—senza né testa né coda—
girano a turbine
e i colombi cambiano strada
col becco spalancato.
Il racconto della nonna
col vecchio cattivo che succhiava
il sangue ai bambini buoni
si sta avverando
e dietro alla mia porta
c'è un toro cogli occhi freddi
che m'aspetta.
Vorrei solo che correndo dietro alla luna rossa
dirupasse tutte le vostre case
e vi facesse scappare per strade e paesi
e che tutti quanti
diventaste d'un colpo emigranti.

II

Tigri elemosinanti.
M'avete dato solo morsi nell'anima.
È da quando emigrai che
che non vedo una luna piena
e le donne che torcevano gli occhi per me
hanno ora figli a vent'anni
Gli amicuzzi d'un tempo
sghignazzano con le gengive marcite
e le pietre che mi tiravate addosso
si son tutte smanciate.
Rimasero senza risposta
le chiamate del bimbo dietro ai pipistrelli
che sbattevano come ciechi
alle insegne delle cantonate

Begging Tigers

Our bells have almost stopped.
Flags flailing
out of their poles
—without heads or tails—
swirling in a storm
and the pigeons change course
their beaks wide open.
My grandmother's tale
with the mean old man who sucked
blood from good kids
is coming to pass
and behind my door
stands a bull with icy eyes
waiting for me.
I only wished he chased after the red moon
destroyed all of your houses
and made you escape along streets and towns
and that all of you
suddenly became emigrants.

II
Begging tigers.
You only bit chunks of my soul.
Not since I left home
have I seen one full moon
and the women who stared after me
now have twenty-year-old kids.
Old childhood friends
grin now with rotten gums
and the stones you used to throw at me
have turned to sand.
The calls the child threw at the night bats
all went unanswered
they used to smack like blind things
against the street corner signs

e stridevano come le donne
alle quali stava partendo il marito
e guardavano le strade
come lampade fulminate.

and screeched as women
whose husbands got ready to leave
and then looked down the streets
like shut-off lights.

Al padre, a Zurigo

Il vento soffia sulle tue spalle
vòlte a non far spegnere il lampione
impiccato al mandorlo
che ti fa luce stanotte
e sbatte come il battaglio
della chiesa grande,
senza tregua.

I tuoi occhi in quest'altalena
son più spiritati
dei buoi scappati
la notte dalle mandrie
quando nessuno vede niente
e le donne all'alba
si mordono disperate le zampe.

È' la notte che ti scappai per il paese
quando il tuo forcone, girando nell'aria
come la ruota d'una trebbia,
si fermò nella mia spalla
e i chiodi dei tuoi scarponi
s'affrettarono a calpestare
il sangue che serpeggiava (sguisinava)
sulla loppa
che formava garofani.
"I figli cattivi non crepano mai."

Ora stai piantato su una sedia
col testone alto
come il re delle tue battaglie perdute
e ti chiedo se hai fatto
bene a emigrare (ultimo scherzo
che combinasti ai tuoi "belli")
in questo paese dall' erba ricamata,
"Oh, ma perché me lo chiedi sempre?
non ti basta come la coscienza mi batte

To My Father, in Zurich

Wind blows on your shoulders
turned so as not to put out the streetlight
hanging on the almond tree
that brightens you tonight
and beats without rest
like the knocker
on the main church.

In this seesaw your eyes
are more spirited
than runaway oxen
abandoning the herds
when no one sees anything
and in the morning desperate
women bite their own feet.

It's the night I ran through town
when your pitchfork, flailing in the air
like the wheel of a wheat harvester,
came to rest on my shoulder
and the nails from your boots
hurriedly stumped on
the blood that was snaking (squishing)
on the chaff
piled as carnations.
"Mean kids never die."

Now you are nailed to the chair
with a high back
like the king of the battles you lost
and I ask if you did right to emigrate
(the final joke you pulled on your "loved" ones)
to this land of carpetlike lawns,
"Oh why do you keep on asking?
Isn't it enough that my conscience claws
night and day?"

notte e giorno?"
Chini il capo e alzi il pugno
per chiarirmi che qui ci muori
solo se ti ci ammazzano alle
spalle.

Bending the head you raise the fist
to make it clear that here you die
only if they kill you behind
your back.

Portateci sulle coscienze voi che siete rimasti

Qui non ci manca il pane.
I nostri figli frequentano le scuole
e sono gli ultimi della classe.
È venerdì di Pasqua e i cantieri
sono aperti. Soffia il favonio
e stralunano gli occhi a cavallo scappato
i capisquadra. Si gonfiano di rabbia
le mascelle dei guidatori.

Come sono rossi a quest'ora
i garofani dei vostri balconi
s'attorcigliano come serpenti
colle bocche spalancate
e le donne dietro alle finestre semichiuse
soffiano menta e petali di rose.

Voi come ogni anno
vi sbattete la coppola a mezza pancia
mentre vi girano un crocefisso nel quartiere.
Vi fa paura il rosso che ci cala
sopra le ossa
il suo sguardo giallastro senza vita.
E le vostre bocche, che non cantano mai,
ora cantano tutte.

Credete che son più vivi gli emigrati?
I loro occhi son più aggufati
d'un cristo scannato
e il sangue è secco appassito
anche se gli camminano i piedi per le strade.
I chiodi glieli appesero
i martelli della recessione e le spine
—spine che penetrano nel fegato—
le raccomandate (con ricevuta di ritorno—
sennò "si perdono"—) dell'ufficio
degli stranieri.

Keep Us in Your Conscience You Who Are Left

Here we don't go without bread.
Our kids go to school
and are last in their class.
It's Good Friday and factories
are open. Sirens blow
and the bosses show up bleary eyed
like runaway horses. The operators' jaws
tighten with anger.

How red are your carnations
at this hour of the day
they wind around like open-mouthed
snakes
and the women behind half-opened windows
blow mint and rose petals.

Like every year, you
beat your hats against the belly
as the crucifix moves through the neighborhood.
You are afraid of the red that drops
on your bones
and that jaundiced stare without life.
And your mouths, that never sing,
now are all singing.

Do you think the emigrants are more alive?
Their eyes are more owllike
as of a gored Christ
and the blood is dried hard
even though his feet keep moving along the streets.
The nails were driven in
by the hammers of recession and the thorns
—thorns that pierce the spleen—
are the registered letters (with return addresses
otherwise they might "get lost") from the
Immigration Office.

Loro non ci vogliono e voi non ci volete.
Dunque perché non ci ammazzate?
Ammazzateci tutti una mattina
mentre ritorniamo.
Una mattina presto
quando il sole è ancora insonnolito
e gli uccelli gorgheggiano sui rami.
Con le teste nascoste nelle botti
come contro i "ridderî"[8] che risalgono il fiume
dateci due schioppettate a tradimento
e addio emigrati.
A quale perditempo potrebbe venire in mente
ch'esistevamo pure noi—scarto di gente?

They do not want us and you do not want us.
So why don't you kill us?
Kill us all one morning
while we come back
early one morning,
when the sun is still half asleep
and birds chirp on the branches.
With heads hidden behind barrels
as if against seagulls that fly upstream
fire a couple of gunshots at our backs
and goodbye immigrants.
What timewaster could imagine
that we too existed—discarded people?

Agli

I

Per non partire avrei venduto
anche la gola. Quanto ho zappato coi piedi
su tutte le strade secondarie
sperando che non mi vedessero
gli occhi vostri di dragoni.
Ma il mio corso è fatto
come le settimane di Pasqua
—di stazione in stazione—
e colpi d'ago ai fianchi
a ogni inciampo.

Eppure quando partì il mio ultimo treno
c'erano bimbi che ridevano
alla piazza delle scuole
e trecce d'aglio alle finestre
bianche di calcina.
Lo sapevate ch'era un serpente
senza ragione il mio treno.
E io vi avrei uccisi tutti per
l'invidia, voi che restavate
in paese con le sgangherate risa
sotto i balconi e gli occhi furbi
alle ginocchia delle donne
che stendevano panni.

II

Quanto hanno danzato
queste risa sgangherate.
M'assaltano la notte per il petto.
Avrei voluto non nascerci
in questo paese. Avrei voluto
che il mare coprisse le vostre
teste con tutta la zagara e gli ulivi
in una mattina di sole—a tradimento.
Rinunciare a questa parlata, magra
come i cani che ammazzate nelle

Garlics

I

So as not to leave I would have sold
even my throat. Barefooted I hoed
every side road
hoping your dragon eyes
wouldn't find me.
But my path is drawn out
like Easter week
—station by station—
and needles fit in my flanks
each time I stumbled.

And yet when my last train pulled away
there were laughing kids
in the school yard
and garlic strung on the windows
white as plaster.
You knew that my train
was a snake without reason.
And I would have killed you all
out of envy, you who stayed behind
in town with blaring laughter
beneath the balconies and sly eyes
on the knees of the women
who hung out the laundry.

II

O how much that
blaring laugher danced about.
At night they grab my chest.
I wanted not to be born
in this town. I wanted
the sea to cover your heads
with orange blossoms and olives
on a day full of sunshine—in betrayal.
Better not speak, bone-skinny
like the mongrels you kill

trazzere. Ma è autunno anche qui.
E soffia aria sulle foglie.
E aspetto che gli anni passino
per venire a contare assieme
a voi i voli delle rondini in piazza
e sulle case.
Ma cala il sole e s'affievolisce sempre più
questa speranza.

on the cow paths. But it's fall even here.
Wind blows on the leaves.
And I wait for the years to pass
to come back and measure with you
the swallows' flight over the squares
and over the homes.
The sun is setting and this hope
gets weaker and weaker.

→ Alida Airaghi (b. 1953)

Alida Airaghi's biography can be divided into three periods. The first, naturally, consists of the early years of her professional development between 1953, the year of her birth, and 1978; she spent these years between Verona, her birthplace, and Milano, where she studied (receiving a degree in philosophy and classical literature) and participated in political and cultural debates. The second period, between 1978 and 1992, is her Swiss period in Zurich, which was particularly important for her poetic work, since it was there that she developed a rapport with her mentor, the intellectual Siro Angeli, who later became her husband. The third period of her biography began in 1992, marked by her return to Italy, where she continued to publish poems and contribute to journals and newspapers in Italy and Switzerland. Her publishing debut took place in 1984, when she was included in the Einaudi anthology *New Italian Poets*, edited by Walter Siti. The volume that gained her a wider audience was *Rosa rosse rosa* (*Rose Red Pink*, 1986), prefaced by an illuminating essay by Giovanni Giudici. During those years Airaghi taught Italian courses organized by the Italian consulate in Zurich for the sons and daughters of Italian residents. Inspired by the Italian cultural ambience in Zurich in which she and Siro Angeli were immersed, Airaghi published a volume of five stories with the title *Appuntamento con una mosca* (*Appointment with a Fly*, 1991). She also contributed to various Swiss journals, such as *Bloc Notes*, as well as Italian ones. In 1992, after the death of her husband, Airaghi left Zurich and went to live with her two daughters between Verona and Lake Garda. Four years later, in 1996, *Il lago* (*The Lake*) was published, which is a collection of poems inspired both by the lake of Zurich and Lake Garda. This collection was followed by *Sul pontile* (*On the Deck*) and *Nell'acqua* (*In the Water*) in 1997, then by *Litania periferica* (*Peripheral Litany*) in 1998, reprinted in 2004. Her later poems are gathered in *Un diverso lontano* (*A*

Different Distance, 2003) and *Frontiere del tempo* (*Frontiers of Time*, 2006) and the anthology *Nuovi poeti italiani 6* (*New Italian Poets*, 2012).

Airaghi's beginnings, as evidenced by the Einaudi anthology *New Italian Poets*, point to a mature poet. The selection consists of four sections: "L'appuntamento" (The Appointment), "La mosca" (The Fly), "La fotografia" (The Photograph), and "Spaccato coniugale" (Conjugal Cross-Section). The first section, "The Appointment," covers the various components of a dwelling (the carpet, the door, the mirror), personifying them, giving them consciousness and the power of reflection. The result is a parody of a life limited to the four walls of a dwelling, a life based on appearances. Each of the various items shows a characteristic of such a life: the humble carpet is, in almost a masochistic way, someone who suffers in silence from being stepped on; the door functions as a protector who safeguards the objects and the secrets of the house, preventing them from running out into the streets; the mirror, though flat and passive, represents a temptation for the guests who stop to admire their reflection in it. In spite of the ironic attitude of the poet, the outcome is a strange sense of the fragility of the individual, fearful to venture out of the protective cocoon and comforting routines. "The Fly" is a short prose piece presaging the future, longer one entitled *Appuntamento con una mosca*, which came out in 1991. In a limpid style, the author recalls a childhood experience by setting up a contrast between the affection and love of her mother, reachable only through the imagination and appearing as a fly that comes to class to comfort the poet, and the harshness of the nun who is her teacher. In this short prose narrative, Airaghi shows a capacity to draw the conflicts between appearance and reality and private and social living. The third section, "The Photograph," returns to the form of dialogue with objects. Here, it is an ambiguous dialogue not with the person of the photograph, but with the truncated image frozen in time (like the form, Pirandello would say, that contrasts with life), which memory preserves like a camera.

The fourth section plays on the ambiguity of the title, "Conjugal Cross-Section." The poems present a cross section, in a critical and ironic vein, of the life of a couple, a couple whose relationship is falling apart because of monotony, misunderstanding, and lack of communication. The last pieces are about female characters from Greek epics and tragedies, such as Iphigenia, who deludes herself regarding her father's intentions, Penelope, who labors only for her cloth, and Antigone, who is overcome by sorrow. For these compositions, Airaghi adopts loftier language and longer verses. Flow and harmony are interrupted by punctuation breaks and frequent enjambments, suggesting an element of underlying dramatic tension. These pieces later became a section of their own in "Classiche" (Classical Things).

Several poems from the Einaudi anthology reappear in *Rose rosse rosa* in 1986, which gets its particular tone from its opening section. These poems, like the most famous of the group, the frequently anthologized "Abbaiata della sposa di passeggio" (Barking of the Promenade Wife), are marked by a strong feminist perspective in defense of the dignity of women and mutual respect in relationships. The language becomes more concrete with respect to previous publications, the tone harsher. The voice is not that of a character, albeit mythical, but that of the poet in a more transparent way. The discourse takes on more openly a tone of fight, protest, and vindication. In addition, the inclusion of the earlier poems, scattered throughout the new collection, gives the new book the quality of a poetic biography, of a psychological journey with cultural and political overtones. It is a trajectory of maturation in a discontinuous key, as the agrammatical combination of the title shows. The name of the flower typically associated with women is followed by the color typically connected with revolt, followed by the adjective that connotes issues particularly related to women.

Following the death of Siro Angeli, and during the short period thereafter that she still spent in Zurich, Airaghi styled poems dealing with lake imagery, compositions that would later be accompanied by poems pertaining to Lake Garda. The two lakes compose a sort of diptych. One side offers winter landscapes, ice, frost, colorlessness, all buried in monotones of grey or white. These elements express solitude, stark sentiments, and the difficulty of forming relationships, social or intellectual, in a place that has become strange and hostile. On the other side are the landscapes of Lake Garda, inspiring sentiments of peace, freedom from worry and trouble, and an ability to sedate negative feelings of anger or rebellion. The rhythm is more ample, the vocabulary less harsh. The reprint of this volume evidences the success of the collection and represents a culminating point in Airaghi's poetics.

Le pareti

da *Nuovi poeti italiani*

Di quale altro colore,
—che non si perda l'essenziale che sono
lisce, senza bisogno di niente?
Gente diversa ama appendervi quadri,
abbracciarvi rampicanti, fare ombra
con lampade astratte. Ma è gente
che le teme, vuole sentirsi
indispensabile anche a loro:
che non hanno bisogno di niente.
Le ho lasciate come sono, bianche.

The Walls

from *New Italian Poets*

Of what other color—so as not to lose the essence that is
smooth, without needing anything?
Different people love to hang books,
clinging crawlers, create shadows
with abstract lamps. But it's people
who are afraid of them, want to feel
indispensable even to them:
who have no need of anything.
I left them as they were, white.

Gli spigoli

Impietosi stabiliscono confini, delimitano spazi:
gli spigoli, rigidi guardiani del solido,
sanno il diritto dell'aria che occupano
e da padroni mi marchiano
a sangue quando dispersa mi giro intorno,
cercando un posto al mio corpo.
Implacabili a ferirmi, io goffa inconsistenza
nel loro pieno, mi riducono alle mie ossa,
battuta e immobile, non esisto.

The Corners

Without pity they establish borders, limit spaces:
the corners, rigid guardians of solidity,
knowing the correctness of the air they occupy
and as proprietors they scrape me
raw when out of balance I move around,
searching a spot for my body.
Relentlessly striking me, the clumsy inconsistency
of their wholeness, they reduce me to slivers,
beaten and still, I don't exist.

Le tende

Le tende non ci sono, per questo occupano
tanto spazio. Ospiti che arrivano
portando in dono cioccolatini, si guardano
coi volti di chi attende qualcosa,
tetri si chiedono cos'è che manca
in questa casa. Sono a disagio,
si fingono disinvolti davanti alle finestre,
ma ogni tanto ticchettano sui vetri, fanno
un cenno ai vicini che li spiano.
Non ci sono le tende, la loro inesistenza
riempie le stanze.

The Curtains

There are no curtains, that is the reason they
occupy so much space. Arriving guests
bring chocolate gifts, look at each other
with faces that seem to expect something,
smugly they ask what is missing
in this house. I am embarrassed,
they move disinterestedly in front of the windows,
but every once in a while they knock on the glass, nod
to the neighbors who are spying them.
There are no curtains, their nonexistence
fills up the rooms.

Il letto

Dormo sull'orlo, di fianco.
Inutile è il resto che si offre;
lo ingombro di altre cose,
lenzuola che non mi somigliano
coperte che non sono me.
Io amo i margini mi piace
stare scomoda. Ai corpi
simulacri, ai fantasmi
che si litigano millimetri di spazio
"state buoni," protesto,
ma loro "fatti in là!" ingrati
roditori cui ho ceduto anche il letto.

The Bed

I sleep on the edge, on my side.
The rest that offers itself is useless;
I fill it up with other things,
bed sheet that don't resemble me
covers that aren't me.
I love the edges I like
to be uncomfortable. To the fake
bodies, to the ghosts
who fight over every inch of space
I protest, "be good,"
and they, "move over!" ungrateful
rodents to whom I've yielded even the bed.

Il tavolo

Attenta a questo tavolo,
che a detta del padrone di casa
ci si può mangiare in due.
Attento al piatto al bicchiere
che non tintinnino
che non ti spaventino il cuore
toccandosi.

The Table

Watch out for this table
on which, according to the homeowner
two can eat.
Watch out for the plate for the glass
so they won't clink together
and frighten your heart
as they touch.

NOTES

1. *Cinq* is Swiss slang for, less politely, a wop.

2. See Jean-Jacques Marchand, "La letteratura dell'emigrazione italiana in Svizzera," in *Lingua e letteratura italiana nel mondo oggi*, ed. Ignazio Baldelli and Bianca Maria Da Rif, 1:457–59 (Florence: Olschki, 1991).

3. Rolf Mäder, "Autori italiani emigrati in Svizzera," in *Il pane degli altri*, ed. Rolf Mäder, 7–8 (Bern: Francke, 1972).

4. Jean-Jacques Marchand, "Quando gli immigrati italiani si fanno poeti e scrittori," in *Lingua e letteratura italiana in Svizzera*, Atti del convegno tenuto all'Università di Losanna, 21–23 May 1987, ed. Antonio Stäuble, 65–74 (Bellinzona: Casagrande, 1988); Marchand, "La letteratura dell'emigrazione italiana in Svizzera"; Giovanna Meyer Sabino, *Scrittori allo specchio. Trent'anni di testimonianze letterarie italiane in Svizzera: Un approccio sociologico* (Vibo Valentia: Monteleone, 1996).

5. Gabriella Madrassi, "Riflessi ed immagini quotidiane nella narrativa degli emigrati in Svizzera nell'ultimo trentennio," in *La letteratura dell'emigrazione. Gli scrittori di lingua italiana nel mondo*, ed. Jean-Jacques Marchand, 39–49 (Turin: Edizioni della Fondazione G. Agnelli, 1991).

6. *Alpini*: a corps of Italian mountain soldiers.

7. Giuseppe Scalarini (1873–1948) was a socialist and pacifist caricaturist whose drawings were published in the newspaper *L'Avanti* between 1911 and 1928.

8. *Uccelli marzaioli*.

The United States

The United States

PETER CARRAVETTA

From this the poem springs,
that we live in a place that is not our own.

Wallace Stevens

A general introduction to the question of writing in one's native language while residing for long stretches of time in a foreign country is faced with a complex web of critical issues, not least being the relationship, besides that between poet and language, of time and place, origin and destination, and the give and take of negotiating a position, or a poetics, in the ever-unfolding spectrum of cultural values. The interpreter is called upon to stake out a mobile critical field within which these relationships can be metaphorically mapped out, and at best offer an itinerary among other possible ones. On the premise that, historically, poetry is an art form that essays to transcend its own materiality, the following remarks are couched within a broad continuum that begins with Calypso's gift of immortality to the traveler and ends with the locus where the *poiesis* in effect occurs.

In book 5 of the *Odyssey*, when the nymph-goddess Calypso is informed by Hermes of the nonnegotiable decision by Zeus to let Odysseus go from the island of Ogygia—for "Destiny still ordains that he shall see his loved ones, / reach his high-roofed house, his native land at last" (127–128)—the "lustrous" queen's complaint goes on to list the fact that she "welcomed [Odysseus] warmly, cherished him, even vowed to make the man immortal, ageless, all his days . . ." (150–151), though in the end she reluctantly acquiesces to the will of "storming Zeus."[1] When we meet Odysseus for the first time, we find him on the beach "sitting, still, weeping . . . for his foiled journey home . . . unwilling lover alongside lover all too willing" (167–173). Though informed of the unexpected outlook, Odysseus is still distrustful of Calypso's change of heart, and he reiterates his desire to go back to Ithaca. She reminds him of the dangers ahead and, making one last attempt even against the will of Zeus, begs him to "stay right here, preside in our house with me / and be immortal" (230). But Odysseus stands his ground; suggesting that there may be something greater even than love, and the love of a goddess at that, he says: "Nevertheless I long—I pine, all of my days— / to travel home and see the dawn of my return" (240–243).

Calypso's unaccepted gift of immortality is mentioned again in book 7 when, after eighteen days at sea, Odysseus lands at Phaeacia and is eventually introduced to the court of Alcinous. Recognized by Queen Arete, Odysseus is compelled to tell of his most recent provenance, the home of the daughter of Atlas who "took me in all her kindness, / welcomed me warmly, cherished me, even vowed / to make me immortal, ageless, all my days," although, he hastens to add with pride, "she never won the heart inside me, never" (294–297). The sentiment of wanting to return home— *nostos*—recurs a third time when Odysseus is finally persuaded to tell the whole story of his misfortunes, at the beginning of book 9: "So nothing is as sweet as a man's own country, / his own parents, even though he's settled down / in some luxurious house, off in a foreign land / and far from those who bore him" (37–41). Just a minute before, he had said: "Mine is a rugged land but good for raising sons— / and I myself, I know no sweeter sight on earth / than a man's own native country" (30–32).

Unlike Achilles, for whom achieving immortality was the very reason for being, even at the price of having to die to attain it—indeed, that was the only way of becoming immortal, dying in battle—Odysseus wishes to accept his mortality as long as he can go home, to his *domus*, to his family, to his land.[2] One would have to surmise that our hero cares more about *being in a place* he can call his own than about *becoming in time* a model for everyone; or, otherwise stated, he leans more toward personal satisfaction than perennial transfiguration.

But is this entirely true? Is not the immortality of the hero founded on fame, from the Greek *kleos*, Latin *fama*?[3] That is to say, on renown among people, or mortals? And is not *fama*, derived from speaking (Latin *fari*), which includes rumor good or bad, that discourse which continues to be woven about the hero not only in his time, but *through* the generations? And do we not have a long-standing tradition in the West whereby literature primarily, first oral then written, permits and confirms the tales of the hero, his/her reputation, his/her embedding in the cultural memory of a people, a group, and in more recent history, a nation, a profession?

No need to summon Petrarch, or Shakespeare, or even Dorian Gray on this score. After all, have poets not always sung, and sought, the universal, immortal, transhistorical essence of the human condition? At least the lyrical ones?[4] And if this is the case, what difference would it make *where* they reside—at home or abroad? Or *when* the poetry is sung/written (and often read)—in the community or everywhere over time? Which brings us to a key word in our opening paragraph: What is and where is the *locus* of poetry? Many poets in this anthology will struggle with this debacle throughout their careers. Calypso's gift of immortality presents a double bind for our paradigmatic hero: Remain in the absolute present of the domain of the goddess, and you will even physically live forever; try to return to your place of provenance, among mortals, and you too shall die.

Signaling a major epochal shift from the archaic to the historical age, Odysseus brings consciousness to the fore and leaves the world of Achilles behind. The master wielder of language, the wily rhetor, *polytropos*, does not renounce *nostos*, the return to origin. He does not wish to *ex*-ist forever as an outsider, in as foreign a place as Calypso's heaven can be; he will accept mortality as the only path to immortality, without having to die in battle. He will tell of his deeds in the first person, as a survivor, not as a victim of fate or the enemy's sword: He will not be narrated by others. The first-person utterance embeds itself in the third-person construct of the gods and of the heroes. We must then reframe the critical paradox: The poet's immortality seems to be dependent upon his/her linguistically embodied deeds among mortals, through social memory. And language (in general, but as used by poets in this particular context), in a perturbing analogy with war, seems to be inextricably bound to circumscribed places (cities, regions, nations) and times (traditions, diasporas, events). This is quite a predicament, for the gift brings with it an obligation, and acceptance entails a renunciation. We are thus confronted with great categorical issues: identity, belonging, death.

Traditionally, these critical *topoi* have inspired countless readings bent on demonstrating that what happens to one during a journey, and what life and activity are realized in the place of destination, are inevitably tinged either with nostalgia and loss or, alternatively, when it comes to the interaction with persons and situations in the new domain, that there must be some imperfection, alienation, or inauthenticity lurking in both deeds or writings. For the unspoken assumption generally is that what is "real" and "true" can only come from the place of origin, the *madre patria*.[5] Identity itself has been construed as based on the locus of prove-nance, on the auroral moment of genesis. By the same token, critics, writers, and most intellectuals have long held that this "real" or "true" can only be expressed in a "native" tongue. But the question that then arises immediately is whether there exists some transcendental connection between place of birth and place of speaking, or poetizing, ignoring which would reveal some irreparable fracture or condemn the writing to some form of incompleteness. As we will see, whether we consider the poet as warrior, emigrant, or self-imposed exile, a more contemporary version of the archetype would shift the focus from the origin to the journey and the destination, or better yet, to the oases or bivouacs or plateaus in which life actually takes place.[6] Even when the destination happens to be the origin.[7] Thus the yearning for recognition remains, no matter where the poet happens to be.

These complex psychological and philosophical questions need to be anchored to three factors, namely *language, reality*, and *history*. For poetry is a fact of language primarily, much more so than other forms of linguistic expression or genres, such as prose fiction, journalism, autobiography, epistolary, or scientific writing, wherein the main objective is communication, that is to say, where the language must speak of something else and foreground a tendency to univocity, to an established coincidence between word and thing. Poetry, on the other hand, is essentially polysemous, multivocal. Now historically we have had two major tendencies in poetry: one which seeks the unsayable, the immortal, the self-contained *nous*, and the other which seeks to renew the very language of the tribe[8]—in more technical terms, a lyric afflatus and an experimentalist bent. Not that one could not go without the other, as demonstrated by Dante, or Pound, or basically any great poet. In brief, however, the lyric poem becomes the quintessential mode of poetry, embodying a full-fledged metaphysics or pure fantasy. This, at least, is the wisdom we acquired about the meaning of poetry through the likes of Leopardi, Hölderlin, Coleridge, Mallarmé, Jiménez, Stevens, on the philosophical side. On the other side, during nearly a century of systematic avant-gardism (and spurred by structuralist poetics), poets challenged the medium and only secondarily concerned themselves with communicating anything outside the poem itself. Self-referentiality of the text has been the name of the game. Thus in the later twentieth century we were typically confronted with the critical task of either assessing degrees of swerve from a supposed standard of communication or else searching for some kind of mostly undesired referentiality. In either case, this left ample space for interpretation.[9]

These dominant critical approaches have of course met with great difficulty in explaining why there has been a parallel, though most recently devalued, tradition of poetry which, though never forgetting itself as a fact of language, that is, as being ultimately a rhetorical construct, has been deeply concerned with what lay *outside* of itself, namely the world of the *res* and humans *de carne y hueso*, or even the worlds of the imagination and myth. I am talking about the epic tradition, from Homer's works through Virgil's, and then, to name some paradigmatic exemplars, despite their obvious differences (that is, even when they become anti-epics), the *Divine Comedy*, the *Lusiads*, *Paradise Lost*, *Don Juan*, *Jerusalem*, *Contemplations*, the *Laus Vitae*, the *Cantos* and *The Waste Land*. When it became obvious that a poem could contain both, the lyric and the epic mode (the distinction having become fuzzy or critically reductive), in American culture the label was changed to "the long poem." In the twentieth century, in which the lyric competed with its desecrating, combative other, the avant-garde poem (although often one school overlaps with the other), we can track how the poetry of reference, or of allegory, or of *the other* lost its purchase on the aesthetic preferences of Euroamerica, and nearly vanished. In the Italian panorama, after Gabriele D'Annunzio, there is precious little to suggest that a poet could do both, seek the immortal gift of gods and tradition, while dealing with the predicament of mortality.[10] In the American context, Whitman, on one hand, and Poe, on the other—representing, respectively, and, again, grosso modo, a poetry about the world, and a poetry about language—were in part relegated to the attic, as we witnessed the rise and dominance of personal, sentimental, experimental, and formalistic creations through the early part of the twentieth century. It is only with the post–World War II neo-avant-gardes that we are witness both to some serious challenges to formalism and poetry for poetry's sake, and also some bona fide attempts to speak about the world, indeed speak the world, through poetic language, as the diverse poetics of Olson, O'Hara, the Beats, and what elsewhere I called the "hyphenated poets" can attest. In key moments, a few of the Italophone poets here presented will exhibit this tendency of reframing the real through a post-avant-garde syntax, as they will also attempt to recapture and readapt a shortened and more focused version of the long poem, or what in Italian is called the *poemetto*. But they will by and large stay away from that other trunk, which is still linked to the epic mode, albeit in a subterranean fashion: the political poem.

Yet it cannot be denied that something always slips out or exudes from the poetic text, and harks toward the "real" world, if for no other reason than as readers/listeners we engage the poem, and establish a connection after a fashion, whether as dialogical pole, dialectical negation/appropriation, or more figuratively as a dancing partner. Thus, saying that poetry is a social fact or experience means that place, tradition, and ideology are necessarily key components of any poetic enterprise. Moreover, being that as *langue* it is but one more social code, poetry must willy-nilly bow down to history, for there is such a thing as change or development over time, whether we call it *Kleos*, or Tradition, or simply refer to a specific school, habitus, or institution. When the values of a society are no longer as clearcut as they were (or so we were told in school) in Homeric times, it stands to reason that notions such as *nostos*, *oikos/domus*, *xenos*, and *metexis*, are either forgotten, irrelevant, or profoundly altered, taking on often unrecognizable masks. In brief, the relationship of the poet to recent historical developments, both inside poetry and outside in the world, surges to the foreground as a function or parameter we must take into account.

We can illustrate these relations by means of a diagram. We have four poles, set against the wavy axis of timelessness/historicity:

The usefulness of this semiotic parallelogram, which we will flesh out as we progress, is to help us when we turn to the texts of the anthologized poets, in order to locate a starting point toward a general interpretation of the situation of writing in a language when actually living in a country where that language is not dominant. Each of the apexes is marked by its own specific inner tension. Apex A situates the long-standing tradition of the immortality topos, whether of the hero, the poet, or the sojourner. From Homer to very recent days, this quest can be realized either through death, or in a place that is not one's own. The tension here is between the missing specific place, the *domus* of the origin, and *any* place, the cosmos, because not dying would require leaving the world of history for that of timelessness. Apex B would represent Apex A's dialectical opposite, as we have seen, where home is the writer's home country, or region, or actual existential domain, but also the place where he or she can exist as a mere mortal, and therefore subject to the ravages of time and the unpredictables of history. The tension is owed to the displacement created by having home away from the origin.

These two apexes are bisected by the critically necessary (to avoid facile dichotomies or logical oppositions) included third field, which is

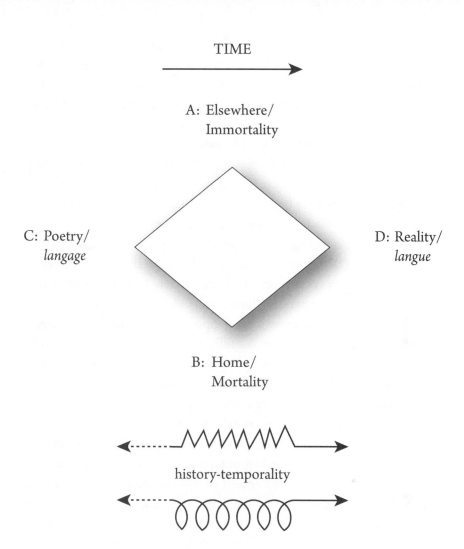

TIME

A: Elsewhere/
Immortality

C: Poetry/
langage

D: Reality/
langue

B: Home/
Mortality

history-temporality

itself of a double nature and thus requires two separate poles. We have seen that poetry can be understood in terms of writing as a fact of language *qua* human language, independently of which national code it happens to be embodied in. This aspect discloses the potential for poetry to be fundamentally a speaking of being, or the expression of the *nous*, or even the *je ne sais quoi* much sought and rarely attained by all works of art. This is most evident in the lyric poem, and one would think it is spontaneously related to Apex A. However, poetry is also, inescapably, a *fact* of language *as* a physical/physiological act deeply rooted in the realm of the existent, the world of the empirical, and therefore given to us as measurable semiotic code that is bound to a specific language, as Italian, English, or Swahili, indeed, to a national or, better, a regional tongue. To foreground this distinction, Apex C must have as a counterpart Apex D, and in order to differentiate between the two senses of what is meant by *language*, I use the two standard terms long employed in structural linguistics, the French *langage* (or *linguaggio*, in Italian) and *langue* (or *lingua*). It stands to reason that a poem that addresses in no uncertain terms events of the world of which it, as a *langue*, is itself part, would gravitate toward this pole. As always, semiotics prepares the canvas for hermeneutics. With this critical gyroscope we hope to sketch a map of the problematic territories inhabited by the Italophone poets of the United States.

Underlying or hovering over the entire enterprise is the knotty issue, mentioned at the outset, of the writing in a language that is not the one of the land, society, or country in which the writing comes into existence. Though it is true that often the Italian poets of America do some of their writing while traveling to or working temporarily back in Italy, it is a working assumption here that they are fully aware—indeed often painfully so—that they are American residents, whether legal aliens or naturalized citizens or at any rate not, or not any longer, *italiani purosangue*, their personal disclaimers to the contrary notwithstanding. (Unless they consider living in a different country for four decades a mere extended vacation!) This will complicate the picture, and often to keep a balance we will refer to a second and already worked-out critical frame, that provided by Deleuze and Guattari on the concept of deterritorialization,[11] and then only on the basis of a small sampling of texts. Finally, for reasons of space, we cannot offer an equal number of representative poems for each poet, especially since some have published more than others.

Among the Italian poets writing in the United States today there is little trace of the laconic and pain-riddled verses of first-generation immigrants, whose struggle with displacement, deterritorialization, and alienation was not a mere rhetorical trope but embodied deep personal and existential predicaments, and in which language is used to express directly what the poet feels with little mediation or metaphorical attenuation and sublimation.[12]

"Classical" Italian emigration, the great exodus that began in the 1880s, had all but ended by the 1970s, so in our recent memory we find no major voices bemoaning the loss of origin or swearing to the "return," or *nostos*, in any of its traditional configurations. Most Italian poets in the United States do not wish, as we will see, to be called immigrants. In fact, in one of those ironic and often tragic reversals of history, it is Italy which today is an immigrant country. The phenomenon has produced some brutally explicit and existentially profound verses, such as by the Albanian-Italian poet Gezin Hajdari: "Little by little I am being consumed / in the empty dank rooms / denouncing my voice / hidden in the rocks / that's why I call out to my Shade / killed in another country / by stones among the stones."[13] Or consider some lines from a poem titled "Para teorizar" by Clementina Sandra Ammendola, a poet who, though born in Argentina, felt she was "returning" to Italy in the early 1990s: "to migrate is to arrive, is to search / is also to leave and to postpone. / It is changing one's reality / without being a stranger to harsh solitude. / It is like changing a soul / from one body to another, but / freedom, absence / with what means can they be contained?"[14]

Yet, surprisingly, aspects of this predicament can still be read in some poems by the older generation, such as Tusiani, Piazza Nicolai, Provenzano, Del Duca, and perhaps some of my own. We could group them under the aegis of Immigrant poets, not least because they were actually emigrants, in a traditional sense of the word. I consider Rimanelli, who had become persona non grata in the literary establishment of late 1950s Italy, the only exile.[15] The rest are expatriates (or dispatriates[16]) whose texts exhibit, as we will see, varying degrees of sociopolitical incompleteness, symbolic nomadism, existential emptiness, identitarian incertitude, philosophical skepticism, and occasionally Pirandellian humor.

This preliminary hermeneutic is not incompatible with a different approach proposed a few years ago by Paolo Valesio. In an article that appeared in *Yale Italian Poetry*, Valesio holds that Italian poets abroad could also be read as belonging to one of four "tribes," namely: "the ancient community of Italian poets in Italy (the metropolitan poets), the historical community of generally or generically American poets . . . the old-tribe of Italian-American poets . . . and finally the new tribe of expatriate poets, in America and elsewhere."[17] The ancient community clearly denotes what makes up the Italian literary canon, which in our diagram would mean "home," or the symbolic *domus* against which the poets of the fourth category, the expatriates or, as Valesio elsewhere called them , the Italophone poets, are measured. A case can be made that for many Italophone poets the tendency to the "return," the Ulyssean *nostos*, is toward this ancient community, Italy as Ithaca. But this is where the issue of immortality *through* poetry resurges, and much more work must be done to understand how deterritorialization impacts this dynamic. The Italophone poets, however, can be further subdivided into those who work on language as the human capacity *to say*, in Italian *dire*, roughly Apex C, where as we will see we could group Ballerini, Moroni, in part Gulli and De Palchi, and some of my own early work; and those who through poetry intend to *say that*, or *speak about*—in Italian, *dire di*—to which belong the rest, and that correspond to our Apex D. This group can be further subdivided in terms of the *what* they speak about: Tusiani, Tanelli, Piazza Nicolai, Fontanella, some texts by De Palchi, Surliuga, Carrera, and myself, and certainly the dialect poets Provenzano and Del Duca, seem to be concerned with the world out there captured in its shifty and slippery boundaries, often manifesting skepticism about any one universal statement we might make about our society; alternatively, they are engrossed in the constitutive search for some authentic self, foregrounding the identitarian component in one of its many iterations, psychological, social, generational, and so on. Much of this we can read in Surliuga, Mobile, Marchegiani, and Saccà, but with greater stress on the emotional, as well as Valesio, but with a marked focus on spirit.

If we were to add that some have chosen to write *also* in English, in virtue of the ineradicable, co-enabling, bond between the *langage* of poetry to the *langue* of the new (or other, or foreign) locus of existence, then some of the above poets can also be grouped among the "old tribe of Italian-Americans," a category that would present us with the daunting critical prospect of figuring out what their relationship to the *domus* actually is, for—to borrow a felicitous phrase from Fred Gardaphé—their writings manifest Italian signs (as excerpts from the Italian *langue*, as references, symbols, and so on) in American streets (the concrete or actual, not symbolic or memorable, *domus*, the place where they actually dwell).[18] In an ideal continuation of Gardaphé's work, we would have to split Valesio's "old tribe" further and generate a new grouping which, owing precisely to the fact that they write directly in English, can constitute the American Italian poets, such as Ballerini, myself, Carrera, Rimanelli, Tusiani, and Condini, among those presented in this anthology, but could include the likes of Pasquale Verdicchio and Justin Vitiello. Indeed this perspective, which some actually resent or reject, has spurred a discussion on the hypothetical status of the identity of American Italians, itself problematic and opening up to other and broader sets of considerations. Yet apart from this, these six poets should furthermore be considered *American poets*, to the degree that there is an established practice of identifying a writer by the language and country in which he or she writes. This raises the connected and critically complex question of potentially belonging to two canons at the same time, a situation which wreaks havoc on the simplistic college-department-based critical mythologemes of pinning a poet to one country (usually on the basis of a birth certificate), one language (the idealist myth that one can only write in one's native tongue), and one activity (the academic-populist dictum whereby one cannot be a poet and a critic at the same time). Unsurprisingly, the avatars and watchdogs of the "ancient community" on both sides of the pond have been rather ungenerous toward these indefinable, heterological, and polymorphic creatures. Until further mapping is provided, until a claim and a sort of Duchampian three-way threshold is conceived to prevent these border guards from exercising the inclusion/exclusion privilege, we might say their fame is that of restless wanderers in the deserts, over the seas, and through the canyons of the possible. But that is another chapter.

It is interesting, however, that for these Italophone poets, who walk and talk the American streets, America is registered and recognized only insofar as being made up of signs of a greater universalism, one whose symbology can only find adequate or exclusive expression in their *other tongue*, the one that, as long as there exist nation-states, identity cards, and geographical barriers, is now deterritorialized and thus exist only in the mind. It is remarkable that this condition is not seen by most of the poets here collected as representing a possible political conduit or force, or, as Deleuze had suggested, as effecting a critique of the immortal homeland canon by dint of its sheer psychological, geographical, and cultural distance, myth and drive of *nostos* notwithstanding. And it is unfortunate that often in the search for pure expression and identity, the poets forget where they are actually living and residing, and where they may meet up with the possibility that ends all other possibilities. But much more frequently the gift that Calypso wanted so much to give the mortal *polytropos*, the status of a god, is not traded in for a home that our poets are painfully aware is no longer their home, or even their idea of home. Being poets, home is in their language, a language that is itself uprooted and vagrant, easily taken to be as strange to the ancient community as it sounds foreign to the present community. These poets, in their different ways all migrant poets, have put an end to the myth of origin or of necessary return to reclaim an anchoring identity: Like existence itself, their poetry is always on the move and lives a plurality of lives.

Joseph Tusiani (b. 1924)

Joseph Tusiani, professor emeritus of Lehman College, City University of New York, came to the United States in 1947, when he was twenty-three years old, and became a naturalized American citizen in 1956. Tusiani is a poet in four languages, a critic, and a translator of Italian classic poetry into English verse. His translations include Michelangelo's *Complete Poems*, Boccaccio's *Nymphs of Fiesole*, Luigi Pulci's *Morgante*, all of Machiavelli's verses, Tasso's *Jerusalem Delivered* and *Creation of the World*, Leopardi's *Canti*, and other anthologies. He is the author of several collections of verse in English, among them *Rind and All* (1962), *The Fifth Season* (1964), *Gente Mia and Other Poems* (1978), and *Collected Poems 1983–2004* (2004). His poetry in Latin includes *In Exilium rerum* (1985), *Carmina latina* (1994), and *Carmina latina II* (1998). He has composed poetry in Italian, such as *Peccato e luce* (*Sin and Light*, 1949), *Odi sacre* (*Sacred Odes*, 1957), and *Il ritorno* (*The Return*, 1992). He has also written fourteen collections of poems in his native Gargano dialect, among them *Làcreme e sciure* (1955), *Tìreca tàreca* (1978), *Bronx America* (1991), and *Li quatte stagioni* (1998). He has written an autobiography in three volumes, *La parola difficile* (1988), *La parola nuova* (1991) and *La parola antica* (1992). Tusiani has won the Greenwood Prize and the Alice Fay di Castagnola Award, and in 1963 he was asked by President Kennedy to record his poetry for the archives of the Library of Congress.

A precocious, voracious reader, and musically inclined since before his *laurea* (BA) from the University of Naples, Joseph Tusiani's literary background is steeped in the classics and in the major authors of the Italian canon. However, he has been rather indifferent to the experience of either the neo- or historical avant-gardes, and has not devoted much attention to committed poetry. Of writers included here, he has the greatest number of translations from Italian into English to his credit, and has written several books in his new adopted language.[19] Tusiani's work is eminent proof of the psychic split that emigration brings at all levels, from the familial to the social, from the professional to the cultural. A professor of Italian at Lehman College in New York for more than four decades, he has been, until relatively recently, rather isolated among his fellow Italian writers of America. His work is particularly interesting for the evolution of his conflicted relationship to *both* Italy and America, both of which he has deeply loved, ever aware of being at once an outsider and an insider, a condition which has caused him an inner restlessness and yearning for a higher unifying locus. Between the two great canons of English and Italian, in order not to feel that he would not be able to express the whole of his self in either, he tried, successfully at the formal level, to go back to his first "natural" language, the dialect of San Marco in Lamis, in the province of Foggia, and, at the same time, back to the first "cultural" language of all of Europe and of European America, Latin, in which he wrote voluminously and for which he also achieved international recognition.[20] Thus we are dealing with a quadrilingual poet fully aware that something always risks *not* being said, or not being said properly.[21] About his return to dialect, he wrote: "To go back to dialect is perhaps a liberating *nostos*, a return to a virginal seeing and feeling. Dialect admits no decoration, so the expression becomes pure and genuine, I would say *elemental*."[22] But is this really true? Are the feelings and ideas developed later in life, and in another tongue, necessarily less pure? In terms of our starting critical parallelogram, this situation may make some think that Tusiani is deeply concerned with the semiotics of Apex D: *Langue*/Reality. But it should not surprise us to find, in his extensive production, questions concerning the mortality/immortality dyad, and the strategies devised to accommodate the self-doubting, identity-troubled, language-besieged self-definition of the poetic Self. Tusiani's poetry speaks about a sorrowful sense of *déracination*, which explains why he threw himself into English in order to re-root himself in the new culture, only to realize that seeds and tendrils in his psyche were, to use Deleuze's term, rhyzomatically shooting up and spreading in other regions of his linguistic-cultural unconscious. Deterritorialization is no mere theory; it refers to a deep psychological-cultural shift that complicates the life of the writer in subtle ways. The impact of this condition on his sense of identity has found expression in the often-cited poem written directly in English from *Gente Mia*: "Two languages, two lands, perhaps two souls . . . / Am I a man, or two strange halves of one?"[23]

As a result, beneath the impeccable prosody, one hears in each of the four languages a striving for completeness, for belonging, for unity which is constantly undermined the moment the poet's consciousness takes into account temporality as much as spatiality. His natural tendency will turn out to be the emulation of the song of the great lyrical poets. Tusiani's poetry is not socially, politically, or ideologically marked, except in the sense that, taken diachronically, it becomes explicitly a saga of the life of the first-generation immigrant. His native country, the "ancient community," has practically ignored him for the longest time, except at the very regional level, in northern Apulia. But his parabola would raise the separate issue of what comprises a national canon (in this case, the Italian one), for until only a few decades ago dialect poetry was either excluded or considered "marginal" literature. A similar fate attended Tusiani's production in English, for as much as he became an expert in the Anglo-American literary and cultural tradition, often exhibiting in his texts hyperperfect prosody, he has not been studied in English and American Studies departments. Until Italian American studies came into its own in the 1990s as a de facto ethnic and cultural studies area of research, and quickly realized the stature of this poet, we can surmise that Tusiani has consistently felt he was an outsider, someone from elsewhere, a foreigner, an Other. With multiple offshore anchorages at point D: *Langue*/Reality, his poetry is stretched problematically between precarious moorings in A: Elsewhere/Immortality, and B: Home/Mortality.

Semplice analogia

da *Il ritorno*

Noi siamo, amore, come le formiche
che, industri e lente nella pigra estate,
chicchi trascinano e opulenze aurate
a ciechi nascondigli e zolle antiche:
pensano a lunghe lugubri giornate
su di una terra senza sole e biche
quando, tra le intemperie nemiche,
vivranno di risorse accumulate.

Ed anche noi, così, portiamo, amore,
i ricordi più belli al nostro nido,
onde scaldarci in fosche e gelide ore.
Attingeremo al gran tesoro interno
e, se buio perduri il cielo infido,
avremo noi l'estate, altri l'inverno.

Simple Analogy

from *The Return*

We are, love, like the ants,
that industrious and slow in the slothful summer,
drag golden riches and kernels
into blind hideouts and ancient turf:
well they foresee long, lugubrious days
on a land with no seeds and no sun,
when, in harsh and hostile weather,
they will live from resources amassed.

And so we, too, my darling, bring
the most beautiful memories to our nest,
to warm ourselves in gloomy glacial hours.
From our great inner treasure we will draw
and, if the treacherous sky still dark remains,
we will have summer, others winter.

Notturno

Forse fra tante lievi
lontanissime luci,
tu per la prima volta questa sera,
o astro senza nome,
l'infima terra scorgi.
Per giungere al mio sguardo
trilioni d'anni ha percorso il tuo raggio,
serenamente ignaro
d'imperi e civiltà risorti e spenti;
ed altri sguardi, o placido
punto nell'universo,
tra milioni di secoli vedranno
il brillare di questo
tuo attimo celeste.
Oh, tale è la distanza
fra te, mia nuova benvenuta stella,
e il tacito pianeta che m'accoglie.
Fra quanti quatrilioni d'anni-luce
ti arriverà il ricordo
di questa mia presente umana sera?
Quante altre civiltà, quali altri imperi
saranno nel frattempo
risorti e spenti ancora? E del minuscolo
granel di polvere, un giorno chiamato
sospiro d'uomo e febbre di potenza,
che rimarrà? Sei bella,
intanto, o tersa notte, assai più bella
se per quello che sei ti guardo e godo.

Nocturne

Maybe among so many
faint, faraway lights,
for the first time this evening,
O nameless star,
you discern this earth so low.
To reach my gaze
trillions of years your ray has traveled,
serenely unaware
of empires and civilizations risen and spent;
and other eyes, O quiet
point in universe,
millions of centuries from now will see
the sparkle of this celestial instant of yours.
Oh, such is the distance
between you, my new welcome star,
and the silent planet that shelters me.
In how many quadrillions of light-years
will the memory of this, my present human evening
finally reach you?
How many civilizations and empires
will in the meantime
have risen and fallen? And of the minuscule
speck of dust, one day called
breath of man and thirst for power,
what will remain? Right now you are so beautiful,
O limpid night, so much more beautiful
if but I watch and enjoy you for what you are.

L'indirizzo

Oh, puntiglioso Iddio!
Quando meno Lo aspetto
dinanzi me Lo trovo
travestito da uccello o raggio o fiore
o come primo verde in secco pruno.
Non mi concede neppure un minuto
per poter dubitare
e poterLo scordare.
Qualunque strada io prenda,
da qualunque montagna o mare o cielo,
sempre inquieto torno
al mio primo indirizzo,
Via dell'Antica Fede, Numero Uno.

The Address

Oh, punctilious God!
When I least expect Him
I find Him right before me
disguised as a bird, a sunbeam, a flower,
or as the first greenness on a still dry bush.
Not even one minute He grants me
to doubt him
and maybe forget all about Him.
Whichever road I may take,
from whichever mountain or sea or sky,
restless, I always go back
to my first address,
Avenue of the Old Faith, Number One.

Lo specchio

Come fragile sfera di cristallo
serro il tuo viso tra le mani e sogno.
Chi mi vedesse estatico a fissare
i tuoi occhi di verde tenerezza
mi crederebbe intento
ad indagare il mio futuro incerto
nella tua pura luce che non muta.
Com'è facile errare!
Più non mi preme alcun futuro evento
se qui resti con me, se ancor carezza
la mia trepida mano il fior che sei.
E il presente che scruto,
fissandoti ansioso:
l'uomo che un dì non ero ed oggi sono,
il cuore che non più pulsava ed ora
è ritmo che scandisce
un canto fino a ieri sconosciuto.
Chissà che cosa pensò Adamo un giorno,
fissando Eva negli occhi!
Chissà che cosa, alla fine del mondo,
vedrà l'ultimo amante in uno sguardo!

The Mirror

Like a fragile crystal ball
your face I clasp in my hands, and dream.
Seeing me in rapture gazing
into the green tenderness of your eyes
one might believe me intent
on inquiring about my uncertain future
within your pure immutable light.
How easy it is to err!
No longer future events upon me weigh
if here with me you remain, if my trembling hand
still fondles the flower that you are.
It is the present that I probe,
gazing at you anxiously—
I, the man who once was not, and am today,
the heart that had ceased to be, and now
is rhythm scanning time
into a song until yesterday unknown.
Who knows what Adam thought one day
gazing into Eve's eyes!
Who knows what, at the end of the world,
the last man in love will see in a glance!

La lettera ma 'mpustata

da *Bronx, America*

Gargane mia, te scrive questa lettera
pe' ffàrete capì che, dallu iurne
che sso' partute, me vì sempe 'nzonne
come ve 'nzonne allu zite la zita,
come vè 'nzonne allu figghie la mamma.
Me sònne che mme trove, come pprima,
ammeze la Padula e, sse mme cride,
te diche pure che sente sunà
la campana 'la Cchiesia de Sant'Antóne
e, quanne annòsele dda voce santa,
che pozze fà? tegne nu nùdeche 'ncanna
che ssule chi è emigrante pò capì.
Te scrive sempe, ma tutte li lettere
non te li 'mposte, ché pésene assà,
e llu pustere ce mettesse a rrire
se lli dicesse che vogghie mannà
na lettera lu iurne a nna Muntagna.
L'ha' cumpatì: iè mmerecane nate
e non capisce che ssi' mmegghie tu
de tutte quiddi ch'ànne studijate.
Dunqua, Gargane mie, Gargane belle,
te scrive questa lettera pe' ddicete
che, doppe quarant'anne de 'sta Mereca,
na cosa sola è certa: quasa quasa
me pare che non zo' manche partute
e cche ddu bastemente l'ej sunnate
o viste inte li libbra de lla scola.
Ma po' ce penze e ma'accorge che face
peccate se tte diche na buscìa:
sope ddu bastemente ce so' state,
inte sta terra so pure sbarcate,

The Letter Never Sent

Dear Gargano, I write this letter to you
to make you see that, from the day I left,
you never fail to come into my dreams,
as the beloved comes to a lover's dream,
and as a mother comes to a son's dreams.
I dream I'm there—down in the Marsh again—
as long ago, and if you can believe me,
I'll also tell you that I hear the toll
Of the bell of St. Anthony,
and when I listen to that sacred voice,
what can I do? An emigrant alone
can know the lump that rises in my throat.
I always write letters to you, but then
don't mail them all because they weigh too much,
and the mailman would laugh at me
if I told him I wanted to send
a letter to a Mountain every day.
You have to sympathize: He's an American,
and doesn't understand that you are better
than all the people who went to school.
So, my Gargano, my beautiful Gargano,
I'm writing you this letter so you'll know
that, after forty years of this America,
one thing alone is definite: It seems
almost as if I had never made that trip,
and the ship sailed only in my dreams
or in the books I loved to read in school.
But then I reconsider, and realize
it would be a sin for me to tell you a lie:
Indeed, I did sail once upon that ship,
and I did come ashore upon this land,
and now three quarters of my life are gone.
In every letter that I wrote to you

e tre quarte de vita so ppassate.
In ogni lettera che tt'eje scritte
e ppo' non eje 'mpustate, quanta vote
t'eje ditte 'ncumpedenza come passé
inte sta terra la iurnata mia.
Embè, mo tte lu diche n'ata vota.
Fatije come ttutte quante l'ati,
ma l'ati ce repòsene cuntente;
invece i' me face sti dumanne:
"Pecché so nnate? pecché so partute?
pecché non zo' rrumaste pure i'
sope ddu bbelle Monte risciurute?"
Gargane mia, iàvete che durmì!
Penze a ddi stelle fute fute e bbelle
e tutte quante me pàrene fatte
a fforma de nu bastemente chijne
de povere emigrante come me . . .
Lu vi', lu vi', che mmo me vè lu chiante
comme ddu iurne allu pórte de Nàpele?
E allora è megghie che me ferme qua . . .
Non mi prolunghe . . .'Ntante tu ssalùteme
tutte li strate 'lu paiese mia,
pure l'appartamente ricche e bbelle
che ci hanne frabbecate tutte quante,
e—requijemmaterna—ddi cappelle,
ah, li cappelle de llu Campesante
ddova dda santa de Mamma Lucia
stà sutterrata cu la crona 'mmane . . .
Cara Muntagna mia, sti duje uuasce,

and never mailed, how many times
in confidence I told you how I spend
the hours of my day upon this shore.
Well then, I'll tell you what I said once again.
I go to work like everybody else,
but other people go to sleep content;
instead, I ask myself these selfsame questions:
"Why was I born? Why did I ever leave?
Why didn't I stay behind with all the others
on that beautiful Mountain in full bloom?"
My dear Gargano, there is no sleep for me.
I think about your teeming, glorious stars,
and to my eyes they all appear to be
in the shape of an ocean liner filled
with crowds of poor immigrants like me . . .
You see, you see, now I can feel the tears,
as on the day I stood in Naples's harbor.
It might be better if I stopped right here . . .
I won't go on . . . But you must say hello
to all the streets and alleys of my town,
even the rich and beautiful apartments
that everybody has erected there,
and—*requiem aeternam*—to the chapels too,
ah, the chapels in the cemetery
where my devout Mamma Lucia is buried
with her hands still closed upon the rosary . . .
Of these two kisses, my dear Mountain, one

iune è ppe' gghiessa, l'atu jè ppe' tte.
Cu ttant'affette e amore,
        Tusijane.

La lettera mai imbucata—Gargano mio, ti scrivo questa lettera / per farti comprendere che, dal giorno / in cui son partito, mi vieni sempre in sogno / come viene in sogno al fidanzato la fidanzata, / come viene in sogno al figlio la mamma. / Sogno di trovarmi, come prima, / in mezzo alla "Palude" e, se mi credi, / ti dico pure che sento suonare / la campana della chiesa di Sant'Antonio / e, quando ascolto quella voce santa, / che posso fare! mi viene un groppo alla gola / che solo chi è emigrante può comprendere. / Ti scrivo sempre, ma tutte le lettere / non te le imbuco, ché pesano assai, / e il postino si metterebbe a ridere / se gli dicessi che desidero mandare / una lettera al giorno ad una Montagna. / Lo devi compatire: è americano nato / e non comprende che sei migliore tu / di tutti quelli che hanno studiato. / Dunque, Gargano mio, Gargano bello, / ti scrivo questa lettera per dirti / che, dopo quarant'anni d'America, / una cosa sola è certa: quasi quasi / mi sembra che non sono nemmeno partito / e che quel bastimento l'ho sognato / o visto dentro i libri della scuola. / Ma poi ci penso e mi accorgo che faccio / peccato se ti dico una bugia: / su quel bastimento ci sono stato, / su questa terra sono anche sbarcato, / e tre quarti di vita sono passati. / In ogni lettera che ti ho scritto / e poi non ho imbucato, quante volte / ti ho detto in confidenza come trascorro / in questa terra la giornata mia. / Embé, ora te lo dico un'altra volta. / Lavoro come tutti quanti gli altri, / ma gli altri si riposano contenti; / invece io mi faccio queste domande: / "Perché sono nato? perché sono partito? / perché non sono rimasto anch'io / sopra quel bel Monte rifiorito?" / Gargano mio, altro che dormire! / Penso a quelle stelle folte folte e belle / e tutte quante mi sembrano fatte / a forma di un bastimento pieno / di poveri emigranti come me . . . / Lo vedi, lo vedi, che ora mi viene il pianto / come quel giorno nel porto di Napoli? / E allora è meglio che mi fermi qui . . . / Non mi prolungo. . . . Intanto tu salutami / tutte le strade del paese mio, / anche gli appartamenti ricchi e belli / che si sono costruiti tutti quanti, / e—requiem aeternam—alle cappelle, / ah, alle cappelle del camposanto / dove quella santa di Mamma Lucia / sta sepolta con la corona in mano . . . / Cara Montagna mia, questi due baci, / uno è per lei, l'altro è per te. / Con tanto affetto e amore, Tusiani. (Translated by Tommaso Nardella)

is meant for her, the other one for you.
With all my everlasting love,
        Tusiani.

Ce sta nu cante

Ce stà nu cante che m'unneja 'mpette
come nu mare che ce stennerica
sope na scuma gghianca de merlette
e non fa cchiù penzà a tempesta antica,
e quistu cante iè lu 'ndijalette
de dda Muntagna (Ddì la bbenedica)
che mme dà pace e no mme dà recette,
me dà tremente ma m'è ssempe amica.
Inte 'sta bbella scjema de parole
ce scròzzene fulìmmije frustere,
ce annetta cullu core ogni penzere.
Inte quest'acqua che addora de sole
faciteme annijà, come ce anneja
inte la luce l'ùtema mureja.

C'è un canto—C'è un canto che m'ondeggia nel petto / come un mare che si distende / sopra una schiuma bianca di merletto / e non fa più pensare a tempesta antica, / e questo canto è il dialetto / di quella Montagna (Dio la benedica) / che mi dà pace ma non mi dà requie, / mi dà tormento ma mi è sempre amica. / / In questa piena di parole / si disperdono fuliggini straniere, / si netta col cuore ogni pensiero. / Dentro quest'acqua che odora di sole / fatemi annegare, come annega / dentro la luce l'ultima ombra. (Translated by Tommaso Nardella)

There Is a Song

There is a song that surges deep inside
and it's an ocean heaving to extend
over a spotless lacework of white tide
that brings thoughts of old storms to sudden end.

This song's the dialect spoken on the side
of that blessed Mountain, forever a godsend,
that gives me peace, yet leaves me unsatisfied,
that makes me suffer, but is still a friend.

Swept by this flood of words, no foreign,
no alien shadow ever will endure,
every thought is cleansed, the heart is pure.
Within this water scented by the sun,
let me be drowned, as the last black of night
is drowned within the flooding of first light.

→ Nino Del Duca (b. 1924–2010)

Nino Del Duca was born in 1924 in Naples and has been living in the United States since the 1970s, "his body in America and his heart in Naples." He writes a weekly commentary for and contributes occasional poems to *America OGGI*, the largest Italian-language newspaper in North America. He studied art, popular culture, literature and music, and has held lectures and readings in numerous schools and universities. He has recently published a collection of his dialect poetry, *Io stongo 'e casa 'America.*

Octogenarian Nino del Duca reminds us of the classic immigrant from the time before the majority of the poets presented here took jet planes to cross the Atlantic. Of the working class and without the formal education of the poet-professors, his poetry is clearly close to the people, and living in the United States this means a strata of society most would define as *ethnic* in all permutations of this word-concept. His tradition is that of the *cantastorie*, the storyteller of small towns or crowded Neapolitan neighborhoods, whose analogues in America served the same function of cementing and entertaining the working class in clubs and weekend social gatherings as in the once-thriving but most recently nearly gentrified Little Italies. His poetry displays, in its candid ironies, the wisdom of the ancient proverbs, the wit of the survivor of many wars and travels, the no-nonsense assessment of how people of different social classes are bound to think, and the sardonic realization that there is after all a general way of the world, an overall sense to life—the big picture, in other words. Very little analysis is required for a poem like "The Grandfather," where the referentiality, the descriptors, the storytelling acquire metaphoric and symbolic value precisely because of their directness and stark contrapuntal disposition.

Is there an overall message contained in his populist vernacular song? Yes, the major waves of Italian immigration to the United States are historically over, a social and cultural truism we will see echoed by other poets in this collection, who will ask the reader not to think of Italian writing in the United States as the writing of the "classic" emigrants. These days, Italians come here as tourists, investors, professionals, and they are clearly content with themselves (unlike those of us who arrived many decades ago). Speaking in the register of the *vox populi*, Del Duca seems to be saying that we immigrants have worked and raised ourselves to a previously unknown level of comfort and security, so all should be well. However, the last stanza of "The Grandfather" begins with the adversative conjunction *ma*/but, signaling the entrance of an afterthought, and is almost said sotto voce: maybe an echo of ancient shame? Not necessarily, though what the poet feels must be expressed is a new order of problems, perhaps less dramatic than those of decades ago when families were divided across oceans and states, but no less unsettling: there is now a different break in communication, a new split, as members of the family speak a new, different, language, American that is, thus raising a cultural, and perhaps affective, barrier *within* the same family. There is a split at the beginning, as with all experiences of *having to* leave family and country, and there is now, a generation later, a split at the end, of a different nature, of course, but a separation nonetheless, no longer as traumatic, yet leaving a "bitter taste in his mouth."

Of course Del Duca, in league with the tradition of much dialect poetry in Italy, is capable also of poking fun at an overcommodified, hysterical modern lifestyle, as in the poem "Hypopastemia," with predictable comic conclusions. The creativity of his native dialect emerges full force in "The Peppers," where once again drawing on an everyday repertoire of situations, the poet picks on one element and weaves the entire fable around it, perhaps showing that this "natural" use of dialect—as opposed, say, to that of Rimanelli and Tusiani, which is clearly a "cultured" version—still retains great expressive potential.

This poet is clearly rooted in his very native *langue*/reality and has much to say about the fact that he has lived in two different homes, or countries, the adopted one remaining psychologically external. So we can situate his overall poetic between Apex D: *Langue*/Reality and Apex B: Home/Mortality, where the latter is imbued with the shadows of Apex A: Elsewhere/Immortality, the elsewhere of his new country and life.

[Although the intention was to present living poets of the Italian Diaspora, we deeply regret that during the gestation of the volume Nino Del Duca passed away in 2010.]

'O Nonno

da *Io stongo 'casa 'America*

Mò ca l'Italia è 'na Nazione 'nzista
l'emigrazione è un fatto occasionale.
Chi vene ccà, ce vene cchiù pe' sfizio,
pe' vedè 'o munno, o tanto per cambiare.

Mò gli italiani veneno redenno
con le scarpe di cuoio ben lucidate,
fanno i turisti, lucidi e alliffati
e chi tene intenzione 'e se restà
tiene in tasca l'assegno di papà.

Cert'è ca quanno 'o nonno mio emigraie,
partette cu 'o dolore dinto 'o core
e 'a valigia 'e cartone arrepezzata,
ma cu 'a certezza ca cu 'e braccia forti,
faticanno se fosse fatta strada.

E accussì è stato, e 'o nonno mò se guarda
tutte e nupute suie, già sistimate,
cull'uocchie allere chine 'e cuntentezza.

(ma cu 'a vocca 'nu poco amariggiata,
pecchè so' sangue suio, sangue italiano,
ma parlano sultanto americano . . .)

Il nonno—Or anche l'Italia è una nazione di dritti / l'emigrazione è un fatto occasionale. / Chi viene qui, ci viene più per divertimento, / per vedere il mondo, o tanto per cambiare. / / Adesso gli italiani vengono col sorriso / con le scarpe di cuoio ben lucidate, / fanno i turisti, puliti e alla moda / e chi ha intenzioni di restare / ha in tasca l'assegno di papà. / / Di certo quando mio nonno emigrò, / partì col dolore nel cuore / e la valigia di cartone rattoppata / ma con la certezza che con le braccia forti / lavorando si sarebbe fatta strada. / E così è stato, e il nonno ora si guarda / tutti i suoi nipoti, già sistemati / con occhi allegri pieni di contentezza. / / (Ma con la bocca un poco amara, / perchè sono sangue suo, sangue italiano, / ma parlano soltanto Americano . . .)

The Grandfather

Now that Italy is a modern nation
emigration is only occasional;
those who come here come out of curiosity,
to see the world, or to do something different.

Now Italians come here smiling,
with shining leather shoes;
they act like tourists, well dressed
and he who has intention to stay
has his father's check signed in his pocket.

It is true that when my grandfather emigrated,
he left with a heart full of sorrow
and a patched-up cardboard suitcase,
but he was certain that with his strong arms
and hard work, he could find his way in life.

So it was, and now the grandfather
looks at his grandchildren (already established)
with cheerful eyes, full of happiness.

(But with a bitter taste in his mouth,
because they are his blood, Italian blood,
but they only speak English . . .)

Hypopastemia. Una malattia facile da curare

Nu miedeco, dal quale sono andato
(soffro 'e vicchiaia ...) per un accertamento,
m'ha ditto, ma cu 'a faccia sorridente,
ca è asciuta fore n'ata malatia.
Tiene un nome difficile e un po' strano,
Se chiamma l'Hypopastemia.

Dice che quando il corpo è deprivato
di un elemento basico, essenziale,
ne risente l'umore e la salute.
Chi ne è affetto diventa assai depresso,
se fa nervuso e fa 'na faccia 'e fesso.

Colpisce sopratutto gli italiani
quando (per caso o per necessità)
vanno ad un pranzo, e nel menù previsto
'a pasta non è inclusa int' 'o mangià.

Pare 'na cosa 'e niente, ma i dottori
che hanno scoperto chesta malatia
dichiarano concordi che 'a mancanza
d'a pasta nella dieta giornaliera,
offendendo sia il gusto che i costumi
dell'italica gente, che n'e adusa,
determina n'effetto assai curiuso:
pure si tu te si abbuffata 'a panza
di molte cose, nun te si saziato:
"E cumme fosse che non hai mangiato."

Però sta malatia non è maligna
anzi, volendo dire 'a verità,
quasi quasi m'è pure un po simpatica
pecchè, cu 'a scusa che ne sono affetto,
dico a mia moglie: Cara, sto malato ...

Hypopastemia: A Disease Easy to Treat

I went to see a doctor for a checkup
now that I'm getting old
and he told me with a grin
that there's a new disease going around—
it has an unusual name, hard to pronounce:
it's called hypopastemia.

He said when a basic, essential element
is missing in the body,
it affects your entire health and well-being.
Symptoms of this illness include depression,
bad nerves, and a doltish face.

This disease affects Italians primarily,
when (by chance or fate)
they go to dinner and looking at the menu,
they learn there is no pasta to eat.

It may seem like nothing at first,
but in fact all the doctors
studying this disease agree that
a pasta deficiency in their diet—
such offence to their taste and their tradition—
is intolerable to Italians who are
so used to it and must now deal
with this peculiar trait:
Even if your belly is stuffed with all kinds of food,
you still aren't satisfied—it's as if you didn't eat.

On the other hand, this isn't a bad disease.
To tell the truth, I've gotten to like it.
Sometimes I pretend I'm feeling its symptoms, and
I tell my wife, "Honey, I'm sick!"

tengo n'attacco di Hypopastemia,
famme nu piatto 'e vermicelli a'vongole,
io me mangio . . . e me passa 'a malatia.

(maggio, 1993)

Hypopastemia—Un medico dal quale sono andato / (soffro di vecchiaia . . .) per un accertamento, / mi ha detto, ma con la faccia sorridente, / che c'è una nuova malattia. / Ha un nome difficile e un pò strano, / Si chiama l'hypopastemia. / / Dice che quando il corpo è privato / di un elemento basico, essenziale, / ne risente l'umore e la salute. / Chi ne è affetto diventa molto depresso / s'innervosisce e sembra stupido in faccia. / / Colpisce soprattutto gli italiani / quando (per caso o per necessità) / vanno ad un pranzo, e nel menù previsto / non è inclusa la pasta nel cibo. / Sembra una cosa di niente, ma i dottori / che hanno scoperto questa malattia / sono concordi nel dichiarare che la mancanza / di pasta nella dieta giornaliera, / offendendo sia il gusto che i costumi / dell'italica gente, che ne è abituata, / determina un effetto molto curioso / anche se tu ti sei abbuffata la pancia / di molte cose, non sei sazio, / è come se tu non avessi mangiato." / / Però questa malattia non è maligna, / anzi, volendo dire la verità, / quasi quasi mi è anche un po' simpatica / perchè, con la scusa che ne sono affetto, / dico a mia moglie: Cara, sono malato . . . / ho un attacco di hypopastemia / fammi un piatto di vermicelli alle vongole, / così mangio e mi passa la malattia.

I've got an attack of hypopastemia!
So fix me a dish of vermicelli with clam sauce."
And as I eat, the illness goes away.

(May 1993)

’E puparuole

Ogne matina, quando esco d’ ’a casa,
passo pe’ ’na puteca ’e fruttaiuolo.
Sta all’angolo d’ ’a strada, e tene spase
frutte e verdura in bella mostra, ’a fora.

È ’na festa pe’ ll’uocchie stà puteca,
so’ mille tinte, tutte in armonia,
ma chella ca cchiù attira l’attenzione
è l’esposizione ’e tutte ’e puparuole.

Quanta culure: russe, verde, gialle . . .
Tutte ’nzieme so’ comme ’na pittura,
ogne tinta s’accorda cu chell’ata,
ognuna e ’nu culore differente,
ma stanno bbuono aunite, cumme frate.

E io penzo (e me fa male stù penziero)
pecchè l’Umanità nun è accussì?
Pecchè ce appiccecammo inutilmente?
“Tu si russo! Io sò verde! Chillo è giallo!”
trasfurmanno in tragedia ’e cose ’e niente . . .

Nuje stamme tutte dint’a stessa cesta,
(n’coppa ’a ’sta Terra ca se stà sfascianno
pecchè ’a trattammo troppo malamente)
e invece ’e ce fà bbona cumpagnia
gudennece ’o miraculo d’ ’a vita
ca Dio ce ha data pe’ ce a fa’ campà,
ce guardamme ’e travierzo uno cull’ato
cercanne ’e mezze pe’ ce ’ntussecà.

L’avessema capì ca simme eguale,
farce capace ca ’a semmenta è ’a stessa,
e accussì cumme stanno ’e puparuole
dint’ ’a ’na sporta: una armunia ’e culore,

The Peppers

Every morning, when I leave home
I pass a fruit store.
It is at the corner of the street, and exhibits
all of the vegetables, well presented, outside.

It is a feast for the eyes, this store;
there are thousands of colors, all in harmony,
but what catches the most attention
is the exhibition of all of the peppers.

So many colors: red, green, yellow . . .
All together they are a painting,
each hue is matched with the others,
each one has a different color
but all together they look fine, like brothers.

And I think (I feel sad, thinking so)
why is humanity not like them?
Why do we fight uselessly?
"You are red!—I am green!—He is yellow!"
We transform little matters into tragedy . . .

We are all in the same basket
(on this earth that is collapsing
because we treat it so badly . . .)
and instead of being together in good company
enjoying the miracle of life
that God gave us to live,
we look at one another with suspicion
figuring out more ways to be unhappy!

We should understand that we are equal,
that our seeds are the same,
and just as those peppers stay in the basket
in harmony of color, so

ce avessema scurdè de' pregiudizie
e campà 'nzieme in pace e fratellanza . . .

(e pe' nun fà fernì 'e scassà 'sta cesta,
trattanno 'a Terra cu nu poco 'e crianza!)

(luglio, 1990)

I peperoni—Ogni mattina, quando esco di casa, / passo davanti a un negozio di frutta. / Sta all'angolo della strada, e mostra / frutta e verdure in bell'ordine, fuori. / / È una festa per gli occhi questo negozio, / sono mille colori tutti in armonia, / ma quella che più attira l'attenzione / è l'esposizione di tutti i peperoni. / / Quanti colori: rosso, verde, giallo . . . / Tutti insieme sono come una pittura, / ogni colore si armonizza con l'altro, / ognuno di un colore diverso / ma insieme stanno bene, come fratelli. / / E io penso (e questo pensiero mi fa star male) / perchè l'Umanità non è così? / Perchè litighiamo inutilmente? / "Tu sei rosso! Io sono verde! Quello è giallo!" / trasformando in tragedia una cosa di niente . . . / / Noi stiamo tutti dentro la stessa cesta, / (su questa terra che si sta sfasciando / perchè la trattiamo troppo male) / e invece lei è buona compagnia / godiamoci il miracolo della vita / che Dio ci ha data per farci campare, / ci guardiamo di traverso uno con l'altro / cercando i mezzi per avvelenarci. / / Dovremmo capirlo che siamo uguali, / renderci conto che il seme è lo stesso. / E così come stanno i peperoni / dentro una cesta: un'armonia di colori / ci dovremmo dimenticare dei pregiudizi / e vivere insieme in pace e fratellanza . . . / / (e per non farla finire di sfasciare questa cesta, / trattando la terra con un po' di buone maniere!) /

should we forget all the prejudices
and live together in peace and brotherhood.

(And to avoid a complete collapse of the basket,
begin to treat the earth with some respect!)

(July 1990)

Io

Io, ca so'nato addo nu'muorzo 'e pane
'mpastato 'e sole, te pò fa felice
e campo int' 'a 'na terra ca m'è amica
ma nun è chella ca me fa sunnà.

Io, ca me sento allero si 'a matina
veco 'n'auciello 'ncielo sfrennesià
e nun me 'mporta si cu 'e mmane accise,
aggia tirà 'a carretta pe' campà.

Io, ca penziere brutte nun ne faccio
pecchè ho fiducia nell'umanità,
e penso ca si pure esiste 'o male,
'o bbene, priesto o tarde, triunfarrà.

Io me sento cuntento, so'felice,
m' 'a piglio alleramente, e 'nc'è 'o pecchè:
"Io voglio bbene 'a tutto quanto 'o munno."

(. . . pure si spisso 'o munno, ch'e 'na palla,
avota e gira . . . e me và 'ncapo a me).

Io—Io che sono nato dove un pezzo di pane / impastato con il sole, ti può fare felice / e vivo in una terra che mi è amica / ma non è quella che mi fa sognare. / / Io, che mi sento allegro se la mattina / vedo dalla finestra un uccello sfrecciare in cielo / e non m'importa se con le mani rovinate / devo tirare il carretto per vivere. / / Io, che non faccio brutti pensieri / perchè ho fiducia nell'umanità, / e penso che anche se esiste il male / il bene, prima o dopo, trionferà. / / Io mi sento contento, sono felice / me la prendo con allegria, senza motivo, / "Io voglio bene a tutto il mondo intero." / / (. . . anche se spesso il mondo, ch'è una palla, / gira qua gira là . . . mi casca sulla testa). /

Me

I was born here where a piece of bread
soaked with sunshine can make you happy
and I survive in a land that is friendly
but it's not the one that spurs me to dream.

Here, I feel happy if in the morning
across the sky, I can see a bird that streams
and I don't care if with my hands so ruined
I have to pull a cart to earn a living.

Here I've had no really ugly thoughts
because I've a faith in humanity,
and I think that if there is some evil here
sooner or later, the good will make the scenes.

I feel so content, and I'm happy
I take it lightly, and there's a reason why:
"I love the whole world."

(... Even if the world, which is a ball,
sometimes rebounds and hits me in the eye).

-→ Giose Rimanelli (b. 1925)

Giose Rimanelli was born in Casacalenda, in the Molise region, on November 28, 1925. He attended Catholic school in Apulia, but at age seventeen he found himself involved in the antifascist urban guerrillas that besieged Italy during World War II. He traveled through Europe and in South and North America, and sojourned in Paris. Professor emeritus of the State University of New York at Albany, where he taught Italian for over four decades, he has had a most prolific writing career. Among his novels and travelogues are *Tiro al piccione* (1953, 1991), *Peccato originale* (1954), *Biglietto di terza* (1958, 1999), *Una posizione sociale* (1959, reprinted under the title *La stanza grande*, 1996), *Graffiti* (1997), *Molise Molise* (1979), *Il tempo nascosto tra le righe* (1986), *Detroit Blues* (1996), *Dirige me Domine, Deus meus* (1996). In English he wrote the novels *Benedetta in Guysterland* (1993), which won the American Book Award from the Before Columbus Foundation in 1994, and *Academia* (1997). In more recent years he wrote, in Italian, the intellectual autobiographies *Familia* (2000), *Discorso con l'altro* (2000), and *Il viaggio* (2003). To this activity he added writings in theater, journalism, art criticism, and literary criticism, in both languages. He also composed the comedies *Tè in Casa Picasso* (1961) and *Il corno francese* (1962); the ballet *Lares* (1962); the critical anthology *Modern Canadian Stories* (1966); the essays in *Tragica America* (1968); the scholarly anthology *Italian Literature: Roots and Branches* (1976); and the narrative monograph *Fratianni e la follia* (2004).

In the area of poetry, Rimanelli, a scholar of Provençal and Latin poetry, has cut a unique figure with *Carmina blabla* (1967), *Monaci d'amore medievali* (1967), *Poems Make Pictures Pictures Make Poems* (1971), and *Arcano* (1990). An accomplished musician, he composed a songbook in his native Molisan dialect, *Moliseide* (1990, 1992) and wrote *Alien Cantica* (1995), *I Rascenije* (1996), and *Moliseide and Other Poems* (1998), the last a volume that collects all his published and unpublished poetry in his native dialect. He is the author, moreover, of the suites *Sonetti per Joseph 1994–1995* (1998) and the trilingual *Jazzymood* (1999). He published a collection of translations from the Molisan dialect and Provençal, *Gioco d'amore amore del gioco* (2002), and the more experimental *Versi persi per S* (2004). Together with Luigi Fontanella he wrote the *tenzone Da G. a G.: 101 Son(n)etti* (1996), and with Achille Serrao the sonnets *Viamerica/Gli occhi* (1999).

Rimanelli, who immigrated to the United States in 1960, is perhaps the most complex of all the Italian writers in this anthology. More widely known as a narrator,[24] he had already reached the top of his literary career in Italy in the 1950s with four solid novels. However, the publication of a book of his reviews, *Il mestiere del furbo* (approximately, *The Profession of Con Man*) (1959) in which he dared to expose a host of underhanded power plays, preferential treatments, and other wretched practices of the intelligentsia at the time, resulted in his being ostracized and practically cut off from publishing anything else.[25] Having become persona non grata in Italy, he might actually be the only real exile in this mix, in the sense that he was forced out of Italy on pain of public attacks and shameful retaliations. He thus began a second life and career and, like Tusiani, Ballerini, Carravetta, Carrera, and Condini, embraced the new world and decided to write creatively in English as well. With a solid and varied background, ranging from the classics to medieval studies, music, folklore, and comparative literature, a translator and endless experimenter with all literary forms, Rimanelli also continued to write in his native dialect from the Molise region. And it is in this language to which, like Tusiani, he turns to with greater intensity late in his career, that he constructs *Moliseide*,[26] made up in great part of ballads and songs. Rimanelli exhibits a Joycean penchant for irony and parody and an exuberant creativity as he compels his native vernacular not so much to mimic or evoke original or "authentic" modules and patterns (which would make him sentimentally nostalgic and reminiscent of emigrant writing of earlier decades and/or lesser poets), but to an elevation and metamorphosis through forms, rhymes, and rhetorical devices that come mostly from other traditions, primarily the medieval and early humanist jongleurs, the Provençal poets, and itinerant monks, as well as from the rhythms of jazz and the blues.

This cultural production presents formidable problems of interpretation. For if it can be argued that the "return" to the "real" mother tongue—the great majority, perhaps all, of these Italian poets spoke a dialect before they learned standard and then literary Italian—may acquire the sense of an ideological rebuff to the homogenizing, monotonous, and alienating speech of television and urbanized propriety, then one can claim, as many critics have said of Rimanelli as well as of other Italian vernacular poets, that they thus regain a directness, an expressiveness, and the chance of reviving buried treasures. But it can also be said that poets typically shape and polish their vernacular with the armamentarium of consummate artists, in a sense reenacting the Dantean creation of a *vulgari eloquentia*. In brief, Rimanelli does not go "down" to a supposedly "natural" Molisan, or use dialect like Provenzano and De Luca, rather, he raises "up" from the trenches of his personal memory a local variation of Italian and proceeds to mold it, like a sculptor, to suit his cosmopolitan and translinguistic consciousness. How else to explain Molisan, in which one finds words from several different languages and patterns from altogether different traditions? We should rather consider whether and how the poet *uses* this medium because he is essentially in love with words, music, and play.[27]

This brief sketch points to the problem of figuring out exactly what is the poet's relationship to his native land, and to the great themes we have been using as our guidelines, given that the dominant influence of the troubadours places the onus on, if I may be allowed, form above content, on the signifier rather than the signified, let alone the referent. In fact, in *Moliseide* wordplay carries the day, making it maddening to attempt even a fair rendition in English, since the text is overladen with "paronomasia, anaphora, assonance, consonance, internal rhyme, alliteration, chiasmus, homeoteleuton, couplets (coblas capfinidas), tercets, refrains"[28] and the dominant trope of repetition, from the phonetic to the structural. The potential "message"? That perhaps despite his recurring references to themes such as love and distance, memory and death, the poetic persona is ever just a step away from skipping on to the next surface, or sound, or gesture, perhaps manifesting his deeply felt existential split and unmoored *Lebenswelt* by simply playing around with it or, again, perhaps, by being superficial in some as yet unexplored Nietzschean mode? A deep-seated sensibility to change, to shifting frames, to seek ever new surroundings, pervades his work in general. There is no stability either in life or in art, but rather than dwelling in the throes of nostalgia or gloomily wade in the anxiety of the uprooted, to which he is extremely sensitive nevertheless, Rimanelli anchors his poetics in the writing experience itself. In an intellectual autobiography, *Familia*, he comes to terms with his condition: "And today there is no road of return / for this man, except with his / writings. The words expatriate or / expelled or exile or emigrant don't / make sense anymore for the writer: / they have become metaphor, in / so far as for him—as Adorno early on / understood—his home is in the end only / and uniquely writing."[29] The poet is then clearly aware of a double exile, first from his land of origin, and then from any one language he chooses to inhabit, as that home he found in the *writing* of poetry can be embodied in several different idioms.

One might thus conclude that, for Rimanelli, lucky is the man who has special, memorable, encounters *strada facendo*, especially if they are light-hearted: "Ignis! / *Dum vinum potamus, te Deum laudamus.* / Ignis! *Saxon genitive.* / Pardon, genital. Which is to say: *In Hoc Signo* / IGNIS! / / Fill this: / the glass!" (215). He is clearly of *this* world, buckling established mythologemes, and covering humors from melancholy jazz to word games. We might situate his poetics in the neighborhood of Apex D: *Langue*/Reality, in the sense that he adapts to and interfaces with the great variety of idioms and genres encountered along the way, but clearly he is keenly aware of the beckoning of Apex B: Home/Mortality, and its ironic relation to Apex C: *Langage*/Poetry.

L'Italia è una terra lunga

da *Carmina blabla*

L'Italia è una terra lunga
una terra luuuuuunga
da camminare

Mio padre tornava da fuori
noi ragazzi non sapevamo da dove
si toglieva la giacca e le scarpe
si metteva col dito a girare
un globo di terra e di mare
che lui chiamava   il MONDO

L'Italia è una terra lunga
una terra luuuuuunga
da odiare

Mio padre   "Portami da bere, O,
che ho sete arretrata!"   diceva
studiandosi inquieto sudato
quel Globo di terra e di mare
L' acquae   è nel buco del muro
nell'anfora afosa   di rame
Mia madre la prende   riprende
col vento la nebbia la pioggia
paziente   modesta   un po' strana
al pozzo artesiano
      Non basta maialla sete

L'Italia è una terra lunga
una terra lunnnnnga
da vedere

Adesso che tutti sappiamo
soltanto girare la sfera
a lui viene sete o terrore

Italy Is a Long Country

from *Carmina Blabla*

Italy is a long country
A very very long country
To cover on foot

My father   was coming home
we were boys and knew not from where
he'd take his jacket and shoes off
he'd use his finger to start roaming
over a globe of lands and seas
that he'd call   the WORLD

Italy is a long country
a very very long stretch of land
to want to hate

My father   "Hey, bring me something to drink,
for I am parched!"   he used to say
while uneasy and sweating he'd
study that GLOBE of lands and seas
The water   is by the hole in the wall
in the sweltering copperamphora
My mother takes it   again and again
whether in the wind the fog the rain
patiently   modestly   a bit weirdly
to the Artesian well
        It is never enough   for the thirst

Italy is a long country
a very very long country
to get to see

Now that we all know
only how to spin the globe
he feels thirst or terror

sempre in avanzo   sui ritorni
prepariamo la brocca più alta
che finisce col prenderefiori
        Non mancano mai   al balcone

L'Italia è una terra lunga
una terra lunnnnnga
da possedere

"Non c'è acqua nemmeno"   diceva
"se la conosco Oh se la conosco!
Ma cammina   cammina   E cammina
ti trovi sempre di fronte alla sete
fin che uno si accorge   il DESERTO
non ha fine o principio
        se ci preme sul petto"

L' Italia è una terra lunga
una terra lunnnnnga
come il rancore

Prendeva il treno o il cavallo
anche il camion quando passava
dicendo"Oggi arrivo fino al mare"
Stava fuori tre giorni
anche un mese
e quando tornava   sempre stanco
abbruttito   le sue tasche sapevano
di sabbia e acqua di mare

Siamo saliti sulla collina più alta
        una domenica mattina
        per vedere dov'era arrivato   mio padre
        Il mare non era là dietro
        e un pastore ci disse   indietro
        salire sull'altra collina

L'Italia è una terra lunga
una terra lunnnnnga
come il mal di cuore

in abundance   going back
we ready the tallest pitcher
but it ends up being filled   with flowers
         There's always flowers   on the balcony

Italy is a long country
a very very long country
to want to own

"There is not even water"   he used to say
"if I know it, oh yes, I know it!
And so walk and walk   And walk
and you are always facing the thirst
until you realize that   the DESERT
has no end and no beginning
       if it presses upon your bosom"

Italy is a long country
a very very long country
like an ill-feeling

He used to take the train or the horse
often the truck when he passed by
saying"Today I'll go as far as the sea"
He would stay out three days
even a month
and when he'd come back   always tired
soiled   his pockets had the taste
of sand and seawater

       One Sunday morning we climbed
       the tallest hill
       to see how far my fatherhad traveled
       But there was no sea to be seen
       and a shepherd told us   go back
       climb up the next hill

Italy is a long country
a very very long stretch of land
like a heartsickness

"L'Africa o l'America
ecco cosa ci vuole"
e sempre col dito girava
quel globo di terra e di mare
per trovare la terra   che ci voleva
Siamo cresciuti nel buio
di un soldo di terra   che non basta
alla sete   l'Italia è una terra lunga
una terra luuuuuunnnnnnga
da dimenticare
Ora è venuto in America
mette i bulloni alle macchine
Ha un giardino un garage le piante
tutta l'acqua che vuole negli idranti
È diventato più giovane ed esperto
più quieto più tondo un po' bolso
          "L'America   è fatta di acqua"
          dice appena ridendo   ai nuovi che vengono
          ma pensa a quella che manca al paese
          (*o l'hanno poi messa al paese?*)

e alle donne scomparse che un tempo
pazientimodeste   un pò strane
prendevano l'acqua coi secchi
al pozzo artesiano.

L'Italia è una terra lunga
una terra lunga
da ricordare

(Detroit, 1959)

"Africa or America
that's what we need"
and always with his finger he'd spin
that globe of lands and seas
to find the landthat was needed
We grew up in the darkness
of a patch of land   which is hardly enough
for the thirst   and Italy is a long country
a very very very long stretch of land
to have to forget

Now he came to America
he screws bolts onto cars
He owns a garden a garage some plants
all the water he needs in the hydrants
He became younger and smarter
more quiet more pudgy slightly feeble

>"America   is made up of water"
>he says faintly smiling   to those just arriving
>but he is thinking of its lack in the town
>(*did they ever bring water to the town?*)

and to the bygone women who once
patiently   modestly   uncannily
would draw the water with their pails
from the artesian well

Italy is a long country
a very long country
to have to remember

Dóce è a vóce sìje

da *Moliseide*

Dóce è a vóce sìje cuànne me pàrle
da chiàte d'àccue dóv'ìje me spècchie.

Dóce è a vóce sìje cuànne me coglie
u tiémbe ch'aje misse pe' rèccòglie.

Dóce è a vóce sìje cuànne me svèscte
a sére che m'èddòrme pa' fètìje.

Dóce è a vóce sìje cuànne me suónne
ch'è fènùt' ù mùnne, ce sém'èmbìse.

Dóce è a vóce sìje cuànne me dice
Ch'amóre è sule cuille che ce rèscte.

(Albany, 1983)

Dolce è la voce sua—Dolce è la voce sua quando mi parla / dallo specchio d'acqua dov'io mi specchio. / Dolce è la voce sua quando m'accorgo / del tempo che ho impiegato per raccogliere. / Dolce è la voce sua quando mi svesto / la sera che m'addormento per la fatica. / Dolce è la voce sua quando sogno / ch'è finito il mondo, che siamo sospesi. / Dolce è la voce sua quando mi dice / che l'amore è solo quello che ci resta.

Soft Is Her Voice

from *Moliseide*

Soft is her voice when she speaks
From the water pond I see myself in

Soft is her voice when I realize
How long it took to get back home

Soft is her voice when I undress
At night dead tired from work

Soft is her voice when I dream the world
Has ended, and we're hanging from a string

Soft is her voice when she tells me
That love is only what remains

(Albany, 1983)

A vije du Molise

Quanne t'èzzìcche a i vrìte du penziere
e fóre chiagne 'u sole, ze fa notte,
'u sanghe te ze chiàtre, sié sctrèniére:
a vie da terre tije dónde sctà?

Chiàne te fié li cunte: dunduléje
'u tiémbe ch'è pèssàte 'nnanz' è ll'uócchie;
'ngànne te zómb' 'u córe: nazzèchéje
'a ddóre du Molise, che vuó fà?

A vije du Molise è dóce dóce,
z'èllònghe pe' li munti e 'ngòpp'ì hiùme;
ze védene i pèische fatt'è cróce
e u córe z'èddecréje, vò chèndà.

Siénde 'nè vècchie vóce che te chiàme
d'ù scurdèle da fónde, da li frùnne;
ù suónne è sctàte luónghe, 'nu sctréfùnne.
mè mó sié rèmenùte pe' rèstà?

Molise, Molise: sié càrde e surrise;
me sò 'mbambèlìte de càlle, de frìdde;
Molise, Molise: sié hiùre e serrìse,
'sctu córe me vàtte, te viéngh' è vèscià.

(Termoli, 1983)

La via del Molise—Quando ti accosti ai vetri del pensiero / e fuori piange il sole, si fa notte, / il sangue ti si ghiaccia, sei straniero: / la via della terra tua dove stà? / Piano ti fai i conti: dondola / il tempo ch'è passato innanzi agli occhi. / In gola ti salta il cuore: ondeggia / l'odore del Molise, che ci puoi fare? / La via del Molise è dolce dolce, / s'allunga per i monti e sopra i fiumi. / Si vedono i paesi fatti a croce / e il cuore ti s'inebria, vuol cantare. / Senti una vecchia voce che ti chiama / dal buio della fonte, dalle fronde. / Il sonno è stato lungo, come sprofondare, / ma adesso sei tornato per restare? / Molise, Molise: sei cardo e sorriso; / mi sono stordito di caldo, di freddo. / Molise, Molise: sei fiore e sorriso. / Il cuore mi batte, vengo a baciarti.

The Road to Molise

When you draw near the window of your thoughts
and outside the sun weeps, and darkness falls,
your blood turns into ice, you are a stranger:
the road back to your land, where can it be?

Slowly you start to count: The time gone by
before your eyes begins to waver.
Your heart a lump in your throat: Molise's
scent sways gently along, what can you do?

The road to Molise is sweet as honey;
it stretches across mountains, over rivers.
You can see the towns in the shape of crosses
and the heart rejoices, wants to sing.

And you hear an ancient voice that calls you
from the dark of the fountain, from the branches.
The sleep has been too long, the deepest sinking,
but now that you've come back, will you remain?

Molise, Molise: you're thistle and smile;
I've become dazed with heat and with cold.
Molise, Molise: You're flower and smile,
my heart runs wild, I'm coming to kiss you.

Ballata di Joe Selimo

sanità
santità
pane poco
e libertà

Sono nato in una stanza
piccolina come il mondo.
Ho girato e rigirato
per trovare un altro mondo.
Alla fine, rassegnato,
ho sposato l'emozione.

Sono stato lungo tempo
come appeso a un lampione.
Sono andato lungo il mare
osservando i miei stivali.
Alla fine, rassegnato,
ho sposato l'emozione.

Sono stato con l'amore
ricercando il solo amore.
Il dolore del dolore
è cercare il vero amore.
Alla fine, rassegnato,
ho sposato l'emozione.

Ho volato sopra i monti,
ho nuotato sotto i mari.
Ho mangiato pietre e sale,
ho scavato nel mio cuore.
Alla fine, rassegnato,
ho sposato l'emozione.

Ho goduto, ho ricordato
le stranezze, le emozioni:
punti d'oro, grumi vivi
sia l'amore che il dolore.

Ballad of Joe Selimo

sanity
sanctity
a bit of bread
and liberty

I was born inside a room
that is small as the world.
I went far and I went wide
to find myself another world.
In the end I gave up
and got married to emotion.

Now for ages I have been
as if hanging from a streetlamp.
I went out along the sea
looking closely at my boots.
In the end I gave up
and got married to emotion.

I have been alone with love
looking for the only love.
The real sorrow of the sorrow
is the search for the true love.
In the end I gave up
and got married to emotion.

I have flown over the mountains,
I have swum under the seas.
I have eaten stones and salt,
I have dug deep in my heart.
In the end I gave up
and got married to emotion.

I've enjoyed, I've remembered
both the vagaries and the passions.
Points of gold, living lumps,
There was love there was sorrow.

Alla fine, rassegnato,
ho sposato l' emozione.

La mia vita è in nessun luogo:
sono un alito nel mondo.
La passione mi travolge,
mi rigenera di fuoco.
Alla fine, rasssegnato,
ho sposato l'emozione.

Ho deposto il mio cappello
ad un chiodo del balcone.
Vedo il cielo, il mare, i monti:
spesso sogno l'altro mondo.
Alla fine, rassegnato,
ho sposato l'emozione.

Sono chiuso in una stanza
piccolina come il mondo.
Rido e danzo, a volte piango,
sono intenso come il mondo.
Alla fine, rassegnato,
ho sposato l'emozione

> sanità
> santità
> pane poco
> e libertà

(Pompano Beach, 1984)

In the end I gave up
and got married to emotion.

Now my life is in no place:
I'm a breath across the world.
And as my passion bowls me over,
it renews me with its fire.
In the end I gave up
and got married to emotion.

I went out to hang my hat
on a nail out on the balcony.
I see mountains, sea and sky,
I often dream the nether world.
In the end I gave up
and got married to emotion.

I am shut inside a room
that is small as the world.
I laugh and dance, at times cry,
I'm intense as the world.
In the end I gave up
and got married to emotion.

> *sanity*
> *sanctity*
> *a bit of bread*
> *and liberty.*

Gli occhi

da *Viamerica*

Occhi radiosi della tua natura
Su cui passate sono le visioni
Della tediosa insonnia e la calura
Bigia e il represso strido d'orazioni,

L'alito in albis verso l'agra altura
Glaucoma / Elicona d'ossessioni
Repressioni in cordate d'insicura
Ascesa, quasi un pianto d'oblazioni,

Mio Signore, tra ferita e sutura
E il ragionare nella bocca riarsa
Del toscano Milton e il cieco Oméro.

Occhi radiosi, canto, mia fattura
Nel tempo aggiudicato. Se pur scarsa,
Santa è la tua luce in spero non spero.

(Pompano Beach, 1996)

The Eyes

from *Viamerica*

Resplendent eyes of your own true nature
Across which have transmigrated visions
Of tedious sleeplessness and gray temperature
And the repressed shriek of supplications

The breath in albis up the dour high pasture
Glaucoma / Helicon of obsessions
Repressions in long rope climbs of unsure
Ascent, almost a weeping of obligations,

My Lord, between the wound and suture
And the reasoning in the parched throat
Of sightless Homer and of Tuscan Milton.

Resplendent eyes, song I did nurture
In the allotted time. And though remote,
Holy is your light whether in hope or ruin.

Sonetto

Abbiamo fame di cose essenziali,
Chiaro invoca l'ottimo Loi; e tu il fiato
Hai reso parola, riti nuziali,
Isola e mito poeta rinato!

L'alito antico di voglie natali,
Lacerti epifanici e ansia, di passato
Evocato sudore, fatica, ali
Calve di tempo . . . Ogni intacca hai contato.

Aria di casa senz'altra mal'aria
Int'a nu juorno e sole, com'io credo,
Viamerica, Achì, a new sound, koiné.

Amara comm'ô ffele a vita, e varia
Nova però, se credi com'io vedo.
O calascione sona ? Mena me' . . .

(Pompano Beach, 1996)

Sonnet

A hunger after all that is essential
Cries out praiseworthy Loi: and you have breath
Honed into word, into connubial
Invocations poet reborn! island and myth.

Lost ancient sigh of our natal
Longings, anxiety, epiphanic
Ends, past evoked—time-shorn wings, sweat and toil . . .
Counting as you did each notch and nick.

A homey air without more evil air
Inside a sunny day, as I believe,
Viamerica, Achille, new sound, koiné.

A life bitter as gall, yet strange and rare,
New, if you've come to believe what I perceive.
The calascione's playing? Well, what do you say . . .

→ Alfredo De Palchi (b. 1926)

Alfredo De Palchi, from Verona, Italy, lives in New York City. He was associate editor and then editor of the literary magazine *Chelsea* from 1960 until it ceased publication in December 2007. His work is collected in the following books, some in Italian, some in bilingual Italian/English editions, and some with translations into English and/or Veronese dialect: *Sessions with My Analyst/Sessioni con l'analista* (1970); *Gentile animale braccato* (1983); *Mutazioni* (1988); *The Scorpion's Dark Dance/La buia danza di scorpione* (1993); *Anonymous Constellation/Costellazione anonima* (1997); *Addictive Aversions/Le viziose avversioni* (1999); *In cao del me paese* (2001); *Paradigma* (2001); *Paradigma—tutte le poesie: 1947–2005* (2006); *Dates and Fevers of Anguish* (chapbook, 2006); *Contro la mia morte* (chapbook, 2007).

Born in Legnago, Verona, Alfredo De Palchi came to the United States in 1956, arriving on Columbus Day, at the age of thirty, after having endured a harsh adolescence and, in the wake of the postwar chaos, a trumped-up accusation that translated into five years of imprisonment. Released in 1951, he lived mostly in Paris before making New York his adopted permanent home. De Palchi's poetry is antiestablishment, anti-militaristic, vitriolic and sarcastic at times, marked by an ironclad will to remain free from and untrammeled by the hypocrisies and panaceas with which the dispensers of unrealistic justice and virtues continue to plague the world. In a way, De Palchi does not see a great chasm between living in Italy or in the United States insofar as that "vile merry-go-round of the world" is, mutatis mutandis, everywhere playing the same schizoid and inhumane tune. Yet there are differences between the reality he knew in his youth, gathered in a book published nearly forty years after most of it was written, *La buia danza di scorpione* (1993), and that of his other books, especially *Sessioni con l'analista* (1967), *Anonymous Constellation/Costellazione anonima* (1997), and *Addictive Aversions/Le viziose avversioni*

(1999). In the collection, which (re)enacts his years of anger and bile at the prospect of being, in the flower of youth, condemned to a dank cube deprived of all human dignity, De Palchi develops a biting, uneven, unadorned style in which he symptomatically distorts habitual semantic associations, giving his verses a "singular deforming sprezzatura."[30]

The probing of the human condition continues in *Sessione con l'analista*, with a lean, stark, ever piercing language sketching the ills of society and the unexemplarity of our cultural venues. Texts dedicated to his leaving Italy lack all "the anguish and trepidation of departure, to which much migration literature had accustomed us," as we find in De Palchi a "mixture of feelings of escape, freedom, evasion, infused with an apathetic detachment, as a sort of foretold splenetic distrust toward what the new world might/will offer him."[31] And, in fact, when we turn to the section titled "Reportage," his description of New York is violent and devastating, paralleling the poetical critique of American culture by some of the Beat poets. In New York, rather than a dream, he experiences a nightmare of human wrecks, a catalogue of the sick, the torpid, and the rotten, a procession of the intoxicated, freakish, infested bodies and embodiments of a society that is not really an ideal and bears no promise for anyone. So the poet absorbs and rejects, accepts and denies, revealing a mechanism that Luigi Fontanella, himself caught between two worlds, considers a "typical psychic procedure" of "uprooted" poets whose words are at once a "refuge" and an "abandonment."[32] In this sense, De Palchi's poetic experience would exemplify a "double exile," which we saw emerge also from time to time in Rimanelli and Tusiani, and which will reappear in different form in other poets further down.

It should not surprise then that in *Anonymous Constellation* De Palchi exhibits a wry, skeptical, disenchanted sensibility and continues to make use of a "terse, unadorned language . . . which proceed[s] by what seem inconsequential analogies, yet are linked by a firm coherence of ideas and concepts."[33] And these ideas reveal that humankind is "scum on two legs," a debased cosmic creature who is better understood as unnamed, indeed anonymous, as there appears to be no hope, for in the end "the most cunning / decides" (63). It is hard to ignore an intertextual reference to Odysseus's "Nobody, that's my name" (9:410), and who will survive precisely through cunning. And like Odysseus, the poetic persona's only respite, perhaps a necessary counter pulsion, comes from a barely restrained lustful thirst for life. Present already in *Sessione*, this vector finds its most elaborate concretion in the erotic poems of *Addictive Aver-*

sions, and which, as always in love poetry, betray a profound awareness of its canonical obverse, namely death. Eros seems to be the only way to annihilate both time and thought and ward off the shadows mean. And it is through love as eros that De Palchi recognizes the "only secure subject" of his "existential turmoil." And it is in this context that "the reader may perceive," in this poet still writing only in Italian after half a century in the United States, "his erotic poetry [as] an attempt to do away with displacement and difference."[34]

Referring back to our initial critical model, De Palchi's poetry is certainly not seeking immortality either theological or cultural, and the *elsewhere* could be anywhere once alienation and noncommunication have flayed any trust in the human condition. We could say that his work oscillates between C: Poetry/*Langage,* and D: *Langue*/Reality, with a very lucid sense of the *how* the poetic persona perceives and reads the world. This bilateral relation finds its precarious fulcrum in B: Home/Mortality. But "home" is reduced to the poet's own carnal existence and mortality experienced metaphorically as at once meaningless, because of human stupidity, and meaningful, because of erotic possibilities. Most of the poems do not bear titles.

Al calpestio di crocifissi e crocifissi
sputo secoli di vecchie pietre
strade canicolari
il pungente sterco di cavalli immusoniti
in siepi di siccità

  (al gomito dell'Adige allora crescevo
  di indovinazioni rumori d'altre città)

e sputo sui compagni che mi tradirono
e in me chi forse mi ricorda

[1947–51]

from *The Scorpion's Dark Dance*

At the trampling of crosses upon crosses
I spit out centuries of ancient stones
dogday roads
and the piquant dung of horses sulking
in the hedges of drought

> (at the elbow of the Adige I grew up
> on guesses, rumors of other cities)

and I spit on the buddies who betrayed me and
inside me on those who may remember

Le sacre du printemps

da *Sessione con l'analista*

(Il diamante raschia il solco
iniziale—nebule / gas
liquido fuoco / magma / condensamento

la genesi—materia
rivolgimenti indurimenti centrifughi di polvere
gas / fuoco liquefa glaciali rocce
e ancora rassodamenti / vapori
una goccia / la genesi lunga—nella goccia
una spora si crea / un commentario della genesi /
gocce si addensano in mari—spore / microbi

altro esce dall'acqua
evoluzione:
alghe pesci millepiedi ali
le forme grottesche

imperfezione
genesi senza punto evoluzione senza punto
solo materia—la nemesi

[1950]

The Rite of Spring

from *Sessions with My Analyst*

(The diamond needle scratches the initial
groove)—nebulae / gas
liquid fire / magma / condensation

genesis—matter
centrifugal dust upheavals hardenings
gas / fire melting glacial rocks
hardening once more / vapors
a drop / genesis enduring—in the drop
a spore creates itself / a commentary on genesis /
drops become seas—spores / microbes

something else comes out of the water
evolution
algae fish millipedes wings
grotesque forms

imperfection

pointless genesis pointless evolution
only matter—the nemesis

Il vento sibila tra lo steccato e sbatte
il bucato appeso sul cortile, i vetri sporchi.
Non so cosa fare: chiudo gli occhi e fumo;
Vorrei telefonare alla ragazza; voglio
mettere il capo dentro il vaso di terracotta e urlare
il fallimento della mia divisione di uomo o denudarmi
sulla scala del fuoco e lasciare che il vento
a bocca di lupo geli
questo corpo martirizzato—
ogni oggetto animato o inanimato è donna,
la fogna luminosa dove sta in agguato il mio sesso
di topo ossessionato.

[1960]

from *Addictive Aversions*

The wind swishes through the fence and whips
the laundry on the clothesline, and the dirty windows.
I'm out of sorts; I shut my eyes and smoke;
I'd like to phone my girl; I want to put my head
inside the terracotta jar and scream
my failure at my divided self
or undress on the fire escape and let
the wind with its wolf's mouth freeze
my martyred body—
each animate or inanimate object is a woman,
a luminous sewer where my sex lurks,
a rat obsessed.

Nota—la mente stermina
nell'atmosfera desertica dell'asfalto
con il vapore, il bollore in sospensione
all'altezza della fronte; vedi—l'acqua persevera
e penetra da uno strato
all'altro nel penetrale del sottosuolo
così compatto e così capace di purificarla goccia
per goccia lentissima a salire alla fonte
di pietra; dovrei riflettere sul perché.

     Come definirti ora
che defluisci con le onde della sera innestata
ancora alla vampa del sole che adagio
si abbassa sulle piante stese tra case
e rocce,
        come esclamare aspramente la vergogna
intanata come l'embrione del male
perenne nelle corsie del sangue;

ti hanno declamata "dolce"
io ti chiamo "sublime," il chiasso della terra
il mostro del vivere in mezzo
al verde brutale, acido

il silenzio nel silenzio del silenzio.

                              (1997)

from *Paradigm*

Look—the mind is immense
in the desert atmosphere of asphalt
with steam, the boiling suspension at the level
of the forehead; see—water perseveres—
and penetrates from one layer
to the other in the penetralia of subsoil
so compact and so capable of purifying it drop
by drop and rising slowly to the source
of stone; I must reflect on the cause.

      How to define you now
that you flow down with the evening waves still
connected to the blaze of the sun, which slowly
darkens itself on the plants extending among house
and rocks,
      how to exclaim the shame bitterly
lodged like the embryo of evil
perennial in passages of blood;

they've proclaimed you "sweet"
I call you "sublime," the noise of earth
the living monster among
the brutal green, acid

the silence of silence in silence.

da *Costellazione anonima*

Sono
      —questo il punto / idea connettivo—
l'unto dell'acqua l'insettivoro petrolio
sigillato da eruzioni
pozzi sotto il fondale, l'oceano grasso
di corpuscoli, plancton che funziona
con premura per i crostacei
per il pesce cui serve ad altro pesce
e avanti secondo l'inevitabile alimento
e grossezza—coriaceo predatore, secco
rogo di pinne dorsali e pettorali
su peduncoli o trampoli
da suggerire trace di membra
e la spina un tubo
di cartilagine: il coelacanth
non estinto

                              [1970]

from *Anonymous Constellation*

I am
        —here's the point / connecting idea—
watery grease insectivorous oil
sealed by eruptions
wells under the bottom, the ocean fat
with corpuscles, plankton
functioning with zeal for crustaceans
for fish serving other fish and so on
and so on according to size and the inexorable
food chain—tough predator, dry
fire of dorsal and pectoral fins
erect on pedicles or stilts
implying traces of limbs and the spine
a gristly tube: the coelacanth
not yet extinct.

La storia nei libri innocua nulla
insegna e nulla imparo dalle esterne vicende
rifacimenti d'interiori
conseguenze
       l'oggi imita l'ieri
e limita il domani—che importa
vi è sempre scempio
o altra pulizia altra sicurezza
altro esempio

l'acqua riflette su ogni evento anche
il meno plausibile
e il più lurido fiume stagno
superficie scivolosa di schiuma verse
in sé concentra la nettezza
concentrica
del passero zampe aggrappate al filtro
del buco—ad ali stese pare spicchi
il volo ma staccarlo
è un peso annegato di sete.

Innocuous history teaches nothing
in books and I learn nothing from external events
reenactments of interior
issues
        today mimics yesterday
and limits tomorrow—what does it matter
there's always carnage
or another cleanup, some other assurance
a different example

water reflects on every event, even
the least plausible
and the dirtiest river the shallow
pool, slithering surface of green scum
sucks into itself the sparrow's
concentric
terseness his claws hooked to the drainhole
—with stretched wings as if for
flight but the takeoff
is weight drowning of thirst.

Vergogna, io? Di questa tridimensionale
vita che mi mena di ruota
in sedia e viceversa,
che compie scempiaggini giorno
dopo giorno sempre più breve
bestemmiato dal mio disdegno e che si oscura
in un lavoro di demolizione—oltre questo
non uno spiraglio di luce ma una corsia
ininterrotta di uomini che si aggirano:
la fortuna è di resistere questi volti
imprecisi

non vi è esito, sono
una catena di subdole origini
ordigni ordini fantasie
che posseggono già l'estinzione
una poltiglia di fango, un fastidioso silenzio
sulla brace di chi ancora vive—
io / che assisto al crescendo d'ogni alba
alla sera non sono che il semplice
shock dei due estremi.

Who me, ashamed? Of this three-dimensional
life that shuttles me from chair to
wheels and vice versa
completing its absurdities day
after day ever shorter
cursed by my disdain and darkening
in the work of demolition—beyond all this
there's no shaft of light but an unbroken
passage of wandering men:
it's my luck to resist these vague
faces

there's no way out,
I'm a chain of insidious origins
orders mechanisms fantasies
already charged with extinction
gruel mud, tedious hush
laid on the coals of the still living—
I / witness of each morning's crescendo
at night I am no more than the simple
shock between two extremes

→ Orazio Tanelli (b. 1936)

Like Rimanelli, Orazio Tanelli is from the Molise region. He arrived in the United States in 1961, at age twenty-five. After his college degree, he taught foreign languages in high school. He is the author of five books of poetry, one of which is also in dialect. Tanelli has worked in that penumbra between the academics and the working class, a situation that has allowed him to reach a broader Italian American audience, especially as editor of *La Follia di New York* and *Il Ponte Italo-Americano*. His poetry is deeply rooted in the tradition to the point that, more than emulate, he seems to imitate some of the canonical writers, and when some of them are named Giosuè Carducci, Giovanni Pascoli, or, most explicitly, Gabriele D'Annunzio, there are huge risks to the enterprise. Perhaps Tanelli can best be compared to the first or earlier generations of immigrant poets who, confident of their *liceo classico* education, could muster a decent line and deploy iconic lexemes to raise the text to what certain dominant sectors of society qualified as "poetic." In this sense, if we could momentarily ignore their respective politics, in terms of style, Tanelli's poetry can be read next to that of Arturo Giovannitti, Rosario Ingargiola, or Umberto Liberatore, whose best work dates to the 1920s and 1930s. Tanelli's entreaties and invectives recast what political activists may have actually uttered, yielding the unsettling feeling that the rhetoric of left and right of the 1930s can easily be updated to appear in the poetry of some Italian-American poets of the 1970s and 1980s, when it was acceptable to scream in favor of one's ethnic identity, visibility, and empowerment. Still, in decrying injustice against one's kin, there is a logic to falling back on one's original or reclaimed identity. Consider the poem "To the Italian Emigrants," where we read: "Be proud / of your name! / Don't hide / your identity! / Be not ashamed of your origin! / . . . / / Our brothers / have died / on the electric chair . . ." and some had been lynched, and so on. The populist streak, perhaps more easily detectable in the English version, sets the stage for exhortations to readers to continue in the footsteps of their forefathers—with locutions such as *"genio italico,"* which no one would use after the 1970s or the 1980s—that is, fight with pride in order to avoid the bitter fate of those Italians who were hanged or discriminated against or who "drown[ed] in the Mississippi."

Reading through his omnibus collection *Canti d'oltre oceano* (*Songs from Beyond the Ocean*) (1994), one notices that it is replete with well-meaning sentiments, nostalgia for his hometown like no one else in this gathering, personal regrets of things "not done," and a nearly contemptuous view of America, unless it is to extol some of its more universal symbols. In his texts emerges a critic of any and all social upheavals of the twentieth century, and a lament for a tidy, long-bygone pastoral world that most likely never existed. Or he may be retroprojecting in the mode of what Sartre would have called "bad faith." Part of this may be due to the fact that Tanelli looks at the society about him through a personally fashioned, timeless, moralizing eyepiece, so ultimately no real-world distinction between left or right is possible. In Tanelli's texts ideals are brought to rarefied, often intolerable abstraction, while the diction ignores the multifarious ways in which Italian, and the language of Italian poetry in particular, have developed in the past half a century.

Tanelli is thus the most traditional, nostalgic, personally and socially bitter poet in this collection. This poetic is concerned with the troublesome A: Immortality/Elsewhere locus beaming down on the abject B: Home/Mortality frame, the latter being glorified despite the impossible return, not simply to the geographical home, but the by-now fictive past of the *domus* or origin. In this perspective, he exhibits a totally alienated sense from what perhaps should matter most to a poet, the tenuous link between C: Poetry/*Langage* and D: Reality/*Langue*.

Contadino

Quel sentiero che mena al cimitero
seminato d'antichi ricordi
giganteggia nella tua mente
come i pioppi del nostro vallone
e i grattacieli di New York.
Tu venisti a questa terra
con muscoli d'acciaio;
ora torni magro e ignaro
alla parca mensa del paese natio
rinunciando ai sogni del domani.
Non ti trattiene il volto sereno
della Statua della Libertà
né i figli e i nipoti
che qui lasci in mezzo a indigeni!
Al tuo ritorno il paese
ti farà festa e là, nella cantina,
brinderai per me con i nostri amici.
Dall'alto della torre cilindrica
un'infinita nostalgia
si diffonderà fino ai campi
profumati di lupinella e di fieno:
quelle terre ricoperte dalle acque
del lago Occhito
le terre che hai arato per tanti anni
non sono più tue.
Tu porterai nel camposanto
quel dollaro che non ti è servito
in questa terra di nostalgia e di pianto.
Io ti ammiro e ti lodo
ma non ti posso seguire.
Per me altri destini decise il cielo
se allora la mamma piangeva
dicendo al figlio di non partire . . .

Farmer

That path leading to the cemetery
sown with ancient memories
towers in your mind
like the poplars of our valley
and New York's skyscrapers.
You came to this land
with muscles of steel,
and now you return lean and unknowing
to the frugal table of your native town
forswearing tomorrow's dreams.
You're held back
neither by the serene countenance
of the Statue of Liberty
nor the children and grandchildren
you leave here among the locals!
When you get back the town
will bid you a happy welcome
and there, in the tavern,
you will drink a toast to me with our friends.
From the top of the cylindrical tower
an infinite longing
will spread as far as the fields
fragrant with sainfoin and hay:
those lands covered by the waters
of Lake Occhito
the lands you plowed for so many years
are no longer yours.
You will bring in the cemetery
that dollar that was useless to you
in this land of longing and tears.
I admire you and praise you
but cannot follow you.
The heavens chose another destiny for me

e seguire il suo sguardo nel firmamento
stagliato da nuvole minacciose,
quando nella valle del Fortore
il pianto della mamma
aveva sapore d'eternità.

if back then a mother wept
telling her son not to leave . . .
and follow her gaze in the sky
crossed by threatening clouds,
when in the Fortore valley
a mother's tears
had the taste of eternity.

Agli emigrati italiani

Siate orgogliosi
del vostro nome!
Non nascondete
la vostra identità!
Non vi vergognate
della vostra origine!
Non rinunziate
alla vostra nazionalità!
Non cercate
una pagina nella storia
per imprimervi il vostro nome!
L'epopea di questa delinquenza
è il labirinto della discrimazione
della violenza odio e demenza.
Non vi fidate
della falsa luce della storia
che si diffonde sui dementi geni
e sugli assassini eroi!
I nostri fratelli
sono morti
sulla sedia elettrica
sono finiti
nella camera a gas
sono stati impiccati
col cappio al collo
sono stati uccisi
in pubblica piazza
sono stati condannati
da corti prostituite
sono stati cacciati
dalle scuole per ingiuste ragioni!
I nostri fratelli
hanno lavorato
nelle miniere di carbone
e sono stati ingiustamente
chiamati mafiosi!

To Italian Immigrants

Be proud of your name!
Do not conceal
your identity!
Do not be ashamed
of your origins!
Do not renounce
your nationality!
Do not look
for a page in history
to print your name on!
The epic of this villainy
is the labyrinth of discrimination
of violence, hatred, and insanity.
Do not trust
the false light of history
that spreads over insane geniuses
and murderous heroes!
Our brothers
have died
on the electric chair
they have ended up
in the gas chamber
they have been hanged
with nooses
around their necks
they have been killed
in public squares
they have been condemned
by corrupt courts
they have been expelled
from school for unjust reasons!
Our brothers
have worked
in the coal mines
and they have been unjustly
called *mafiosi*!

I nostri fratelli
hanno costruito questi grattacieli
e sono stati ingiustamente estradati!
Emigrati italiani,
lavorate per la giustizia
e per la libertà
amate i vostri figli
e fateli studiare!
Figli degli emigrati italiani,
seguite il retaggio dei vostri padri!
Nipoti degli emigrati italiani,
amate la nostra bella Italia!
Un giorno preferirete camminare scalzi
sulle pietraie dei nostri fiumi
piuttosto che annegare nel Mississippi
indossando dei pazzi i lussuosi stivali!

Our brothers
have built these skyscrapers
and have been unjustly extradited!
Italian emigrants,
work for justice
and freedom
love your children
and make them study!
Children of Italian immigrants,
follow the heritage of your fathers!
Grandchildren of Italian immigrants,
love our beautiful Italy!
One day you will prefer to walk barefoot
on our stony riverbeds
rather than drown in the Mississippi
wearing the luxurious boots of madmen!

Il linguaggio dei defunti

Un uomo si perde fra gli indigeni
e cerca un sasso
per scolpire una statua.
Il fischio del vento muore
fra le querce silenti
e spazza via il profumo del fieno
che si diffonde
fra le acacie e le stoppie.
La notte tu guardi la luna
che disperde le ombre tra i pini
e cerchi le ginestre
fra tanto oblio.
Il silenzio
è il linguaggio dei defunti
che fremono nelle tombe
ma non temono la morte.
Quest'esule molisano,
rapsodo randagio,
ascolta la voce che proviene dal cimitero
ma non ritorna per l'esigua eredità
ora che nella vigna solatia
fioriscono i cardi,
pungono le ortiche.
Ma l'ape ancora
succhia il mosto,
la farfalla si posa
sulla violacciocca
prima che la neve
ricopra il Matese.

The Language of the Dead

A man gets lost among the natives
and looks for a stone
to make a statue.
The whistling of the wind dies
among the silent oak trees
and sweeps away the smell of hay
that spreads
amid the acacias and the stubble.
At night you watch the moon
that scatters the shadows among the pine trees
and look for the brooms
within so much oblivion.
Silence
is the language of the dead
that chafe in their graves
but do not fear death.
This Molisan exile,
vagabond rhapsodist,
listens to the voice coming from the cemetery
but does not go back for the small inheritance
now that in the sundrenched vineyard
the cardoons are blooming
and the nettles sting.
But the bee
still sucks in the must,
the butterfly alights
on the gillyflower
before the snow
blankets the Matese.

La terra di nessuno

Sono voluto entrare
nella lontana frontiera
della terra di nessuno.
Sono qui un eroe
che cerca la morte
riceve medaglie d'onore.
La linfa fluisce
da remote radici:
il tacito morire delle foglie
languisce nello stupore autunnale.
Qui sono ombra fra le ombre,
un piccolo povero cuore.
Qui manca la speranza
di nuove aurore.
La vita si è fermata
al bacio di addio.
Le lacrime rapprese
in grumi di rinunzie
sono il guscio del mio silenzio
la doglia del mio perduto amore.
Uno strano destino
mi ha spinto a salire
sul calvario dell'emigrazione.

No-Man's-Land

I decided to enter
no-man's-land,
the faraway frontier.
Here I am the hero
who seeks to die,
who gets medals of honor.
The lymph flows
from distant roots:
the silent dying of the leaves
languishes in the autumnal wonder.
Here I am a shade among the shadows,
a small wretched heart.
Here there is no hope
of new dawns:
Life stopped
with our farewell kiss.
The tears congealed
in clumps of resignation
are now the shell of my silence
the grief of my lost love.
A strange destiny
has prodded me to climb
the Calvary of emigration.

→ Paolo Valesio (b. 1939)

Paolo Valesio was born in 1939 and studied philology at the universities of Bologna and Rome before coming to the United States in the mid-1960s, where he continued studies in linguistics at Harvard before taking a post at Yale University for most of his career. He is the Giuseppe Ungaretti Professor in Italian Literature at Columbia University. He has been a fellow of the Center for the Humanities at Wesleyan University, a fellow of the Guggenheim Foundation, and a fellow of the Whitney Humanities Center at Yale University. The author of numerous critical essays and articles on language and literary theory, the history of ideas, and poetics, and of books such as *Novantiqua: Rhetorics as a Contemporary Theory* (1980), Valesio has also written two novels, composed one collection of short stories, a novella, and a drama in verse, which has been staged in Italy. He is the author of fifteen books of poetry, including *Prose in Poesia* (1979), *Dialogo del falco e dell'avvoltoio* (1987), *Le isole del lago* (1990), *La campagna dell'ottantasette* (1990), *Analogia del mondo* (1992), *Every Afternoon Can Make the World Stand Still: Thirty Sonnets 1987–2000* (2002). A selection of his earlier poetry appeared in English as *Nightchant* (1995). On his creative work, see the critical anthology edited by Victoria Surliuga, *Analogie del mondo. Saggi su Paolo Valesio* (2008). Committed to the study and practice of poetry, Valesio has founded and coordinated from 1993 to 2004 the "Yale Poetry Group." He founded and directed the journal *Yale Italian Poetry*, which has now become the annual *Italian Poetry Review*, co-published by Columbia University and Fordham University.

Paolo Valesio's poetry offers an altogether different perspective in the rich panorama thus far sketched. His first collection, *Prose in Poesia*, points clearly to what he did *not* wish to do: follow in the quickly canonized lyrical tradition of the hermetic poets of the 1930s and 1940s, or of the "Fifth Generation" of the energetic postwar 1950s. Moreover, he did not seem to want to dawdle in the debris left by the neo-avant-gardes by the end of the 1970s, and he certainly steered clear of political literature. Valesio's poetry can be usefully understood as representative of a poetics of the witness—*testimonianza*—testimony to the micrology of existence, attendant upon a tireless questioning of the very reason for our existence. Thus Valesio *intends* to communicate, he is highly referential, his words denote as much as they inevitably connote, and one might also see his early books as a *pris de conscience* of the fact that the individual enters in a relationship with the world without necessarily understanding why, for there seems to be no solid ground to any perennial truth, not even the reassurance of a God. So from early on we go through a series of live sketches, *quadretti*, in which the poetics of testimony is slowly compounded with what we might call a poetics of acute directed listening, as if eavesdropping, *origliare*, to the reality about us, a keeping the metaphoric ear to the ground to record the most minute manifestations of the illogic yet ever sensual presence of being in the world.

In the poetry of the 1980s and 1990s, the poet's *I* is unabashedly brought to center stage on the page, as the reader begins to perceive what might be called a self-effacing and confessional demeanor, a purging and a cleansing in a relentless search for some deeper, or higher, understanding. In what we might call a third stage, Valesio is better understood as a theological or mystic poet. In this context, one can read in *Piazza delle preghiere massacrate* the movement from the apperception of the instant of revelation toward the assessment of the immanence of creation, and the felt need to share this epiphany with others, as in "Lungo una strada di campagna." In the collection *Volano in cento*, the poet recovers traditional poetic forms such as the *dardo*, literally a *dart*, a religious ejaculatory prayer, suitable to a confessional and participatory poetry profoundly aware of the divide between the self and the Divinity. The return to tradition can be seen also in *Every Afternoon Can Make the World Stand Still*. In the sonnet "Origins," the poet is not speaking about anything geographic or historical or social, but, true to his calling, searches rather inward, in his *soul*—a word Valesio resemanticizes against half a century of pointed rejection of Christian-sounding speech by the majority of his Italian peers—and quite disarmingly emulates the *stilnovisti*, echoing both Dante and Petrarch: "It was love who first moved me / and shook me from my shadowed life . . ., / before the Logos before the Universe / . . . Now on the road / I plod, fall, crawl, proceed on bent knees / and live a borrowed life" (my translation).

At least in his writings, there is no pining for *nostos* in Valesio, unless by that we mean the Italian—and actually, as in Tusiani and Rimanelli, the entire Western—*literary* tradition. On the social-geopolitical level, we can say that residing in America is, as for many of the younger poets we will see, nearly incidental: "Going to and coming from the United States is no longer . . . a conversion, is no longer the dramatization of a great tragedy, it is no longer an initiation rite."[35]If we read slowly through Valesio's now sizeable production, and attempt to map out his poetological itinerary, we can provisionally assert that his poetry is not so much concerned with Apex C's treatment of poetry as *langage*, as with its dialectical counterpart, Apex D, in which the *langue* is required to speak, register, capture reality, in terms of its givenness in conversation as well as through subtle grafts from the canon. On the vertical axis, A: Elsewhere/Immortality, the references in Valesio's poetry do not necessarily seek a vaunted immortality, but they do speak of the divinity, the gift that is life itself, and, better yet, the mystery that it sparks the sentient being to seek. Thus the *elsewhere* where the very mystery of the immortality (say, of the soul) can be sought can actually be *anywhere*, as it occurs in everyday epiphanies. As a result of and complement to this strong A/D field, at the opposite pole, B: Home/Mortality, there is no longer a fatherland or actual geographical home to yearn for, as the *domus* for the poet, acutely aware of the existential possibility of the end, once again can also be literally anywhere. And he had long ago decided that this locus can only exist in the mother tongue, the Italian language, and that becomes the ultimate place to dwell.

Puerta del sol

da *La rosa verde*

1.

       A questa sbarra, chi mi ha sospinto—
a questa porta del ritorno?
Sono tornati, al Mercato
di San Michele, i sussurri
dei garofani: rossi? bianchi? rosa?
(il bacino ramato del sole
tanto sbalza e scintilla che non posso—
non che vedere—nemmen nominare
i colori).

2.

       Chi viaggia e vaga resta condannato
a ripetersi immobile.
Quanti anni, per scoprire il nome
del fiume che ci intorbida e ci porta!
E dopo, tanti altri anni logorati
(il rame che s'inarca è divenuto
grigio e freddo—toccato dalla sera)
per capire: la vita era anche mia.
E qual è il passo prossimo?

3.

       Lo indica una Voce
che chiama un'idea viva;
traudita nel mercato,
più forte che i sussurri
dei fiori, è questa una Voce
dipinta su un cartiglio:
"*Rosa, ancilla cordis mei*".
Queste parole non posso enunziare,
queste parole non odo annunziare.
Ma mi aiutano a rivendicare
(io che non posso benedire un'anima
e nemmeno pregare per la mia)
la dignità silente dello schiavo.

Puerta del sol

from *The Green Rose*

1.

> Who has ushered me to this gate—
to this doorway of the return?
The whisperings of the carnations have returned
to St. Michael's Market: are they red? white? rose?
(the bronze basin of the sun shimmers and sparkles so
that I cannot, let alone see, even name
the colors).

2.

> He who roams and wanders is doomed
to traveling over and over in stillness.
Oh, so many years to learn the name
of the muddling river that bears us along!
And then, so many other weary years
(the arching bronze has turned gray and cold—
touched by the night)
to understand: Life was mine as well.
And what is the next step?

3.

> A Voice points the way
calling forth a living idea;
half-heard at the marketplace,
stronger than the whisperings
of the flowers, this is a Voice
painted on a cartouche:
"Rosa, ancilla cordis mei."
These words I am unable to pronounce,
these words I do not hear announcing.
And yet they help me vindicate
(I who cannot bless a soul
nor pray for my own)
the silent dignity of the slave.

4.

      La *Gran Via* odorosa di polvere
è piena di luci cattive.
La cammino pensando a una sera
quando esclamai: "Vale più il cuore, sempre,
che la mente"; la fece impallidire
di furia—uscì sbattendo,
non la rividi più.
Ero nel giusto allora,
ma non avevo ancora
pagato le monete del mio corpo—
la multa dei soldi roventi
dentro, nei solchi della pelle, ardenti—
prima di dire "cuore".

5.

      Adesso ho spogliato ogni panno
di volontà e di controllo;
e del pensiero ho perse
perfino le parole.
Servo fedele io,
servo al fedele.
Dovunque egli spinge io muovo.
Sono il minimo dito del mio cuore.

                              (Madrid)

4.

  The *Gran Via*, scented with dust,
is filled with malignant lights.
I walk it recalling the night
when I exclaimed: "The heart, always,
is more important than the mind." She
grew pale with rage—door slammed,
I never saw her again.
I was right then,
but I had not yet paid
with the coins of my own flesh—
the fine of coins burning
in the furrows of the skin, aflame—
before saying the word "heart."

5.

  Now I have shorn all layers
of will and control;
and I have lost even
the words for my thoughts.
I, the faithful servant,
servant of the faithful.
Wherever he leads I follow.
I am the smallest finger of my heart.

       (Madrid)

La tentazione

       Forse passai la vita respirando,
giornata dopo giornata,
gli odori di un'alba non mia.
Viene sopra di me la tentazione
della disperazione:
io e la vita mia,
mai ci siamo incontrati. Ma poi penso:
queste albe, qualcuno le ha mandate;
queste albe, qualcuno
le deve accogliere.

The Temptation

       It may be that I've spent my life
breathing in, day after day, the scents
of dawns that were not my own.
Upon me comes the temptation
to despair:
Me and my life,
we never did meet. But then I think:
These dawns, someone sent them;
these dawns, someone
has to welcome them.

Il pasto dell'avvoltoio

da *Dialogo del falco e dell'avvoltoio*

Morire è facile.
Ma essere sepolti: è un'arte filosofica.
Bisogna farsi seppellire
col vestito del dì delle nozze.
Tu riaffermi la linea di una vita
con un solo vestito buono
dallo sposalizio alla terra.
Sperando che così ritroverai—
al taglio decisivo, e sopra l'ultima
lama della luce di coscienza—
i padri dei padri dei tuoi padri.
Le madri dovrebbero
sopravvivere ai figli per poterli
piangere degnamente. Solo esse
esperte in corruzione delicata
in cure morbide
in vizio dolce dei figli,
solo le beneficamente corrotte
sanno fare il corrotto sul cadavere.
Il vestito all'antica è un argine di stoffa.
Ma non è semplice
la vita che così muore.

Troppe radici terrose
s'intralciano a fiore di terra.
Caccia alle nicchie libere,
gara di cadaveri ammonticchiati
che attendono i turni.
Tutta la terra dunque è sconsacrata
da cupidigia di picchetti e pali.
Territorio vien da terrore.
La spada scava terra
poi subito scava il collo.

The Vulture's Feast

from *Every Afternoon Can Make the World Stand Still*

Dying is easy.
But being buried is a philosophic art.
A man ought to be entombed
in his wedding day apparel.
You avow the course of a lifetime
with just one good suit
from wedding to funeral.
With the hope of finding then—
at the decisive breach, and on that final
blade of the light of consciousness—
the fathers of your forefathers' fathers.
Mothers should outlive
their children so as to properly
mourn them. For only they
understand the subtlety of the passing,
the tender care and
the habits of nourishment of children,
only they, charitably aged, know how to wail over the body.
The traditional garments are fabric retainers.
Yet it's not a simple matter
for a life to pass away.

Too many earthen roots
entangle just above ground.
The hunt is on for available nooks,
piles of corpses waiting their turn.
Earth itself is thus profaned
by greed for posts and stones.
Territory comes from terror.
The spade digging the soil
Digs then right into the neck.

The Parsis say:
the earth is sacred—
therefore it cannot be polluted

Dicono i Parsi:
la terra è sacra—
dunque non può essere polluta
dal cadavere;
l'acqua è sacra—
       e non può essere
intorbidita da carcasse;
il fuoco è sacro—
dunque non può esser profanato
bruciando un corpo;
l'aria è sacra—
non può essere offuscata da ceneri.
Quale luogo, allora, al cadavere?
La tomba semovente che preclude
tutti gli elementi, li taglia
fuori dalla sua angusta volta buia:
l'avvoltoio.

      A volte penso il contrario:
terra e acqua
fuoco e aria—
sono tutti polluti e bruttati,
nessuno degno più di ospitare
l'unico simulacro di purezza:
il corpo umano.
Ma—
mentre cammino lungo il viale grande
(Bombay ai piedi sotto la collina)
osservando le Torri del Silenzio
comprendo di dover tornare
alla chiara visione dei Parsi:
l'avvoltoio.
Angusti pozzi profondi
torri rovesciate
dentro il ventre dentro la terra.
Là sono gettati i cadaveri.
E su tutte le palme intorno,
gli avvoltoi ristanno.

with cadavers;
the water is sacred—
so it cannot be fouled
with carcasses;
the fire is sacred—
therefore it cannot be profaned
by a burning corpse;
the air is sacred—
it cannot be darkened by ashes.
Where, then, is the place for the dead?
In the self-propelled tomb that rules out
all the elements, that shuts them off
in its narrow black vault:
the vulture.

       Sometimes I think the opposite:
earth and water
fire and air—
they are all polluted and soiled,
no longer worthy of hosting
the only simulacrum of purity:
the human body.
Yet—
as I walk along the wide avenue
(Bombay at my feet below the hill)
observing the Towers of Silence
I realize I must return
to the lucid vision of the Parsis:
the vulture.
Narrow deep wells
upturned towers
inside the womb inside the earth.
There, corpses are discarded.
Perched atop the palm trees all around,
the vultures wait.
Large, coppery, bald,
with necks shunted into their shoulders.
The vultures are naked philosophers

Grandi, cùprei, calvi,
con i colli incassati tra le spalle.
Gli avvoltoi sono filosofi nudi
(mostrano quanto assurdo
sia il filosofo vestito).
Gli avvoltoi sono critici:
prima d'ogni altro membro,
ingoiano gli occhi.

      Nel loro stomaco
la morte si purifica,
la ruota si riavvia.

(showing how absurd
the robed philosopher is).
The vultures are critics:
before any other part,
they swallow the eyes.

     In their viscera
death is purified,
the wheel keeps going round.

Il confronto e il bilancio

Qualche volta pronunzi ad alta voce
quando sei solo, la parola "vita";
e ti appaùri, vedendo la foce
del fiume che ti scorre tra le dita.

"Vita" più "tua": che congiunzione atroce!
Ti ricordi di come l'hai tradita
e sei rimasto in libertà feroce
che forse è prigionia Villa Sfiorita.

Vita: tu la vuoi stringer fra le mani
come una coppa azzurra, o il diamante
dello sguardo di un cuore dominante

che plachi il mare che tranquilli il vento
delle passioni, e goda ogni momento
nella teoria dei templi quotidiani.

The Comparison and the Balance

You utter the word "life" in the quiet air
from time to time, when no one is about;
and you grow fearful, seeing the delta where
the river that runs through your fingers empties out.

"Life" plus "your": the words join wretchedly.
the thought of your betrayal fills your head.
You're left in a wild freedom, which may be
your Villa Sfiorita, a prison instead.

Life: You would like to take it in your hands
just like a sky-blue goblet, or the diamond
of the look of a dominating heart that stays

the rolling seas and stills the howling winds
of the passions, and that savors every moment
in the procession of the temples of the days.

Origini

Amore è stato il primo movimento
che mi ha riscosso dalla vita oscura,
ma non era profondo: giù in pianura
scorreva in sensuale malcontento.

Amore è stato il primo movimento,
prima del Logos e dell'universo.
dunque il mio amore era un fuoco perverso
e non ha resistito al forte vento

che ha spento lui e me. Adesso arranco
cado striscio procedo sui ginocchi
vivo una vita in prestito. È severo

il giogo? No, non sono troppo stanco.
ho il peccato—e la meta—innanzi agli occhi.
Soltanto in questo viaggio sono vero.

Origins

It was Love who moved my soul at first
and shook me from my shadowed life, although
he wasn't profound: He scoured the plains below
in discontented sensuality.

It was love who moved the souls initially,
before the Logos and the world. In youth
love was a flame of wickedness, in truth
no match for the fierce wind that forcefully

extinguished him and me. Now on the road
I plod, fall, crawl, proceed upon my knees
and live a borrowed life. Does it chafe me then,

the yoke? No, I'm not too wearied by the load.
With the sin—and the destination—before my eyes,
only on this journey am I genuine.

Pagus

da *Piazza delle preghiere massacrate*
Per Cathy e Bill

Vi sono, nella terra dei pagani,
tanti angoli dolci e riparati.

In uno di questi, un uomo
si appresta alla vigilia
del Giorno di Ognissanti:
la festa dei fantasmi e dell'autunno.
Dispone in un cestello
alcune larghe foglie
di vita declinante
il cui consuntivo colore
ha lasciato nell'anima una traccia,
e due o tre piccole zucche
indurite e lucenti di lacca.

Stamattina, ogni cosa gettata
sotto i suoi occhi lo incanta.
È lo spirito della contemplazione
che lo chiama?
Sì, ma è anche la stanchezza
che gli ha striato i capelli
e rallenta ogni suo movimento.

Queste ricurve attenzioni,
valgon come preghiere?
Non lo sa né il pagano né il cristiano
e l'uno
all'altro si rimette.

Pagus

from *Piazza of the Massacred Prayers*
For Cathy and Bill

> Out there in the lands of the pagans,
> There are many a sheltered and pleasant nook.

> In one of these, a man
> is prepping: 'tis the evening
> before All Saints' Day:
> the feast in autumn and of the ghosts.
> He arranges in a basket
> some broad and wilting leaves
> whose turned color
> has left a trace upon his soul,
> and two or three smallish pumpkins,
> hardened, and shining as of lacquer.

> This morning, whatever catches
> his eye enchants him:
> Is it the spirit of contemplation
> that beckons him?
> Yes, but it is also the weariness
> that's thinning his hair and
> slowing down his each and every step.

> But such meticulous care,
> Is that the same as praying?
> Neither the pagan nor the Christian
> really does know,
> and they look at each other for the answer.

Alba

Siamo tentati
(sul piccolo pensiero io albeggiavo
mentre mi risvegliavo),
siamo tentati di inventarci un dio—
in gola o nel cervello o dentro l'inguine
o perfino nel cuore—
per convincerci che la vita umana
non sia poi tanto vana.

Ma sono tutti modi per tentare
di non udir la voce di una bocca
che non appena si apre
viene invasa di terra
(così che il suono di lei
è morbido e grigio e sfacente):
è la voce di Dio l'inevitabile
il cui ricordo per noi

è che la vita umana
è atrocemente strana.

Dawn

　　　　We are prone
(this tiny thought dawned on me
while I was waking up),
we are prone to invent ourselves a god—
in our throats or brains or in our loins
or even in our hearts—
so to reassure us that human life
is not so vain after all.

　　　　But these are all attempts
to avoid hearing the voice
from a mouth filling with earth
the moment it opens
(so that the sound of her voice
becomes soft and gray and weary):
It is the voice of God we cannot avoid
reminding us that

it is human life
which is atrociously strange.

Dardo 7: Contra Platonem

da *Volano in Cento (Poesie 1999–2001)*
(*Symposium, 203b*)

Se Eros nasce dalle furtive nozze
di Povertà e Ingegno in giardino
quale mai dio scugnizzo e fosco
(dio-demone della mia vita)
nasce dal congiungimento
del Silenzio e la nuda dei boschi,
la Nulla?

Dardo 7: Contra Platonem

from *Volano in Cento (Poems 1999–2001)*
(Symposium, 203b)

If Eros is born of the stealthy nuptials
of Need and Talent in the garden,
then what sort of dark creepy god
(heaven and hell of my life)
is born of the coupling of Silence
with that naked creature of the woods,
Nothingness?

Dardo 40

Basta che la parola
"santo" sia menzionata
e subito mi metto
sull'attenti mentale
e fantasmi s'affollano entusiasti
effusivi
di ammirazione e rimpianto

Dardo 40

As soon as someone
mentions the word "saint"
I immediately switch
to mental alert—
as crowds of ghosts enthusiastically
pour out
admiration and regrets

Dardo 99

Allora quando in una cittadina
nobilesca e volgare nella notte
nell'istantissimo
in cui volgi la faccia
a una vetrina lucente
  (21,59
   ma quando abbassi l'occhio sul tuo polso
   son già le 22)
cade, prima della serranda
di ferraglia, quella della luce spenta
che segnala l'inizio
del commerciale silenzio—
in questa coincidenza
del tuo sguardo con quello spegnimento,
solo allora cominci a sentire
il taglio terracielo aperto
alle 8,46 di ieri
sopra le Gemelle di Manhattan.

Dardo 99

So when in a genteelish and coarse
provincial town at night
in that very moment
when you turn toward
the shining store window
> (it's 9:59 p.m.,
> but by the time you glance at your wrist
> it is already 10)
even before the lowering of the metal shutters
you see the lights go dim
signalling that business hours are over—
in this co-occurrence of your glance
and that shutting of the lights,
only then do you begin to feel
the skyearth slash opened up
yesterday at 8:46 a.m.
over the Manhattan Twins

→ Luigi Ballerini (b. 1940)

Poet, essayist, and translator Luigi Ballerini was born in Milan in 1940. He divides his year between New York and Los Angeles, and teaches modern and contemporary Italian literature at the University of California, Los Angeles. His books of poetry include *eccetera. E* (1972); *Che figurato muore* (1988); *Che oror l'orient* (1991), winner of the 1992 Feronia Prize; *Il terzo gode* (1994) and its American edition, *The Cadence of a Neighboring Tribe* (1997); *Shakespearian Rags* (1996); *Uscita senza strada* (2000); *Uno monta la luna* (2001); and *Cefalonia* (2005), winner of the 2005 Brancati Prize. He has written extensively on avant-garde literature (see *La Piramide capovolta*, 1975) and contemporary visual art and poetry, as well as on gastronomy, as in his editions of Pellegrino Artusi's *Science in the Kitchen and the Art of Eating Well* (2003) and Maestro Martino's *Book of the Cooking Art* (2004). A number of his publications have been realized in cooperation with artists. Among them are *La parte allegra del pesce* (with Paolo Icaro, 1984), *Leggenda di Paolo Icaro* (1985), *La torre dei filosofi* (with Eliseo Mattiacci and Remo Bodei, 1986), *Selvaggina* (with Angelo Savelli, 1988), *Una più del diavolo* (with Marco Gastini, 1994), *Navi di terra e di mare* (with Marco Gastini, 1999), *Vademecum per il Carro solare di Eliseo Mattiacci* (2004), and *The Unyielding Machines of Lawrence Fane* (2006).

The poetry of Luigi Ballerini, who came to the United States after a brief stay in London in his mid-twenties, is born out of the ashes of the last great neo-avant-garde movement in Italy, the *Novissimi*. From his first book, *eccetera. E*,[36] we infer that the poet seems to have accepted that language, whether of society in general or of tradition in particular, is in our epoch reified, misused, abused and banalized. As a result, he sets out on a tireless search for a language which is basically concerned with itself, sounding its potential for *suggesting* sense, casting off into the uncharted seas of "the possible, and not the known, toward something yet undefined."[37] Ballerini's poetry quickly evolves into an oracular style that challenges the idiomatic and the codified demotic grammar of the tribe,[38] breaking the logical or expected sequences in order to raise awareness of the fact that language can literally do its own thinking, or rather, that a new thought can be sparked by a rearrangement of the habitual syntactical and semantic patterns of the *langue*. In *Che figurato muore* the poetic persona, in the tradition of Apollinaire and Mallarmé, is definitely not interested in representation, narration, description, "or even escape from the world. Poetry must definitely choose to be somewhere else, and write itself *instead* of writing the world, in place of an inadequate reality, *despite* the coercion of grammar."[39] One way of avoiding the cliché and the unthinking language of the "they say," what Heidegger had characterized as the inauthentic chatter, the "averageness," of everyday conversation (see *Being and Time*, par. 27), is to focus on the minor parts of speech— conjunctions, prepositions, but also adverbs—rehabilitating them after the destruction of syntax performed by Marinetti, and forcing them to accept the weight of a resemanticization which compels us to think the *langue qua langage*, short-circuiting the opposing apexes C and D in our model, as in "the footprint of nameless / catches when by surprise" (63), and "An excluded wound / blanches in this here" (59). Deeply steeped into the avant-gardes, Ballerini is here also showing a profound assimilation of the challenging work of Gertrude Stein. Or consider the section "The barely of almost" (68–87), whose epigraph is taken from Cavalcanti, a longtime companion of Ballerini's in the severity of his vision and the torment he endured in the knowledge that meaning vanishes or diminishes once it is represented, or portrayed (hence the title, which means "once represented, it dies"). The effort to write a *non-sense* poetry is made explicit when he cites a phrase by Guillaume d'Acquitaine: "I'll write a poem of pure nothing" (91).

But is there such a thing as writing about nothing? Does nothingness not compel the mind to think of something all too often cloaked in metaphor or masked in self-deceit, namely death? And in fact, as the poet writes in a short essay contained in the book *Che figurato muore*, "The Oar of Odysseus," "Death is the ultimate and inimitable object of poetic imitation" (131). Interestingly, yet unsurprisingly, Ballerini delves into the presumed second journey of Odysseus *after* his return to Ithaca. But, once again, with a critical gesture reminiscent of Dante's invention of this second journey away from the *domus* into uncharted seas in search of ultimate knowledge, or immortality (see *Inferno* 26), Ballerini envisions

Odysseus the mariner undertaking instead a journey over land and in which, consistently with his predilection for *depistage*, "some other way-farer" will mistake his oar for a winnow fan. Misunderstanding, equivocation, delimitation, and upstaging of meaning are the preoccupations of this poet who finds no respite in irony, dares to ride the dangerous rhetoric of sarcasm, refuses parody, and tenders no deals to a world of simulacra and repetition of the indifferent.

In *The Cadence of a Neighboring Tribe* the poet moves into a third stage, one in which a semblance of ratiocination emerges and standard language seems to return, but only at the level of syntax, for at the semantic level there persists a dark pursuit of estrangement, of unforeseen associations, and constant perturbing questioning: "Shouldn't a language / chafe in the bones, among the fingers of the mating call, / the myth of splashing and healing?" (25). Here reality makes sense only insofar as language can evoke what has never been said of it before; no concessions are made to the predictable, reassuring, yet deeply alienated platitudes of socialized discourse. This entails making subtle yet exacting use of rhetorical devices such as hyperbaton, hypallage, enallage, and so on. As a result, there is little that can be called historic, geographical, cultural, according to the common usage of these words, and therefore nothing peculiarly "Italian" in the sense of identity, or geohistory, or homecoming in this poetry, outside of the grand obvious truth that it is *in* Italian and *about* the Italian language and its poetic possibilities. The struggle here is with language, *langage*, itself, with the gift given to humans: That it is the national semiotic code called *Italian* is, as the Schoolmen would have it, just "an accident of substance," and it is never to be taken for granted, because even the mother tongue—ironically given in French, "*la langue maternelle*" (see the poem of the same title below)—"stabs you in the back."

Now if syntax is slowly accepted though constantly pushed to the limit to make it bespeak its own metapoetic reality, to utter the fact that language, as *langage*, is the alpha and omega of poetry, and is constantly shifting, tripping, deviating, and suggesting, in a Heraclitean flux, the half-life of expressive possibility, then the same should be possible in other national languages, that is, by entering the syntax of an other *langue*. In Ballerini's case, he turned to English, as in the hauntingly beautiful *Shakespearean Rags/Stracci Shakesperiani*, and Milanese, with the wry *Che oror l'orient*. The rediscovery of, or retreat to, Milanese, the language of his childhood and adolescence, suggests that the poet is finally ready and willing to let the speaking subject roam the scene of being *back in* the language of the origin, much as writing in English establishes a profounding into the language and culture of the destination. Yet, once again, we find no external references, no identifiable calendars or topographies, no recognizable ideologies, no nostalgias, only an inkling of what might be called feelings and a tone that subtly absconds with ancient resentments. The last collection of Ballerini's writings, *Cefalonia*, signals another phase of his parabola, as he abandons verse for a prose drama, this time explicitly referencing a specific tragic event that occurred during World War II, and which relates, we may suppose, to the author's psychological autobiography, as well as to the issue of what goes into historical account and accountability. In this latter sense, the poet has regained—we may say, returned to, and accepted—the socioempirical referent present in every act of language, whether as *langue* or *langage*.

In terms of our critical quadrilateral, Ballerini's poetry, even in its constant evolution and rigorous experimentation, hovers around C: Poetry/Language (as *langage*). It is metapoetic by virtue of focusing on itself while rarely mentioning that it is doing so; it also dwells in the domain of C, the *langue* of reality and history, but only in order to constantly upstage it. Moreover, Ballerini's poetry is concerned with A: Immortality/Elsewhere, only to tame its diametrical opposite, D: Mortality, or Death. Yet even here, without any concern for a fatidic return home, it is a poetry about existing, being language, and "saying language" (in Italian, *una lingua dicente,* to avoid a perhaps too easy association with American "language poetry," with which it shares but a few traits); home is *in* the language, and whether the poet is physically in Italy or America or Tierra del Fuego seems relatively irrelevant.

Da: La parte allegra del pesce

da *Che figurato muore*

inclemente dilata il ragno impuro,
la cerniera distratta che declina
lo strame dell'azzardo, l'orologio
d'inchiostro, lo schiaffeggio
della vena morta, e impeccabile,
tibia o carrubo, crepita nell'esca,
incline alla ruga e alla commedia,
alla fattura che scava di soppiatto
sotto il filo bruciato, come tosse,
retino, fuga o zanna, come goccia di rame
tra le piume gelate della corsa.
E come spugna si liquefà nel taglio,
nella gobba del fiuto, della novena,
nella chioccia infedele di uno stile
caparbio, disabitato, di una spinta
che trebbia il bagnato di sangue

From: The Cheerful Part of the Fish

from *Represented, It Dies*

inclement dilates the impure spider,
the abstracted hinge declining
the debris of hazard, clock
of ink, smack-in-the-face
of the lifeless vein and, impeccable,
tibia or carob, crackles in the bait
inclined to wrinkle and comedy,
to the evil spell that slily digs
under burnt up thread, like cough,
screen, escape or tusk, like a drop of copper
in the frozen plumes of chase.
And liquefies like a sponge in a cut,
in a hump of scent, of novena,
in the faithless hen of a vacated
style, of a headstrong shove
that flails the bathed-in-blood

Selvaggina [brano]

se a bruciapelo un angelo di tigre
mette in gioco la calza, il guanto duro
dell'inseguimento, e scolma dai piovaschi
l'accaduto, la cenere dispersa, il burro
scampato all'alibi, alla scena madre,
il grido si fa più identico, più oscena
e magra la ribalta: ma io nella carne
ho già scritto la mia vocazione indiscussa,
la scheggia che abbaglia, la selvaggina
che ingabbia la recita dei versi. O da noi
mille volte umiliata sirena dei mari del sud,
o allarmata sutura, o miele impareggiato,
risponde alla tua voce un impervio equinozio,
un disguido, alla tua pelle un intrico
di azzurre altalene: ma io mi sarei fatto
vedere da te sano di mente, ellittico, immortale,
intonsurato cavaliere errante

Game Birds [excerpt]

if at point-blank that angel of a tiger
were to barter his socks, the stiffened glove
of pursuit, and from rain-showers drains
the event, the dispersed ashes, the butter
rescued from an alibi, from the crucial scene,
the cry becomes more equivalent, the footlights
leaner and more obscene: But I have already written
in my flesh my unquestioned vocation, the dazzling
splinter, the game birds that cage the recital
of verses. O mermaid of the South Seas
whom we have vilified countless times,
o alarmed suture, o unparalleled honey,
your voice is echoed by an impervious equinox,
a mistaken destination, your skin an intricacy
of azure seesaws: I would have shown myself to you
mentally sound, elliptical, immortal,
untonsured and knight-errant

imitazione del sogno

da *Il terzo gode*
per Remo

> Je suis celui que je vois par Celui qui me voit
>
> Edmond Jabès

succederà un veleno, un'indulgenza priva
di simmetria, di astuzia, succederà una lingua
camuffata o leggermente scolpita, un'ipotesi
di tramestio, succederà un puntiglio, una discesa
in salita (col rischio che corre di rovinarsi),
succederà una cantilena di traverso, una sbirciata,
un vocativo illustre, un'agnizione a prezzo
di concorrenza. Sopra pensiero, guardando
dall'alto verso il basso, vittima dell'uso,
dello specchio, di questo euforico arricchimento

succederà in una cornice religiosa, denigrante,
incline a riprodursi nei sensi pubblici, nei verbi
equinoziali, succederà perché l'idea dell'ordine si leghi
ai primi spasmi del coro, agli incendi, alle piume
che si ritraggono, ai grembiuli, alla breve cautela
dell'ira, succederà per la maschera inquieta che aguzza
il respiro, che ne suppone la scossa, la rimonta,
l'inospite ironia. Succederà perché l'asso pigli tutto
e accolga la svista prematura, l'imitazione del sogno,
del quesito: di sasso in sasso, di barca in barca

succederà dopo il latrato che ci ripopola e prima
dello scongiuro, del partito preso, succederà
nell'ombra di un proscenio che si mangia la coda,
che si sorpassa da un luogo all'altro del corpo,
da un corpo all'altro, e nel luogo del corpo a corpo,

imitation of the dream

from *The Third Enjoys*
for Remo

> Je suis celui que je vois par Celui qui me voit
>
> Edmond Jabès

a poison will occur, an indulgence devoid
of symmetry and cunning, a language will
occur, camouflaged or slightly sculpted,
a hypothesis of hustle and bustle, a spite
will occur, an uphill descent (running
the risk of ruin), a sideways sing-song
will occur, a glance, an eminent vocative,
a shock of unsold recognition. Frowning
upon bequests and losing thought, a victim
of habits and mirrors, of euphonic increase

it will occur in a religious setting, in jeers
inclined to reproduction, in the public senses
and the verbs of equinox, it will occur
again to tie the idea of order to choral
spasms, to fire and retracting feathers,
to aprons and the brief caution of wrath;
it will occur through restless masks that
whet the breath and the jolt, the comeback,
and paint the barren irony of sleep. It will
occur so that the ace can take it all and
welcome the unripe oversight, the imitation
of dream, of query: and rock to rock

boat to boat, it will occur after the howl
repopulates us and before the incantation
of a salacious goal, it will occur in the shade
of a stage eating its tail, overtaking itself
from limb to limb, from one limping body
to the next, in the place of a hand-to-hand

succederà nel bello messo in luce, in olio, in abisso,
messo e rimesso, nel bello del ballo, del birillo,
nel bello in ascolto e nelle dita insonni per acquisto,
per somiglianza. Ma come pura ipotesi di accanimento,
come cipria e chimera pieghevole del fondo

combat, it will occur in beauty and display,
in oil, in chasms played over and over,
in the beauty of the dance, of the skittle,
of listening to fingers sleepless from
stalling or marauding; it will occur as pure
hypothesis of doggedness, as mutilated
powder and pliant chimera of depth

la langue artificielle

per Paola

colpisce a tradimento, sgrana
le maglie lavorate, il ferro,
cesure di un assenso a coda
di volano, a scivolo, a scacco
matto, scagiona chi è scampato,
chi funge da vescovo, irrompe
da ogni buco, da ogni episodio
tagliato, mette a nudo il fiele,
stravolge l'ordine d'arrivo:
un uomo solo al comando (nella
pienezza del proprio isolamento)

si spaglia con astuzia latente,
con imbeccata, confluisce in varo
suggella l'ipotesi di un altro
gancio, di un altro pronostico
ma per diffondere, per riciclare
rimorsi differiti (rilancio del
pastiche, della cavia), naufraga
per diluire la fine del canto:
è anche un dormire che azzecca

s'intarsia di assedi, di scarichi,
spolvera magre aporie, riaccende
il tangibile oggetto, la delega,
la sua farinosa tortura, ma quando
implode, alla prima stazione, nel
comminare-mutare, nell'alleviare
le some, le lune sommarie. Rimuove
formule indegne di contromarcia,
di alfabeto (a ummo a ummo), risale
a più acconce ossature: da leone,
da gambero. E se per asola intende
l'insopprimibile *glib*, la tesi
del *bric-à-brac* che coccola

la langue artificielle

for Paola

stabs you in the back and husks
the knitted wool, the iron, breaks
in a trilled, checkmated assent
and its flywheel tail; acquits
the survivors, those acting
as bishops, bursting forth
from every corner, from every
slice; lays bare the bile,
upsets the order of arrival:
one man alone in the lead
(in the wealth of his isolation)

comes apart with latent cunning
and, prompting, flows into the
launching; seals the hypothesis
of another hook, of another far-
reaching forecast, recycling
deferred remorse (the revival of
pastiche, of guinea pig); founders
and dilutes the end of the tune:
a slumber, also, that hits the mark

inlaid with siege, with dumping,
dusting hesitant wits, relighting
the tangible, the proxy, the starchy
torture, only to implode at the
first stop, in the threat / mutation,
in the cutback of sums, of summary
moons. Represses formulas worthy
of reverse gear, of an alphabet
(for wise guys only), retracing
a more suitable framework: the lion's
or the shrimp's. And if by eyelet
we mean the unsuppressible glib,
the thesis of bric-a-brac that

progetti acuminati, che conta
i sassi in tasca o li succhia
       potrebbe dal bosco arditamente
uscire, fusa, svergognata, che sa
di primizia, di rapina, potrebbe
ostinarsi in questo idillio di spade
ingoiate in extremis, come novene
o esagoni di miele, col dito alzato,
potrebbe, succube, tornare al banco
degli imputati, di quelli che dicono
mezzo cammino oppure mezza montagna
intuendone appieno le conseguenze

cuddles whetted plans, and sucks them
        might from the woods boldly come
forth, molten, unashamed, tasting
of first fruit, of robbery, might
brazen forth in this idyll of swords
swallowed in extremis, like novenas
or honeyed hexagons. Cowering, with
fingers raised, might go back to
the defendants' block, to those who
say halfway there or half the hill,
fully aware of the consequences

→ Ned Condini (b. 1940)

Ned Condini, writer, translator, and literary critic, was the recipient of the PEN/Poggioli Award for his versions of poet Mario Luzi (1986), and of the Bordighera Prize for his rendering of Jane Tassi's *Andsongsongsongless-ness* (2002). Short stories and poems of his have appeared in *Translation, New York, The Mississippi Review, Prairie Schooner, The Partisan Review, Mid-American Review, Negative Capability, Italian Americana, Chelsea Review, YIP Review, The Village Voice,* and *The Litchfield Review.* He has translated Ben Jonson's plays and adapted *The Malcontent,* by John Marston. Other publications include the plays *Malcolm X* and *Sabbath* and the poetry collections *Rimbaud in Umbria* (1994) and *quartettsatz* (1996). In November 2002, Condini placed first in the Winning Writers War Poetry Contest in New York. In October 2004, Chelsea Editions published his selection of Giorgio Caproni's poetic works, *The Earth's Wall.* For the Modern Language Association, Condini edited an anthology of modern and contemporary Italian poetry, *Yet Fire Is All.* In May 2005, Condini was awarded the John Reid Fiction Prize in New York, and in January 2006 the first prize in the short fiction contest of Writers of North Carolina in Asheville. His most recent published work is *La morte e la fanciulla* (2005). After that, he worked on a play, *The Debt.*

Of Piedmontese origin but a naturalized American since 1976, Condini is another bilingual poet a discussion of whose work in English we must, as for the other Italian expatriate poets we labeled American Italian, defer to another time and place. His Italian production could be approached as a modernist venture into the incoherence or ironies of existence, and this not only at the personal but also at the geographical and historical level. Never coy or melodramatic, he exhibits rather a stoic wisdom rooted in a clear-headed honesty, a rare sincerity about his loves and his delusions, suggestive of a deeply elaborated inner detachment. The title of his collection *Rimbaud in Umbria*[40] is indicative of this poetic wisdom: *Apparte-*

nance is no longer a geographical, cultural, or familial issue, in fact it is not even a linguistic one. As Franco Borrelli quite aptly observed, "One is completely off course if in approaching Condini's poetry . . . [one] expects to find nostalgias or, worse, emigrant tears."[41] In the new country, Condini records and partakes in the natural and the social manifestations of America, but he is clearly conscious of the fact that existence is one and unique and that after all the journeying, he is at home in his own self only: "[I]n the solitary walk of an antinuclear bunch. / I had brought the city / in my heart all those years: I had fled / Ithaca only to return" (56). The Ithaca metaphor is not Homeric, and Condini is not nostalgic about Italy; rather, the toponym is of a Heideggerian stamp, meaning that he has been where he is, or that home is where he is at the moment, whereby the return, the *nostos*, is actually to constant self-awareness of his being there, we might even say, to the complex of his *Erlebnis*, his lived experience.

After a long silence, with *La morte e la fanciulla*, Condini gives us his best mature poetry. Like Tusiani and Carravetta before him, he has Americanized his first name, from Nereo to Ned. That may be a fact to explore in itself. His ideal interlocutors are Rilke, John Berryman, and the great Greek writers of antiquity, and his verses echo the "torrid and hard" music of Schubert. There is no doubt that the poet is now profoundly "American," to the point of personalizing his new country and wishing "to marry her," perhaps in an attempt to stave off the inevitability of the receding, dying origin, the "motherland," and accept his mortality in the new *domus*, where the passing and generating continues independently of time and history. I make this observation on the ground that Condini is keenly aware of being in the world *with others*, for death is everywhere, acknowledged and confronted at both the existential and the sociopolitical level, as the reader gathers from the anguished references to the tragedies of the Congo, Somalia, Indonesia, and Iraq, culminating in the concrete and symbolic horror of September 11, 2001. But by referencing tragedy, is this poet a nihilist? Not necessarily, and the stoicism that seems to circulate in some of his texts is not tantamount to a poetics of hopelessness either, insofar as acceptance of the inevitable, or what has been irretrievably committed, does not automatically signal an incapacity to look for where choice and agency can be translated into a life-affirming perspective. Where, in the impossibility of immortality, does the poet look? To love, one is tempted to say, naturally. Yet the turn toward the original life-drive is not understood as power over nature or sheer possession, but rather as its opposite, as founded on relinquishing things, letting go of one's chains, focusing rather on that being with others, or with the other, that recalls Gianni Vattimo's notion of a "weak modality of being," a letting oneself live and be lived.

From this sketch it would then appear that Condini's poetry is actually very much involved in the effective reality of the world, and will negotiate the proper register and tonality of the C apex, the *langue* of *both* origin and destination, as attested by his more recent production, entirely in the American idiom. And he is certainly also gravitating toward Apex B, the *home/mortality* pole of our interpretive model, with the very crucial distinction that home is not a geographical, cultural, or national location, but rather—and in this he also manifests traits typical of Apex C: Poetry/*Langage*, but without metapoetic references—a place in language (as *langage,* precisely) itself, the expression of being as *being there,* the place where as humans we have since always *been.* Thus the poet speaks to a most human consideration whose relevance is ontologically prior to the sociohistorical subdivisions into nations and cities and ideologies, exposing the arbitrariness of (arguably culturally and psychologically necessary) myths of immortality, identity, origin, and originality, focusing instead on the journey, which is existence itself.

Daniele

da Rimbaud in Umbria

Lo vedo: non avrebbe mai potuto
tollerare i miei modi al matrimonio.
Ero il padrino, e le morsi un orecchio;
da Gemignano, pieno di alcol, dissi:
è Parmigiano questo, o Rinso? Poi
lo risputo sul tavolo, mi soffio
il naso nel foulard—mi spuntò un grugno.

Decollo in un reattore per califfi:
su, giù in picchiata, strapazzando il cosmo
di Keplero, tornando alla sorgente,
Eufrate, Nilo, Tigri . . . ancora infisso
a sogni, volteggiante in cumuli.
Tornato a Terra Piatta, incespicai
nel buio, odorai sangue, e all'improvviso

la belva si strofina contro me,
fuoco negli occhi. Là mi riconobbi:
il trógolo, i letarghi, sconsolante
spreco: inglobò il dolore di vent'anni.

Prima sentii le zanne nella tana,
poi il pelo mi crebbe, si fletterono
i muscoli. Non mi trattenni più,
ruggii il tremendo ruggito del leone.

Daniel

from *Rimbaud in Umbria*

I see: She could have never tolerated
my manners at the wedding. Her godfather,
I bit her ear; at Gemignano's, high,
I said: Is this Parmesan cheese or Rinso?
spat it out on the table, blew my nose
into a scarf—and developed a snout.

Later, my takeoff on a regal jet:
up, down in spirals, treading Kepler's cosmos
back to the source, Nile, Tigris, and Euphrates . . .
impaled on dreams, swimming in thunderclouds.
Back to vile earth, I fumbled in the dark,
smelling the blood, until all of a sudden

I rub against the beast, fire in his eyes.
I recognized myself at last: the trough,
inaction, wretched waste come to no good,
totaling the collapse of twenty years.

At first I felt my fangs grow in the den,
my hair turn into a mane, my muscles bulge.
I could not stop my anger anymore,
I let out a lion's terrifying roar.

Vassar College

da *quartettsatz*

Adesso i rami là sono folti di ali
e ogni casa è una bacca che brilla
nell'aria tersa di ottobre.

Vorrei tornare a Sproul Hall
alle sue guglie al nido
del "college" salvo in un alveo di foglie.

Su volte di pino dardeggia
la cappella smaltata di Vassar
e nubi in stole amaranto
perdonano tutte le fughe. Anche la mia.

Vorrei tornare a Sproul Hall
alle sue radure ai suoi pub
pregni di risa e fumo al sapere
battuto come musica sul cuore.

Vassar College

from *quartettsatz*

Branches there are alive with wings,
each house a berry glowing
in the crisp October air.

I'd like to go back to Sproul Hall,
its spires, the college nest
safe in a niche of leaves.

On aisles of pines shines
the stained-glass chapel of Vassar
and clouds in amaranth stoles
forgive all escapes, even mine.

I'd like to go back to Sproul Hall,
its clearings, its pubs pulsating
with laughter and smoke, to knowledge
beaten like music on the heart.

Com'era verde la mia vallata

da *La morte e la fanciulla*

Pausa dove la vipera
guizza sull'erba arsa di Paestum;
con l'occhio della mente stravedi
gli Argonauti; evoca poi ciliegi
bianchi da spezzare il cuore,
lucciole prendere fuoco in amore,
Val San Martino—supremo Olimpo mio.
Deliziato tendi così l'orecchio
da udire quasi una voce paesana.
Illusione. Non chiama nessuno.

I paesaggi ammalianti, catene di monti,
i ponti, le torri, e ineffabili
vedute da segreti sentieri
in quella terra litigiosa, un tempo
eco di passi divini—tutto sorge
dentro di te volendo dire Lei—
che è cieca, muta, e sorda.

How Green Was My Valley

from *Death and the Maiden*

Picture a viper darting
along parched grass in Paestum;
with the mind's eye flesh out the Argonauts,
cherry trees in heartbreaking white, the golds
of fireflies in heat—Saint Martin's Valley,
my high Olympus. So enamored, strain
your ear longing to hear
a native voice. Dreamer. No one is calling.

The haunting seascapes, ranges, bridges, towers
and ineffable views on treasured lanes
in that bickering land that once resounded
with the steps of the gods—all rise within you
to mean her, who is deaf and mute and blind.

Presto comincerà la mia ordalia

Su per il cielo s'arrampica la luce.
Mi vesto indeciso, triste mi giro a guardare
la stanza vuota. Per poco ti vedo ancora.
Un solo partire, tanti rincrescimenti.
Penso a tutto quello che hai fatto per me
e mi vergogno: che cosa ho fatto per te?
Mele verdi in cambio di ametiste.
Eppure devo salpare. Questo è un paese
che soffoca. Addio, amica mia.

At Dawn My Long Ordeal Will Begin

Light crawls up the sky. Dawdling I dress,
turn around saddened to look at the empty room
and for an instant seem to see you still.
A single parting, beleaguering regrets.
I think of all the things you did for me
and am embarrassed: What did I do for you—
green apples back for amethysts.
And yet I have to sail. This country
is choking me. Farewell, my friend.

Il cigno di Rilke

Diventerò là il cigno di Rilke dopo
il tuffo nell'acqua, che in adorazione
e contentezza si chiude dietro di lui
in doppia scia? Prima, che goffo cammino!
come gestanti a un parto ancora incompiuto,
disorientate dai rischi del desiderio . . .

Ma come il cigno, quando abbiamo finito
e ogni parola canta e significa quel che intendiamo,
lasciar andare, non più calcare la terra
che ogni giorno ci regge nel timore,
tuffarci nell'acqua, e più che mai consapevoli,
silenziosi e regali lambire la corrente.

Intimations

There, will I ever become Rilke's swan
after his dive into the water, which
in worship and content draws back past him
in streams on either side. Yet before! what
a clumsy walk like laboring through work
that's still undone, hobbling along through hazards
of desire . . .
     But swan-like, when we're done
and each word sings and means just what we wanted,
then to let go, no longer feel the ground
we stand on frightened every day, to fall
into the water, and infinitely aware,
silent, imperial, acquiesce to glide.

Il lago di Woodcliff

La nebbia sale leggera dal lago come schiuma
e mostra il blu sotto solo a strisce sconnesse.
Ma più lontano s'aprono spiazzi di oro
e, poco dopo la curva, fuochi di foglie
di quercia illuminano l'orizzonte grigio
di vite rinchiuse. Un'improvvisa

malinconia ti colpisce non sai da dove
mentre il peana delle foglie s'apre maestoso allo sguardo:
è la tua giovinezza che s'invola, l'inverno già vicino,
o stai cadendo come cade natura,
e senti il tuo corpo sciogliersi in fiamme, i capelli
presi in questa lattea bruma che annega il cuore.

Non sei il ragazzo di Grimm che scordò di tremare
di fronte alla Morte, ma oggi in silenzio mentre guidi
cerchi il viso di uno che una volta era tuo amico:
non vuoi rattristarti perché discendono le foglie.
Sei il loro rosso e oro, com'eri il loro verde.
Così ogni viaggio contiene la meta nel suo seme.

Lasciala ancora, Tu che plasmi e io cerco,
verde come la visione vergine di una bambina.
Foggiala in acqua, chiarità che schiva colori,
ma con l'idea, nascosta, dell'arcobaleno.
E con questi gialli ancorati in lei come soli
di colma saggezza, ogni mattino
sia la sua andata un saluto all'inverno.

Pausa per l'albero scarnito a geometrie
di linee, lo stelo d'erba fatto
lama d'acciaio, la ghianda che sotto cumuli
di neve dorme, ma cresce in bellezza pura.
Conta la spinta interna, non primavera.

Woodcliff Lake

Tenuous the fog rises over the lake,
showing the blue underneath in ragged streaks only.
But in the distance a flowering of golds
is coming into view and, round the corner, fires
of oak leaves stir the limited horizon
of our restricted lives.

A sudden melancholy strikes you from nowhere
as the paean of leaves majestically swells:
Is it your youth that's fleeing, winter approaching,
or are you falling with the fall of nature,
feeling your limbs go up in flames, your hair
caught in this milky mist that drowns the heart.

You're not the child from Grimm who forgot to shudder
at the sight of death, but your ride today is a silent
search for the face of someone who was your friend:
You do not want the fall of leaves to grieve you.
You are their gold and their red, as you were their green.
So every journey contains the seeds of its end.

Let her be green, you Mover that I'm seeking,
once more with a child's fresh vision.
Let her be water, clarity stripped of colors,
but with the idea of rainbow in it.
And with these yellows anchored in her like suns
of ripened wisdom, may

her ride every morning be a salutation to winter.
Pause for a tree reduced to a geometry of lines,
a blade of grass made into a blade of steel,
an acorn resting under feet of snow
but growing into a thing of utmost beauty.
The yearning is the essence, not the Spring.

Così, così, la tua faccia

Così, così, la tua faccia:
una maschera d'odio, il tuo riso
stravolto in scherno, le rughe
fitte fino a spegnerti gli occhi,
i capelli un arruffo, le spalle
rivolte in sfida al mondo intero.
Contro il tuo stesso volere, tutto
in te negava amore—l'indigenza
mai svelta dal cuore, la pietra
che cercava di uscire
dalle sue cieche pareti. Papà,

so che è un insulto dire: ti conosco.
Piantarti un cuneo nella carne.
Ma ho imparato a studiarti, sai,
e rinnegato le apparenze.
Senza una mano che lo smuova, il sasso
propagginato a terra
non può che supplicare verso il basso.

Just So, Your Face

Just so, your face: a mask of hatred, laughter
distorted to scorn, wrinkles so thick
they swallowed up your eyes, your hair a tangle,
your shoulders turned in defiance to the world.
Against your will, everything past in you
refuted love: The gruesome years of indigence
never uprooted from your heart—a stone
struggling to shatter its night-mantled walls.

Dad: It's an insult to say that I know you.
To drive a wedge into your flesh.
But I have learned to study you, to unmask
appearances. No hand lifting it upward,
the stone embedded in the earth pleads downward.

⇀ Nino Provenzano (b. 1944)

Nino Provenzano was born in Castellammare del Golfo, Sicily. He is vice president of Arba Sicula, a New York based international organization that promotes Sicilian culture in the world. His passion for poetry, which blossomed early in his childhood in Sicily, has accompanied him throughout his life. He has presented his poetry at universities such as St. John's, Hofstra, Stony Brook, Fordham, and Montclair College in New Jersey, and at other venues such as the World Congress of Poets for Poetry Research and Recitation. For his poetry, he has received numerous awards in Italy, Canada, and the United States. He has delighted his audiences with his humorous and often heart-rending poems that speak of the plight of the immigrant, and the difficulties of finding a harmonious modus vivendi in American society. A bilingual anthology of Provenzano's poetry titled *Vinissi*, with translations by Gaetano Cipolla, was published in 1995 by Arba Sicula. He works in Manhattan and lives on Long Island with his wife Josephine and their three daughters, Patricia, Catherine, and Rosanne.

On nearly the same wavelength as Del Duca, Provenzano writes in a Sicilian dialect and exhibits greater formal control of the medium, both in the handling of the line and in the use of rhetorical devices. Also somewhat isolated and little known among the literati, his poetry addresses not so much the popular as the commonsensical, with some profound insights as revealed in "Not a Word," where the poet reminds us, as would any linguist, that words can indeed create moods and be soothing, but also cut throats and, worst of all, especially for a poet, be "bland, stale, bitter." But he goes one over, into the broader semiotics of communication: "[A] glance, / a smile, / a facial expression, / . . . / define / with silent certainty / romances, / brotherly relations among people, / tales about peace." In short, signs and gestures can communicate as well, and often in fact words are not necessary at all, as we may get by with "just a glance. / All without speaking." But Provenzano is also capable of a reasoned poetry, well balanced within a consciously crafted stanzaic disposition, and prone to meditation, as he attempts to grasp some essential truth possible only in the great economy of the poetic text, as in "It Was February" or in "The Inheritance."

Still, when it comes to a poem about immigrants, the traditional polarity between native home and adopted one resurfaces, dressing the topos of being uprooted with strong identitarian traits, expressed in the cogent metaphor of having one's flesh torn out, and suggesting moreover that the experience burns a permanent scar in the psyche. Here Provenzano speaks, foremost, as an Italian immigrant, one of the last members of the greatest peacetime exodus in modern history, as one of those who *had to* leave Italy between 1880 and 1970. But it wouldn't be too much of a stretch to say that he is speaking as, and for, those 250 million people who at the beginning of the new millennium are roaming the planet in search of a *real* abode, forever caught between what is no longer theirs, and what cannot ever feel to be theirs, remaining therefore suspended between (at least) two worlds. In this dynamic, a value to explore is the fact that now the poet's world—home, family, dreams—is always traveling with him, having found the *domus* within. Another, hardly less important, value is the humility experienced upon realizing that somehow *we are all migrants*, we are all in the same metaphorical and existential boat, "Blacks, Whites, and Arabs, / with Jews and Christians too, / and many more," as he writes in the poem "There Will Always Be Emigrants."

In terms of our critical map, by persisting in writing (thinking, singing) in his literally native idiom, Provenzano is certainly retaining "the language whence he came," and is certainly adding "to America's own history," so his poetics covers a melancholy patch between pole D: *Langue/Reality*, and pole B: Home/Mortality. The poems here come from his book, *Vinissi*.

Senza paroli

da *Vinissi*

Si li paroli
fussiru tutti duci,
duci, comu lu meli,
ni l'agghiuttissimu tutti,
comu li calameli.

Ma, tutti li lingui,
su fatti di paroli,
grevi, duci, amari.
o paroli tagghenti
usati pi scannari.

E quantu paroli,
chi quasi sempri
nun c'è bisognu usari . . .

Picchì

'Na ucchiata,
un surrisu,
un'espressioni
di l'occhi,
di la facci,
un gestu,
'na stritta di manu,
n'abbrazzu,
'na calata di testa;

discrivinu
cu silinziusa cirtizza
rumanzi amurusi,
rilazioni fraterni fra populi
storii di paci,
prumissi fatti di lu cori,
di lu cori chi taci.

Not a Word

from *I'd Love to Come*

If all the words were
oh so very very sweet
like honey,
we would gulp them all down,
like candy

Unfortunately, languages
are made of bland, stale, bitter
words, or words
sharp like knives
and used to cut throats

And how many words are there
that we hardly have
any use for . . .

Because:

a glance,
a smile,
an expression of the face,
a glint of the eye,
a gesture,
a hand squeeze,
an embrace,
a nod of approval,

define
with silent certainty
love stories,
brotherly relations among people,
tales about peace,
promises that come from the heart,
the silent heart.

Gesti, signali,
misurati sulu
cu lu metru di lu silenziu.

Un silenziu
chi s'allarga
cu l'unna di lu mari,
di l'aria,
purtannu
missaggi aspittati
nutizii spirati,
paci addisiati.

Senza paroli.
Sulu cu l'occhi.
Senza mai parrari.

Senza parole—Se fossero tutte dolci / le parole / dolci come il miele / l'inghiottiremmo tutte / come caramelle. / / Ma tutte le lingue / sono fatte di parole, / insipide, dolci, amare; / o parole taglienti / usate per scannare. / / E di quante parole / spesso non ce n'è proprio bisogno . . . . / / Perchè / / Un'occhiata, / un sorriso, / un'espressione / degli occhi, / della faccia, / un gesto , / una stretta di mano, / un abbraccio, / annuire col capo / / Descrivono / con silenziosa certezza / romanzi amorosi, / fraterne relazioni tra i popoli, / storie di pace, / promesse fatte dal cuore, / dal cuore che tace; / / gesti, segnali / misurati solo / col metro del silenzio, / un silenzio / che s'allarga / con l'onda del mare, / dell'aria, / portando / messaggi aspettati, / notizie sperate, / pace desiderata. / / Senza parole. / Solo con gli occhi. / Senza mai parlare. (Translated by Giuseppe Turriciano)

All gestures and signs
measured
with the meter of silence.

A silence that radiates
with the waves of the sea,
of the air,
bringing
awaited messages,
desired news,
yearned-for peace,

All without a word.
Just a glance.
All without speaking.

Biddizzi scanusciuti

'Na ciura di biddizzi scanusciuti
nasci a li voti dunni un ti l'aspetti
'nfacci a lu mari 'ntra scogghi puntuti
o 'nta muntagni fra spini e ruvetti.

Spunta macari dunni chi nun chiovi,
o 'ntra la valli ch'è fangusa e scura,
ma si la so' biddizza tocca e movi
nun mi dumannu s'è di razza pura.

Cusì è quannu leggiu 'na puisia,
osservu un quatru o attentu 'na canzuna,
viu 'na scultura, 'na fotografia:
si c'è biddizza l'arma sinn'adduna.

Biddizza, è virità chi sula veni,
varca limiti umani e si prisenta
davanti a l'occhi di cu ci apparteni,
di cui la cerca e suspirannu attenta.

Di chista virità, di st'arti, iu vivu
l'essenza di lu meli so' sprimutu
e cu l'effettu etericu arrivu
'nta un munnu di biddizzi scanusciutu.

Bellezze sconosciute—Un fiore di sconosciuta bellezza / nasce a volte dove non te l'aspetti, / in fronte al mare tra scogli irti / o in montagna tra spini e roveri. / / Spunta anche dove non piove / o giù nella valle fangosa e scura. / Ma se la bellezza tocca ed emoziona / non mi domando s'è di razza pura. / / Così è quando leggo una poesia, / osservo un quadro o ascolto una canzone; / vedo una scultura, una fotografia: / se bellezza c'è, l'anima se ne accorge. / / Bellezza è verità che da sé viene. / Varca i limiti umani e si presenta / davanti agli occhi a cui appartiene, / di chi la cerca e sospirando ascolta. / / Di questa verità, di queste arti, io vivo / spremendo l'essenza del suo miele. / E con l'effetto etereo arrivo / in un mondo di sconosciuta bellezza. (Translated by Giuseppe Turriciano)

Unrevealed Beauty

A flower of unrevealed beauty
can grow at times where you least expect it:
on groggy sea cliffs, or broken rocks,
or on mountains among thorns or brambles.

It can appear where it never rains
or in the deep dark muddy ravine.
But if its beauty touches and moves me
I do not ask if its breed is pure.

And so it goes, when I appreciate a poem,
admire a painting or applaud a song,
revere a sculpture or contemplate a picture;
without being told, the soul knows what is beauty.

Beauty is a truth that arrives serenely;
it transcends reason, and materializes
before those to whom it belongs,
rewarding their anticipation.

Of this truth, of this art, I drink
the essence of the squeezed nectar.
And lifted on ethereal wing
I enter into a world of unrevealed beauty.

Era febraiu

Era febraiu, un iornu friddulusu
c'era lu suli però nun quariava.
Un'autobussu ia pagghiri susu
siguia la strata per si firmava

pi lassari e pigghiari passaggeri.
A un certu puntu, acchiana un'omu anzianu.
Avia 'nmazzu di rosi frischi e veri
e s'iu assittari cu ddi rosi 'mmanu.

A specchiu ad iddu c'era un giovanottu
chi taliava ddi ciuri e l'ammirava
cu gran curiusità. E poi di bottu
dissi all'anzianu: "Eu puru l'accattava

s'avia li sordi, ma haiu sta cartulina,
oggi è San Valintinu e a la me zita
ci portu sulu sta cosa mischina.
Ma ni vulemu beni pi la vita!"

L'anzianu l'attintau, fici un surrisu
poi si susiu, e misi chiddi rosi
'mmanu a ddu giovanottu,chi surprisu
dissi "Mancu pi sonnu! No sti cosi!

No, nun l'accettu, nun sunnu pi mia!
Eu lu dicia tantu pi parrari!
E lei soccu ci porta dunni ia?"
L'anzianu dissi "Un ti prioccupari,

portali tu sti rosi a la to' amata
ed iu a me muggheri lu va cuntu
chi ti li detti a tia, sarà priata.
Iu scinnu a sta firmata, sugnu iuntu."

L'autobussu firmau, l'omu scinniu,
senza mancu vutarisi narreri,
cu li manu vacanti sinni iu.
Passau ddu latu di lu marciaperi.

It Was February

It was a cold day in February
the sun was out but it had little warmth.
A bus was moving uphill
along the road and stopping

to let on and off its passengers.
At one point an elderly man got on
holding a bouquet of fresh fragrant roses
and sat with the roses in his hands.

Across from him sat a young man
who gave the flowers a wistful survey.
Then suddenly he tells the man
"I would have bought them also

Had I had the money. But I have this card.
It is St. Valentine's Day, and to my fiancée
I'm bringing only this miserly card.
But our love is stronger than life itself."

The gentleman listened and smiled.
Then he got up and placed the roses
in the hands of the young man, who startled said
"No! I cannot accept this.

No! It is out of the question!
I . . . was only making conversation.
And you . . . what will you bring to her?"
The gentleman said: "It is all right.

You take these roses to the one you love
and I'll tell my wife
I gave them to you. She'll be elated.
I'm sure. I'm getting off. This is my stop."

The bus stopped, and the man got off
without even glancing back.
He left empty-handed.
He crossed to the other side.

Nino Provenzano 1243

ddu giovanottu incredulu siguiu
cu l'occhi a dd'omu e nun ci parsi veru
quannu a distanza vitti chi spinciu
'na grara . . . e trasiu 'nta un cimiteru

Era febbraio—Era febbraio, un giorno di freddo. / C'era il sole, però non riscaldava. / Un autobus se ne andava su / seguendo la strada, ma si fermava / / per lasciare e prendere passeggeri. / Sale a un certo punto un uomo anziano. / Aveva un mazzo di rose fresche, vere; / e si sedette con quelle rose in mano. / / Di fronte a lui c'era un giovanotto / che guardava quei fiori e li ammirava / con grande curiosità. Subito ad un tratto / disse all'anziano: "Io pure li avrei comprati / / se avessi avuto i soldi, ma ho questa cartollina; / oggi è San Valentino e alla mia fidanzata / porto solo questa cosa meschina. / Ma ci vogliamo bene per la vita!" / / L'anziano l'ascoltò, fece un sorriso. / Poi si alzò e mise quelle rose / in mano a quel giovanotto, che sorpreso / disse: "Neanche a pensarci. Non queste cose! / / No, non l'accetto, non sono per me! / Io dicevo così, tanto per parlare! / E poi, dove va lei cosa porta?" / L'anziano disse : "Non ti preoccupare. / / Porta tu queste rose alla tua amata; / quando lo racconto a mia moglie, / che le detti a te, ne sarà contenta. / Io scendo a questa fermata. Sono arrivato." / / L'autobus si fermò, l'uomo scese / senza neanche voltarsi indietro; / se ne andò con le mani vuote / passando all'altro lato del marciapiede. / / Quel giovanotto incredulo seguì / con gli occhi quell'uomo e non gli sembrò vero / quando a distanza vide che spinse / un cancello . . . ed entrò in un cimitero. (Translated by Giuseppe Turriciano)

That young man, still stunned,
followed the man with his eyes and
could not believe it when at a distance
he saw the old man push a gate and enter a cemetery.

L'eredità

Una curiosità di niatri umani,
è chidda di sapiri lu futuru.
Ma semu sempi anziusi pi dumani,
chi trascuramu lu prisenti puru.
Nun fussi megghiu si cu senzi sani,
taliamu ad oggi, e a lu passatu puru?
Chi lu passatu, cu fatti pruvati
'nsigna la storia di l'umanitati.

La storia di l'America è saputa.
Cincucent'anni e sù ducumintati.
La vecchia Europa, a funnu è canusciuta
pi lotti, 'ntrighi e regni di papati,
Siddu sapiri chisti cosi aiuta
a farini chiù saggi addivintati.
Com'è chi ognunu sapi pocu o nenti
Di storia propria e di li so parenti?

Finu a me nunnu haiu notizi chiari,
e di so patri qualcosa l'haiu 'ntisu.
Lu nunnu di me nunnu, pochi e rari,
su li notizi e di dubiusu pisu.
Lu nunnu poi di chissu, 'un c'è chi fari,
nenti si sapi e a lu scuru sta misu.
E chi si parra, mancu ducent'anni,
Persa è la rera comu su mill'anni.

Mi fa gran rabbia si ci ragiunamu,
sapiri stori di regni e rignanti
chi nun ni vennu nenti, e li sturiamu
narre' di vinti seculi distanti.
Mentri li cosi nostri li 'gnuramu.

The Inheritance

We humans have a great curiosity
about the future. We just have to know.
But we sometimes so worry for tomorrow
that we forget to worry for today.
Would it not be much better if we looked
at both the present and the past, instead?
The past, indeed, with facts already proved,
can teach to everyone the history of humanity.

America's own history is known:
five hundred years of it well documented.
Old Europe has been known for all its struggles,
its kingdoms, the intrigues of all the popes.
If knowing all these things can be of help
to make each one of us a wiser being,
how come so few of us know anything
of our own story and of our own kin?

Of my grandfather I know many facts.
Of his own father I have heard some things.
Of my grandfather's old ancestors, few
are the facts I know and quite uncertain.
But beyond him there's nothing there to know.
Nothing remains, all's hidden in the dark.
We're only reaching back two hundred years
and it's as if a thousand years had passed.

It drives me crazy, if I stop and think
that I know stories of great kings or realms
that date back twenty centuries or more
and they're not even relatives of mine!
And we don't know meanwhile our histories.

Ah! Quali gioia! Eu fussi triunfanti
d'iri sei, setti seculi arrè 'nfunnu
e rintracciari lu decimu nunnu!

Com'era? Longu, curtu, grossu, siccu?
Era schirzusu, si sciarriava mai?
'Ntra la so'sucita' faceva spiccu?
E di pulitica si 'ntricava assai?
Era un patriota? Era scarsu, riccu,
o era occhi Pasquali passa guai?
Socch'era era, iu ni fussi gratu
sapiri d'iddu e l'autri lu passatu.

Un libru ci vulissi e poi sfugghiari.
Truvari puru ritratti e li dati
di li me avi, e leggiri macari,
fatti di vita a sceni già passati.
Certu chi mi putissi diliziari,
dicennu a li me figghi, "Ccà, taliati!
Chista è la storia nostra propria e vera,
lu filu drittu di la nostra rera".

"Perdiri 'un s'avi, e vogghiu chi scriviti
appressu a chidda mi la storia vostra.
Cusì a li figghi passalla putiti.
L'aviti a fari! Picchì vi dimostra,
quannu custumi e lingua mantiniti,
chi fati onuri a la Sicilia nostra.
Terra d'amuri e canti di l'aceddi,
conca di suli e di picciotti beddi.

L'eredità è patrimoniu, è beni,
a cui va data la giusta attenzioni.
E specialmenti ccà cchiù si ci teni,
chi semu genti di tanti nazioni.

What joy I'd feel! I would be in my glory
if I could go back seven centuries,
and find my father's tenth grandfather.

How was he? Tall or short, or heavy or thin?
Was he congenial, did he have some fights?
Was he a man of substance in his day?
Was he involved at all in politics?
Was he a patriot? Was he poor, rich?
Was he some kind of bungler or a fool?
No matter what he was, I would be grateful
to know his story and that of my folks.

I'd like to have a book so I could find
portraits and dates and other things as well
about my own ancestors. I would love
to read facts about their lives, live through their scenes.
I think I would be very pleased to say
to my own children, "Now, here look at this!
This of our lives is the true history:
the straight and true line of descent."

"You must not lose it! I want you to write
your histories in it after my own
so to your children you may pass it on.
This you must do because it demonstrates,
when you retain the customs and the language,
that you pay homage to our Sicily,
that land of love where birds forever sing,
that sunny land where handsome youths abide."

Our heritage is wealth, a patrimony,
which must be given care as it deserves,
especially in this land where we're many
of many different nations joined together.

Si ognunu sarva di d'unni pruveni,
usi, custumi, lingua e tradizioni,
agghiunci a chista storia Americana
n'autra perla 'nta la so' cullana.

L'eredità—Una curiosità di noialtri umani, / è quella di voler sapere cose future. / Siamo sempre ansiosi per il domani, / che trascuriam il presente pure. / Non sarebbe meglio che coi sensi sani, / Guardassimo al presente ed al passato? / Che il passato, come si sa / insegna la storia dell'umanità / / La storia americana è a tutti nota. / Cinquecent'anni e ben documentati. / La vecchia Europa a fondo è conosciuta: / intrighi, lotte, stragi e papati / e a saper queste cose aiuta / a diventare più saggi. / Perchè allora ognun sa poco o niente / della loro storia, dei propri parenti? / / Fino a mio nonno ho notizie chiare, / e di suo padre qualcosa l'ho inteso. / Del nonno di mio nonno poche e rare, / son le notizie e di dubbia qualità / Del nonno di costui, niente da fare, / niente si sa e così rimane nell'oscurità. / E sol si tratta di duecento anni, / ma è buio fitto come fosser mille anni. / / Mi fa gran rabbia se un po' ci pensiamo / sapere più storie di re e di regnanti, / che parenti non son, e li studiamo / fino a venti secoli distanti. / Mentre le nostre cose le ignoriamo. / Ah! quale gioia! Sarei trionfante / di ritornar a sette secoli fa e non in sogno / a rintracciare il decimo mio nonno! / / Com'era? Alto, basso, grasso, secco? / Era scherzoso, ed era in risse assai? / E nella società faceva spicco? / E di politica s'interessava mai? / Era patriota, era povero o ricco, / o era un Pasquale passaguai? / Comunque fosse, io ne sarei grato / conoscere di lui e d' altri il passato. / / Un libro ci vorrebbe per sfogliare. / Trovare pure ritratti e dati, / dei miei avi, e legger magari, / fatti di vita e scene già passate. / Certo che mi potrei divertire, / a dire alle mie figlie: "Qua, guardate! / Questa storia, o meraviglia, / è il fil diretto della nostra famiglia. / / Perderla non dobbiam e voglio che scrivete / appresso la mia la storia vostra. / Così ai figli passarla potete. / Farlo dovete perchè vi dimostra, / quando costumi e lingua mantenete, / che fate onor alla Sicilia nostra. / Terra d'amore e di canti d'uccelli, / conca di sole e di 'picciotti' belli. / / L'eredità è patrimonio, un bene, / a cui va data la giusta attenzione. / E specialmente qua più ci si tiene, / che siamo gente di varie nazioni. / Se ognuno serba da dove proviene, / usi, costumi, lingua e tradizioni, / aggiungierà a questa storia Americana / un'altra perla nella sua collana."
(Translated by Calogero Cascio)

If everyone retained the uses, customs,
traditions and the language whence he came,
it would add to America's own history
another pearl to grace her worthy necklace.

E ci sarannu sempri l'emigranti

L'emigranti partiu,
partiu pi chidda fami
chi nun s'astuta,
inchennusi la panza.
Sinn'iu assitatu
di vidiri giustizia,
ma no di na giustizia
ch'è fatta di la liggi.

Partiu cu rabbia 'ncori,
ntra l'occhi l'amarizza,
comu s'avissi
pi qualchidunu stizza,
na stizza e un odiu.
Ma contru cui e chi?
L'amici? La famigghia?
La terra sua?
E no! Chisti 'un si toccanu!
Chisti su' parti di la carni viva!

Ma allura st'odiu
di d'unn'è chi arriva?
Fu forsi la pulitica,
cu li puliticanti
chi quannu ch'ai bisognu
vasi li manu a tanti?
O forsi fu ddu mali
tirribili suciali,
chi fa suvirchiarii,
cuntrolla tuttu,
'nnomu di un idiali
e chi simina luttu?

Ma l'emigranti parti
e pi lu viaggiu sonna.
Viri la terra sua
chi unn'è chiù schiava

There Will Always Be Emigrants

The emigrant left his home,
driven by a hunger
that cannot be sated
by filling up his belly.
He left thirsting for justice,
but one that is not made
by laws written in books.

The emigrant left home
with bitterness in his eyes,
as though he were upset
with someone he knew not.
He felt anger and hatred.
Against whom? Against what?
His friends? His family?
His homeland?
Oh, no!
Those are untouchable,
they're part of him as his own flesh.

So then where did this anger
come from? Perhaps it came
from all the politics,
against politicians whose
hands you must kiss
when you're in dire need!
Or maybe it was rooted
in some social disease
that makes abuse of power,
and can control all things
in the name of an ideal
that can reap only death!

And so the emigrant leaves,
and in his journey dreams.
He sees his dear homeland
in slavery no more.

Nino Provenzano   1253

e pi li strati
senti genti cantari
mutivi assai diversi.

E sonna la campagna
sutta d'un celu friscu ed azzurrinu
e un suli d'oru.
Viri n'anticu arvulu d'alivu
e sutta ci su' genti
nivuri, bianchi,
arabi, ebrei, cristiani
e tanti autri.

Su' tutti addinucchiati
e cogghinu l'alivi
pi poi mettili tutti
dintra na granni cesta
senza funnu a forma di cori.
Su' tutti addinucchiati . . .

E ci saranno sempre gli emigranti—L'emigrante è partito, / partito per quella fame / che non si spegne, / riempiendosi la pancia. / Se n'è andato assetato / di vedere giustizia, / ma non per la giustizia / ch'è fatta dalla legge. / / Partì con la rabbia nel cuore, / con l'amarezza negli occhi / come se avesse stizza per qualcuno, / una stizza, un'odio. / Ma contro questo o quello? / Per gli amici? Per la famiglia? / Per la propria terra? / E no! Questi non si toccano! / Questi sono parti della carne viva! / / Ma allora quest'odio / dove ha origine? / Forse fu la politica / con i suoi politicanti / e le cui mani baci / costretto dal bisogno? / O forse fu quel male / terribile, sociale, / che fa soverchierie, / controlla tutto, / nel nome di un ideale / e che semina lutto? / / Ma l'emigrante parte / ed in viaggio sogna. / Vede la terra sua / non più schiava, / e per le strade / sente gente cantare / motivi assai diversi. / / E sogna la campagna / sotto un cielo fresco ed azzurrino, / e un sole d'oro. / Vede un antico albero d'ulivo / sotto il quale stanno varie genti: / neri, bianchi, / arabi, ebrei, cristiani / ed altri ancora. / / Sono tutti inginocchiati, / a raccogliere le olive / per metterle tutte / dentro una grande cesta / senza fondo, e a forma di cuore. / Sono tutti inginocchiati . . . (Translated by Calogero Cascio)

And in the streets he hears
his people singing songs,
with many different tunes.

He dreams of open fields
beneath a cool blue sky,
and a brilliant golden sun.
He sees an olive tree
under whose ancient branches
are gathered many people,
blacks, whites, and Arabs,
with Jews and Christians too,
and many more.

They are all kneeling down
gathering olives.
They're placing them inside
a large basket with no bottom
shaped like a human heart
They all are kneeling down . . .

↘ Luigi Fontanella (b. 1943)

Luigi Fontanella, born in Salerno in 1943, lives on Long Island, where he is professor of Italian language and literature at the State University of New York, Stony Brook. Poet, novelist, and literary critic, he has published more than twenty-five books. His most recent volumes are *Ceres* (1996), winner of the Orazio Caputo Prize; *From G. to G.: 101 Sonnets* (together with Giose Rimanelli, 1996); the novel *Hot Dog* (translated by Justin Vitiello, 1998); *The Transparent Life and Other Poems* (translated by Michael Palma, 2000); *Terra del Tempo e altri poemetti* (2001), winner of the Circe Sabaudia Prize, S. Andrea Prize, Minturnae Prize, and the S. Nicola Arcella Prize; *Angels of Youth* (translated by C. Lettieri and I. Marchegiani, 2001); *Azul* (2001); the books of criticism *Storia di Bontempelli* (1997), *La parola transfuga. Scrittori italiani in America* (2003); *I racconti di Murano di Italo Svevo* (2004); *Pasolini rilegge Pasolini* (2005); he also published an anthology of his poetic work with facing English translations, *Land of Time. Selected Poems: 1972–2003* (2006). Fontanella is the editor of the international literary journal *Gradiva*, and director of Gradiva Publications in Stony Brook, New York.

Fontanella presents unique poetological and writerly traits. He arrived in the United States after his Italian *laurea*, and he completed a doctorate at Harvard. His poetry is inhabited by a poetic persona among the most restless, dissatisfied, melancholy, even angry of this entire collection of Italian poets in the United States. Like a Dantean character, Fontanella lives the condition of uprootedness and loss as if it were a damnation, but unlike what happens to Dante the pilgrim, his constant search for meaning and grace does not lead up the terraces of purgatory toward immortality, or the native *domus*. Thematically, in fact, the journey is a dominant frame of reference in his texts, and for all the various embodiments he tries there seems to be no satisfying or appeasing reason for the impossibility of a return to his Ithaca. This significantly affects his style and the metaphors and symbols thereby generated. As a late modernist who is no longer attracted by the polyglot furnaces of the early twentieth century, his poetry tends toward a middle register that does not disdain spoken, journalistic, and diaristic tonalities, punctuated at strategic moments with highly literary references. When it comes to *what* the words and phrases refer to, the reader can easily perceive how he objectifies his "feelings and thoughts through a profuse multiplicity of details and impressions concerning the world of everyday reality"; in short, he seems to be working on "a kind of subtly camouflaged autobiography in verse and a search for personal identity."[42]

This tendency is clearly perceivable in his earlier books,[43] where the titles alone give away the struggle he is waging with a sense of unitary self not subject to the objective correlatives that define so much of our lives. And this may be the best way to approach a substantial body of work in which each book represents a stage, an observation point, even metaphorically—but not so much—a port from where to look again back to the provenance, and around to see where one has arrived. One of his books is titled, very emblematically, *Round Trip.* A study of the imagery and of the precise locations either described or alluded to, will yield an inventory of references to airports, stations, planes, trains, boats, and cars, and with that to anxieties about leaving, sleeplessness, returning, traveling, and feeling that life is transparent, aleatory, swishy, and elusive, if not altogether untouchable. A full critical study would therefore have to describe, map, and plot a network of topoi consisting of (1) incertitudes about the meaning and value of place where the poetic persona happens to be; (2) the recording of the detachment of a never-ending procession of passersby indifferent typically to the poetic persona; (3) the distinct sense of being incomplete, unfulfilled, untethered when it comes to belonging to any one place—city or nation—in the world; (4) the sad realization—registered in the text whenever the poetic persona realizes, upon reflection or simply by being reminded by a flash, a drop of water, a glance—that there is always another place *over there* (a spatial diffraction); or (5) that there was a different world *back then* (temporal dissonance); or, yet again, and most complex, (6) that there is both a potential and necessary life to be fulfilled *right here* as well as an existence to be revealed and lived *right now*; and, finally, (7) that there is no place one can call home even when one does actually return to the *domus* of ancestors, because a part of one's being has been lost during the previous trip, or else is left waiting for the poet at the place he is returning from. Quite a complex existential predicament.

Fontanella therefore is probably the one poet in this group who writes the most about traveling and, though himself not an immigrant in the traditional sense—a label he has objected to and rejected in the past, preferring that of exile or expatriate—he often evokes some of the personal and poetological dramas of the earlier generation of Italian emigrant poets in America.[44] Indeed, in his critical work he has only late in his career shown a particular interest in the poetry of the earlier Italian poets who have had to relocate to the United States. He also reminds us of the problematic of deterritorialization of the speaker/writer, that is, the condition of *spaesamento* of who is writing in the idiom of a major literature but is geoculturally removed from it. For Fontanella, one way of dealing with this condition is to Italianize his America, to dwell body and soul in whatever can be expressed in that native tongue while living in this here place, which is now his home independently of the nation-state called Italy and its juridical boundaries. One would have to go outside the critical grid I established in the introduction and come up with the notion-recently floated among some cultural critics—of a *glocal poetics*, which would allow us to account for the back-and-forth, zigzag movements of Fontanella's poetics, a poetological dynamics which, incidentally, may be perceivable as well in Valesio, Moroni, and Livorni. But that would risk ending up with an acritical, superficial generalization, for the notion of glocal simply restates that the individual is always pinned within some universal parameter of sorts, one grounded upon the alogical, abstract, polarity global *versus* local, or local *within* the inescapably global. This can be said of anyone and everyone, and downplays the manifold role of time, the irreversibility of history, and the subject's belonging to a given, and not just any, society. It would not do justice to the specificity of the poet's protean struggle with language (Italian) and location (the American Northeast). Searching for the elusive stable structure, in his more recent work Fontanella finds it in the least visible and tangible of elements: time. This allows him to voyage through a plenum within which he can account for his own existence, made up "of so many selves," without any abstracting logical or sociological preoccupation. But with *Terra dei tempi* (*The Land of Time*) he attains his most haunting creation, as he selects poems from his previous books in which the dominant topos is precisely time or, better, human temporality. All entries here come from his personal anthology. Even more profound is the struggle with transitoriness in *Bertgang. Fantasia Onirica* (2012), where history, dream, and mythological personae create a new register, yet ever more fully immersed in the grand Italian lyrical tradition.

We could then hypothesize that Fontanella's poetics extends, "stuck halfway in-between," as he writes in "Shop of Fools," along the axis B–D, that is, not drawn to carve a pure language or design a metapoetics, nor any longer tempted by the lure of immortality by actually preferring the elsewhere (the alien status in what would be a fictive paradise), he works rather in the dynamic endless spaces disclosed by the native *langue*, which allows him the freedom to face and address a world of objects, situations, and reflections, or even worlds made up of "transparences," and home, the *domus*, as the anywhere he happens to be, where he can confront his own mortality, continually.

La vita trasparente

da *Terra del tempo*

Apre la città le sue strade,
corrono biciclette senza persone,
alla finestra s'affaccia
e sparisce un volto di donna,
le vetrine offrono sessi
per ogni stagione,
giro di vite:
balla una coppia agile e magra
nella piazza deserta,
la corsa degli uomini,
agita chiome il bosco
in controluce,
passi su foglie
e solchi di fango duro,
viale d'autunno
carrozza regale
pioggia di rugiada
e di carta:
la vita trasparente.

The Transparent Life

from *Land of Time*

The city opens its streets,
bicycles go by riderless,
a woman's face in a window
appears then vanishes,
shop windows offer fetishes
for every season,
lives turning,
a slender agile couple dances
in the deserted piazza,
the race men run,
the hairy woods shivering
against the grain of light,
footsteps on leaves
a furrow of stiff mud,
avenue of autumn
royal coach
rain of dew
and paper—
the transparent life.

Il mercato dei pazzi

Non tanto il tempo
mutilato la generazione
arrivata prima
che pensa di trasmettere
gli stessi idoli.
Un falso mercato dove agli odori
antichi si sovrappone la presente
tristezza. Insopportabile.
E parla questa lingua
imbalsamata fuori dal vecchio e dal nuovo
rimasta a metà
come loro, monadi pietose.

(Little Italy)

Shop of Fools

Not so much the crippled
time the generation that
arrived before
thinking to pass on
its own idols.
A synthetic shop where amid
age-old smells the present sadness
overwhelms. Intolerable.
And it speaks this
embalmed language neither old nor new but stuck
halfway between
like them, these pitiful monads.

(Little Italy)

In viaggio

In viaggio tutto si disunisce e disgrega
il desiderio si tinge di bianco
e dilaga lentamente sul foglio
come una caldaluce pomeridiana.
Fuori
la velocità inebria gli oggetti
e conforta l'inerzia l'ebbrezza l'abbandono
a un sogno infinito.
Più che altro è questa
disperazione del niente la pietà
verso tanti se stessi
il terrore calmo di scoprire che forse non altro è
la vita

Traveling

While traveling everything is disrupted and dispersed
desire is dyed white
flooding slowly onto the page
like a warmlight afternoon.
Outside
speed intoxicates objects
and consoles inertia inebriation abandon
to its infinite dream.
More than anything else there is this
desperation of nothingness
compassion for so many selves
the calm terror of discovering that perhaps life is
nothing but this.

A Francesco Paolo Memmo (II)

Ciò che resta è questa oscurità
puntuale e immutata della notte
arma sospesa che vacilla
e si frantuma di fronte ai miei sogni
o fa palizzate ai ritornati desideri
alle amene illusioni
alle mie scombinate chimere: ecco,
pensare, ad esempio, alle cose
che avresti potuto intraprendere
oggi vent'anni fa.
Perché dunque mi parli di treni
perduti, amico mio?
Si perde davvero il treno?
Per quanto mi riguarda
ci sono sempre rimasto dentro, io.

For Francesco Paolo Memmo (II)

What remains is this punctual and immutable
darkness of the night,
suspended force that trembles
and shatters before my dreams
or fences off the resurgence of my desires
my comfortable illusions
my disorderly fantasies: So,
think, for example, of all the things
that you could have undertaken
today twenty years ago.
Why do you speak, then, my friend
of missed trains?
Does one really miss a train?
I for one
have always remained on board.

Terra del tempo

C'invase la stessa luce compatta
a tagli sui numerosi tornanti
fino alla scrigno finale: il nostro
paese del tempo arroccato lassù
in una sua forte e flebile demenza
"le stradine hanno ancora l'acciottolato antico"
e l'insegna sbilenca del Presepe
ancora un invito
sempre più irraggiungibile, irreale
irrelato. Poi un ennesimo vicolo
mai attraversato ma forse
da te già prefigurato. Anch'esso
ci avrebbe portato all'antico Castello
ne conoscevamo ormai ogni anfratto
o avello, ogni minaccia
di precipizio nello sprofondo.

Ma d'improvviso
sbucammo su una piazzola sguincia
a strapiombo sul mare
una ragazza seduta su una seggiola
accecata dal sole e dal vento
giocava silenziosamente a carte
di fronte a quell'azzurro immane, io
facevo fatica ad accettare una tale
disposizione naturale, tanto flagrante
da sembrarmi messinscena predisposta
angolo d'infanzia reinventata
e dunque non osai rivolgerle parola
temendo che quella visione
potesse di colpo svanire
forse le avrei chiesto soltanto
di condurci per mano
in quel suo regno d'acqua e di vento
in cambio degli occhi
che non ci sarebbero più serviti.

Land of Time

Pervaded by the same dense shafts of light
over the countless twists and turns
on our way to the final treasure chest: our
town of time fortified there on the hill
in a powerful and feeble madness
"the little streets still have their ancient cobblestones"
and the crooked Nativity sign
still reads as an invitation
though ever more unreal, unreachable,
unconnected. Then a passage you may have previously
envisioned before but never before traversed.
That path would have led to the Castle too
by now we knew every burrow
and lair, every threat of
plummeting into the chasm.

But suddenly
we came upon a small sloped piazza
with a sheer drop to the sea
a young girl blinded by sun and wind
was sitting on a chair
silently playing cards
before that enormous sweep of azure, while
I had difficulty in believing
such a natural pose, so deliberate
that it seemed to me a staged scene
a corner of childhood imagined anew
and so I didn't dare speak to her
fearing that the vision
might suddenly vanish
perhaps I only wanted to ask her
to take us by the hand and lead us
into her kingdom of waters and wind
in exchange for our eyes
that would serve us no more.

Infine il Castello scempiato
rimasto a metà dal vecchio frantumato
e dal nuovo incapace a rinascere
o riproporsi ad altro destino
un po' pateticamente
come quei disegni sui muri
chissà da quali mani dipinti
che vanno sfumando col tempo.
Siamo come questi murales, pensai,
che vanno sbiadendo un poco ogni anno.

Più tardi volli tornare sulla piazzola
ma la ragazza cieca mariposa era scomparsa
e con lei svanito tutto l'infantile armamentario.
Chiesi a un tale, che m'era stato indicato
come proprietario, se una casa sbrindellata
lì nei pressi fosse in vendita:
m'era messo in testa di comprarla
quella scassata bicocca.
Ci saremmo venuti periodicamente
a ricomporre qualche brandello
dei tanti noi stessi disseminati
in quella Terra del Tempo, lassù
dove il calendario
riporta sempre l'identico giorno
e ogni giorno è una pagina bianca
da riempire con le stesse parole.
Il nostro quaderno
è rimasto aperto su un tavolo
di fronte a una finestra a picco sul mare
su di esso batte impavido il sole
imbiancando ogni volta quella pagina
su cui ostinatamente noi ritorniamo
a scrivere lo stesso dettato:
O azzurra memoria che si consuma in se stessa!

Di ritorni dunque è fatta la vita
o agra ballatetta,
di false ripetizioni, vecchie e nuove,

Finally, the ruined Castle
suspended between the crumbling old
and the new, unable to resurrect itself
or claim a new destiny
how pathetic
like the images on its walls
painted by an unknown hand
fading with time.
We resemble those murals, I thought,
a little fainter year after year.

Later I wanted to return to the small piazza
but the blind girl the *mariposa* was gone
and with her had vanished all her whimsical accoutrements.
I asked a fellow, whom I was told was the owner,
if that shabby house nearby
was for sale:
I had gotten into my head the notion
of buying that rundown shack.
We would return there from time to time
to reassemble a few shards
of our many selves scattered
in that Land of Time, up there
where the calendar
always displays the same day
and every day is a blank page
to be filled with the same words.
Our notebook
remained there on the table
by a window overlooking the sea
where the intrepid sun beats down on it
blanching over and over again that page
to which we stubbornly return
to rewrite the same inscription:
O self-consuming azure memory!

Thus, life is composed of returns
O bitter little ballad
of false repetitions, new and old,

come nei piccoli passi, incerti e pur certi
della nostra bambina-staffetta
che di colpo vince ogni malattia del tempo
e va sicura incontro al vento
rifiutando la mano
di chi l' ha portata fino lassù.

like the small steps, unsteady yet sure,
of our child-messenger
who suddenly overcomes every malady of time
and strides confidently against the wind
rejecting the hand
of the one who led her there.

La città celeste

Per Pascal D'Angelo
e per tutti gli italiani emigrati in America

Questi luoghi sono stati i vostri cammini,
quelle lotte-speranze i nostri dolori,
diverso il mare visto dalla riva
da quello visto dentro un bastimento.

Questi luoghi sono stati i vostri mulini
a vento. Non fummo noi a fare quel viaggio:
fu lui a portarci lontano, quando in chi viaggia
lontano e vicino scompaiono.

Questi luoghi sono stati i nostri respiri,
l'estraneo ch'è in noi cancellò ogni sorte,
ogni Macondo. Il falso esilio di oggi
una coorte di sogni dentro e fuori il nostro mondo.

Questi luoghi sono stati i nostri mattini.
La città galleggiante non vi interessò
ma solo il cuore diviso fra l'appena passato
e un futuro presente solo nella mente.

Questi luoghi sono stati i nostri destini,
voi che seguiste il cammino del sole
ignari di ciò che vi avrebbe aspettato, a cominciare
dal nome irrimediabilmente storpiato.

Questi luoghi ci sono ormai dentro e vicini,
qui dove tutto e nulla avrebbe rimescolato
le carte del gioco e del bisogno, trasformato
in un coacervo l'inganno, la nostalgia, il sogno.

The Celestial City

For Pascal D'Angelo
and for all the Italian immigrants in America

These places have been your pathways,
those struggle-hopes our pains;
seen from the shore the ocean is different
than when seen from a boat.

These places have been your windmills.
We didn't go on that voyage:
It took us away, when for the traveler
the near and the far disappear.

These places have been our sighs,
the stranger in us cancelled every fate,
every Macondo. Today's false exile
is a cohort of dreams within and without our world.

These places have been our mornings.
The floating city did not interest you
but only the heart divided between the recent past
and a future present only in the mind.

These places have been our destinies,
you, who followed the path of the sun,
unaware of what was awaiting you, starting
with a name hopelessly mispronounced.

Today these places are inside us and near,
here where everything and nothing would mix
the cards of game and need, transformed
into a pile of deceit, nostalgia, dream.

Il ramo dell'albero

Il ramo dell'albero
è una mano verde che si tende
verso la finestra. Vorrei
allungare la mia e
intrecciati come due adolescenti
camminare insieme per la via.

The Branch of the Tree

The branch of the tree
is a green hand extended
toward the window. If only I could
outstretch mine,
like two adolescents
we'd walk together arm in arm
down the road.

→ Adeodato Piazza Nicolai (b. 1944)

Adeodato Piazza Nicolai was born in Vigo di Cadore, in the province of Belluno, Italy, in 1944, and emigrated to the United States, to the outskirts of Chicago, in 1959. He is a teacher, poet, critic, and translator. He has a bachelor of arts degree from Wabash College and a master of arts degree from the University of Chicago. He worked for thirty years as a steelworker at the Inland Steel Company, in Indiana, then retired in 1996. He now lives in Padua, Italy.

Nicolai has published poems, translations, and essays in various Italian and American reviews. He is the author of three collections of poetry, *La visita di Rebecca* (1979), *I due volti di Janus* (poems and translations, 1980), and *La doppia finzione* (1988). Glauco Cambon prefaced a selection of Nicolai's dialect poetry in the autumn 1987 issue of *Forum Italicum*. Nicolai translated the dialect poetry of nine poets from the Friuli Venezia Giulia (among them Pier Paolo Pasolini and Biagio Marin), which appeared in the anthology *Dialect Poetry of Northern and Central Italy* (2001), while some of his own poems written in Ladino were included in the trilingual poetry anthology *Via Terra: An Anthology of Contemporary Italian Dialect Poetry*, edited by Luigi Bonaffini. From Italian into English, he has translated poetry by Giulia Niccolai, Silvio Ramat, Emanuele di Pasquale, Luciano Troisio, and others, as well as individual books by Luigina Bigon, Cesare Ruffato, Marilla Battilana, and Mia Lecomte. He has also translated from the English into Italian poetry by Erica Jong, Gwendolyn Brooks, Nikki Giovanni, Rita Dove, Maya Angelou, and Alice Walker. A book of dialect poetry, *Diario ladin*, translated by the author into both Italian and English, came out in 2000 under the sponsorship of the Union Ladina del Cadore de Medo. In 2006 he published a study on the literature of the Dolomite region around Belluno. He recently edited and translated an anthology of African American women poets, *Nove poetesse afroamericane* (2012). His own forthcoming book of poems is titled *Apocalisse e altre stagioni*.

Adeodato Piazza Nicolai is one of the five true immigrants to the United States in this selection; he left Italy to find employment as a steel worker in Indiana in his youth, and it was only in his mature years that he turned to poetry. Not being affiliated with a scholastic or academic institution meant producing a poetry literally in the vats of the foundries, his words and lines being raw and direct and endowed with a Pasolinian expressiveness lacking in most of the other authors. "Iron City" conveys this in a most trenchant way. As Nicolai got older, he dedicated more and more time to poetry, trying different forms and registers. At a certain point, rooted as he was by then in America, he turned to English, though not for long. Finally, he had to dig deep into his origin and find the lifeline of his creativity, which resides in his native Ladino dialect of northeastern Italy, in the Veneto region.

The rediscovery of Ladino was facilitated by his return home after four decades away. Here our author had to deal with another problem, the Italian language itself, which was hardly the same one he had learned as a schoolboy before emigrating. Equally important, since his *nostos*, his most recent production is thematically concerned with the values and the sensibilities of the historically recent but psychologically deep past, which are constantly challenged, once again, by a postmodern Italy significantly different from the Italy of the 1950s and early 1960s. In this sense, his poetry bears a strong social consciousness component that reminds us that though this poet is firmly planted on the ground where he lives, he is also aware that the patch beneath his feet is never neutral territory. In fact, it is paradoxically strange. The fact that he chose to write in a regional dialect in a sense further alienated the poet from the native country, whose language is by now, regional inflections notwithstanding, more standardized and much more supple in accepting new koines, foremost Anglicisms and technobabble. Turning to dialect here would then mean, above and beyond any psychological motivation, not only a lateral, political move, but also a vertical, historical thrust into a realm where perhaps some coherence can be found, and a sense of identity recovered, or at the very least reconstituted. Thus Nicolai finds Ladino empowering, though a critical examination would reveal, at the level of the themes and fields of reference, that for the poet social reality is pointed toward an unpromising future, onto which he can foist, as a counterpoint, a clear nostalgia for times and values that modern Italy is ignoring or trampling upon. One might even go as far as to say that often Nicolai is angry at the total lack of concern, in his first but now actually *third* "home," for any ethical principles or social concerns among his peers. In those moments, his civic spirit transforms him into an engagé poet with a strong populist afflatus, the voice of an everyman who can point his finger at the endless procession of scandals, abuses, and idiocies that go on in our sophisticated cities and at all levels, but mostly in the social circles of the upper hierarchies.

In his early poems, Nicolai did speak about America, and marginally about his travels, especially in his very first book, but in the later poems, the Italy he had perhaps constructed for himself during his stay abroad is no longer what it was, or what he thought that it was, a long time ago. The self-erasure he experienced in Indiana is renewed when he is back in Padua. We can therefore say that he gravitates uneasily toward the poles B: Home/Mortality, and D: *Langue*/Reality, at the same time. Nicolai's experiments, understood as lived experiences, as living the language-being-territory complex—which he undertook in three languages in order to make sense of the world, and the intense and sustained efforts put into translating (itself an activity that requires a constant crossing over in order to attribute a meaning to the language/reality nexus in an elsewhere) indicate the recognition that home is a place you never can really return to: This emigrant is forever on the way to somewhere, including his own inner self, but a place from where he can nonetheless verbalize his perception of a decaying civilization.

Città di ferro

da *La doppia finzione*

1.

Mostri la carta d'ingresso,
è messicano la guardia stasera.
Passi il cancello, là dove certa
è la morte. Nell'auto la musica
tenta assordire, ma invano,
sia tonfi di schiacciaferri
che grida di ruote di locomotive.
Sicura la morte, tu viaggi
affiancato dai fari una strada
abissale—mancano i pioppi adornanti
quei viali che adombrano tombe.
I neo-soldati ancora ficcano
nei magiafuochi degli altiforni
rottami di diurne battaglie:
certa la morte

2.

Qualcosa di serio trafora l'aria.
Fredda, vulturna è stasera la luna.
I camionisti bisbigliano e girano
mentre l'Azteco, più persistente del mito,
quest'ora scherza con noi
quasi emersi sommersi da sterco notturno.
Sui prati d'asfalto nastri di ferro
pare sorridano ai numi; lungo i binari
lastre di ghisa su barche piatte
credono attendere ignaro scultore.
Statue-lingotti appena usciti dai forni
stanno ignorate a disvelare
magro rossore difforme, diffuso: vano
traforo e scade a bava, stasera, la luna.

City of Steel

from *The Double Fiction*

1.
Showing your work badge,
tonight the guard is Chicano.
You enter the gate, where death
is certain. In the car, music
attempts in vain to wipe out
the poundings of steel rolls,
the screeching of train wheels.
With sure death, you travel
a hellish road, escorted by spotlights
—no cypresses embellish the side
roads shadowing graveyards.
Neo-soldiers still ram inside
the fire-chewing blast furnace
steel scraps from our daily battles:
death is assured.

2.
Something serious pierces the air.
Cold, vulture-like the moon is tonight.
Truck drivers whisper and walk around
while the Aztec, stronger than the myth,
tonight jokes with us, almost
floating submerged in the dung of the night.
On fields of concrete steel coils seem
to laugh at the gods: Along the tracks
steel plates on flat railcars seem
to be waiting for some unknown sculptor.
Ingot-statues just out of the ovens
stand ignored as if to unveil their
pale redness unformed, diffused: A useless
drilling; tonight the moon is drooling.

3.

Puoi navigare, guidato da stella
più spesso raccolta
da fitte coltrine di nubi,
l'antica zattera? Tu, mezzaluna,
stai zitta misura dell'uomo *faber*
lanciato mangiato dalle vetture
lungo la strada che imbocca all'inferno
dov'è padre eterno il dolore,
ma il formicatore lo nega e lega
con certa fattura: lavoro è pane
per dimagrire la fame. Certo il sudore
poi nell'anticamera dell'altoforno
resiste un graffio insistente di grillo.

4.

Guardi la tua pienaluna
covata nel pozzo incrinato.
Sorride a labbra dell'uomo
che falcia con fauci d'industria
la terra sua vita: certo l'inferno
qui dove gufi lunari
stanno piccioni, superbi.
Se vieni, gabbiano,
sull'orlo d'un fosso
t'attende un nido
di becchi affamati—
covo irradiato da vampe votive
rigurgitate dai forni nel lago.
Deposita un pesce scavato dal brago.

5.

per Martin Luther King Jr.

Da mesi non parli, tu cara mia
piccola luna; ingolfa il budello
quel puzzo d'inferno, per noi dirottati
fra eterni rottami dove la musica
batte un martello sul cuore. A stento
strascinano, schiavi all'industria

3.

Can you navigate, guided by a star
more often than not buried
behind a thick curtain of clouds,
the ancient raft? Half-moon, you
are the mute measure of *homo faber*
propelled and eaten by automobiles
along the road leading to hell
where pain is God-the-Father,
but the ant-man denies it and wraps
it up in a receipt: Work is the bread
that staves off hunger. Sweat is forever
while in the chamber of the blast furnace
a cricket's scratching continues, resisting.

4.

You stare at your full moon
nested in the polluted pond.
She smiles with man's lips
that sever with industrial jaws
life-giving earth: Hell is certain
here where like lunar owls
stand arrogant pigeons.
If you land, seagull,
on the edge of the black hole
a nest is waiting for you
full of hungry beaks—
a cove lit up by votive flares
spewed from ovens into the lake.
Deposit a fish pulled out of hell.

5.

for Martin Luther King Jr.

For months you've said nothing, my dear
tiny moon; that hellish stench plugs
up the gut, for us who have been derailed
amidst timeless scrap where music
pounds on the heart like a hammer.
They can barely drag themselves along

che inghiotte la sera. Se l'ape
fa cera, da cenere l'uomo ma
Prometeo liberato sarà segno il sogno
e un popolo avrà la sua terra
dove la notte sarà cerchio rotto.

6.
Quasi gravida, tu scherzi in colma notte
questo maggio che commenta sul materno
con balocchi più balordi del Barocco,
piena luna. Dalla terra tutto il giorno
abbiamo colto folte erbacce credo in vano
dove un giallo spreca spesso il sempreverde.
Presso i vetri di cucina, nella siepe,
quattro becchi appena emersi stanno aperti
all'oltreazzurro dove un merlo ponga il vermo
nell'imbuto e poi ritorni a sorvolare.
Inattesa dal Cadore si fa voce la mia madre.

the slaves to industry that swallows the night.
If bees make wax, man arises from ashes but
freed Prometheus signals the dream and
a people shall inherit their corner of earth
where night becomes the broken ring.

6.
Nearly pregnant, you tease us at midnight
like Mayday commenting on motherhood
with baubles crazier than the Baroque,
you full moon. This whole day we picked up
lots of crabgrass from the garden but
in vain, where yellow wipes out the evergreens.
Near the kitchen window panes, in the bushes,
four beaks just emerged stand wide open
to the sky-blue where a blackbird will deposit
a worm in their trough then take off again.
From Cadore, unannounced, my mother calls.

Solitudine

Scovando per più di quaranta stagioni
mai stanco dell'ombra nascosta nel fosco
sonnecchi. Dal bosco
non spiazzi che pigne, non cogli che funghi,
non segni che larve di semi,
ma *Koiné* non cola: disfiorano poche memorie
lassù tra le crode e un gergo impietoso
serpeggia quaggiù: fosse ramo tra il muschio.
Il grumo s'affonda nel sottoletto
scavato da talpe, da nevi e radici
ma nulla riscatta, nessuno risponde—
soltanto sta un sole impiccato tra i rami.

Solitude

Digging for more than forty seasons
never tired by the shadow concealed in the mists
you doze off. From the woodlands
you shove only cones, find only mushrooms,
trace only the larvae of seedlings,
but Koiné won't come: memories blur
high on the rocks and a meaningless mumble
snakes down to the plain: were it a branch in the mosses.
The bundle sinks in the pine floor
furrowed by moles, by snows and by roots
but nothing resolves, nothing responds—
there's only the sun, dangling from the branches.

Sequenza dell'autocancellamento

La meridiana segna l'ora
nel suo tipico modo segreto.

Virginia Woolf, *Orlando*

1.0
al punto dell'autocancellamento
guardare né davanti
né indietro ma qui
dove il nulla fiorisce.
Svuota il tuo cervello,
non ricordare il salmone
che lotta per aria
e qualche appiglio che tiene
in questo momento:
semplicemente lasciati andare

1.1
"Il suicidio non porta dolore,"
così dice la canzone. È più
duro partire per luoghi
sconosciuti
con la certa probabilità
che ri ripeta
di nuovo, sempre di nuovo

1.2
La morte lenta dal fumo
e non nel mare,
così desidero andare avanti.
E non importa dove
mi aspetta la fine . . .
i denti dell'anima mia
che stridono con insistenza
vogliono farmi capire
com'è più facile
il cogitare del fare

Self-Erasing Sequence

> The meridian marks the hour
> in its usual cryptic way.
>
> Virginia Woolf, *Orlando*

1.0
At the point of self-erasure
look neither forward
nor backward but here
where nothingness blooms.
Empty out your brain,
do not recall the salmon
that grapples for air
and something to hang on to
for the time being;
simply let yourself go

1.1
"Suicide is painless"
said the song. It's
hard to leave for
lands unknown
when there's a clear chance
of having to do it again,
over and over again

1.2
Slow death by smoking
and not by water,
that is how I wish to move on.
Where I will end
does not matter . . .
the teeth on my soul
unendingly screech
trying to remind me
that it's easier to think
than to do

1.3

La stufa non fa per la mia testa.
Ho provato anche il tubo
con l'ossido di carbonio.
Per paura di mollare
aggrappati al domani
che si fa piombo.
Non c'è premura
di regredire nell'utero
a forma di stanza
che sembra fatto per te

1.4

La furia nel cervello si fa più selvaggia
dei giri del nostro pianeta—
Ho tentato il ritorno al tuo focolare
purtroppo i mattoni non c'erano più;
a vele spiegate
ho nuotato controcorrente
là dove il fiume era già morto.
Sapere, ecco ciò che conta:
e allora sia fatta non la Tua
volontà ma solo la mia
di essere perpetuamente
disfatto e rifatto . . .

1.5

Non conoscendo
come andare,
dovrei forse
rimandare.

1.3
My head in the oven won't do.
I've tried the hose blowing
carbon monoxide.
Afraid of letting go,
hang on to a tomorrow
that turns into lead.
There is no hurry
to reenter the womb
shaped like a room
made especially for you

1.4
The roar in my head grows wilder
than all the rotations of earth—
I tried to get back to your hearth
but the bricks were all gone;
I swam upstream
unfurling the sails there
where the river was dead.
Knowledge, that's what counts
So then let not Your will be done
but only my own
to be endlessly
undone and redone . . .

1.5
Not knowing
how to go,
perhaps I should
refrain.

Ancora una volta

Ancora una volta guidami, madre.
Non so più salpare: adesso è gobba
la luna, un mare liscio s'increspa
a burrasca, la luce rosicchia le cime
dei pini, stornelli zitti sullo steccato.
Ancora una volta s'aggruma la nebbia
dove il mio sangue ribolle, impietrisce.
Perché m'hai svelato il sentiero adesso
privo di ponti gettati dalle tue mani?
Domani riprendo la strada da te sigillata
nel parto: temo e desidero un varco,
una sosta, la pura mattina ma non c'è
scampo. Palpeggio le mura del labirinto
convinto di non riscattare l'uscita
così la giostra sta ferma, non sa ripartire.
Insegnami, madre, di nuovo a morire . . .

Once Again

Guide me once again, mother.
I've forgotten how to sail: The moon
is hunchbacked, the smooth sea
gets ready to storm, light nibbles at
the tips of the pines, mute crows on the fence.
Once again the fog is curdling
while my blood boils, turns to stone.
Why did you show me the path that is
now devoid of the bridges your hands had laid?
Tomorrow I walk again the road sealed
by your parturition: I fear and wish for a gap,
a short pause, a perfect morning yet there's
no way out. I palpate the labyrinth's walls
knowing there will be no exit, and so the
merry-go-round stands still, won't start up.
Teach me, mother, again how to die . . .

De primavera

Adés l'erba crese, i dí se slarga,
n saor stranbo me bianda la lenga
ma no l capiso. Sentòu su na bancia
scolto n cucù scónto tra i rame:
la soa lamentéla quasi me tocia
anche se l cianta na storia diversa
dai miei sentimenti che se remena.
Me sento strano. L viado ch'ei fato
scominthia de nuou. Tornòu a ciasa
me sento storto come n careto
sentha na ruoda. Tanto é canbiou
da cuanche ero bocia. Puoche sea
vare, semena cianpe, porta le torse,
parcura le vacie e neanche i vecie.
I fior salvarghe me brusa i ocie,
authiei contente me fa crepà l cuor.

Adesso cresce l'erba, i giorni si allargano, / un sapore strano mi bagna la lingua / ma non capisco. Seduto sulla panchina / ascolto un cuculo nascosto tra i rami: / il suo lamento quasi mi tocca / anche se lui canta una storia diversa / dai miei sentimenti che si smuovono. / Mi sento strano. Il viaggio che ho fatto / incomincia di nuovo. Ritornato a casa / mi sento sbilenco come un carro / senza una ruota. Tanto è cambiato / da quando ero ragazzo. Pochi segano / i prati, seminano i campi, portano il fieno, / accudiscono le mucche e nemmeno i vecchi. / I fiori selvatici mi bruciano gli occhi, / uccelli felici mi fanno scoppiare il cuore.

Of Springtime

Now the grass grows, the days expand,
a strange taste whets my tongue
but I don't understand. Still on a bench
I listen to a cuckoo hidden in the branches:
his lament nearly touches me
although he sings a different story
from the feelings that rumble within me.
I feel strange. The journey I finished
begins again. Returned back home
I stand crooked like a cart
without a wheel. Much has changed
from when I was young. Few cut
the fields, seed cornfields, gather hay,
raise cattle or take care of old folks.
Wild flowers burn my eyes,
happy birds shatter my heart.

Gioco frisbico

Perdonami Giulia, non ho saputo resistere
la tentazione di questo gioco frisbico.
La copertina del tuo volume *La misura
del respiro* mi ha preso-mesmerizzato—
Nella cassa del giogo, nella
mis-u(su)ra del res-piro. *Todo*
son mato *ten*+denti a frisbarsi,
(D)is tratti di as + p + etti, dist-r-atti
i pro pri stru-menti (dementi) . . .
Ora saprai misurare la follia di questa
mia mente polifonica, la pazzia del pluri
linguismo . . . e pensare che già Polifemo
aveva visto il tutto con solo un occhio . . .

Frisbee Game

Giulia, forgive me, I could not resist
the temptation to play this frisbic game.
The cover page of your book *The Measure
of Breathing* grabbed / mesmerized me—
by the strangling of the thorax, in the
mis-us-age of res-piration. When all is *sum
mat*ed up our ten-dance to frisbeesation,
(D)is tracted by as + pects, dis-rupt-eenth our
(demential) in-strumindations . . .
Now you can measure the craziness of my
polyphonous mind, the madness of my
plurilinguism . . . and to think our own Poly
phemus might have seen it all with one eye . . .

⇻ Irene Marchegiani

Irene Marchegiani, born in Pescara and raised in Florence, professor emerita of Italian language and literature at California State University, Long Beach, is currently the coordinator of student teaching in the Department of European Languages, Literatures, and Cultures at the State University of New York, Stony Brook. In collaboration with Charles Jernigan, she has translated Torquato Tasso's *Aminta* (2000), which was awarded the prestigious "Diego Valeri" Monselice Prize in 2002. With Carol Lettieri, she has translated other volumes of poetry, including *The Star of Free Will* by Maria Luisa Spaziani, *Angels of Youth* by Luigi Fontanella, and *Promises of Love* by Plinio Perilli. She is coauthor of the literary reader *Incontri attuali* and the Italian textbooks *Crescendo* and *Percorsi*. Marchegiani has written articles on Giacomo Leopardi and on contemporary Italian literature, with a particular emphasis on women writers. She edited the volume of poetry *Land of Time* (2006) by Luigi Fontanella, and edited *The Poetics of Place: Florence Imagined* (2001). She has published her poems in various poetry journals, in Italy and in the United States, and in 2004 she published *La vita in cerchio*, her first collection of poetry. She is member of the editorial boards of the literary journals *Gradiva* and *Journal of Italian Translation*.

Irene Marchegiani's poetry speaks about self and Self, about love and loss in a continuous exhortation not to lose sight of the immanent belonging of human beings to a world of emotions, of sensations, or to feel and recognize emanations from the things and places seen and deeply internalized. Nature, the world itself, speak to this poet directly, through her skin, and her texts are consequently tight and direct, with light echoes of the great lyrical tradition. A poetry that aspires to be Poetry turns concentric, recasting "the worn words" to give them a new vibrancy on the basis of the poet's unrepeatable experiences, highlighting her being a woman, facing the challenge of saying what can only come out in a bittersweet song, as she writes in a poem not included in this selection: "To find / so I may say I love you / two signs sculpted / on the stones of history / eternal hieroglyphics painted in the marble / ... / The universe becomes a point / and then hides in my heart." This poetry is a poetry of desire, reflecting "a solar temperament," as Maria Luisa Spaziani once observed, which tempts and exorcises, which dances and animates, which in short is about Life. A celebration of life is the reverse of locus B: Home/Mortality, and the emphasis extends to pole D: *Langue*/Reality.

La vita in cerchio

da *La vita in cerchio*

Mi porto dentro
cumuli di strade
rattrappite al sole aggrovigliate
d'una città consunta
perse e poi passate
piazze imbrunite e un po' disfatte
giardini d'inverno
confinati di muri e di respiri

Arrivammo un giorno
su questa terra
dilatata
ancora senza nome
si fa piccola ora e si restringe

Vi trovammo un sorriso
e l'abbraccio celeste d'un cielo
ci volavano in cuore
farfalle racchiuse
ali leggere della libertà

Noi vagabondi
d'illusioni
per sempre corriamo
sul bordo d'una vita
a cerchio contratta
Ma perso è il canto e il segno dell'inizio

Life in a Circle

from *Life in a Circle*

I carry within
the heaps of streets
of a worn-out city
numbed by the sun and entangled
streets lost and gone
darkened piazzas a little undone
winter gardens
bounded by walls and breaths

One day we arrived
on this expanded
land
still unnamed
now it's getting smaller as it contracts

Here we found a smile
and the celestial embrace of the sky
in our hearts there flew
butterflies in their folds
the light wings of freedom

Vagabonds of illusion
forever we run
on the edge of a life
contracted in a circle
But lost are the song
and the sign of the beginning

Nuova mitologia

Cosmo: parola d'ordine
li mise fuori
fratello e sorella
la Notte e il Vuoto
l'istinto mistico di Eros
l'amore orgia che porta al sapere
guardia nazista del Tempo doloroso
che ancora non era
misurato
a pause di pace e di delitti

Il Vento e la Notte separò
decisione d'àrbitro dittatura
d'arbítrio crudele conquista
—chirurgia per i poveri penosa—
e sprofondava intanto
Erebo del pensiero, Logos
sedotto e abbandonato
baratro dell'Ade
isolato immenso vuoto
oblio d'amore e creazione
Restò questo niente, in nome della storia

Funamboli del cielo perplessi e stupiti
solo un momento
d'equilibrio e certezza
una pausa
tutti—si passeggia e si sosta
su questa corda tesa male e malintesa
fra due spicchi di luna
sul Cosmo sospesa

New Mythology

Cosmos: A watchword
expelled them
brother and sister
Night and Void
the mystic instinct of Eros
the love-orgy that brings to knowledge
the Nazi guard of a sorrowful Time
not yet measured
by intervals
of peace and crimes

It separated Wind and Night
an arbiter's decision
an arbitrary dictatorship
a cruel conquest
—a painful surgery for the poor—
while thought in Erebus
collapsed,
a seduced and abandoned Logos
chasm of Hades
isolated boundless void
oblivion of love and creation
This nothingness remained, in the name of history

Puzzled and astonished tightrope walkers in the sky
only a moment
of balance and certainty
a pause
all of us—we stroll and we stop
on this poorly fastened rope poorly understood
between two crescents of the moon
suspended over the Cosmos

Oggi ti narro un racconto

Oggi ti narro un racconto,
amico fragile e tenero:
pensavo la vita come fosse
un largo passaggio
da un sogno ad un altro

credevo amore
—stupefatto e magnifico—
era nato dal respiro lieve d'una dea
sui tuoi occhi cullati dal cielo

Ma stasera lo sento
anche il niente è cessato
e solo la terra rinasce umida
di sangue e di sterile seme impastata

ed io finisco
quando ancora non conosco
né tregua o misura.

Se non vuoi toccare almeno un miraggio
o il coraggio ti manca di aggrapparti alla luce
allora a noi solo resta in eterno
un tempo smisurato di morte

Today I Am Going to Tell You a Story

Today I am going to tell you a story,
my fragile and tender friend:
I thought life was like
a large passageway
from one dream to another

I believed love
—astonished and magnificent—
was born from the gentle breath of a goddess
over your eyes lulled by the sky

But tonight I feel it
even nothingness has ceased
and only the earth is reborn moistened
with blood and kneaded with sterile semen

and I come to an end
without having known
either respite or limitation.

If you won't touch at least a mirage
or you lack the courage to cling to light
then all we have left forever
is an endless time of death

→ Peter Carravetta (b. 1951)

Peter Carravetta is Alfonse M. D'Amato Professor of Italian and Italian American Studies in the Department of European Languages, Literatures, and Cultures at Stony Brook University, New York. He was born in Calabria and migrated to the United States at age twelve. He has BA and MA degrees from City College/CUNY, and a PhD from New York University. Founding editor of *Differentia, review of italian thought* (1986–1999), he has published five books of criticism, including *Prefaces to the Diaphora: Rhetorics, Allegory and the Interpretation of Postmodernity* (1991), *Del Postmoderno. Critica e cultura in America all'alba del duemila* (2009), and *The Elusive Hermes: Method, Discourse, Interpreting* (2012), and coedited *Postmoderno e letteratura* (1984) and *Poeti italiani d'America* (1993). He has translated into English Martino Oberto's avant-garde opus *Anaphilosophia* (1993; bilingual edition). Carravetta is also the author of seven books of poetry, including *percorso masticato* (1974), *delle voci* (1980), and *The Sun and Other Things* (1997). A selection of his Italian poetry is now available in *L'infinito (poesie scelte 1972–2012)* (2012).

It is necessary here to switch to the first person. I came to the United States, to the Bronx to be exact, in the early 1960s, bringing with me the memory of some classic poems from the Italian canon—some *terzine* from Dante, and bits and pieces of Leopardi, Manzoni, Carducci, Pascoli, and D'Annunzio—and, as I stated elsewhere,[45] echoes of the "peggiore ottocento," which they fed grammar school children in those days. The fact is I began my career as a poet in the English language, at City College of the City University of New York, and rediscovered Italian years later when I went to study at the University of Bologna, in 1973–74. There I witnessed firsthand the waning fires of the last true neo-avant-gardes, the *Novissimi* and the *Gruppo 63*. My first book of poems, *percorso masticato* (1974), literally a "chewed" or even "ruminated" journey, takes its title from a verse by Edoardo Sanguineti, and intends to show a poet's birth and growth, with poems about youth written in everything from rhymed quatrains to open-form texts about what I saw in the, to me, "new country" (I was born in the deep South, near Cosenza), to incoherences about political ideologies, and mostly about the meaning of existence. As I was absorbing the variety of styles and the revolutions in poetics—which in some unsettling way reminded me of similar developments in American poetry I was already acquainted with, from Pound and Eliot through Williams, Olson, O'Hara, and Ginsberg—I made efforts to avoid the weight of the tradition which, however, I was simultaneously studying. Thus some poems were written in a conversational, occasionally mock-ironic, style—as in the poem "Lettera a Betteloni," included in this selection—which allowed me to focus on *what* the language referred to, as for instance the abysmal distance between modern Northern Italian urban life and my little pre–Industrial Age native town, which started receding from my artistic concerns. And I also had a first opportunity to see my adopted home, America, from the outside. Upon my return to New York, I wrote two books in English, *Existenz*, and the first draft of what much later became *The Sun and Other Things*. But in 1978 I went back to Italy to finish my doctorate and lived in Milan for three years. I thus resumed writing in Italian. In *delle voci* (1980) I resolved to create a persona, Humanus, to inscribe a background choral investigation into all sorts of limits and possibilities, creating and giving space at the same time to several voices, literally, and therefore different styles, collected in the book in several suites of four poems each. In this work one finds (I can say this without qualms, three decades later) a tormented weave through the destruction of syntax and the destruction and recomposition of words, polyglottism and dialect, existential yearnings and ontological, depersonalized, antilyrical experiments. After each suite, the quasi-epic song of Humanus reemerges, printed in italics to set it off as the overarching or underlying Voice, now plural—title means "some voices" and "of the voices"—seeking to give body and consistency to the searching persona.

I then continued for a while on the path to what I would call ontological poetry, poetry wherein the language speaks Being, or some form of transcendental illumination. For example, in *dialogy v*,[46] I attempted a dialogical modality where forms and ideas took center stage. Here the language was flush with echoes, rhythms, and lexemes from all corners of the inexhaustible canon of Italian literature. This vein continued until and through the first part of *metessi* (*1980–1989*), but by the late 1980s, now working regularly and living in New York, my adopted and by-now true home, I also underwent a third poetological metamorphosis. I thus began to work with the language as it was available, the conversational register, and cultivated a dialogical, even epistolary form, questioning the social reality of our times (whether American or Italian making no difference), questing still for a sense of the universe amid countless epiphanies and ever surprising, when not shocking, human endeavors. Perhaps that is why I titled the personal selection of my Italian adventure *L'infinito*, literally *Infinity*.

Trying to be consistent with the critical model I devised in order to situate the poetics of the Italian diaspora contained in this anthology, I would say I went from Apex D: *Langue*/Reality as I was mastering the language/culture of Italy, to Apex C: Poetry/*Langage*, or poetry itself before reality, back to Apex D: *Langue*/Reality. I believe I kept the vertical axis A–B, the relationship between Elsewhere/Immortality and Home/Mortality, as a constant watermark, addressed by and large indirectly. I wrote only a few poems about being two or more people in one, with two languages, two traditions, and so on, and always through a quasi-mythological persona, Humanus or Helios. I know that, to the degree that it is humanly possible, I have consciously tried to keep the two worlds separate and distinct, otherwise I would not have been able to write in the two languages (I don't know how my fellow bilingual and multilingual poets have handled this particular plight of their artistic lives, surely an intriguing topic to investigate). But for this anthology, which gathers Italian writing by people who do not ordinarily live in the country called Italy, or who have lived the greater part of their adult lives outside the country in which they were born and partly educated (though the age at which the poets came to the United States is a key factor to consider in any more sustained analysis), I have chosen a few poems which do in fact speak of place, of being in melancholy worlds real or recalled, maybe of being (or having been made to feel) an American in Italy and an Italian in America, always "out of place," so to speak, a widely reported affliction in these postmodern times and certainly a feeling all emigrants, expatriates, exiles, refugees, and nomads of all stripes know all too well. Whether as a poet I have succeeded, however, and what meaningful symbols or messages are embedded into my production, is not my place to say. The English versions are of course my own.

Lettera a Betteloni

da *L'infinito (poesie scelte 1972–2012)*

caro collega:
ti comunico che, fortunatamente,
l'idea di volere la poesia (indi: tutto)
semplice, senza orpello, nuda—
è andata dispersa o dissipata
nella polvere di qualche biblioteca.
mi dispiace davvero, ma pensa—
ora che ci puoi vedere davvero come
siamo—che se non ci fossero
i cosmetici, e l'etichette, e la pompa,
e le assurde tradizioni, ognuno,
ti pare? vedrebbe l'altro—
e per intero!!!

assunto—fatto irrazionale—
su cui si vive: l'atomo, con una nuvola di
elettroni e nucleo al centro,
è più vuoto che materia.
sicurezza: la materia è compatta—
scoprire o capire ch'essa è
piena di vuoto può dare le vertigini
(scusa per l'inciso).

poi, se capitassero davanti
a uno specchio, o sull'argine
di uno stagno calmo, vedrebbero
se stessi—capisci?—
e non vorresti mica che il suicidio
di massa anticipi la schizofrenia o
la bomba H a distruggerci, no?
—saluti a tutti—

(Bologna, 1974)

Letter to Betteloni

from *Infinity (Selected Poems 1972–2012)*

Dear Colleague:
I writing to inform you that, luckily,
The idea of wanting poetry (therefore everything)
Simple, bare, with no frills—
Has been lost or wasting in
The dust of some library.
I'm really sorry about that, but think—
Now that you can see us for what we really
Are—that if there were no such things
As cosmetics and etiquette and pomp,
And all absurd traditions, everyone,
You know, could actually see everyone else—
And fully!!!

Assumption—an irrational fact—
About life: The atom, with a cloud of
Electrons and nucleus at the center
Is more emptiness than matter.
Reassurance: Matter is compact—
To discover or understand that it is
Full of void can give vertigo
(Pardon the digression).

Then, if they chance in front
Of a mirror, or on the edge
Of a calm pool, they would see
Themselves—get it?—
And you wouldn't in the least wish that
Mass suicide anticipate schizophrenia
Or the H-bomb in destroying us, would you?
—Regards to everyone—

(Bologna, 1974)

Vissuto

mi significa su i quadranti un
quarto di secolo o meglio d'ora ma pensa
      è già di troppo è gratuito come
      scartabbellare il barbanera l'atlas
ma sono testi come piroglifici fu detto
cercane la logica e impazzisci cerca e cerca
sono teste palabras munte rifratte et citera
      mettiamocela dunque tutta
      tutta bisogna mettercela
la storia madre sarà di qualsia
notula credessere il padre dunque
adameva prole moltiplicante
      tutti vogliono divenire or
      bene divenire noi vogliamo
e in tutta coscienza perché non sfon
dare le tesmoforie del pensiero
perché chiedere e non suvviarsi
ad espungere il morbo e l'orbo e
l'arcano trapezio della canoscenza
dell'ultima farsa quasi foss'un
      rinascere continuatamente
ripensa a te stesso nel mondo
ripensare lo stesso nel mondo

(Chicago, 1976)

Real Life

the quadrants mark me out as being
a quarter of a century or maybe hour old yet
      it's already too much it's gratuitous
like skimming an atlas an almanac
but these texts are cut by fire it was said
look for their logic and you go crazy search and research
they are heads palabras milked fragmented and what not
      let's then give it all we got
      everything we got we got to use
history mother will be of anywhich
notation believe-being the father therefore
adameve offsprings multiplying
      everyone wants to become so
      well becoming we do want
and in all fairness why not break
through the feasting laws of thought
why ask and not undertake to
expunge the diseased and the bereft
and the arcane geometry of knowledge
of the ultimate farce as if it were an
      endless recreation
think again of yourself in the world
think again what's the same in the world

Adolescenza

il sole qui non brilla ma squaglia fonde
tale volte la neve lo spirito l'alluce
brutali stagioni eccessi norma
recessi / decessi / fughe / menzogne e
nelle mani la spada la moneta nelle mani
sorriso per angeli tristi frecce dei graffiti
trappole grappoli d'umano

mi sono fermato / formato / tra queste sfingi
tecnoillogiche perfettamente luride e ricovo
nel curiosare peccaminoso dell'adolescenza
inzuppandomi di scostumi e di mitemi e di
questo viscidume sterminato rio

strabicano qui le bolge
il volto diaccio al vetro ai tarli ai tanfi
all'argenteo fiato della lumacaglia
ai poderosi vagiti del leviatano
all'ossessione transustanziante
della propria scheda
del proprio anonimato
            o dio caso e causa
o tuniche del veltro
o squami del drago e
di bisanzio di corinto
e dei sassoni la corteccia

questa macchia cicatrice del secolo
questo squarcio nel peritoneo della collettività
questo buco nero della modernità
questo grigiore dell'umano cosmo
questo truce silenzio dell'animo vagante

spurgatorio seducente
dove topi parodiano le etnie
ed affamati scannano sofisti
e pitagorici ed eroi televisivi
e rodono i cavi comunicanti nelle macerie

Adolescence

the sun hereabout is hardly shimmering
yet often it melts even smelts the snow the spirit your toes
brutal seasons extremes are the norm
hideaways / deaths / escapes / lies and
in your hands the sword money in your hands
smiles only for sad angels graffiti arrows
booby traps clumps of humanity

I have lived / known these technoillogic
perfectly lurid sphinxes and hideouts
for the sinful experiments of adolescence
soaking myself in mythologies the uncouth
and this endless exterminating slime

here the moats squint and congeal your face
before scarred glass and pangs and stench
about the musty breath of the muculent
over the whimpering vibes
        from the mercurial siege
        of the leviathan
        of one's file and number
        and benumbing anonymity
oh chance the god the cause
of the tunics of the greyhound
the scales of the dragon
the ground remains of Corinth
and Byzantium and the Saxons

this stain and scar of the century
this gash in the peritoneum of society
this black hole of modernity
this grey lucor of the human cosmos
this sordid silence of the vagrant spirit

seductive purgatorial run-off
where the rats parody the ethnos
and ravenously butcher sophists and
pythagoreans and television heroes

Peter Carravetta   1321

e corrodono stagionate e stagionali ideelogiche
e non distinguono fra rogna a carogna
e stridono ciecamente nel pavido tepore imperante
stridono annaspano e grattano l'anima
nel Bronx
gli uomini-topo

(The Bronx, 1970–75)

and chew on the cables linking the heaps of rubble
and corrode the seasonal and seasoned idealogies
and distinguish not between scabies and carcass
and shriek blindly in the sullying ebbs of pavid drafts
they shriek and gasp and scrape the soul
in the Bronx,
the rat-people

(The Bronx, 1970–75)

Ad perpetuam rei memoriam

per Romilio Iusi

> Tu sì de lluocu ed io de ccà te viu,
> Sona chitarra mia, sona chitarra!

Ciardullo

de chiru chi pariti
è mìeglju'nne parramu:
amu fattu due vie
due vite dui munni—
ce sunu cose cùn ze dìcianu e
ù'nne capiscìssimu de neente

arrassusìa sapìssiti chiri ccaju fattu
se mèriche mèriche:
me vrusciàssiti!

e me cummene cumu aju fattu
ogni bota chi minne viegnu:
rirìre cuzzettijare e ppue
a'bbe dire chire cosicedde strane
chi ce pigliati gustu quannu vè'ccuntu

cumu s'ùn ce fùossi intrae de vue:
mmienzu na neglia pàrica me viju:
a'dduve guardu guardu
si cuozzi eìrtu o si vadduni ppennìnu
a'ri spuntuni dduve se jocava:
è sulu nu ricùordu, daveru,
me pare moni cchiù cumu nu suonnu

e'ppue me diciti: pecchì 'un ce stai,
ricògliate, chissa e'ra casa tua
ca ccàni mo' se stà de patreternu!

ma ca ce signu e me sientu ccu'bue
ca n'àverramu 'e dire facimu 'ncuna cosa insieme:
jamu a trovare a chiru parente o puru

To the Eternal Memory of Things

for Romilio Iusi

> You are from there and I from here can see you,
> Play on my guitar, play on!

> Ciardullo

of what you seem to me
it is better not to say:
We have traveled two roads
two lives two worlds—
there are things none's supposed to tell
and we wouldn't understand one another at all

heaven forbid you'd learn of things I've done
roaming through that there America:
surely you'd lynch me!

so it behooves me to do
what I've always done at each of my returns:
nod and smile and then
tell you those weird little facts
that you so much desire for me to tell

I feel as if I weren't among you
I feel as if I were treading in a fog:
Wherever I rest my eye
up the ragged peaks or down by the ravine
or by the alley corners where we used to play:
It is only a memory, really,
more and more it feels it's been a dream

then you say to me: Why don't you stay,
come back to this your home
life is like heaven around here!

but that I am back and fall in with the bunch
that we should say let's do this or that
go visit that old relative or maybe

jocàmu a'ru paddune o conzàmu chiru carru
mangiamu sutta a' cerza fissijamu u'prìevite . . .

sapiti ca minne vaju fra nu pare e' juorni
sapiti c'un ce staju cchiù de casa:
'n cuntu!

ed è accussì chi me tocca de campà':
cumu nu strambu chi vena e sinne vani:
na vota chi tinne'sì ghjutu
—ca si fujutu o ti'nnaru mannatu—
nun pue dire cchjùni a'duv'è chi t'appartene . . .

e'ppue in verità capisci pecchìdi
tinne vai notte e jùornu si pizzi pizzi
se dìcia cumu nu remita
nu pazzu o nu spirdu

(Lappano, 1975)

Alla perenne memoria delle cose—Di quello che mi sembrate / è meglio non parlarne: / abbiamo fatto due strade / due vite due mondi: / ci sono delle cose che non vanno dette e / del resto non ci capiremmo affatto // non sia mai sapeste di quante ne ho combinate / su e giù per l'America: / mi gettereste al rogo! // e mi conviene fare come ho fatto / ogni volta che ritorno: / ridere annuire e poi / a dirvi di fatterelli strani / che tanto vi divertono a sentirli // ma è come se non ci fossi tra voi: / mi sembra di vagare in una nebbia: / ovunque io posi lo sguardo / su per questi picchi o giù lungo i valloni / agli angoli dove si giocava: / è solo un ricordo, veramente, / mi sembra adesso più come un sogno // e poi mi dite: ma perché non rimani, / ritòrnatene, è questa casa tua / e qui si sta ormai da dio! // ma che ci sono e mi sento come uno di voi, / che dovremmo dirci facciamo delle cose insieme: / andiamo a trovare quel parente o anche / giochiamo al pallone aggiustiamo quell carro / mangiamo sotto la quercia sfottiamo il prete . . . // sapete bene che tra qualche giorno me ne devo andare // sapete che non vivo più qui: / non c'entro! // ed è così che devo campare: / una volta che te ne sei andato / —che sei scappato o ti hanno cacciato fuori— / non puoi più dire dov'è che appartieni . . . // e poi invero capisci perché / te ne vai notti e giorni da luogo in luogo / si dice come un eremita / un pazzo un fantasma.

play soccer fix that there old cart
eat under the oak tree pick on the priest ...

you know I have to leave in a few days
you know I don't live here anymore:
I don't matter

and so this is how now I have to live:
like a stranger coming and knowing he has to leave:
once you are gone away
—whether you fled or were forced out—
you can no longer say where you belong:

and then in truth you grasp the reason why
night and day you go from place to place
people have called you a hermit
a lunatic a ghost

(Lappano, 1975)

sentinella

Quali voci per le vie
a quest'ora? E' l'ottobre
dei carbonai, la nebbia
E' l'ora di lasciare
la lampada e guardare
Senza rimpianto il sonno.

Franco Fortini

quali voci per le vie
alle tre? è marzo
e s'avventano giovinastri
nello spazio senza ombre

notte delle voci vissute
in te coabito
e lo spot le matite gli scaffali
fedeli compagni mi sono
non come il sonno
un limbo altro che ci contiene

si riporta la mente piano piano
ai rapaci verbi e i corvini sostantivi
e poi silenzi strozzati di
questo vastissimo pianeta ideologico
che da secoli sconsacra
le catabasi le sonde uranie
le irritabili coscienze
con scabrosi desideri
con storpiate piante
con lupigno orgoglio
e implausibili complotti rimbalzanti sotto i portici
alle tre del mattino nella città medioevale

Sentry

Whose voices do I hear in the streets
at this hour? It's the October
of the coal workers, of the fog
It's time to turn away
from the lamp and look
with no regrets to sleep

Franco Fortini

Whose voices are these I hear in the streets
at three in the morning?
it is March and raucous youth wade
into shadowless spaces

night of living lived voices
in you I dwell
with pencils bookcases clip-on light as
my loyal and dependable companions,
unlike sleep, a different limbo
that holds it all.

the mind hauls slowly back
the vulture-like verbs the screeching nouns and
then the chocked silences over this immensely
vast planet of ideologies
for centuries it's been cursing
catabases interstellar probes
fretful consciences
with rude desires
with warped plants
with lupine pride
and unlikely plots that bounce off the porticos
at three in the morning in the medieval city

è l'ora di sorvegliare il tempo
che nel buio ammalia voci
lampada e la finestra
       ora di pensare
       agli echi
       di questa geremiade
       del vivente

                       (Bologna, 1978)

the hour has come to keep an eye on time
which in the darkness bewitches voices
and desk lamp and the window as well
      it is time to think
      about the echoes
      of this jeremiad
      of the living

(Bologna, 1978)

Lettera

per E.S.

> E passate così, per vie terrene!
> Chi osa? Chi vi prende? Chi vi tiene?
>
> G. D'Annunzio

a.
questi non sono tempi
da introspezioni sibilline
dalla voce hai capito
che qualcosa non
vanno anzi molte cose
cioè,
            Humanus,
non deliberano
né fondi sono i suggerimenti
le tappezzerie dei sentimenti
i violacei traviatissimi
redentori,
            Humanus,
indecenti, lei disse,
infami turiferarii mondi
da fendere un mollusco una scimmia
questi tempi
commentabili solo perché
non è data all'epoca passione
che non sia anche a te a noi
suprema falcidiante malapena

b.
poi c'è chi ti descrive per filo
e per famelici segni
la propria trasparenza
tempi di ginepri, che vuoi?

Letter

for E.S.

> And you just go by like this, on earthly grounds?
> Who dares? Who takes you? Who holds you?
>
> G. D'Annunzio

a.
these are no times
for sibylline questions
from the voice you gathered
that something is
actually many things are wrong
that is,
                    Humanus,
there is no resolve
no depth to the suggestions
the carpeting of sentiments
the purplish highly corrupt
redeemers,
                    Humanus,
indecent, she called them,
disgraceful contaminated adulators
piercing mollusks monkeys retirees
times, these,
remarkable really because
there are no longer passions
which are not for you for us
supreme debilitating evil fate

b.
then there are those who describe
in detailed famished letters
their own diaphaneity
the juniper age, what else?

aquile e lettere minuscole
doveri intangibili
tuttavia necessari,
               Humanus,
sdrammatìzzati
ché le firme agognano
le voci e il senso
insegue il ritmo del cosmo

c.
e certo tu lo sai
non farmi ridescrivere i perimetri
gli appunti a mente
e i ricatti di tapini cinquantenni—
i fantasmi ci sono li conosci
lo dicono tutti le nonne i libri
persino gli epistemologi
sì che basta alterarsi
i passi le varianti i temi
le multe insomma,
               Humanus,
lo spettro dell'animo non è
non è mai stato
una finzione
una creazione dell'intelletto preistorico
una creatura dal desiderio assopito,
               Humanus,
gli specchi sono franti
e i mostri i mostri
lei lo sa n'è certa
le maschere l'hanno posseduta

d.
quasi che gli uomini non ci fossero
e in lor presenza chiamali come sai
indicibili indecenti—
spirito sincero altero

eagles and puny writing
irrelevant duties
somehow necessary,
        Humanus,

put off the drama
for the signatories are thirsty
for a voice and meaning
is chasing the rhythm of the world

c.
and of course you know that:
do not let me redraw the contours
the entries for the mind
the blackmailing of wretched fifty-year-olds—
ghosts do exist you know them
everyone says so grandmothers books
even epistemologists
the steps the variations the topics
the summons in short,
        Humanus,
the specter of the soul is not
never has been
a fiction
an invention of prehistoric mind
a creation of dormant desires,
        Humanus,
the mirrors are shattered
and the monsters the monsters
she knows it she's sure
the masks possessed her

d.
as if men did not exist
and when about call them by their names
unspeakable indecent—
proud and sincere soul

inconfondibile preda,
                    Humanus,
non suicidarla,
non lasciare che le parole
smettano di viverla

(Milano, 1984)

unmistakable prey,
           Humanus,
do not suicide her,
do not let words stop
giving her life

                         (Milan, 1984)

Meditazione su Pasolini

Pier Paolo, hai scritto delle belle pagine, sai,
parli di giustizia, classi sociali, la perfida ignavia
dei tuoi pari e maggiori e maggiormente minori
e sei, ahimè, un sorpassato!
> Un gusto letterario satrapico e menegreghista
(chiamali bicipiti di seppia)
>> ha deciso di non ascoltarti, di deriderti,
>> di non capire che
>> res sunt nomina
>> e che hai toccato delle corde spiacenti
>>> anzi very troubling ones
o miseri borghesotti di due soldi
sì, tu, pirla della madonna
>> (ma non faccio falsi regionalismi,
>> avrei potuto scrivere—sapete, sono anche americano!—
>> you stupid suburban bastard)

dunque,
avete capito, maledetti architecnici
nembi sgambetti ululii polari e intasati

mi devo inventare in altro linguaggio
(i miei amici, questo, non lo sanno)
ti ho già citato altrove, ricordi,
ho detto a chiare lettere
> *Ho sbagliato tutto*
Annettendo sfacciatamente all'indicibile tua predestinazione

"Smetto di essere poeta originale,"
> —eri, e lo ignoravi, un vero avanguardista e ingenuo—
"un sistema stilistico è troppo esclusivo,"
e poi scrivesti che adotti schemi letterari collaudati
"per essere più libero" aggiungi
tu e la tua fottuta libertà:
>> sempre di quella parli,
>> anche quando la gente che ce l'ha
>> non la prezza che a perderla del tutto,

Pasolini Meditation

You know, you wrote some really good pages, Pier Paolo,
you speak of justice, social classes, the perfidious apathy
of your equals and betters but mostly inferior
and you are, alas! a has been!
     A satrapic don't-give-a-hoot aesthetic
(call them cuttlefish biceps)
       has decided to stop listening to you, to laugh at you,
       and insist on not seeing that
       res sunt nomina
       and that you struck some unpleasant chords
         actually very troubling ones
oh you wretched two-bit puny-bourgeois
yes, you, goddamn shmucks
       (but I am not playing on pseudomulticulturalism
       I could have written—you know, I am also Italian!—
       stronzi pirla provincialotti)
so then,
you understand, you cursed architechnics
rainclouds trick kicks jammed up polar howlings

I must reinvent myself in another language
(my friends are not informed of this)
and I have already cited you elsewhere, remember,
I said loud and clear
     I did it all wrong
Shamelessly admitting to your unspeakable doom

"I am going to stop being an original poet,"
       —you were, unawares, a true yet naive avantgardist—
"a stylistic system is too exclusive";
and then you wrote that you adopt well-proven literary schemes
"in order to be more free" you add
you and your fucking freedom:
       That's all you ever talk about,
       even when the people who do enjoy their freedom
       don't value it till they lose it altogether

Peter Carravetta   1339

francamente ci rompevi
col tuo anticlassicismo e pseudopopulismo ...
(adesso grandi masse sono infine libere, ma
dubito che si riconoscano nella *tua* idea di libertà ...)
in ogni caso
termini con consueta autoironia
(sai, da qui ti si vede in controluce)
e cioè naturalmente per ragioni "pratiche ..."

ecco,

adesso mi hai costretto
    davvero
        a smettere di
  scri
     vere
  poesie

almeno in questa irreale tua lingua o sogno
d'irritrovabile futuro

(New York, 1990)

frankly you were really a pain
with your anticlassicism and pseudopopulism . . .
(now some in great numbers are finally liberated, but
I doubt they see themselves in *your* idea of freedom . . .)

at any rate
you end with your typical self-irony
      (you know, from here we can see you against the light)
and that of course for "practical" reasons

there,

now you have really
      forced me
            to stop
   writ
        ing
poems

at least in this your unreal language or dream
of an impossible future

                    (New York, 1990)

Gli insegnanti di New York

ai miei studenti del Master's

Avevano detto loro che la diversità
È auspicabile giusta legittima infatti
Verbo pedagogico politico
Peraltro "possibilitante"

Avevano detto loro che il multiculturalismo
E' incessante inevitabile pure necessario
Discorso dell'alterità altrui e comunque
        Degli ultimi arrivati e "del domani"

Avevano detto loro che la "differenza"
E' la norma filosofica e critica ed etica
Paradigma di futuro illuminato e di certo
        Salvaguardia "delle minoranze"

Avevano detto loro che le lingue straniere
Sono da far conoscere a tutti i livelli
Metodo di contattare e contrattare con gli stranieri
        Esuli rifugiati ed "emigranti a vario titolo"

Poi invece politici e mediaclasse e la massa
Dispersa nell'exurbia americana
Decretarono per voto consenso incompetenza
Che la nuova pedagogia all'atto pratico
Insegnasse a costo di minacce penali e contrattuali

Che essere americani vuol dire
Identità specifica speciale non contaminata
Monoculturale monolingue monolitica
        Non hanno aggiunto apolitica
          acritica acefala . . . ma non si è d'accordo
          se ciò sia un bene dire o meno

Comunque gli insegnanti di New York
Sono molto infelici
        Infatti in molti sono disillusi o indignati
        E parecchi hanno già cambiato mestiere . . .

New York Teachers

to my MA students

They had told them that diversity
is desirable legitimate legal in fact
the political pedagogical verbum
      and moreover "enabling"

They had told them that multiculturalism
is the constant inevitable even necessary
discourse of others' otherness and concerned with
      the newly arrived and "tomorrow's"

They had told them that "difference"
is the norm in philosophy criticism ethics
paradigm of enlightened futures and for sure
      safeguard "for the minorities"

They had told them that foreign languages
ought to be known at all levels
method to contact and engage the foreigners
      exiles refugees and "other immigrants"

And then instead politicos middle class and
scattered masses in American exurbia
decreed by vote consensus or incompetence
that the new pedagogy would concretely teach
under threats both penal and contractual

that being American means essentially
a specific exceptional uncontaminated Identity
that is monocultural monolinguistic monolithic
they neglected to add apolitical acritical
brain dead . . . though no one can say
whether this is a good thing to mention, or not

At any rate the teachers in New York
are generally unhappy
      in fact many are disillusioned or angry
      while others have already traded jobs . . .

Mentre altri, pochi, abbassano la testa, afferrano
I loro programmi, e continuano indefessi a credere
Che vale la pena battersi per la mente dei giovani

(New York, 2003)

but the rest, a few, lower their heads, grab their syllabi
     and continue tirelessly to believe
the minds of the young are worth the fight

                         (New York, 2003)

→ Alessandro Carrera (b. 1954)

Alessandro Carrera was born in Lodi, Italy, in 1954. In 1980 he received his *laurea* in theoretical philosophy from the Università degli Studi in Milan, with a thesis on text and music in the works of Arnold Schönberg. In 1987 he came to the United States as a *lettore*, a lectureship position sponsored by the Italian Ministry for Foreign Affairs. In that capacity, he taught Italian language and literature at the University of Houston, New York University, and McMaster University. In 2001 he was named director of Italian studies at the University of Houston, where he is now full professor. His collections of poems are *La resurrezione delle cose* (1988), *La ricerca della maturità* (1992), *La sposa perfetta/The Perfect Bride* (1997, translated by the author and D. F. Brown), *L'amore del secolo/Love of the Century* (2000, translated by the author and L. A. Stortoni), *Lode all'isterica* (2000), *La stella del mattino e della sera* (2006), and most recently *Poesie per paraurti* (2012). He has published the novel *La torre e la pianura* (1994) and the short stories *A che punto è il Giudizio Universale* (1999), while his novella *La vita meravigliosa dei laureati in lettere* (2002) went through seven reprints. He has been the recipient of the Montale Poetry Prize (1993), the Arturo Loria Prize for short fiction (1998), and the Attilio Bertolucci Prize for literary criticism (2006) for his collection of essays, *I poeti sono impossibili* (2005). Carrera has published extensively in the fields of literary theory, continental philosophy, and music criticism. He has also written *La voce di Bob Dylan. Una spiegazione dell'America* (2001) and edited and translated into Italian Bob Dylan's *Chronicles, Volume 1* (2005), *Lyrics 1962–2001* (2006), and *Tarantula* (2007).

Carrera's early book of poetry, *La sposa perfetta*, was published with facing-page English translation in 1992.[47] It displays immediately a sense of amused detachment and irony, employs a long or narrative line, and is definitely referential; it is a book *about* America, the first of a trilogy. Carrera's poetry records the encounter between self and reality, and much like a travelogue it sketches a busy mosaic of fortuitous situations and the perplexing questions they generate in the mind. A cosmopolitan Italian mind will find endless contradictions in the American hinterland, but the poet is not chasing about the *differance* between being American and being Italian; rather, he essays to frame and then reframe for his own inner landscape the moments when a wondering ego meets up with a not always reassuring and coherent society tout court.[48] Some of the topics that circulate in his texts are relatively familiar to those who have had to relocate at some point in their lives, for the expatriate poet realizes that his identity is now potentially split and linked to a new signifier in a new code, and that in view of this, or perhaps because of this condition, there surges a deep awareness that there is no direct connection between language and world. This will inform Carrera's poetics later when he begins writing directly in English, as in *Love of the Century*, as if before this abyss the poet must at least reconnect the new signifiers with the new signifieds, that is, the referents in the new "home."

As a poet concerned with the signifieds in the broader sense of the possible meanings generated by the world about and around him, Carrera will move toward a poetic diction that wishes to communicate, which means also that Carrera conceals no rhetorical tricks other than the occasional anaphora to stress the absurdity of certain situations and the inevitable tendency toward the objective correlative. And through that, at a thematic level, he manifests early on a disenchanted view of his new society, as in the poem "Ulysses Arrives in California," or the other segment of the suite, number 9, titled "Ulysses Meets Andy Warhol in Hades."[49] In the "Farewell," he begins to roam the past, and we find lines that clearly point to a sane and somber realism: "In the Fifties I also marched against NATO. / Some friends were communists, / I wasn't too sure, but we talked about it: / Working twelve hours at night / Makes freedom of thought a luxury" (110). Indeed!

In *La ricerca della maturità* (1992), which is about his youth and his father's post–World War II Italy, the poet, perhaps now a substantial geohistorical distance from his origin, returns to the past and weaves the personal and the social, reframing and conjoining the traditions of labor struggles with idealizations only partly and patiently to be realized. The key to a reading of this collection is to begin by gathering the lexemes that refer to working-class environments, from night shifts to warehouses, from factory strikes to anxious and polarizing encounters around worksites, everyday household sacrifices, leftover weapons from the war, bicycles, radio broadcasts, the struggle to get an education, the sour air of the *periferia* (which is not exactly the same as the American suburb), the recent installation of a telephone line, card playing, tobacco, railroad yards and trains, trains, lots of them, which will become an iconic presence in much of Carrera's poetic production.

In *The Love of the Century* we find a greater variety of stanzaic forms and metrical patterns, with intercalations of speech fragments both from circumstances as well as from the recesses of memory, and it is not always clear who the speaking persona is. This Italian poet living and working in the United States for the past twenty-five years is not that interested in issues of belonging, of nationalist identity, of comparing and contrasting the two countries and cultures, nor in acritical claims to special filiation and heritages. As a result, the text is now strewn with references to myth and to philosophers and scientists, while descriptions of daily occurrences launch quickly into existential reflections. Thus when the poet, in a post-9/11 world, returns "home" to consider the reality of present-day Italy, we do not hear the angry and disappointed political consciousness of the first book, but are alerted to a "Brave New World" (81–94) that, as can be read in the poem here reprinted, "Khalid Arrives in Bologna," is a not-so-tragicomic description of current racism and xenophobia in Ithaca: When the main character finally quips, "[W]e simply went the wrong way," the narrating persona can only too sadly respond, "[L]et me tell you how way off you were" (84). The conclusion is an elegy to Victoria, his woman, his love, who is perhaps the one to confer sense to a quantic universe always already on the verge of collapsing upon itself, but perhaps also the real incarnation of that "perfect bride," the woman, the Beatrice function, who allows the poet to connect past and present, and is, in Dantesque mode, "vehicle for elevation, capable of liberating us from the most fleeting human rubbish . . . dispenser of health and salvation."[50] She has accompanied the poet since the beginning of his poetic adventure, and has represented for him a *domus* in the erring of existence, in its very breathing, *pneuma* even before *spiritus*.

But from this to conclude that "home is where the heart is" would be doing an injustice to this prolific and multifaceted writer. For there is no omniscient God, for Carrera, to collect everything up in one volume. The poems in *Stella del mattino e della sera*, for their tactile social consciousness, may make some think of Pasolini, but without nostalgia, or resentment, or the finger pointed toward a presumably homogenous bourgeois pact. The poet appears to accept his role as witness, as that sensorium that registers the dramas of the more recently uprooted immigrants from the third world coursing through Italy, and the incoherence of a postmodern society torn off any logical hinges. He is therefore much more humble than a "civic" or "committed" poet might be, but his mock-ironic statement, or conclusion, "blessed be he who writes," suggests rather critically that those who for half a century have taken to the much-cited Adornian quip whereby the poet's home is his language may be due for some radical rethinking. To dwell in language only, almost to the exclusion of any pretense to speak the world, to occupy oneself with the *langage* or work the chosen *langue* to its formal limits, may indeed yield valid and occasionally stupendous aesthetic results (for example, philosophical in Ballerini and Moroni, spiritual in Valesio, emotional in Saccà), but also exposes the poet to the lure and risk of a pseudo immortality, a transhistorical, nonsocial, self-referential creation which really only addresses simulacras and specters, and in those less endowed, mere psychological projections.

Carrera's poetics can be said to tend at least toward the two loci at once, one at Apex B: Home/Mortality, and then at Apex D: *Langue*/Reality, where the links the *langue* establishes with reality, whether in a "here" (America) or a "there" (Italy), or, in the end, "anywhere" (as the two places reverse their perspective with each trip), hark to a deeper sense of being toward death—understood not only in terms of the explicit referents in his text—the poet's father, his past, his immediate existence, his *madrepatria*—but also, and perhaps more important, as a perception of the dwindling possibilities for the human condition as a whole to make sense, since societal relations do not seem to pay much attention to history, to the political project, to any value which transcends the here and now. The poems included in this collection about the injustices and racism that the new immigrants experience ought to make that clear. The poet is no longer in either Ogygia or Ithaca and may not care to choose one over the other any longer; he may be satisfied to land once in a while in Phaeacia and, like the man of many tropes, watch from the sidelines the show the current king or czar or president or John Doe proclaims, sadly conscious that when neither intellect nor soul has believable coordinates to hold onto, we are at the mercy of virtualities and indirections, and to recall a title by Richard Milazzo, we are like a "circus in a fog."[51] His very last book, whose title translates into "bumper sticker poems," epitomizes this condition. Drawing on a tradition that in recent times includes Antonio Porta and Paul Vangelisti, Carrera collected commonplaces, indeed clichés, typically palmed off as pseudowisdom in the great media outlets, at elegant parties, in the front office of the dean or the dentist or the mainstream destitute, making at the same time painfully evident that even the liberating poetics of the "object trouvée" has had its day. The poet, then, can at most aspire at being a wandering ethnographer.

Buongiorno, sono il vostro pilota

da *La sposa perfetta*

Buongiorno, sono il vostro pilota.
Sapete, certe volte non so chi sono.

Ma voi chi siete? Perché siete qui?
Dove volete andare?
Cosa credete di fare?

Sono sempre il vostro pilota.

Ditemi dove siamo, sono tre giorni che volo.
E' l'Arizona sotto di noi? E' il Kansas?
E' l'Oklahoma, il Nebraska? E' la Tierra del Fuego?
Qui dall'alto vedo solo il sole
raccogliere nei laghi le sue monete d'oro.

Durante questo volo non dovrete preoccuparvi
delle interferenze dei radioamatori.

Durante questo volo non dovrete preoccuparvi
di avere sbagliato volo.

Durante questo volo non dovrete preoccuparvi
della natura umana.

Durante questo volo non dovrete preoccuparvi
della polvere da sparo
perché è già stata inventata dai cinesi.

Buongiorno, sono il vostro pilota.
Fidatevi, non ne avete altri.

Buongiorno, sono il vostro pilota.
Voi no.

Good Morning, I Am Your Pilot

from *The Perfect Bride*

Good morning, I am your pilot.
You know, sometimes I don't know who I am.

But you, who are you? Why are you here?
Where do you think you're going?
What do you think you're doing?

I am still your pilot.

Tell me where we are, I have been flying
for three days. Is it Arizona below us? Or is it Kansas?
Is it Oklahoma, is it Nebraska? Is it Tierra del Fuego?
From up here I can only see the sun
collecting golden coins from the lakes.

During this flight you won't have to worry
about the interferences of CB's.

During this flight you won't have to worry
that you took the wrong flight.

During this flight you won't have to worry
about human nature.

During this flight you won't have to worry
about gunpowder
because it was already invented by the Chinese.

Good morning, I am your pilot.
Trust me. I am the only one you have.

Good morning, I am your pilot.
You are not.

Il vagone dei ferrovieri

Ho una brutta stampa appesa in casa
che ai miei ospiti non piace.
È un vagoncino rosso della Union Pacific,
qui in America lo chiamano Caboose,
ultimo di dieci carri merci
che seguono la curva dei binari
su una prateria di cespugli di saggina.
Oltre il quadro
il treno va, continua a andare,
si perde nella spugna del muro
verso un sole tramontato ad occidente del pittore
e che manda luci postume, ubriache.
Paul F. Detlefsen, dice la placchetta,
The Red Caboose.
I ferrovieri ci andavano a mangiare
scodelle di fagioli, a fumare e bere whisky.
La locomotiva è piccola in distanza,
non riesco a distinguere il tipo.
Avrà un nome eroico e familiare
come il *General* di Keaton, e comunque
manda un fumo strepitoso e dritto
che si mischia col colore viola polvere
delle nuvole avanzanti le colline.
Sento gli uomini passarsi la voce
in fila sulla cima dei vagoni.
Li vedo tirarsi le bretelle, scacciar mosche,
scherzare coi neri cappelli a visiera.

"Nessuno può distruggere le stazioni."
È una cosa che ho scritto una volta e non sapevo perché.
Mi ipnotizzava come qualcosa di morto e sicuro,
mi sembrava vera
come un congresso di metereologi
di cui solo metà ha portato l'ombrello,
vera come il cartello all'ingresso

The Red Caboose

There's a cheap print in my living room
my guests don't like.
A Union Pacific red wagon—*caboose*
they call it here in America,
last of ten freight cars
in a line curving with the tracks
down the tumbleweed prairie.
Beyond the painting
the train is going, it keeps going
getting lost in the sponge of the wall
toward the setting sun that shines drunk, posthumous,
west of the painter.
Paul F. Detlefsen, reads the plate,
The Red Caboose.
The railroad men, here, ate their plates of beans,
smoked, drank whiskey.
The locomotive is tiny in the distance,
I can't make out the model
though it must have a heroic, familiar name
like Keaton's *General*. Anyway,
the smoke rises straight
and mixes with the dusty purple clouds
coming from the hills.
I can hear the men shouting,
I can see them jumping along cars,
stretching their suspenders, flicking flies away
and joking in their peaked black caps.

"Nobody can destroy stations."
Something I wrote once not knowing why.
The sentence hypnotized me like something
that was dead and sure. It seemed true
like a conference of meteorologists
only half of whom brought umbrellas,
like the sign at the entrance

di qualche città di guerra, Dresda, Coventry,
dopo che gli aerei si furono sgravati.

Una sera presi un treno a Siracusa,
facevo il folksinger allora.
Finito un altro festival,
gruppi rock, una compagnia di teatro Kathakhali.
Gli indiani si erano mangiati tutto il riso,
i musicisti rock si erano portati via tutti i soldi.
Ricavai le spese e il teatro greco.
Nell'Orecchio di Dionisio un disc-jockey mi assordò
con le sue graduatorie personali
e con il music business che fa schifo.
Verso Catania, corridoio dopo corridoio,
fantasticavo di essere in un plastico,
forti motrici sulle montagne coniche,
merci che scendevano dondolanti allo smistamento.
Quando ancora mi attaccavo alle vetrine
i treni più belli, più cari erano i Märklin.
i Rivarossi traboccavano dagli scaffali,
pochi avevano i Fleischmann,
e io ero orgoglioso di possederne uno.
Non avevo scambi. Avere scambi era da ricchi,
spenderci soldi era scelta morale.
Eracle al bivio, la via in discesa della virtù,
la lenta salita del conforto.

Entrai nel vagone postale.
Mio padre contava sacchi di lettere,
pacchi tesi contro le corde come seni dentro vestiti.
Non riuscivo a andare avanti,
la mia cuccetta era due carrozze in testa
ma non mi muovevo, mi ero fissato
che il treno corresse più di me.
Non posso dormire, papà, raccontami ancora
la storia dell'aereo americano
che mitragliò tutto intorno alla stazione, al tuo paese,
e non la prese mai.
È ancora là, l'ho vista,

of some war-torn city, Dresden, Coventry,
after the airplanes had dropped their loads.

One evening I took a train from Siracusa,
I was a folksinger then.
Another festival over,
rock bands and a Kathakhali theatre company.
The Indians had eaten all the rice,
the rock musicians had taken away all the money.
I got my expenses and Greek theater.
In Dionysius's Ear a disc jockey deafened me
with his personal top ten
and with music business—such a drag.
Toward Catania, corridor after corridor,
I pictured myself in an HO train-table landscape,
powerful engines on cone-shaped mountains,
freight cars rolling down to the shunting yard.
When I used to press my nose against shop windows
the most gorgeous, most expensive trains were the Märklins.
The Rivarossis were falling off the shelves,
but few had the Fleischmanns,
and I was proud of owning one.
I had no switches. I thought it was for rich boys.
To spend money on a switch was a moral issue,
Hercules at the crossroad, virtue's downhill path,
comfort's gentle rise.

I stepped into the postal wagon,
my father counting sacks of letters,
packages pressing against the ropes like breasts.
I couldn't go any further,
my couchette two cars ahead,
but I couldn't make a move, convinced that
the train was going faster than I was.
Dad, I can't sleep, tell me again
of the American airplane over your village
machine-gunning all around the station,
and never hitting it.
The station is still there, I saw it

sempre uguale dalla fine della guerra.
È adesso che sembra bombardata, vecchia, inutile,
ma nessuno l'ha distrutta.
Vedi papà che mi ricordo la tua storia,
vedi che mi sembra vera
come una tavola d'oro anticamente incisa
da cui ci raggiunge
una splendente profezia dimenticata,
vera come una sentenza giusta
che tutti decidono entusiasti di non applicare.
Devi essere qualcuno nella vita, ragazzo mio.
Devi aver servito qualcuno,
devi aver fatto fuori qualcuno,
oppure sarai solo qualcuno
sulla strada da Carlsbad a Whites' City
coi piedi sporchi e una borsa di tela
come la vagabonda dagli occhi infossati
che scendeva la via del serbatoio
e non ci credeva che le davo un passaggio.
Se n'era andata di casa da dieci anni.
Mendicava, trovava. Non mi raccontò la sua storia.
Non le avrebbe fatto nessun bene, così disse.
Voleva sapere cosa prova
una donna che si chiude in una grotta.
Aveva sentito
che le grotte di Carlsbad
erano bellissime.

Al distributore mio padre serviva da bere.
Mi chiese se quella era la mia ragazza.
No, gli dissi, è una zingara.
Non ci sono zingari in America, disse lui.
In America ci sono palle da biliardo
smangiucchiate come tasti di pianoforte,
ci sono piatti speciali
in ristoranti senza niente di speciale,
ci sono pelli di serpente
essiccate con gran cura ed esposte alle verande dei motel.

unchanged since the war.
It is now that the station seems bombed, useless,
but not destroyed.
You see, Dad, I remember your story,
you see, it seems true to me,
like an ancient, carved gilded table,
from which some shining
forgotten prophecy reaches us,
like a just verdict which
everyone cheerily decides to ignore.
You must become somebody, my son.
You must serve somebody,
you must take out somebody.
If not, you will only be someone
on the road from Carlsbad to Whites' City,
dirty feet and a canvas bag,
like the drifter with the deep-set eyes,
coming down the road by the water tank.
She couldn't believe that I wanted to give her a ride.
She had left home ten years before.
She begged, she scraped, she didn't tell me her story.
It wouldn't do her any good, she said.
She wanted to know what it is like for a woman
to seclude herself in a cave.
She had heard the caves
of Carlsbad
were beautiful.

At the filling station my father was serving drinks.
He asked me if she was my girlfriend.
I said no, she's a gypsy.
There are no Gypsies in America, he said.
In America there are billiard balls
as worn as piano keys,
there are specials
in restaurants that are not special at all,
there are snakeskins
carefully desiccated and displayed on motel patios.

Gli zingari scelgono la strada. In America non si sceglie.
Si sceglie forse in paradiso?
E se il paradiso per qualcuno fosse orribile,
ci sarebbe mai di meglio?
L'aria crepitava secca, avevo ancora sete,
c'erano tre ore prima di El Paso.
Devi esser qualcuno nella vita, figlio mio.
Devi esser così bravo
da lasciarci disgustati.

Ebbi paura quando misero la bomba alla stazione di Bologna.
Qualcuno poteva distruggere le stazioni, dopotutto.
Vedi, papà, nemmeno la tua storia era più vera.
Quante vicende da allora, quante persone.
A volte ho nostalgia di quando
appena vestiti e mandati nel mondo
ci alzavamo a separare il bene e il male.
Molti poi hanno gnaulato come cani,
molti sono spariti come code di topi in un muro,
molti hanno negato al canto del gallo,
molti hanno strozzato il gallo.
Io ho riscritto un Ecclesiaste personale.
Trovo un tempo per fuggire e uno per per tornare,
un tempo per scegliere e uno per alzare le spalle,
e mi guardo passare dall'uno all'altro
in una obliosa, vellutata privatezza.
Il centro della vita è una cosa polverosa
e provvisoria, una stazione di pianura
costruita in fretta e che nessuno abolirà,
un bambino nato troppo presto,
una casa abusiva
in un quartiere mal battuto dalle guardie.
Quanta luce dalla mia finestra, quante scie nel cielo.
Mi sfilo, mi addormento, invecchio.
Mi scrivono amici che in Italia
l'unica cosa che conta
sono i soldi.
Si vede che ce n'è.

Gypsies choose the road. You don't choose in America.
How could you choose in Paradise?
And if Paradise were horrible for someone,
who could find something better?
The air was dry and crackling, I was still thirsty
and it took three hours to get to El Paso.
You must become somebody, my son.
You must be so good
To make the rest of us disgusted

After they bombed the Bologna station I was scared.
Someone could destroy stations after all.
You see, Dad, your story is true no more.
So many things happened, since then, so many people.
Sometimes I have nostalgia for the time when we,
just dressed and arrived into the world,
stood up to tell right from wrong.
Many, later, howled like dogs,
many disappeared like mousetails in the wall,
many denied at cockcrow,
many strangled the cock.
I rewrote a personal Ecclesiastes.
I find a time to flee, a time to come back,
a time to take a stand, a time to shrug.
And I look at myself, passing from one time to another
in an oblivious, velvet privateness.
The center of life is something dusty
and temporary, a station in the plains
built overnight whom no one will suppress,
a child born too soon,
a house built on restricted lots
in a neighborhood police rarely patrol.
So much light at my window, so many vapor trails in the sky.
I unravel myself, I fall asleep, I grow old.
Friends are writing me.
They say in Italy now
only money counts.
There must be plenty of it.

Infine tocca a me,
la tua storia è ancora vera.
Ti faccio nascere, papà,
è il mio racconto che è truccato.
Ti apro in due come un romanzo
di cui so già la fine, e sono io.
Ti faccio attraversare
le massicciate d'amore, colpa e pena.
Vi sfrecciano treni senza stazioni,
angeli di uno stracolmo paradiso,
olandesi volanti ubriachi di ferro e di scintille.
Un giorno arriverò sull'ultimo vagone,
sul rosso Caboose dei ferrovieri
alla stazione intatta
fatta d'aria e d'orari.
Qualcuno mi dirà che sono cambiato,
qualcuno mi dirà che niente cambia,
tutto rimarrà come non l'avevo mai lasciato.
Ma siamo nati insieme. Quando sei morto
ho respirato con i tuoi polmoni.
Un giorno risorgerai,
un giorno mi sentirò mancare il fiato.

And now it's my turn,
your story still rings true.
I give you birth, Dad,
it's my story that's made up.
I open you in the middle like a novel
whose ending I already know, and it is me.
I help you crossing
the ballast of love, guilt, pain,
where trains without stations are whizzing,
angels of an overcrowded paradise,
Flying Dutchmen, drunk with iron and sparks.
Someday I will get off that last car,
the Red Caboose of the railroad men,
at the untainted station,
made of wind and schedules.
Someone will say that I have changed,
someone will say nothing changes,
everything will be as I never left it.
But we were born together. When you died
I breathed with your lungs.
Someday you will rise,
someday I will be out of breath.

Khalid arriva a Bologna

da *La stella del mattino e della sera*

In un'isola tagliata col coltello, città del vostro Sud,
orecchini d'osso pendevano dai lobi di quattro mie sorelle
d'altopiano. Gente in tuta puzzava di benzina e proteggeva
i motori dalla sabbia. Io mangiavo in pentolini scrostati,

seduto sul gradino della strada, sporco di catrame e pesante
degli attrezzi. Corso via da casa, di furia e di tempesta,
ricordavo il sole rompersi a grani tra stuoie di stecche,
i quartieri svenati, marci, morti, e le colline disboscate.

Donne ridevano un riso che spariva, la strada incanalava
un vento d'olio, grasse navi suonavano motori con sordina.
Quattro mogli perdute, fiamme dei miei occhi, mi lanciarono
caute un'occhiata, senza farsi vedere a voltarsi per me.

> Dicevano che il nostro bar era la base dello spaccio,
> dava scandalo ai bambini della scuola qui vicino.
> Hanno raccolto le firme, un migliaio, e a mia figlia
> chiamata in questura le han detto di chiudere un mese.

> Clienti da vent'anni mai più visti, e loro si son presi
> tutto il bar. Adesso la gente fa l'arco quando passa,
> tira i bambini che non guardino, e a parte quattro
> o cinque pensionati non viene più nessuno che conosco.

> L'altro giorno ero seduta pensierosa, uno m'ha fissato
> e poi m'ha detto: "Hai l'espressione di mia madre."
> Dove vanno d'inverno, quando chiudo? Dove dormono? Non so.
> Ci son taxi che li portano in campagna, avranno i loro posti.

Era l'ora che ogni stretto è Gibilterra accesa. Gli occhi
mi bruciavano di ossidrico, nuvole pesanti, lente gocce
calde, mosche che friggevano sui neon, ma poi una sorella
si è fermata, e mi batteva il cuore a guardarla da uomo.

Avrà avuto sedici anni, una goccia di aranciata le colava
dalla bocca, le braccia un paio d'ali di cotone rammendato,

Khalid Arrives in Bologna

from *The Morning and Evening Star*

On an island cut with a knife, in one of your southern cities,
bone earrings hung from the lobes of four sisters from my mountains.
People in overalls smelled of gas, and protected the engines
from the sand. I would eat in scraped aluminum pots,

sitting on the curb, dirty with tar, heavy with tools—
a runaway, full of rage and fury. I remembered
the sunshine breaking into beads between the slats—the neighborhoods
were gutted, rotten, dead, and the hills—razed.

Women laughed a vanishing laughter, the street channeled
an oily wind, fat ships played their engines with a mute.
Four women I'll never marry, four flames in my eyes, cast
cautious glances at me, making sure no one noticed.

> People said our bar was the center of a drug ring,
> and that it gave scandal to the children of the nearby school.
> They collected signatures, a thousand, then the police
> called my daughter in, told her to shut down for a month.
>
> Customers of twenty years disappeared, and they
> took over the joint. Now people keep at a distance,
> pull their children away so they don't look inside. Apart
> from four or five retired people, the usuals no longer drop by.
>
> A couple of days ago I was sitting and thinking. One of them
> stared at me and said: "You look like my mother." Where do they go
> in the winter, when I close? Where do they sleep? I don't know.
> Cabs take them to the country, they must have a place somewhere.

It was the time of day when every strait is a flame-red Gibraltar.
Oxyhydrogen burned my eyes. Slow, black clouds—warm raindrops—
flies fried on the neon lights, then a sister stopped by,
and my heart beat fast when I looked at her like a man.

She could have been sixteen, a drop of orange juice ran down
her chin. Her arms, wings of patched cotton. The soles

e chiare le piante dei piedi. Non posso comprarvi né
adesso né mai, non fissatemi negli occhi che mi ammazzo.

Faccio il turno di notte, mi offrono da bere, non devo
stare in piedi né seduto, il bar non tiene sedie, fanno
apposta così non perdo tempo, ma io so stare in piedi,
non mi stanco a stare in piedi, cammino su sterrati

e sull'asfalto, scalcio i sassi che a voi vi fanno male,
ascolto, porto orecchie grandi e fini, di giorno tenetevi
l'Europa, la notte è quando l'Africa va in cielo. Città
del vostro Nord, spaccato come vetro, mi fermate?

> *Poi è passata la volante e gli ha detto di spostarsi.*
> *Ha strisciato due macchine e sono corsi fuori dalle case*
> *a picchiarlo e gridargli parole, lui diceva che pagava,*
> *a settembre gli fanno il processo. Ha ammazzato qualcuno?*

> *Balbettava, lo tastavano dovunque, gli hanno tolto le scarpe*
> *con quel freddo, fatto aprire la bocca, cercavano*
> *droga nascosta tra i denti, può darsi che ci fosse,*
> *quando spacciavano i soliti italiani nessuno protestava.*

> *Io non sono il loro angelo custode. E poi non gli importa*
> *di noi, argomenti non ne hanno e non mi chiedono mai niente.*
> *Mi fa pena vederli tutti in fila, a dieci a dieci a bocca*
> *aperta, i poliziotti che gli abbassano la lingua con le pile.*

Spero che mio padre sia vivo, che le sue mogli dicano
di lui che è una montagna d'uomo, che battano i piedi
nel ballo e che il pozzo delle capre non sia asciutto,
che beva il suo latte e che comandi, scuotendo il bastone

di padre cacciatore, padre mungitore, padre di bastoni
e di montoni—tu che ballavi tra le pergole con il passo
dei vincitori, fammi scendere un poco nel tuo sonno,
è più forte del mio. Mi perdoni? E io, io ti perdono?

Dammi del latte bollente, signora, scaldami sul fuoco
una brioche e quattro uova, l'harissa ce l'ho io, metti
un cucchiaio di olio d'oliva che anche quello mi dà caldo,
fammi spargere il pepe nel latte, al venerdì una birra,

of her feet—white. I can't buy you women now,
not now not ever. If you stare at me I'll kill myself.

I work the night shift, they offer me to drink, I am not allowed
to stand, I am not allowed to sit, there are no chairs in the bar
so that I don't waste time, but I know how to stand,
I'm never tired of standing, I can walk on asphalt

and dirt roads, I can kick stones that would hurt your feet,
I listen, my ears are good and big, in daytime you can have
your Europe, but it is at night that Africa reaches to the sky—
cracked as glass as I am, can your northern cities stop me?

> Then the police came and told him to move.
> He had scratched two cars, people ran out to watch,
> to beat him up, to call him names, though he cried he would
> pay. They'll try him in September, did he kill anyone?

> He stuttered, they patted him all over, it was freezing
> but they took his shoes off, pried his mouth open
> to look for drugs between his teeth. There may have been some,
> but when the pushers were Italian, nobody complained.

> I am not their guardian angel, and they don't really care about us,
> they have nothing to tell me, they never ask me anything.
> It pains me to see them all lined up, ten by ten, their mouths
> open, cops pressing down their tongues with flashlights.

I hope my father is still alive, I hope his wives will say
he is a man like a mountain. I hope they stomp their feet when they dance,
that the well is not too dry and the goats have water to drink.
I hope he drinks his milk and gives orders, shaking his stick—

stick of a hunting father, goat milking father, father of sticks
and rams—you who would dance under the vines with the steps
of a conqueror, let me descend in your sleep, it is stronger than mine.
Do you forgive me? And I, do I forgive you?

Lady, give me some hot milk, heat me up a bun
and four eggs, I've got the harissa. Put in
a spoonful of olive oil, that too will help warm me up.
Let me sprinkle pepper on my milk, let me drink a beer on Friday,

non dovrei ma è festa al mio paese il venerdì, un giorno
le quattro sorelle mi arrivano a casa, un giorno porto voi
che non siete mai nati, che per morire siete troppo fini,
che avete muri e non avete casa, che avete fuoco

e non avete caldo, che insegnate con i pugni il vostro canto,
un giorno voi sentite il mio, vi porto sull'Atlante
e vi do ali, e voi direte: "Abbiamo soltanto sbagliato
la strada," e io vi dirò: "Di quanto l'avete sbagliata."

I shouldn't, but back home Friday is a holiday. One day
the four sisters will arrive at my doorstep, one day I will
take all of you—you who were never born, who are too
delicate to die, who have walls but no homes, who have fire

but are cold, who teach songs with your fists,
one day you'll hear me sing. I'll take you to the Atlas Mountains,
I'll give you wings, and you will say, "We just took
the wrong turn," and I will say, "You don't know how wrong."

Porca Italia in Piazza della Scala

1.

Porca Italia gridava la minuta filippina in un cappotto troppo corto
  in Piazza della Scala che le avevano rubato il portafoglio i
    documenti

il permesso di lavoro porca Italia sotto l'acqua di dicembre
  senza ombrello il foulard che le cadeva dai capelli quasi bianchi

porca Italia con la faccia contro il muro dopo il chiosco dei giornali
  uscita presto presi i mezzi se n'è accorta quando è scesa giù dal
    tram

la gente non sa bene cosa fare stanno intorno mani in tasca
  non si riesce a dirle niente non c'è un vigile a pagarlo appena
    sente

la parola polizia è porca Italia con più furia testa al muro
  una donna sui quaranta sciarpa grigia voce roca dice assurda

vuoi qualcosa da fumare sta impacciata come a dire ci ho provato
  ma lo stesso è porca Italia al monumento a Leonardo al palazzo

del Comune alla Scala che bisogna rinnovare al coro del Nabucco
  e viva Verdi al consolato filippino che ti tratta come straccio da
    lavare

2.

adesso basta fare cerchio adesso basta almanaccare le sue vie
  seguila davvero nel toccarsi il fazzoletto che non va per la
    questura

non denuncia nessun furto adesso è Dio che l'ha punita lei lo sa
  che cosa ha fatto e torna a piedi sotto gli archi gli omenoni

ha le chiavi di una casa in viale Maino dove l'edera tormenta
  le facciate adesso vedila che è un'eco in faccia al muro

senza gli occhi senza un'isola di mare in quella stanza la signora
  l'ha sgridata il letto gli angoli la polvere lei manco che l'ha vista

Damn Italy in Piazza della Scala

1.

Damn Italy the small Filipino woman was shouting—wearing a coat
   too short for her
      in Piazza della Scala, that they stole her wallet her papers

her work permit damn Italy in the December rain
      no umbrella and kerchief falling from her whitening hair

damn Italy her face against the wall past the newsstand she left home
   early
      she took public transport she found out just as soon as the
         streetcar was gone—

people don't know what to do they hang around with their hands in
   their pocket
      you can't talk to her no policeman around when you need one
         she just hears

the word police and it's damn Italy with more fury—her head banging
   against the wall—
      a woman in her forties grey scarf hoarse voice says absurdly

d'you care for a cigarette then looks around awkwardly as if saying
   well I've tried
      but all the same it's damn Italy to the Leonardo monument to
         the City

Hall building to the Scala that has to be renewed to the choir of
   Nabucco
      and viva Verdi to the Consulate of the Philippines that treats you
         like a filthy rag

2.

now stop hanging around stop guessing her ways
      follow her now that she readjusts her kerchief and doesn't go to
         the police

does not report that she was robbed now it's God who's punished her
      she knows
         what she's done she walks home under the arches the caryatids

e la vasca che era tale e quale a prima ce n'è tante senza un'isola
    sugli autobus che chiudono un po' gli occhi "ma ci vedi o non
        ci vedi?"

la signora gliel'ha detto chiaro e tondo e quando lei è stata sola
    ha fatto quella cosa col cuscino che ha arrabbiato il Dio del cielo

adesso vedila davvero senza carte senza borsa
    che si muove clandestina in questa bella bella casa

3.

deve sfare quel che ha fatto l'hai seguita nella camera da letto
    dei padroni l'hai sentita aprire federe e cuscini tirar fuori dalle
        piume

un crocifisso fatto d'ossa di gallina una catena di legnetti bastoncini
    annodati a fil di refe gusci d'uovo sbriciolati carte con stampate
        brutte cose

fuori fuori tutto la signora non ha visto non s'è accorta che le stava
    a venir male ma Dio da dentro il vetro ha allungato la sua mano
        dal suo

cubo antiproiettile con due dita come ladro s'è preso il permesso
il passaporto il portafoglio porca Italia la signora porca Italia

il Dio dei ladri la minuta filippina adesso disfa quel che ha fatto
    mette tutto in un sacchetto della spesa a mezzanotte in mezzo

a un campo brucia tutto e prega in fretta Nostra Lady di Turumba
    Nostra Lady del Viaggio Sicuro Santa Rosa di Lima Cuore
        Immacolato
di Maria San Lorenzo Ruiz che fu martire in Cina e prega porca Italia
    tutta l'anima il suo cuore porca Italia una grazia porca Italia una
        grazia.

she holds the keys of an apartment in Maino Street where ivy tortures
    the façade now look at her she's an echo against the wall

she has no eyes she has no island in the sea there's a room where the
    signora
        yelled at her because of the bed the corners and the dust she
            didn't even see

and the bathtub that wasn't getting any cleaner there's so many of
    them with no island
        on the buses when they try to close their eyes "are you blind or
            what?"

the *signora* told her straight and when she was alone she did that
    something with the pillow that made God up in Heaven very
        angry—
now see how she really looks—with no papers and no purse,
    going like an illegal alien through the rooms of that beautiful
        beautiful home

3.
she must undo what she's done—have you followed her in the
    masters'
        bedroom have you heard her open up the pillowcases and
            take out

a crucifix made of chicken bones a chain of wooden sticks
    tied together with yarn and crushed eggshells and ugly stuff
        printed on paper—

out, out, everything out, the *signora* didn't see didn't understand what
    evil
        was coming down on her but God outstretched his hand from
            inside his glass

from his bulletproof glass cube with two fingers like a thief got hold of
    her permit
        her passport her wallet damn Italy the *signora* damn Italy—

oh God of thieves—now the little Filipino woman is about to undo
    what she's done

she puts everything in a grocery bag and at midnight outside
the city

in an empty field she puts fire to it she prays hastily she prays Our
Lady of Turumba
Our Lady of the Safe Journey Saint Rosa of Lima Mary's
Immaculate

Heart Saint Lorenzo Ruiz who was martyred in China and she prays
damn Italy
with all her soul with all her heart damn Italy have mercy damn
Italy have mercy.

Sidi che parla italiano

Sidi che parla italiano a New York
        racconta l'Italia come lui l'ha trovata
come Annibale a destra della Spagna
        impestata di lombardi e di romani.

Sidi che parla francese e italiano
        racconta di come ha imparato la lingua
di come gli è servita sulle strade nei
        cantieri e sulle lunghe lunghe spiagge.

Sidi che l'inglese non lo parla e sulla
        Quinta saluta nei negozi in italiano
gli viene un'idea e mi chiede ma
        il libro dei morti qui dove si trova?

Ci vuole un po' a capire che dice le pagine
        bianche, l'elenco dei vivi. Che vivi,
che vivi mi ride guardandosi in giro,
        qui l'unico vivo era quel mostro

del novecentotrenta innamorato
        in cima a quella guglia.
Mah! Mestiere ce l'ho sulle dita,
        sarà ora di metter famiglia

prima di perder lo sputo e la vena,
        Sidi ha già cambiato argomento,
ma serviva mettersi in ghingheri,
        la vista valeva la pena.

Ha visto gente che si è spenta
        per la sete che sembrava una
candela smozzicata. Il barcone
        era fermo, i pellegrini squagliati,

c'era niente da pensare, ti scuotevi
        come pazzo e nelle orecchie ti rombava
il coro immenso di quelli rottamati
        sulla riva. Alla fine era il caldo

Sidi Speaking Italian

Sidi speaking Italian in New York
   tells of how he found Italy
—like Hannibal to the right side of Spain—
   plagued by Lombards and Romans.

Sidi who speaks French and Italian
   tells of how he learned the new language
and then put it to use on the streets, working
   in construction and along the endless beaches.

Sidi who doesn't speak English and on
   Fifth Avenue says hello in Italian to the shopkeepers
gets an idea and asks me, wait a minute,
   where do you find the Book of the Dead in this place?

It takes some time to realize he's talking of the
   white pages, the Book of the Living. What living,
what living says he, laughing and looking around,
   the only living being in this place was that monster

of the nineteenthirties, madly in love
   on top of that needle over there.
Well, I've got my skills on the tip of my fingers,
   better to marry me a wife

before I lose my spit and my blood
   —Sidi has already moved to another subject—
but it wasn't for nothing that I got so dressed up,
   this sightseeing was worth all the trouble.

He has seen people dying out
   of thirst, looking like the flayed end
of a candle. The big boat
   didn't move, the pilgrims melted away,

nothing to think about, you'd shake
   like a madman and the rumble in your ear was the
enormous choir of the ones who'd been left
   on the shore like wrecks. In the end, it was the heat

a muoverti sul mare, o così ti pareva.
            Non sto ancora tanto bene, fa Sidi,
sono un tronco di cera, quando spegni
            la candela e quella fusa che è colata

sembra un albero tagliato, le radici
            ancora forti eppure è morto.
Ma il libro dei morti, dallo qua che
            cerco un nome, fra dieci milioni

un paesano, in viaggio insieme da
            Dakar a Gibilterra, io per Spagna
e Pirenei, lui non lo sapeva, ma
            l'America, diceva, l'America mi gira.

Sidi che parla francese al telefono
            adesso piange a occhi bassi
l'orecchio appeso alla cornetta
            calcando un marciapiede della Quinta.

Tutto ha trovato sul libro dei morti,
            l'amico che esplode il suo nome,
sei qui, come hai fatto a arrivare,
            mi sono sposato, com'è che è l'Italia,

anche tu, quante magliette taroccate,
            combiniamo stasera che devo partire.
E poi che ha messo giù mi dice
            che questa è davvero la valle dei morti,

dove i vivi ci vengono uno a uno
            per star pronti il giorno che saremo
tutti assieme, bianchi e neri
            che saremo, a sentircela cantare.

that shifted you on the waves—or so it seemed.
            I am not feeling very well, Sidi says, not yet.
I am a trunk made of wax—you extinguish
            the candle and all the melted wax

looks like a tree that's been cut down, its roots
            are still strong—but the tree is dead.
But the Book of the Dead, give it to me, I'm looking
            for a name, one in ten million,

a countryman, we traveled together from
            Dakar to Gibraltar, I was heading to Spain
and the Pyrenees, he did not know, but
            America, he would say, America suits me fine.

Sidi who speaks French on the phone
            now cries, keeping his eyes low,
his ear hanging from the receiver,
            feet planted on a sidewalk on Fifth Avenue.

He has found everything in the Book of the Dead,
            his friend who blasts Sidi's name up in the air,
are you here, how did you get here,
            yes, I got married, how is it Italy,

how many fake T-shirts, together, you and me,
            let's hook up tonight before I must leave.
As he puts the phone down he tells me
            that this is really the valley of the dead,

where the living come one by one
            to be ready for that day we'll all be here,
together, black and white,
            that's what we'll be, to face the music.

Beato chi scrive

da *La mosca di Milano*

Beato chi scrive,
chi morde la sghemba gommina
e consuma la mina,
chi scambia le lingue e i cognomi,
chi allinea pensieri,
se fosse un raccolto di pomi,
chi canta il poema africano
del suo parrocchetto che squilla,
la nota che trilla
dall'ultima ottava del piano,
chi conta le anse e le dune
della polvere a cui tornerà,
chi ignora moltissimo e sa,
adesso lo sa.

Beato chi traversa
il display del processore,
che spacca quel vetro di sale
che preme i suoi fogli d'amore,
chi trova un momento a tirare
una riga e rifare il totale,
beato chi si sveglia
in qualsiasi città dove è voluto,
beato chi ci parte fra un minuto,
una calza bucata e un principio di tosse,
beato chi prova
col dito bagnato
il calore del ferro
da stiro sull'asse,
beato chi paga le tasse,
chi sospira sul cagnetto che possiede,
chi tenta il torrente col piede,
chi spanna gli occhiali e ci vede,
adesso ci vede.

Blessed Is He Who Writes

from *The Fly of Milan*

Blessed is he who writes,
who bites the worn-out eraser
wearing the lead,
who trips over tongues and surnames,
who gathers his thoughts
like a bushel of apples,
who sings the African poem
his parakeet's squeaking
—the high tone trilling
from the piano's last octave—
who counts the coves and dunes
of the dust to which he will return,
who knows very little yet he knows,
now he knows.

Blessed is he who runs through
his computer windows,
crashing the salty screen
that weighs heavily on his love letters,
who finds only a minute to draw
a line and rearrange the figures,
blessed is he who awakens
in any city where people still want him,
who is leaving right now for that town
with holes in his socks and coming down with a cold,
blessed is he who checks
with a wet finger
the hot bottom of the iron
on the ironing board,
blessed is he who pays taxes,
who gets sentimental about his puppy,
who tests the water with his toes,
who wipes off his glasses to see,
and now he sees.

E vede una cosa da nulla,
un falso carattere a stampa,
una lucciola cacchina,
appena una fiatata di spessore,
beato chi è amico
di quell'informatore
che gli porta le soffiate che poi scrive,
se poi le sta a guardare
e sa benissimo che appena
le ha lasciate a refolarsi alla ventata
cercare di tenerle
e dire in giro sono mie
è come respirare
una cicchina già fumata.

And he sees nothing special,
a tricky typo,
a firefly stain
the width of a breath.
Blessed is he who befriends
the snitch who brings him
the leaks he then writes,
if later he keeps on staring at them
fully aware that soon
they dry in the wind as he
tries to hang on to them for a while
telling people they are mine
would be like breathing through
spent cigarette butts.

⇥ Mario Moroni (b. 1955)

Mario Moroni, born in 1955, is professor of Italian at the State University of New York at Binghamton. He has published six volumes of poetry, *Dall'assoluta attualità* (1979) *I racconti* (1985) *La composizione del tempo* (1988) *Paesaggi oltre* (1989) *Tutto questo* (2000), *Le terre di Icaro* (2001), and *Icarus' Lands* (2006), translated by E. Di Pasquale, and a DVD, *Reflections on Icarus' Lands* (2006), with composer John Hallstrom. Moroni has also composed one volume of poetic prose, *Brevi storie dell'ospite assente* (2002). His poems have appeared in numerous magazines and several anthologies, including *Poesia Italiana Oggi* (1981), *Viaggio al termine della parola* (1981), ... *a cominciare da zeta* (1986), *Le radici della poesia* (1987), *Poesia italiana della contraddizione* (1989), *Poesaggio* (1993), *Scritture di fine Novecento* (1998), and *Akusma* (2000). He is also author of three books of criticism: *Essere e fare. L'itinerario poetico di Antonio Porta* (1991), *La presenza complessa* (1998), and *Al limite* (2007). He coedited *Italian Modernism* (2004), *From Eugenio Montale to Amelia Rosselli* (2004), and *Neoavanguardia* (2009). Mario Moroni began his poetic activity in the mid-1970s, experimented with visual poetry and mail art, and published in such key journals as *Squero, Steve, Cervo volante,* and *Anterem,* at a poeticological conjuncture in which, having "journeyed to the end of the word,"[54] Italian poetry was trying to restart anew. *I racconti,* in fact, shows evidence of the influence of the last of the true neo-avant-gardists, namely Adriano Spatola, who himself had begun to move on to a poetry that was "self-sufficient, not closed in itself but resolved in a conscious organism."[55]

In Moroni, we find a long line with repeating, almost hammering phonetic stresses, with a rediscovered sense of the potential of syntax, semantically depersonalized and yet, precisely owing to this recurring, almost obsessive fixation with objects and situations exfoliated to deepest essentiality, one gets the feeling that subjectivity is being tacitly reintroduced. As Paolo Valesio pointed out,[56] Moroni's particular rhetoric of *repetitio* introduces a *ruminatio*, a sort of reflective, philosophical excavation, a returning to the depths that implies a refining of the poetic *materia*. And what is being talked about is the relevance of time to the construction and meaning of both the text and the world. This is visible in Moroni's *La composizione del tempo*,[57] in which we can register a nomadism of the objects and the affects of a seemingly endless recitation: "now you seek the traces / the table on which you mark the passage / papers or magnets to manage the event / ... / remember: words, silences, intervals" (26). In essence, Moroni's poetry before his coming to the United States was working on the threshold of what has been called *dicibilità*, the capacity of the text to relate not so much *to* the world as *saying* the world, in a sense making his an ontological poetics that could be analyzed in Heideggerian terms, as the speaking of language qua *langage*.[58] In this sense, his early poetry does show some affinities, at least at the level of poetological intentions, with the poetry of the younger Ballerini.

But it is in Moroni's next book, *Le terre di Icaro*,[59] written in *terra straniera*, in Calypso's cave, that the referent, the "real world" elbows, nudges, and heaves, and finally irrupts into the text. Although some of the tonalities of the earlier work remain, the versification is now based more on actual speech patterns, the syntax recovers the full panoply of the system of the *langue*, and the themes bring Moroni in the company of the other expatriates: "Can it be said here it was us, in the photo, / on the map or place. Will they / say here we have been, yesterday" (16). Paradoxically, against the annihilation of the subject present in his first two books, the ones written while still in Italy, the speaking *I* emerges now starkly in virtue of its no longer being housed entirely *in* language as *langage*, perhaps the effect of a parallax possible only when there is that deterritorialization vis-à-vis not only the land but also the culture, the speech, the *alveus* of the Italian poetic tradition. The poem "Parlare" harps on the perception of the world from a window, subjecting it to repeated phenomenological passes, ending with a sense of the difference between *I* and world, floating in the immeasurable distance between logos and topos, the utterance itself and the array of events prisoners of situated time, or a particular *place*.

Moroni's poetic voice metamorphizes as he *rediscovered* the world once in the United States, being in this not unlike Livorni. This well-known phenomenon creates a split in the poetic psyche but also discloses the possibility of a new poetics, one that *reterritorializes* the heterogeneous surroundings not necessarily in a social or political vein,[60] but in a new or different "intensive utilization of language." Again, like many a poet in this collection, the issue of rediscovering language as *langue*, and of sensing a chasm between sign and reference, is palpable. This condition discloses spaces more apt at showing the point of contact between poet and world, that is, more predisposed to inscribing pain, sorrow, loss, doubt, memory, as well as, and perceivable in other poets gathered here, playfulness, ironies, and detachment. Finally, Moroni makes manifest what can be called the knowledge of the nomad, which is markedly different from that of the migrant or the exile.[61]

In terms of our hermeneutic model, Moroni's poetry, in traveling from Time to History, and therefore in abandoning the immortality of the timeless text, has abandoned the search of Apex C: Poetry/*Langage*, and moved toward the axis between Apex D: *Langue*/Reality, and Apex B: Home/Mortality, where, as he writes in "Cinque terre," which follows, the questions about a possible dwelling "are routes"—for "there is no answer."

Il luogo segreto

da *Tutto questo*

Cosa voleva dire mio padre
quando indicava quell'angolo
in un pomeriggio dalla luce ferma,
nello spessore di quel silenzio,
lui ormai perso nella paralisi dei suoni,
dei verbi. Cosa voleva dire indicando
quel punto, luogo di nascita, d'infanzia.
Cosa c'era di così segreto da guidarmi lì,
portarmici a gesti, nella sospensione
della parola, nel luogo delle uova.

Quel luogo sepolto, dentro l'arena
dei segreti, di ciò che non era stato detto.
Era l'archivio delle cose, l'ultima informazione,
nell'aria della voliera, nel recinto della memoria.

Seguirlo fino a lì, oltre il cancello,
per un segreto che solo lui conosceva.
Cosa c'era nelle uova, sotto
le foglie secche, oltre il tempo consumato.
Voleva passarlo a me quel piccolo segreto,
quel modo di ritrovare il luogo, di ritornare.

The Secret Place

from *All That*

What did my father mean
when he pointed to that corner
one afternoon of still light,
in the heft of that silence,
he already lost in the paralysis of sounds,
of verbs. What did he mean by pointing
to that spot, place of birth, of infancy.
What was so secret that led him to guide me there,
to bring me there with gestures, with the words
dangling, to the place of the eggs.

That place buried, inside the arena
of secrets, of what had not been said.
It was the archive of things, the final indication,
in the aviary's air, in memory's enclosure.

To follow him there, beyond the gate,
for a secret that only he knew.
What was in the eggs, under
the dry leaves, other than the time gone by.
He wanted to pass that little secret on to me,
that way of again finding the place, of returning.

Terra, questa terra

da Le terre di Icaro

terra, come esiste
questa terra che torna
in mente in ore diverse
ed oltre la casa
come l'uomo si sveglia
dice solo parole
tornano solo parole
ragionando il respiro
gli odori che sono suoi

anche dietro gli anni
negli anni pubblici
non sai quanto lunghi
non sai quanto veri
capaci di dare il senso
di uno sguardo chiuso
quasi respiro e voce
molte voci, dietro gli anni
che chiare e raccolte
scendono in strada

come si sanno, le cose
che udite come ombre
solo sapere la voce
come ombra, incredibile
raccolta con alcuni segreti
con i toni, ancora occhi
che sembrano chiusi, invece
solo si levano lenti

ancora la voce, una voce
giorno, nel giorno che viene
quasi sempre respiro, adesso
e parole che sotto il fiato
restano e danno spessori

Land, This Land

from *Icarus's Lands*

land, how does this land
exist remembered
at different hours
and beyond the house
like a man awakening
says only words
and only words return
the breath the reasoning
the scents that are his

even after the years
the years in the public eye
you don't know how long
you don't know how true
capable of making sense
of an impenetrable look
almost a sigh a voice
many voices, which clear
and self-contained after these years
takes to the road

how does one know the things
which heard as shadows
are known by the voice
like a shade, incredible
gathered with some secrets
with the tones, eyes that still
seem closed, but instead
are only rising slowly

again the voice, a voice
day, in the coming day almost
always brings breath, now
and words that under the breath
remain and give breadth

e rivissute, come tessuti
in parte sospesi e sogni
senza stupire, certi
che come stagioni intorno
come parole riposte
come mai è stato detto
nessuno attende nulla
senza attese non accade
e come rami che sporgono
ed entrano dalla finestra
stretti tra i vecchi timori
di freddo e carne secca
tavole consumate e frutta
che ingombrano il vento
e le parole, ora si trema

non so se è la voce
ora e come prima
a parlare del gran campo
del contatto dei corpi
ora si sfugge alla presa
e tutto uscirà dal fondo
come se tra gli alberi
non detti ci fossero gli anni

tavole secche e rimosse
che sono parole ed oltre
anche vento e colori
ma più secchi
forse o solo tempo
tempo per vedere
e tempo per ascoltare
necessità, voglie, senso
cose in acceso silenzio
in strade, più in là

and are relived, like fabrics
partly unused and dreams
which no longer astonish, sure
that like seasons around
like words put away
as never said before
no one expects anything
without waiting it doesn't happen
and like branches that reach out
and enter through the window
tightly between the old fears
of the cold and dry meat
consumed tables and fruit
that hinder the wind
and the words, now we tremble

I don't know if it's the voice
now and as before
speaking of the great field
of the contact of the bodies
now one escapes the grip and
everything will vanish from the bottom
as if among the trees what
was unsaid were the years

dry and removed tables
that are words and more
even wind and colors
but drier
perhaps or only time
time to see
and time to hear
necessity, desires, sense
things in glowing silence
on the roads, farther on

Le Cinque Terre

1.

I tuoi occhi che pongono la domanda,
le domande: a quante ho già risposto?
A quante non ho saputo, potuto. Qui
siamo al limite del giardino, tra la collina
e le piccole strade, percorsi in cui si potrebbe passare
molte volte senza riconoscerli. È segno che le domande
possono essere come quei sentieri,
che le risposte sono percorsi?

2

Per ora ci sono solo sedie vuote, bianche,
al limite del giardino, è da questo luogo
che inizio a risponderti, esporre una frase
e più frasi. Queste circondano la collina,
i gradini che si perdono su rocce, questo lo sapeva
il poeta che per tracciare una vita segnò un solco
nell'acqua. Questo rimane, ora: navi che percorrono linee,
tracce marine che attendono altre spiegazioni.

3.

Tenendo gli oggetti appesi
tutti nella mente, al muro,
che pendono e si aprono, producendo suono.
Piena d'aria è la notte
e sempre rivive il pensiero
di come sia, cosa sia
una stagione diversa da questa.
Come dare l'immagine di un'altra stagione,
il suo clima, il perché essa appare sempre
nello spazio, stesso luogo di adesso,
ma vista in un altro momento
in cui io non ci sarò.
È possibile parlarne?

Cinque Terre

1.

Your eyes that ask the question, the questions:
how many have I already answered?
Many I have not answered, could not. Here
we are at the garden's end, between the hill
and the small roads, routes one could often
pass by and not recognize. Is it a sign that
the questions are like those paths,
that the answers are routes?

2.

For now there are only empty chairs, white,
at the garden's edge, and it's from this place
that I begin to answer you, to expound a phrase
and more phrases. These surround the hill,
the steps that lose themselves on rocks; this was known
by the poet who in tracing a life dug a furrow
in the water. This remains now: ships that travel lines,
marine traces that await other explanations.

3.

Holding them suspended
in the mind, on the wall, the objects
hang down and open up, making sounds.
The night is full of air
and life comes back thinking
again of how, of what
a season different from this is.
How does one give flesh to another season,
its climate, why it always appears
in the space, the same place as now,
but seen at another moment
where I won't be.
Is it possible to speak of it?

4.

La superficie dell'acqua e quella delle domande
si equivalgono?
Ogni metro quadrato pieno di parole.
Non c'è risposta.
Ora solo tagli nella roccia, a solchi, a squame,
squamatura delle pietre che simula quella dei pesci.
Sono loro, i pesci, a mandare gli ultimi segnali,
elettrici, notturni, sulle superfici sparse, lungo le coste.
Parlo di loro o di noi, adesso?
Non c'è risposta.
Ora si va per linee oblique.
Solo segnalando una dimora c'è obiettivo,
esistenza di singoli o tracce del loro andare
e venire, che formano disegni, a squame, a tagli
come quelli nelle rocce, fenditure della memoria,
innesti che il tempo ha fatto
qui nei vari ripiani, gradini della mente
che costeggiano le cose. La risposta dipende
dalla loro consistenza: quella delle coste, delle fenditure,
ferite che spesso lasciano spazio alla luce

4.

Is the the surface of the water and that
of questions the same?
Each square yard is full of words.
There is no answer.
Now, you cut only scales or grooves in the rock,
scaling the stones fish-like.
It is they, the fish, who send the last signals,
electric, nocturnal, on the scattered surfaces, along the coasts.
Am I speaking of them or of us now?
There is no answer.
Now the traveling follows oblique lines.
Only in pointing out a dwelling is there an aim,
the existence of individuals or traces of their coming
and going, that make designs, like scales, cuts,
cracks in the memory, like those in the rocks,
grafts that time has made
here in the various terraces, steps of the mind
that run along things. The answer depends
on their consistency: that of the coasts, of the fissures,
wounds that often leave room for the light.

Il pastore in transito

da Giacomo Leopardi

1.

Sopra le mille e mille luci
di città deserte e mille villaggi, ora
tutte riunite le greggi meccaniche
le greggi alate, a quale voce
ho diritto io, pastore
nelle vesti di capitano di bordo,
io pastore, capitano di vascello
seduto solo per un attimo,
quale voce risiede e presiede
qui, nel luogo della luna,
nel punto d'osservazione
ormai liberate tutte le greggi,
da lungo tempo, ormai.

2.

Io, partito dai villaggi del sale,
porti smarriti di cui oggi
si legge sui libri o sulle mappe,
partito dai deserti quando
l'Asia era altra Asia,
quando le mattine non erano ancora
esplose nelle viscere
sotto i fuochi dei mortai, degli dèi.
Nell'avventura di una lingua
soffusa, mai del tutto scritta,
io, sospeso nella sera a guardare
e meditare, quale luogo oggi
per quei pensieri, quali sogni
di nascita, quali di morte?

3.

Tutto il mio errore ora
è nella carta elettronica,
a cavallo di oceani, lasciati

Shepherd Going Through

after Giacomo Leopardi

1.

Above the thousand upon thousand lights
of deserted cities and thousand villages, now
the mechanical flocks the winged flocks
have now gathered, what voice
do I have a right to, I shepherd
in the guise of a crew captain,
I shepherd, captain of a vessel
sitting only for an instant,
what voice resides and presides
here, in the moon's dwelling,
at the point of observation
now that all the flocks are freed,
for a long time, now.

2.

I, departed from the salt villages,
lost ports that one now
reads of in books or on maps,
departed from the deserts when
Asia was another Asia,
when the mornings had not yet
exploded in the bowels
under the fire of the mortars, of the gods.
In the adventure of a suffused
tongue, never wholly written,
I, suspended in the evening, looking
and meditating, what place today
for those thoughts, which dreams
of birth, which ones of death?

3.

The whole of my erring now
is on the electronic map,
straddling oceans, having left

i deserti e gli armenti
e le carovane ormai viaggianti
a ottanta miglia l'ora.
Ora la luce notturna, buio e grigio
per contemplare, come ripensare a te,
luna? Dove va il mio breve corso?
Con il vento che spira in coda,
che insegue le foglie, spezza
le memorie, e il tuo corso
sempre immortale, dove va?

6.

O luna, io nei miei infiniti passaggi,
impossibile adesso perfino sedere
sulle erbe ed ombre, con il vecchio fastidio
che ritorna e assale le cose,
ma ancora ho motivo di pensare
che più felice non sono
nel volare tra le greggi di nuvole,
più felice non sono, eppure vivo
e passo tra stagioni ostili
e laghi ghiacciati perché, o luna,
forse era vero: in quale stato io sia
passo la vita a vivere, ma questo
non è condanna se forse funesto è il giorno;
ma è da quel giorno che io vivo tra i vivi
e andando passo, nel capire
le ragioni del pianto,
non mirando all'altrui sorte,
trovo la strada da pastore e passeggero
ormai non più atteso, eppure in movimento
tra i due mondi che s'incontrano adesso
nel punto più alto della notte.

the deserts and the herds
and the caravans by now traveling
at eighty miles an hour.
Nocturnal light now, dark and gray time
to contemplate, but how to recall you again,
moon? Where does my short path lead?
With the wind that blows from the rear,
that chases after leaves, breaks
memories, and your always
immortal path, where does it go?

6.
O moon, I in my endless crossings,
impossible now even to sit
on the grasses and shadows, with the old bother
that returns and seizes things,
but I still have reason to think
that happier I am not
when I fly among the flocks of clouds,
not happier at all, and yet I live
and go through hostile seasons
and frozen lakes because, o moon,
perhaps it was true: In whatever state I'm in
I spend my life living, yet this
is no punishment though the day be ominous;
but it is from that day that I've lived among the living
and by going along I cross, in understanding
the reasons for weeping,
not looking at others' fates,
I find the shepherd's road and of the passenger
now no longer expected, and yet in motion
between the two worlds that meet now
at night's highest point.

→ *Bruno Gulli (b. 1959)*

Bruno Gulli, born in Calabria, has lived in the United States since 1985. He has studied literature and philosophy in Venice, Italy, and then in San Francisco and New York, where he completed a doctorate at the CUNY Graduate Center in 2003 with a dissertation on the ontology of labor titled *An Art Hidden in the Forest of the Earth: The Ontology of Labor between Economy and Culture*. A revised version of his dissertation is now published as *Labor of Fire* (2005). His work in political philosophy continued with *Earthly Plenitudes: A Study on Sovereignty and Labor* (2010). He teaches philosophy at Long Island University and at Kingsborough Community College, in Brooklyn. He has published poetry in various journals and anthologies. He also published two chapbooks of poems: *Lines of Another Research* (1988) and *Figures of a Foreign Land* (2001).

Bruno Gulli is a philosophical poet in the tradition of Parmenides, Hölderlin, Michaelstaedter, and Stevens, but he is also political like Pasolini, and the texts easily reflect the schism between Being in its elusive showing/concealing and the concretions of what Heidegger calls the *Dasein* , actual being-there, in real political social history. He writes of the ontological aspect of existence, as in "Hölderlin's Window," included here, where we read: "Nothing but being remains / When / In the strong silence persisting / Unheard / The planes of time shift / And thought appears / In all its brightness: / The plane of memory / And the absent other—the future." Here we pick up an implicit critique of our entire Eurologocentric globalization project, where the revelation casts its light on the flattening of the past and the loss of hope, as futurity, Heidegger's *Zukunfheit*, is definitely lacking. It is therefore pessimistic, as attested by these lines: "War and blood and death / Reign all over. / The world sees no light. / Neither in the sweatshops in Pakistan / Or Thailand, nor those in New York / Or California does the void of time bring / New being."

This poet is clearly working along the horizontal axis of our critical model, connecting Apex C: Poetry/*Langage* to Apex D: *Langue*/Reality, that is, the ontological to the ontic, the metaphysical to the historical-existential.

La finestra di Hölderlin

Non c'è altro che l'essere
                    Quando
Nel silenzio che non passa inascoltato,
Tanto è forte,
Si spostano i piani del tempo
E il pensiero appare
In tutta la sua lucentezza.
Il piano della memoria
E l'altro assente del futuro.
Ma rari sono momenti e modi
Della consolazione.
Noi da un lato il pensiero
Dall'altro la parola
Nel vuoto del tempo
Con affanno cerchiamo.
La quiete era prima
Dopo sarà la quiete.
Dietro la finestra questa luce nuova
Esuberante della natura
Calda della sera
Vuoti e freddi ci trova
Nel tempo dell'indifferenza
E ci ravviva.

Forse un pensiero nuovo
Dalle foreste e dai monti,
Forse dalle affollate stazioni
Delle grandi metropoli
Un viso eterno e giovane,
Ma nello sguardo antico,
Rinnova le passioni, il fuoco
Che il cielo della sera accende.
Eppure semplici sono abiti e modi.
Qui sul treno che va downtown
E si perde nei boschi infuocati
Dal nuovo sole,

Hölderlin's Window

Nothing but being remains
                    When
In the strong silence that goes not
Unheard
The planes of time shift
And thought appears
In all its brightness:
The plane of memory
And the absent other—of the future.
But moments and modes
Of consolation are rare.
We anxiously seek
Thought on one side
The word on the other
In the void of time.
Quiet was earlier
Later there will be quiet.
Behind the window this new light
Exuberant with nature's
Warmth in the evening
Finds us empty and cold
In the time of indifference
And revives us.

Perhaps a new thought
From the forest and mountains,
Perhaps in the crowded stations
Of forlorn cities
A young yet eternal face,
Ancient in its gaze,
Renews our passions, the fire
Kindled by the evening sky.
Yet simple are dress and manners.
Here on the city-bound train
That vanishes into the woods
Set on fire by the new sun,

Negli angoli remoti della terra,
Semplici sono i discorsi,
Ma alti e veri,
Discorsi tra paria e dei,
Di come guerra ovunque
E sangue e morte regni.
Luce non vede il mondo.
Né negli sweatshop del Pakistan
O della Thailandia, né in quelli di New York
O della California porta il vuoto del tempo
Essere nuovo. Ridono a Washington, Londra,
E nelle altre capitali. Né per le strade di La Paz,
Né tra le macerie a Bagdad l'essere è nulla.
Non si accorge quel riso

                        Che si dice democratico

Della nuova libertà che viene,
Scende come lava dai monti,
Fiume che rompe gli argini.
Del futuro è l'essere che viene
Assoluto e libero, dalla fronte ampia.
Immensi spazi reca con sé.
Come un nuovo dio, schiaccia
Sotto i piedi nudi e forti
Tempie di falsa intelligenza.
Nuove città sorgono dappertutto nel mondo,
Nuovi centri di vita. Al crescente rumore
Di festa, al libero andirivieni di gente
Il dono della schietta parola inatteso
Si aggiunge, il presagio, che è memoria,
                        Dei lumi.

Alla solita finestra stanco ritorno
Come chi per lunga assenza
Per estenuante cammino
E laboriosa ricerca
Perduto della mente abbia la forza,
Del corpo il senso, a cui il riposo
Perfino sembri azione e sforzo.
Né celi tu la tua presenza, pensiero.

In the remote corners of the earth,
Conversations are simple,
But lofty and real,
Conversations between pariahs and gods,
On how war and blood and death
Reign all over.
The world sees no light.
Neither in the sweatshops in Pakistan
Or Thailand, nor those in New York
Or California does the void of time bring
New being. They laugh in Washington, London,
And the other capitals. Neither on the streets of La Paz,
Nor among the rubble in Baghdad is being nothing.
The laughter that calls itself democratic
                                        Doesn't see

The new coming freedom
That flows like lava down the mountains,
A river that breaks its banks.
The absolute and free being which is coming,
With a wide brow, comes from the future.
It carries with it immense spaces.
Like a new god, it crushes
Under its bare strong feet
Temples of a false intelligence.
New cities arise everywhere in the world,
New centers of life. To the crescendo of festivity,
To the free coming and going of people
The unexpected gift of a genuine word
Adds itself, the presage, which is memory,
                                        Of enlightenment.

To the usual window, tired, I return
As one who after a long absence
After an exhausting journey
And a laborious search
Has lost his mental strength,
His bodily sense, one to whom even rest
Appears to be action and effort.
Nor do you, thought, hide your presence.

Il sonno è giusto in queste circostanze.
Avvolge nel crepuscolo i muri trepidanti
Delle case, il suono dei nostri passi,
La solitudine.
     In questo vortice
Della memoria e di ciò che a eguale stato
Aspira trova i suoi elementi il lavoro.
Al risveglio, la luce del pensiero,
Un nuovo sole, inonda spazi eterni.

           (New York, 2003)

Sleep is good in these circumstances.
It envelopes in the twilight the trembling walls
Of houses, the sound of our steps,
Solitude.
          In this vortex
Of memory and of that which to equal status
Aspires, labor finds its elements.
Upon waking, the light of thought,
A new sun, floods eternal spaces.

(New York, 2003)

Preparazione e nascita

Death is not this master

E. Levinas

Ho imparato che spesso
È doloroso il ritorno
E deve esserlo
Di noi stessi a noi stessi
Del lavoro al lavoro
Della vita e del tempo
All'assente presenza
Dell'atomico moto
Di tumulto e di caos
Del tempo che siamo:
nunc stans.

Ora assorto sedendo
Dentro i monti nei boschi
Di faggi e di pini
Che hanno visto i briganti
Contro stati nascenti
E signori oppressivi
Fra due mari chiarissimi
Spazio certo del nascere
Di violenza e tragedie
Ancora eterno
E sempre nuovo
Copre i tempi negati
Veloci e insieme lenti
Fra l'inizio e la fine.

Dirompente fiato
Immenso fuoco—
E noi? Poter restare
Abbandonati e nudi
Su questa terra cruda
A sognare una vita diversa?

Preparation and Birth

Death is not this master

E. Levinas

I've learned that often
It's painful to return
As it must be
From ourselves to ourselves
From labor to labor
From life and time
To the absent presence
Of the atomic motion
Of unrest and chaos
Of the time we are:
nunc stans.

Now sitting thoughtful
In the mountains in the woods
Of beeches and pines
That saw the brigands
Against rising states
And oppressive lords
Between two bright seas
Certain space of birth
Of violence and tragedy
Still eternal
And ever new
Covering denied times
Both quick and slow
Between beginning and end.

Explosive breath
Immense fire—
And yet, can we still stay
Abandoned and naked
On the crude earth
Dreaming of a different life?

Tempo diverso del nascere
Pluriverso del fare comune
Nell'insolitudine vera
Di terrene plenitudini
Dentro l'essere che è
E non può non essere
(mentre il nulla non è
Ed è necessario che non sia)—
Sognare una vita diversa?
Costruirla ogni volta
Fuori da questo immenso
Silenzio, nel giusto mezzogiorno
Di apparente stasi
Nelle notti stellate
Del probabile ritorno.

(New York, 2003–2006)

Different times for birth
Multiverse of common doing
In the true insolitude
Of earthly plenitudes
Within being that is
And cannot not be
(Whereas nothingness is not
And it is necessary for it not to be)—
Dreaming of a different life?
Building it constantly
Out of this immense
Silence, in the just noon
Of apparent stasis
In the starry nights
Of a probable return.

(New York, 2003–2006)

⇥ Ernesto Livorni (b. 1959)

Ernesto Livorni, born in Pescara, is professor of Italian and comparative literature at the University of Wisconsin, Madison. He came to the United States in 1984 and obtained his doctorate in comparative literature from the University of Connecticut in 1990, with a thesis on Dante and Pound. He taught at Yale University from 1988 until 2000. Livorni has published three collections of poems, *Prospettiche illusioni* (1977–1983) (1987), *Nel libro che ti diedi. Sonetti* (1985–1986) (1998), and *L'America dei padri* (2005). He is preparing another collection, *Onora il padre e la madre (Honor Thy Father and Mother)*, for publication. His poems have appeared in numerous journals in Italy (*Tracce, Anfione—Zeto, Frontiera, La Voce dell'Emigrante, Quaderno, Steve, Ricerca Research Recherche*) and the United States (*Forum Italicum, Polytext , Antigones, VIA: Voices in Italian Americana*). Livorni's scholarly publications include *Avanguardia e tradizione: Ezra Pound e Giuseppe Ungaretti* (1998) and more than forty articles on medieval, modern, and contemporary Italian, English, Italian American, and comparative literature. He also translated and edited Ted Hughes's *Cave-Birds: Un dramma alchemico della caverna* (2001) and is currently editing essays and poems by Giovanni Pascoli. Livorni is the founding editor of *L'Anello Che non Tiene: Journal of Modern Italian Literature*, which began publication in 1988, and was the coeditor of the review *YIP: Yale Italian Poetry* (1997–2000). He is on the editorial board of *Italica* and served on the editorial boards of *Italian Culture* and *Ricerca Research Recherche*. He was the vice president of the American Association for Italian Studies (2000–2006) and served on the Modern Language Association Executive Committee of the Division on Seventeenth-, Eighteenth- and Nineteenth-Century Italian Literature.

In *L'America dei padri*, his most recent book, Livorni is clearly straddling the two worlds and is strongly referential, though perhaps owing to his background in and great knowledge of the tradition—which counterbalances his work inspired by the avant-gardes, as represented by the poem "Hysteron Proteron" in this selection—he elects to couch his journeying in classical forms such as the sonnet, the ballad, and the epistle. Right from the incipit, one becomes aware of how Livorni threads and weaves his song of the soul through geographical and historical tapestries, entering the tormented *alveus* of memory, of inexplicable events, of endings and beginnings that have no closure and no identifiable origins. In a poem we could not include here he writes: "Two months he traveled before arriving / and the year even my grandfather, his son, / has forgotten: what difference / there was between the Marulli elms / and those great sequoias / soon even he forgot. / The arrival was not at all triumphal, / in fact, if the truth be told, he never even / realized he'd arrived."[52] A more detailed analysis, however, would also reveal the co-presence of a tendency toward the spiritual, toward a Power that might help in understanding this bleak and melancholy scenario of indifference, of abuses, of desperation. On the topic of not-being-home, of living elsewhere, the poems included in our small sampling speak most eloquently about the process of dealing with the rift and the sequence of thoughts and questions in search of some form of mediation, some understanding that would quell the anxiety or worse fear of getting a nonanswer, or a question in return.

Livorni's poetry is more concerned with the place of destination than with the place of origin, but it has already acknowledged that the new home is not fixed, is not a replacement, and in fact, and most unsettling, often it is not even recognized. Perhaps it is always to be sought. It speaks of the elsewhere without an explicit concern for immortality either divine or human, although that option is not barred from some unforeseen disclosure. This may be grasped in the unmistakable echoes of the *langue* of the tradition that mark his texts, embodied in a melic voice, instancing a presentiment of mortality generated by the awareness that home is actually now the journeying itself. Much like Carrera, but perhaps less stoic, Livorni dwells in the wandering, though his poetic line does retain a more musical, melopoetic, even mythic tonality. No one can say that deterritorialization here is not felt, described, and belabored. In section XV of *L'America dei padri*, reproduced below, we read: "Perhaps you would say that the hardest exile / is the one you suffer when home, / land, longtime friends you leave / and, having crossed the river and sea, you go. / ... / Perhaps you would say that the hardest exile / is the one you suffer quietly in dreams / or in sleepless nights," when the previous life "belongs neither to you nor others any longer." Though properly speaking an expatriate, Livorni takes the existential and symbolic condition of the exile very seriously.

But only up to a point: There being no pining for *nostos*, there is clearly no yearning for a home "back there," or "back then," but more like a melancholy reconstituting of the world as being lived. His "Ode to America" is one of the most beautiful and passionate songs to that still undecipherable and relentlessly contradicting continuum called America. We might add that, of the four traits of the language employed by the estranged, dislocated writer, which are vernacular, vehicular, referential, and mythic, Livorni's poetry can be read as beginning with the vernacular and the referential in order to alight upon the mythic, "on the horizon of cultures," which permits "a spiritual or religious reterritorialization."[53]

But there is another possible itinerary, as is often warranted when before a real poet. The poet's belonging may be sought in that transversal phenomenon implied in the very creation of language, in reaching deep beneath national languages, beneath, that is, territorialization and social boundaries, and experience and explore the very coming into being of the human possibility to speak, as is the case with children. Whether "Hysteron Proteron" was in part motivated by the fact that the poet in his early adulthood had to basically relearn another language (with all attendant mythologies, nuances, nursery rhymes, and so on, including considering the learning patterns of an offspring), and thus be reborn, the fact remains that the uprooted poet not only fertilizes his store of semantic spora and rhyzomatic tendrils, but also sharpens his receptors and perhaps hoists up a few more antennas to record and to listen to the very *pneuma* of existence, the word of life into its very coming into being.

In this perspective, anchored to the Apex D: *Langue*/Reality, (and with an ear to keep the *langage* of the tradition, Apex C, alive), his poetics extends between the problematic Apex A: Elsewhere/Immortality, keenly aware of the nonbelonging implicit in the "any place," and the just as problematic Apex B: Home/Mortality, where once again the negative of one term of the dyad, in his case, not-home, informs the tension issuing from the other, the possibility that ends all possibilities.

X

La pioggia picchiettava leggera
i fumi delle metropolitane
che dai fondi tombini a New York
ci salivano in gola a esalarci;
e la pioggia insinuava un gran freddo
colando sulle vetrate riflesse.

La gente passava, le teste flesse,
senza notare che tutto quel freddo
ci saliva in gola per esalarci
coi fumi delle metropolitane;
e la pioggia ci picchiettava leggera
sotto i fondi tombini a New York.

from *The America of the Fathers*

X

The rain tapped lightly
the smoke from the subway
that from the deep sewers of New York
was rising in our throats to exhale us;
and the rain suggested a deep cold
dripping from windows reflected.

People passed by, their heads tilted,
without noticing that all that cold
was rising in our throats to exhale us
with the steam of the subway;
and the rain tapped lightly
beneath the deep sewers of New York.

XIV

      New York di notte è un sassofono
che tinge il cielo di velluto blu
con le vetrate slanciate ed opache
dei grattacieli senza tetto, sfida
perenne nello spazio che s'incaglia
tra i reticoli di strade ed avenues,
dai quali invano una fuga o soltanto
un rifugio parziale cerchiamo;

      un sassofono d'ottone
che si distende nella notte gialla
di luci intermittenti a Manhattan
in un'orchestra di taxi che vanno
(la metropolitana in sottofondo)
tra le dita nere di minoranze
etniche, nelle radio alternative,
sulla pelle bucata di ambulanze.

      New York di notte è un sassofono
che tinge il cielo di velluto rosso
nella rabbia calpestata ai margini
dei fuochi ad Harlem, nelle metaforiche
gabbie del Bronx e dello zoo parte
siamo anche noi del Village e di Broadway
non restano che i gatti disperati
mentre annusano polvere e siringhe;

      un sassofono in luminescenza
sotto i riflettori di quel concerto
di cui la musica mi balla vene
martoriate dal pulsare sudore
e pianto nell'iridescenza solita
del giorno che s'alza ancora fatidico
come un pendolare che voglia suonare
quest'ultima nota prima dell'alba.

XIV

New York by night is a saxophone
that tints the sky blue velvet
with the tall and opaque windows
of skyscrapers without roofs, perennial
challenge in a space stuck
among the intersection of streets and *avenues,*
from which an escape or even
a partial refuge we vainly seek;

a brass saxophone
that stretches through the night yellow
from the intermittent lights of Manhattan
in an orchestra of taxis that move
(the subway as background)
through the black fingers of ethnic
minorities, on the alternative radios,
on the punctured skin of ambulances.

New York by night is a saxophone
that tints the sky red velvet
in the rage trampled at the edges
of fires in Harlem, in the metaphorical
cages of the Bronx and the zoo—a part
we are too—of the Village and on Broadway;
nothing is left except the hopeless cats
sniffing dust and syringes;

      a saxophone luminescent
under the flood lights of that concert
where the music danced in my veins
tortured by the pulsing sweat
and crying in the usual iridescence
of the day that arose still prophetic
as a commuter who wants to sound
the last note before dawn.

Esilio

Forse diresti che il più duro esilio
è quello che soffri quando la casa,
la terra, gli amici di sempre lasci
e, varcato il fiume e il mare, vai.

Forse diresti che il più duro esilio
è quello che soffri quieto nei sogni
o nelle veglie notturne: la madre,
la terra ed ogni brandello di quella
vita trascorsa, di quella che ormai
a te o ad altri più non appartiene.

Ma forse quel giorno che venne infine
a separare la notte dall'acqua,
la notte che ci avvolge senza tempo
e nel più fondo segreto nasconde;
forse quel giorno non giunse ferino,
eppure immerso di luce negli occhi?

Son certo che il pianto che primo fuse
noi e la terra, sigillo sicuro
fu al primo distacco, con dolore
che ancora ci marchia, chissà per quanto!

Forse diresti che il più duro esilio
è quello che segna i giochi d'amore,
li forza, li stringe come una rete
senza più varco e con le maglie infitte.

Forse diresti che il più duro esilio
è quello che segna ogni tuo errore
ed a sera ti pesa più degli anni
e non sai come librarti nell'aria
più fresca senza quei sensi di colpa
che ogni mattino ti svegliano ansanti.

Ma quel giorno che viene infine
a conciliarci col freddo e col buio,

Exile

XV

Perhaps you would say that the hardest exile
is the one you suffer when home,
and land, and longtime friends you leave
and, having crossed the river and sea, you go.

Perhaps you would say that the hardest exile
is the one you suffer quietly in dreams
or in sleepless nights; mother,
the land and every shred of that
life lived, that life that now
belongs neither to you nor others any longer.

But perhaps the day that came at the end
to separate night from water,
the night that covers us without time
and in deepest secret hides;
perhaps that day arrived savage,
yet immersed with light in your eyes?

I am sure that the cry that first fused
us with the land, sure sign
of the first separation, with pain
that still marks us, who knows for how long!

Perhaps you would say that the hardest exile
is the one marked by love's whims,
he pushes them, pulls them like a net
without an opening, the threads meshing in.

Perhaps you would say that the hardest exile
is the one that marks your every mistake
and each night weighs on you more than years
and you don't know to balance yourself in a fresher
air without the sense of guilt
that each morning wakes you anxious.

But that day comes at the end
to reconcile us to the cold and darkness,

col buio che ci avvolge senza tempo
e nelle più fonde segrete scende;
forse quel giorno non giunge tremendo,
seppure sommerso in un fato cieco?

       Son certo che il riso che presto fonde
noi e la terra, sigillo sicuro
sarà a quel distacco, con dolore
che già ci marchia, e chissà per quanto!

darkness that covers us without time
and in deepest secret descends;
perhaps that terrible day will not arrive,
even if submersed in a blind fate?

      I am sure the laughter that soon will fuse
us with the land, sure sign
it will be of that separation, with pain
that already marks us, and who knows for how long!

Ode all'America

America qua, America là,
dov'è più l'America del padre mio?

Rocco Scotellaro

XXIII

L'America terra che accoglie, come puttana
pronta per tutti; l'America come conquista
col fascino di frontiera sperduta.
L'America terra d'acquisto,
l'America terra che prostra, come padrone
che sfrutta; l'America nuova Terra Promessa
come un viaggio senza ritorno.

L'America grande Babele,
crogiuolo di razze e di religioni,
di lingue culture e disperazioni,
di luci la notte su strade deserte
e fredde vetrate di grattacieli,
non guglie slanciate di cattedrali!

L'America t'offre le luci per accecarti
senza sapere, ti nutre e ti spinge a sperare
senza il coraggio d'amare la vita,
senza né raggio né piena catarsi,
ed ogni sogno dura una notte.

L'America ride tra le cortine velate,
ti succhia le labbra come pompelmi,
poi prende, ti gira e lenta ti fotte.
L'America asciuga ogni goccia del mare,
te le ficca negli occhi, ti forza a sognare,
ti spinge da dietro come per gioco,
ti sparge benzina e ti dà fuoco.

America   America   America
L'America scende senza più senso
finché Atlantide la chiameranno;

Ode to America

> America here, America there,
> Whatever happened to the America of my father?
>
> Rocco Scotellaro

XXIII

America land that welcomes, as whore
ready for everyone; America as conquest
with the fascination of the lost frontier.
America land of accumulation,
America land that prostrates, as master
that exploits; America new Promised Land
as a journey with no return.

America grand Babel,
crucible of races and religions,
of languages cultures and despairs,
of lights at night on deserted streets
and cold skyscraper windows,
no raised cathedral spires!

America offers you the lights to blind yourself
without knowing, nurtures you and pushes you to hope
without the courage to love life,
without either gleam or full release,
and every dream lasts a night.

America laughs through hidden curtains,
she sucks your lips like grapefruits,
then takes, turns you and fucks you slowly.
America dries up each drop of the sea,
sticks them in your eyes, forces you to dream,
pushes you from behind as if for fun,
splashes you with gasoline and sets you on fire.

     America   America   America
     America descends without any more sense
until they will call her Atlantis;

L'America come leggenda è come uno sputo
che si dilata; l'America terra di mito,
terra di rito, ti guarda con gli occhi
di un bimbo anemico, senza più sangue,
senza più rabbia, senza più nessuna speranza
e celebra inerte idoli danzanti
come l'ombre intorno al fuoco che presto divampa.

America as legend is like a spitwad
that spreads; America land of myth,
land of ritual, she looks at you with the eyes
of an anemic child, with no more blood,
with no more rage, with no more hope
and inertly celebrates dancing idols
as the shades around a quickly burning fire.

Sonetto della rimembranza

Per Mila

XXXV

E tua sorella suona ancora il piano
e tuo nipote rincorre i tuoi passi
nella casa dove ho lasciato te
e il palpito ansioso del tempo andato.

E tu per le stanze ogni giorno vivi
quel sogno che condividemmo e ancora
come un martello il chiodo mi tempesta
l'anima, il cuore, il petto, tutti i giorni.

Senz'altro t'avrà sorpreso incontrarmi
negli angoli di memoria, fiutando
persino l'atmosfera che avvolgeva.

Forse riderai se ti dico
che subito così ora m'accade,
mentre ti penso, e chissà se lo sai.

Sonnet of remembrance

for Mila

XXXV

And your sister still plays the piano
and your nephew runs in your steps
in the house where I left you
and the nervous throb of time gone by.

And in those rooms each day you live
that dream that we shared and that still
like a hammer the nail, pounds
my soul, my heart, my breast, every day.

It will surely surprise you to meet me
in the corners of memory, scenting
even the enveloping atmosphere.

Perhaps you will laugh if I tell you
that suddenly it struck me, while thinking
of you, and who knows if you know.

Hysteron Proteron

Per Isabella Maria

> L'unica occasione di osservare il linguaggio umano
> *in statu nascendi* ce la offre il bambino

Karl Bühler

        Carponi traccia
l'ignota lettera dell'alfabeto
antico la tua sagoma
                          caracollante:
poggio ferma la pianta del mio piede,
mi guardi e non favelli,
               afferri con perizia
infante il dorso di quel libriccino.

        Volteggio sui braccioli del mio trono,
trotterellando
                  "Chiocciolina" chiedo
(la cerca qui comincia:
                        là dove la finisci)
"t'affascina il dorso od il risvolto
della preda ambita che per ben tre
volte" (tre le mostro con le dita)
"in balìa del tuo balocco
                          precipita?"

        Trattengo il risguardo come il respiro,
con la coda dell'occhiello raffermo
l'innocente gualcire del tuo gesto
subitaneo: *As We Know*, risuona
il titolo.
            As We Know:
parentesi del senso condiviso,
come fosse il discorso
Hörstummheit
           l'apertura

Hysteron Proteron

For Isabella Maria

> The child offers us the only chance
> to observe human language *in statu nascendi*
>
> Karl Bühler

Crawling on all fours your
                              caracoling
profile traces the unknown
letter of the ancient alphabet:
I plant my foot sole still,
you look at me and do not speak,
                              you grasp with infant
skillfulness the spine of that little book.

I whirl on the arms of my throne,
toddling
                    "You little snail" I ask
(the quest here begins:
                              where you end it)
"does the spine or jacket fascinate you
of the avid prey which three
times" (three I show her with my fingers)
"at the mercy of your plaything
                              precipitates?"

I hold back the book flap like my breath,
with the corner of the eyed title I strengthen
the innocent rumpling of your sudden
gesture: *As We Know*, resounds
the title.
                    As We Know:
parenthesis of the shared meaning,
as though discourse were
Hörstummheit
                    the aperture
to the understanding

alla comprensione
                              senza parola.
              T'accomiati cinguettando,
ballonzoli
                     bid   bid
                                        ancora *bird*
descrivi un panoramico pannello
insinuando con la lingua
                                   pan   pang
l'altrui
                     terreno: rifuggi il convito
a cui t'invoco
                                   (per te è un gioco,
As We Know)
              pain [pê]   *pain   paint*
potessi capirti
                     ca-tto   ca-tto
totalmente contenere la mia
tentacolare presunzione tenera
e viva, evviva! tu non saresti
je
              nemmeno per gioco
                                   jeu   jeune
je ne
        je n'est sain
pas   je ne sais
                            plus
parler   palier   pallier
              Nelle tue braccia spalancate
s'accartoccia la mia persona:
        pa!   "a pa"   pape!
Volgo indietro lo sguardo
a questo processo all'irraggiungibile
afasìa del non logoro logo,
il tuo fato diviene la metatesi
afflata della mia istante

                    without words.
        You take leave twittering,
you trip along
                    bid   bid
                              again *bird*
you trace a panoramic panel
insinuating with your tongue
                         pan   pang
the other's
                    ground: you shun the feast
I entreat you to join
                         (for you it is a game,
As We Know)
              pain [pê]   *pain   paint*
if I could understand you
                         ca-tto   ca-tto
totally contain my
tentacular, tender presumption
and live, long live! you would not be
je
         not even in jest
                         jeu   jeune
je ne
        je n'est sain
pas   je ne sais
                    plus
parler   palier   pallier
         In your wide-open arms
my person crumples up:
         pa   "a pa"   pape!
I turn my gaze back
to this progressing trial of the unreachable
aphasia of the not yet worn out logos,
your fate becomes the inspired
metathesis of my instant

metastasi:

         pa'   *pape!*

               l'apostrofe

che mi deduce
attrae nell'apocope del tempo:
babbo   *babble* *Babel*
    L'avvento separa dei figli i figli
padri dai padri antichi;

              cosí m'ingiungo:
il mio etimo sia il tuo,
la tua faticità la mia.

metastasis:

    pa' *pape!*

        the apostrophe

which deduces me

attracts in the apocope of time:

babbo   *babble* *Babel*

  The coming separates the children fathers

of the children from the ancient fathers;

        thus I enjoin myself:

my etymon be yours,

your phatic speech mine.

→ *Annalisa Saccà (b. 1954)*

Annalisa Saccà holds a doctorate from New York University and is a professor of Italian at St. John's University, in New York. She has published three books of poetry, *Il tempo del grano* (1993) *Nominare Delfi* (1999), and *Dove non è mai sera/Where Evening Never Falls* (2006), and a book on Italian postmodernism, *Significando Simulacri* (1992), with emphasis on author Pier Francesco Paolini. She has published in several academic and literary journals.

Grounded in the classics, especially Greek, Saccà's poetry reverberates with the echoes of the great Italian literary canon, and has absorbed and made hers the high points of romanticism and hermeticism. By temperament, her early poetry manifests a solar quality, a Mediterranean afflatus delicately modulated. At a certain point, however, the tragic loss of her partner changed her voice to bring forth a powerful, sustained lyrical ode to love and loss. As far as I know, Saccà has not written much about either departing from Italy or arriving to the new continent, perhaps taking the position, which is shared by a few of the poets in this gathering, that the location, or physical/existential situation of the poet, is not that important after all, considering the levels of urbanization and the standards of living of the countries, which are nearly equal, cultural differences notwithstanding. Moreover, for this poet as for many others who have never relinquished the great tradition—which is another way of saying, poets who have been relatively indifferent both to the seismic shocks of the avant-gardes and the minefields of political and civic poetry—poetry is essentially a musical orchestration of words, the eminent achievement of human language tout court, the magic fusion of feeling and voice. In that sense, hers is a most eloquent lyrical expression, capturing subtleties of great psychological, emotional, and aesthetic power.

Mindful that a poem should sound "like a poem" and therefore be concerned with the link between *langue* and *langage*, Saccà's poetry conjoins the two halves of the polar opposition of Apex A and Apex B, namely immortality, accorded the poet, or the poet's love, in an *elsewhere* which may or may not be home, and mortality, which gives power to the song about a lost real love, again independently of any notion of a *domus* or dwelling: Love, song, loss, all exist in the untouchable reality of poetic time.

da *Dove non è mai sera*
Per Franco,
che risplende nell'ombra della mia solitudine

i.
Vorrei parole
per piangere i miei morti
per non udire il grido di dolore
vorrei parole
per trattenere i volti
per non sentire l'orrido del cuore.

Vorrei parole per spogliare il tempo
che vela il sentimento e la memoria
vorrei parole
timide carezze
per rivivere il sogno un'ora ancora.

Vorrei parole
per restarti accanto
ora che scivoli via dal mio universo
vorrei parole
esuli e rimpianto
per non perderti ancora nell'immenso
velario d'ombra.

Vorrei parole
per strapparti alla terra
ricamarti
per asciugarti il volto col mio cielo

per raccontarti
destino mio mia carne mio signore
vorrei parole
all'infinito.

ii
Sii in me
sembianza di una notte smerigliata
fiaba che brucia i vesperi del cuore

from *Where Evening Never Falls*
For Franco,
who burns bright in the shade of my solitude

i
I seek the word
to weep for my dead
not to hear the screaming of pain
I seek words
to hold back the faces
not to feel the dread of the heart.

I seek the word to unclothe time
that veils feelings and memory
I seek words
timid caresses
to relive the dream an hour more.

I seek the word
to stay beside you
now that you are sliding away from my universe
I seek words
of exile and regret
not to lose you again in the immense shadowy curtain.

I seek the word
to tear you out of the earth
to embroider you
to dry your face with my sky.

to speak of you
my destiny my flesh my lord
I seek words
endlessly.

ii
Be in me
semblance of a frosty night
a fable that burns the vespers of the heart

alito di giardino orlato invito
nell'ora della cenere il dolore

Sii in me
lacrima dolce scavata d'universo
preda soave stordita di risvegli
di danza che trascorre morbido il giorno
e piana il gioco d'aride venture

Sii in me
col fiato giocoso di memorie
con l'impeto lo sguardo la carezza
l'ardore del deserto il primo fiore

Sii in me
illimitato canto
nel palmo della mia
consuetudine

iii
Mi eri quercia ondulata
incanto d'ali
che guarda lo stupore del sereno
mi eri pane
che morso a prima sera
scioglie la fame del dolore
e pieno
il grido veste come rete l'ombra.
Mi eri sete che gioca coi deserti
mi eri carne che scorre nelle vene
mi eri voce ultimo pensiero
tu m'eri canto
interminato seme
che oggi muove sotto le ginocchia il buio
al cimitero

iv
Voi che tornate a splendere sui passi
se avessi colorato d'incertezza
inerme il manto che scandiva i giorni

embroidered breath of a bordered garden invitation
sorrow in the hour of the ashes

Be in me
a sweet tear carved out of the universe
a soft prey stunned by awakenings
by dancing that lives out the day softly
and smoothes the play of burnt out ventures

Be in me
with the playful breath of memories
with the urging the glance the caress
the ardor of the first flower of the desert

Be in me
unending song
in the palm of my
consuetude

iii
You were for me a willowy oak tree
enchantment of wings
who looked at the astonishment of a serene sky
you were bread for me
that bitten early in the evening
dissolves the hunger of sorrow
and the scream fully clothes as a net the shadow.
You were my thirst playing in the deserts
you were my flesh flowing in my veins
you were my voice my last thought
you were song for me
unending seed
that under my knees today moves the darkness
at the cemetery.

iv
You who return to glow on the footsteps
if I had colored with uncertainty
the helpless cloak that ticked the days

dopo molte ombre
io delle spoglie e del fragore inquieto
avrei smorzato di terrazze bianche
pallido il riso
e in un tramonto di quercie che si piega
nell'alito profondo delle nevi
avrei coperto
di ritorni il canto
che scivola le rive del pensiero
come un abbraccio
bacio dell'arcano
che di antichi preludi e di cordami
spande
i miei resti
nelle brune lanterne della pena

v

C'è qualcosa nel sonno d'un uomo
che muove la donna
l'innocenza d'un bimbo crucciato
che allenta la presa
il volo di palpebre mute su onde distanti
che non conoscevano il cuore.
E la donna che è cuore lo sa
lei tace lei madre
e vigila l'uomo ragazzo
nel sogno che dura lo spazio d'un mondo.
Non basta che un gesto a svegliarlo
ma attende
e nel sonno lo vede fanciullo
che scivola vergine il volto del sangue
nei pensieri banditi alla donna.
Ma il risveglio trafigge l'abisso
affiora il ricordo dolente del corpo
e col capo chino lui cerca la donna
che è sorte
e che tace il destino dell'uomo.

after many shadows
I would have extinguished with white terraces
the restless rumblings
and the remains
of your pale smile
and in a sunset of oak trees that bows
in the deep breath of snows
I would have covered
with returns my song
that slides the shores of thought
like an embrace
a kiss by the arcane
that spreads
over my remains
ancient preludes and twinings
in the somber lanterns of sorrow.

v

There's something in a man's sleep
that moves a woman
the innocence of a worried boy
that lets go
the flight of silent eyelids on distant waves
that the heart did not know.
And woman who is heart knows it
she's silent, a mother
and keeps an eye on the man-boy
in the dream that lasts the beating of a world.
A gesture is all that's needed to awaken him
but she waits
and in the dream she sees him a child
that slides the face of blood untouched
in those thoughts forbidden to women.
But the awakening pierces the abyss
the sorrowful memory of the body resurfaces
and with his head bowed he seeks the woman
who is destiny
and does not voice the fate of man.

vi

Le mie parole non saranno pietra
che chiama sulla strada del ritorno
il pellegrino e adorna
le sponde del finito.
Né saranno grido
che insegue il calice e il rancore
per schiudere un incanto sospirato.
Le mie parole sono di confine
son sabbia di paesi sconosciuti
che il mare prende
vecchio gioco segreto
e copre eterne
di solitudine e oro celeste

vi

My words shall not be stones
that beckon to the pilgrim
on the returning journey
and adorn the shore of the finite.
Nor will they be a scream
that pursues chalice and rancor
to disclose a longed-for enchantment.
Mine are boundary words
they are sand from unknown regions
that the sea takes up
—an old secret game—
covering them with celestial gold
and eternal solitude

⇥ Victoria Surliuga (b. 1972)

Victoria Surliuga was born in London, grew up in Turin, and studied in the United States from 1991 to 1995, then moved there permanently in 1998. She is associate professor of Italian language and literature at Texas Tech University. She specializes in contemporary Italian poetry, has edited a collection of Giampiero Neri's prose (*La serie dei fatti* [The Series of Events], 2004) and has written a monograph on Neri (*Uno sguardo sulla realtà, l'opera poetica di Giampiero Neri* [A Glance at Reality: Giampiero Neri's Poetry], 2005). She has published six collections of poetry, *Risposte del silenzio/Answers of Silence* (1994), *Allergia alla notte* (Allergic to the Night, 2000, with an introduction by Paolo Valesio), *Forbici* (Scissors, 2006), *Donne* (Women, 2009), and *Plastica/Plastic* (2010), as well as the chapbook, *abbandono* [abandonment] (2003).

The poetry of Victoria Surliuga clearly shows the evolution of a rich sensibility that seeks definition in an unstable cosmos of forces and voices, of unpredictable situations and spontaneous illuminations. The collection *Allergia alla notte* contains poems in which the poetic persona struggles to grasp some deeper sense of existence even as it continually bumps up against non-sense, that is, the indirection of meaning in the world, to which the response is both an acceptance and an irritation, a growth of the self and a weighing down of the consciousness as it explores deeper and hidden recesses of thought. Consider the imaginary dialogue with Anne Sexton: "But we are already alienated: / there is no road back in this mode of consciousness: / Anne, we are outside of time and space and look on / our beings who pretend to say / what no one cares to hear" (18), though even her own writing is found to be, in merciless self-analysis, "useless, and lacking meaning" (19). It is a poetry of emotion, of questing, of feeling the world coupled to the realization that people have few if any answers, and where, if anything, "Hope, Love, Reason" (51) are basically a calvary.

The collection *Forbici* shows a qualitative step forward toward a more lean and nuanced rhythm, a more sophisticated verse and stanza structure, and definitely achieves the impersonal self so crucial to a broad community of poets during the past century or so. The title of the collection, which means "scissors," suggests that the operation being conducted concerns a cutting off of, and possibly a doing away with, various forces, values and psychological blockages, which metaphorically reveal the contradictions and inconsistencies of people and culture encountered along the way. The references to the condition of an uprooted poet are not overly dramatized but they do give voice to a sentimental yearning to keep within view the locus of an age—childhood? adolescence?—that is temporally marked. Certainly the dialogical relationship with the mother discloses a host of possible temporalities. Thus the loss is in time, as well as in space, and yet, perhaps owing to absence, to yearning for an incomplete communication, fact and fantasy can coexist. Proof of this may be gleaned in the poem "Plastic," which clearly accepts the "return of the witches."

It appears that for Surliuga becoming a poet is in itself a full-time pursuit, and the objects and memories she brings to the speaking persona point to a widening, depersonalizing horizon. Surliuga is working between Axis D: *Langue*/Reality, and Axis B: *Home*/Mortality.

america

da *Forbici*

1.

forse un giorno
sulla soglia di casa
avrei raccolto
un bambino in fasce
stretto in braccio
per attraversare
un campo minato

> foglie marroni nella piscina
> una superficie su cui glissare
> fino al trampolino pronto
> all'esplosione di mille ciabatte
> di spugna oltre agli alberi

in palio una casa in periferia
con giardino e vicini dai calzoni
bianchi seduti composti a tavola

> non basta
> tornare a casa
> chiudersi a doppio
> giro di chiavi
> guardare il buio
> tutte le sere

2.

mio padre guidava
mia madre sbucciava le mele
io guardavo dal finestrino
immaginando

> lungo una lettera C dalle punte aguzzate a sinistra
> dei due estremi interrotti mancava la memoria
> a vent'anni la prima svolta a trent'anni la seconda
> il resto si sfumava negli occhi non vedenti

america

from *Scissors*

1.

perhaps one day
on my doorstep
I'd pick up a baby
in swaddling bands
hold it tightly in my arms
in order to cross
a minefield

>   brown leaves in the swimming pool
>   a surface to glide on
>   to the springboard waiting
>   for the explosion of a thousand sponges

slippers beyond the trees
a suburban house's the prize
with backyard and neighbors in white
pants sitting properly at their table

>   it's not enough
>   to go back home
>   and bolt the door
>   looking at the darkness
>   every night

2.

my father was driving
my mother was peeling the apples
i was looking outside the window
daydreaming

>   along a letter C with sharp left-leaning serifs
>   at the truncated edges memory was missing
>   at twenty the first turn at thirty the second one
>   the rest was fading away in the blindfolded eyes

mio padre ci insegnava il croato sulla spiaggia
vuk era lento gli piaceva l'orologio meccanico
erika aveva il gommone però a vuk cadeva il costume
nel tirarlo su con noi mentre suzanne nuotava
il y a une meduse così le aveva toccato la gamba
pestavo formiche nell'erba dove c'era una cicala secca

       spingevo da sempre l'anima sui gomiti
       come facevo con la valigia piena di libri

3.
le porte dell'ascensore liberty
non si chiudevano del tutto
in via valfré 17 gennaio 2004
ho sudato un po' nel cappotto
il terreno poteva sparire
l'ascensore saliva in diagonale
roteavano a lato i piani
porte vecchie contrapposte
torino trasuda sempre morte

ero un'ospite seduta sul davanzale
con i piedi a penzoloni
mia madre si è buttata
per anni dalla finestra
ma i fili della biancheria
sono stati il suo telone

4.
da bambina camminavo
sulle ali degli aerei
a volte infilavo un braccio
nel tritacarne sull'ala destra
impassibile mio padre
mi tirava per la bretella
e chiudeva il finestrino

gli aerei sfondano le case
per prendere quota
attraversano gli attici

my father would teach us croatian on the beach
vuk was a slow learner he liked the mechanical watch
erika had the dinghy but vuk would lose his swimsuit
every time we pulled him up and suzanne was swimming
il y a une meduse that's how he managed to touch her leg
i'd stomp on the ants in the grass where a dead cicada lay

      since always i pushed down my soul with my elbows
      like i did with my suitcase full of books

3.
the doors of the art nouveau elevator
did not close properly
in via valfrè on january 17, 2004
i was sweating a little in my coat
the ground could disappear
the elevator was going up on a slant
floors were swirling on the sides
old double facing doors
always turin exudes death

i was a guest sitting on the windowsill
with my feet dangling
my mother had thrown herself
out the window for years
but the clotheslines
were her safety net

4.
as a child i used to walk
on the airplanes' wings
sometimes i would slip my arm
into the meatgrinder on the right-side wing
unperturbed my father
would pull me back by my suspender
and close the window

airplanes crumple houses
when they take off
they go across the attics

mentre al primo piano
la portinaia taglia
una fetta di torta
i passeggeri abbassano
i finestrini in un colpo
per una boccata d'aria
passando sulla mongolia

5.
se la costa del texas si aprisse sul lago maggiore
potrei uscire di casa e sedermi sulle panchine
vedere uno spazio chiuso e una scheggia di cielo
non i dodicimila chilometri tra i continenti

tempero le matite sperando che diventino remi
posso sfogliare per anni seduta a scrivere
sempre dirò le cose sbagliate a mia madre al telefono

while on the ground floor
the doorkeeper is cutting
a slice of cake
the passengers lower
their windows rapidly
to catch some fresh air
flying over mongolia

5.
if the coast of texas would look out onto lago maggiore
i could go out of the house and sit on the benches
gaze into a closed space and a splinter of sky
and not the ten thousand kilometers between the continents

i sharpen my pencils hoping they will turn into oars
i can skim for years on end while i sit and write
always i say the wrong things to my mother on the phone

Plastica

da *Plastica*

a cinque anni
guardavo dalla finestra
le streghe in un comizio
mia mamma mi salutava
prima di uscire

andavo in cucina
a staccare la testa
della barbie
mangiavo una fetta di crostata
bevevo una tazza di latte

più tardi le streghe venivano
a prendersi la testa
lasciata sul balcone

Plastic

from *Plastic*

sitting on my bed
when i was five
i saw the witches in
a meeting from my window
my mother said goodbye
before leaving

i went to the kitchen
to pull off barbie's head
i ate a slice of cake
i drank a glass of milk

later the witches returned
to take the head
left on the balcony

→ Giorgio Mobili (b. 1973)

Giorgio Mobili was born in Milan, Italy, in 1973. In 1999 he received his *laurea* in Italian language and literature from the University of Pavia, with a philological thesis on Paolo Volponi's *Il Pianeta irritabile*. He came to the United States in 1999 and obtained his doctorate in English and comparative literature from Washington University in 2005. He now teaches humanities and Spanish at California State University, Fresno.

The author of several academic essays on modern and postmodern literature and film, Mobili has written the book *Irritable Bodies and Postmodern Subjects in Pynchon, Puig, and Volponi*. His Italian poetry has appeared in journals such as *Gradiva, Steve, L'Immaginazione, Ore piccole*, and *Offerta special*. His poetry was also featured in the anthology *1°non singolo: Sette poeti italiani*. His first book, *Penelope su Sunset Boulevard* was published in 2010 by Manni Editori. Mobili published also in English in periodicals such as *The Tipton Poetry Journal, Pank*, The *Hiram Poetry Review*, and *Gradiva*; and his first Spanish-language collection (*Última salida a Ventura*) is forthcoming.

Mobili's poetry manifests an original combination of syntax and lexical choices in part dictated by an approach to reality that draws heavily on film sequencing, travel, and the constant repositioning of the experiencing/writing persona. Far from lyrical temptation and intimism, he is rather more existential in questioning not so much the instant as the frame or the sequence that unfurls before our eyes. For this reason his lines recover the tempo necessary to tell a sequence of perceptions by harnessing the ductility of Italian syntax, something which he has felicitously mimicked in his own English renditions. The poetry in *Penelope su Sunset Boulevard* explores regions in the continuum of this poet's deterritorialization in which the juxtapositions between the new world and the old are subtle, not shrill, nor are they always easily identifiable, activating the chambers of a sensibility that bonds with the real world only to express possible meanings of existence, in other words, "transporting the whole upon a collective proscenium."[62] This is achieved, moreover, through an agile linking of quotidian scenes the poet chisels out from the fluff and blur of life with recollections from classic *topoi*—as present, for instance, in Homer, Dante, and Montale—and unabashed gut reactions to the broader picture within which we live, beginning with (and citing from poems not included in our selection), "the undoing [*sfascio*] of our recent years" ("Mr. Lang rewrites the *Odyssey*," 30), the fact that "there is no longer a pressing need, / day after day, to do and undo things" ("Penelope on Sunset Boulevard," 10), because today "paralysis embraces us, and the syntax of things . . . escapes and diffracts in a net of curving patterns / from which nothing is left out" ("Customs," 44), so that perhaps the Ultima Thule is to welcome "the free road toward the electrifying realm / of the imaginary" ("State of Siege," 48).

Many references point to the incoherence, if not aberrations, of our social life as Westerners, whether in Italy or the United States, but also to a world that is postmodern to a fault, where everything has been tried, said, done, and twice over at that. Yet this may also embody, inevitably, the coming apart of the poet's world, one that, itself riddled with contradictions and incoherence, was still somehow manageable within his native *langue* and within the geohistorical *domus* called Italy. But once in the great expanse of America, the crack between word and reference requires that the poet move up from exclaiming or saying to the more layered possibilities offered by telling, leveraging a known distinction in hermeneutics between the first two meanings of the ancient word *hermenéouin*, which are "to say" and "to tell" or "narrate."[63] Poetry here reclaims the temporality of experiencing and engages often dormant strata of sensibility, not simply of the author's other, which is discounted (psychoanalysis *docet*), but of the others, the actually existing humans he encounters along the way and who allow him to sketch a canvas of the vastness of this new planet. By the sheer catalogue of places the poet names where he came face to face with existence itself against the inalterable declinations of sea and prairie, and most significantly of the sunsets and the evenings, home here is, then, not a mere geographical location, but a temporal *situs*, a place where the *logos* exists as *logoi* seeking to grasp and bind some deeper sense to life itself. Questions that occasionally arise do not really want an answer, sentences that frame like a movie camera, artful mix of polysyndeton and asyndeton, and a springing if anxious rhythm that often float the syntagms like a torrent furnish further support to this reading. The reader can enjoy the rich syntax the poet weaves in tying several points together, but without preaching, without reassuring solutions, without either hope or despair. There seems to be only *ex-sistere*, erring.[64]

On the basis of our initial critical grid, we may situate Mobili's poetry between C: Poetry/*Langage* and B: Home/*Mortality*, but a home grounded in the journey itself.

Molo 39

Da *Penelope su Sunset Boulevard*

Prima o poi si ha l'occasione di emendare
La scarsezza di un approccio secondario
Al suono spastico dei bufali di mare:
Corpi senz'arti, è vero, ma con corazza
E cuore di materiali idrorepellente.

Questo inaudito affronto acustico
(quasi il lamento a doppio filo del reale)
Fece pensare a un'impossibile apertura
Oltre le scorie di una magra colazione:
Prima, cioè, che le invaginazione dello spirito
Ritornassero a saldarsi col mattino.

Pier 39

From *Penelope on Sunset Boulevard*

Sooner or later everyone gets a chance
To amend the scarcity of a secondary approach
With the spastic sounds of ocean buffalos—
Issued from limbless bodies, true, but with heart
And armor of waterproof material.

This unheard of acoustic insult
Aping the dual wailing of the real
Reminded me of a brush with something open
Beyond the clutter of a meager breakfast—
Before, that is, the soul's interstices blended
Again against the morning.

La città degli angeli

Non può morire senza un'ultima asserzione:
ma anche scrutando oltre lo scherzo
non decifrava indizi nelle orbite di lei,
nulla di quella insufficienza
di quel furore iconoclasta consumato
durante una settimana estiva di vittorie
ininterrotte sul panno verde di Durango.

Cieco alla misura esatta del bisogno
non fu mai tale da raschiare fino
al fondo degli eventi;
affabile malgrado ogni evidenza
serbava il suo dolore in una fiala
mentre ancora navigava
tra gli sputi e le gratelle dei tombini.

Ora, allungato sul selciato
sente il cielo (o perlomeno
la sua viscosa incarnazione urbana)
ungere come scolo sulla pelle
in attesa dello schianto che comunemente
annuncia la bianchissima incoscienza

Travolta dalla logica pietrosa del suo cosmo
di scappamenti e delinquenza spicciola
lei sporge un volto troppo piatto
per il lutto, più disposto
alla cautela, o al tradimento

Eppure, sono ancora le parole
ad offrire lo spiraglio
di una tregua, in quel rallentamento ultimo
del tempo e delle cose—
ma non raggiungono nessuno
per via di quello strano assopimento
che come sempre sigilla
gli orecchi che presentano il disastro
chiudersi intorno a un essere vivente.

City of the Angels

He could not die without one last pronouncement:
but as he looked beyond the jest into her eyes
he read no trace of that deficiency of life
they held in common, nothing of
the crumbling of the idols they contrived
while on a short summer blast
over the green expanse by Durango.

Purblind to the exact measure of his needs
he was never one to dig down to the bottom of events;
well-meaning in the face of all the evidence
he kept his grief sealed in a vial while
maneuvering through the spit and sewer gratings.

Stretched on the pavement, he can now
feel the sky (or, should we say,
its hazy urban incarnation)
cascade like sand upon his skin
no doubt in preparation for the crack
that ushers in blinding white foolhardiness.

Swept away by the rocky logic of his universe
of petty escapades and scoundrel feats,
she turns a face not really prone
to mourning but, rather,
to caution or betrayal.

Still, it only words that can muster
a glimpse of a truce,
that ultimate slowdown
of time and things:
And yet, they reach no one,
as predictably a strange drowsiness
blocks all ears that sense disaster
closing in on a living being.

Fuori

Il coroner è giunto a esaminare
la traccia algebrica confusa ed inesatta
di due cadaveri da prima mal disposti
su questa piana abbottonata a pozzi
e trivelle, all'incalzare della sera.

Dopo un'anamnesi del tutto lacunosa
schediamo il silicone e i chioschi di tamales
tra gli ànsiti di una vegetazione inerte,
mentre la macchina di sabbia e firmamento
continua ad inibire con tenace indifferenza
la normale peristalsi di un rapporto.

Che cosa resta, allora, se non un'insegna esausta,
sperare nel neon pallido di una parola intera
che ancora ronzi, appesa a un cavo flaccido
contro la griglia di raffronti e insenature;

punta tutto su un delirio prematuro
che traligni da quel solco prefissato dal destino
come una breve sospensione del ricatto.

Cedere tutto, insomma, per un pomeriggio fuori.

Outside

The coroner has finally arrived
to sort out the algebraic evidence of
two confusing, ill-positioned remains
across this plain stretched taut by wells
and rigs in the far corner of the evening.

After we certify the inaccurate anamnesis
we file away tamales stands and silicon equipment
amidst the gasps of an inert vegetation,
while the mechanics of sand and sky
persists with indifference to compress
the normal peristalsis of romance.

What's left, then, but to bet on a mirage,
the pallid neon of a tangible pronouncement
that may still buzz, slung on a flaccid cable,
against the grid of blueprints and collations;

to wager on a premature delirium, away
from the pre-established furrow of our fates,
like momentarily suspending an extortion . . .

Giving everything up, in brief, for one last afternoon outside.

1. Homer, *The Odyssey*, trans. R. Fagles (New York: Penguin, 1996). All references are to this edition.

2. One may also say, somewhat maliciously, yet accurately from a postcolonial perspective, that Odysseus wanted to regain his scepter, return to power. He was, after all, mythologemes comparing him and his Latin successor Aeneas to the emigrants notwithstanding, a king, as some of the writers presented here will point out.

3. For reasons of critical expediency we must unfortunately ignore the connected theological, philosophical, and biological perspectives on immortality. Here we take it as a general critical figure with which to discuss relations between language, existence, society, and creativity.

4. On the fundamental pulsion to timelessness in lyric poetry, see my article "Tuning in / to the Diaphora: Lyric, Metaphysics, and the Reasons of Allegory," *RLA Romance Languages Annual* 6 (1994): v–vx.

5. This notion combines the differentiating subset of "*mother* tongue" and "*father*-land," not an insignificant fact for anyone writing in Italian outside of Italy proper.

6. See my essay "Migration, History, Existence" in *Migrants and Refugees*, ed. Vangelis Kyriakopoulos (Athens: Komotini, 2004), 19–50.

7. Half of the *Odyssey*, in fact, deals with what happens when Odysseus is back at Ithaca. Though the hero does in the end succeed in getting his family and kingdom back, he is at first unrecognized (and unrecognizable) and appears to be alienated from everyone, being at ease only with the swineherd Eumeus. This has bearing on the interpretation of Italian writing by authors who "return" to Italy after a considerable absence.

8. I am aware that this may sound reductive, but given the space constraints, I cannot introduce another and just as important tradition, one that speaks in the first person about given states of affairs in a society. Historically, this has been characterized, in different countries and in specific social circumstances, as pedagogical, moralistic, civil, and finally political or engagé poetry. Occasional references to these modes of poetizing will of course appear throughout my analyses.

9. Sometimes too much, to the point that an entire generation of critics (in the later twentieth century) would end up saying that the basic quality of a poem is that of being ambiguous. This is not critically useful at all, as it eschews the interpreter's responsibility to take a stand on the probable sense of a poem, and the possible meanings it may carry. A critic is a mediator, so hermeneutic risk is always involved. See on this my book *Prefaces to the Diaphora* (West Lafayette, Ind.: Purdue University Press, 1991), and my article "Take a Stand, Again: On the Ethics of Critique," in *Italian Cultural Studies 2001*, ed. A. Tamburri, M.S. Ruthenberg, G. Parati, and B. Lawton (Boca Raton, Fla.: Bordighera, 2004), 13–33.

10. This is in part owed to over half a century under the hegemony of Crocean aesthetics, which never considered poetry as having anything to say about the real world. But there may have been two additional reasons: first, the fact that societies, through gradual fragmentation, were no longer thought as being homogeneous, and second, the unleashing of the age of irony, psychoanalysis, and the mass media.

11. Gilles Deleuze and Félix Guattari, *Kafka: For a Minor Literature*, trans. D. Polan (Minneapolis: University of Minnesota Press, 1986).

12. For an extensive sampling, see the monumental anthology edited by Francesco Durante, *Italoamericana*, vol. 2 (Milano: Mondadori, 2005), of which an English version is slated for publication by Fordham University Press.

13. From A. Ramberti and R. Sangiorgi, eds., *Le voci dell'arcobaleno* (Santarcangelo di Romagna: Fara Editore, 1996), 29 (my translation).

14. Ibid., 31.

15. Rimanelli had published a book in 1959, *Il mestiere del furbo*, in which he exposed all the politicking that goes on behind the scenes in the world of publishing houses and literary prizes. See note 25.

16. On the notion of *dispatrio*, see the recent collection of papers in F. Sinopoli and S. Tatti, eds., *I confini della scrittura. Il dispatrio nei testi letterari* (Isernia: Cosmo Iannone, 2005).

17. Paolo Valesio, "Introduction: 'Who Says Words with My Mouth,'" *Yale Italian Poetry* 1 (2001): 11–22.

18. Gardaphé's book, *Italian Signs, American Streets* (Durham, N.C.: Duke University Press, 1998), deals with the evolution of Italian American writing in English, and the different contexts and strategies of expression each generation adopted or invented.

19. For a collection of essays that explore different periods of his life while focusing on particular works, see Paolo Giordano, ed., *Joseph Tusiani: Poet Translator Humanist—An International Homage* (West Lafayette, Ind.: Bordighera, 1994).

20. As he says explicitly, "O Latina loquela, tu / lex et ars mihi pura," cited in J. T. Kirby, "The Neo-Latin Verse of Joseph Tusiani," in Giordano, *Joseph Tusiani*, 188.

21. In Tusiani's three-volume autobiography, as well as in some critical essays about his work, there emerges the critical juggernaut of whether writing in one language about experiences that took place in the context or culture of another country where a different language is spoken does not risk making a given text a "translation" of emotions, and furthermore risk, in the critical vocabulary of another generation, working in a constant state of "inauthenticity" and "estrangement."

22. Cited in Luigi Bonaffini, "La poesia dialettale di Tusiani," in Giordano, *Joseph Tusiani*, 145. But after further analysis, Bonaffini shows how Tusiani's dialect is "twice removed" because besides there having been a geographical distancing from the birthplace, that dialect is actually practically extinct, its reality marking rather an absence. Ibid., 149. With this goes the analysis of poems in which, at different times, the poet claimed he was and remained a "true Sanmachese," as if he had never left! Clearly it is a "belonging" of the mind at this stage, a necessary fiction, an emigrant's utopia.

23. Joseph Tusiani, *Gente mia and Other Poems* (Stone Park, Ill.: Italian Cultural Center, 1978).

24. Alberto Granese writes: "In the course of his narrative production Rimanelli has employed a great many of the literary conventions of the novel: historical (*Tiro al piccione*), social (*Peccato originale*), adventure (*Biglietto di terza*), psychological (*Una posizione sociale*), fable (*I vecchioni*), police thriller (*I giovanoni*), academic (*La macchina paranoica*), oral (*Graffiti*), liquid (*Benedetta in Guysterland*), autobiographical (*Molise Molise*), and essayistic (*Gli accademici* or *Il cavallo a tre gambe*)." "Su/per Rimanelli. Studi e testimonianze," *Misure critiche* 65–67 (October 1987–June 1988).

25. For information about this "case," as well as various studies on different aspects of Rimanelli's work, see Sebastiano Martelli, ed., *Rimanelliana* (Stony Brook, N.Y.: Forum Italicum Publishing, 2000).

26. Giose Rimanelli, *Moliseide*, trans. Luigi Bonaffini (New York: Peter Lang, 1992); abridged version, *Moliseide and Other Poems*, ed. and trans. Luigi Bonaffini (New York: Legas, 1998). Both editions contain translations of the vernacular into Italian as well.

27. "Rimanelli understands that the troubadours' game of love is in fact a love of the game, a fixation on literary wordplay, and that the true object of their passion is not woman, but language itself." Bonaffini, Luigi, "Rimanelli and the Language of Desire," introduction to *Moliseide*, xxix.

28. Ibid. The playfulness and the rigor at once of rehabilitating forms from the past is seen also in some smaller collections, such as *Sonetti per Joseph. Poesie 1994–1995*. See especially the plurilinguistic sonnet *"tenzone"* with the Neapolitan-dialect poet Achille Serrao, in Giose Rimanelli and Achille Serrao, *Viamerica (The Eyes)*, where the poet accepts his destiny as chanteur of what Rebecca West, in her introduction, likens to Montalian *occasioni*: "That's how my memory remembers / When gazing deep into her lustrous gaze / I discerned consolation, love, fibers / Of exile reduced to the purest gaze / . . . / This life of mine has become a drumskin, / It rumbles at times, at times it's a torch holder, / But without you a fistful of cyanide" (21).

29. Cited in Sante Matteo, *Borderlines. Migrazioni e identità nel novecento* (Isernia: Cosmo Iannone, 2007), 241. Translation by Sante Matteo.

30. Luigi Fontanella, *La parola transfuga. Scrittori italiani in America* (Florence: Cadmo, 2003), 186.

31. Ibid., 204.

32. Fontanella uses the words *profuga* and *transfuga* (ibid., 210), to indicate that the poetic word in De Palchi (and to some degree in the other expatriate Italian poets) becomes bearer of something paradoxical, insofar as the poetic construct on one hand acquires the status of the poet's asylum, the only possible destination for a "refugee," yet, on the other, this sanctuary signifies at the same time an act of betrayal, a "going over to the other side," as it were. A definitive chasm between language (origin) and *appartenance* (destination) is thus disclosed. For an earlier discussion on this linguistic and existential juggernaut, see Paolo Valesio, "Il nuovo tribalismo," *Alfabeta* (May 1987): 12–13, and "I fuochi della tribù," in *Poesaggio. Poeti italiani d'America*, ed. P. Carravetta and P. Valesio (Treviso: Pagus, 1993), 255–290. See also in this same collection Peter Carravetta, "Poesaggio" (9–26, 211–214). In English, see by Paolo Valesio, "The Writer Between Two Worlds: Italian Writing in the United States Today," *Differentia* 3–4 (Spring–Autumn 1989): 259–276.

33. Alessandro Vettori, "Introduction" to *Anonymous Constellation*, ix.

34. Ibid., xiv. See also Vettori's critical essay "Il carcere come metafora nell'evoluzione poetica di Alfredo De Palchi (1993–1999)," *Quaderni di Hebenon* 6 (October 2000): 42–55.

35. See Paolo Valesio, "The Writer Between Two Worlds." In this sense, Valesio's experience as embodied in his poetry practically invalidates Deleuze's theory about deterritorialization, as the two societies, of Italy and of the United States, are much more alike than they are different (different national languages and traditions notwithstanding), while the technological and economic strides of the past thirty or so years (whereby living in two countries is now almost possible) whittle down the formerly epic drama of the separation between *elsewhere* (Ogygia or Phaeacia) and *home* (Ithaca).

36. Luigi Ballerini, *eccetera.E* (Milano: Guanda, 1972). See the reviews by Adriano Spatola in *Tam Tam* 3–4 (1973) and Tibor Wlassics in *Il Verri* 4 (1973): 214–223.

37. Beppe Cavatorta, *Strade Maestre e l'isola che non c'è* (New York: Agincourt Pamphlet, 2002), 6.

38. For example, consider the 1992 book *Uscita senza strada ovvero come sbrinare una bandiera rossa* (Palermo: Edizioni della Battaglia), in which the hypallage in the title turns a standard locution inside out. The normal expression in Italian is "strada senza uscita," which literally means "road without an exit," or what in idiomatic English we refer to as a "dead-end street." Reversing the position of the two nouns forces the reader to imagine what an "exit without (a) road" might be like. The same occurs with "sbrinare," typically associated with defrosting something, but here instead of, say, a fish, a red fish, the object is, surprisingly, a red flag, a clear reference to the communist banner. Perhaps there was implicit a message to bring that ideology out from the congealment of the (official) left perceived at the time.

39. Alfredo Giuliani, foreword to *Che figurato muore*, by Luigi Ballerini (Milan: Scheiwiller, 1988), 15.

40. Condini published this book using his Italian given name, Nereo, which he changed to Ned when he started publishing in the United States.

41. Franco Borrelli, review of Ned Condini, *Rimbaud in Umbria*, in *America Oggi*, November 7, 1993.

42. G. Singh, *World Literature Today* 65, no. 4 (Autumn 1991).

43. In particular in Luigi Fontanella, *Simulazione di reato* (Bari: Lacaita, 1979); and *La vita trasparente* (Venice: Rebellato, 1978).

44. See his cited study *La parola transfuga* (2003), which explores the life and poetry of Emanuel Carnevale and Pascal D'Angelo, among others.

45. Carravetta and Valesio, *Poesaggio*, 214–215.

46. Peter Carravetta, *dialogi v.* (Parma: Edizioni Tam Tam, 1978).

47. For a brief analysis of this book, see Peter Carravetta, "Introducing the Poetry of Alessandro Carrera," *VIA Voices in Italian Americana* 2, no. 2 (1991): 157–163. *La sposa perfetta* was republished with some revisions in 1997.

48. In a poetic statement published in Carravetta and Valesio, *Poesaggio*, 218–221, Carrera remarked on the strangeness of his new habitat in Texas, on his personal and professional isolation, and on the efficiency as well as the anti-intellectualism of American institutions, which nearly made him nostalgic for the "fratricidal brawls" of Italian cultural debates. He clearly acknowledges that, as an Italian, he "has nothing in common with the descendents of the thousands who arrived at the end of the nineteenth century, from Aci Trezza to the port of Galveston, without any hope of returning, bringing along the nothingness of the sea and a dialect which no one outside of themselves spoke. Even if perhaps I would like to be identified with them, I can't" (221). On the other hand, he also noticed how Italians arriving in Texas at the end of twentieth century lived in a "state of colloidal suspension," a jealously garded existence much "preoccupied with not having their children become too American" (220).

49. In *Poesaggio*, Carrera had observed, concerning the overuse or abuse of the symbolic identification with Ulysses by many poets residing abroad: "Let's not overdramatize. He is a comfortable Ulysses who takes the plane twice a year to spend Christmas

and Ferragosto in Ithaca, and then returns to that huge Calypso cavern which is America, where all desires are satisfied except the essential ones" (219).

50. Alessandra Giappi, *Poesia* 19 (July–August 2001): 72.

51. See Richard Milazzo, *Circus in a Fog: Poems 2005–2006* (Venice: Sottoportego Editore, 2009).

52. Ernesto Livorni, *L'America dei padri* (San Cesario di Lecce: Manni, 2006), 9.

53. Deleuze and Guattari, *Kafka*, 23.

54. Renato Barilli, *Viaggio al termine della parola* (Milan: Feltrinelli, 1979). In this small and important anthology, Barilli was making the case for a poetry ideologically committed to splintering language asunder, fragmenting and exploding the minimal units of language down to phonemes and graphemes, ending in the in-between terrain of visual and concrete poetry.

55. Adriano Spatola, *Various Devices*, trans. P. Vangelisti (Los Angeles: Red Hill Press, 1978); there are no page numbers, but the quotation is in the short introduction by Spatola, "A Vaguely Ontological Aspiration," originally in *Tam Tam* 2, 1972 (again without pagination).

56. Paolo Valesio, "Postface" to *Tutto questo*, by Mario Moroni (Salerno: Oedipus, 2000), 67, 73.

57. Mario Moroni, *La composizione del tempo* (Modena: Edizioni del laboratorio, 1987). Within the canon of Italian poetry, I consider this one of the best books of the 1980s, a true heir to the great and, to date, not adequately studied poetry of Adriano Spatola.

58. In this sense Giorgio Patrizi, in his preface to Moroni's *La composizione del tempo*, spoke of an "allegorical" aspect of the text, "which reveals the double *evenemenzialità* of the world" (7), that is, first, the cyclic reutilization of myth, and then the original, unrepeatable givenness of fact, of the event that follows other events. But this "allegorical" dimension has not been explained further, perhaps because it is inconsistent with a focus on language *qua* language.

59. Mario Moroni, *Le terre di Icaro* (Castel Maggiore: Book Editore, 2001). A bilingual collection of Moroni's poetry carries the same title, *Icarus's Land*, trans. E. Di Pasquale (Como: Lieto Colle, 2006), although it is actually a translation of another of his books, *Tutto questo* (2000), but includes some previously unpublished material. That the poems are gathered under the aegis of Icarus is in itself worthy of a deeper study: Is America the land of impossible dreams? Are the new settlers, the recently arrived exiles, expatriates, immigrants destined to have their dreams, their American dream, come crashing down?

60. See Deleuze and Guattari, *Kafka*. Of the three characteristics of a "minor literature"—which is what Italian writing in America is, despite the reservations expressed by many (including Carrera and Valesio)—namely, deterritorialization, politicalness, and the transsubjective or collective values that it must necessarily take on, this last one can help explain why Moroni falls into the "school" or "category" of an *Italophone literature*, independently of what his personal style might be and how he negotiates his alienation.

61. See Gilles Deleuze and Félix Guattari, *A Thousand Plateaus*, trans. B. Massumi (Minneapolis: University of Minnesota Press, 1987): chapter 12, "Treatise on Nomadology," 372, 380, 381.

62. Fabio Pusterla, "Il revox di Giorgio Mobili," in Giorgio Mobile, *Penelope su Sunset Boulevard* (San Cesario di Lecce: Manni, 2010), 5.

63. See Peter Carravetta, *The Elusive Hermes: Method, Discourse, Interpreting* (Aurora, Colo.: Davies Group, 2012), 160–161.

64. "What the poet represents in this book is truly a world, or rather, a way of relating to the world: to the complexity, the contradictoriness, the painful elusiveness of a multifaceted reality, elusive and yet piercing, striated by anxiety and perversity, and yet still at times illuminated by a light that hurts." Pusterla, "Il revox," 7.

Venezuela

Venezuela

MICHELE CASTELLI

The Italian population in Venezuela increased dramatically following World War II and continued to climb over the ensuing decade up to the fall of the dictator Marcos Pérez Jiménez and the subsequent election of Rómulo Betancourt, the first Venezuelan president elected democratically in the twentieth century. The official records of the Ministry of Foreign Affairs show that in 1958, there were about 180,000 Italian immigrants, and that these numbers decreased considerably as some of them returned to Italy and others relocated to other countries, such as Canada. Currently, the Italian consulate estimates—accounting for individuals of the first, second, and third generations—that about 205,000 residents hold Italian passports, a number that would total more than a million if it were to include residents of Italian descent. This substantial community is highly integrated into the country, and it has made significant contributions to its economic, social, and cultural development.

Among the artistic spheres in which Italians have been active in Venezuela, literature is of particular note. Venezuelans of the colonial era were aware of Boccaccio's *Decameron*, and, especially from 1892 to 1915, thanks to the review *El Cojo Illustrado*, authors such as Carducci, Pascoli, Ada Negri, and Gabriele D'Annunzio became well known. The latter had a great impact on Venezuelan poets of the first half of the last century.

A key figure in the diffusion of Italian prose and poetry was well-known maestro Edoardo Crema, a scholar from Padua who, born in 1892, resettled in Caracas in 1927 and remained there until his death in 1974. Crema was the founder of the Department of Humanities and Education of the Central University of Venezuela, where he became the first professor of Italian. His main accomplishment was due perhaps to his introduction in Venezuela of a critical approach influenced by Croce's theories based on esthetic values as fundamental for artistic creation. During his long university career, Crema published works on Dante, Petrarch, and

Ariosto, among others, and established a lasting interest in studies related to Italian culture and civilization, a legacy carried on by some of his students, such as Marisa Vannini, author of a famous book called *Italia y los italianos en la historia y en la cultura de Venezuela* (*Italy and Italians in the History and Culture of Venezuela*). In more recent years, the professorship at the university, which functions as the main center of diffusion of Italian culture, has been led by Lucia Veronesi, whose principal goal has been to give a decisive boost to the teaching of Italian, and by Michele Castelli, who has focused on dialect studies and on the linguistic behavior of Venezuelans of Italian descent, particularly those from Molise. Castelli also initiated the study of such regional poets as Nicola Iacobacci and Raffaele Capriglione.

Poets and writers of the diaspora in Venezuela are now treating different themes in their works, though still focusing on Italy and Italian identity. Among these there is Gaetano Bafile, director and founder of the daily *La voce d'Italia* (*Italian Voice*) and author of *Passaporto verde* (*Green Passport*), which compiles the most important editorials covering significant moments in the history of Italian immigration to Venezuela. He also wrote a novel denouncing a barbaric event that took place during the dictatorship, the violent killing of seven Sicilians in 1955. There is also Giuseppe Domingo, who has promoted in the editorial market an autobiographical novel titled *Famiglia nostra* (*Our Family*), which tells the story of his Sicilian family in Venezuela. Filippo Vagnoni, a somewhat different figure, has produced works like *Talión* (*Retaliation*) and *Flores para dos tumbas* (*Flowers for Two Graves*), both written in Spanish. Two other poets, both characterized by a deep sensibility, must also be mentioned. They are Vittorio Fioravanti and Valeriano Garbin, whose literary achievement shall be clearly exemplified in this anthology.

⇥ *Vittorio Fioravanti (b. 1936)*

Vittorio Fioravanti was born in Taranto on April 13, 1936, the first child of Remo Fioravanti, an officer in the Italian air force, and Clara Grasso Fioravanti, a schoolteacher. His wife, Marlene Müller Velasquez Fioravanti, is Venezuelan. After living in several Italian cities and in Germany, Fioravanti settled in Venezuela in 1966. His background is varied. He pursued studies in scientific fields, including nautical studies, but never completed his university degree. Instead, he accumulated ample experience in graphic design and radio and television production and has been assistant director for a multicultural magazine, *Incontri* (*Meetings*), as well as for radio and television agencies, including Radio Deportes (Sports Radio) and Venevisión.

Fioravanti has had a number of leadership positions and significant political posts. He is active in sports organizations, a promoter of Italo-Venezuelan sport centers, founder of the Apulian Association in Caracas, and representative of the Venezuelan Italian Emigration group in Buenos Aires, Argentina. He is also the Venezuelan representative to the Italian information agency in Sao Paolo, Brazil. He is also the recipient of several honorary titles and medals such as the Cavaliere dell'Ordine della Repubblica Italiana (Knight of the Italian Republic), and he has won several literary prizes, including first place in Nuestra Libertad in Valencia in 1986 and first place in the international competition Italia Mia, sponsored by the Ministry of Italians in the World. He has also been recognized as one of the major graphic artists in Venezuela and has published works in numerous literary magazines. His website, with information on his published work, is at www.vittoriofioravanti.it.

Razza mediterranea

Siamo il seme disperso
frammenti d'una diaspora estesa
Siamo gli scampati oltre il muro
dell'orto franatoci intorno

Razza bastarda
fuggiamo da sempre
lungo i sentieri più incerti
delle patrie scelte soffrendo
sui biglietti d'un viaggio
ormai senza ritorno

Sopravviviamo
forti del dolce coraggio
d'una donna incontrata
quasi per caso
appena all'angolo di un'ora
della nostra vita
Sopravviviamo
forti anche dei figli
del nostro esilio

Razza testarda
ci cerchiamo con gli occhi
l'alito d'aglio
le mani stanche e sporche
ripulite ogni sera
e quelle poche parole restate

Siamo un'Italia antica
copia sbiadita d'una fotografia
l'ombra del campanile
che attraversa a tentoni la piazza
lungo le stesse pietre
le foglie frementi sull'albero
di una strada di periferia
l'acqua rossa dell'unico fosso

Mediterranean Race

We are a seed dispersed
the fragments of a far-flung diaspora
We are the ones who have escaped beyond the walls
of the garden that crumpled around us

A bastard race,
we are always fleeing
along paths paths more and more uncertain,
suffering in chosen homelands
on one-way tickets for a voyage
without return

We survive
made strong by the gentle courage
of a woman met
almost by chance
in the corner of an hour
of our life
We survive
strong through the children
of our exile

A headstrong race
seeking each other with our eyes,
garlic on the breath,
our hands tired and dirty
rewashed every evening,
and these few words that remain

We are an ancient Italy
a faded copy of a photograph
the shadow of a belltower
that gropes through the same piazza
over the same stones
the leaves quivering on the tree
in a peripheral street
the red water from a common ditch

Vittorio Fioravanti   1485

Siamo in quel grido allo stadio
la stessa gente

      Siamo un'Italia remota
l'eco di quel violento '45
Siamo i reduci dei due fronti
la rivincita d'una guerra persa
      Qui siamo l'emigrazione
le rimesse e i risparmi
l'eco di quel grido allo stadio
un'immagine fatta e disfatta
d'arduo lavoro e di sacrifici
di scontri e nemici
Siamo un volto rassegnato
uno sguardo rivolto al buio
dell'integrazione

C'è una voglia in noi
crescente come la spuma
d'una calda mareggiata
morbida come il volo lento
d'un gabbiano steso nel vento
      le ali aperte
sul fragore della risacca
      C'è in noi violento
il rimpianto di quelle scogliere
nostalgie di filari di viti
di tristi ulivi contorti
di case bianche di gesso
d'una preghiera resa in coro
nel segno della croce
nel lancio d'un pallone di cuoio
calciato al centro dell'oratorio
e c'è il sapore delle domeniche
e la tua giovane voce
il tuo pianto Mamma

We are there in the cry of the stadium
the same people

We are a remote Italy
the echo of that violent '45
We are the veterans, surviving on two fronts
the revenge of a lost war
          Here we are the emigration
the money sent back and the money saved
the echo of that cry in the stadium
an image made and unmade
of arduous work and sacrifice
of clashes and enemies
We are a resigned face
a glance turned toward the darkness
of integration

There is a will in us
cresting like the wave
of a warm and heavy sea
smooth like the slow flight
of a seagull streched out in the wind
its wings spread
in the roar of the sea-spray

          It is violent in us,
the regret of those cliffs
the nostalgia for the rows of grapevines
for the sad, contorted olive trees,
for the houses white with gesso
for a prayer rendered in unison
in the sign of the cross
in the pitch of a leather soccer ball
kicked into the center of the oratory
and this is the flavor of Sundays
and your youthful voice
and your cry, Mama

Sangue mediterraneo
ci abbracciamo in incontri
concertati per crederci uniti
               strette di mano
tra i brindisi accesi e le risa
la pasta ancora fumante
               bandiere spente
e un canto assonnato
un sospiro d'assurdo

E in fondo al salone
col tricolore appeso
               intanto
di lá della vetrata aperta
oltre la vallata e i monti
al di lá di tutta quell'acqua
che ci divide dal passato
c'è un'Italia diversa
               cosí cambiata
vibrante e moderna
perversa nei suoi nuovi costumi
               quasi straniera
che oramai ci ignora

                              Caracas, estate 1996

Mediterranean blood
we embrace in matches
in meetings
organized as a means of believing ourselves united
a clasp of hands
among the bright toasts and the laughter
and the pasta still steaming hot
extinct flags
and a sleepy song
an absurd sigh

And in the back of the room
the tricolor hanging
in the meantime
beyond the panes of the glass door
beyond the valley and the mountains
far beyond all that water
which divides us from the past
there is a different Italy
so changed
vibrant and modern
so perverse in its new customs
almost foreign
that now ignores us.

Caracas, summer 1996

Andarsene via

Pietre immobili
cerchiate di strida d' uccelli
la torre dell' orologio
fermo nel tempo
d'una vendemmia sfumata

Andarsene via
dalla dura sventura
di non trovare un padrone
con tutti quegli anni
persi in attese umilianti
tenuti a bada dai cani
senza un impiego onesto
la parte più forte
di tutta una vita
lasciata lungo i muri
d'una fabbrica chiusa
dietro le scritte
della nostra rabbia
gli stivali della legge
e ancora i cani

Andarsene via
dall'avversa disgrazia
di non essere mai nessuno
di non trovare ascolto
di passare ormai inosservati
sotto gli occhi di chi
non ti ha mai guardato

Andarsene
lontano dalle finestre aperte
senza più madre
senza più donne
via dalla piazza di casa
dall' orologio fermo nel tempo
dal ballo del santo

To Go Away

Unmoved stones
encircled by the cries of birds
the clock tower
fixed in the time of
a disappearing harvest

To go away
from the harsh misfortune
of not finding a patron
with all these years
lost through humiliating delays
kept at a distance by dogs
without honest employment
the greater part
of an entire lifetime
left along the walls
of a closed factory
behind the writings
of our rage
the boot of the law
and the dogs, again

To go away
from the unfortunate disgrace
of not being anyone, anymore
of not being listened to
to pass unobserved, all the while
under the eyes of one
who has never looked at you

Go
far from the open windows
             without a mother any longer
             without any more women
go from the piazza of the house
from the clock fixed in time
from the dance of the saint

che non ti ha protetto
via dai ciottoli del paese
dagli alberi visti crescere
dal sole oltre il colle
via dai tuoi morti
con una croce segnata
in fretta sulla tua fronte
via dalle pietre immobili
da quelle strida d'uccelli
via dalle frane e dai fossi
oltre il fango ed il pianto
   via da casa
   lontano
oltre il rimorso

   Andarsene via
prima di cadere innocenti
tra le strette di certa gente
che ti manda con uno sguardo
   gli occhi negli occhi
e ti ritrovi con un'arma
tra le dita che hanno cercato
invano un lavoro
   muto in agguato
per uccidere un uomo

      Caracas, gennaio 1997

who has not protected you
go from the cobblestones of the town
from the trees you watched growing
from the sun beyond the hills
go, away from your dead
with the sign of the cross, made in haste
across your forehead and chest
go from the unmoved stones
from the cries of birds
from the landslides and the graves
beyond the mud and the lament
go from the house
      far
beyond remorse

Go away
before falling innocently
in the grasp of certain people
who send you with a look
eyes in the eyes
and find you with a weapon
clasped in your fingers that have
looked in vain for work
mute in ambush
to kill a man

                          Caracas, January 1997

Me n'andrò

Quando sarà il momento
spento lo sguardo
farò un gesto di rassegnazione
e me n'andrò
sbiadita memoria
di parole perse
lungo mura immerse
nell'acque immote
della laguna

Me n'andrò
senza ascoltare pianti
senza un addio
chiuso in me stesso
al di là dell'estrema luce
dell'ultima nota sospesa
lontano
senza rabbia oramai
come un esausto gabbiano
su un lembo di sabbia
senza più un grido

Così me n'andrò
senza un urlo
ignorando ogni appiglio
senza un gemito
muto
spoglio
senza neanche
lasciar dietro di me
una scia di rimpianto

Gondola nera
scivolando nel vuoto profondo

I Will Go

When it will be that moment
the gaze spent
I will make a gesture of resignation
and I will go
a faded memory
of words lost
along the wall immersed
in the stagnant waters
of the lagoon

I will go
without hearing cries
without a goodbye
closed within myself
beyond the extreme light
suspended in the last
distant note
without rage now
like an exhausted seagull
on a stretch of sand
without another cry

Thus I will go
without a wail
ignoring every plea
without a moan
mute
bare
without even
leaving behind
a trail of regret

Black gondola
gliding in the deep void

dove non c'è più nessuno
dove tutto svanisce

Da sempre e per sempre
in eterno

Caracas, settembre 1999

where there is no longer anyone
where all vanishes
for ever and for ever
in eternity

Caracas, September 1999

Un uomo solo

Eccolo accanto a me
un uomo solo
con una birra scura davanti
come un cavallo in piedi
il feltro a tappargli dentro
pensieri e grida

Parliamo a gesti divisi
dalla sbarra del bar
fra sorrisi e strette di mano
e le ceneri di due sigarette
indicando le cose col dito
con scarne parole e verbi
espressi nel modo infinito

Quest'uomo solo
ogni sabato delle sue notti
pugni avvezzi al contatto
del gelo e la calce
sogni rotti in frantumi
due fessure colme d'iridi
rese oscure dall'ombra
covata sotto il sole tondo
d'una terra lasciata alle spalle
Mi parla di mare
di scogliere e di schiuma
d'aranceti e di reti stese
di vele bianche e di barche
rastremate
come le anche svelte
sotto le nere gonne
delle donne del suo paese
Ha voce roca
un suono rozzo che evoca
la contorta corteccia
d'un vecchio ulivo
affiora da un pozzo

A Man Alone

Here next to me
a man alone
with a dark beer in front of him
standing like a horse
the felt to stop up what is inside
thoughts and cries

We speak with divisive gestures
from the barrier of the bar
among smiles and handshakes
and the ashes of two cigarettes
indicating things with a finger
with spare words and verbs
espressed in the infinitive

This solitary man,
all his Saturday nights
fists accustomed to contact
with frost and quicklime
dreams broken, shattered into bits
two cracks full of rainbows
rendered dark in the shadows
smoldering under the round sun
of a land left behind.

He speaks to me of the sea
of its reefs and of its spray
of its orange groves and of its spread nets
of white sails and tapering
boats
as the slender hips
under the black dresses
of the women of his land

He has a hoarse voice,
a broken sound that evokes
the twisted bark
of an old olive tree

colmo di nostalgia
ha lo sguardo che s'apre
su orizzonti lontani a occhi chiusi
che spazia distese marine
come un cieco gabbiano

Così conosco
quest'uomo mediterraneo
in un sabato notte
della sua inane esistenza
la sciarpa di capra alla gola
e la vista che fugge via
oltre il boccale spumoso
oltre i rutti, il fumo e le teste
oltre Stoccarda e i confini
alpi rocciose e vaste pianure
che lo separano da troppo tempo
dal muretto franato
attorno all'orto incolto di casa.

Caracas, giugno 2003

flowering out of a well
full of nostalgia
He has a gaze that opens itself
with closed eyes onto far-off horizons
that cover the expanse of the sea
like a blind seagull

So I know
this Mediterranean man
on a Saturday night
of his mundane existence
the goat-sash at his throat
and the fleeting vision
beyond the foamy tankard
beyond the belching, the smoke and the faces
beyond Stuttgart and the confines
rocky alps and vast plains
that have separated him for too long
from the collapsed wall
around the unkept garden of his house

Caracas, June 2003

Silvia

Il soldato era da tempo
a bocca in giù
nel fondo nero del pozzo

Nel buio c'erano gli scarponi
e le braccia legate sul dorso
ma lo sapevano i partigiani
che ce l'avevano buttato dentro
per nasconderlo morto

Noi s'attingeva l'acqua ignari
due volte al giorno
al mattino e alla sera
da oltre un mese ormai

Da quando eravamo scappati
da La Spezia e le bombe
sganciate a grappoli dagli alleati
ogni notte sul porto e le case
rase al suolo con l'Arsenale

Fuggiti via dall'ansia
dalle macerie e gli agguati
cercando di sopravvivere
come animali feriti
in un borgo lontano dal mare
nell'aspera Garfagnana

Fuggiti via
da una morte straziante

C'era invece il tedesco
ucciso nel pozzo infetto
e Silvia—che non aveva
ancora detto una volta
mamma—

Silvia

The soldier had been there for a while,
mouth facing downwards,
in the pitch-black bottom of a well

In the dark there were boots—
and arms tied behind the back—
but they knew, the partisans
who'd thrown him inside
to hide the dead body

Unaware, we drew water
from the well
two times a day,
in the morning and in the evening,
for more than a month

From the time we had escaped
from La Spezia
and bombs
released in clusters by the Allies
every night in the harbor
and the houses
razed to the ground with the Arsenal

Fleeing the anxiety,
the rubble and the ambushes,
seeking to survive
like wounded animals
in a village far from the sea
in inhospitable Garfagnana

Fleeing
a harrowing death

Rather, it was the German
killed in a polluted well
and Silvia—

consunta di febbre e di pianto
come un fiorellino appassito
si spense nell'abbraccio muto
d'una madre impotente
di salvare i suoi figli

Caracas, settembre 2003

who had not yet said
"mamma," not even once—
consumed by fever and by crying
like a budding flower, withered,
expiring in the mute embrace
of a mother powerless
to save her children.

Caracas, September 2003

→ *Valeriano Garbin (b. 1937)*

Valeriano Garbin was born in Schio, in the Veneto region, in 1937. He now resides in Venezuela. His first collection of poems was published in 1970 with the title *Il Batticuore* (*The Excitement*), which was featured in the prestigious Premio Bergamo poetry prize competition. In 1974, Garbin published *Gli occhi della Civetta* (*The Owl's Eyes*), a collection that was illustrated by Emilio Crivellato. A year later Garbin published another book of poems called *Amori* (*Loves*), illustrated with the works of a well-known lithographer, Pio Penzo. After Garbin moved to Venezuela in 1976, he published *La calida vida* (*The Warm Life*), with photos by Pietro Mattioli. *Tierras vivas* (*Living Earths*) came out in 1978 and contained illustrations of sculptures by Giorgio Sferra, and 1979 was the year of *El viento, la luna, el sol y el agua* (*The Wind, the Moon, the Sun, and the Water*), featuring twelve original drawings by the great master Braulio Salazar, winner of a national prize in Venezuela. In 2000 Garbin published *Venezuela Enamorada* (*Venezuela in Love*), illustrated by Dileyde Vásquez Sánchez, who also contributed nine drawings to *Raices Entregadas* (*Transferred Roots*). In 2001 Garbin participated in the forty-ninth Venice Bienniale with some poems, and in 2004 he edited the volume *Petrarca in Venezuela* (*Petrarch in Venezuela*). The poems that follow are unpublished as of this writing.

Le ceneri di Lia

Le ceneri di mia moglie sono disperse
nelle serene, dolci, calde, acque del Caribe
onde libere e incontaminate da mille colori
dove i gabbiani grandi come alianti
volano girando intorno al giorno,
fenicotteri sfrecciano penetrando l'universo,
magiche rosse garze accendono l'aurora e il tramonto
per garantire il sogno d'eternità
e la visione interiore di Dio
e dove i cormorani si lanciano come meteoriti
in tuffi di mistero.
Le ceneri della madre di Stefano, Sabrina e Andrea
scintillano con il loro canto di stelle
tra i vergini coralli e il silenzio di arcobaleni.
Fu il giorno dei Re Magi
generosa forza del bello, del degno d'essere generosi
dell'offerta, giorno simbolo
di sacrificio e dolcezza, delicatezza e vigore:
personalità convinta, fresche vene di Lia
combattiva energia sorridente
creatrice di vite degne d'essere vissute.
Trasformata in altare
la barca si muoveva lentamente
come sciolta gondola in laguna.
Con le bandiere e gli inni
il "Va, pensiero sull'ali dorate"
per una meditazione, per l'esistere
per l'avvenire
per purificare il mondo e le persone
penetrò i solchi di smeraldo e turchese
per i piccolissimi luminosi soli
protetti da tropicali petali e danzanti rose
memorie, sentimenti, sacrifici, generosità.

Lia's Ashes

My wife's ashes are scattered
in calm, sweet, warm Caribbean waters,
free and unpolluted waves of a thousand colors
where seagulls large as gliders
fly circling around the day,
flamingos burst like arrows through the universe,
magic red herons climb the sunrise and the sunset,
vouchsafing the dream of eternity
and the inner eye of God,
and where cormorants hurl like shooting stars
into whirlpools of mystery.
The ashes of the mother of
Stephano, Sabrina, Andrea
sparkle with the song of the stars
among the virgin corals and the silence of rainbows.

It was the feast of the Three Kings
and the generous strength of beauty,
the dignity of being generous,
the feast of the Gift, the day that is symbol
for sacrifice and sweetness, tact and vigor.

The fresh veins of Lia, a woman with conviction,
combative, smiling, energetic,
who created lives worthy to be lived. . . .
Transformed into an altar,
the boat moved slowly
like a gondola undocked in a laguna.
With banners and hymns—

Va, pensiero, Go, thought, on golden wing,
for a meditation, for existence,
for the future
to make the world and its people pure,
it drifted through furrows of emerald and turquoise
through minuscule luminescent suns,
protected by tropical petals and dancing roses,
memories, feelings, sacrifices, generosity.

Valeriano Garbin 1509

Le valli di Caracas

Valli come stelle filanti
s'intrecciano sotto l'imponente Avila
colorate, esuberanti, primaverili
contraddittorie, eclettiche, felici
e guardano indifferenti colline
di suggestione scottante
e accecanti verità,
ardui simbolismi
di sopravvivenze e attese deluse.
Valli come avvenimenti
guardinghe a Caracas
per nuovi pericoli
d'inconcludenti promesse
giovani valli che corrono su e giù
benedicendo la natura
invocando l'uomo e il futuro.
Primaverili valli di cemento e ranchitos
tra tristi ostinati colli
che non lasciano cadere le speranze
contro la rinuncia, contro la fuga.
La notte trasforma tutto
in pacifico presepio d'amore.

Caracas Valleys

Valleys like ranks of stars
crisscrossing under the great Avila
colored, exuberant, springtime,
contradictory, eclectic, happy—
they look up at the indifferent hills
with their hints of conflagrations
and blinding truths
and harsh symbols
of survival and disappointed waiting.
Valleys like events
in Caracas are wary and watch
for new dangers and
vague promises.
Young valleys running up and down,
blessing nature,
invoking Man and The Future.
Springtime valleys of concrete and *ranchitos*
among the stubborn hills,
whose hopes do not fail
against surrender and flight.
Night transforms everything
into peaceful creche of love.

Svegliati

Aspettando e sperando, un altro anno è fuggito
con violente raffiche di minuti come rapidi treni:
delusioni, utopie, ingiustizie. Morte.
L'immensa umanità nuota sopra barche affondate
cammina su sentieri insanguinati
vola tra nuvole che incendiano roveti di spine.
Non ha pane né risaie né vigneti
non ha canna da zucchero né frutteti
la sempre più povera e numerosa gente.
Non ha più nemmeno la sua ombra
le case con finestre arrampicate una su l'altra
sulle colline senza panorama.
Nessuna emozione, né sorriso in Santa Chiara.
Un altro anno si è sgretolato
con la stagione delle piogge
nudi i piedi pazienti come tombe
della gente imbrogliata, spaventata
soffocata, abbagliata, stordita
anche dai fuochi artificiali
della sagra della Misericordia.
La terra non è più la terra
e la rosa non è più la rosa né i sogni i sogni.
Solo l'inutile morte, per la povera gente
è ancora l'inutile morte e i giorni un fiume
che gioca a cascare di gradino in gradino
di corsa come schiuma di versi.
Svegliati!, svegliati!, creatura, abbandonata umanità,
scalda il tuo cuore addormentato
aprilo al sole
e scuoti l'albero del tuo corpo
carico di desideri e speranze
e vibra amore amore amore.

Awake

Waiting and hoping, another year has fled.
Minutes squall by like rapid trains:
illusions, utopias, injustices. Death.
All of humanity is drowning over sunken ships,
walking on bloody trails,
or flying through a burning bramble patch of clouds.
No bread, no rice fields or vineyards,
no sugar cane, no orchards
for the always poorer always more plentiful people.
Windowed houses with nothing to look out on,
piled one atop another,
no longer own even their shadows.
No excitement, no smiles in Santa Chiara.
Another year dissolves
in another rainy season.
The feet are bare, patient as graves
for confused and frightened people,
smothered, blinded, stunned
by even the Santa Misericordia
celebration fireworks.
The land is no longer the land,
nor a rose a rose, nor are dreams dreams.
Only useless death, for the poor,
still has some use. The days are a river
tripping swiftly from slab
to slab like the froth of verses.
Wake up, wake up! Forsaken creature, poor humanity,
warm your sluggish heart
and open it to the sun.
Shake your body like a tree
laden with hopes and desires.
Set love a-quiver, amore, amore, amore.

Contributors

Luigi Bonaffini is professor of Italian language and literature at Brooklyn College. His publications include *La poesia visionaria di Dino Campana* and translations of books by Campana, Mario Luzi, Giose Rimanelli, Attilio Bertolucci, Pier Paolo Pasolini, and many other contemporary Italian writers. He has edited five trilingual anthologies of dialect poetry and has translated widely from various dialects. He coedited *A New Map*, a bilingual anthology of migrant writers in Italy, and is the editor of *Journal of Italian Translation*.

Joseph Perricone is professor of Italian and comparative literature at Fordham University. He has written critical studies on Italian literature as well as film, including work on Grazia Deledda, Vittorio Bodini, Ardengo Soffici, Guido Gozzano, and Federico Fellini. He has translated numerous works by novelists such Grazia Deledda, Giuseppe Berto, and Arrigo Boito and poets such as Ferdinando Russo, Mario Novaro, Sergio D'Amaro, and Cristanziano Serricchio.

Adria Bernardi received the 2007 Raiziss/de Palchi Translation Award to complete *Small Talk*, a translation of poetry in the Romagnole dialect by Raffaello Baldini. Her translations include Rinaldo Caddeo's *Siren's Song*, Gianni Celati's *Adventures in Africa*, and Tonino Guerra's *Abandoned Places*. She is the author of two novels, *Openwork* and *The Day Laid on the Altar*, and a collection of short stories, *In the Gathering Woods*. A collection of essays, *Dead Meander*, is forthcoming.

Novella Bonaffini is a neurologist living in Rome. She translated several dialect poets for the anthologies *Dialect Poetry of Southern Italy* and *Dialect Poetry of Central and Northern Italy*.

D. F. Brown is a native of the Missouri Ozarks who now lives in Houston, Texas, where he teaches writing.

Michael F. Capobianco is professor emeritus of mathematics at St. John's University. He has been writing and translating for more than forty years and has published ten books and several award-winning short stories and poems. He has translated poems in the Neapolitan and Trentino dialects. He is now teaching Mandarin Chinese.

Barbara Carle is a poet, translator, and critic. She has published three bilingual volumes of poetry and three books of translation and has written numerous articles on Italian poetry and translation. She teaches Italian language, literature, and cinema at California State University in Sacramento.

Peter Carravetta is Alfonse M. D'Amato Professor of Italian and Italian American Studies at Stony Brook University. Founding editor of *DIFFERENTIA: review of italian thought* (1986–1999), he has published numerous books of criticism, including *Prefaces to the Diaphora: Rhetorics, Allegory and the Interpretation of Postmodernity* and *After Identity: Perspectives in Italian American Culture*, as well as seven books of poetry and a number of translations.

Alessandro Carrera is director of Italian Studies and graduate director of World Cultures and Literatures at the University of Houston. He has published extensively in the fields of Italian and European literature, literary theory, continental philosophy, and music. He is the author of many books of poetry and fiction and is the recipient of the Montale Poetry Prize, the Loria Prize for Short Fiction, and the Bertolucci Prize for Literary Criticism.

Michele Castelli received a degree in foreign languages and literatures from the University of Bari. In 1967 he moved to Venezuela, where he taught Spanish and Latin American literature in the Instituto Luigi Einaudi of Caracas. He is now head of the School of Humanities of the Central University of Venezuela. Among his publications are *Poesias* and *La piedra azul turqi*, a translation of Nicola Iacobacci's *La pietra turchina*.

Gino (Carmine) Chiellino, born in Calabria in 1946, is interested in intercultural literatures. Among his latest works are *Interkulturelle Literatur in der Bundesrepublik, Parole errant, Ich in Dresden*, and *Landschaft aus Menschen und Tagen*.

Gaetano Cipolla has translated several authors from the Sicilian: Giovanni Meli's *The Origins of the World, Don Chisciotti and Sanciu Panza*, and *Moral Fables and Other Poems*; Vincenzo Ancona's *Malidittu la lingua/*

Damned Language; and Antonino Provenzano's *Vinissi/I'd Love to Come.* He is a professor emeritus of Italian at St. John's University.

Paul D'Agostino is an artist, writer, and translator. He holds a Ph.D. in Italian literature and is adjunct assistant professor of Italian at CUNY Brooklyn College, where he also works in the art department. He writes in and translates among a number of different languages, primarily Italian, German, French, Spanish and English. He is an assistant editor of the *Journal of Italian Translation* and co-founder of the art blog *After Vasari*.

Celestino De Iuliis was born in Campotosto, Abruzzo, and emigrated to Canada at the age of six with his parents. He studied mathematics and Italian literature at the University of Toronto. In 1981 he published a collection of poems, *Love's Sinning Song.* He has translated works by Maria Ardizzi, Michel Tremblay, and Dario Fo. He is at present completing a new terza rima translation of Dante's *Divina Commedia.*

Emanuel di Pasquale was born in Ragusa in 1943 and came to America in 1957. He is the author of several books of poetry, among them *Genesis, The Silver Lake Love Poems,* and *Out of Stars and Sand and Other Sicilian Poems.* He is the translator of Dante's *La Vita Nuova* and Paolo Ruffilli's *Dark Room.* He has won numerous awards for his poems and translations alike.

John DuVal received the the 1992 Harold Morton Landon Translation Award for Cesare Pascarella's *The Discovery of America* and the 2006 Raiziss/de Palchi Award for Pascarella's *Tales of Trilussa.* His latest books of translation are *Voices of a Continent,* with his daughter Kathleen DuVal, and *The Song of Roland.* He teaches literary translation in the University of Arkansas Creative Writing Program.

Gil Fagiani is the author of several poetry collections, including *Rooks, Grandpa's Wine,* and *Serfs of Psychiatry.* His translations have appeared in the *Journal of Italian Translation* and other journals, as well as in Francesco Durante's anthology *ItaloAmericana: Storia e Letteratura Degli Italiani Negli Stati Uniti.* He is associate editor of *Feile-Festa: A Literary Arts Magazine.*

Jason Laine coordinates the Italian language program at Pennsylvania State University. In addition to teaching language and culture courses, he is interested in online learning and technology implementation in the language classroom, Italian cinema, and contemporary Italian poetry.

Andrea Lombardi obtained his doctorate in comparative literature and theory of literature at the University of São Paolo. He is a professor of literature at the Federal University of Rio de Janeiro and coordinates the blog Eticadaleitura, which features essays on Hebraism, the ethics of reading, and migration.

Rosemary Manno is a poet, artist, and lover of foreign languages and the natural world. Her work has ?appeared in numerous chapbooks, magazines, and anthologies. Her forthcoming collection is entitled *Marseille*.? She lives in San Francisco.

Jean-Jacques Marchand was born in 1944 of an Italian mother and Swiss father. He studied in Switzerland and Italy and was a full professor of Italian literature at the University of Lausanne (1983–2006) and visiting professor in Rome and in several European universities. He has published more than a hundred studies of the Italian literature of the Renaissance and of the nineteenth and twentieth centuries, above all the literature of Italian emigration in the world.

Gabriel Cacho Millet is an Argentinian journalist and writer. He has been a Spanish citizen since 2006 and has lived and worked in Rome for many years. Besides Dino Campana, Cacho Millet has translated Luigi Pirandello, Jorge Luis Borges, Rafael Alberti, and Primo Conti. He has also edited previously unpublished short stories, poems, and essays by Emanuel Carnevali. He is the author of many theatrical pieces and essays as well.

Adeodato Piazza Nicolai has published poems, translations and essays in various Italian and American reviews. He has written three collections of poetry: *La visita di Rebecca, I due volti di Janus*, and *La doppia finzione*. He translated nine dialect poets of the Friuli Venezia Giulia that appeared in the anthology *Dialect Poetry of Northern & Central Italy*, and he has translated into Italian poems by Erica Jong, Gwendolyn Brooks, Nikki Giovanni, June Jordan, Rita Dove, Maya Angelou, Alice Walker, and Elizabeth Alexander.

Elis Deghenghi Olujić teaches Italian literature and children's literature at the Juraj Dobrila University of Pula (Croatia). She is the author of dozens of reviews, prefaces, and articles. Her main field of interest is the literature of Istria-Kvarner and the writings of Italians living in Croatia and Slovenia. She has published more than ninety articles focusing on the analysis and criticism of the work of authors from Istria-Kvarner. She is a member of the editorial board of the Fiume journal *La Battana*.

Elizabeth Pallitto received a PhD in comparative literature from the Graduate Center of City University of New York. She has published translations from the Italian of poetry by Campanella, Velardinello, Fioravanti, and Iraqi exile Thea Laitef, and from the Turkish of Murathan Mungan and Birhan Keskin. In 2007, she published the first English version of Tullia d'Aragona's 1547 *Rime*, entitled *Sweet Fire*. Her articles, translations, and poetry have appeared in *The North American Review* and *Journal of Italian Translation*, among other journals.

Michael Palma has published two poetry chapbooks, *The Egg Shape* and *Antibodies*; two full-length collections, *A Fortune in Gold* and *Begin in Gladness*; and an online chapbook, *The Ghost of Congress Street*. He has translated the work of Guido Gozzano, Diego Valeri, Maurizio Cucchi, Franco Buffoni, and Sergio Corazzini, among other modern Italian writers. His translation of Dante's *Inferno* was published in 2002 and reprinted as a Norton Critical Edition in 2007.

Joseph Pivato is professor of literary studies at Athabasca University, Edmonton. His research focuses on Italian Canadian writing. His publications include *Contrasts: Comparative Essays on Italian-Canadian Writing* and *Echo: Essays on Other Literatures*. Among other collections, he has edited *The Anthology of Italian-Canadian Writing* and *Literatures of Lesser Diffusion*.

Gaetano Rando is honorary senior fellow in the Faculty of Arts, University of Wollongong, Australia. He has written extensively on Italian Australian studies. His recent books are *Celluloid Immigrant: Italian Australian Filmmaker Giorgio Mangiamele*, *Literary and Social Diasporas: An Italian Australian Perspective*, and *Emigrazione e letteratura: Il caso italoaustraliano*. He has also translated Rosa R. Cappiello's seminal novel *Paese fortunato* (*Oh Lucky Country*).

Robert Testa Redy is a teacher who lives in Vancouver, British Columbia.

Graziella Sidoli holds an M.Phil. in comparative literature from New York University. She is the founder and editor of *PolyText* and has published translations and articles on translation theory in the United States and Italy. She teaches Spanish language and literature at Sacred Heart Preparatory School in Greenwich, Connecticut.

Laura Toppan wrote her master's thesis on Mario Luzi's Dantism, then continued to explore Luzi's work in its relationship with French symbolism at the Sorbonne (Paris IV) with a doctoral dissertation. The results of this research have appeared in various Italian and French journals. She is now working on the literature of migration, in particular the poetry of Gëzim Hajdari and Božidar Stanišić. She teaches in the Department of Italian Studies at the University of Nancy 2.

Serge Vanvolsem (1946–2011) was a professor of Italian linguistics, director of the Center for Italian Studies at the Catholic University of Leuven, and a distinguished scholar of the Italian language and it diffusion in the world. He was also a member of the Accademia della Crusca and was recently named Commendatore dell'Ordine della Stella della Solidarietà Italiana. He was a tireless organizer of conferences and symposia. Among his books are *L'infinito sostantivato in italiano*, *Gli spazi della diversità*, and *Identità e diversità nella lingua e nella letteratura italiana*.

Justin Vitiello has published numerous scholarly articles and translations of medieval, Renaissance and modern Italian, Sicilian, and Spanish poetry. His books include *Il carro del pesce di Vanzetti*, *Confessions of a Joe Rock*, *Sicily Within*, and *Poetics and Literature of the Sicilian Diaspora: Studies in Oral History and Story-Telling*.

Brief Biographies of the Poets

Acquavita, Vlada (b. 1947). Born in Capodistria, Slovenia, Acquavita has long lived and worked in Buie d'Istria, Croatia, though she studied French letters in Zagreb and translation in Trieste. Her poetry collections of note include *The Wild Road and Other Elysian Songs* and *Mystical Herb Grove: Medieval Sentences*, which received a prize from Istria Nobilissima.

Airaghi, Alida (b. 1953). Born in Verona, Airaghi studied philosophy and literature in Milan before moving to Zurich in 1978, where she sharpened her poetic practice by working closely with Siro Angeli, her mentor and eventual husband. *Rose Red Pink* is an early book that was quite successful in the 1980's. It was followed in subsequent decades by collections such as *The Lake*, *In the Water*, and *Peripheral Litany*.

Aliberti, Antonio (1938–2000). Born near Messina, Italy, Aliberti relocated to Buenos Aires in 1951, where he published nearly twenty books of poetry in Spanish and one, *No Greater Sorrow*, in Italian. An essayist, literary critic and journalist as well, Aliberti edited an international poetry publication, *Zum-Zum*, from 1979 to 1983 and published a Spanish edition of Dino Campana's *Orphic Poems* in 1986.

Alziati, Cristina (b. 1963). Born in Milan, Alziati lives in Berlin, where she edits the journal *Guerre & Pace* and writes poetry in Italian. Her work has been featured in *Poesia*, *L'Ospite ingrato*, and *Annuary of Poetry 1991–1992*.

Andreoni, Giovanni (b. 1935). Born in Grosseto, Andreoni emigrated to Australia in 1962, where he found work in various universities as a lecturer in Italian language and literature. Now retired and living in New South Wales, Andreoni continues to write novels, short stories, and poetry.

Ardizzi, Maria J. (b. 1931). Born in Legnano, in the province of Teramo, Ardizzi studied in Rome before moving to Toronto in 1954. She has written for newspapers and magazines, and her fiction writing has met with great success since her first novel, *Made in Italy*, won the Ontario Arts Prize in 1982. She has written several other novels and a bilingual collection of poetry, *Conversation with My Son*.

Avolio, Alberto (b. 1949). Born in Fagnano Castello, Avolio moved to Australia with his family in 1955. He is a professor of biomedical engineering at the University of New South Wales. His poems, mostly in Italian but occasionally in dialect as well, pertain to individual and group identities, his early life, and the transition from old to new worlds. He lives in Sydney and is an active figure in the Italo-Australian community.

Ballerini, Luigi (b. 1940). Born in Milan, Ballerini lives in New York and teaches Italian literature at the University of California in Los Angeles. An essayist, translator and poet, his collections include *Eccetera, The Cadence of a Neighboring Tribe*, and *Cefalonia*.

Barlessi, Ester Sardoz (b. 1936). Born in Pula, Croatia, Barlessi writes prose and poetry in the local dialect and in Italian. Her published works, often melancholic and sentimental, include *And Between a River, Fears and Hopes*, and *Voyage On a Cloud*.

Biasiol, Adelia (1950–2000). Born in Dignano d'Istria, in Croatia, Biasiol published her first book of poetry, *First Flights*, in 1968. Thereafter she published regularly, locally as well as abroad, and received significant critical recognition through honors granted by Istria Nobilissima. *A Subdued Voice*, from 2004, is a collection containing all of her works.

Biondi, Franco (b. 1947). Born in Forlì, Biondi moved to Germany in 1965 and currently resides in Hanau. He writes novels, short stories, and essays in Italian and German. Works of note include *Passavanti's Return, The Tarantula*, and *The Traffic Jam*.

Bogliun, Loredana (b. 1955). Born in Pula, Croatia, Bogliun completed a doctorate in social psychology at the University of Ljubljana, Slovenia. She currently teaches sociology in the Department of Literature and Philosophy at Pula University. She writes poetry in Italian and in the dialect of

Dignano. Her collections include *Dry Walls*, *The Little One*, and *About the Buzzard*.

Bosi, Pino (b. 1933). Born in Tolmino, in the province of Gorizia, Bosi emigrated to Australia in 1951. He has worked for various Italo-Australian and Anglo-Australian newspapers and magazines, including *La Fiamma*, and has published novels, short stories, poetry collections, biographies, and essays. Among his volumes of poetry are *I'll Say Good Morning* and *Thirteen Continents and a Rocket/Magi Lost*. He lives in Melbourne.

Bufano, Alfredo (1895–1950). Though he claimed to have been born in Guaymallén, in Mendoza, Bufano was actually born in Apulia. He held various jobs in Argentina while writing essays, poems, and translations, and published his first book of poetry, *The Undecided Traveler*, in 1917. He wrote for several reputed journals, including *Caras y Caretas* and *Mundo Argentino*, and worked as a teacher.

Campana, Dino (1885–1932). Born in Marradi, near Florence, Campana was an estranged youth who left Italy for Argentina in 1907, allegedly bringing along only a gun and a copy of Whitman's *Leaves of Grass*. In Buenos Aires, Campana composed verses channeling his Mediterranean origins through the culture and history of his surroundings. *Orphic Poems*, first published in 1914 as *Canti Orfici*, is his major work.

Caporossi, Franco (b. 1930). Born in Segni, near Rome, Caporossi moved to Benghazi, Libya, as a child. Upon returning to Italy, he studied at a college of Italian Fascist Youth, then at a technical institute before engaging in military service and emigrating, in 1956, to Belgium, travelling extensively for work thereafter. His poetry collections include *The Skies of the North*, *The Voice of Thought*, and *Afterwards*.

Carducci, Lisa (b. 1943). Born in Montreal, Carducci studied education and taught French for many years. She writes poems, short stories, novellas, and essays, and her work has appeared in French and Italian. She is also active in art, theater, and broadcasting. Some of her works in poetry and prose are *Landscapes and Paintings*, *Seasons of Love*, and *Classified Affair*.

Carrera, Alessandro (b. 1954). Born in Lodi, Carrera studied philosophy in Milan before emigrating in 1987, when he began teaching Italian language and literature in various American universities. He is currently associate professor and director of Italian studies at the University of Houston. He has won a number of prizes for his prose, poetry, and criticism, and he is the Italian translator of works by Bob Dylan.

Carravetta, Peter (b. 1951). Born in Calabria, Carravetta came to the United States when he was twelve. He is a professor in the Department of European Languages, Literatures and Cultures at Stony Brook University. A writer, critic and translator, Carravetta has published six books of poetry, including *Existenz, The Sun and Other Things,* and *Otherwise.*

Chiellino, Gino (b. 1946). Born in Carlopoli, in Calabria, Chiellino has been living in Augsburg, Germany, since 1970. A professor of comparative literature at the University of Augsburg, Chiellino writes in German, primarily, with a general focus on the theme of the foreigner. His poetry collections and other works include *Desire for Language, Errant Words,* and *Living in Languages.*

Concas, Lino (b. 1930). Born in Gonnosfanadigia, in the province of Cagliari, Concas received a degree in philosophy before migrating to Melbourne in 1963. A retired Italian language teacher who continues to write, Concas has published a number of volumes of poetry, including *Ballad of Wind, Half a Man,* and *The Man of Silence.*

Condini, Ned (b. 1940). A native of the Piedmont, Condini became a naturalized American citizen in 1976. He is a writer, translator, literary critic, and recipient of various prizes and distinctions, including the PEN/Poggioli Award and the Bordighera Prize. His short stories and poems have appeared in many different publications.

Continanza, Marcella (b. 1940). Born in Roccanova, near Potenza, Continanza has been living in Germany since 1986, currently in Frankfurt. She writes prose and poetry in Italian, and she is founding editor of the journal *Vietato Fumare* and *Clic! Donne 2000.* Her collections include *Feathers of Angels, Nocturnal Roses,* and *Passage with Two Voices.*

Coreno, Mariano (b. 1939). Born in Coreno Ausonio, Coreno relocated to Melbourne in 1956. His poetry, in both Italian and English, has appeared in various newspapers, journals, and anthologies. His published volumes include *Cry of Love, Beneath the Sun*, and *Passing Stars*.

Costa, Giovanni (b. 1940). Born in Vizzini, Sicily, Costa emigrated in 1962, eventually arriving in Montreal, where he taught Italian and French and established the Italian program at Concordia University. He has published many academic papers in Italian and French, and his poetry has appeared in *Alternanze Alternances Alterations* and *Beyond the Horizon*, among other publications.

Damiani, Alessandro (b. 1928). Born in Sant'Andrea Jonio, Calabria, Damiani relocated to Croatia in 1948. Having worked in journalism in Rome beforehand, he worked for *Panorama* and *La Voce del Popolo* in Fiume. A writer of novels and poetry, Damiani has published numerous books including *The Wings of Time, Roman Notes*, and *From Pontus*.

Del Duca, Nino (b. 1925). Born in Naples, Del Duca came to the United States in the 1970s. He is a journalistic and creative contributor to *America OGGI*, North America's most prominent Italian-language newspaper. He recently published a collection of poems in dialect, *Io stongo 'e casa 'America*.

De Oliveira, Vera Lúcia (b. 1958). Born in Candido Mota, de Oliveira is professor of Portuguese and Brazilian Literatures at the University of Lecce. In addition to many academic publications, her creative works include *Pieces, Time of Suffering*, and *In the Heart of the Word*.

De Palchi, Alfredo (b. 1926). A native of Legnago, near Verona, De Palchi came to the United States in 1956 following years of imprisonment and some time living in Paris. A resident of New York City ever since, he edited the literary magazine *Chelsea* from 1960 until 2007. His poetic works include *Sessions with the Analyst, The Scorpion's Dark Dance*, and *Anonymous Constellation*.

Di Giovanni, Severino (1901–1931). Born in Chieti, Di Giovanni had aspired to a career in teaching until Fascist authorities forced him to flee Italy in 1923. Settling in a town west of Buenos Aires, Di Giovanni espoused revolutionary ideals that he promoted in *Culmine*, an anarchist newspaper that he headed from 1925 to 1931, when he was executed by firing squad.

Di Stefano, Enoe (b. 1921). Born in Rovereto, in the province of Trento, Di Stefano earned a teaching diploma before emigrating to Sydney in 1949, where she worked for the Italian language newspaper *La Fiamma* as well as other media outlets. Di Stefano has published a number of volumes of poems, including *Terra Australis, Mine and Not Mine*, and *The Itinerary*.

Dobran, Roberto (b. 1963). Born in Pula, Dobran moved to Gorizia, Italy, after spending some time in Ljubljana, Slovenia. He has worked as a journalist and in rehabilitation centers, and some of his poetic works have appeared in *Panorama*. His collections include *Implosions, Departures*, and *Global Plaque*.

Fioravanti, Vittorio (b. 1936). Born in Taranto, Fioravanti moved around Italy and Germany before settling in Venezuela in 1966, where he works in graphic design and radio and television media. He has been honored as Knight of the Italian Republic and is widely recognized for his work in graphic art as well as literature.

Fontanella, Luigi (b. 1943). Born in Salerno, Fontanella studied in Italy before emigrating and completing a doctorate at Harvard. He is professor of Italian at SUNY Stony Brook. A novelist, literary critic and poet, he has published dozens of books and is the editor of *Gradiva*, an international journal, and the president of Italian Poetry in America.

Garbin, Valeriano (b. 1937). Born in Schio, in the Veneto region, Garbin relocated to Venezuela and published his first volume of poetry, *The Excitement*, in 1970. His numerous collections, including *The Owl's Eyes, Living Earths*, and *Transferred Roots*, are collaborative publications featuring works by various artists and illustrators.

Genovese, Andrea (b. 1937). Born in Messina, Genovese moved to Milan in 1960. His first collection of poetry, *Essential Odyssey*, appeared in 1964. Writing primarily in Italian and dialect, Genovese began writing in French as well after moving to Lyon. In addition to a number of books of poetry, Genovese has also published two novels.

Giambusso, Giuseppe (b. 1956). Born in Riesi, Sicily, Giambusso relocated to Germany in 1974 and currently resides in Fröndenberg. He writes poetry in Italian and is an editor of pedagogical materials for Italian language instructors. His books of poetry include *Beyond the Horizon* and *Departures.*

Grohovaz, Gianni (b. 1926). Born in Fiume, Grohovaz is a poet and journalist who came to Canada in the 1950s. One of the founders of *Corriere Canadese*, the major Italian paper in Canada, Grohovaz has also been involved in broadcasting. He has published a number of nonfiction prose works as well as two volumes of poetry, *To Recall the Things I Remember* and *Words, Words As Grains of Sand.*

Guidi, Anna Maria (1926–1994). Born in Rome, Guidi studied English language and literature at the British Institute before moving to Sydney in 1954. A poet and translator who wrote in Italian, English, and Romanesco, Guidi had her work published in anthologies, magazines and journals in Italy, India, the United States, and Australia.

Gulli, Bruno (b. 1959). Born in Calabria, Gulli has lived in the United States since 1985. He studied literature and philosophy in Venice, then in San Francisco and New York, and he currently teaches philosophy at Long Island University and Kingsborough Community College. His two published chapbooks are *Lines of Another Re-Search* and *Figures of a Foreign Land.*

Jelicich, Marianna (b. 1976). Born in Capodistria, in Slovenia, Jelicich lives and works in Buie d'Istria, in Croatia. She studied at the University of Trieste. Her poetry has appeared in such journals as *La Battana* and *Semne,* and her collections include *Ethereal* and *Possible Scenarios.*

Lattmann, Silvana (b. 1918). Born in Naples, Lattmann settled in Zurich in 1954. Her first poems appeared in 1978, in an anthology published by Mondadori, and were followed by a number of well-received collections, including *The Stories of Ariano, The Voyage,* and *Fire and Memory.*

Livorni, Ernesto (b. 1959). Born in Pescara, Livorni came to the United States in 1984 to pursue a doctorate in comparative literature at the University of Connecticut. He teaches at the University of Wisconsin. He has published three collections of poems and a number of scholarly essays and books.

Lucchesi, Marco (b. 1963). Born in Rio de Janeiro, Lucchesi is currently a professor at the Federal University of Rio de Janeiro. A poet and translator,

Lucchesi has published several volumes of poetry, including *Sphere* in 2004, as well as Portuguese editions of works by Eco and Vico. He also translates from Russian and German.

Marchegiani, Irene (b. ca. 1950). A translator, critic, and writer of creative works as well as Italian-language textbooks, Marchegiani is coordinator of Student Teaching for European Languages at SUNY Stony Brook. Her first collection of poetry, *Life in a Circle*, was published in 2004.

Marchig, Laura (b. 1962). Born in Fiume, Marchig became a key figure in the revival of Istrian poetry in the 1980s. She studied at the University of Florence and now works in theater and as chief editor of the journal *La Battana*. Her collection *Narrating Men* won first prize in the Istria Nobilissima competition in 1988.

Marretta, Saro (b. 1940). Born near Agrigento, Marretta studied education before resettling, at the end of the 1960s, in Switzerland, where he taught Italian language and culture before transitioning to a school for interpreters, teaching in Zurich as well as in several other European cities. His collections of poetry include *The Double Truths* and *Swiss Allegro*.

Martini, Lucifero (1916–2001). Born in Florence, Martini was drafted into the army in 1941 and briefly imprisoned in 1943, after which he joined the partisans. He moved to Fiume in the 1950s and worked for several periodicals there while publishing numerous books, including *The Sign of the Sea*, *Algae Aroma*, and *Shards of Time*.

Mastropasqua, Corrado (b. 1929). Born in Cimitile, in Naples, Mastropasqua completed his studies of medicine in 1953, becoming a doctor in the Italian navy until emigrating to Canada in 1961. While working as an anesthesiologist in Montreal, he helped establish an Italian theater group. A bilingual collection of his poems, *Ibrido*, was published in 1988.

Minuto, Ermanno (b. 1929). Born in Savona, Minuto traveled extensively as a businessman before settling in Brazil in 1987, where he began writing poetry, primarily in dialect, upon retiring. Among his most recent works is a collection of prose writings, *The Bitter Taste of Berries and Other Stories*, published in 2005.

Montagna, Giovanni (1905–1991). Born near Pavia, Montagna received a diploma in business. A writer, editor, translator, and teacher, Montagna was also known as an ambassador of Italian culture, living and working in many European cities before settling in Brussels for several decades. Works of note include *On the Emilian Way* and *Codex*.

Moroni, Mario (b. 1955). Moroni, an assistant professor of Italian at Colby College, has published verses in a number of different journals, magazines, and anthologies in the United States and Italy. He has also published a volume of selected poems, *The Lands of Icarus*, as well as a book of poetic prose.

Nicolai, Adeodato Piazza (b. 1944). Born in Vigo di Cadore, in the province of Belluno, Nicolai came to the United States in 1959. A teacher, translator, critic, and poet, he has published three collections of poetry: *Rebecca's Visit*, *The Two Faces of Janus*, and *The Double Fiction*.

Petricarini, Romano (b. 1934). Born in Fermo, in Le Marche, Petricarini moved to Vancouver in 1967, where he began to publish poems in newspapers and magazines. His work includes the collections *The Slingshot Kids*, *From My November Notebook*, and *One of You*.

Piccolo, Fruttuoso (b. 1953). Born in the Veneto, Piccolo has been living near Hanover, Germany, since 1972. He writes poetry and experimental texts in German and Italian. His published work includes *Ten Years Between Two Worlds*, *Harlequin Guest Worker*, and *Through Language Another Self*.

Pizzi, Giancarlo (b. 1950). Pizzi grew up around Novara before moving to Milan, where he eschewed poetry for political engagement until 1977. In 1982 he relocated to Mexico, then returned to Europe a year later, settling in Paris and continuing to write in Italian. His works include *Last September* and *Clotted Blood*.

Provenzano, Nino (b. 1944). Born in Castellammare del Golfo, in Sicily, Provenzano now lives and works in New York. He is vice president of Arba Sicula, an organization that promotes Sicilian culture around the world. His bilingual anthology of poetry, published in 1995, is called *Vinissi*.

Ramous, Osvaldo (1905–1981). Born in Civitaveccchia, in Fiume, Croatia, Ramous published his first collection, *Wind Over the Pond*, in 1923. After retiring from his post as director of the Dramma Italiano di Fiume, Ramous published a number of books of poetry, including *Night's Wine*, *Medea's Awakening*, and *The Seagulls on the Rooftops*.

Rimanelli, Giose (b. 1925). Born in Casacalenda, Molise, Rimanelli is considered something of a complicated, exiled figure among Italian writers in the United States. His novel *Benedetta in Guysterland* won the American Book Award in 1994.

Saccà, Annalisa (b. 1954). A writer, translator, and literary critic, Saccà is professor of Italian at St. John's University in New York. She writes for several different academic and literary journals, does translation work in a number of different languages, and has published two books of poetry, *The Time of the Grain* and *Naming Delfi*.

Salabè, Piero (b. 1970). Born in Rome, Salabè has lived in Germany since 1995. He writes poetry and prose in Italian, German, and Spanish, and works as a critic and translator of South American literature. His first collection of poetry, *I Am Preparing the Room*, appeared in 2000.

Salvatore, Filippo (b. 1948). Born in Guglionesi, in Molise, Salvatore emigrated to Montreal in 1964. He teaches Italian literature at Concordia University. He writes in Italian, French, and English, though his poetry is primarily in Italian. His books include *Suns of Darkness, Fascism and the Italian in Montreal*, and *Science and Humanity*.

Sanna, Salvatore A. (b. 1934). Born in Oristano, in Sardinia, Sanna relocated to Germany in 1958 and lives in Frankfurt, where he co-founded and is now president of the German-Italian Union. He is also the founding editor of the journal *Italienisch*. He has published four collections of poetry.

Schiavato, Mario (b. 1931). A native of Quinto di Treviso, Schiavato moved with his family to Dignano d'Istria in 1943. In 1948 he moved to Fiume and began working in publishing. A writer of poetry since the 1980's, Schiavato has published several collections, including *Istrian Poems, Time's Voracity*, and *A Different Country*.

Scotti, Giacomo (b. 1928). Born in Saviano, near Naples, Scotti moved to Istria in the postwar years. He was a journalist for *La Voce del Popolo* and published his first collections of poems in the 1960s. Notable works include *Flag of Salvation, The Color Orange,* and *Looking for Secret Rivers.*

Sepe, Franco (b. 1955). Born in Fondi, Sepe studied psychology at the University of Rome before moving to Germany in 1979. Since 1995, he has been a lecturer of Italian language and culture at the University of Potsdam. His works include *Little Berlin Elegies, Autobiography of the Five Senses,* and *Investigations of a Castle.*

Siurliuga, Victoria (b. 1972). A professor of Italian language and literature at Rice University, Siurliuga is a scholar and poet with a number of critical and creative publications to her name, including two collections of poetry, *Answers of Silence* and *Allergic to Night.*

Strano, Luigi (b. 1913). Born in Castellace di Oppido Mamertina, Strano emigrated to Sydney in 1929. He writes in Italian, English, Calabrian, and Latin. Among his dozens of published works are *Forbidden Poems, The Creatures of the Woods,* and *Rocky Is the Path: Memoirs.*

Tanelli, Orazio (b. 1936). A native of Molise, Tanelli arrived in the United States in 1961. He worked as a language instructor and as director of *La Follia di New York* and *Il Ponte Italo-Americano.* A poet in Italian and in dialect, his primary collection is *Songs From Beyond the Sea.*

Tedeschi, Pietro (1925–1998). Born in Reggio Emilia, Tedeschi migrated to Australia in 1952, where he eventually took up writing and contributed articles to *La Fiamma,* an Italian-language newspaper, for many years. Tedeschi published two autobiographical novels, *Shirtless* and *B53.*

Totaro, Paolo (b. 1933). Born in Naples, Totaro resettled in Australia in 1963. With degrees in law and music, he has held various jobs, including work with arts councils and universities, continuing all the while to write in Italian and English and play chamber music. One of his short stories won the Premio Letterario 2 Giugno competition in 1993.

Tremul, Maurizio (b. 1962). Born in Bertocchi, Slovenia, Tremul won first prize in the Istria Nobilissima competition in 1979 for his first collection,

Love as Life. Tremul's other collections of poetry include *Fragments for a Crisis* and *Refractions.*

Tusiani, Joseph (b. 1924). A native of the Gargano, Tusiani came to the United States in 1947 and was naturalized in 1956. Professor emeritus of CUNY Lehman College, Tusiani composes verses in English, Latin, Italian and Gargano dialect. His collections include *Rind and All, Carmina Latina,* and *The Difficult Word.*

Valesio, Paolo (b. 1939). A native of Bologna, Valesio studied linguistics and literature at various universities in Italy and the United States before assuming his current post as Giuseppe Ungaretti Professor in Italian Literature at Columbia University. He has published criticism, prose, drama and poetry.

Wilcock, J. Rodolfo (1919–1978). Born in Buenos Aires, Wilcock was as a polymath, wanderer, and literary figure who associated with Borges, Bioy Casares, and Silvina Ocampo. After relocating to Rome in 1958, he began to write in Italian, publishing collections such as *Common Places* and *34 Love Poems.*

Zamaro, Silvano (b. 1949). Born in Cormons, in Gorizia, Zamaro relocated to Edmonton in 1976. His poetry has appeared in Canada, Italy, and the United States. In 1988, his collection of Italian poems, *Highway to the Moon,* won the Bressani Prize for Poetry.

Zanier, Leonardo (b. 1935). Born in Carnia, Zanier found himself in Morocco and French Switzerland before settling more permanently in Zurich. His publications as a poet appeared in the following decades and include collections such as *Semen and Blood, Traces,* and *Big Feast.*

Zanini, Eligio (1927–1993). A native of Rovigno d'Istria, Zanini is considered a pioneer in dialect poetry of the Balkans, publishing his first collection, *Ashes,* in 1966. Subsequent collections include *Conversations With the Seagull Philip in the Corner of Paradise* and *With the Prow to the Wind.*

Compiled by Paul D'Agostino